GOD,
REVELATION
AND AUTHORITY

Volume V

GOD WHO STANDS
AND STAYS

Part One

GOD, REVELATION AND AUTHORITY

Volume V

GOD WHO STANDS AND STAYS

Part One

Carl F. H. Henry

WORD BOOKS, PUBLISHER
Waco, Texas

God, Revelation and Authority
Volume 5
God Who Stands and Stays
Copyright © 1982 by Word Incorporated.

Library of Congress Cataloging in Publication Data

Henry, Carl Ferdinand Howard, 1913–
    God who stands and stays.

    (God, revelation, and authority/Carl F. H. Henry; v. 5)
    Bibliography: p.
    Includes index.
    1. God. I. Title. II. Series: Henry, Carl Ferdinand Howard, 1913–   God revelation, and
authority; v. 5.
BR1640.A25H45 vol. 5 [BT102] 230'.044s [231] 82–10968
ISBN 0–8499–0320–3
Printed in the United States of America

Unless otherwise specified, Scripture quotations are from the
Authorized or King James Version of the Bible.

Quotations from the Revised Standard Version of the Bible (RSV),
copyrighted 1946, 1952, © 1971, 1973 by the Division of Christian Education of the National
Council of the Churches of Christ in the U.S.A., are used by permission.

Quotations from *The New English Bible* (NEB), © The Delegates of
The Oxford University Press and The Syndics of The Cambridge
University Press, 1961, 1970, are reprinted by permission.

Quotations from Today's English Version of the Bible (TEV), ©
American Bible Society 1966, 1971, 1976, are used by permission.

Quotations from the *New American Standard Bible* (NAS) are copyright
© 1960, 1961, 1963, 1968, 1971 by The Lockman Foundation.

Quotations from *The New Testament in Modern English* (Phillips) by
J. B. Phillips, published by The Macmillan Company, are © 1958, 1960, 1972 by J. B. Phillips.

Quotations from the New International Version of the Bible (NIV),
published by The Zondervan Corporation, are copyright © 1973 by
New York Bible Society International.

Quotations from *The Jerusalem Bible* (JB), copyright © 1966, by
Darton, Longman & Todd, Ltd. and Doubleday and Company, Inc., are
used by permission of the publisher.

Quotations identified LB are from *The Living Bible Paraphrased*
(Wheaton: Tyndale House Publishers, 1971).

Contents

Preface

AS ORIGINALLY PLANNED THIS WORK was to comprise only three volumes. But exposition of the fifteen theses on divine revelation (epistemology) that followed Volume 1 in itself required three volumes, and expounding the doctrine of God (ontology) required two more. This expansion to six volumes has been harder on me than on my readers. Now fifteen years after it began in Cambridge, England, at the conclusion of my editorship of *Christianity Today*, this writing project finally comes to an end.

One or another chapter was presented during short teaching terms or special lecture series on campuses both in the United States and abroad. Many of the overseas engagements were made possible in my role as lecturer-at-large for World Vision International.

Besides those campuses mentioned in prefaces to earlier volumes some of the content of these concluding volumes was presented during teaching terms at Asian Center for Theological Studies and Mission in Korea, Asian Theological Seminary in the Philippines, China Evangelical Seminary in Taiwan and in a lecture series at Union Biblical Seminary in India. Short-term courses here at home were offered at Columbia Graduate School of Bible and Missions, South Carolina; Denver Conservative Baptist Seminary, Colorado; Fuller Theological Seminary, California; Gordon-Conwell Theological Seminary, Massachusetts; C. S. Lewis Institute, Maryland; New College/Berkeley, California; and Regent College, Vancouver, Canada. Other presentations included lecture series at Alma College, Michigan; Carolina Study Center, North Carolina; Cornell University, New York; Covenant College, Tennessee; George Fox College, Oregon; Milligan College, Tennessee; Newberry College, South Carolina; Northwest Nazarene College, Idaho; Pepperdine University, California; University of Hawaii, Honolulu; University of Virginia, Charlottesville; Virginia Baptist Pastors Conference at Bluefield College; Western Conservative Baptist Seminary and Western

Evangelical Seminary, both in Oregon. Still other series were given in Kobe, Japan, attended by faculty and students of five cooperating evangelical institutions and in Vail, Colorado, at the Theological Vacation Conference for Lutherans, a lively program that included Professor Paul Holmer of Yale University and Dean Krister Stendahl of Harvard Divinity School. Special series were also given in my home community of Arlington, Virginia, at Cherrydale Baptist Church and at Little Falls (Presbyterian) Church; C. S. Lewis Institute sponsored the former.

The chapter on "Revelation and Culture" was given in preliminary form as the tenth anniversary address of the Japan Evangelical Theological Society and in final form as the retiring president's address to the American Theological Society. The material on "Justice and the Kingdom of God" in the final volume was presented at the Conference on Recovery of the Sacred at Notre Dame University, as well as at an informal meeting of U.S. congressional aides in the Senate Office Building, and during a Christian education lecture series at Coral Gables Presbyterian Church, Florida.

It is gratifying indeed to see the serious theological interest that these volumes have stimulated in many circles and in many parts of the world. Earlier portions of the English edition have gone into a fourth printing. The first two volumes have appeared also in Mandarin and the first three in Korean; a German translation is in process.

January 1, 1982   CARL F. H. HENRY

Note: Full information on all sources cited in the text is given in the bibliography at the end of this volume.

Introduction: God Who Stands and Stays

VOLUMES I THROUGH IV in this series have concentrated on *God Who Speaks and Shows;* the fifth and sixth concluding volumes concern *God Who Stands and Stays.* The earlier writings focused mainly on religious epistemology, that is, on the problem of knowledge and the fact of divine revelation as the answer to the question of how we know God. These later volumes emphasize ontology or metaphysics; they probe the nature of the self-disclosing God whom man may know and worship and serve. Such examination is the very lifeline of theological inquiry. God's existence is the foundational biblical doctrine; from it flow all other Christian principles and precepts.

Contemporary man seems to have lost God's address. But that is not all. He is unsure how to pronounce God's name, and, at times, unsure even of that name, or whether, in fact, God is nameable. But since most human beings still claim to "believe in God," the question of whom or what they worship remains both important and contemporary. An ironic feature of the late twentieth century, of course, is that while literate Westerners laugh at primitive worship of sticks and stones, they themselves do obeisance to the brick and plastic of materialistic technology. Revealed religion has always known that when man denies supreme allegiance to the eternal living Lord he inevitably worships some contemporary counterfeit. Man's character is ultimately defined by the character of his god.

We have already established that while man the spiritual vagabond may be confused about God's identity and address, God in self-revelation confronts him continually in an amazing variety of ways. God stands eternal and majestic. But he is neither inactive nor speechless; he speaks and acts. Successive cultures have their half-day, and except for the perpetuity lent them by anthropologists and historians, they fade, along with their gods, into oblivion. The false gods are always destined to become gods that *were,* gilded idols of the past whose imagined existence has given way.

I am is the exclusive hallmark of the God of the Bible. The self-revealing God stands—before successive civilizations arose, before mankind was, before the world itself was—as the *I am.* He is eternally the God who is *there,* the God who *is,* the incomparable *I am.* Dietrich Bonhoeffer, supposedly in the interest of vital personal faith, remarked that the God who "is there" does not exist; eager to reinforce the point, Hans Jürgen Schultz observes: "God tells us that we must live in his presence as men who exist without God" (*Conversion to the World,* p. 60). But if these commentators profess at this point to echo the God of the Bible, it would be helpful if they would adduce chapter and verse. For God's ontological "reality" is independent of man's personal decision. He has being in and for himself.

Is revelation or is the eternal God the basic axiom of the Christian system of truth? For Karl Barth revelation often seems to be the foundational Christian axiom. He writes, for example: "God's revelation has its reality and truth wholly and in every respect—i.e., ontically and noetically—within itself" (*Church Dogmatics,* I/1, p. 350). Yet in some passages he implies— if not asserts—that the doctrine of the triune God is the primary axiom; if we do not know God as triune, he insists, we do not know the living God (I/1, p. 347). There is no need, however, to elevate revelation as ontically, and not simply noetically, prior. As Gordon H. Clark indicates, "the eternal God precedes his acts of revelation in time" (*Karl Barth's Theological Method,* p. 94). The living God is the original Christian axiom, both ontically and noetically, for God discloses himself in revelation as the God who is eternally there.

God who is is the ultimate Who's Who, God who introduces himself. He is the standing God before whom every knee shall bow "in heaven and on earth and under the earth" (Phil. 2:10 ff.). He is the eternally living God, nothing less, nothing other. Inviting us to lifelong rendezvous with the reality of realities, he bids us fallen creatures to make ourselves acceptably at home in the Stander's presence. *God who is* calls a halt to the religious inventions, to the prodigal flight from spiritual reality that intellectual vagabonds defend as the enterprise of enlightened modernity. Behold "the beauty of the Lord" writes the Psalmist (27:4). "Let not the wise man glory in his wisdom," exhorts Jeremiah, "neither let the mighty man glory in his might, let not the rich man glory in his riches: but let him that glorieth glory in this, that he understandeth and knoweth me, that I am the Lord, which exercise lovingkindness, judgment, and righteousness, in the earth: for in these things I delight, saith the Lord" (Jer. 9:23–24).

God who is, we shall contend, is *God who stands,* and *stays.* God who independently "stands" is the personal sovereign containing in himself the ground of his own existence; God who "stays" governs in providence and in eschatological consummation of his dramatic plan for man and the world.

The term "stand" carries far greater and more profound meanings and implications than ordinary conversation would suggest. In fact, the massive

Oxford English Dictionary devotes almost 15 pages to the meanings and uses of this one word. The self-disclosed God, this One who "stands," exists forever in a self-specified condition free of external determination; his reality, purpose and activity are not contingent on the universe. He continues steadfast, unimpaired and immutable. Not only *He* stands, but also *His Word;* He remains and his truth as well holds good and abides valid. Jesus admonished in the lonely wilderness temptation: "Worship the Lord your God, and serve him only" (Matt. 4:10, NIV; cf. Deut. 6:13) and he stressed that "Man does not live on bread alone, but on every word that comes from the mouth of God" (Matt. 4:4, NIV; cf. Deut. 8:3). Though no man stand with us, though the fury of evil assail us, *God who stands* pledges himself to stand with his own. Emboldened by God's standing presence and Word, Luther with his "Here I stand" not only renounced the renegade world but also faulted the stumbling church. God stands—and only those who stand in, with and under him will withstand his judgment of and upon prodigal mankind and nations.

Theologians and philosophers have spoken of God in diverse ways, sometimes in keeping with and sometimes in variance from the inspired teaching of the scriptural writers. In representing the God who speaks and shows, traditional Christian theology has often used the term *substance.* While this word may readily acquire connotations unserviceable to revelational theology, it does have acceptable uses. In their flight from the category of divine substance, current alternatives that depict reality only in terms of impersonal processes and events are hardly appropriate to the being of God.

The ancient Greeks used the term *ousia* (being) in various senses; the Latins used *substantia* (substance) as an equivalent. But these terms, being or substance, may imply simply an immanent *ground,* rather than an independent, transcendent Creator of the universe. God is not the primary or contributive being of all things. The basic meaning of substance is to *stand under;* substance is that on which all else depends but which itself depends on nothing. The self-revealed God is the transcendent source and support of the space-time universe. God is substance in the several senses of living self-subsisting divine nature and of standing under or being under all other reality as its creator and preserver. God is not a spiritual substratum or psychic core in which divine perfections inhere. The substance of God is, in the primary sense, nothing other than God himself; the divine substance is not an essence distinguishable from divine personality or from the divine attributes but is the very living God. God is therefore substance as existent reality, as opposed to nonbeing, or mere appearance and shadow.

Most theologians have held that necessary existence must be predicated of God if one is to honor the biblical revelation. Some contemporary philosophers consider the notion of necessary divine existence to be absurd, however, asserting that the relation of essence and existence must always be contingent. Schubert Ogden asks whether "the traditional assertion of God's necessary existence really is the only way in which the God of Holy Scripture can be appropriately represented" (*The Reality of God,* pp. 121 ff.).

Ogden concedes that "God is understood by Scripture to be the necessarily existent" and as "both Alpha and Omega, the ultimate source and end of whatever is or could even be" (*ibid.,* p. 123), and grants that "one . . . can scarcely claim to interpret Holy Scripture if he simply abandons its affirmation of God's necessary existence" (*ibid.,* pp. 122 ff.). But he criticizes evangelical theism for depicting God as in every respect "necessary and as lacking in all real internal relations to the cogent beings of which he is the ground" (*ibid.,* p. 124). Ogden assumes that the premises of process philosophy explain the relations between God and the universe more satisfactorily than do those of biblical theology. He claims that "the Scriptural witness to God can be appropriately interpreted only if his nature is conceived neoclassically as having a contingent as well as a necessary aspect" (*ibid.,* p. 122).

Over against this modern tendency to trap aspects of the divine nature in the space-time continuum, evangelical theology affirms God's *aseity;* that is, it declares that the universe is not necessary either to divine being or to divine perfection. God stands free of such dependence; he alone, moreover, stands completely and intrinsically independent of the created order. Schleiermacher rightly emphasizes man's feeling of absolute dependence on God as integral to authentic religious experience, although his pantheistic premises tended to distort this emphasis. Creation is not an absolute necessity for God, nor does the universe exhaustively reveal him. God has power to create or not to create, and could have created—had he willed—another kind of universe. He stands free of the universe both as its voluntary creator and voluntary preserver; he stands at ease, as it were, independent of external command. He is the Lord who exercises sovereignty over his entire creation and stands free of dependence on the external realities which owe their being and continuance to him. He is the self-revealed Creator who is the source and support of all finite substances and structures.

As the divine substance or being, moreover, he as voluntary Creator stands above and behind and under and in all created reality. We are able to depict the universe as reality only because God has given it a substantiality or real existence different from his own substance. Except for its preservation by God who stands and who stands by his creation, all creation is vulnerable to nonbeing. God is the God who underlies all phenomena, not as the permanent substratum of things, nor as a necessary aspect of them as though the universe were a mode of his being, but as the free originator and preserver of all qualities which, because they are other than God, do not have their existence in themselves. He voluntarily constitutes the essence or substance of the universe, and gives it its specific character.

God *stands under* the universe, therefore, as the self-sufficient God whose place of standing or position or station is that of transcendent sovereign. He stands fast; he is not in process, in a condition of change, in motion toward perfection. At the same time he does not lifelessly "stand model" for cosmic observation, like some antiquarian artifact. He is, as we shall stress, God who stoops and stays, and as we have already stressed, God who speaks and shows. He is the eternally active God. The emphasis that God *stands* must not encourage the thought that he is an inactive deity, for the God who stands is the self-same God who speaks and shows. God who stands is not an indifferent and static divinity like the impersonal or remote gods of many ancient philosophers. Only through God's revelational initiative and activity, through his self-speaking and self-showing, do we know that and how he stands. As sovereign unchanging Lord and Creator he acts and speaks; he creates and redeems and judges, he reveals and manifests himself, he comes in Christ. In the sovereign selfhood of Godhead in interpersonal communion he maintains eternal fidelity in love. He is the steadfast God, not a vacillating sovereign. He stands and neither falters nor stumbles. He is secure in himself, God who stands fast when all else seems or is insecure. Scripture reveals the fall of angels and the fall of man; only Satan dare hope for a divine fall (Matt. 4:8 ff.) and only mutinous man dare think of the death of God, of darkness that extinguishes the Light (John 1:5, NEB). God who stands is unfallen, is invulnerable to assault, as even atheists learn in their time of final reckoning. As Satan knows even now and will finally acknowledge when bound by the victorious Christ (Rev. 20), God's standing or repute is beyond reproach.

Not only does God *stand under* the universe, but in a classic sense he alone *understands* it. The misunderstanding both of man and the world and of God who stands—and as it were, stands under the universe as source and support, cause and conserver—is avoided only if we recognize that in the primary sense God also *under-stands*. When we speak of divine understanding, insofar as the self-revealed God of the Bible is in view, we mean much more than divine omniscience, although God indeed knows the end from the beginning. By *under*standing we mean—not as some process theologians would have it, that God in the past knew less than we know today—that God plans and decrees the world and man, and that because he ordains the future he knows all contingencies. He does not leave in doubt the final triumph of good and the final doom of evil. He does not leave in doubt the eternal bliss of the elect in Christ; in earthly political affairs human leaders may "stand for election" but in the kingdom of God they stand by God's election.

The modern "secular understanding" of God is woefully in error because it sacrifices divine transcendent being and knowledge. If man properly knows God he will *under*stand him; man either stands under divine revelation and looks up to it, or resorts to revisable conjecture and vain imagination. Only as God manifests himself and as the truth of his revelation determines our affirmations do we truly know him. In Shakespeare's *Two Gentlemen* we find a clue to the biblical understanding of the Divine Understander: "Why, stand-under; and under-stand is all one" (Act 2, Scene 5, line 31). God is not only infinite Mind, but as Sovereign he disposes the future and stands under all creaturely knowledge. In this context we must discuss both God's rational attributes, including his wisdom, foreknowledge and omniscience, and his moral perfections. God is Light, and only in his

Light do we see light. Were God not to command light to shine there would be only darkness. Because he commanded Light to shine, to walk in his commandments is to walk in the Light.

Modern technological civilization takes a perverse turn when it inverts relationships involved in human understanding. When man forgets his creatureliness and thinks of himself as standing over and as overstanding the universe, confidence in his own gnosis exalts human rationalism above divine reason and eclipses the doctrine of divine understanding. In biblical theology true understanding of God and of his Word requires that the creature stand under the epistemic priority of the Creator.

The shift of epistemic center from God to man accommodated the existential, phenomenological and behavioral perspectives in which man becomes himself the creator of an experienced world that no one else can share with him. The deobjectification of God, as Karl Barth promoted it, led to his dialectical emphasis that God's perfections are not universally or objectively knowable; instead God is said to be revealed only internally in personal response to a supposed transcendent interpersonal confrontation. It is not surprising that this internal reorientation of revelation would deteriorate to Bultmannian existentialism. Minimizing the transcendent being of God, Bultmann concentrated instead on man's self-understanding in faith, which he gratuitously viewed as a response to God's inner confrontation in his Word. But the notion that the experienced reality of God was thus dramatically preserved soon gave way. The supposed relation between man and God was soon transformed into an inner tension with man's sense of unconditional obligation—that is, into a conflict between the "I may" and the "I ought." Or it became simply a description of the relationship between man and his neighbors to which traditional theological language was deployed. Such "understanding of God" denied any transcendent reality beyond happenings in our own existential experience.

From secular philosophers and even so-called secular theologians one now often hears that God is an incomprehensible idea for contemporary man—moderns allegedly find the idea of God unthinkable and meaningless. Much of this portrayal misjudges the epistemic predicament of secular man and in fact involves a basic and needless compromise with radically secular views. To be sure, the intellectual postulates of naturalistic theory leave no room whatever for the supernatural except as myth. The secular humanist does indeed declare every doctrine of a transcendent God to be false and irrelevant. But such declaration requires at least some comprehension of the meaning of deity. Biblical theology insists that even the most radical secularist in his thinking and doing reflects some elemental awareness of God's claim upon human life, and that every man—the secular humanist included—has enough vital knowledge of God to invite divine judgment upon his personal rebellion. God stands and understands, and no man can escape God's full comprehension of human thought, motive and act, nor escape responsibility for them when God stands in judgment. The fact that God stands strips away any excuse for making the secular misunderstanding of reality normative; indeed, the secular misunderstanding is unable to sustain any norms whatever. It is not the case that the "meaning of God" is dead for contemporary thought, any more than that God is himself dead, although secular theologians readily accommodated themselves—as did Paul van Buren in *The Secular Meaning of the Gospel* (pp. 102 ff.)—to existential and naturalistic prejudices about reality and human experience while attempting to salvage a case for values in lieu of God. The problem of contemporary society is not modern man's inability to know or to acknowledge God, nor his total lack of awareness and knowledge of him, but his unwillingness to acknowledge as sovereign the God who *stands* over all.

Skepticism concerning commitment to God by those outside the churches stems in part from the virtual obliteration of theistic claims from the public schoolroom, in part from the spiritual atrophy and intellectual softness of a generation preoccupied with material and secular concerns, and in part from uncritical tolerance of others' religious views that denies ultimate allegiance to any view. The truth is that material priorities have emptied rather than filled the lives of the affluent, and that naturalism is an unworkable philosophy even for its proponents. Numbers of people—most notably university students for whom God has become vital—are still finding spiritual reality at a time when life for others has turned sour. Contentious academic attacks on the truth of the Christian religion are now less common, and for good reason the case against theism has little persuasive intellectual power. There is no reason, however, why the data that commend the truth and power of God should be ignored.

God *stoops*—that too becomes a dramatic reality through his sovereign initiative and self-disclosure. *God who stands*—the eternal *I am*—condescends to create a finite universe inclusive of humans made in his rational and moral image to know, worship and serve him. He condescends to redeem a renegade humanity and a fallen cosmos. He condescends to make himself known and through inspired envoys to republish his holy purposes to man in revolt. He condescends to provide redemption for sinners through the incarnate Logos, the eternal Word become flesh. He condescends to go to the cross—to death on the cross—in holy covenantal love.

By his own incomparable way of stooping, God voluntarily forsakes his sovereign exclusivity; he condescends to fashion the planets and stars in their courses, the creatures in their diverse habitats and man in the likeness of his personal Maker. His stooping was not to something beneath his dignity, not to something degrading or unworthy (Rev. 4:11), but a stooping that manifested the outgoing righteousness and love of God who stands. In the heavens themselves he set the sun that canopying the earth as the center of his creative and redemptive plan rises and sets as a daily commentary on God's condescension; amid stars bending in their downward courses and descending into the night sky he planted the Southern Cross. In creation God stoops to fellowship with man who bears his image; as the Logos becomes flesh, God himself assumes man's nature, and as the sinless Substitute gives himself freely for the redemption of the lost. ". . . The Son of man came not to be ministered unto, but to minister, and to give his life a ransom for many" (Matt. 20:28). ". . . I lay down my life. . . . No man taketh it from me, but I lay it down of myself" (John 10:17–18a). Scripture declares that God stands, but nowhere states that he runs; the only intimation of running occurs in the parable of the prodigal son, where the Father hastens to embrace the returning penitent.

God reveals his nature not in intelligible propositions alone nor only in miraculous deeds; he reveals himself supremely in Jesus Christ, whose life and death and resurrection are cognitively and propositionally interpreted by the inspired Scriptures. God stoops to state his purposes in our language and thought-forms which he first fashioned that we might think his thoughts after him, commune with him and serve him. His stooping is a continuing disposition; after stooping to welcome the penitent prodigal home, he stoops to lift the devout believer ever closer to his own heart and toward the moral image of the crucified and risen Redeemer. God stands majestic and incomparable, yet he does not stand alone. In self-accommodation, he who stooped to freely fashion the world of celestial bodies and creatures stoops to speak to man and to act in his behalf, stoops to proffer and provide redemption, stoops to embrace the penitent to his bosom as an adopted son. There is in God's stooping nothing of the wickedness and deceit that so often characterize sinful man, who stoops to depravity and deception. God cannot be felled by us, or humiliated, but he can and does bring his adversaries to naught. The day will come when as the agent in final judgment he weighs human works and neglected opportunities for grace on the scale of divine righteousness. But as of today he still stoops to save, and heaven's glories remain accessible to those who repent. Man who has forfeited his standing by creation may still find new standing in Christ because the stooping God proffers grace to contrite sinners.

God *stays*—this we know also on the basis of the selfsame condescending self-revelation granted us by God who *stands* and *stoops*. Social critics may write of a runaway generation or of a runaway world, or of mankind on the run in a technocratic society, but God is no runaway God. Creation six "days" in the making is for him no hit-and-run affair; still preserving and governing it, he will eventually, perhaps soon, climax his sovereign purpose in the endtime vindication of righteousness and the doom of evil.

God is the supreme Stayer. He stays with his creation though man flaws it. He stays himself from destroying it when man falls in Eden. But as the Geneva Bible (1560) puts it, "None can stay his hand" (Dan. 4:35), a translation that survives even in some modern versions (RSV; cf. also David's word, "They came upon me in the day of my calamity; but the Lord was my stay," 2 Sam. 22:19, RSV). In writing about his first hearing before the Roman magistrate when "no man stood with me, but all men forsook me," Paul adds: "Notwithstanding the Lord stood with me, and strengthened me; that by me the preaching might be fully known, and that all the Gentiles might hear: and I was delivered out of the mouth of the lion" (2 Tim. 4:16 ff.).

God supports, steadies and sustains man and the world, preserving his scarred creation for a redemptive purpose. Those who speak of nature as unpatterned and of history as chaotic see the external world only in terms of man's rebellion and of the consequences of sin, for nature and history are both under God's ultimate jurisdiction. God remains and participates in his fallen universe by preserving and governing it, while he yet calls mankind to decision. Were it not for his staying power, man and the world would crumble into dust and disappear into nothingness. God stays with the fallen world and not only transcendently preserves it but also maintains a settled presence and activity in it. He preserves and limits the regularities of nature and determines the times and boundaries of nations (Acts 17:26). He remains the cosmic stay to the very end, holding out when all else gives way, keeping created realities in their fixed limits even while he decides both span of years and terminus of time. By staying the final judgment he shapes a season for repentance (Rom. 2:4); he lends a pause for mercy before God who stands deliberately brings human history to a halt. God who stands and stoops and stays will then finally vindicate eternal righteousness throughout the cosmic and creaturely world, and transform it into a new heavens and a new earth. Fallen man who overstays his opportunity for grace will find the righteous God staying to judge human presumption no less than human rebellion.

Even now, daily, hourly, moment by moment, God who stays makes not simply a "one-night stand" but a stand to the finish against evil. He does not stand aside to abandon or ignore the fallen world. He holds his ground against the enemy and his legions. Satan and unrighteousness he will bring to a halt; he will stand the devil on his head by fully vindicating right and dooming evil. Even now God arrests sin's power and redemptively reverses its inroads. Someday the righteous Lord will summon us into his presence and never will God stand taller than when the impenitent wicked stand trial and he acquits the penitent on the ground of Christ's substitutionary death alone, while he condemns the perverse who have spurned the proffer of redemption.

God will reign in full and final triumph when death is conquered and Christ the Victor restores all things to the Father's authority (1 Cor. 15:28); righteousness will once again prevail throughout the created sphere, and evil will meet its decisive doom. Only that which has its stay in God who *stands, stoops* and *stays* will abide, and abide forever.

These volumes have deliberately deployed everyday terms like *stands, stoops* and *stays, speaks* and *shows* as a bridge to contemplation of the doctrine of God. Many persons find the technical vocabulary of professional theologians forbiddingly abstruse. Others see in the use of Latin predications like the *aseity* of God a dogmatic desire to box God into ancient constructs. Even the mention of divine omnipotence raises the eyebrows of some atomic and nuclear experts, while in a technological age the theme of divine omniscience seems quite unimpressive to some computer specialists. We must nonetheless consider the theme of divine essence and attributes in depth, and in doing so cannot avoid using traditional language and concepts. That is all the more the case if we think about God in a way that interacts with the Bible—with its declarations about him in Hebrew, Aramaic and Greek—and with the influential views of past ecclesiastical interpreters as well as of contemporary scholars who range themselves for or against the evangelical heritage.

If technical terms must at times therefore unavoidably intrude into our treatment of the doctrine of God, then so be it. The modern sciences, after all, abound with technical language appropriate to each field of study, and the advanced learning centers are crammed with scholars whose mastery of complex data qualifies them for the space age. Why should intelligent Christians shun a specialized grasp of the content and implications of biblical learning, and insist on only a sidewalk discussion in one-syllable words? The term Zen may seem less complex than the name Yahweh, but even young people interested in religious rationalization of amorality need to grasp some of the technicalities of Mahayana Buddhism to confer an aura of intellectual respectability upon their misconduct. The Christian lifeview likewise cannot be divorced from the Christian revelation of God. The good news of salvation in Jesus Christ can be stated so simply that no elementary school child will miss its content and life-claim; the truth about the living God is so profound even in its simplicity, however, that no philosopher has any basis or reason for demeaning the Christian revelation as simplistic.

The doctrine of God is unquestionably the most important tenet for comprehending biblical religion. The Bible leaves in doubt neither the absolute uniqueness of the self-revealing God nor the specific features that comprise Yahweh's incomparability. It was primarily because Israel's self-manifesting God differed definitively from the gods named by the other ancient religions that the Hebrews knew revealed religion to be normative. To be sure, no biblical writer or book professes even on the basis of revelation to give a complete, systematically elaborated doctrine of God. This obtains not merely because their knowledge of God on the basis of special revelation was progressive, as indeed it was, and even less because the inspired writers held contradictory and divergent views of the living God, for they did not. It obtains, rather, because God who speaks and shows, the living God known by word and deed, disclosed himself in the moving midst of the dynamic history of his chosen people, and not in abstraction from their world fortunes. Yahweh made known his thoughts and purposes in grace and judgment in the history of a people who were proffered redemption in a wider world that universally spurned its sovereign Maker and Lord.

Neither the Old nor the New Testament gives us a systematic definition of God, but each contains many statements about God grounded in divine revelation. God sovereignly makes known his glory in every new manifestation of his personal presence and power. There is no extended argumentation that God is; rather, God declares himself in his works and words: "Who has performed and done this, calling the generations from the beginning? I, the Lord, the first, and with the last; I am He" (Isa. 41:4, RSV). "Thus says the Lord, the King of Israel and his Redeemer, the Lord of hosts: 'I am the first and I am the last; besides me there is no god' " (Isa. 44:6, RSV). "Hearken to me, O Jacob, and Israel, whom I called! I am He,

I am the first, and I am the last. My hand laid the foundation of the earth, and my right hand spread out the heavens; when I call to them, they stand forth together. Assemble, all of you, and hear! . . ." (Isa. 48:12 ff., RSV). Later passages often state in precise didactic form what is earlier implicit in God's self-manifestation, for example, that the personal living God (Ps. 36:10) is to be contrasted with human persons (Hos. 11:9); is Creator of all, transcendent above time and space, not to be pictorialized or localized (Ex. 20:4); is determiner of the destiny of nations who makes ancient Israel his special possession (Ex. 19:15 ff.); is everlasting King of Zion and of the world (Isa. 52:7, cf. 37:16); is the Holy One (Ps. 7:10; Isa. 40:25; Hab. 3:3) given also to grace and mercy (Ex. 34:6; Ps. 103:8; Isa. 54:8).

While the New Testament doctrine of God is deeply rooted in Old Testament revelation, it also stands in significant respects on its own independent ground in view of the supremacy of the revelation in Jesus Christ, the fuller gift of the Spirit, and the role of the inspired apostolic teaching. For the Bible as a whole, however, God is the infinitely perfect Spirit who freely reigns as Lord and Light and Love, and to whom all men and things owe their origin and continuance, and whose Messiah-borne mercy shapes the sinner's only ground of enduring peace and joy.

The world of our day has too much in common with the world of biblical times to think that God's revealed character and purpose gradually lose relevance. God is still addressing human spiritual revolt wherever and however it occurs. *God who speaks* and *shows* solicits an obedient faith amid modern civilization at bay; God who *stands, stoops* and *stays* remains our only transcendent hope and our only trustworthy support.

1.
The Reality
and Objectivity of God

THE SELF-REVEALED GOD IS the God who *is,* not a god who *may be,* or a god who *was,* or is yet *to be.* To affirm the living God in biblical perspective is to assert his eternal objective being: "He that cometh to God must believe that he is . . ." (Heb. 11:6).

That God stands, and stands forever, means that any suggestion of the fate of God, or the death of God, is an impudent slander; not God, but the universe, has contingent existence; not God, but man, is fallen; not God, but theology that speaks of the death of God, is due for interment. God objectively confronts man in an existence independent of the world. His reality is not suspended upon the existential decision of finite creatures; rather, he thrusts upon humans the inescapability of individual personal response to his claims upon them.

In expounding the doctrine of God recent neo-Protestant theology sacrificed this insistent scriptural emphasis on God's existence and objectivity. Both existentialism and positivism made the rejection of God's objective existence an imperative, but for different reasons. While existential theology repudiated God's objective existence on the assumption that man's encounter with spiritual reality is essentially *personal-subjective,* logical positivism did so by elevating *empirical verifiability* as the criterion of all meaningful theological affirmations and, to nobody's surprise, declared that God had failed the test.

To be sure, highly important differences distinguished logical positivist from existentialist interest in religious concerns. The logical positivist outlook is essentially antifaith, whereas the existentialist intention is often profaith. For the latter, God is real only in the decision of faith; for the former, the logical positivist, God is a nonsense syllable devoid of all meaning; only in the faith of the unenlightened is God real. Logical positivism presumes to reduce all claims for the objective existence of a supernatural deity to private mythologies or to psychological projection. Existential theology, on the other hand, develops a theory of the nonobjectivity and nonexistence of God, supposedly to promote the transcendent reality of God.

Both approaches despoil any rational case for theism by unjustifiably erasing all valid cognitive knowledge of God. Alongside their shared confidence in the nonexistence and nonobjectivity of God they focus theological discussion solely on the internal significance of religious faith. Existentialist theologians expound man's authentic existence in relation to God who becomes real in man's inner response; humanist philosophers emphasize the psychological vitality and integrating function of the God-idea in subjective experience; logical positivists consider the God-idea disintegrative. Existential theology views God as the Absolute Subject whose transcendent confrontation engenders new being for all who personally exercise faith; positivist theory allows the nonsense God-idea no subjective functional role in human experience. For different reasons and with different intentions, both outlooks abandon those rational supports for God's existence and objectivity through which evangelical Christian theology has historically maintained the reality, meaning, and significance of God. Instead, they affirm the nonexistence and nonobjectivity of God, and set the discussion of God contextually in a cognitive vacuum.

Dialectical-Existential Theology

Dialectical and existential expositions of religious knowledge deliberately rejected the subject-object schematization of knowledge affirmed by medieval theology and modern philosophy. A philosophical and theological revolt against subject-object distinctions was already underway in the mid-nineteenth century. Influenced by Kant, Ritschl in the late nineteenth century deprived theology of any objective knowledge of God-in-himself, and confined faith in God to value-judgments. In deference to Kant's notion that humans have no cognitive knowledge of things-in-themselves, he demeans knowledge of God-in-himself as an intrusion of Aristotelian or other speculative philosophy into scholastic and then into Protestant theology, and, in turn, of Greek and scholastic ideas into evangelical theology. Science, by contrast, was believed to provide constitutive knowledge of the external world; despite their oft-revised hypotheses, scientists were not disposed before the turn of the century to doubt that their formulas ontologically describe nature.

Søren Kierkegaard (1813–1855), in important respects the precursor of Karl Barth, understandably rejected the idealistic premise of man's direct identity with the Absolute Mind. Kierkegaard tried, commendably, to rescue the significance of the human self from Hegel's rationalistic submerging of the individual in the Absolute. But he tried to do this by substituting subjectivity for objective knowledge of the transcendent God, a proposal no less calamitous for evangelical faith than was Hegel's error. Kierkegaard asserted inner subjectivity as the sole way of grasping spiritual reality, and withstood the contention that all existence can be rationally comprehended. The transcendence of existing beings by each other, he held, implies an inner subjectivity impervious to objective thought. The transcendent eludes our conceptual categories; the God-man's mediation of the transcendent Kierkegaard held to be completely distinct from reason and experience. Existence is mediated only by direct confrontation and passionate inward response, by relations of faith, and not through any system of ideas or external observation.

It may be the case, as Thomas F. Torrance contends (*Theological Science*, p. 4), that Kierkegaard's championing of subjectivity was "never intended to mean the abrogation of objectivity." The Danish philosopher's immediate objective was doubtless to criticize the speculative metaphysics of Hegel, which rationalistically postulated and substituted the Absolute for the living God of the Bible. But Kierkegaard's alternative requires a highly vulnerable theory of faith as a leap in a cognitive vacuum. Personal decision is not for him a consequence of recognizing truth, but an essential element in recognizing it. Kierkegaard held that the object of theological knowledge is Truth in the form of personal, active Subject and that we can know this Truth only in a way appropriate to its nature as Subjectivity. This "way appropriate" turns out to be a nonpropositional person-trust devoid of any claim to universal validity and conditioned on individual decision.

World War I disturbed long-standing theories of meaning even as it overturned many long-accepted patterns of social life. The existential orientation of life marked a break with the subject-object modeling of experience; the whole development of modern existentialism, as Paul Tillich notes, sought to "cut under the subject-object distinction" (in *Theology of Culture*, p. 92). Tillich himself insisted: "Theology must always remember that in speaking of God it makes an object of that which precedes the subject-object structure and that, therefore, it must include in its speaking of God the acknowledgment that it cannot make God an object" (*Systematic Theology*, Vol. I, p. 191).

The subject-object distinction was at first conceded to be both proper and necessary in the physical sciences. But only in our knowledge of *things* was a sharp distinction of subject from object held to be valid. Elsewhere existentialists considered such distinction of subject and object to be philosophically outmoded and false: *I-thou* knowledge was held to be essentially different from *I-it* knowledge. They were not alone in pressing the distinction; Bertrand Russell, hardly a religious thinker, did not use the words "thou knowledge," but he distinguished "knowledge by acquaintance" and promoted two kinds of knowledge that recalled the "twofold truth" of medieval philosophers.

Nowhere, neoorthodox theologians contended, is the subject-object contrast more essential and indispensable than in the divine-human encounter. The aim of dialectical and existential theologians was, as we said, to reinforce the significance and worth of *personal-spiritual* existence in the context of modern *impersonal-scientific* interpretation which strives to encompass all reality within its explanation. The mathematical-quantitative explanation of reality stresses what is repeatable; the unique it considers an oddity that scientific uniformity will eventually engulf. The human self here gains significance only through universally verifiable features; individuality, personal decision and subjectivity are "off limits" scientifically. Yet if a person is as he "thinketh in his heart" (Prov. 23:7), then the inner decisions of the self somehow constitute or shape its nature. If individual response to invisible spiritual realities defines human destiny, then we must find the meaning and worth of the human person in a realm of *I-thou* personal relationships irreducible to *I-it* impersonal relationships. To prevent man's personal significance from being swallowed up in impersonal objectivity—a wholly legitimate and necessarily Christian concern—modern theologians propounded their dialectical and existential theories. Later we will see why the effort of both dialectical and existential theology, while aiming to correlate the human self and the reality of God, was not only self-defeating but a costly liability to twentieth-century Christianity. But first we shall note how their rejection of the existence and objectivity of God—ventured, as they saw it, in order to promote God's reality in correlation with the significance of the human self—involved the downgrading and dismissal of knowledge "about God."

Dialectical and existential theologies emphasized that God is always the Subject who confronts us, and therefore is never the object of faith. Although he moderated his position somewhat in later works, Barth insistently maintained this emphasis in his earliest writings. Emil Brunner and other dialectical theologians shared the view as did Rudolf Bultmann and other existentialist theologians. The deobjectivizing of God became their major theological concern long before dialectical and existential tenets attained maximal influence in Europe. The fact that God is not an impersonal object, but is personal Subject, they turned into a necessary contrast between objective knowledge and personal knowledge. Martin Buber contended that person-to-person relationship with God precludes speaking *about* God (*I and Thou*, pp. 33 ff.). Bultmann took the same tack: "If by speaking 'of God' one understands *to talk 'about God,'* then such style of speaking has no sense at all" ("What Sense Is There to Speak of God?", p. 213). Speech about God, Gustaf Aulén held, can be regarded as objectifying only when we deal with the history of doctrine about God (*The Faith of the Christian Church*, p. 3).

Over against the traditional subject-object schematization of knowledge, existential philosophy insisted that the experient's own decision must from the outset be included in the knowledge-situation. Existentialists assigned such high priority to human decision and interpretation (Bultmann's term was "life-relation") in expounding personal reality, that they superimposed the existential conceptuality even upon the Bible. Thus they obscured the objective existence of the God of the Bible. God was said to be grasped only in immediate internal decision in an act of faith or new self-understanding. Affirming the nonexistence and nonobjectivity of God became the necessary prerequisite for that existential faith-decision by which the reality of God was declared to be exclusively knowable.

To be sure, the idea of a presuppositionless observer is fictional; no observer is ever totally free of presuppositions. But the necessary inclusion of the interpreter in the knowledge-situation, as existentialism saw it, requires an abrogation of the distance between the knower and the known. The exclusion of the self's personal decisions in establishing the nature of the object, the distinction of subject and object, the striving after objectivity, are all rejected so that reality may instead be experienced in its inner confrontation of the subject related directly to individual response.

The final result of theology of this kind was very different from what its exponents actually intended. By concentrating on divine subjectivity, they unwittingly forfeited the reality of God along with their deliberate surrender of God's objective existence. More radical disciples began to "demythologize" the transcendent reality of God, reducing God to an aspect of intrapersonal human relationships. Bultmann strove inconsistently to salvage "objectivity" for God's act over and above his existential reduction of theology to human self-understanding. "If speaking about God's act is to be meaningful," said Bultmann, "it must indeed be not simply a figurative or 'symbolic' kind of speaking, but must rather intend a divine act in the fully real and 'objective' sense" (*Kerygma and Myth,* Vol. 2, p. 96). We must remember, nonetheless, that the existential "transcending" of the subject-object distinction inevitably confers whatever absoluteness the religious reality has through the decision of the interpreter. According to Jean-Paul Sartre, Christian existentialists like Gabriel Marcel share with atheists like Heidegger and himself the insistence that "existence precedes essence, or, if you prefer, that subjectivity must be the starting point" (*Existentialism and Human Emotions,* p. 13). But, as John Warwick Montgomery pointedly remarks, "'transcending the subject-object barrier'. . . inevitably produces, not an experience with higher reality, but a falling back into subjectivism" (*Where Is History Going?,* p. 191).

When one thus obscures the distinction between the decisions of one's own psyche and any objective reality outside one's self, subjective psychologism readily takes over. The case for the reality of God, if one rests it simply on my "being claimed" and my "self-understanding," quickly falls upon hard times as rival explanations account for "the transcendent reality of 'God'" by subjective postulation and not in terms of external factuality at all. Herbert Braun, for example, connected the transcendent internal "address" simply with the moral tension of the "I ought" of conscience and the "I may" of radical faith; a social relationship between man and his neighbors then replaces the relation between man and God. Paul van Buren, once aligned with "death of God" theologians, dismissed Bultmann's emphasis on the transcendent reality of God as a vestigial remnant of supernatural theism whose logical supports existentialism had presumably eroded. Existential theology led beyond the denial of the objective existence of God to the unwitting loss of his reality as well.

But the rejection of the subject-object distinction in interpersonal knowledge relationships ran into increasing philosophical counterattack upon dialectical-existential positions. Schubert M. Ogden pointedly identified the declaration that objectifying thought and speech about God are excluded as either an empty assertion or as itself an instance of such objectifying thought. "It is one thing to acknowledge God existentially as eminent Subject or Thou, but it is quite another to lay down the general principle that only by thus acknowledging him can one know him concretely as God" (*The Reality of God,* p. 83). Ogden is right in principle when he contends that "there is as much reason for God to be the object of the objectifying thinking and speaking of theology as for him to be the eminent Subject whom I can know as *my* God here and now only in my existential understanding of faith" (*ibid.,* p. 83).

Charles Hartshorne likewise rejected the theory of the nonobjectivity of the divine Subject. It assumes, he declares, that God must be regarded as wholly subject on the erroneous premise that divine simplicity precludes any ability on our part to discriminate distinct facets of divine being (*The Logic of Perfection and Other Essays in Neoclassical Metaphysics,* pp. 3 ff.). Contrary to Tillich's claim that the denial of God's existence protects the radically exceptional reality of Being-itself, Hartshorne notes that "there is as much reason to keep the word 'existence' as the word 'being' which he (Tillich) employs" ("What Did Anselm Discover?", p. 325, n. 2).

The whole biblical relationship of belief to objective reality and factuality was improperly inverted by existential philosophers. Existentialists distorted the requirements of biblical thought by their emphasis that the objective existence of God is antithetical to Christian experience and abrogates the need for personal decision. What existentialism demeans in the traditional view as a kind of objectionable "striving for security" actually involves a correlation of personal trust with indispensable cognitive elements. The evangelical call to decision presupposes the external objective reality of the self-revealed God whose disclosure is not merely a matter of immediate punctiliar confrontation enlisting naked faith. Rather, the God of the Bible discloses himself and his purpose objectively in world history and also in the sequence of special redemptive acts climaxed by the life and work of Jesus of Nazareth; he universally addresses mankind through human reason and conscience and especially in the prophetic-apostolic Scriptures. Oscar Cullmann insists, and rightly, that the distinction between the objective on the one hand and personal faith and decision on the other is not rooted, as many neo-Protestant theologians contend, in "an 'unconscious,' antiquated philosophy" that separates object and subject and that existentialist and other theologians influenced by Heidegger have outdated, but rather "is the plain and simple New Testament concept of faith as it is developed especially clearly in Paul. *The act of faith itself requires this distinction,*" emphasizes Cullmann, if we are to understand faith in the true biblical sense (*Salvation in History,* p. 321).

No one could have spoken more pointedly and prophetically than did Leonhard Stählin in the last century when he warned that the denial of objective knowledge in religious faith by Kant and Ritschl turns religious truth into mere subjective valuation. Whoever expounds the Christian view of God in a cognitive vacuum forfeits the knowledge credentials of evangelical faith. "Christian faith," Stählin emphasizes, "involves a theoretical element, *notitia:* without that, in fact, it would not actually exist. It rests on, or contains within itself, the conviction that its object exists really, objectively. . . . Were the certain assurance of the objective reality of that to which faith is directed to vanish, faith itself would vanish with it. . . . To oppose religion to theoretical knowledge, in other words, to the knowledge of objective realities, leads accordingly to the destruction of religious faith, by robbing it of the objective truth which is its very life" (*Kant, Lotze and Ritschl: A Critical Examination,* pp. 266 ff.). However much Hegel erred in resolving religion into philosophy, he saw more clearly than Kant that meaningful religion must stand in positive relationships to theoretical truth. Ritschl's theology already incorporates the emphasis that God is not known in his self-existence. In deference to Lotze's theory that things are known in phenomena, however, Ritschl stressed that God is disclosed in his effects, but even this knowledge, he held, is practical and moral rather than theoretical. Faith knows God not as "self-existent," but in his active relation to the Kingdom; knowledge of God is correlated with human trust (cf. *Theologie und Metaphysik,* pp. 8 ff). Although diverging in many directions, Ritschl's followers retain his insistence on the practical nature of faith-knowledge as opposed to metaphysical-knowledge of God.

The biblical emphases that "in the beginning God created the heaven and the earth" (Gen. 1:1) and that "he that cometh to God must believe that he is, and that he is a rewarder of them that diligently seek him" (Heb. 11:6) invert the existentialist demand for transcending "the subject-object schema," for these emphases clearly indicate that authentic faith has God's external, objective existence as its presupposition. That man is "addressed" in his own existence requires first and foremost not that his decision shall creatively shape or contribute to the nature of reality but that he must listen. Indispensable as personal commitment is, man is not excused from striving for objectivity. His commitment may be little more than self-assertion or self-delusion if its decisive ingredient is the self's inner response. Either man's faith takes place in a context involving what is truly and objectively the case or all talk of religious reality and knowledge capsizes into subjective confusion.

The reality of God therefore rests upon the logical precondition and revelational factuality of his existence, an existence not dependent upon my personal perception of him. William Hordern rightly insists: "There is a legitimate way to speak 'objectively' of God. . . . When John says that 'God is love' (1 John 4:16), he is, in the normal meaning of the words, 'speaking about God' " (*Speaking of God,* pp. 156 ff.). The Psalmist writes concerning God: "If I make my bed in hell, behold, thou art there" (Ps. 139:8). Yet if one would anywhere volitionally rule out God and prefer to believe in his nonreality it would be in Hades. The objective existence of God is in truth integrally fundamental to the religion of the Bible. Whatever philosophical considerations may motivate those who insist upon the nonobjectivity and nonexistence of God, to deny God's objective existence is to contradict a basic premise of revelational religion. As James Moffatt commented on the epistle to the Hebrews almost a half century ago: "Belief in the existence of God is (for the author of Hebrews) one of the elementary principles of the Christian religion" (*The International Critical Commentary: Hebrews,* on Heb. 11:6). In his aptly titled book *The God Who Is There,* Francis Schaeffer observes that "we are surrounded by a generation that can find 'no one home' in the universe," whereas the Christian knows "the personal God who is there" (*The God Who Is There,* p. 157). Against the new theology's denial "that God is there in the historical biblical sense" (*ibid.,* p. 145), he insists that "Christian faith turns on the reality of God's existence, His being there" (*ibid.,* p. 133).

In short, the living God is objectively existent; he is the God who stands, the eternal "I Am" (Exod. 6:6). Jesus identified the "I Am" as "the God of Abraham, and the God of Isaac, and the God of Jacob. . . . the God . . . of the living" (Matt. 22:32), not simply as God encountered individually and internally only in existential response.

In earlier generations those who assigned God less objective existence than even a grain of sand were acknowledged atheists. More recently, a cadre of neo-Protestant theologians have insisted that the denial of God's objective existence is the only way to preserve his reality. Neoorthodox theologians held that God as a reality encounters man only on the occasion of personal spiritual response or decision in a cognitive vacuum that implies God's nonobjectivity and nonexistence. But their misguided emphasis on the supposed cognitive vacuity of religious experience played into the hands of logical positivists who not only rejected the objectivity and existence of God, but stressed the meaninglessness of religious sentences as well. No less than dialectical and existential theologians, logical positivists contended that theology is nonobjectifying. They did so, however, for very different reasons. Because theological assertions differed in content from empirically verifiable statements, assertions about God were declared nonscientific non-sense affirmations that lack any and all meaning. Logical positivism stressed the nontruth character of God-talk rather than its "person-truth." Dialectical and existential theologians emphasized the noncognitive decision-oriented nature of theological claims; accordingly they exempted faith-affirmations from any need for rational justification. Exploiting this dialectical-existential correlation of divine revelation with inner decision independent of universally shared truth, logical positivists took the next step: they affirmed the merely private or subjective significance of religious assertions.

If Kantian thought in some respects shaped dialectical and existential perspectives, Kant's critical philosophy also made itself felt in much of the debate that issued in logical positivism. Kant's theory of knowledge vexed Western thought with questions about the concept of existence. On the one hand, Kant tried to vindicate the objectivity of human knowledge over against Humean skepticism. What gives objective validity to our knowledge of things, argued Kant, is the nature of the human mind itself: man's cognitive faculty supplies a priori categories or forms through which our otherwise chaotic sense impressions are transformed into universally valid knowledge. On Kant's theory, causality and substantiality are among these innate forms.

But if this is the case, then it becomes difficult to see—as Kant at times would have us believe—that things-in-themselves existing independently of our knowledge are the *cause* of our sense impressions, or even that they objectively exist. Kant theorizes that the human mind contributes causality and substantiality to our knowledge experience. The innate elements that constitute knowledge cannot be made an object of independent investigation, for knowledge is a combination of the categories with sensation. We are told that concepts without perceptions are empty while perceptions without concepts are blind. The critical philosophy, therefore, answers Humean skepticism with its epistemology that precludes objective truth about the thing-in-itself. The phenomenal gains universal validity and objectivity only by being subsumed under the necessary forms of human thought. There is no objective knowledge of any reality outside of and independent of human consciousness, no knowledge of the nature of objects considered in themselves. What we know we know only under the conditions of (the innate forms of) time and space, and only as structured by *a priori* categories supplied by the human knower. What the human mind knows, says Kant, gains its universal validity and necessity from the circumstance that all human reason is universally structured in the same way, that is, by a transcendent ego or schema of knowledge.

Statements which affirm independent existence, such as that the world *is,* must therefore leave in doubt the metaphysical reality of the subject; for Kant, the thing-in-itself can never become an object of experience. Since he restricts all real knowledge to sense experience, and presupposes the constitutive activity of the human mind, no way remains to know that the thing-in-itself exists independently and objectively. The existence of external things is always an inference from inner perception, and this inner perception presumably is effected by an outer cause. Yet Kant considers cause itself to be an innate form of knowing. Consequently, the source of our impressions can hardly be located in external causation.

In the second edition of the *Critique* Kant supported the idea that phenomena are more than mere ideas and representations. "The simple but empirically determined consciousness of my own existence," he wrote, "proves the existence of objects in space outside of me"; moreover, determinations of my existence in time are possible only on "the supposition of the existence of actual things which I perceive outside of myself." If space and time are forms of perceiving, and exist only in the mind itself, then Kant here seems deliberately to compromise his theory or momentarily to abandon it. Yet by things "outside of me" Kant probably refers to things outside the body, but not outside the mind; the things outside my body are the objects of science. Nonetheless, as Stählin points out, on Kant's

premises "a conclusion from inner perception and phenomenon to the existence of the thing-in-itself is not merely, as Kant concedes, uncertain and
doubtful, but *unjustifiable*, yea, *impossible*" (*Kant, Lotze and Ritschl*, p. 25).

While Kant asserts the objective existence of things and distinguishes
them from subjective impressions in view of the necessary connection that
prevails among objects of experience, his theory of knowledge wholly disallows the objective existence of God. While Kant holds that the idea of
God is a necessary conception of reason, he rules out any conclusion that
God actually exists as an external metaphysical reality. Knowledge is assertedly a joint product of the innate categories and sense experience; our
knowledge is therefore subject to laws that prevent our knowing anything
beyond sensations. Since no object congruous to the idea of God can be
presented to the senses, no rational basis remains for asserting God's objective existence. Not even the universality and necessity of the idea of God
establishes a rational basis for inferring his actuality.

Kant cannot concede the existence of things-in-themselves, because he
restricts our knowledge to our mode or way of representing things; we
know nothing outside of this mode, not even that sensations are *caused*
by noumena. Not only is cause a Kantian thought category; reality and
existence likewise are innate categories and therefore must not be extended
to the noumenal or thing-in-itself. For Kant, then, the thing-in-itself or
noumenal is only a limiting concept of negative significance. If inference
to the noumenal were possible, then not only knowledge of its bare existence but of its nature and constitution also would be possible. "To maintain
that the categories are the necessary forms of the thinking function of
the understanding would be absurd, if one were at the same time to represent the understanding as not bound to these forms. On the contrary,"
says Stählin in his assessment of Kant, "it is as incapable of temporarily
discarding the necessary forms of thought, for the purpose of undertaking
an act of thought beyond the limits imposed by its own nature, as the
senses are incapable of intuiting anything apart or aside from the forms
of intuition, namely, space and time. . . . The Kantian criticism thus necessarily involves the abolition of the thing-in-itself . . ." (*ibid.*, p. 275).

It is at this point that European philosophy made the transition from
the thing-in-itself to the nonego, and from the transcendental schema to
absolute idealism. Over against the idealistic option formulated by Hegel,
Kierkegaard and the existentialists tried to rescue significance for the individual self by asserting the subjectivity of knowledge of other selves. The
logical positivists, on the other hand, built on Kant's insistence that the
content of valid knowledge comes from sense experience alone and that
God is but a regulative idea or subjective postulate. Bertrand Russell and
G. E. Moore, for example, each reflected in his own way Kant's emphasis
that there is no road from essence to existence, from concept to reality.
No way is open, presumably, to turn existence into a predicate or attribute;
truths of reason are separated by a great gulf from truths of facts. No
a priori reasoning can establish the nature of what *is*. Empirical verification alone, positivists said, can validate as meaningful (i.e. either true or
false) any statement about metaphysical entities.

Only affirmations which are in principle open to falsification by scientific empiricism were considered to be meaningful assertions; except for logical or mathematical tautologies, all assertions not empirically verifiable are held to be meaningless "non-sense" statements. Consequently, only propositions that belong to the natural sciences picture the real world truly; only what is scientifically confirmable can be true. Aside from the merely tautological propositions of formal logic and mathematics (which convey no knowledge of how things are), the only knowledge we have, so it was asserted, comes from external percepts refined by the methodology of science. Since meaningful statements require falsifiability by external perception, the positivist denies in advance that theological claims can be true. Logical positivists, in short, stressed the *non-meaningful* character rather than the *person-truth* nature of theological claims concerning an object whose nature as immaterial and invisible Spirit falls necessarily outside the competence of scientific methodology. Since assertions about God cannot be tested by the prescribed empirical methodology, they are discussed as linguistic expressions whose meaning must be cognitively vacuous.

While the positivist effort to discredit metaphysics is now generally conceded to have failed, on many university campuses in Europe and America it registered for half a generation an influence erosive of interest in ontological concerns. Some theologians tried to protect the objectivity of theological assertions by insisting that theology is a form of science whose statements are in principle empirically falsifiable in view of their "eschatological" or end-time verifiability. John Hick and I. M. Crombie stressed that religious beliefs can finally be verified in man's postmortem life. William T. Blackstone comments that such future verification could not assure the cognitive status of present religious claims, and in fact rests on the disputed assumption that there is an afterlife (*The Problem of Religious Knowledge*, pp. 16, 122 ff.). The decisive objection to the emphasis that theological claims are "eschatologically" verifiable by scientific requirements is, as Schubert Ogden notes, that it views statements about God's being and nature as somehow "an actual or potential object of our ordinary sense perception" (*The Reality of God*, p. 76). No less disconcerting is its needless forfeiture of rational supports for the case for theism in the present time when all humans desperately need to know the truth about God.

Swayed by positivist dogma concerning the nonconceptual status of theology, some writers tried to validate religion in functional or psychological terms. R. G. Braithwaite, for example, asserted that religious statements have no specific intellectual content but express personal "adherence to a policy of action"; in other words, they reflect an orientation of will. They express the asserter's "intention to follow a specified policy of behaviour. . . . A Christian's assertion that God is love" should be understood, Braithwaite contends, as a declaration of "his intention to follow an agapeistic way of life" (*An Empiricist's View of the Nature of Religious Belief*, pp. 13 ff.). R. M. Hare held that theological affirmations express no cognitive truth about objective reality and involve no rational explanation of things as they really are; instead, they reflect an inner attitude or "blik" toward the world (*New Essays in Philosophical Theology*, p. 101). Paul van Buren

likewise contended that the Christian message ventures no cognitive statements about God; instead, it expresses toward life a "historical perspective"
or human posture that is subject to empirical verification or falsification.

While on the surface positivist theory aimed only to promote a legitimate
validation of knowledge-claims, its underlying bias discredited as cognitively irrelevant all theological statements about supraempirical reality.
Positivism contended that it is as meaningless to say that God is infinite
as to say that he is finite; as meaningless to say he is immutable as to
say he is changing; as meaningless to say simply that he is as to say he
is Spirit. But its erosion of historic Christianity's assertions about the objective character of divine reality had no solid basis. Christians themselves
insist that the distinctive theological claims simply do not lend themselves
to such empirical falsification or verification, and that they cannot and
must not be restated in language identical with that of the physical sciences. Positivists superficially oversimplified the realm of truth and meaning. They themselves were unable to agree on their verification principle.
Ogden aptly notes that most theologians repudiate positions that require
man in his need for truth to live "by the bread of science alone. . . . They
have resisted the pretensions of a narrow positivism, in the conviction
that 'true' and 'false', as we actually use the words, have legitimate applica-
tions beyond the limits prescribed" by the champions of ordinary sense
perception (*The Reality of God,* p. 109). But their tenets not only shrank
the criteria of truth in a way that cancels in advance the reality of a transcendent God; they thwarted the possibility of doing science as well.

Against positivist dogma a vigorous counterattack was mounted on two
fronts: first, criticism of its arbitrary and restrictive knowledge-theory, and
second, demands that affirmations of the reality of God be tested by a methodology actually appropriate to theological truth-claims. Many analytic
philosophers joined Stephen Toulmin's protest (*An Examination of the
Place of Reason in Ethics*) against the positivists' imperious narrowing
of reason and meaning. Truth must indeed be one, and must be universally
valid, but it need not be established—nor can it—by applying to all of reality
a methodology that is relevant to only certain elements of that whole. Truth
is validated or invalidated only by criteria of credibility appropriate to
its particular object.

The early positivist demand that cognitive meaning be withheld from
statements incapable of empirical falsification boomeranged. Positivists
were themselves insisting on the intelligibility of many assertions that
violated this very criterion. No influential philosopher today holds this
indefensible view. Even A. J. Ayer, England's leading champion of "Vienna
Circle" notions, modified his own early positions.

Disengagement from the verifiability theory was provoked by its consequences, its ambiguity, and its self-destructive nature. If the theory
"proved" anything about metaphysics, it "proved" far too much to please
its own advocates: the demand for sense-verifiability, if valid, reduced to
unintelligible nonsense not only assertions about God and the supernatural,
but also affirmations about justice and love and human rights, statements

about psychological referents such as the self, memory experiences and the will, references to past historical events, and even to the so-called laws of empirical science.

How can we equate verifiability and meaning, critics asked, since we investigate the meaning of *words* but verify *propositions* as true or false?

No less vexing was the growing confusion over the theory itself. To the positivist complaint that metaphysicians talk nonsense, Wittgenstein early added the further contention that they also misunderstand the logic of language; Ayer compounded logical positivism with philosophical analysis. In later years Wittgenstein discarded the analytic theory of meaning and Ayer finally shifted the basis of his repudiation of metaphysics from logical impossibility to empirical skepticism.

But more embarrassing still was the self-refuting character of the verifiability-theory. Its test of meaning discredited the theory itself as nonsense since it is neither tautological nor empirically verifiable. Any theory of knowledge or of reality that cannot get underway without begging the question is suspect; the validity of conclusions can only be commensurate with the logical adequacy of the foundations on which those conclusions finally rest. Denial of any basis of truth and meaning to all nonempirical claims invalidated the positivistic theory itself by positivistic criteria.

To require that an assertion about God the divine Spirit be empirically falsifiable (or formally analytic) was to force upon that assertion an inappropriate canon of verification. Spiritual realities are neither empirically falsifiable nor verifiable. Hegel said (specifically of Kant): "Who could ever have imagined that philosophy would deny reality and truth to the *intelligibilia*, simply because they are destitute of the temporally and spiritually determined matter of sense?" (*The Science of Logic,* Vol. II, p. 21). To insist on empirically establishing propositions in formal logic and mathematics would be less arbitrary than to insist, as a condition of cognitive significance, that supra-empirical realities be empirically falsifiable. Counterfeit reasons for unbelief sooner or later are summoned to court. No view of reality can satisfy the demands either of reason or of experience if, on the basis of prejudiced criteria, it prelabels assertions about God's being and nature as cognitively vacuous. The bold attempt of logical positivism to discredit Christian supernaturalism on the basis of empirical verifiability-theory abruptly thrust aside as futile and useless the centuries-long debate over God's reality and nature, whether carried on between the great world religions, by divergent schools of philosophy, or by the theology of revelation.

The unfavorable contrast that credits scientific statements as objectifying and discredits theological statements as nonobjectifying and nonsensical is prejudiced on both counts. The claim that science deals with impersonal things does not in and of itself prove that scientific statements define objective reality. Science copes only with what is sensorily perceived and not directly with objective structure. In the physical sciences, objectivity or nonobjectivity turns upon supra-perceptual considerations, no less than does the determination of whether theological assertions are nonobjectifying. To insist, therefore, that metaphysical claims are necessarily nonobjectifying would at the same time disqualify all scientific statements that presume to characterize objectively real structures. Theological thought does indeed differ in method, and theological language in content, from the methodology and terminology of modern science. But that fact in no way establishes theological reflection as inherently nonobjectifying. Ogden insists and rightly that "Theology is in its own way scientific; . . . its statements in their most proper part are assertions about God and his action; and . . . the justification of these assertions, so far as they are rationally justifiable at all, can only be a metaphysical justification" (*The Reality of God,* p. 98).

Nor does the evident fact of disagreement among theologians finally decide what is cognitively true, any more than does disagreement among scientists. Theological speculation and reflection, like scientific reflection, is not to be credited or discredited simply according to current philosophical fashions; the evidence is indispensable, and the test of logical consistency wholly appropriate. Among empirical scientists the main expectation of scientific progress depends upon continuing revision of their theories. Consequently they hesitate to impose absolute claims upon empirical limitations, and avoid the prideful arrogance of naturalistic theorists who would illicitly attach the prestige of empirical methodology to antisupernaturalist dogma.

The whole weight of historic Christianity opposes the recent concessions by many theologians to existential or positivist theories that approve of the noncognitive character of religious claims. There is no sound basis for positivist pretensions that would limit meaningful assertions to mathematics and the empirical sciences. Yet the widening withdrawal of philosophers from positivist commitments has not issued in any new wave of metaphysical theory or philosophical theology. Marxists and neo-Thomists energetically affirm rival descriptions of the metaphysical reality, and some neo-Christians have revived process theology as an alternative. Many scholars probe the epistemological possibility of metaphysical assertions only formally. The distinction between philosophy as theory and philosophy as activity or critical analysis is, however, now acknowledged to be arbitrary, inasmuch as anyone who declares the role of philosophy to be the clarifying of linguistic meaning acts on a philosophical theory. In an essay on "The Metamorphosis of Metaphysics," John Wisdom, while asserting the value of metaphysics as both illuminating and misleading, continues to reject its role in superempirical description (*Paradox and Discovery,* 1965).

This strategic situation disengages philosophy and theology from their longstanding interest in the existence and reality of God. Instead of emboldening the positivist disavowal of all metaphysical assertions as nonsense, the exasperating contradictions of modern philosophers and theologians ought to have encouraged a new probing of divine revelation and of metaphysical affirmation based on an adequate theory of religious knowledge. Neo-Protestant theology had regrettably forfeited the possibility of this alternate option by its devastating anti-intellectual compromises of historic Christian theology.

Modern theology has gone into costly debt to secular philosophy. The carrying charge has been the loss of special divine revelation as a rational category involving valid truth about the living God. Theology followed modern rationalism in assimilating Christianity to speculative theism, which first diluted the principle of special revelation into general revelation and then finally surrendered both to human insight. This trend, which got underway with Aquinas's deferment of an appeal to revelation, was stimulated by Descartes, and found its boldest expression in Hegelian idealism in which man participates directly and immediately in the divine mind. Hume and Kant had set severe limits to the metaphysical competence of human reason by radically removing God from rational knowability. Kant's epistemology excludes any possibility of divine revelation either in external phenomena or in internal experience. Dialectical and existential restatements of Christianity failed to overcome Kant's radical break with intelligible divine revelation. Despite their efforts to promote faith, recent modern theologians could therefore offer a choice only between two unrewarding alternatives: either *metaphysical affirmation* on the basis of rationalistic speculation, or *metaphysical agnosticism* on the premise of noncognitive revelation.

Behind the loss of intelligible, objective divine revelation lay the growing Continental insistence on the subjectivity of God. Supposedly Christian theologians, declaring that God's reality is to be known only in personal confrontation and nonconceptual decision, repudiated objective knowledge of the God of the Bible. How much of this twentieth-century development was indirectly encouraged by Ritschl whose theology reigned during the last quarter of the nineteenth century is often overlooked. Over against Kant's denial of all metaphysical knowledge, Ritschl honored Lotze's emphasis that God is revealed in his manifestations. At the same time, Ritschl insisted that we never know the thing-in-itself—a clear concession to Kant—but know the thing only in its effects. No doubt Ritschl intended to espouse knowledge of an objective God grounded in God's revelational activity, particularly in Jesus of Nazareth through whom we know God as Redeeming Father. But Ritschl's dichotomy of science (all truth and no value) versus religion (all value and no truth) undermined the revelational truths basic to evangelical orthodoxy.

His theory of religious truth (that revelation kindles not theoretical knowledge but personal value-judgments leading to obedience) correlates the revelation of God with our moral response and excludes universally valid cognitive knowledge of God in his objective existence. Thus Ritschlian theology prepared the way, in part at least, for the dialectical-existential emphasis that personal awareness of God's reality requires a rejection of his objective existence. Barth and Bultmann both correlate revelation with divine subjectivity and individual response. While God is said to disclose himself, revelation nevertheless is no longer a mental concept but is connected with obedience; God's divine disclosure of truths, that is, communication of valid information about himself and his will, is forfeited. Thus the response-oriented theology contended that the living God is revealed personally, not propositionally or intelligibly in universally shareable truths. All external disclosure of God in nature and history is rejected—all rational revelation also, even to the very prophets and apostles who profess to speak God's thoughts and words. The case for the living God was completely concentrated in direct personal confrontation and response, and the biblical witness was deployed in support of this confrontation.

What positivists were saying against philosophical statements about God's existence, transcendence and other divine qualities—presumably on the ground of verifiability-theory—the anticonceptual theologians were saying presumably on the ground of the intrinsic nature of divine revelation.

If the attachment of Christianity to speculative idealism encouraged logical positivists to impugn theology as imaginative nonsense, certainly the detachment of special revelation from valid universal truths offered no effective resistance to the secular derogation of metaphysics. Forfeiture of all objective, cognitive disclosure of transcendent and supernatural reality led on to the God-is-dead theology which proceeded to surrender God himself as a transcendent reality. Empirical verification by the scientific method was declared the decisive modern criterion of knowledge. The death-of-God movement in the United States gained impetus mainly among scholars conditioned by the anticonceptual kerygmatic theology of the Continent. Van Buren's dismissal of Christian confidence in revealed knowledge of the transcendent God prepared for his reduction of Christianity to an alternate "secular theology" (*The Secular Meaning of the Gospel*, pp. 199 f.). By invoking the test of empirical perception used by modern physical science, van Buren denuded supernatural theology; yet not even the most broadly stretched concept of empirical verification will validate the values of love and freedom that he definitively connects with Jesus and retains as the heart of the Gospel (*ibid.*, pp. 106, 171). While van Buren professes to justify a permanent role for the values he associates with the Nazarene, the Cambridge anthropologist Edmund Leach, in his 1967 Reith Lectures, wholly ignored Jesus and urged contemporary scientists themselves to "play God" (*A Runaway World?*).

That neo-Protestant theology strenuously insisted on God's reality must not mislead us, however, since "reality" is capable of multiple meanings. Humanists and logical positivists speak not of God's ontological reality but of the functional significance of the God-idea. Nowhere does the Bible separate the reality of God from his intelligible self-revelation, from his action in the external world, from the factual truth of his objective existence. While the biblical writers insist that God for us is appropriated only by faith they insist just as firmly that God objectively exists and acts outside ourselves. Throughout Scripture God is declared to exist in and for himself, irrespective of man's subjective decisions. Modern existential assertions about God, however, were predicated on an explicit rejection of such divine objectivity and existence, and of valid cognitive information about the supernatural world.

Neo-Protestant theology had tried to reinforce the meaning and worth of spiritual-personal reality despite the scientific-technological context of contemporary Western civilization. Our vastly expanded scientific insights, expressed in quantitative mathematical formulas, dwarf man as an individual to a speck of dust in the immense galaxies, a frail reed amid the powerful forces of the cosmos. Existential theology championed man's personal significance by emphasizing his private subjective life in the midst of the objective reality of the world. Although nature was routinely reducible to formulas of predictable, controllable behavior, man, it stressed, could not be assimilated to this world-process. Asserting his will over against nature, he finds distinctive transcendent selfhood. I-Thou knowledge is not reducible to I-it knowledge, said existentialists. I-Thou knowledge is truth of a different order, personal and subjective. The subjectivity of God, it was said, can be known only in personal response or inner decision. As the reality of God was located outside the realms of objective existence and universal reason, so also was reality of the individual man; in his faith-decision man transcends the impersonal world of scientific objects, so readily known in mathematical routines, and finds his own authentic existence in responsive trust alone apart from cognitive knowledge.

In thus separating faith from rational validity and objective reality, and centering it instead in inner existential decision, neo-Protestant theology lost the reality of both God and man in subjectivity, and risked entirely the loss of shared meaning. Both atheistic existentialism and logical positivism, and, in turn, death-of-God theology, disparaged the transcendent God as a phantom that even recent theologians declared void of objective existence, and of which they disclaimed cognitive knowledge. Existential theology thus proved self-destructive. If the event involved in the process of revelation is not an objective reality, can it be other than simply a change in man's subjective consciousness? What reality has God if his objective existence serves only as a threat to faith? What reality has man if his authentic existence or new being requires trust drained of valid knowledge?

Some counter-theory is necessary if we are to avoid an unwitting personal nihilism and the loss of the meaningful existence and reality both of God who succumbs under a thousand qualifications and of the human self. Such a counter-theory can point in either of two directions. One is evangelical theism with its emphasis on the objective reality of God and of the world as his creation. The other is radically secular theology which deplores the withdrawal of man from objective existence as the requisite of spiritual decision and affirms that only the reality of the world must be restored to faith as an objective concern. To rescue contemporary man from nihilist consequences of a subjectivized religious reality, radical secular theology emphasizes the reality of the world as an object of faith, and focuses human decision and action upon the cosmos and history.

The concentration of dialectical-existential theology on inner divine revelation had led to a divorcement of the world and the social order from God-response. Karl Barth launched kingdom-concerns into the stratosphere of superhistory; Rudolf Bultmann, on the other hand, located revelation wholly in the essentiality of the individual and expounded the meaning of existence not in relation to the world but over against it. Only in the punctiliar moment of response to vertical revelation, in a wholly private internal divine encountering of the isolated individual, is revelation a reality. Authentic self-understanding arises in segregation from the world, history and society.

In opposition to this unhistorical and individualistic emphasis, critically radical theology stresses the objective reality of the world. Man's bodily concerns no less than his spiritual response are related to the spheres of creation and redemption. Humans live in a social order, and their world of decision includes not only internal private historicity but also the panorama of events that requires a response at social frontiers. The objectively real world makes pressing claims upon human decision. But radical theology lifts these cosmic-historical concerns to priority, perpetuates a cognitive vacuum in respect to divine being, and leaves in doubt the objective existence of the transcendent supernatural. Only in the service of this world is man said to serve God, only in loving his neighbor is he said to love God. God speaks, we are told, not in the inner arena of isolated subjective response; he speaks today in the external world—in revolution, in demonstrations and riots, in the picket lines and wherever else the status quo is challenged and a new earth is in the making. Authentic existence is to be found only in bold social involvement and the forced changing of the inherited structures.

The irrelevance of the reality of God to social renewal was bluntly affirmed by Leon Watts, area program counselor for the New York City presbytery of the United Presbyterian Church. In *Renewal* magazine, of which he was associate editor, Watts asserts as a "somewhat tenuous proposition . . . that the existence or the nonexistence of God, belief or nonbelief in God, are not crucial and critical to our times" (September-October, 1969, issue, p. 13). In this view, he adds, "that the existence or the nonexistence of God is immaterial and irrelevant, those who center their energies upon defining the existence are just as irrelevant as those who seek to deny the existence of God. It just does not matter. This assumption . . . places reconciliation in a revolutionary context" (p. 16). Watts thus detaches the problem of human reconciliation from the reality of God, gives reconciliation a wholly secular and sociological sense, and commends a revolutionary approach to social change.

However important social engagement is, to rest it on such theological nebulosity is self-destructive. The current secular restoration of a social dimension of objective existence to man's experience is now often ambiguously and hence vulnerably correlated with spiritual sanctions. Having been told that God speaks, we are nonetheless disallowed cognitive knowledge of who or what God is, and not told in valid truths precisely what he is alleged to say. Despite the commendable secular concern for human rights, the secular evolutionary theory can guarantee neither universal nor enduring human rights, nor can it provide norms for definition. Secular religion lacks revelational criteria to distinguish the divine from the demonic in its promotion of social revolution; the notion of good violence soon loses moral answerability. Its sponsors fall into such curious contradictions as repudiating coercion or force in international affairs while endorsing it in domestic matters. Secular theology is a reaction to a reaction, and hence it has no stable future. Contemporary theology will sooner or later channel into equally objectionable correctives, including extreme forms of mysticism and pietism. The one truly hopeful and promising alternative to theological prodigality is a return to the secure foundations of biblical theism.

Alarmed by the existential evaporation of the reality of God, even some dialectical theologians have reemphasized the existence and being of God as an indispensable Christian tenet. But the departure from the evangelical insistence on God's objective intelligible self-revelation weakens this welcome adjustment of belief.

Despite early strictures against the rational conception of divine being, Barth later asserted that being and existence can be ascribed both to God and to the creation without any disparagement of the uniqueness of God: "The Existence of God," he writes, "is the criterion of general existence. . . . The objective reality of all beings apart from him is such that it can also be conceived as not existing . . ." (*Church Dogmatics*, III/1, pp. 5 ff.; cf. pp. 350 ff.; cf. *Fides quarens intellectum*, p. 154). Barth seems here to withdraw the emphasis on God's Subjectivity which by compressing revelation into personal response excludes universally valid knowledge of him. But even the later Barth affirmed that only an internal miracle of grace, only special revelation, renders man's concepts of God cognitively adequate. The existence of God, then, is not an affirmation ventured on the basis of general revelation, nor does special revelation constitute it a universally valid truth. Helmut Gollwitzer likewise—asserting that "it is a sign of grace that we can predicate the words 'being' and 'existence' both of God and the creation, without detriment to their *totaliter aliter* in the two references" (*The Existence of God as Confessed by Faith*, p. 211)—deprives the assertion of God's existence of any basis in general revelation and connects it with personal conviction grounded in internal divine confrontation.

Do such formulations really overcome the loss of God's objective existence that issues from the dialectical-existential emphasis on God as Subject? We know God, to be sure, only through his self-revelation; what we may say authoritatively about God depends on his self-disclosure. This precludes our speaking objectively of God-in-himself as a verdict that he exists wholly apart from any and all divine relations to mankind. God is indeed the Subject behind whom we cannot thrust ourselves, whose secrets we cannot penetrate. God's revelational self-disclosure is therefore the heartbeat of Christian knowledge. Evangelical theists share Barth's complaint against medieval scholastic distortion of the living God into the immovable object of Greek metaphysics. Recent Continental theology was formally right, moreover, in rejecting speculative "proofs" of the reality of God, and in reasserting the centrality of divine revelation. The Bible centers the case for supernatural theism in God who reveals himself; nowhere does it seek to establish God's existence through inferences from the world or from man's inner experiences.

But more must be said, for existential champions of divine-human encounter repudiated rational metaphysics on presuppositions that distorted the scriptural understanding of both revelation and reason.

God's existence is indeed not simply a conceptuality borrowed from the creation, a semantic conferment projected back on the Creator. With a bit of caution we may even say with Gollwitzer: "In the sense our 'is' propositions have elsewhere, God is not" (*The Existence of God as Confessed by Faith,* p. 206). God's objectivity is not akin to that of inanimate objects; his existence is not reducible to that of dependent creatures. The Bible warns against confusing God's reality with that of man-made images (Exodus 20) or with created things (Romans 1). Evangelical theology insists on this vast difference between God and creatures, God and the world, as much as idealistic, pantheistic, and humanistic theories abridge it.

But God *is,* for all that. Hebrews 11:6, for all the misguided derogation of this text as the "most Greek passage in the New Testament," is nonetheless a safer guide through this controversy over God's existence or non-"existence" than most recent German theology. The text in Hebrews yields not an inch to an existential theology that would dismiss God's objective being as rationalistic speculation and allow God who *is* only a mythological function in expounding the subjectivity of human existence.

The Christian says *God is* to emphasize not simply that *more than the world is,* but that *other than the world is,* and indeed, that *only because God is, the world that need not be, and would not be, is.* In Gollwitzer's words, "In the face of this disproportionality between the being of God and the being of the world the wonder of the creation consists precisely in the fact that he, who alone 'is' from eternity to eternity, calls into being that which is not . . ." (*ibid.,* p. 210).

Only by recognizing God's objective existence and objective revelation can we fully honor the biblical emphasis on God's disclosure in the cosmos, history, conscience and Scripture itself. God's universal or general revelation is thus seen as integral to his intelligible self-disclosure and as correlated with the scriptural understanding of revelation, and not submerged in internal noncognitive confrontation and response. To insist that I-Thou relationships demand an affirmation of God's non-"objectivity" and non-"existence"—that is, that God is a Being whose existence is not objectively ascertainable—arbitrarily imposes upon the Bible the novel modern theory that God's reality is a subjective existential phenomenon only. Gollwitzer correctly protests Ferdinand Ebner's emphasis that we cannot speak of God as the object of faith's knowledge. In Ebner's words: "To speak of God in the third person means to speak 'as if he were not there'" (*Das Wort und die geistigen Realitäten,* p. 220; cited by Gollwitzer, *The Existence of God as Confessed by Faith,* p. 212, n. 2). Not to define "faith's knowledge" in relation to God's objective and intelligible self-disclosure is to subvert the teaching of the Bible. Only the reaffirmation of God's objective disclosure, in nature and history, and in the prophetic-apostolic conceptions and propositions of Scripture, can preserve even Barth's highest intentions when he writes: "God is who He is in His works. He is the same even in Himself, even before and after and over His works, and without them. They are bound to Him, but He is not bound to them. . . . In His works He is revealed as the One He is" (*Church Dogmatics,* II/1, p. 260). Evangelical theology has every reason and duty to challenge the compromise of God's objectivity and existence inherent in existential and dialectical religious theory.

We must therefore move far beyond an elemental recognition that all that we properly say of God must have its basis in his own revelation, to the exposition of God's objective being; we must move, in short, from epistemology to ontology, from threshold considerations to theology proper. The essential theological confession *that God is* means little unless we can affirm *what* or *who God is.* Existence merely as such is a nebulous if not meaningless term. A dog exists. Even hallucinations exist; they are real. Devotees of various religions claim their gods exist. The god some naturalists adduce exists as a part of the universe. The important concern therefore is not simply whether God exists, but what is God?

Through revelation he is self-disclosed as the God who is before and beyond as well as in his revelation: he is God who *is,* not merely God who comes or God who becomes. "He that cometh to God must believe that he is and that he is a rewarder. . ." (Heb. 11:6). Neither our cognitive belief nor our trustful response constitutes his *is*-ness; rather, his *is*-ness legitimizes our belief and requires our response. The whole of theology aims to say *nothing less* and *much more* than that *God is.* "I believe in God. . ." is the indispensable foreword in the lifeline of theological exposition. What comprises theology is the delineation of this one divine Reality, the objective existent God, and of the implications of his revelation of himself. Only because the word and deed of God provide an objectively intelligible revelation of God and his purposes are we justified in contemplating his being and perfections, and, indeed, are we obliged to do so. Otherwise, instead of venturing broad and impressive generalities about God's existence, or fashioning high rhetoric about God's perfections, we had best let well enough alone, and maintain discreet silence. In the absence of intelligible objective revelation all assertions about the objectivity and existence of God must sooner or later collapse into subjectivity. Nonconceptual alternatives to evangelical theism simply prepare the way, however contrary may be their intention, for secular theologians who, like Paul van Buren, insist that dispensing with the existence of God does no violence to the essence of Christianity (*The Secular Meaning of the Gospel*). Precisely the opposite is the case: to forfeit the objective existence of God is to forfeit Christianity, to malign truth, to stifle love, to shrivel hope, to make a mockery of faith.

What Christianity claims above all else to know on the basis of the prophetic-apostolic word and of the incarnation of Christ is the revelation of *God.* The God of the Bible is the timeless "I Am" (Exod. 6:3, NEB). He is God eternal: "Before me there was no god fashioned nor ever shall be after me. I am the Lord, I myself . . ." (Isa. 43:10 f., NEB). He is Elohim who calls the world into being. "Thus says the Lord, the creator of the heavens, who is God, who made the earth and fashioned it and himself fixed it fast. . . . I am the Lord, there is no other" (Isa. 45:18, NEB). "Hear me, Jacob, and Israel whom I called; I am he; I am the first, I am the last also. With my own hands I founded the earth . . ." (Isa. 48:12 f.). He is Yahweh who manifests his redemptive presence and power. To Moses he declares, "I am the God of your forefathers, the God of Abraham, the God of Isaac, and the God of Jacob" (Exod. 3:6). . . . "I am with you" (Exod. 3:12).

Psalm 139 proclaims "the God who is there" not simply as an existential affirmation, but as the self-revealed ontological presupposition of man's existence and destiny. "Thou hast beset me behind and before, and laid thine hand upon me. Such knowledge is too wonderful for me; it is high, I cannot attain unto it. Whither shall I go from thy spirit? or whither shall I flee from thy presence? If I ascend into heaven, thou art there: if I make my bed in hell, behold, thou art there. . . . If I say, Surely the darkness shall cover me; even the night shall be light about me. . . . For thou hast possessed my reins: thou hast covered me in my mother's womb. . . . My substance was not hid from thee, when I was made in secret, and curiously wrought in the lowest parts of the earth. Thine eyes did see my substance, yet being unperfect; and in thy book all my members were written, which in continuance were fashioned, when as yet there was none of them. . ." (Ps. 139:5–8, 11, 13, 15–16). The notion that God is real for man only on the condition of subjective responsive trust makes a shambles of these verses. The objectively existing One is inescapably real even in hell, where man would be least likely to welcome intensive encounter with the living God. Even before birth, and before self-consciousness, before conception itself, the objectively real God works out his providential purposes in the created order. The self-revealing God is God who *is*; our being and reality are conditioned on his being and reality, and not vice versa.

2.
The Being and Coming and Becoming of God

FROM THE VERY FIRST the Bible designates God as the transcendent ground of the universe. It depicts him as the eternal Sovereign who voluntarily comes to create the world and man, and comes also to redeem and to judge his creation. Yahweh not only announces a prospect of salvation, but in dramatic fulfillment of his prophetic promise God also becomes what he was not, namely, the God-man of Nazareth.

When revealed religion speaks of God's essential being, of his "coming" in condescension, and of his "becoming" in history, it differs profoundly from secular philosophy which frequently uses similar terms to portray divine Reality. We must therefore expound the basic differences between Christianity and contemporary views in regard to God's being, coming and becoming.

Long after Moses and the Hebrew prophets declared Yahweh to be the self-revealed creator and preserver of the cosmos, the ruler of men and nations who acts personally in history for the salvation of his people, the early Greek sages were still trying to discover the one permanent principle of unity and being that could explain the world's diversity and change. These ancient philosophers considered divine being and divine becoming to be absolute antitheses. They disagreed among themselves as to what constitutes a rational explanation of the universe; in the absence of revelation some conceived the necessary first principle in hylozoistic terms, others in material or mechanical, and still others in mental terms; a few dispensed entirely with any insistence on immutable being (*ousia*) and instead affirmed the ultimacy of temporal change or becoming (*genesis*). Greek philosophers struggled ingeniously with the problem of the one and the many, but, for all their ingenuity, they found no satisfactory answer.

Greek philosophy got underway in the sixth century B.C. with Thales (636–542 B.C.). At that time the Milesian school of nature-philosophy, concerned mainly with identifying the basic stuff of the world, defined the immutable ground of the universe in nontheistic terms. Thales proposed water as the ultimate source from which all else supposedly evolved, Anaximander projected an infinite indeterminate matter, and Anaximenes suggested air or mist.

The Eleatic philosopher Parmenides (c. 475 B.C.) totally denied the reality of becoming, however, and declared that immutable being is the first principle and, indeed, is all there is. Zeno later became his disciple, although Parmenides' immediate successors tried to explain change rather than to dismiss and deny it. Yet despite its insistence that being is the ultimate explanatory principle Greek philosophy from the fifth century onwards evidenced no knowledge of Hebrew monotheism. Alongside his dismissal of the world of change and diversity as mere appearance, Parmenides' postulation of changeless being involved acceptance of an impersonal unifying first principle.

Some thinkers, who on the other hand emphasized change or becoming, discerned the supernatural only dimly. Heraclitus (525–475 B.C.) identified the one original element of the universe as fire, and affirmed that everything changes except the law of change; this law he designated *Logos*. Empedocles, Anaxagoras and Democritus reaffirmed diversity by expounding rival theories of pluralism. Empedocles considered the elements both immutable and qualitatively different; Anaxagoras rejected the belief that anything comes into being or is destroyed; Democritus explained all existence in terms of atoms and empty space. According to Democritus and Leucippus, the universe is divided into an infinity of immutable and indivisible fragments of matter that change only in their external spatial relationships; they considered the atoms to be unchangeable except as to position.

The classic Greek philosophers in turn expounded a role for both being and becoming, but related them unconvincingly in a variety of revision-destined alternatives. Certain of their emphases show some similarity to the teaching of Moses that the universe has its ground in a supernatural mind. Their representations of being, however, and of its relations to the world and man, differ from Hebrew theism in many respects, not only in regard to the nature of God, but also in the striking absence of any doctrine of creation, sin, redemption, and God's salvific activity in history. Plato distinguishes between being or the world of thought and becoming or the world of sense; as John Burnet puts it, only the objects of thought are said to *be,* while all else is *becoming* and cannot be said to *be* at all (*Greek Philosophy. Thales to Plato,* p. 126). In his proposed course of study for the Academy, as set forth in the *Republic,* Plato promotes the soul's continuing contemplation of being rather than of becoming, although he does guide the philosopher into, out of, and back into the cave (Book VII). Plato also contrasts becoming with not-being and ascribes it "a place intermediate between pure being and the absolute negation of being" (cf. *The Republic of Plato,* Book 5, 477). By so doing he makes becoming a mixture of the real and the unreal, a mixture that escapes unreality insofar as it partakes of the real. For Plato, eternal Ideas are immutable logical essences to which he subordinates the sphere of change; in the *Timaeus* he contrasts, as two coexisting realms, that which "always is and has no becoming" with "that which is always becoming and never is."

Aristotle conceived being or primary substance as consisting not of universal Ideas but rather of concrete individuals or substances that develop from potentiality to actuality. Metaphysics, he held, is concerned with "being *qua* being"—being in general—not with beings in particular (*Metaphysics*, Book 4, Chapter 1, in *The Works of Aristotle*). The Prime Mover and formal cause of all change in the world, he said, is itself unmoved (*The Works of Aristotle: Metaphysics*, Book 4, 256a). Aristotle's philosophy, in which the Unmoved Mover coexists with a world of change in passage from potentiality to actuality, is sometimes said to anticipate the "open future" affirmed by contemporary process theology. Yet Aristotle's determinism in no way regards the world, as a whole, to be evolutionary; Aris-. totle considers the same species to have always existed. Even more strenuously the ancient scholars resisted any view of dynamic process in which change is the very essence of reality and constantly transforms itself into what is qualitatively different.

Plotinus subsequently resorted to divine emanation in order to correlate the realm of timeless being with that of changing phenomena: for him change and succession characterize a level of emanation lower than the divine One. Like Plato, Plotinus considers the temporal to be an imperfect image of the eternally perfect.

In formulating their doctrine of God many medieval theologians—Jewish and Islamic philosophers as well as Roman Catholic Scholastics—were influenced by the Greek philosophical controversy over being and becoming. In regard to this important medieval development we will only note for the moment the immense influence of Thomas Aquinas' *Summa Theologica*. In it he orients the doctrine of the immutability of the God of the Bible to Greek philosophical motifs and develops theistic doctrine more in Greek than in Judeo-Christian biblical categories.

From ancient through medieval times, and even into the early modern period of philosophy, most Western systems have assigned priority to being and have given only a subordinate rank to becoming. Yet the history of secular philosophy, as Milič Čapek remarks, has been notably "dominated by the antinomy of Being and Becoming" ("Change," in *The Encyclopedia of Philosophy*, Vol. 2, p. 76). Because ancient and medieval philosophical rationalism failed to relate the eternal and the temporal realms satisfactorily, the problem was bequeathed to modern thinkers. In discussing ultimate reality, the moderns tended to obscure the relevance of God-in-his-revelation even more than had the medieval scholastics. The boldest of the early modern efforts to adjust the antinomies of being and becoming took the form of pantheistic monism. This was developed in different ways, all indebted in one or another respect to ancient conjectural notions such as Parmenides' Being, Plato's Ideas, Aristotle's Prime Mover or Plotinus's One. Yet the monadology of Leibniz, the pantheism of Spinoza and the idealism of Kant and his followers all tried to coordinate the eternal and the temporal, the changeless and the changing. Hegel, by emphasizing both the Absolute's timelessness and the historical character of reality, stimulated the rise of conflicting schools of thought that on the one hand affirmed the eternal immutability and perfection of the universe, and on the other the dynamic nature of all reality. At the end of the nineteenth century F. H. Bradley disputed the view that change and time are real and once again championed static monism.

The widespread philosophical notion that immutable eternal being requires repudiating the temporal and the changing as illusion prompted a reactionary counter-movement. Reaffirming finite existence, change and diversity, it disputed the very existence of timeless immutable being. And now, profoundly interested in the themes of time, change and succession—which are among the most persuasive aspects of man's introspective and sensory experience—the modern scientific era concentrates on transitory phenomenal reality and is prone to dismiss the supernatural as myth.

The impact of earlier empiricists like Locke, Berkeley and especially Hume, and of Kantian and post-Kantian idealists, all of whom considered sense experience decisive for cognitive knowledge, eroded any rational basis for affirming the supernatural. The controversy over being and becoming thus soon tilted strongly in favor of process and change; indeed, as Čapek observes, "the reaffirmation of change and the exploration of its structure is a salient feature of contemporary thought" ("Change," *The Encyclopedia of Philosophy*, p. 78). Secular philosophy today still dialogues over being and/or becoming in the setting of Parmenides and Heraclitus, or of Hegel or Marx and Dewey, while it largely ignores the biblical alternative posed by Moses and Isaiah and by Jesus and Paul. Besides traditional Thomistic expositions, Paul Tillich's doctrine of being—or being itself (*esse ipsum*) as he characterized it—was aggressively promulgated in neo-Protestant circles. Thinkers who granted even limited importance to the biblical doctrine of the God of creation can no longer affirm ultimate being without affirming also the reality of the finite universe.

Defining God as the "Ground of all being"—the ultimate or absolute or unconditioned that transcends everything concrete and finite (*Systematic Theology*, Vol. I, p. 211)—Tillich stressed that God is not "a being alongside or above others" but rather is "being-itself" (*ibid.*, p. 236), "the power of resisting non-being" (*ibid.*, p. 236). Tillich's promotion of being-itself as the only nonsymbolic statement that we can make about God soon proved futile, however; his very denial that our predications about God's nature are literal soon drove him to compromise claims for the literal objective reality of being-itself (Vol. II, p. 9).

Specially noteworthy is Tillich's denial that divine revelation uncovers the true deity. Such a premise would presuppose a personal God, a reality that Tillich disallows; for him divine personality is only something symbolic. Like earlier secular philosophers Tillich bases his argument for divine being instead upon philosophical reasoning: ". . . if we speak of the actuality of God, we first assert that he is not God if he is not being-itself.

Other assertions about God can be made theologically only on this basis" (Vol. I, p. 238 f.). One can readily understand why Tillich expounds and even exaggerates similarities between Platonism and Christianity (Vol. II, p. 23) and in fact regards Plato's views as the key to a proper understanding of Christianity (Vol. I, p. 163). While Tillich does indeed emphasize revelation that functions through the divine *logos* indwelling man, his conception of revelation is more like existential intuition. As Kenneth Hamilton observes, Tillich disallows any unambiguous revelation by God (*The System and the Gospel. A Critique of Paul Tillich,* p. 67).

We object to Tillich's exposition not because he insists that philosophers from Parmenides to Hegel have necessarily been preoccupied with ontology, and that all sound theology must be ontologically informed. We object, rather, to his conjectural analysis of "the structure of being" that forfeits the rational content of divine revelation, lacks authoritative basis in God's self-disclosure, and grossly misconceives the being of God. As Hamilton says, "when God is called the infinite power of being to resist the threat of non-being, a most definite content is given the word *God*—a content derived wholly from the definition of God as being-itself over against finite existence. There is no evidence to suggest that the Christian message about God revealed in Jesus Christ, or any other specifically Christian statement, enters the picture at all" (*The System,* p. 123). Taken on its own merit, the notion of being-itself is not a self-evident or necessary conception; Tillich's distillation of absolute being by philosophical analysis depends not upon logical demonstration but more upon creative and conjectural revision of features borrowed from the Judeo-Christian view and even more from traditional secular metaphysics. The difference is like day and night between a view that founds its analysis of the human situation upon an obedient hearing of divine revelation and one that proceeds from human initiative, investigation and illumination. To hear it said that being-itself is not simply "one being among others" may sound to undiscerning evangelicals like the music of heaven; but when Tillich insists that God precedes the subject-object structure of being he actually echoes not the cadences of eternity but rather the familiar cadences of Kierkegaard.

Moreover, much as Tillich denies being a pantheist in the sense of identifying God with the universe, he implies nothing less than pantheism by his monistic view of reality. God cannot be conceived without the universe of which he is the ground. Charles Hartshorne notes that Tillich considers the doctrine of God's pure actuality to be erroneous (*Systematic Theology,* Vol. I, pp. 84, 153) and "wishes to transcend the old theology of God as Being in the exclusive sense (negative of becoming) . . . by recognizing, 'symbolically' at least, a polarity in deity (or in being-itself) of infinite *and* finite, potential *and* actual, fixed being *and* becoming" ("Tillich's Doctrine of God," in *The Theology of Paul Tillich,* ed. by Charles W. Kegley and Robert W. Bretall, p. 166). It is curious, of course, that, for a time at least, Tillich presumed to speak literally of being-itself but only symbolically of being-in-process. Actually, his view places all affirmations about God beyond intelligible reach; on the basis of his own premises Tillich must exempt symbolic predications about God from logical tests, and hence, one would think, from logical significance as well.

Also resisting the contemporary reduction of all reality to natural processes and events are a number of process philosophers; they hold that God is literally a personal deity whose being is immutable in some respects but changing or growing in others. This view, for which Schubert Ogden became a prominent spokesman (*The Reality of God and Other Essays*), has links to such earlier conceptions as Henri Bergson's *élan vital,* Alfred North Whitehead's metaphysics of events, and C. Lloyd Morgan's emergent evolution. It has gained support from a limited circle of mediating scholars who claim to speak broadly for Judeo-Christian heritage and who promote process theory in diverse forms as the best alternative to the evolutionary naturalism of Karl Marx, Samuel Alexander and John Dewey.

The mediating stance of process theology has two dangers, however: it forfeits the vitalities of revelational theism, and it vulnerably exposes the case for theism to naturalistic evolutionary theory. Naturalistic philosophers have long made use of Charles Darwin's theory of evolutionary origin and development to undermine quasi-supernaturalism. Despite the limits of empirical observation, particularly in respect to past origins, and despite the basic questions that continue to challenge philosophical Darwinism, the theory of organic evolution has become virtually an unquestioned assumption of contemporary biology. Most of the theory's champions correlate it with naturalistic cosmological beliefs even though if valid it need not entail atheism. Radical secularism has elevated the notion that all reality is explicable by natural processes to unparalleled prominence in Euro-American classrooms. Aggressively promulgated as official dogma in communist East Europe, organic evolution has gained almost the status of quasi-official academic doctrine in much of the noncommunist Western world. Not simply the inherited theism of Christian and Jewish orthodoxy but modern philosophical expositions of eternal changeless being as well struggle against engulfment by this secular preoccupation with the realm of becoming. Naturalistic scientism tends to encroach without being decisively challenged wherever God in his revelation is obscured. No less in scientific than in other circles one nonetheless finds eminent scholars and specialists who affirm the reality of a supernatural mind and will upon which everything depends for existence and continuance (cf. *Horizons of Science: Christian Scholars Speak Out,* C. F. H. Henry, ed., San Francisco, Harper & Row, 1978); this commitment they consider credible on the basis of Judeo-Christian revelation.

Inner weaknesses and contradictions beset secular philosophical notions of ultimate being, and metaphysicians are admittedly embarrassed by the striking differences between rival views predicated on philosophical reasoning. Not more than one—if that—of these numerous conflicting theories can be true. The self-revealing God of the Bible stands in judgment upon secular metaphysicians whose misrepresentations routinely polarize the principles of being and becoming and provoke the rise of unmeritorious alternatives and counteralternatives. Discussion of divine being is conditioned in biblical revelation by the intelligible self-disclosure of the Lord and Creator of the universe. The legitimacy of what we may say about God's being, essence, nature, substance, attributes, or whatever else, stems solely from the living God who makes himself known and from the divinely inspired Scriptures that characterize the finite universe as the creation of the self-manifesting supernatural God. In short, the Bible speaks of being and becoming on its own terms and in its own way, and orients these conceptions in a manner strikingly different from that of secular philosophy.

Karl Barth criticizes the Roman Catholic Scholastics for investigating the knowability of God *in abstracto*—that is, apart from revelation—and for following the road of natural theology to arrive at God as creator (*Church Dogmatics,* II/1, p. 80). The Bible knows only the self-revealing God as creator; it accommodates no division in the divine unity of the transcendent Revealer-God whom it knows simultaneously as "Creator and Lord." Roman Catholic theology delays treatment of God-in-his-revelation until it first self-reliantly arrives at the existence of God, and then applies the term "God" to that for which it adduces no revelational authority but only philosophical argumentation based supposedly on empirical observation; by doing so it detaches the knowability of God from the indispensable necessity of divine revelation. Concerning this scholastic approach Barth says: "When we ask questions about God's being, we cannot in fact leave the sphere of His action and working as it is revealed to us in His Word" (II/1, p. 260). Again: "Every statement of what God is, and explanation how God is, must always state and explain what and how He is in His act and decision. There is no moment in the ways of God which is over and above this act and decision" (II/1, p. 272). Legitimate pursuit of God's "essence" does not sunder God's being from his activity of revelation, for it is in the act of revelation that God makes known to us his inner being and reality.

The philosopher who seeks to trace observable processes and events back to basic entities moves on a very different track, and in the opposite direction from the prophet who attests God's self-disclosure as Creator and Lord. Both may contend that they affirm ultimate reality or being only in terms of a causal activity. But the conjectural approach that delays or sets aside consideration of the self-disclosing God will reach conclusions about ultimate being devoid of all distinctive features discernible through divine self-disclosure alone. Philosophical hypothesis has no authoritative basis for equating some preferred first principle with the living Revealer; whatever it says of God while it excludes divine revelation has no necessary connection with the God of the Bible. If it is God's self-disclosure, however, and the scriptural revelation that determine our concept of God, then we are no longer speaking of "God in general," of some deity built on conjectural premises.

For good reason, therefore, Barth set the whole philosophical pursuit of being over against the supernatural Lord who gives himself to be known and is known by us on the basis of divine revelation. To evaporate the revelation of the living God by a conjectural doctrine of divine being, as done by many post-Reformation Protestant philosophers of religion no less than by conventional Roman Catholic Thomists in the tradition of ancient Greek metaphysicians, carries a costly toll. The divine being arrived at independently of God-in-his-revelation is always some god other than the one living God, or an altered vestige of the true God, one that conforms to biblical theism only where it secretly or unwittingly borrows from the scriptural heritage. The metaphysician who believes he can, by his own ingenuity, spy out the secrets of the sovereign transcendent Lord, who is as free to hide from the obtrusive curiosity of his creatures as he is to reveal himself and his purposes, is a victim of professional egoism. He seems unaware that knowing God is a divine gift, is at very least the common grace of God and an awesome and undeserved privilege for man the creature, a possibility that God himself grants and preserves in sovereign freedom. The assumption that man can and does speak authoritatively about God apart from divine revelation is what spawns the diversity of gods espoused and extolled by competing philosophers. The Bible, on the other hand, sets out with the living God as Creator, Lord, Judge and Redeemer. He moves toward man in personal self-disclosure. Nowhere does Scripture encourage human attempts to authenticate the being of God by first dissecting the universe and then standing upon the being of the world or the being of mankind. A doctrine of God that reverses the direction of the biblical pattern for accepting the reality of God is not to be welcomed by proponents of divine revelation as if it were an aid to faith, or even as a secondary fall-back position.

While from the standpoint of revelation criticism must be levelled against rationalistic expositions of divinity-in-general, biblical religion does not for that reason entirely disallow discussion of God's being. Some neo-Protestant theologians profess to honor revelational theology by decrying any and all consideration and expositions of the being of God. But as Barth observes, "if the Word of God forbids the question of God's being as a particular question, or leaves us in doubt about this particular question, it means that it gives us no real revelation of God." The Word of God "as true revelation does not remain silent on the particular question of God's being—quite apart from the fact that it is in its entirety one single answer to that question. . . . We shall be guilty of an omission which will recoil on us if we hurry over the statement that God is . . ." (*Church Dogmatics*, II/1, p. 259). Some commentators unfortunately have disparaged Hebrews 11:6, stigmatizing its emphasis on God's existence (". . . he that cometh to God must believe that he is . . .") as a deep intrusion of alien Greek philosophy into the New Testament. But such a verdict rests upon the unacceptable assumption that to show interest in the premise that "God exists" is unbiblical.

Yet what is evangelically acceptable is not being-in-general, that is, being as an abstract philosophical construct, through which finite being is considered analogous to infinite being. What interests evangelical theism, rather, is the being of God as God has made himself known in his self-disclosure.

But we must also note that Barth's decision-oriented view of revelation, disavowing any divine communication of valid propositional truths, precludes significant affirmations about God's transcendent ontological nature. To be sure, Barth insistently protests the notion that we know only God's activity, and not God himself: "in the light of what He is in His works it is no longer an open question what He is in Himself" (*Church Dogmatics*, II/1, p. 260); "God is not swallowed up in the relation and attitude of Himself to the world and us as actualized in His revelation" (*ibid.*, p. 260). For all that, Barth charges that the failure to begin and to develop discussion in terms of God's revelatory acts is "the fundamental error which dominated the doctrine of God of the older theology and which influenced Protestant orthodoxy at almost every point"; moreover, he repudiates any effort to deduce the content of revelation "from the premises of formal logic" (*ibid.*, p. 261). But what evangelical theologian sought to derive the content of revelation from the premises of logic? Barth implies that reliance on deductive logic evaporates any dependence on divine revelation and instead requires theologizing on the basis of self-communing reasoning. But theological reliance on formal logic seems hardly to lead, as Barth thinks, to an eclipse of revelation and to a contemplation of divine being in the confederacy of false gods. Actually, the revelation of the triune God, on which Barth himself insists, can be significantly maintained only if divine revelation is intelligible and by expounding its content without resorting to paradox and logical contradiction.

More specifically defined, the revelatory relationship that Barth requires for authentic knowledge of God's being involves both the internalizing of divine revelation in person-to-person confrontation, and the nonobjectification of its content. Barth tells us that we cannot speak of God's "being in and for Himself but in His being within this relationship" (II/2, p. 6), a relationship "outside of which God no longer wills to be and no longer is God, and within which alone He can be truly honoured and worshipped as God" (*ibid.*, p. 7).

If, however, as evangelical orthodoxy insists on the basis of the biblical representations, God's revelatory activity includes the divine disclosure of truths about God (valid information that stipulates the meaning of God's redemptive acts and unveils information also concerning God's transcendent selfhood and his divine goals) then no need arises for such rigid distinction between the self-revealed God and God-in-himself (since in self-revelation God conveys objectively valid knowledge of his eternal nature and will).

Barth thinks that God's being can be known only internally as a faith-response to personal sporadic revelatory confrontation. He writes: "What God is as God, the divine individuality and characteristics, the *essentia* or 'essence' of God, is something which we shall encounter either at the place where God deals with us as Lord and Saviour, or not at all" (*ibid.*, p. 261). In other words, however much Barth stresses that faith to be significant must be a response to God in his revelation, he does not allow us to speak of God in himself in terms of universally sharable truths, but only

in the context of personal faith. The event of God's revelation, Barth emphasizes, "is in no sense to be transcended" (*ibid.,* p. 262); it not only occurred
in the past but occurs also in the present, and in this event God discloses
who he is, namely, the merciful Lord who communicates himself to us
in grace. Barth emphasizes that God "is not only to be found alone in
His act, but is to be found alone in His act because alone in His act He
is who He is" (II/1, p. 272). "With regard to the being of God, the word
'event' or 'act' is *final,* and cannot be surpassed or compromised. To its
very deepest depths God's Godhead consists in the fact that it is an event—
not any event, not events in general, but the event of His action, in which
we have a share in God's revelation" (*ibid.,* p. 263). That "God speaks as
an I" seems for Barth wholly to vindicate the claim that trustful response
puts us fully in touch with God's inner spirit (*ibid.,* p. 267). Yet if God is
"to be found alone in his act" and if confrontational revelation involves
no communication of valid propositional information and no objectifying
theological truth, then what cognitive basis remains for speaking about
God as he transcendently is?

Precisely because and only because Barth misdefines God's revelation
as self-communication known only internally in obedient response, can
he limit the content of divine revelational activity to grace and hence identify "the being of God" as "the one who loves" (*Church Dogmatics,* II/1,
pp. 272 ff.). Such exposition not only dwarfs the intellective content of revelation, but also requires subjecting other features such as righteousness
and wrath to the supremacy of love. Evangelical orthodoxy, on the other
hand, emphasizes the equal ultimacy of all divine attributes in the nature
of God.

Barth does indeed argue that "every individual perfection in God is nothing but God Himself and therefore nothing but every other divine perfection" (II/1, p. 333). His primary affirmation about God, however, is that
God is "the One who loves in freedom," a tenet he expounds by subsuming
under love all other divine "perfections," righteousness included. "All His
perfections," writes Barth, "are the perfections of His love" (II/1, p. 351).
To say that love is the being, essence and nature of God (II/1, pp. 279 f.)
is one thing and is not in question; to say that every intervention of divine
being in action is love (II/1, p. 281) is quite another matter and has no
biblical warrant (cf. John 3:18). Not even Barth's vivid insistence that God
supremely publishes his inner nature in Jesus Christ—an emphasis essential to every Christian theology—escapes his biased correlation of mercy
and wrath, nor is it allowed to supply objective ontological knowledge of
God as he transcendently exists.

Having discussed the being of God we focus now on the coming of God.
This transition in no way involves a complete change of interest, for unless
God in sovereign freedom comes in self-revelation we have no definitive
basis for speaking of God at all; we have indicated, moreover, that revelation must be intelligibly communicable to be cognitively significant. The
coming of God therefore speaks of his self-disclosure; in and through that
revelation he declares what we are authorized to say concerning the living

God. The Book of Revelation describes God's divine nature as "he which is and which was and which is to come" (Rev. 1:4, 8; 4:8). The divine name given in Exodus 3:14 ("I AM THAT I AM"; Septuagint: "I am he who is") is thus expanded to correlate that being of God with his presence and coming—an emphasis already implicit in Exodus: "I am that I am. . . . I will be with thee" (cf. *God, Revelation and Authority,* Vol. II, p. 219 ff.). Austin Farrer calls this phrase "the most tortured piece of Greek" in the Book of Revelation (*The Revelation of St. John the Divine,* p. 61), but to concentrate on the grammatical difficulties of the passage at the expense of its theological importance is, of course, lamentable. Greek pagan sources refer to "Zeus who was, Zeus who is, and Zeus who will be" (Pausanias, *Descriptions of Greece,* x.12.5) and the shrine of Minerva (Isis) at Sais bears the inscription "I am all that hath been and all that is and shall be" (Plutarch, *On Isis and Osiris,* 9). But the biblical reference to God "who is to come" cannot be tapered to such statements. While Hebrews 13:6 indeed characterizes Jesus Christ as "the same yesterday, today and forever," Revelation notably connects "who is to come" with the decisive eschatological reign and kingdom of the Lord and of his Christ (11:17). It anticipates the coming eschatological reign of the living God who acts in history and whose reign at last wholly fulfills and replaces the phrase "who is to come": "We give thanks to thee, Lord God Almighty, who art and who wast, that thou hast taken thy great power and begun to reign" (Rev. 11:17, RSV; the KJV follows inferior texts that retain the phrase "and art to come").

If we view God's being biblically, the coming of God can only indicate personal divine relationships to the created finite universe. God does not "come to himself"—far less "come to self-consciousness" through cosmic evolution—but relates himself condescendingly and contingently to man and the world as sovereign creator, preserver, redeemer and judge. The Greek verb *erchomai,* which has the meaning of "to come" and "to go," is therefore specially appropriate to depict such voluntary divine activity. The God who is eternally "there" ventures to originate and maintain the cosmos of man, and through his presence and power to work out his purposes in the realm of created reality.

Ancient pagans included prayers in their cult rituals through which they presumed to summon deities to appear in fulfillment of worshipers' desires. In the Bible, however, God as the sovereign creator and redeemer of man and the world appears on his own terms and in his own way. God who takes the initiative in self-revelation is not at the command of his creatures. The voluntary coming of God in sovereign determination, in personal presence and act, the coming of God in his Word, the coming of Messiah, the coming of God's Spirit, and the eschatological coming of God belong to the heart and substance of both Old and New Testaments.

Alongside his inner triune life of resplendent self-sufficiency, God's coming signals broadly his being-for-others that rises from his sovereign decree to create a universe with man in his image and to provide redemption for fallen sinners. Divine condescension characterizes his manifold relationships, a condescension evident in his creation of the universe out of nothing as a contingent reality that he ongoingly preserves alongside himself. It is seen in his self-revelation whereby he crosses the frontier between himself and the created world to make himself known to man. It is seen in the prophetic-apostolic Scriptures that articulate the divine claim and command in intelligible, inspired human words. Divine condescension is seen in God's mercifully promised redemption for rebellious mankind, in his incarnation in Jesus Christ and the mediator's death upon the cross, in his universal calling of sinners to repentance and the still open invitation to enter the kingdom of God. It is seen in his providential preservation of the faltering regenerate church in the midst of an ungodly world, in his hearing and answering of the prayers of his people, in the "season for repentance" built into God's historical judgments in anticipation of a final assize of the nations. It will yet be seen in a crowning consummation of human destiny in the end-time reward of the righteous and of righteousness.

Where do secular expositions of primal being reflect any genuine awareness of God's condescending coming? These conjectural systems are total strangers to the realities of his sovereign creation of the cosmos, his unparalleled incarnation in the Babe of Bethlehem, his powerful regeneration of sinful penitents and his irreversible final doom of the wicked. They are separated by a vast gulf from the Revealer who makes himself known personally in divine disclosure. They are unfamiliar with what even the unlearned and unlettered learn from a casual reading of the Bible: that God in his freedom and good pleasure condescendingly decrees to create a universe, one in which finite man is capstone as divine image-bearer. It is a universe in which God reveals himself in multiple ways for man's benefit, one in which he mercifully declares himself the friend of fallen and disgraced Adam. It is a universe in which God involves himself in incredibly costly ways for the rescue of sinners, one in which he establishes covenant with a chosen though unfaithful people. This is a universe that he proposes to salvage for all things good and godly, in which he ventures personal relations not only with the community of faith but also privately with its individual penitents. It is a universe in which he showers his Spirit upon believers as a sample of their coming glory.

As early as patristic times theologians have acknowledged God's accommodation of human limits and needs to be a central feature of divine revelation. Ford Lewis Battles, noted Calvin scholar, asserts that Calvin in *The Institutes* made this recognition of divine accommodation a central feature of his interpretation of Scripture and of his theological exposition ("God Was Accommodating Himself to Human Capacity," pp. 19–38). God's revelation through nature and in man is an accommodation, as is the revelation through Scripture even in its "scaled-down" language. Divine condescension and accommodation are dramatically involved also, Calvin avers, in God's incarnation in Christ, and in the sacraments that present invisible spiritual realities in visible form. Yet we must not extol Calvin's emphasis on divine accommodation as the one main feature of his theology and subordinate all other concerns to it, as some critics tend to do, in order to range Calvin on the side of scriptural errancy. God's accommodation in divine disclosure by no means precludes us from speaking properly and truly about spiritual realities. Calvin himself cautions us, as Battles notes, "to seek after a definition of divine accommodation which neither repudiates the anthropomorphisms of Scripture in our quest of pure Spirit, nor clings to the anthropomorphic mode of thought and worship as ourselves, veiled by flesh, to lose sight of God. In the divine rhetoric accommodation as practiced by the Holy Spirit so empowers the physical, verbal vehicle that it leads us to, not away from, the very truth" (*ibid.*, p. 37).

Twentieth-century theology has revived the theme of the coming of God in contexts that set aside the cognitive authority of the Bible and in formulations that compete and conflict in numerous ways with scriptural representations. Two such developments are the dialectical-existential schemas by Karl Barth and Rudolf Bultmann and the theology of the eschatological coming of God by Jürgen Moltmann and Wolfhart Pannenberg.

The early Barth absorbed the future into the revelational manifestation of the Christ-Presence; even where Barth later escaped Bultmann's subjectivizing of revelation he denied to revelation a role in the horizontal timeline of history that historians investigate. Existential interpretation of God's transcendent coming to meet man in internal revelational encounter gained widening influence through Bultmann's teaching and writing. For Bultmann, God's coming in Christ is "the Revelation of the divine reality in the world" (*Theology of the New Testament,* Vol. 2, p. 34); Jesus' coming is an internalized "eschatological event" (*ibid.,* p. 37). Bultmann thinks the "historicizing of eschatology" was "introduced by Paul" and "radically carried through by John" (*ibid.,* p. 38); in actuality, he holds, the judgment that Jesus brings "is no dramatic cosmic event, but takes place in the response of men to the word of Jesus" (*ibid.,* p. 38). Bultmann transforms Jesus' saying about the coming of the Son of Man into statements by the early church about his arrival or advent in an inner eschatological occurrence (*Theology of the New Testament,* Vol. 1, pp. 29 ff.). He appropriates Paul's emphasis that life in Christ is a present reality to support a theory that Jesus in his coming-and-going is the Revealer or transcendent Word in whom God sporadically confronts individuals internally. Obedient response to such confrontation lifts us to authentic selfhood, Bultmann avers, but it sheds no light on God's transcendent being.

The coming of God has emerged also as the central motif of the eschatologically oriented theology of Moltmann and Pannenberg who set human hope in the context of the future of God behind which the world lags and toward which history moves. Instead of viewing God supernaturally above man and as vertically and internally addressing him, whether in dialectical confrontation or in existential encounter, Pannenberg and Moltmann see external history as a sphere of divine revelation and God's eschatological history as the hope of mankind. Here the language of transcendence is redirected into the future of God—God ahead of us as the goal of man and the world; futurity becomes the controlling theme of theology, and this horizon of the future permeates all history and all Christian faith. In a significant comment Carl E. Braaten says: "A crucial difference between secular futurology and Christian eschatology is this: the future in secular futurology is *reached* by a process of the world's *becoming.* The future in Christian eschatology *arrives* by the *coming* of God's kingdom. The one is a *becoming,* the other a *coming*" (*The Future of God. The Revolutionary Dynamics of Hope,* p. 29). Theologians of the future bluntly deny—as did Barth and Bultmann before them—the fatal hypothesis of modernist theology that the kingdom of God arrives by accelerating processes already latent in history.

Moltmann and Pannenberg nevertheless stress a one-layer view of reality that avoids the traditionally sharp distinction of supernatural and natural, though they emphatically look to the end—to the future of God—as the decisive key to the past and present. But this formulation tends to disadvantage and threatens to disqualify even the singular resurrection of Jesus which they declare to be definitively anticipative of the end, inasmuch as they set aside all other factors proleptic of the end. So definitive is the future coming of God that not only is the cognitive significance of Christ's first coming handled reductively, but even the gospel accounts of his birth and ministry are minimized. For that matter, in charting eschatological specifics Moltmann and Pannenberg often shroud the discussion of Christ's second coming in ambiguity. The strong emphasis on the future coming of God tends therefore to dwarf the becoming of God in its legitimate and indispensable biblical dimensions. Moltmann speaks of a "coming" God rather than of a "becoming" God, the distinction being required by his notion that God will exist only in the future. Pannenberg conceives eschatologically the reality of God whom he considers a being having only qualified existence: "In a restricted but important sense God does not yet exist. . . . God's being is still in the process of coming to be" ("Theology and the Kingdom of God," in *Theology and the Kingdom of God,* p. 56). In distinction from process theologians, Pannenberg emphasizes "the coming One" rather than "the One becoming," but he nonetheless confers ontological priority on the future of God. While the futurist theologians invert the dictum that "he who controls the past controls the future," the Apocalypse disputes their dictum that "he who controls the future controls the past and the present," and affirms instead the God "who is and who was and who is to come" (Rev. 1:4).

We have spoken of the being and of the coming of God as central Christian affirmations. Now we must emphasize the becoming of God as no less biblically central. To be soundly scriptural any exposition of God must deal with all three: God's being, God's coming and God's becoming. In the Christian view divine becoming is a climactic reality that contrasts at once with ancient Greek notions of abstract being and becoming, and with modern process philosophy misconceptions of divine becoming that postulate change in the very nature of God.

Many secular philosophers have conceived being and becoming only as exclusive antinomies or antithetical alternatives. Others, in correlating being and becoming, have stood ready to partition even the essential nature of God, viewing some aspects of divinity in terms of being and others in terms of becoming. Once prominently discussed by ancient Greek metaphysicians, the doctrine of divine becoming currently holds new interest because of a revival of process philosophy. But secular exposition distorts the incomparably unique place that the theology of the Bible ascribes to divine becoming as, for example, when process philosophy aims to preserve a transcendent deity essentially implicated in the universe. Where God's coming in intelligible self-revelation is obscured or misconceived, God's becoming is bound to be misunderstood.

A fundamental problem confronting ancient Graeco-Roman intellectuals, we noted earlier, concerns the relationship between the eternal world and the spatio-temporal world, that is, the realms of being and becoming. For the Greek philosophers God in one way or another becomes the world or some aspect of the world—whether in a context of materialism, idealism or pantheism—even if only as the intrinsic principle of cosmic meaning and order. Stoicism equated God with the world, neo-Platonism envisaged the world as the necessary form of God's objectification, and for the early modern pantheist Spinoza the mathematical network of nature was God. Numerous modern idealistic schools of thought at the end of the nineteenth and beginning of the twentieth century similarly characterized the whole universe as divine. Empirically oriented thinkers like Henry Nelson Wieman, who earlier in this century sought to bridge between naturalism and theism at the developing frontiers of an evolutionary universe, considered emerging aspects of the cosmos to be divine.

The notion that God becomes the world, or that the cosmos should in whole or in part be considered divine, is from the biblical point of view unthinkable and profane. Graeco-Roman philosophy, and later German philosophy also, did not hesitate to contemplate deity in a visible cosmic manifestation or emanation. But the second commandment prohibits graven images not alone because man-made idols are mute alongside the living God, but also because the divine Creator is not to be confused with the created universe. Worship of carved stones or sticks as a locus of divine presence fundamentally conflicts with the doctrine that God is immaterial and invisible Spirit. The Hebrew "holy of holies" contained no material representation of God whatsoever.

The same Greek world-wisdom that readily identified God with the cosmos or with some aspect of the world, or as its intrinsic ground, and did so in violation of Hebrew revelation, also ruled out in principle what is central to the New Testament revelation of God, namely, the doctrine of divine becoming so forcibly stated in the prologue of John's Gospel: *The Word became flesh* (John 1:14). Yet the New Testament so centrally and strenuously insists on the exceptional and incomparable incarnation of God in Jesus Christ that it deplores as deceivers (2 John 7) and strangers to the living God (1 John 2:23) all who deny that God has come in the flesh. That *man* might be divinized was for disciplined Greek and Roman thought within the range of possibility; that God should assume human nature was out of question. As Hermann Kleinknecht comments, "the idea of God becoming man was always alien in the Gk. world. The distinctively Gk. experience of God demands that we assume the divine mode of being, not that God assume the human" ("*Theos:* The Greek Concept of God," *TDNT,* 3:78). In the Bible, however, God's coming—the divine movement toward the universe in creation, revelation and redemption—gains its climactic center in God's becoming, that is, in his extraordinary divine condescension and assumption of human nature. "In the beginning was the Word. . . . The Word was made flesh" (John 1:1, 14)—this is the only doctrine of divine becoming authorized by Scripture, and at once ranges the Bible against both the whole realm of secular philosophy and the world of nonbiblical religions.

The biblical link between the being of God and God's coming and becoming is the promised and expected Messiah: "He that should come" (Matt. 11:3). As Johannes Schneider puts it, the gospel statements that focus on Jesus' coming to mankind are at "the very heart of the early Christian message of salvation" (*Erchomai, TDNT* 2:668). Schneider stresses, moreover, that the sayings in which Jesus speaks in the first person of his coming derive from his messianic self-awareness and reveal his certainty of the divine mission on which his coming rests. The words "I am come" (Matt. 5:17, 10:34 ff.; Mark 1:38, 2:17; Luke 5:32, 12:49 ff.) and "the Son of Man is come" (Matt. 20:28; Mark 10:45; Luke 9:56, 19:10) that have their setting in the sending God who gives his Son (Matt. 15:24; Luke 10:16; John 9:7) ring with global good news. In the Fourth Gospel Jesus designates God six times as "the Father who sent me" and nineteen times as "he who sent me"; this sending is the presupposition and corollary of his coming to save the lost. The same Gospel emphasizes that Christ's coming has for its goal the rescue of the world from its destructive alienation from God (John 3:16 ff., 12:47). The fundamental fact of the Gospels and the Epistles is not that multitudes came to Jesus or even that the disciples and early Christians did so, however requisite such human response is for personal salvation, but rather that God came in Christ (2 Cor. 5:18 ff.) and that history moves toward Christ's eschatological coming and the kingdom of Messiah. The distinctive feature of the awaited second coming is that Messiah comes suddenly (Mark 13:36; 1 Thess. 5:2). In the interim, however, between Christ's first and second advents, Christ continually comes to his followers in and through the Holy Spirit (John 14:18, 23; Col. 1:27), so that even now Messiah's coming maintains in unbroken continuity a spiritual relationship that anticipates his future visible presence.

The prologue of John's Gospel contains two majestic affirmations concerning the Logos of God. The first dramatic declaration is that "In the beginning the Word was." For this "wasness" of the Word John uses the verb *ēn* (from *eimi,* to be), which is fully appropriate to eternal being and carries no necessary suggestion of "coming into being." As Leon Morris says, "the verb 'was' is most naturally understood of the eternal existence of the Word: 'the Word continually was'" (*The Gospel According to John,* p. 73). But in John 1:14 the prologue makes a second dramatic declaration,

namely, "And the Word became flesh" (RSV), and here John uses the verb
egeneto (from *ginomai*, to come to be). By flesh is meant essential manhood
(cf. "flesh and blood," Matt. 16:17) and not, as William Temple suggests,
"part of human nature" (*Readings in John's Gospel*, p. 12).

Morris finds it noteworthy that John did not say that "the Word took a
body" or even that "the Word became man" (*The Gospel According to John*,
p. 102). For all that, the Gospel forcibly affirms a divine incarnation, assumption by the Word of nothing less than human nature. The statement
does not, however, imply an absolute "becoming" in the sense of canceling
the Word's prior nature. Hence C. K. Barrett says of *egeneto* in John 1:14:
"It cannot mean 'became,' since the Word continues to be the subject of
further statements—it was the Word who 'dwelt among us,' and whose
glory 'we beheld'; the Word continued to be the Word." Barrett thinks the
sense may be that "the Word came on the (human) scene as flesh, [as]
man" (*The Gospel According to John*, p. 138). Morris and Barrett therefore
arrive in different ways at the same emphasis that the Word who preexisted
substantially, and became Jesus Christ in visible historical incarnation,
did not divest himself of divinity when he assumed essential human nature.

It was not deity therefore but the "form of God" that Christ set aside
in his self-emptying servanthood (Phil. 2:3 ff.). As Barth says, "He did not
treat it as His one and only and exclusive possibility. . . . It was not to
Him an inalienable necessity to exist only in that form of God, only to
be God, and therefore only to be different from the creature, from man,
as the reality which is distinct from God, only to be the eternal Word and
not flesh" (*Church Dogmatics*, IV/1, p. 180). In other words, Barth rules
out, and rightly, any absolute inclusion of the Logos in the creature, a
subordination of the Word to the man Jesus that would limit and alter
the divine nature. In his self-humbling the eternal Christ refused to cling
to the form of deity; he assumed the form of a man in order to experience
the ignominious death upon the cross to save sinners (Phil. 2:8). In supreme
condescension God steps into human history as the God-man to manifest
his outgoing love and grace in the person of the Son. To enable penitent
sinners to embrace spiritual life, God comes in the actuality of the man
Jesus to take upon himself in human nature all the consequences of fallen
man's rebellion and shame. Nowhere is this fact stated more precisely
than in the Apostles' Creed: "He descended into hell."

We should note, however, and comment on the fact that the Bible uses
the term *El* for the divine, in explicit contrast with the human: "thou
art a man, and not God" (Ezek. 28:2); "for I am God, and not man" (Hos.
11:9). This mutual exclusiveness of the divine and the human as distinct
ontological entities runs throughout the New Testament no less than the
Old ("we ought to obey God rather than men," Acts 5:29; "it is appointed
unto men once to die, but after this the judgment," Heb. 9:27). Yet this
contrast of the two natures in no way precludes the Christian doctrine of
divine incarnation in Christ Jesus, a doctrine needlessly blurred by such
misleading shorthand expressions as, for example, that "God became man."
To say that "the Word became flesh"—that the second person of the divine

Godhead alongside his eternal nature assumed human nature—differs greatly from the notion that the humanity of Jesus of Nazareth exhausts the total meaning of the being and structure of God. To speak of the fullness of the Godhead dwelling in the God-man Christ Jesus is quite another matter from the impression conveyed by Barth's words, "the human being of God" (IV/1, p. 183), a phrase that can fuel both Jewish and Islamic misunderstandings of incarnation.

Barth can be highly misleading when he writes, for example, of God's becoming a creature: "In the decisive action in the history of His covenant with the creature, in Jesus Christ, He actually becomes a creature, and thus makes the cause of the creature His own in the most concrete reality and not just in appearance. . . . This is how God comes on the scene" (*Church Dogmatics*, III/3, p. 358; cf. IV/1, p. 129).

That God becomes flesh in the sense of assuming human nature, of acquiring manhood indwelt by the fullness of the Godhead (Col. 1:19), is wholly compatible with the emphasis on Jesus Christ as God-man, that is, on this specific Jesus of Nazareth who manifests both divine and human natures. Evangelical orthodoxy affirms that the Logos did not become a human person at all; it follows the Chalcedonian emphasis, that is, one person (divine), two natures (divine and human). But that God becomes "a creature" is quite another matter; to formulate divine becoming in this way makes it seem the absolute antithesis of divinity. To be sure, Barth safeguards what he says against such misunderstanding: "He does not cease to be God," says Barth (IV/1, p. 159); "The deity of Christ is the one unaltered because unalterable deity of God. . . . He humbled Himself, but did not do it by ceasing to be who He is" (*ibid.,* pp. 179 f.). But can Christian theism then afford to inculcate either the impression that God became a creature, or, what it also expressly repudiates, that a creature can become God?

On occasion, but very infrequently to be sure, the Old Testament does use the term Elohim of men but when it does so interpreters differ over the meaning. Psalm 45, dedicated to the king, is a case in point. The King James Version translates the sixth verse: "Thy throne, O God, is for ever and ever; the sceptre of thy kingdom is a right sceptre." The Revised Standard Version reads: "Your divine throne endures forever and ever" (marginal readings: "your throne is a throne of God" or "Thy throne, O God"). The New Testament considers the passage messianic (Heb. 1:8 ff.). In other words, the explanation of the text is not to be found—as by comparative religions commentators (cf. Anton Jirku, *Altorientalischer Kommentar zum Alten Testament,* p. 266)—in the ancient pagan application of divine titles to kings as divine viceregents. Whatever its historical occasion, the psalmist's expression is peculiarly appropriate to the royal messianic line of David (cf. 2 Sam. 7:16, "Your house and your kingdom shall be made sure forever before me; your throne shall be established forever"; cf. Ps. 89:3 f., 29). Because the king of the Davidic line typifies the divine eternal king the writer of Hebrews affirms that the psalmist is speaking prophetically "of the Son." Philip Edgcumbe Hughes observes: "To address the royal messianic personage as God is not without parallel in the Old Testament. Isaiah, for example, proclaims that the coming one who will rule on the throne of David will be called 'Mighty God' (Isa. 9:6), a designation used elsewhere of the Most High (cf. Deut. 10:17; Neh. 9:32; Ps. 24:8; Jer. 32:18); and Jeremiah prophesies that the 'righteous Branch' who is to be raised up for David, and who will reign as king, and who will execute justice and righteousness, will be called by the name 'The Lord [Yahweh] is our righteousness' (Jer. 23:5 f.)" (*A Commentary on the Epistle to the Hebrews,* p. 64).

Somewhat different, however, is the usage in Exodus 21:6, 22:7 ff. and Psalm 82:1, 6; from these passages interpreters conclude that the term *theoi* was applied to judges as a class because in God's name they pronounce judgment in human affairs. In no way can such passages compromise the fundamental Jewish repudiation of polytheism, or the Hebrew conviction that it is blasphemous to regard human beings ontologically as God. Judges may officially serve in the name and role of God and therefore be titled God's representatives and be honorifically called gods. But not even the greatest among them accepted the worship that belongs to God alone and that is due him from judges no less than from others.

Oddly enough Jesus' own comment on Psalm 82:6—a passage that he introduces to emphasize the unbreakable authority of the Bible—seems to complicate the God-man discussion, at least on the surface. In reply to those who accused him of blasphemy and were ready to stone him for claiming oneness with the Father (John 10:30), Jesus referred to this Psalm to show that when speaking of princes or magistrates who rule or judge for God the Old Testament (Ps. 82:6) characterized such persons as gods. Were this emphasis (John 10:34) the climax of Jesus' rejoinder, one might take his words as merely *ad hominem* and perhaps even as an evasion of the prime issue of whether or not he claimed divine metaphysical status. But Jesus' reply soon takes a strategic turn: he sets himself apart, as "the Son of God," from those whom the received canonical literature designates 'gods' because of their representative and interpretative roles. Jesus is not content to take to himself a kind of godhood to be shared pluralistically with others; instead, he presses an absolutely unique claim: "If he called *them* gods *to whom the word of God came,* . . ." he replies, "do you say of *him whom the Father consecrated and sent into the world* 'you are blaspheming'" (John 10:35-36)—indeed, the veritable Word of God enfleshed—"because I said, 'I am the Son of God'?" (ital. sup.). In short, while Jesus acknowledges that Scripture properly applies the divine title in a certain representative sense to judges, he at the same time applies it exclusively to himself in its absolutely unique intention. Jesus' words in no way imply the divinity of all humanity; they emphasize, rather, that the one living God is personally and singularly present and active in Jesus.

Another Johannine passage brings out even more powerfully the connection and contrast between "being" and "becoming" in the life of the Christ of God. In John 8:58 Jesus declares: "Before Abraham was, I am" (KJV) or, as another version translates it, "before Abraham was born . . ." (NEB). The aorist tense used of Abraham suggests, as Morris observes, "a mode of being which has a definite beginning in contrast with one which is eternal" and which the present tense "I am" implies concerning Jesus (*The Gospel According to John,* p. 473). The term *ginomai* used of Abraham is related to the term *genesis;* by derivation the latter indicates what has come into being, in explicit distinction from the eternal and uncreated.

The New Testament doctrine of divine becoming differs in striking ways therefore from that of contemporary process theology. The latter propounds a one layer view of reality more than a clear distinction between the supernatural and the natural, and it speaks of God's becoming in terms of an inner divine necessity of certain aspects of the divine nature rather than in terms of divine voluntarism; its formulation therefore centers elsewhere than in the once-for-all incarnation of God in Jesus Christ. Although process philosophy takes a variety of forms, it invariably rejects the orthodox thesis that the divine nature as such is immutable. It therefore sponsors an alteration of the very form of divinity, no less than of its content. This approach contrasts with the New Testament doctrine of divine becoming, in which Christ does not cling exclusively to the form of divinity, but voluntarily comes in the form of a man to unveil the inmost nature of the unchanging God. Process philosophy imports change and development into aspects of the very nature of God and consequently speaks of a growing God.

The Bible does indeed contain elements of process theology, or rather, of procession theology. But scriptural interest in divine procession has nothing whatever in common with philosophical theories that depict the universe as necessary to God. The Bible focuses instead on the interior life of the Godhead. When modern theology deals with God and process, it often expounds theories of how God intrinsically changes and develops, how aspects of the divine nature supposedly mesh into time-space realities, and how the early church allegedly invented the doctrine of the Trinity. But the New Testament confines the terms "begetting" and "procession" to interrelationships between the persons of the Trinity, even as it speaks of divine "becoming" only in relation to the incarnation. Discussion of divine procession is properly considered therefore under the theme of the Trinity rather than under that of creation and preservation of the world. An antimetaphysical age is reluctant to speak of divine ontology. In the biblical view, moreover, the emphasis on the "only begotten" Son has to do with absolute uniqueness rather than with the notion of derivation. Likewise, when it emphasizes the procession of the Spirit from the Father and the Son, the Bible deals not with origination but with a subordination of office and work.

The biblical revelation of God's "becoming" therefore differs sharply from modern process conceptions. The fact of Jesus Christ as God come "in the flesh" to exegete (*exagō,* John 1:18) who God permanently is, contrasts spectacularly with speculative notions of change and growth in God that preclude our knowing and saying who and what in certain respects God permanently is. The New Testament declares even the crucified and ascended Jesus to be "the same yesterday, today, and forever" (Heb. 11:8).

Any removal of the doctrine of God's once-for-all incarnation in Jesus Christ from centrality in discussing the being and becoming of God, any compromise of the doctrine that Jesus Christ alone is the embodied revelation of God, constitutes an assault on scriptural teaching. The reality of the incarnation of God in Christ is the linchpin of any authentically biblical discussion of divine becoming. Religious philosophers who profess to illumine the divine immutability, infinity and eternality of God in terms of speculative conceptions that mute this doctrine of incomparable incarnation can only distort the biblical view, however much they may deploy Scripture selectively to support partisan expositions. There is every reason to press those who occasionally stress the congruity of some of their conclusions with the Bible to indicate on just what basis of scriptural sensitivity they venture these traditional affirmations about God, and by what divine authority they reject other passages that contradict process philosophy perspectives.

It should surprise us little that James Barr, a leading spokesman for biblical critics, abandons the scriptural view not only of an unchanging but also of an unerring God (*The Bible in the Modern World,* pp. 11, 179) and declares God's nature to be at once imperfect, vacillating and changing (*Fundamentalism,* p. 277). He commends biblical critics and modern theologians for enabling us to escape ancient Greek "misconceptions" that God is essentially perfect, and proceeds to tell us that "Christological orthodoxy has to go too." Indeed, he adds, it may well be that any formulation that would "satisfy our present understanding" of the person of Christ "would be unorthodox or heretical in terms of the ancient discussions" (*ibid.,* p. 172). It is patently clear that the critical rejection either of the reliability of Scripture or of divine incarnation of Christ sooner or later involves a changed conception of God in virtually all of his nature.

In early Christian times Gnostic philosophy ruled out a real incarnation of God in the flesh; today rampant secularism denies and disdains any role whatever for the supernatural. Even subbiblical theologies that insist upon theism balk at the doctrine of divine incarnation. Today a widening chorus of professional ecclesiastics have joined Bultmann (*The Theology of the New Testament,* Vol. 2, pp. 33 ff.) in viewing the incarnation of the eternal Logos in Jesus of Nazareth as only myth (cf. *The Myth of God Incarnate,* John Hick, ed.).

Powerfully pertinent in confronting this broadening denial—even in supposedly Christian circles—of God's singular incarnation in Jesus Christ are the brief letters of John the apostle. The New Testament refuses to compromise the affirmation that "God was in Christ"; it disallows any verdict that denies Christ's fully divine no less than fully human nature. The Bible teaches that from the moment of incarnation a true and permanent union of divine and human natures eventuated in Jesus Christ. John emphasizes not only that Jesus Christ "has come in the flesh" (1 John 4:2, RSV) and that this is he "who came by water and blood" (cf. 5:6), but sets forth also, as a test of Christian orthodoxy, the doctrine that Jesus Christ is "coming in flesh" (2 John 7, translated literally). I. Howard Marshall thinks that these verb tense variations indicate that Jesus Christ has come and still exists "in flesh," in short, that John stresses a real and lasting incarnation (*The Epistles of John,* p. 70). When John refers to the God-man's second advent in terms of "the one who is to come" ('*o erchomenos*), Robert Mounce thinks the apostle avoids using '*o genomenos* (the coming one) as unacceptable "because *ginomai* means 'to become' " and can also substitute for *eimi,* meaning "to be." "John," says Mounce, "would use no word which could imply change in God" (*The Book of Revelation,* p. 68, n. 13). In short, a term applicable to Christ's incarnation in flesh (John 1:14) in the first advent is inappropriate to the second advent.

Denial of the incarnation—often ventured by those who extol Jesus as a good man manifesting remarkable moral integrity and spiritual power—cuts at the very root of New Testament faith. Presumably with Tillich in mind, Marshall comments that the first New Testament confessors of "Jesus is Lord" "would not have accepted 'I regard Jesus as my ultimate concern' (but not as having the metaphysical status of 'Son of God')" as a correct exegesis of the formula (*The Epistles of John,* p. 206). The apostle John labels anyone who repudiates the doctrine that Jesus is Christ come in the flesh not only as a "deceiver" but also as "antichrist" (2 John 7), one who already manifests the spirit of the apocalyptic Antichrist (1 John 2:18). John considers the rejection of Jesus as God's only Son not only a distortion of christology but also a distortion of the doctrine of God (cf. 1 John 2:23, "no one who denies the Son has the Father").

If we are concerned with the themes of God and change, the Bible confronts us on the one hand with a series of mainly Old Testament passages that speak of God's "repentance" and on the other, with a warning in Paul's epistle to the Romans about the dire consequences of human misbelief that finally exchanges the eternal God for an array of ever-changing human idols. Some theologians invoke the so-called repentance passages to reject the doctrine of a fixed divine decree that predestinates only certain individuals to salvation; others appeal to them in order to revise traditional views of God's immutability. Discussion of the repentance passages is reserved for independent treatment. At this point we note instead the use in Romans 1:25 of the term *metallassō*—a derivative of *allassō* meaning to alter, to make otherwise, to change. The verse in Romans deals not with change in the nature of God, but rather with change in speculative human conceptions and reconstructions of God's identity. According to the apostle Paul, those who "exchanged the truth of God for a lie" (the verb *metallassō* means to change for or into, to exchange) merit divine abandonment. John Murray notes that "the truth of God may here mean (1) God's truth—or the truth that belongs to God that God has made known; or (2) the truth that God himself is; or (3) the truth concerning God. Although Murray prefers the first alternative, viz., the truth that God has made known over against man's falsehood, he concedes that the phrase, "the truth of God," may correspond in meaning to "the Creator"; it may, in fact, be the equivalent of God's being, reality and glory, in which case "the lie" would be the worship and service of whatever is creaturely (*The Epistle to the Ro-*

mans, p. 45). The idolatry that puts finite beings in God's place begins by altering God's nature and attributes.

By focusing the intellectual dilemmas of their age in the context of their own speculative schemes, cloistered intellectuals (a vanishing species) often find themselves misled by their very own sophisticated theories. While it is true that the worship of becoming rather than of divine being is an increasingly prominent feature of secular society today, the pagan in the street has little if any interest in technical process philosophy; this academic pursuit preoccupies mainly a small and elite cadre of scholars and seminarians. The contemporary worship of becoming is nonphilosophical and existential in character. Its crassest and crudest forms are seen in the worship of mammon, in the pursuit of sexual gratification as the essence of life, in the reliance on the stars rather than on the God who made them. It fuels and fires the aspirations of multitudes who reach for monetary affluence both because of inflation and despite its erosive power. It tricks gamblers at the casinos, lotteries or race tracks into hopes of a better life. Before developing nations it dangles the lure of affluence by political miracles. It spawns addiction to what is novel in technological gadgetry and even in fashion. It is not God and change but rather change and chance that bracket contemporary desire.

In the forefront of New Testament derivatives of the verb *allassō* stands the term *katallassō,* reconciliation, that speaks of the change God works in his relation to the sinner and in the sinner's relation to him. The Bible insistently reminds its readers that fallen man as God's enemy stands in dire need of a changed nature and of changed relationships; it uncompromisingly demands a change in man and in human society. The Bible therefore has a spirited interest in God and change. But the Bible cannot be detoured into conjectural theories of ontological change in God. It emphasizes instead that fallen man and the fallen universe will be changed (Heb. 1:12), that in the eschatological triumph of God "we shall all be changed" (1 Cor. 15:51 f., 2 Cor. 3:18); we are to fix our hearts on heaven where "neither moth nor rust doth corrupt" (Matt. 6:20) and should "no longer . . . be . . . tossed by the waves and whirled about by every fresh gust of teaching . . ." (Eph. 4:14, NEB). The being and coming and becoming of God are the Bible's main motifs and its discussion of change illumines and brightens the plight of mortals because the Sovereign of the universe does "not change" (Mal. 3:6, RSV).

3.
The Living God of the Bible

THAT GOD LIVES IS at once the simplest and profoundest statement to be made about him, for his life embraces the full reality of his sovereign being and activity.

Both the Old and New Testaments speak of "the living God" (2 Kings 19:16; Acts 14:15). That the Father "has life in himself" (John 5:26) is no figure of speech but a declaration of God's essential being. Pagan gods and idols simply have "no breath in them" (Jer. 10:14). There is no other God but the one living God (Deut. 4:35; 2 Kings 19:15); God alone is God and there is none like him (Ex. 8:10, 15:11; 1 Chron. 17:20; Ps. 86:8, 89:8).

For this very reason the formula for an oath in Old Testament times was "as the Lord liveth," "as God lives," or "as the God of Israel lives." When Hebrews were menaced they used this phrase to present Yahweh as the living One who, in contrast to the lifeless nonexisting heathen gods, evidences his existence and presence in absolute supremacy. Only rebels dispute God's active sovereignty (Jer. 5:12); only fools deny that God exists (Ps. 14:1, 53:2; Job 2:10). By a self-affirming oath, Yahweh himself confirms the dependability of his promises and warnings: "As surely as I live, declares the Sovereign LORD" (Ezek. 17:16, 33:11, NIV).

What God's life is cannot be determined by analyzing creaturely life and then projecting upon deity a vitality that characterizes intricate living creatures. The Bible never depicts life as an observable phenomenon, something known by empirical investigation that enables us to comprehend transcendent divine existence. God's life is not a unique configuration of impersonal processes and cosmic events. Nor is it merely a more durable form of the vitality imparted to lifeless man when God breathed into him "the breath of life, and man became a living being" (Gen. 2:7, NIV) and the bearer of God's image (Gen. 1:26). All conjectural attempts to refine the being of the world and of man into some generalized concept that can be projected upon an imagined deity are more hindrance than help for comprehending the One who through his own self-revelation makes himself known as the living God.

God is "the fountain of living waters" (Jer. 2:13, 17:13), "the fountain of life" (Ps. 36:9). The Father "has life in himself" (John 5:26), that is, originally and absolutely. Christ is "the Author of life" (Acts 3:15, RSV), or, in magnificent brevity, "the life" (John 14:6; Phil. 1:21; Col. 3:4; 1 John 1:2). The agent in the creation of all the forms and structures of the universe was the divine Logos (John 1:3); as the incarnate Logos or God-man he additionally received from the Father the divine prerogative to bestow redemptive life upon the penitent, and resurrection life in the age to come (John 5:26).

God is the incomparable "I am that I am" (Ex. 3:14). "There is no plainer description of the divinity of God," Barth remarks, "than the phrase which occurs so frequently in the Pentateuch and again in the Book of Ezekiel: 'I am the Lord your (or thy) God,' and it has its exact, New Testament parallel in the 'I am' of the Johannine Jesus. . . . In this biblical 'I am' the Subject posits itself and in that way posits itself as the living and loving Lord. . . . He who does this is the God of the Bible" (*Church Dogmatics*, II/1, pp. 301 f.).

The Bible has no twilight zone of demigods and semigods; it knows only the living *theos* and inert and false *theoi*. Unlike much conjectural philosophy, the Bible is not concerned merely with divinity or being in general; its hallmark is the highly particular self-revealed God. It is no happenstance that the definite article is used (*'o theos*) to designate the God of Israel. The Old Testament is well aware that outside Israel both *El*, the generic term for God, and *elohim*, the plural polytheistic term, were in common use throughout the ancient world. In biblical theology, however, the living God as the one and only God wholly fulfills the species *El* and except when referring pejoratively to the pagan gods, the biblical writers use *Elohim* with a singular verb for the one living God. Elohim concretely and fully manifests divine reality. ("Know therefore that Yahweh thy Elohim, he is Elohim, the faithful Elohim, which keepeth covenant and mercy with them that love him and keep his commandments to a thousand generations," Deut. 7:9; "If Yahweh be Elohim, follow him," 1 Kings 18:21, "that this people may know that thou art Yahweh Elohim," 1 Kings 18:37). In these passages Elohim is called God absolutely, the one who alone is essentially divine ("Unto thee it was shown, that thou mightest know Yahweh; he is Elohim; there is none else beside him," Deut. 4:35). The living God claims not only exclusive validity among the Hebrews (Ex. 20:2 f.) but declares himself to be also the only God of the Gentile world and in fact of the entire created universe (Isa. 45:18–23).

Greek, Roman and other ancient civilizations used the term *theos* even of outstanding rulers or emperors whom they worshiped as essentially divine. Homeric mythology postulated living gods that lack eternality but nonetheless outlast man's mortality; the Epicureans ascribed to their gods not nontemporal eternity but unending duration in time. But the Bible provokes debate not only over the authentic nature of divine life, but over that of human life as well. It affirms that God makes known his *vita* on his own initiative and that the *imago Dei* imparted at creation confers upon mankind a creaturely life superior to that of animal existence; in no case, however, has man or any creature a latent potential for divinity. Ancient religious philosophers applied the term *theos* to impersonal cosmic powers; by the easy device of capitalization they then conferred metaphysical status upon the Divine, the Good, the One, and so on. (Modern counterparts are similarly dignified as Space-Time or Being or Ground.) By such postulations God and the cosmos, in part or whole, become identical; certain elements of the world—its supposed intrinsic necessity, irrevocable laws, or evolutionary powers—are considered divine. Instead of acknowledging God as living and transcendent, Greek philosophers—notably Heraclitus and the Stoics—tended to equate God simply with the living essence of the world. But Scripture sanctions neither this ancient Stoic conception of the universe as a psycho-physical divine organism, nor the modern Hegelian regard for man and nature as evolutionary manifestations of the life of the Absolute, nor deity misdefined by process philosophy as the immanent ground of the universe and an aspect of all experience. The biblical God is a transcendent reality who preexisted both the world and man.

Process philosophy professes to overcome a Greek "static" God that obscures the deity's ever-active relation to man and the world. But it also restructures the biblical revelation of the living God and opposes central emphases of scriptural theism. This it does by substituting a necessary divine creation of the universe for voluntary supernatural creation, and by excluding the once-for-all miraculous as a misreading of natural processes. Process theology also considers the universe as God's body, obscuring both the incarnation of God in Jesus Christ and the church as the regenerate body over which the Risen Christ reigns, and strips the grace of God of such decisive historical acts as Jesus' substitutionary atonement and his bodily resurrection from the dead. Process philosophy further dilutes the biblical revelation by excluding propositional conceptual content from God's self-revelation, and by correlating God's salvific activity not primarily with historical redemptive acts but rather with man's inner faith response to an interpersonal divine human encounter. Whatever process philosophers may presume to gain by such alternatives to a "static" deity, their projected reconstitution of God's nature actually deprives deity of major perfections and activities characteristic of the living God of the Bible, and results in a view of the divine that is inadequate philosophically, scripturally, and experientially. The theory that created reality is necessary to God, and is in some respects divine, departs in crucial ways from the biblical revelation of God. On the basis of God's own self-revelation biblical theists reject notions that make the universe God's body and essential to his life; they disavow views that replace the scriptural doctrine of God's primordial creation of graded orders of life, like that of Schubert Ogden, for whom God himself changes as "the ever-present primordial ground" of an evolving universe (*The Reality of God,* p. 210). Ogden's insistence that God exists necessarily, but that his essence is in part dependent upon the universe, is self-defeating, for if God exists necessarily, he cannot be essentially dependent; on the other hand, if God is essentially dependent, he does not exist necessarily.

Far less does the Bible approve such naturalistic notions as that food and water or material factors fully account for man's survival; such nourishment does indeed nurture human life, but it is God who gives (Luke 12:15) and sustains it (Matt. 4:4). However much the twentieth century pursues a higher quality of human life—one that the Bible commends in its own way—the quality of divine life will always transcend the human, unique as it is, and even at its best. Redemption can indeed lift the creaturely life of fallen man to the incomparable human joys of "eternal life" (John 3:16) by providing an imperishable human life fit for time and eternity. But God lives his own distinctive life; an immense ontological chasm separates man who "became a living soul" (Gen. 2:7) and bears the divine image (Gen. 1:26) from the living God who created man and endowed him thus.

The God of the Bible eternally has life in himself. As theologians have sometimes put it, he has *aseity,* or life from and by himself in independent freedom. His essential life does not correspond merely to his personal relations to the cosmos and to human beings. Nor should the life God has in himself be contrasted with the life of creatures by asserting merely that creaturely life exists through his will and purposes. The fact is that though heaven and earth, the work of his hands, shall perish (Ps. 102:25 f.), God himself "endures." He neither became the living God by his creation of the universe, nor did he become the living God at some point in eternity past; he *is* the one living God, and is so eternally. He lives in eternal self-affirmation. His life is all that he thinks, decides, and wills in creative freedom. God perpetually wills and purposes his own being; this being depends upon nothing external to himself yet is not internally necessitated as if he exists forever whether he wills to do so or not. He wills eternally to be himself in the fulness of his independent vitality, and never ceases to be himself. God exists in absolute plenitude and power. He is wholly free to be himself and removes the mystery of his own being by making known his inner nature by voluntary self-disclosure.

The pagan gods cannot help others; they cannot even help themselves. They are mere zeds or zeros: ". . . There is no breath in them. They are worth nothing, mere mockeries" (Jer. 10:14, NEB). The idols are "useless" (Ps. 31:6, NEB). Samuel pleads: "Give up the worship of false gods which can neither help nor save, because they are false" (1 Sam. 12:21, NEB). Jeremiah adds: "Our forefathers inherited only a sham, an idol vain and useless" (Jer. 16:19, NEB).

The living God is to be obeyed because in self-disclosure he has declared his commanding and directive will; the false gods have neither mind nor will; they issue no summons to obedience, nor can they direct human action. "The Lord alone led him (Israel), no alien god at his side," declares Moses (Deut. 32:12, NEB). Jeremiah speaks of the pagan gods which are "no gods"

(2:11); he rebukes Israel's rebellion and apostasy through Yahweh's pointed question: "How can I forgive you for all this? Your sons have forsaken me and sworn by gods that are not gods" (Jer. 5:7, NEB). Isaiah speaks by contrast of the whole earth as full of the glory of the living God (6:3).

While false gods are not authentic divine powers, the Old Testament indicates that through fallen man's imagination they gain a power of attraction in human experience, captivate the will and elicit religious response. Such response not only victimizes adherents; it also evokes Yahweh's displeasure, for Yahweh is a jealous God: "You shall fear the Lord your God, serve him alone and take your oaths in his name. You must not follow other gods, gods of the nations that are around you; if you do, the Lord your God who is in your midst will be angry with you, and he will sweep you away off the face of the earth, for the Lord your God is a jealous god" (Deut. 6:13–15, NEB). Here one must cite especially the Decalogue: "You shall have no other god to set against me. You shall not make a carved image for yourself nor the likeness of anything in the heavens above, or on the earth below, or in the waters under the earth. You shall not bow down to them or worship them; for I, the Lord your God, am a jealous God" (Exod. 20:3–5, NEB; cf. Deut. 5:7–9). The living God is jealous not of false gods as real entities but of the power they exert over those who imaginatively invest idols with ontological existence and volition (cf. Deut. 4:23 ff.).

The God of the Old Testament is indeed a God of social justice, as many expositors today stress above all else, but he is no less prominently the living God who challenges the false gods that lure away man's attention and preempt his energies. This indictment of evil powers gives biblical religion great force in Asia and Africa where invisible spirits wield extensive influence over daily life. It is no less significant for European and American life, however, where secular man despite his intellectual dismissal of a transcendent world places himself in idolatrous relationships to material things and natural processes. Harvey Cox reminds us that "from the perspective of Biblical thought, neither the garden nor the machine can save man . . . . Yahweh creates man to enjoy and attend the garden, but not to sacrifice to it; to make things for his own use, but not to pray to them" (*The Seduction to the Spirit,* p. 300). The passion for things and lust for money have become such a hallmark of materialistic Western culture that tangible realities hold priority among life's values.

The pseudo-divine and the demonic inspirit much of twentieth-century life in both the Occident and the Orient. Non-Christian Formosan workers have a god of the living room, of the dining room, of the kitchen, of the bedroom, of the bathroom. Besides worshiping ancestors and numerous household gods, workers also revere the gods of their profession—farmers, for example, fishermen, merchants, even beggars and prostitutes worship their own special god. The more miserable one's situation, the more gods one will implore. The farmer lacking scientific techniques will worship the sun god, the rain god, the river god. Even rural road workers using modern machinery sometimes refuse to work until or unless they first pray to the local gods.

Surviving in this invocation of invisible spirits is the blurred conviction that the living God is concerned with all human activity. But while subdividing the deity into multiple divinities with a superstitious kind of reverence may preserve regard for the transcendent, this course is ridiculed by the younger generation under the pressures of modern learning. Some students say they have no use for the church simply because they are students; they do not believe in God because disciplines like computer science can solve all problems accurately and quickly. The scientific desacralization of nature helps breed the presumption that science dissolves the supernatural. Only the biblical revelation which banishes false gods and at the same time challenges the myths of modernity such as materialism, scientism, and eroticism avoids human capitulation to naturalism, be it Marxian, secular capitalist, or scientistic.

Some expositors ground the Old Testament case for Yahweh's exclusive divinity in man's internal response rather than in cognitive considerations. Instead of giving an unbiased statement of the Hebrew view, their explanation reflects the influence of the decision-oriented dialectical and existential theology of recent decades, or involves lingering concessions to evolutionary theories of religious development. Obviously the Old Testament account of the living God is not a metaphysical discourse interested only in intellectual delineation; while its proximate interest is knowledge of God, its call to obedient faith in the living and active God stands everywhere in the forefront. But the revelation of the God of the Bible is not subcognitive. Hence we are not reduced to the alternatives of conjectural argumentation on the one hand or personal trust on the other. Of itself the latter would not be decisive for knowing the truth of the one God (even rebellious demons are said to share this, cf. James 2:19).

Only decision-oriented theology can supply a basis for Gottfried Quell's protest that "there is perhaps an excess of rational argument in the complaints of the prophets" and for his disparagement of supposedly "arid, theoretical statements in the later literature" ("*Theos:* El and Elohim in the Old Testament," *TDNT,* 3:89). Quell has in mind specially Daniel 11:36, with its prophetic reference to the willful king who speaks against "the God of gods"; Malachi 2:10 ("Have we not all one father? Hath not one God created us?"); and the statement in Psalm 82:1 that "God . . . judgeth among the gods," that is, among magistrates who rule as his representatives. But these passages are hardly as arid as Quell implies and they surely do not exhaust the cognitive elements through which Old Testament revelation exhibits the one living God.

Kenneth Hamilton thinks that the Hebrew conviction that no God exists other than Yahweh arose as the end-product of a history of spiritual obedience to Yahweh, and emerged "through a long process of education of Israel's imagination rather than a direct appeal to the intellect" (*To Turn from Idols,* p. 18). It is of course the case that an insistent divine demand for faith and obedience accompanies the biblical revelation of Yahweh. But to suggest as Hamilton does that as an intellectual commitment ethical monotheism has no Hebrew roots earlier than the eighth-century prophet Isaiah (*ibid.,* pp. 18 ff.) grounds earlier monotheistic faith extrarationally in volitional response, if not in religious imagination which Hamilton elsewhere depicts as the special domain of the pseudo-divinities. The Decalogue does indeed set the affirmation of Yahweh against other gods (Ex. 20:3; Deut. 5:7) in the context of a call to obedient love, but one hardly does justice to Mosaic representations to say that "it did not matter greatly whether the people believed that the gods of the nations had some kind of independent existence or whether they were pure fictions, empty 'wind' " (*ibid.,* p. 21). Elijah demanded a clear choice between Baal and Yahweh (1 Kings 18:21), a choice that required trust and obedience to be sure, but hardly on that account, as Hamilton would have us believe, one that involved no "illumination of the mind by knowledge" (*ibid.,* p. 20).

Hamilton extends his "volition-centered" interpretation of biblical data to the New Testament as well. He thinks that, discouraged at Mars Hill by "little response from the philosophically minded . . . to Paul's apologetic efforts," the apostle thereafter preached Christ crucified "without regard to the Greek search for intellectual truth" (*ibid.,* pp. 27 ff.) and followed what Hamilton supposes to be the Old Testament precedent of witnessing to God's acts instead of insisting on the intelligibility and reasonableness of faith (*ibid.,* p. 28). Hamilton even deplores any attempt to state religious truth in "cool reason"—that is, in objectively valid terms—as an effort to demythologize (*ibid.,* p. 33), and insists that only "through personal encounter" can we justify a personalized view of the universe (*ibid.,* p. 34). So too when he expounds Paul's comments on eating food devoted to idols as turning on obedience rather than on knowledge (*ibid.,* pp. 14 ff.), Hamilton seems to confuse knowledge that is translated into obedient love with love in the absence of knowledge.

At the very opening of the Bible the Hebrew creation account leaves no room intellectually for other gods, nor does the Decalogue. Although in the Bible, as Hamilton says, "the 'nothingness' of idols is never asserted as a general truth to be known by itself," that is, apart from a summons to worship the living God alone (*ibid.,* p. 20), it hardly follows that the Hebrews did not intellectually know the nothingness and powerlessness of the pagan deities.

In certain important respects the Hebrew monotheistic revelation strikingly differs from Greek philosophical monotheism, one crucial difference being the forefront Hebrew emphasis on worship of Yahweh over against the rather secondary and subordinate role that Greek philosophy assigns to worship. We need not on that account, however, subscribe to Hamilton's thesis that "monotheism as an intellectual system may be said to have been invented by the Greek mind" (*ibid.,* p. 23). Greek philosophers indeed presented their views more rigidly in an orderly philosophical scheme, independently of progressive divine revelation and premised on creative rational analysis which led to many rival expositions. But the Hebrews were not indifferent to concerns of logic and consistency. They did not, however, present their teaching about the one true and living God as a conclusion derived as an inference from the character of the cosmos or nature of man. They traced monotheism, both intellectually and volitionally, not ultimately to the invention of any human mind, Greek or Hebrew, but to the living God's self-revelation.

Some Greek philosophers conceived the cosmic elements and powers as "abstract and inexorable"; whether because of recalcitrance (Plato) or because of pure potentiality (Aristotle), matter itself was thought to be evil and resistant to the divine will. Even ancient Near Eastern astrology and divinization of cosmic as well as astral powers had anticipated some of these features. Near Eastern religions connected cosmic forces with benevolent and malevolent divinities. Zoroastrianism ranged light and darkness against each other as good and evil principles, whereas Platonic philosophy connected matter with evil as an impersonal force.

The biblical writers on the other hand speak of superhuman powers as rebellious personal agents hostile to God's good governance of the world yet ultimately subject to the Creator. Insofar as pagan polytheism had any ontological basis, it came about through the corrupt elevation and idolatrous worship of such spirits, worship that sacrificed the unity of the living God and exalted rebellious creaturely agents or mere cosmic forces to an absolute divine role.

But when Hamilton suggests that the Hebrews "personalized" the cosmic powers, and that Hebrew monotheism was experiential rather than intellectual, he obscures the doctrines of satanology and angelology as well as underestimates the rational revelational basis for biblical monotheism. In a universe that Near Eastern religions populated with gods and intermediary beings, the Hebrews assign a remarkably subordinate role to angelology, one that nowhere reflects polytheism. While it remained for Christianity to give full expression to the fact that "no angel, no prince, nothing that exists, nothing still to come, not any power, or height or depth, nor any created thing, can ever come between us and the love of God made visible in Christ Jesus our Lord" (Rom. 8:38–39, JB), the Old Testament call for exclusive trust in the one Creator and Lord already implies this. By emphasizing that the whole realm of "principalities and powers"—or elemental spirits and energies—is subordinate to the Creator's agency, and that nothing can permanently frustrate the personal action and purpose of the Lord of the universe, Paul stripped cosmic elements and forces of any paralyzing power over mankind and removed the temptation to divinize their elusive mysterious nature. As Hamilton well says, "the antidote to fear of the abstract powers was the concrete revelation in Christ of the living God, the Creator still personally active in his world" (*ibid.*, p. 29).

Writing of "the ambivalence of the being and nonbeing of the gods, of the power and folly of idolatry," Helmut Thielicke says: "The Old Testament attack on pagan gods and idolatry brings out the ambivalence that is their characteristic. They can win power and yet they are empty. Yahweh is the first and the last, and besides him is no god (Isaiah 44:6). Yet in a way that accepts the existence of the gods he can be compared with them and extolled as incomparably superior (Exodus 15:11; 18:11; Psalm 72:18 ff.; 86:8, 93:3; 96:4)" (*The Evangelical Faith,* p. 93). "In comparison with the one true God the gods are impotent, vain and unprofitable (cf. Isaiah 44:8, 2 Kings 18:33 ff.; Jeremiah 16:19 f.)" (*ibid.,* p. 98). In relation to the created universe, they are "entangled" in creation and implicated in "what is created and perishable." In relation to man, "if God is my only Lord, the gods are disarmed and . . . nonexistent. If God is not my Lord, either because I do not yet know him and am outside the covenant, or because, as a weaker brother, I accept him only partially, and my spiritual life is still immature, then there are ethically unredeemed spheres to which God's lordship has not yet extended, and here the beaten gods can fight a rear-guard action and set up pockets of resistance where nothingness can win power over me and come to existence" (*ibid.,* pp. 98 ff.).

This ambivalent status of other divinities than Yahweh is not a result of evolutionary development from polytheism or henotheism to monotheism, but reflects rather the ambiguous ontology of the world of rival powers and spirits. The gods initially gain their standing merely as human conceptions, as products of human thought and imagination (Isa. 44:9–20). As Thielicke says, "this origin of the gods, this feature that they are creature rather than Creator, is the reason for their impotence, their nondeity. . . . As products of men's hands or minds the gods can have no reality independent of man" (*The Evangelical Faith,* Vol. 1, p. 94). When man fashions gods, they are "empty" and "useless" (Jer. 16:19 ff.; 2 Kings 18:33 ff.; Ps. 106:19 ff.; Jer. 2:24) for they cannot respond to man's need (Jer. 2:19). Unlike Feuerbach, the Bible nowhere gives the impression that the gods, as postulations of hope and projections of fears, remain sheer fantasy with no power. These gods somehow do get men in their clutch. In biblical theism Satan and other fallen angels have an objective existence. Although they are only products of idolatrous imagination, the false gods nonetheless accumulate a coercive power that lends them demonic force.

The apostle Paul writes on the one hand of so-called gods (1 Cor. 10:19 ff.) and on the other of "gods many, and lords many" (1 Cor. 8:5). Nowhere does he compromise the fact that the Christian knows that there is only one God, the Father of Jesus Christ (1 Cor. 8:4 ff.), and that faith in the self-revealing living God alone effectively disarms false gods by exposing them as mythical constructs. He unqualifiedly rejects the thesis that the idol "really amounts to anything" (1 Cor. 10:19 ff., TEV), "itself is real" (JB), "really exists" (Phillips), or that idols "are really alive and are real gods" (LB). The Christian must nonetheless be careful not to regard idols as realities or to assign them an actual captivating power, for pagan practice, when properly seen, is nothing less than surrender to demons (1 Cor. 10:18–22). Theological truth must not be sacrificed. But moral sensitivity to weak brethren is nonetheless an issue. Yet the Christian must leave no doubt that those who regard false gods as powers and beings having majestic predicates and attributes pervert and reject the truth of the one living God.

Thielicke, therefore, seems to overexistentialize the Christian response to false gods when he relies on faith alone to cancel their latent power: "Within God's sphere of power, i.e., faith, in which God is the only one for us (1 Cor. 8:6, Col. 1:16 f.), the gods are disarmed and cast into the nothingness of nonbeing. They have no more being or significance for us" (*ibid.*, p. 97). It is true that vital commitment to the alternative, that is, to the God of the Bible, precludes merely adding Jesus Christ to one's household or shelf gods. But atheistic movements also appeal to ideological faith to demythologize not only the false gods, but the one living God as well. And nonbiblical religions often appeal to sheer commitment to exclude the God of the Bible as an alternative.

Yet the Bible, in proffering its revelationally reasonable case for the divine self-disclosure of the living God, strips the false gods of ontological status and leaves no doubt that because of fallen man's perversity it is God only who can now win the battle over the false god (Rom. 1:21 ff.; 1 Cor. 1:21). By disregarding God in his revelation fallen man in a catastrophic repudiation of the created orders changed the truth into a lie; enlightenment rationalism, in turn, discarded the biblical god along with false gods.

The most radical modern cults of self-realization sponsor a contemporary kind of idolatry under the guise of humanistic self-esteem. Selfism elevates the subjective ego as the only god; here the living God becomes the self-exalting ego. Paul C. Vitz alerts us: "To worship one's own self (in self-realization) or to worship all humanity is, in Christian terms, simply idolatry operating from the usual motive of unconscious egotism" (*Psychology as Religion: The Cult of Self-Worship*, p. 93).

Even Erich Fromm's rather moderate work, *The Art of Loving*, declares the god of Christian theology to be an illusion. And in *The Dogma of Christ* he dismisses Christianity as a fantasy compensation for human frustrations and debunks Christian doctrines as childish medieval beliefs. The concept of God, Fromm elsewhere informs us, has developed to the point that man is God; whatever realm of sacredness there is centers in the human self (*You Shall Be As Gods*).

Summarizing the philosophy of one of the recent self-assertion and self-deification cults, Carl Frederick writes: "*You* are the Supreme being. . . . You are IT. Choose . . . Choose to BE what you know you are" (*est: Playing the Game the New Way*, pp. 168 ff.). This mood, as Paul Vitz points out (*Psychology as Religion: The Cult of Self-Worship*, p. 33), is highly reminiscent of the existential atheism of Jean-Paul Sartre: "Life is nothing; it's up to you to give it a meaning, and value is nothing else but the meaning that you choose" (*Existentialism*, p. 58). Here by asserting self-divinity, the renegade human spirit in a mighty counterstroke of rebellion against the living Lord seeks to escape the doom that awaits man as sinner, and the death and nonbeing that must climax human destiny in a world without God.

Otto Baab notes that many biblical passages distinguish the "pure worship of Israel's superhuman and transcendent God" from idolatry by emphasizing that idols are mere personifications and objectifications of the human will. "When the idol is worshipped, man is worshipping himself, his desires, his purposes and his will" (*The Theology of the Old Testament,* pp. 105 ff.). It tells something about man's spiritual deterioration that the Creator who images himself distinctively in man later enjoins the death of any man who murders his like (Gen. 9:6) and explicitly prohibits man from imaging God in created things (Exod. 20:4); fallen humanity, in turn, supremely exhibits its foolishness and futility by exchanging "the glory of the immortal God for images made to look like mortal man and birds and animals and reptiles" (Rom. 1:22). In ancient times pagan Gentiles looked upon their earthly rulers as divine; in modern secular circles, a misguided cluster of intellectuals consider themselves divine.

Kenneth Hamilton comments that although supernatural polytheism and graven images have long been intellectually and culturally unfashionable, Western culture has not by any means discouraged idolatrous imagination, nor excluded subtler manifestations of polytheism. "As happened in Israel," he remarks, "conscious profession of faith in the one God does not prevent the imagination of men's hearts turning them back to worship 'strange gods' " (*To Turn from Idols,* p. 40). The idolatrous imagination which in past centuries shaped graven images, in our time projects equally corrupt and corrupting alternatives to faith in the living God.

Like the fascination that pinups of a bikini-clad beauty hold for the single male, even if she be only an artist's conception with no life in the real world, so the conscious and subconscious projections of a renegade humanity acquire artificial magical compulsion and imagined power. Conferring realism upon the merely imaginary at the expense of objective truth seems more and more to become a deliberate ambition of modern commercialism, a force which routinely commends its products through symbols of status and sex. Imagination elevates creaturely entities into superhuman influences that then take control of human experience. As Hamilton suggests, imagination is an "interior workshop"; here man fashions idolatrous images of God formed internally of concepts and ideas no less than externally of wood and stone (*ibid.,* pp. 54 f.).

Hamilton observes that "the imagination of men's hearts," as the King James Version translates the original language of Scripture (Gen. 6:21; Deut. 29:19; 1 Chron. 29:9; Prov. 6:18; Jer, 23:17; Luke 1:51), reflects the seventeenth-century connection of the term imagination with unreality— that is, "the imagin*ary* rather than the imagin*ative*" (*To Turn from Idols,* p. 29). Seventeenth-century writers assigned to imagination a constructive as well as illusory role.

Hamilton even credits imagination with a superrational capacity to resolve some questions of truth and error (*ibid.,* p. 31) and suggests that in the Christian life "personal decisions must go beyond 'knowledge' and rest on 'love'" (*ibid.,* p. 32, n. 4). Contending that "every philosophical or religious doctrine presupposes" an imaginative picture and images of the real world (*ibid.,* p. 32), he nonetheless emphasizes that we should "labor to make our imaginatively conceived convictions look intellectually respectable" (*ibid.*, p. 39). Quite apart from this somewhat ambiguous image-dependent epistemology that demotes the cognitive elements basic to Christian commitment, Hamilton nonetheless offers incisive insights into the forms of idolatry that currently preempt the devotion of secular Western man and, for that matter, all too often powerfully confront even professing Christians. The modern emphasis on imagination—the human mind's power to call up images—gives new force to the biblical contrast between Christ, the express image of God, and the idols or false images of God. The Old Testament and New Testament alike associate graven images with faithlessness toward God. Throughout the entire biblical era idol-worship was the most characteristic phenomenon of Gentile religion. Nothing so precisely sharpens the contrast between the pagan and Christian concepts of God as the pagan charge that the early Christians were atheists because they neither venerated prescribed images nor had images of their own.

As indicated, idolatry in the Bible involves far more than the worship of man-made images of wood and stone; it includes also the imaginative deification of powers and concepts to elicit supreme allegiance and absolute respect. Unlike ancient Babylonian astrologers, Moses and the ancient Hebrew prophets deplored sun-worship, moon-worship, star-worship and worship of other created elements (Deut. 4:19; Jer. 10:2; Ezek. 8:16). But, as Donald J. Wiseman comments, although the astrologers yielded the cosmos and life to the control of impersonal mechanical fate and drew signs from "the relations of the moon to the sun, eclipses, or, less extensively, from . . . planetary movements . . . their observations were never applied to individuals." Israel, he adds, knew that "direct Divine revelation . . . rendered divinatory techniques unnecessary"; because of their fidelity to monotheism the Hebrews avoided "the polytheistic practises of their neighbors who worshipped planets and stars" ("Astrology," p. 42). In Paul's time, observes G. B. Caird, the polytheistic gods of the Graeco-Roman world had been largely displaced by impersonal law or superhuman elemental spirits; these were thought to control the universe and consequently sapped individual life of meaning and hope (*Principalities and Powers*, p. 51). Augustine argues against pagans who applied astrology to individuals.

The Pauline protest against "vain imaginations" (Rom. 1:21, KJV; cf. JB: "they made nonsense out of logic and their empty minds were darkened") thus gains force against the secular priorities of the modern civilized world no less than against the crude spiritual aberrations of remote primitive tribes. When loosed from the constraints of rational divine revelation, religious imagination plunges man readily into spiritual idolatry; creative imagination confers an imagined reality and dynamic power upon the nonexistent to shape and direct cosmic and human affairs; it becomes the playground of imaginary idolatrous divinities, those sham-gods of both primitive and literate cultures.

Hamilton identifies "relevance," "change" and "liberation" as specially influential contemporary cultic images. These catchwords gain added authority through the modern communications media and the slogans and

clichés of Madison Avenue. The notion of inevitable progress, still somewhat current in contemporary philosophy, and the premium placed on
change both work against inherited and traditional conceptions of God,
truth and the good. If progress and change are the very stuff of reality,
then even deity, as Hamilton observes, must "conform to the idea of progress" (*ibid.*, p. 82). Setting the mood for all things both human and divine,
the "perennial new" nurtures the idea that supernatural Christianity must
yield before novel views of God and Christ; the Bible, it is said, must decrease in value for modern man. "Anything labeled relevant is above criticism, anything labeled irrelevant is beneath contempt. The affirmation
of the supreme worth of relevance becomes an article of faith, and the
pursuit of relevance a cult" (*ibid.*, p. 67). Relevance or immediate appeal
thus displaces even worth and goodness, and tradition is deplored as the
very essence of irrelevance. When the spirit of the age dictates which beliefs are acceptable or unacceptable, their relevance has become "an absolute power."

Thomas J. J. Altizer pontificates that "nothing delights the enemy of
faith so much as the idea that faith is ever the same yesterday, today,
and forever, with the obvious corollary that faith is hopelessly archaic
and irrelevant today" ("Commentary" in *The Religious Situation: 1968*,
pp. 242 ff.). The equally obvious corollary—which Altizer seems blithely
to ignore—is that even Altizer's alternative cannot be permanently relevant.
The cult of the perennially new must anticipate the sudden death of its
own mental offspring. On close reexamination such offspring often gain
a measure of staying power by adopting preferred fragments of inherited
views and parading them in contemporary dress.

Hamilton's protest against relevance sometimes seems overdrawn. After
all, among the virtues of divine revelation and divine redemption is their
relevance for all men in all generations. By contrast many items promoted
as indispensably pertinent to human welfare soon reveal their irrelevance
to human good and destiny. Hamilton himself argues for the permanent
validity of the divine commandment against graven images, a command
which on first thought may seem irrelevant for our day. Basic to the argument of his book *To Turn from Idols,* says Hamilton, is "the contention
. . . that the warning against worship of idols given in the Second Commandment remains very pertinent to our own culture" (*ibid.*, p. 12). Just
as early Christianity recognized the first commandment "to be as pertinent
as ever in the context of contemporary culture" (*ibid.*, p. 27), so, too, nothing
is more urgent for mankind today than to hear Yahweh's call "to turn
from the idols that exercise power over contemporary imaginations" and
to resist "conformity to the pattern of the present age" (*ibid.*, p. 228). What
Hamilton protests, in other words, is the absolutizing of relevance in the
process of demoting all other concerns. "If relevance is absolutized," he
says, "the wholeness of truth is . . . completely inconceivable. . . . All that
anyone needs to know is what is declared to be relevant for contemporary
man . . . and all that is relevant is given in the Perennial New. Relevance
is asserted by repeating slogans and catchwords, thus arbitrarily ruling

out any rational discussion of truth and falsehood, and by-passing by dogmatic pronouncement the delicate, exacting task of trying to examine an issue comprehensively and in its proper context" (*ibid.,* p. 134). What Hamilton does is shift emphasis from the perennially new to living tradition, from catchword-dogmatism to reverence for truth. But unless living tradition is itself subject to a permanently valid norm, it, too, will not escape impermanence. And reverence for truth, important as it is, cannot of itself establish the truth of revelation. Indeed, if personal trust is more decisive for monotheism than are rational considerations, as Hamilton elsewhere indicates, then truth does not seem to matter all that much.

While idols are truly nothing, as Paul stresses (1 Cor. 8:4, 10:19), idolatry is something, and a very serious something—indeed, it is a terrible sin (1 Cor. 10:7; cf. Acts 7:40 ff.; 1 John 5:21). Not only does idolatry eclipse worship of the living God but it also entails bondage to demonic powers that intimidate and dominate the human spirit (cf. Rom. 1:23, 25; Gal. 4:8; Eph. 2:2). "What gives Paul's battle against idolatry its seriousness and what distinguishes it from the rationalistic arguments of Hellenism," Ethelbert Stauffer observes, is the fact that idolatry involves not merely so-called gods that are in themselves nothing, but also a real world of demonic powers (*"Theos,"* TDNT, 3:100).

Early Christianity rejoiced that those enlightened by divine revelation and by the Holy Spirit have the "ability to distinguish true spirits from false" (1 Cor. 12:10). The apostle John affirms that human beings need to assess spirits abroad in the world on the basis of their witness or nonwitness to Jesus Christ (1 John 4:1–3). Just as in his Gospel John emphasizes that the Holy Spirit witnesses to Jesus Christ (John 15:26, 16:49 ff.), so in his First Epistle he stresses that in view of God's self-disclosure in Jesus Christ his Son we must be on guard against idols (1 John 5:20). The church lives by God's leading; false prophets, on the other hand, belong to the "godless world" (1 John 4:4–6). Corrupt religious imagination fashions notions of deity that have no basis in divine disclosure and scriptural testimony.

Only in daily experience can the credal confession of monotheism be put to constant test. Service of the living God requires repudiating all idols— be they the philosopher's deifying of elemental forces of the cosmos (Gal. 4:8 ff.); the political tyrant's imposition of obligations that God disallows (Acts 4:19, 5:29); the secularist's idolatry of mammon ("You cannot serve both God and Money," Matt. 6:24, NIV; cf. Luke 12:19); the glutton's capitulation to appetite ("whose god is their belly," Phil. 3:19); or even the Western tourists' tolerant curiosity about ancient temple idols (2 Cor. 6:16; 1 Thess. 1:9).

The living God calls us from worship of false gods to the permanent responsibilities entrusted to us at creation. The living God is himself the God of life and death (Num. 27:16; Deut. 32:39; Job 12:10; Luke 12:20; 2 Cor. 1:19; James 4:15). Death does not belong to life but contradicts it as its opposite. God governs the book of life in which he inscribes the names of his people (Isa. 4:3) and assures their heavenly felicity (Exod. 32:32; Ps. 69:28; Mal. 3:16) in view of their obedient response to his Word that calls for life-or-death decision (Deut. 30:15–20, 32:47). God reveals himself as the absolute and exclusive God of human existence—as man's creator, preserver, judge, redeemer and companion even in and beyond death (Ps. 23:4, 6, 72:23 ff.). He is judge of both the living and the dead (1 Pet. 4:5). Since life is a gift of God, the Bible does not view death as natural or necessary, but as a consequence of sin. Life in God is indestructible, whereas creaturely life is conditional. God can declare human beings dead ("in your transgressions and sins," Eph. 2:1; cf. Col. 2:13) while they are still physically alive (Matt. 8:22; Luke 15:24) or he can declare them eternally alive even in the face of physical death (John 11:25 ff.; Phil. 1:23).

Eschatological life is of course not wholly new in all respects; in it God contravenes the vulnerabilities of man's earthly existence by arresting and reversing the power of sin. While eschatological life remains somatic, it involves also the indestructible life that God confers in association with the resurrection body. Natural immortality of the soul is not a biblical tenet. Christian belief in the soul's ongoing divine preservation (Mark 1:27) and in bodily resurrection should remind us that the living God alone is the real life-giver.

The resurrection of the crucified Jesus becomes in New Testament context the central historical reality upon which resurrection faith focuses. Christ's triumph over death strips death of its sting (1 Cor. 15:56), that is, of its "power to hurt" the believer (TEV).

The difference between the biblical revelation of bodily resurrection and pagan theories of spirit-immortality involves more than simply realistically rejecting idealistic notions that man's psyche is inherently divine and therefore indestructible. Scripture teaches that sin involves a violent rupture in the created relationship between God and man, and requires a radical negation by divine redemption. The New Testament portrays the resurrection of the crucified Jesus as a threshold event, one that inaugurates the new eschatological age and guarantees the future resurrection of mankind. But the regeneration conferred even now by faith in Christ the Redeemer already involves participation in eternal life (John 5:24, 25; 1 Tim. 6:12, 19). Life, whether creation life, redemption life, or resurrection life, is not a vitality inherent in man, or something that he can develop. It is a supernatural gift. Even now, on the authority of the revealed Word of God and by faith in the substitutionary death of the Savior for his sins, the alienated sinner may enjoy this gift of eternal life (Eph. 2:5 ff.). Cancellation of spiritual death already now in the present frees redeemed man for new daily possibilities of life in the Spirit. The force of physical death is experientially neutralized since the believer identifies himself with the historical death and resurrection of Christ who in his coming final victory will completely abolish physical death. The apostle Paul pinpoints the believer's perspective by the words: "dying, and, behold we live" (2 Cor. 6:9). That the redeemed sinner may in virtue of divine preservation and grace live eternally in God's intimate presence gains its wonder not only from the fact that myriads of creatures are intended by creation to have only brief temporal existence, but also from the fact that the redeemed will forever enjoy the company of the supernatural bestower of creation, redemption and resurrection life, and that God will even express his own proper life in unobstructed spiritual and moral union with all who love him. In other words, the very real facts of day-to-day existence occur within the dynamic relationship the believer already bears to the risen Christ; from the eternal order Christ the Lord is mediating to him love, joy, peace and other virtues distinctive of the age to come.

But God's personal relationships to his creatures, and particularly to human beings, do not exhaust his interpersonal activity, nor do these divine-human relationships take divine priority. Throughout eternity the living God is active within himself, active in unending interpersonal relationships in the Godhead. This fact we discern only on the basis of his self-revelation. What we know of God's attributes and activities is not arrived at through conjecturing some abstract being-in-general, a being that is first contrasted with all finite beings and then dignified as divine and glorified with all the appropriate perfections. The dipolar deity projected by process philosophy is much more abstract than the self-revealed triune God presented in the Bible. Process thinkers, like some rationalistic philosophers before them, thrust an identity upon God that they infer from the functions of the cosmos, the cosmos being gratuitously viewed as his body. All the attributes or characteristics that appropriately belong to his being the God of the Bible makes known in living self-disclosure. Any distinction that we properly make in God we make only if we acknowledge one or another perfection that he, the living, self-revealing Lord, has revealed to man. For Jesus, faith in God is first and foremost faith in the true and living God self-disclosed as holy, loving and merciful, but also as the God of wrath and judgment. The Gospels consequently remind us that God is true (John 3:33), good (Mark 10:18), holy (John 17:11), loving (John 3:16), merciful (Luke 6:36), righteous (John 17:25), wrathful (John 3:36) and so on. These and other emphases recur in the Epistles. Numerous statements bearing on the nature of the living God speak on the unlimited and unrivaled fullness of his perfections: he is "God only wise" (Rom. 16:27), "who only hath immortality" (1 Tim 6:16), and who in brief is the "only wise God" (1 Tim. 1:17; Jude 25). Only because the living God by cognitive disclosure lifts the veil, as it were, on the inner life of the Godhead do we know that from all eternity he decreed to create the temporal universe, proposed the incarnation of the Logos, freely elected fallen sinners to salvation, and much else.

God publishes his holy will to the human race, as the living God relates himself to the forces of the cosmos and the experiences of mankind, hears the prayers of his creatures, providentially governs the fortunes of the redeemed (Rom. 8:28) and sovereignly influences the direction of human history toward the sure and final triumph of righteousness (Rom. 8:29 f.).

In its affirmations about him the Bible does not set before us simply the fact of God's personality and stop there; it implements that fact by maintaining centrality for the living God's personal revelatory disclosure. When John boldly declares "God is love" (1 John 4:8) he is not equating

God with some impersonal power; rather he is characterizing the personal God who is the source and norm of all love (1 John 4:16). When he declares that "God is light" (1 John 1:5) he is not reducing deity to some impersonal aspect of the natural universe; rather he is presenting the self-revealing personal God as the source and norm of all light—natural, rational, moral and spiritual.

In attesting the personal self-disclosure of the living God Jesus frequently used the term *theos* in correlation with *patēr* ("Father"), or the name Father instead of the term God. Yet few turns in the history of thought are stranger than the fact that almost from the beginnings of Western secular philosophy worldly-wise scholars have insisted that one must choose between divine personality and divine sovereignty; God is sovereign but not personal and living, they have argued, or conversely, God is personal and living but not sovereign. All the more ironic is the fact that even Judaism, not because of disbelief but because of excessive reverence, came to avoid the name of Yahweh, so that, as Karl Georg Kuhn remarks, "this name for God continued to exist only as a written symbol, not as a living word" (*"Theos:* The Rabbinic Terms for God," *TDNT,* 3:93). No less ironic is the fact that in the mid-1800s Hegelian modernism disputed God's personality. The living God of the Bible became a conjectural abstraction to be freely manipulated by elitist philosophers.

4.
Methods of Determining the Divine Attributes

ANYONE WHO SPEAKS OF THE perfections of God must show how to identify them and also how to correlate and classify them meaningfully.

Biblical theology affirms God's transcendent disclosure of his attributes, and implies a classification not found in secular philosophical theology. Secular metaphysicians proceed independently of the principle of divine revelation and contribute their own creative conceptions of the character of God.

Secular philosophy and biblical theology have nonetheless significantly influenced each other. As a result the methods by which some theologians and philosophers of religion profess to arrive at and classify the attributes of God are notably similar. Some scholars combine speculative and biblical data in a way that full attention to biblical theology disallows.

Some professedly Christian theologians claim, for example, that any and all attribution finitizes God, that divine existence must therefore be conceived as attributeless. There is obviously then no method of discriminating divine attributes. Only philosophical conjecture could have encouraged such affirmations.

Other theologians have held that we know the attributes of God only by extending to an infinite degree those perfections found to a lesser extent in nature and man. Still others have said that we personally glimpse the divine attributes through individual response to superrational divine-human encounter.

Many philosophers of religion, on the other hand, reflect in their expositions of the divine attributes an unacknowledged, even unrecognized, debt to biblical theism. The vast contrast between Eastern and Western philosophy leaves little doubt that biblical representations have greatly influenced many secular Western portrayals of deity. Once the Hebrew-Christian revelation of God became the living inheritance of the West, even some thinkers in revolt against the biblical characterization of God could formulate no alternative views without at least some dependence upon and influence of the prophetic-apostolic heritage. For this reason statements of the divine attributes even when formulated on the basis of philosophical reasoning and independently of divine revelation at times incorporate revelational emphases inconsistent with a secular rationalistic methodology. Actually, theology and philosophy need not be at odds in their expositions of the attributes of God, nor need their classifications conflict, if due attention is given to God's intelligible self-disclosure.

In identifying the divine attributes scholars have espoused several methodologies:

I. The way of negation (*via negationis*) affirms that any predication of attributes compromises God's perfection and leads in neo-Platonism to the nameless Absolute. In *The Republic* (509 B.C.) Plato held that "the good is not essence, but far exceeds essence in dignity and power." Insisting that creaturely limitations are inapplicable to God, some early Christian theologians held that all predications compromise the divine essence, despite the fact that the Bible ascribes to God such attributes as sovereignty, righteousness, love and omniscience. Some medieval theologians argued that the divine "simplicity" excludes the ascription of particular attributes to God. Mystics employed the method of negation to exalt God above wisdom, goodness, holiness, life, essence, being and even godhead. And Spinoza held that, except for thought and extension, we are ignorant of God's infinity of attributes.

The question therefore arises whether the biblical writers speak only figuratively and pictorially of God, while secular philosophy speaks truly of him. If so, we must face the fact that secular philosophers often widely contradict each other; some (e.g. Paul Tillich) even deny that our predications about God are literally true. Differences in what scholars say about God turn fundamentally upon two ways of conceiving him. One is based on God's intelligible self-revelation; the other rests, instead, upon speculative attempts to define ultimate reality on the basis of perfections found in man and the world, and upon a negation of finite limitations. This latter approach leads readily to the view that all affirmations about God are equivocal; God therefore is unknowable.

The God of the Bible is not, of course, the "Unspeakable," an abstract Idea or Absolute sealed off from all logical and verbal identifiability. If we negate all predication concerning an "Absolute" or an ultimate "Being," then the "Unspeakable" reduces, in fact, to the "Unknowable." Such conjecture obscures the self-revealed God of the Bible and eclipses the Christian doctrine of God; it substitutes unbiblical notions of divinity for scriptural representations of the sovereign God who personally reveals his name and provides for mankind an intelligible revelation of his nature and will.

Theological comments by some church fathers concerning God's supposedly unknowable attributes, most notably by the Pseudo-Dionysius (450–500) do not reflect the scriptural doctrine of the living God who makes himself known, but rather Platonic and neo-Platonic speculations about the divine. A century after the apostles wrote their first epistles, Christian scholars versed in Greek philosophy saw the need of addressing educated Greeks concerning the differences between biblical and Greek views of divine nature and transcendence. Justin Martyr (d. c. 165), welcomed Plato's theism because it insisted on objective morality; moreover, like Clement of Alexandria (c. 184–254), he also accepted some essentials of Platonic philosophy. But Justin was more eclectic than Platonic. While more critical of Platonic thought than were Justin or Clement, Origen (c. 184–254) nonetheless synthesized Platonic and Christian principles into a philosophical theology that exerted continuing influence, especially upon Gregory of Nyssa (d. 394). Contrary to Nicene and ante-Nicene fathers who expounded the doctrine of God in terms of the Scriptures, church fathers familiar with Greek philosophy in some cases readily subscribed to the unbiblical notions that the purity and spirituality of the divine are best maintained by stripping God of all logically meaningful predication.

Pseudo-Dionysius the Areopagite (c. 500), for example, wrote letters and treatises trying to unify neo-Platonic theory with Christian theology and mystical experience. Borrowing the name of one of the apostle Paul's converts (Acts 17:34), this supposed Syrian monk gave neo-Platonism currency throughout Byzantine, Islamic and Roman lands. Appropriating the views of the fifth-century Proclus (410–485), Dionysius held that God transcends all rational understanding, and that all qualities we apply to God are limited forms of expressing the inexpressible. This concept stimulated a growing medieval tradition, especially in the Western Latin Church, that busied itself energetically with communicating the incommunicable. After John Scotus Erigena (c. 810–c. 877), who translated the works of the Pseudo-Dionysius, mystical notions of God gained wide currency in Roman Catholicism.

One of the two great Muslim scholars, the Persian philosopher Avicenna (Ibn Sinā, 980–1037) channeled neo-Platonic emphases into the Arab world, as in a lesser way did the Spanish Muslim Averroes (Ibn Rushd, 1126–98). Medieval Jewish writings, particularly the works of Ibn Gabirol (b. 1021), also reflected heavy neo-Platonic influences. Moses Maimonides (1135–1204), sometimes anachronistically called the Jewish Aquinas, went far beyond thirteenth-century Thomistic denial of human knowledge of the divine essence by insisting that everything that we affirm about God, including his existence, must be construed in terms of pure negation.

However much medieval theology moved beyond its initial methodological emphasis on the *via negationis* in order to emphasize constructive analogy or the *via eminentiae,* the way of negation coincided with neo-Platonic mysticism. This approach of negation sought to emancipate the Absolute from all earthly attributions in the interest of some nameless divinity. The mystics promoted religious exercises that strip human contemplation of all positive ascriptions and declare God to be not only beyond time and space but no less beyond truth and falsehood, and beyond good and evil. Schleiermacher rightly rejected this approach, but on the wrong premise of pantheism, which requires assimilating nature and man to God;

like other mystics he believed that the divine is accessible to all men without mediation, and also that God transcends the bounds of discursive reason. The thesis of mysticism that man, stimulated by divine love, can rise above all structures of experience and knowledge into mystical union with God, draws its inspiration from neo-Platonism, not from the Bible.

II. The way of eminence (*via eminentiae*) seeks to rise by analogy from the creaturely world to positive affirmations about the attributes of God. The way of eminence views the way of negation as but a preliminary activity that denies to God whatever belongs to contingent being; in other words by establishing what God is not, negation prepares the way for affirming what and who he is.

The theory of analogy dates back to Aristotelian philosophy. Aristotle used analogy to signify both proportionality and similarity, although he did not apply it to human knowledge of the Unmoved Mover. Through the influence of Aquinas, foremost scholastic of the thirteenth century, analogy became deeply entrenched in Christian theology as a way of establishing the divine nature. Thomist scholars still aggressively rely on the doctrine of analogy which assigns to God in an eminent degree all perfections found in creaturely existence. Thomists deny that these perfections are to be predicated of God either univocally (in the same sense as applied to the creaturely) or equivocally (in a contradictory sense) but affirm analogical predication. Analogical argumentation takes many forms, but all of them can be comprehended under the two principles of analogy of proportionality and analogy of attribution.

The analogy of proportionality denies that any direct likeness can be predicated between God and creaturely reality, but affirms that terms used of the infinite and the finite involve a relational likeness. But on what basis, critics ask, is it first assumed as a matter of nonanalogical knowledge, that God is infinite? Frederick Ferré asks, moreover, what justifies the basic ontological claim that some relational similarity must prevail between Creator and creature ("Analogy in Theology," p. 95). The analogy of proportionality rests therefore upon secret assumptions about the creature's fundamental likeness to a divine Creator, a premise that philosophical reasoning cannot demonstrate apart from transcendent divine revelation. But once intelligible divine revelation is admitted, a methodology other than empirical analogy is available for arriving at knowledge of God's attributes.

Furthermore, apart from a simultaneous discussion of particular qualities or attributes, philosophers cannot vindicate their insistence simply on a proportionality of human and divine relations. If the analogy of proportionality implies only that qualities must qualify their objects appropriately to the objects they qualify, then we are engaged simply in tautology. In any case, does a relational likeness of goodness when predicated of God and man make sense if its ascriptions to both the divine and the human have no univocal overlap? When thus conceived the analogy of proportionality channels into equivocation and hence into agnosticism.

The Bible affirms not simply that God differs from all finite created beings. It declares also that God is the supremely knowable reality, and is so in view of his intelligible self-revelation and disclosure of reliable information about his nature, purposes and acts. It denies, however, that God is in all respects wholly other than man who bears his image.

The analogy of attribution affirms a likeness between God and the creaturely in specific perfections or attributes in distinction from mere analogical relationships. Ferré cautions against the hidden assumptions that underlie analogical arguments proceeding from God as the prime analogate who perfectly possesses such qualities as goodness, wisdom and love in distinction from creatures who possess these attributes only imperfectly. Such argumentation "presupposes prior nonanalogical knowledge," knowledge without which "human virtues could not be known to be merely imperfect approximations of the divine" (*ibid.*, p. 95). Why, moreover, are only certain, and not all, creaturely qualities thus predicated of God? Does not the appeal to analogy here secretly presuppose in advance certain facts about the very nature of God that it professes to establish only by analogical reasoning? Evolutionary theory disputes the argument of a first cause that infinitely incorporates all perfections in subsequent effects; contemporary science avoids the conception of objective causality, and humanists assume that man is himself the creator of all values. Such alternative emphases do not, to be sure, provide comprehensively adequate and valid explanations. But can insistence on a sovereign and perfect first cause be persuasively presented apart from recognition of God's intelligible self-revelation of his nature? On the analogical approach one could not consistently speak even of divine causality in a univocal sense; the term "cause" falls victim to the same equivocation that erodes other analogical claims for objective knowledge of God. Cause as a previous *event* is not cause as *Creator*.

There is a further problem. If we contend that God perfectly relates to creatures in ways by which creatures only imperfectly relate to each other, then how do we get from claims about knowledge of God's relational activities to knowledge that God is in himself intrinsically good, wise, sovereign, eternal?

The basic difficulty with the analogical method is its denial that the terms used of God and man have univocal meaning. Such denial cannot consistently avoid agnosticism and skepticism. Only the univocal element in attribute-terms can guard their analogical application to God from equivocation. Not even E. L. Mascall's discussion of theological analogy in neo-Thomist perspective (*Existence and Analogy*) fully escapes this difficulty. Hebrew-Christian revelation avoids this epistemological tension between affirmation and negation, anthropomorphism and agnosticism, by stressing the priority of God's intelligible self-revelation of his nature as attested in the prophetic-apostolic Scriptures.

Evangelical emphasis on the priority of special revelation does not preclude general divine revelation in nature and mankind, nor does it exclude a proper use of argumentation concerning negation and divine eminence. But Christianity insists, as Herman Bavinck stresses, that "God is not named on the basis of that which is present in creatures, but creatures are named on the basis of that which exists in God" (*The Doctrine of God*, p. 134). According to Cornelius Van Til there is an orthodox and an unorthodox conception of the way of eminence and of the way of negation. The orthodox view begins with God as archetype and humans as ectypes: "God is not named according to what is found in the creature, except God has first named the creature according to what He is in Himself" (*Junior Systematics*, unpublished lecture notes, p. 152). Unless we recognize that God is the original and man the derivative, negation invariably leads us to an abstract notion of the divine essence, and eminence leads to uncertainty in its determination of God. Hence Van Til criticizes abstract philosophical negation and affirmation over against the concrete way of negation and of affirmation which is found by subjecting human thought about God to God's scripturally-attested self-revelation.

The two paths (negation and eminence) must not in any event be separated by a wide chasm, nor separated from special revelation; within the guidance of special revelation both methods may be employed simultaneously. Here negation and affirmation are made not in view of an empty God-concept, but in relation to the living self-manifesting God who is biblically attested. In this context of God's intelligible self-disclosure, biblically defined, affirmation implies negation, and negation implies affirmation; both are permitted in view of the living God's revelation through which evangelical Christians identify the divine attributes.

III. The way of causality (*via causalitatis*) argues from the world and man as effects to an originating cause or author.

The argument sometimes emerges as a method wholly distinct from the way of eminence. It may proceed, for example, through the idea of causation to ascribe the universe as an effect to its supreme source and author, instead of resorting to analogy to supply positive statements about the divine attributes. Schleiermacher postulated the divine attributes, for example, by the way of "causality"; he excluded the ways of negation and eminence because he considered the feeling of dependence to be the essence of religion, and regarded all distinctions within the deity merely as poetic commentary on this feeling. Although Philo and Plotinus employed the two "ways" and some church fathers (the Pseudo-Dionysius; John of Damascus; Erigena) made them the basis of a twofold negative and positive theology, scholastic theology frequently followed the example of Durandus de S. Porciano who invoked the three "ways": negation, removal of limits (eminence), and causality. Although some formulations of the way of eminence include it, the causal argument is adduced both in connection with and independently of a doctrine of analogy. Philosophical theism has long relied upon the argument from causality in propounding its case for a personal God. But it appears impossible to distinguish absolutely between the method of eminence and the method of causality. Both methods assume that perfections discoverable in the universe are to be referred back to an antecedent divine being who exhibits these perfections superlatively. The way of eminence and the way of causality, comments Bavinck, "are really *one*, and together" may be viewed as "the method of affirmation" over against the "method of negation" (*op. cit.,* p. 134). Both methods pursue natural theology based on philosophical reasoning, and involve no prior appeal to special divine revelation.

Modern empirical science considers the idea of causality empirically questionable, and speaks instead of observed sequences. Kant regarded causality as an innate category of understanding and held that every cause is also an effect. But even if we presuppose the idea of causality on other grounds, its presence in the space-time world does not directly establish its applicability to God.

If God is considered first cause on the basis of philosophical reasoning, then the qualities ascribed to him may indeed agree more or less with scriptural representations, but will hardly coincide with the comprehensive revelation of God's character as given in Scripture. Controversy over whether God is finite or infinite, omnipotent or limited, personal or superpersonal, has long shadowed the argument from causality.

As a method of defining the existence and attributes of God, the attempt to construct the idea of God on the basis of secular metaphysics or natural theology has nothing in common with revealed theology. The causal argument not only fails to take seriously the epistemological significance of God in his intelligible self-revelation, but also formulates its alternative on the premise that man's volitional and epistemic revolt does not demand priority for special divine revelation in acquiring comprehensive knowledge of God in objectively valid form. The theory makes nature and man, not God, its starting point.

The secular empirical approach occurs in numerous modifications and combinations. But it invariably involves confidence in man's ability to arrive reliably at extensive metaphysical knowledge despite his present moral condition. Apart from a biblical counterchallenge by Reformation theologians devoted to revelational theism in view of man's epistemic predicament, its greatest setback came through the rejection by Hume and Kant of all metaphysical knowledge on the supposed ground that human conception does not extend to noumenal realities. Kant asserted that the human knower—and not God—contributes causality and order to the phenomenal world, and that man's moral nature demands only the "regulative" ideal of a supernatural lawgiver and not valid knowledge of an objectively existing deity. Kant's attack on natural theology rested in part on a fallacious theory of knowledge that ruled out any knowledge of noumena, including God. But the empirical appeal in behalf of natural theology, as an alternative to special revelation, rested on an equally objectionable alternative. It should be noted, moreover, that Kant's criticism of the theistic proofs does not depend wholly on his epistemology.

The empirical approach to the doctrine of God dominates Roman Catholic insistence that the Thomistic "fivefold proof" logically demonstrates the existence of God; biblical theology is then imposed on this "proof" as an upper level of information. This priority for philosophical theology as an indispensable preparation for biblical theology unwittingly encouraged modern philosophers to neglect biblical theology and even to revolt against it. Instead of welcoming biblical revelation as the capstone of philosophical reasoning, secular philosophers exchanged the biblical God for philosophically competitive gods. Mediating Protestant theologians moderated the Thomistic claim of logical proof into one of probability that imposes a moral rather than rational obligation of belief. This line of argumentation obscured the high significance of God's self-disclosure addressed objectively to man as a sinner volitionally in revolt against the light of divine revelation.

Many Protestant theologians, influenced by Joseph Butler's *The Analogy of Religion* (1736), ascribed to the empirical method a preparatory role which supposedly arrived—not with certainty but with "high probability"—at a trustworthy though incomplete description of the divine attributes. They then invoked special biblical revelation as an umbrella to lend completeness and certainty not supplied by empirical methodology. Numerous evangelical works on systematic theology fluctuated between special revelation and natural theology, even when the latter's priority was denied, and considered the theistic proofs decisive for establishing not only theism, but in a preliminary way also God's nature and attributes.

Philosophers of religion like Douglas Clyde Macintosh used the empirical method in conjunction with intuitional and pragmatic emphases (*Theology as an Empirical Science, The Problem of Religious Knowledge*), and, in distinction from rational knowledge of God, ventured "tentative" assertions of divine unity, transcendence and personality. Edgar S. Brightman pleaded empiricism in contending that God is finite.

Evangelical theology does not repudiate universal divine revelation in nature and man; rather, it insists on its indispensable importance and priority. But nature and man are not the decisive referents through which we are to characterize the transcendent supernatural. The projection of God from nature and man leads to false gods rather than to the self-revealed God of the Bible.

The Hebrew prophets possessed reliable knowledge of the divine attributes many centuries before secular philosophers projected their several "ways" for identifying the divine nature and attributes. Hebrew theology avoided emptying the God-concept by negation, and affirmed an intimate knowledge of God's attributes not on the basis of tenuous philosophical speculation but in view of God's own intelligible disclosure. The Old Testament made not man or the space-time universe, but divine disclosure the starting point for the doctrine of God. Berkhof protests that empirical methods "take their starting point in human experience rather than in the Word of God. They deliberately ignore the clear self-revelation of God in Scripture and exalt the idea of human discovery of God" and "have an exaggerated idea of their own ability to find out God and to determine the nature of God inductively" (*Systematic Theology*, p. 53).

IV. The way of intuition builds on the premise that the idea of God is innate in mankind and that, apart from prior inference from experience, human beings know some if not all divine attributes through direct cognitive relationships to the living God.

This view differs from the ineffable intuition postulated by mystics who profess to transcend rational criteria; instead, it emphasizes rational intuition. Mystics tend to be pantheists, whereas many rational intuitionists—especially those professing to be Christian—repudiate pantheism.

The father of modern philosophy, René Descartes, believed that human beings innately possess the ideas of God, infinity and substance, a view that gained wide currency in the seventeenth century. While modern empiricism has largely obscured the ontological argument for God—that the innate idea of God implies his existence—the argument has reappeared in our day and is being revived in a variety of forms.

The philosophical emphasis on innate knowledge reaches back into ancient times. In an earlier volume (Vol. 1, pp. 273–394) we traced in considerable detail and evaluated the view that man has innate knowledge of God. Here our concern is the bearing of this approach on discrimination of the divine attributes.

Plato held that eternal truths—including truths about God—are innate in mankind on the basis of a preexistence of the soul and of the mind's present recollection and participation in Eternal Truth. Plato avoided the emphasis of some ancient philosophers that man's mind is a part of God's mind, a view that the biblical doctrine of creation disallows. The soul is not for Plato an Idea in the larger World of Ideas. But underlying his theory is the notion that human intellection participates in a comprehensive divine Mind. Plato's theory of recollection, moreover, does not adequately explain the divergent views of God's nature and perfections held by even the most learned scholars.

Augustine predicated innate knowledge of God on theistic creation and divine revelation: man is a creature specially made in God's image for the knowledge and service of God, and by creation innately bears certain ineradicable truths concerning his Maker. In explaining the participation of man in divine truth and of man and nature in created structures of being, Augustine therefore challenged the Platonic doctrine of recollection on the basis of *ex nihilo* origination; since God is creator of all, all truth is God's truth, and Judeo-Christian revelation involves no necessary conflict with philosophical thinking. Augustine stressed that the revelation of the Creator in the incarnate Logos Jesus Christ and in Scripture corrects and supplements valuable insights in Plato's thought.

Famous for the "ontological argument" (as Kant later named it), Anselm (c. 1033–1109) insists that the idea of God implies God's actual existence. Anselm elaborates this claim in the framework of God's creation of man as bearer of God's image, although he also expounds man's sin and need of atonement. He attaches universal philosophic validity to claims made about God on the basis of general divine revelation. Anselm leaves us unsure about the limits of philosophical argumentation, through which he establishes not only God's self-existence, but also the divine attributes of sensibility (*sensibilis*), omnipotence, compassion, justice and goodness; in fact, Anselm expounds even the doctrines of the Trinity and of creation, and God's mercy as well, on the basis of explication of the a priori God-idea. It is not unusual for scholars to conclude a survey of Anselm's thought with a comment like that of Richard McKeon: "Anselm's faith in the power of reason seems unlimited, as if everything believed were also intelligible, with only one limitation to the exercise of reason—that reason can never attain to complete intelligibility since the data of revelation on which it is employed are inexhaustible" (*Selections from Medieval Philosophers*, p. 148 f.). Yet what needs equally to be said is that once later philosophers divorce reason from God, and confine it to a much more restricted range of interest, human confidence soon weakens also in man's understanding of himself, not to mention in a comprehensive and wise understanding of nature as well; finally, the enterprise of philosophy begins to question more and more the uniqueness and worth of reason.

In later medieval philosophy Anselm's argument was largely eclipsed through the influence of Aquinas who rejected Anselm in favor of the cosmological or causal argument. When Descartes revived the ontological argument, he coordinated it with conjectural rationalism and neglected revelational theism, an approach that indirectly prepared the way for Kant's substitution of innate categories or forms of thought for innate truths. The biblical view that the transcendent Logos of God intelligibly structures all forms of creaturely existence was thus abandoned. Prior to Kant, Spinoza had used the ontological argument, but did so in a context of pantheism; ascribing to human beings knowledge of divine substance and infinity, Spinoza gave these tenets a new meaning. More recently, Karl Barth revived the argument in a context of divine self-revelation (*Fides Quaerens Intellectum: Anselm's Beweis der Existenz Gottes in Zusammenhang seines theologischen Programms.* In line with his view that all human beings are divinely elected to salvation in Christ, Barth deploys the ontological argument to deepening an already implicit Christian faith; its earlier use had been to intellectually persuade the atheist that the universally held God-idea involves the living God's actual existence. Independently of any context of intelligible divine self-revelation, Charles Hartshorne and Norman Malcolm have restated the argument to advance the premise that the concept of God as eternal, self-existent being makes the question of God's existence not one of contingency, but rather one of logical necessity or logical impossibility. Hartshorne then argues that, since the concept of God's existence has not been shown to be self-contradictory, we must conclude that God exists. Critics argue that Hartshorne confuses logical with ontological necessity.

The strength of evangelical theism lies in formulating the case for intuitive knowledge of God in the context of divine self-revelation and the created *imago Dei,* and insisting in view of this on the reality of God as the basic ontological axiom. By divine creation and preservation human beings stand in ineradicable epistemic relationships to God. Man's fall in sin, to be sure, aligns him in revolt against God's continuing revelation, command and claim; man's perverse will dilutes, distorts and suppresses God's general revelation. But that very revelation continues to penetrate man's defenses in ways that maintain cognitive relationships of responsibility to God and to fellow humans. Fallen man's rebellion always dilutes his elaboration of the content of general revelation, even if that dilution occurs through volitional determination and not by ontological or epistemological necessity. Special prophetic-apostolic revelation, that is, the redemptive revelation of the Bible centering in Christ the incarnate Logos, objectively publishes the comprehensive truth about God and his purposes. Although standing in ineradicable cognitive relationships to the living, eternal, holy Sovereign who daily confronts us both in internal and external revelation, fallen mankind can no longer be psychologically sure, apart from special scriptural disclosure, which intellectual representations are authentic or corrupt. Man's fallen condition inclines him to flee from pure religion and turn instead to more congenial alternatives, or to invoke degenerate forms of religion to discredit all religion. The fault, to be sure, lies not in the revelation of the Creator, but in the sinful response of the finite creature who declares his independence of the very Sovereign he presumes to identify. Yet neither empirical observation, environmental factors nor inheritance truly accounts for the ineradicable idea of the living God; no better explanation has been given for the universally held God-idea than that it stems from the divine image implanted in mankind since creation, an image involving responsible relationships to the self-revealing God.

V. The way of dialectical and/or existential divine-human encounter goes beyond the way of negation by affirming a divine initiative in which God mediates redemptive revelation through Christ the Word, such revelation being actualized by responsive human trust. It has similarities to mysticism in that revelation is said to be internal, sporadically repeatable, nonpropositional, and not subject to logical criteria. Dogma or doctrine allegedly stands in the way of God's self-revelation; statements about God's nature, even those of the biblical writers, are considered tentative, fallible pointers to divine self-disclosure known only in internal encounter. Scriptural revelation is repudiated; what historic Christianity cherished as divinely revealed truths and doctrinal revelation becomes merely a human witness to an internal divine-human confrontation.

This dialectical-existential approach jeopardizes a rationally consistent doctrine of God and leads instead to a theology of religious paradox. In earlier statements Karl Barth voiced doubt over the possibility of constructing a doctrine of God. But under the influence of biblical revelation, neoorthodox theologians, especially Barth, have contributed extended expositions that stress God-in-relation-to-man in internal divine-human encounter, rather than God-in-himself objectively and intelligibly revealed. Yet the construction of a comprehensive doctrine of God cannot be consistently fulfilled merely on dialectical or existential premises. Many statements made by neoorthodox writers about the nature of God cannot in fact be derived from a nonintellective divine-human encounter, but are derived instead from scriptural materials and are projected selectively upon the notion of sporadic divine confrontation of man. Both in theology and in ethics the positive assertions of neoorthodox scholars cannot be derived from their principles. Their shift from the objective authority of

Scripture is vulnerable to sacrificing important elements of the biblical teaching about God; moreover, it cannot escape the trap of correlating the content of theology with strange present-day spiritual encounters.

The existential treatment of the divine attributes sets out characteristically from a direct internal divine confrontation of man. Biblical statements concerning God are disallowed the status of revealed doctrine, and become instead fallible testimony to God's interpersonal self-revelation.

Dialectical and existential theologians consider all propositions about and schematizations of the divine attributes but a "pointer" to the self-revealing God, a fallible interpretation of a divine-human encounter in which God is said to make himself known personally and nonpropositionally. They view systematic theology as a faltering human attempt to reflect in propositional terms, for purposes of spoken or written communication, a superrational encounter to which such doctrinal statements merely "witness." They declare the rationally consistent exhibition of the divine attributes to be merely a human construction that lacks revelational legitimacy. Their approach impoverishes the doctrine of God by gainsaying any formulation of God's nature in logically consistent and coherent terms.

Gustaf Aulén describes the Christian view of God as a "tension-filled synthesis" of opposites (*The Faith of the Christian Church*, pp. 106 ff.). Removal of this tension, he avers, falsifies any treatment of the divine attributes. A fundamental difficulty of existential dismissal of the objective biblical revelation here comes to view: existentialism projects upon the nature of God as tension-filled and paradoxical the same epistemic paradox and tension that supposedly characterizes interpersonal encounter with God. Aulén protests replacing "the religious paradox with a metaphysical irrationalism" (*ibid.*, p. 107). But once paradoxic encounter is equated with direct divine self-revelation, this irrational development cannot consistently be avoided, however, except by metaphysical agnosticism. Aulén asserts that it is impossible to arrive at a rationally-constructed concept of God, "but in its stead appears a living figure whose features change and clash one with the other, but whose character nevertheless, as far as faith is concerned, bears the mark of unity, the living God" (*ibid.*, p. 107). Any attempt to exhibit a logically consistent view of God is thus abandoned as an illegitimate concern; instead the dialectical alternative promotes a leap of faith that assertedly grasps the nature and unity of God without rational synthesis.

Appealing to religious encounter, Aulén singles out three basic dogmatic ideas, namely, God's power, judgment and love. From these concepts he derives the whole range of attributes. God's power implies his omnipotence, sovereignty, omnipresence; God's judgment implies his avenging and condemning justice and wrath; God's love implies his goodness, mercy and grace.

Also on the basis of divine-human encounter Emil Brunner expounds the three fundamental notions: God is lord, God is holy, God is love. These dogmatic ideas then canopy the entire range of interests traditionally investigated under the theme of divine attributes.

The encounter-centered approach is obviously incompatible with cognitive claims made about God as he exists outside or transcending his relations to man. Although emphasizing God-in-relations, dialectical theology no longer means by this what the Judeo-Christian movement historically held, namely, that in prophetic revelation and in the inspired scriptures God has revelationally communicated trustworthy cognitive knowledge of himself and of his purposes concerning man and the world.

The displeasure that Brunner voices against conceptions of God-in-himself is directed not only against an abstract conception of deity postulated on the basis of philosophical reasoning, but also against the biblical doctrine of divine aseity or independence. Brunner defines God's essence in terms of activity, the activity of self-communication or self-impartation: "God's being in itself, is His being for us. . . . That is Christian *ontology*, that means the doctrine of God's *being*" (*The Christian Doctrine of God*, p. 192). In Brunner's view, biblical theology leaves no room for the concept of God in himself. He is driven to this position by the assertion that all revelation is relational and nonpropositional, so that we know God only as God-in-encounter. "In Himself," writes Brunner, "God is not the almighty, the omniscient, the Righteous One; this is what He is in relation to the world which he has created" (*ibid.*, p. 247).

In view of this identification of the divine essence with self-communication, Brunner seeks to avoid making the created universe necessary to God as an object of divine self-communication; this he does by appealing to an eternal self-communion and fellowship in the triune divine nature prior to the creation. This approach wedges him into an uncomfortable dilemma. To affirm an eternal ontological Trinity requires abandoning the definition of the self-revealing God only in terms of God-in-relation *to us* and acknowledging the propriety of discussing God-in-Himself. Concerning the following passage from Brunner's pen (*Wahrheit als Begegnung*, p. 33)— "That God from the beginning also in His being in itself would be understood as the God who is for man: that is precisely the meaning of the doctrine of the trinity . . ."—Paul K. Jewett comments that "Here the ice is exceedingly thin" ("Ebnerian Personalism," p. 136.)

It should be noted that (1) the divine attributes are here derived, supposedly, not from objective biblical revelation but from inner existential or dialectical revelational considerations; (2) this derivation cannot really be biblically controlled since the Bible is said to witness fallibly to the encounter, and not vice versa, and that revelational encounter provides its own validation of truth; (3) the attributes lose their status as scripturally revealed predications concerning the divine nature, and become fallible human pointers to a superrational paradoxical reality; (4) the attributes, in the sense in which they are retained, no longer can be said to represent objective metaphysical knowledge concerning the nature of God in himself; (5) the doctrine of God is left in epistemological tension, lacking any claim to coherence and rational consistency; (6) the dialectical theology issues in a nonbiblical compromise of divine attributes by subordinating the wrath of God to his love; (7) the Christian view of God can no longer be indicated by a permanently valid systematic contrast with competitive views, since belief is suspended on subjective encounter or existential decision.

The historic Judeo-Christian treatment of the divine attributes, over against that of dialectical theology, insists that the tension between eternity and time has been bridged by rational revelation. Underlying the divergent approaches are two differing statements of the transcendence of God and of the divine image of God that man bears, only one of which, the traditional, can truly be harmonized with biblical theology.

The dialectical view conceives divine transcendence through a tension-filled epistemology that can be resolved only in a faith-leap. It denies that man as divinely created was endowed with rational forms for comprehending spiritual truths, and condemns him even as a recipient of special divine revelation to metaphysical agnosticism. It considers any rational synthesis of spiritual data a threat to faith. Such views conflict with the consistent representations of biblical theology. They ignore the manner in which the prophets and apostles, in comprehending divine revelation, refer to intelligible revelation, to the image of God in man as surviving the fall, and to propositional special revelation whereby God objectively communicates truths about himself and his purposes. Biblical theology bridges the time-eternity tension through rational revelation, that is, through the divine communication to man of information capable of coherent and consistent rational exhibition. The time-eternity tension is spanned not by an existential leap of faith but rationally in view of a knowledge-relationship that man bears to his Maker on the basis of creation, and more comprehensively on the basis of special revelation.

The implications not only for a discussion of divine attributes, but also for the whole range of biblical and systematic theology, are far-reaching. If knowledge of God's nature and attributes is not suspended upon subjective response, upon God-in-immediate-relations, but is conveyed rather in propositionally revealed truths, then no reason remains why, on the basis of such divine disclosure, man may not possess metaphysical knowledge of God-as-he-is-in-himself, and not merely knowledge of God-in-relation to us. Discussion of the attributes—their number, nature and interrelationships—must then rise not from inferences from religious experience, but rather from exegesis of objective biblical data: moreover, such exposition must respect the fact that special revelation is progressive and moves to a climax in Jesus Christ, and must be systematically correlated with intelligible general revelation in a rationally consistent statement.

Karl Barth is less hesitant than Brunner to defend the legitimacy of thought about God's essence in distinction from his activity, although it is unclear just how a dynamic theology which centers revelation in divine activity but denies its propositional content can permit such a distinction. That God's disclosure is not merely a revelation-in-relation-to-us but an essential disclosure of his inmost being, is Barth's point of beginning. "God's essence and His operation are not twain but one. God's operation . . . is His essence in its relation to the reality distinct from Him, whether about to be or already created. . . . All attributes we can assign to God relate to these acts of His" (*Church Dogmatics* I/1, p. 426).

"It is necessary and important," Barth insists, "to distinguish His essence as such from His operation: in order to remember that this operation is a grace, a free divine decision, also to remember that we can only know about God, because and so far as He gives Himself to our knowledge" (*ibid.,* p. 426). But how does Barth derive this information from nonpropositional divine confrontation?

In some passages Barth distinguishes between "the essence of God as such and His essence as the Operator, the self-manifesting"; by this distinction he defends God's inconceivability and affirms the cognitive inadequacy of all knowledge of the revealed God. While God breaches this inconceivability in a revelation-activity that gives us essential knowledge, such knowledge does not really annul the inconceivability of God's hidden essence.

Barth's relational and nonintellective theory of revelation would preclude any statement about God-in-himself. He tells us: "All we can know of God . . . is His acts. All we can assert of God, all attributes we can assign to God relate to these acts of His. And so not to His essence as such. Although the operation of God is the essence of God, it is necessary and important to distinguish His essence as such from His operation: in order to remember that this operation is a grace, a free divine decision, also to remember that we can only know about God, because and as far as He gives Himself to our knowledge" (*Church Dogmatics,* I/1, p. 426). But Barth violates his own premise that religious knowledge is limited to God's revealing acts and includes no transcendent knowledge by saying that the divine essence transcends the acts, that these acts are free rather than necessary, and that there is more to God than we know. If these latter affirmations are true, then Barth ought to reject his relational theory of revelation and insist that revelation includes propositional knowledge about God's transcendent nature.

Brunner, on the one hand, loses God's essence in his activity, and consequently faces the problem of avoiding a necessary correlation of God with the universe as a presupposition of divine self-communication. Barth, on the other hand, by distinguishing God's hidden essence from his revealed essence faces a different problem, namely how revelation can in fact be regarded as essential knowledge, if we must distinguish a hidden essence and a revealed essence. On what ground can Barth speak at all of divine being independently of God's sporadic revelation?

The prime difficulty with neoorthodox theology is its predefinition of revelation as redemptive self-communication, and therefore as the communication of the divine essence detailed as love. If God is to be known only in and through self-disclosure thus defined—rather than in the divine communication of objective truths or knowledge about God—then we must rule out in advance the idea of incommunicable divine attributes. In its place we are offered the concept of "mystery," or emphasis on divine "sovereignty," buttressed by divine "superiority" to rational concepts. Such pro-

posals lose both an intelligible revelation of God, and the right to speak
with any confidence concerning God's nature whether out of or in relation
to us, since they retain the terminology of revelation while emptying it
of a universally sharable rational content.

Barth sets out from God's self-communication as an activity of love, and
insists that a connection must be established between all the divine perfections and this religious encounter. Even the so-called "metaphysical" attributes, the perfections of almightiness and omnipresence, according to
Barth, are to be derived, as F. W. Camfield puts it, as "radii from the one
center of His love" (*Reformation Old and New;* p. 52). Barth treats the
whole range of divine attributes as perfections of divine love experienced
in God's self-communication in the encounter of faith—whether it be the
attributes of grace, mercy and patience, or those of holiness, righteousness
and wisdom, which reflect God's freedom in his love.

In refusing to discuss divine essence other than so-called divine revealing
activity, the dynamic view of revelation has much in common with American humanism. G. B. Foster and Shirley Jackson Case asked whether the
God-idea possesses simply a functional significance, or if it refers to an
ontological being. For Brunner, the God-idea refers to no ontological reality,
for ideas are irrelevant to God-knowledge; moreover, God for Brunner is
not an "ontological reality" in the usual sense of that term, but is divine
revealing activity that excludes all rational affirmation concerning transcendent essence.

Propositional revelation is a divine communication to man of objective
knowledge of the nature of God as he is, both in his eternal glory and in
his relations to man. Existential encounter, if there be such, would permit
only inferences from experience and can make pronouncements only about
God in relation to his creatures; it cannot discuss God's ante-creation perfections, nor can it move behind relational manifestations of the divine to
assertions about the eternal ontological Godhead. Over against speculative
religious philosophy the neosupernaturalistic emphasis on God's special
redemptive relationship with his people is wholesome. But by discarding
propositional biblical revelation it strips from God's self-manifestation in
his relationships with mankind all valid information about God's eternal
being. Neosupernaturalism permits no distinction between God and God
in relation to the universe and man: it cannot speak of God as transcending
such interpersonal relationships, because it admits inferences only from
the divine-human encounter. God's essence and present activity are viewed
as implying each other: nothing concerning the eternal nature of God can
be affirmed in distinction from his present person-to-person confrontation.
No contrast can in that event be adduced between divine essence and activity. For this reason the neosupernatural formulation of the Trinity cannot
with rational consistency rise above a merely modal triunity to assert that
the Godhead is an eternal ontological Trinity.

Theistic criticism of conjectural notions of divine Being necessarily rejects philosophical speculations about God that disregard special divine
disclosure: it also justifiably disapproves theological statements that con-

trast aspects of God's nature known by revelation with supposedly hidden aspects undisclosed by revelation but about which confident pronouncements are made. But neoorthodox spokesmen deplore appeals to special revelation that define the nature of God as he eternally exists outside the immediate revelational encounter and apart from it. In the end the dynamic approach to God involves not merely the rejection of a conjectural static God, but the loss also of the living God as a permanent and unchanging reality. Only by colossal inconsistency can neosupernaturalism affirm any divine reality that transcends the reality experienced in encounter; it must exhaustively identify experienced divine activity as the divine essence. Rejection of propositional revelation in favor of activistic encounter clouds knowledge of God as he is independent of creation and redemption, ontologic knowledge contained in the biblical revelation.

VI. The way of special biblical revelation declares God himself and his revelation to be the only objective intelligible basis for statements about his nature. Only if God in fact communicates propositional information about himself, as the Judeo-Christian prophets and apostles attest, and only if that information is available to us in a trustworthy record, do we have a confident basis for expounding the divine attributes. Evangelical theism therefore repudiates the effort of secular philosophy to derive a comprehensive analysis of the attributes of God from an a priori metaphysics, whether by intuition, mysticism, empirical observation or philosophical reasoning. The Bible states the content of both God's special and redemptive revelation in objectively reliable form. It provides a basis for distinguishing between God's incommunicable attributes, that is, perfections that are predicable of God alone, and his communicable attributes, or divine perfections shared in some respects by his creatures. Neither Humean, Kantian nor post-Kantian epistemological prejudice that precludes theoretical knowledge of the metaphysical realm, nor an existentially-biased theory of revelation, can be considered normative or decisive for biblical theology.

The comprehensive biblical revelation stands guard against the unnecessary limitation and unnecessary multiplication of the divine attributes. A protest against any and all exposition of divine attributes may proceed from agnosticism, from mysticism, or from theories of paradoxic divine revelational encounter. At the other pole of possibilities, the pantheist Spinoza, for example, contended that God has an infinity of attributes. But due regard for the limitations to which biblical propositional revelation commits us will preserve proper balance in discussing the perfections of God.

In enumerating the divine virtues it makes little difference whether we speak of them as perfections or attributes. Barth took over the term perfections from post-Reformation Protestant theologians, whereas Brunner prefers the term attributes because he considers the term perfection "too closely related to the tradition of the *viae*." But in either case we must define the term in relation or contrast to divine essence and clarify its specifically intended use. Both Barth and Brunner jeopardize defining their terms in a rationally consistent manner. For Brunner, dogmatics consists ideally not in systematically setting forth the biblical data, but rather in reflecting upon revelation on the basis of the fallible testimony of the prophets and apostles; he should be reminded that neither he nor Barth agrees on even so fundamental an issue as whether divine revelation is exclusively redemptive, or both nonredemptive (general) and redemptive (special). Brunner considers the logical ordering of the biblical data about God as a "very unsatisfactory" and "arbitrary" method of arriving at the divine attributes. But what could be more arbitrary and less satisfactory than trying to definitively extract the attributes of the living God of the Bible from a twentieth-century encounter to which the scriptural prophets and apostles are said to witness fallibly—especially since that encounter is declared nonintellective, and twentieth-century European encounters are not necessarily the last word! Brunner's claims that evangelical formulation of the doctrine of God through an orderly presentation of the biblical teaching contradicts the nature and intention of Scripture, and that neoorthodox theology—predicated as evangelicals know it to be upon twentieth-century philosophical prejudices—fulfills the nature and intention of the Bible, surely invert the facts. Neoorthodoxy contradicts the Bible (in any event by declaring it fallible, neoorthodoxy renders insignificant such theological contradiction of Scripture). The fact is that the Bible contradicts neoorthodoxy and stands in judgment upon many of its representations about God and his purposes. Brunner's existential encounter fails to provide an objective epistemology and the leap that he commends from one's religious experience to transcendent ontological reality is seen to be well-nigh impossible. For these reasons Brunner does not persuasively vindicate even the scriptural properties that he considers appropriate to God.

Brunner disparages direct reliance upon the literal teaching of the Bible about God because of its poetical and pictorial language. With sweeping generality he writes: "The ideas of divine attributes, which we encounter in the Bible in poetical or in childlike nonreflective forms as direct testimonies of faith, all point back to God's nature . . . in relation to different particular aspects of the created world" (*The Christian Doctrine of God,* p. 247). Brunner's correlation of divine revelation with inner response provides no epistemological moorings sufficiently objective to rescue his emphasis on God's relational acts as Lord, as holy, and as love, from being assimilated to such merely figurative postulations.

Evangelical orthodoxy holds that the attributes of God are to be determined by a logically ordered exposition of an inscripturated revelation. Neoorthodoxy, by contrast, offers merely the latest of several unstable alternatives when it repudiates in toto the claim that the Scriptures are or contain truth; it considers the Bible merely a fallible reflection on divine revelation. Protestant modernism compromised divine inspiration of Scripture on the ground that the biblical teaching represents a composite of revealed truth and human insight. This assertion brought about colossal confusion and contradiction among eminent liberal scholars as to how and where to distinguish the trustworthy from the untrustworthy. Other

scholars modified the historic evangelical view of progressive divine redemptive revelation by correlating it with conjectural theories of evolutionary religious development; by their many theories and many assaults on
Scripture they sacrificed the unity of the Bible. Critical scholars arbitrarily
manipulated Scripture by selectively conforming biblical data to preferred
speculative premises.

Some scholars held that Scripture is basically a naturalistic vehicle on
which supernaturalism was conjecturally imposed. Others repudiated supernatural prophecy and divine redemption, and rejected the prophecy/
fulfillment motif as the key to the Bible. Others manipulated the seventh-
century Hebrew prophets to make of the sacrificial system a corrupt accre-
tion to the genius of Old Testament religion. Literary critics sought biblical
meanings through etymological rather than theological considerations;
correlating etymological studies with evolutionary premises, they largely
overlooked the fact that word-use rather than word-origin decides word-
meaning.

Any biblically controlled classification of the divine attributes faces two
requirements: (1) it must exhibit God's independence of the created universe, and (2) it must exhibit God's relation to the universe in a way that
makes God accessible to human experience and assures knowledge of him
as he truly is. Any other approach is disastrous for biblical theism. A theology grounded in Scripture will not confuse God-knowledge with world-
knowledge by reducing divine perfections to simply distinctions in the
world of nature, nor will it be limited to apprehending God's activity in
relation to the universe; biblical theology includes also revealed metaphysical knowledge of God-in-himself. Whatever classification of the divine
attributes it ventures, Christian theology must maintain the transcendence
of God without surrendering all ontological knowledge of God. Biblical
theology combines an emphasis on divine transcendence and on an epistemological access provided by God himself in both general and special
revelation. Unfortunately, even some theologians who profess to respect
God's revelation try to classify the divine attributes by speculatively derived
principles or on the basis of supposedly experiential considerations rather
than on the basis of the scriptural data.

In expounding the divine attributes Protestant theology has sometimes
ventured to combine gnosis concerning God's attributes with agnosticism
concerning the divine essence. While some classifications of God's perfections presume to transcend this disjunction of essence and attributes they
nonetheless schematize the divine attributes in such a way that the disjunction still remains even if in a modified form. If our knowledge of God's
divine attributes is so partial that it may be cancelled out by what we do
not know, then the threat of agnosticism is as real as in Thomism where
man supposedly has knowledge of God's existence but not of his essence.
To divide God's nature into what is known and unknown, with the perilous
suggestion that what is unknown is the divine essence or the secret core
of God's being, can only lead to theological skepticism.

Differentiating the attributes as *negative* and *positive* found favor in

102 Methods of Determining the Divine Attributes

ancient times with Philo, in medieval times with John of Damascus, Anselm, Aquinas, Petavius and others; more remarkably, this approach was espoused even by some post-Reformation Lutheran and Reformed thinkers who followed Roman Catholic theologians in the same regard. Such classification turns on "two ways" of supposedly arriving at knowledge of God from nature. The negative attributes, said to be reflected by the cosmos, were assigned to God by stripping away all creaturely limitations; the positive attributes were those perfections in an infinite degree that were mirrored by the universe, whether in man or the world. As theology loosed itself from biblical moorings, and as philosophy divested itself of scripturally mediated presuppositions, these disciplines collapsed into a jumble of disagreement. Some thinkers, for example, interpreted negative attributes, based upon a denial of human limitations to the divine nature, to mean that God is personal; others saw God as either suprapersonal or impersonal. The worst feature of this negative/positive classification of attributes was an avowed reliance on natural theology: thereby it obscured the knowledge of God's perfections available on the basis of scriptural disclosure, concealed man's sinful distortion of general revelation, and reduced study of the nature of God to inferences from the nondivine. A classification that professes to exhibit the divine attributes on the basis only of inferences from the not-God, and that regards it a matter of piety that the divine essence is unknown, cancels the significance of its own delineation of the divine perfections.

Some classifications of the divine attributes appeal to the principle of special divine disclosure given in the Hebrew-Christian Scriptures, but arrange them in a way that needlessly suggests a tension between God as he is in himself and God in relation to us. No doubt the purpose of rigidly contrasting those attributes that God possesses outside of his relations to man and the world with those that he displays in relation to the world is to emphasize a very important fact, namely that biblical theology has no mere relational and antimetaphysical knowledge of the divine virtues; it has, rather, an objectively valid knowledge of them. Problems arise, however, when a particular ordering of attributes suggests that a knowledge of God in himself can be affirmed in advance of or apart from cognitive relations of God to man.

If divine revelation is cognitive and propositional, then God can reveal information about his immanent nature. Because of his intelligible revelation we can speak authentically about both his transcendent being and about his relations to man and the world. Unless proposed divisions of the divine attributes into *natural* and *moral, absolute* and *relative, immanent* and *emanent,* or *intransitive* and *transitive* presuppose this epistemological basis in revelation they are merely conjectural. L. Berkhof protests that all divisions of attributes under two such main heads "apparently divide the Being of God into two parts, first God as He is in Himself . . . and then God as He is related to His creatures" (*Systematic Theology,* p. 56). Descriptive categorizations may unintentionally and needlessly invite confusion. The moral attributes are no less natural and original to God than are other divine attributes, but setting the latter apart may seem to imply that God is in some respects amoral. But such complaints arise only from a surface misunderstanding of the sense in which terms are used. As Henry B. Smith reminds us, "every attribute can be both negative and positive, every one must be both immanent and transient, every one must partake of the qualities of natural and moral" (*System of Christian Theology,* pp. 15 f.). Surely biblical theology does not distinguish some divine attributes as less absolute than others, or some as more relative than others. By observing the technical intention of the terms absolute and relative, we will see that what causes the contrast between them is that God relates himself in distinctive ways to the created universe, including man. Yet to contend for a knowledge of God-in-himself that we possess independently of all divine relations would require renouncing a theology based on divine revelation.

We have elsewhere already expounded God's proper names (cf. Vol. 2, pp. 184–255) and his personal names (cf. Vol. 2, pp. 226–246; Vol. 5, pp. 178–193) on the basis of God's scripturally given revelation. Now we propose to discuss God's attributive names or divine perfections, that is, his incommunicable and communicable attributes.

5.
Relationship of Essence and Attributes

THE RELATIONSHIP BETWEEN divine essence, attributes and activity has long been a major theological concern. During the Middle Ages and the Reformation much theological controversy focused on various aspects of this issue. In the modern period, especially since Hegel's day, philosophers of religion have debated the related questions even more than have theologians, until Karl Barth challenged Roman Catholic theology from an alternative dialectical-existential standpoint.

Protestant theology tended traditionally to adopt Thomistic realism, in line with Aristotelian metaphysics, so that the verdict of medieval theology concerning divine essence and attributes was generally as acceptable to Protestant theologians as to Roman Catholic dogmaticians. But the twentieth century marked a growing revolt against a substance philosophy which assumes that attributes inhere in an underlying substratum.

The question of the relationship between essence and activity has in fact haunted the history of philosophy from its beginnings. Pre-Socratic philosophers divided over the question whether being or becoming characterizes reality. While Plato and Aristotle distinguished an eternal, changeless realm of being, from a temporal, changing realm of becoming, both supported a "substance" view of reality. Plato viewed matter as a formless, unqualified "stuff" that became individuated by participating in the various eternal forms. Aristotle held that the essence or substance of a reality must be distinguished from its attributes and activities. Writing of substance in terms of substratum, Aristotle defines it as "that of which everything else is predicated, while it is itself not predicated of anything else . . . that which underlies a thing primarily is thought to be its substance" (*Metaphysics,* Book 8, ch. 3, 1028 b, 36–1029 a, 1). Yet the highest substance, Aristotle insisted, is not and has no substratum; the highest substance is thought-thinking-thought.

The "realistic" view insists that nonmental substance is the ontological core of all finite entities; it differs from spiritualistic or personalistic views that ascribe the nature of mind or spirit to all reality. Affirming two types of substance, a spiritual and a physical, each of which has its own appropriate attributes or properties, realism becomes the assumed metaphysics of medieval Scholasticism. Spiritual substance is thus said to be the underlying core or being in which the attributes of personality, i.e., self-consciousness and self-determination, inhere. Expounded in these terms, the Trinity was seen as comprising three eternal persons in one divine essence or substance.

Since Hegel's day, however, modern idealists have increasingly attacked the philosophy of substance; they have called for drastic revision of traditional statements concerning the relationship of personality to divine essence, and indeed concerning the relationship between all divine attributes and the nature of God. This shift in perspective has far-reaching consequences. It involves modifications more extended than some thinkers who borrow elements now from one side and then from the other, seem to suspect.

The impact of realistic and idealistic views upon exposition of the nature of God has become an inescapable concern of dogmatics. How shall we view the nature of God? Is it an underlying spiritual substance to be distinguished from its divine attributes or qualities?

One threshold observation should be made. All theistic schools, however they may disagree in relating the nature of God to his activity, affirm the priority of mind in the universe of being. Christian theology, whether realistic or personalistic, agrees on this principle. The starting point of any theology worthy of the name Christian is the denial of any nonmental ultimate, and the insistence that the living God originates and sustains the universe of men and things. The problem of whether cosmic existence is best explained along realistic or idealistic lines, that is, the question of metaphysical dualism or metaphysical monism, remains a second order issue; it is subordinate in importance to the affirmation made by biblical theology at its outset, namely: in the beginning, God.

But the choice between a substantial or personalistic view of reality is nonetheless important. While the issue is discussed here especially in regard to the doctrine of God, it cannot be isolated to this consideration alone; it has implications for other aspects of theology as well. What we say about the relationship of God's activity to divine substance bears also on the relationship of man's conscious activity to his soul, let alone on the relationship of the natural world to the being of God. The problem of substance, therefore, holds significance not only for the doctrine of God, but also for the doctrines of man and of nature.

Exposition of both realistic and spiritualistic metaphysics has usually reflected only marginal interest in biblical theology. Christianity is interested, of course, in revelational rather than conjectural delineation. Emil Brunner blames scholastic realism for misconstruing the nature of the God of the Bible at many points. Thomists, on the other hand, rightly complain that post-Hegelian spiritualistic or personalistic thought has sponsored unacceptable reconstructions of the Christian view of God, and has frequently led to the displacement of theology by secular philosophy of religion. While contemporary Thomists complain that personalism has typically discarded special revelation and miraculous redemption, idealistic philosophers reply that in modern times realism has often been combined with naturalism (as in Ralph Barton Perry's espousal of nonmental "neutral entities"); most idealists, they point out, at least make the priority of mind their starting point.

The controversy over a substantive or spiritualistic view of reality does not therefore reduce to a debate between theism and naturalism, or to a decision for or against special revelation. Representatives can be found on both sides of these concerns. Roman Catholic theologian R. Garrigou-Lagrange (*God: His Existence and Nature*) combined the realistic view with Thomistic theology and Louis Berkhof, the Protestant evangelical theologian, combined it with Reformation theology, whereas Perry, a philosophical realist, was hostile to supernaturalism in any form. The Protestant evangelical Floyd E. Hamilton advocated a spiritualistic view of reality in championing biblical verities; absolute idealists like Josiah Royce and W. E. Hocking, on the other hand, and personalists like Albert C. Knudson, Ralph Tyler Flewelling and Edgar S. Brightman, promoted the spiritualistic view over against miraculous once-for-all revelation and many other central features of evangelical theology. Neoorthodox theologians, notably Karl Barth and Emil Brunner, rejected the scholastic substance view on the ground that it projects a speculative rather than revelational approach to God. Evangelical theologians in turn stressed that these neosupernaturalists themselves promulgated a speculative theory of God's nature that distorts biblical theology.

What then of the compatibility or incompatibility of the substantialist and spiritualist views with biblical theology? The Bible has implications for all questions posed by philosophy, not least among them for that of the substantial or spiritual nature of reality. Does the Christian revelation rule out one or both of these views, or is it committed to some alternative? Does either view, if consistently developed, have implications hostile to essential biblical positions? Does one view fit biblical theology more readily than the other?

That biblical theology frontally affirms a substantialist or realist view of reality can hardly be maintained, or else scholars devoted to revelational theism would have asserted this as a cardinal tenet of Hebrew-Christian teaching. Intelligent acceptance of the essential Christian doctrines has not depended upon the prior establishment of a realist or nonrealist perspective. The community of faith has been able to remain loyal to all minimal requirements of biblical theology without decisively settling this particular issue one way or the other. The Roman Catholic church officially espouses Thomistic philosophy. Some early church creeds incorporate a substance clause (see Philip Schaff, *Creeds of Christendom*, on Epiphanius, pp. 33, 36; the Nicene Creed, p. 57; the Chalcedonian Creed, p. 62 and notes;

and especially the Athanasian Creed, p. 66; etc.). Philosophical considerations have been primary in the advocacy of each view; in relation to the Bible, the main concern has been to demonstrate the harmony of one view or the other with the requirements of scriptural teaching.

To those espousing an Aristotelian-Scholastic-realist approach, proponents of a spiritualist view reply that realism goes beyond what we experience—it affirms a permanent, independent something that is beyond and beneath experience, and that is therefore unverifiable in experience. In countering spiritualist views, whether espoused by absolute idealists or by personalists, the realists reply that the denial of substance results from converting an epistemological predicament into a metaphysical entity; from the acknowledged fact that all our experience of reality is mental it is illegitimately inferred that all reality is mental.

Modern philosophy ranges itself on one side or the other of this controversy. Its founder, Descartes, retained the medieval substance view in which he had been schooled. He affirmed God as the ultimate substance, and in this sense, as the only substance, but Descartes also asserted a plurality of created finite or relative substances dependent upon God for their existence.

Descartes views attributes as the essential quality of substance: thought, for example, is the essence of mental or soul substance, and extension is the essence of physical or bodily substance. Body and mind exclude each other; physical substance is in no way to be identified with mind. In harmony with this view, Descartes distinguished between divine spiritual substance in the nature of God and its attributes or essential qualities.

The idea that God is the only ultimate substance Spinoza developed in a pantheistic direction. He considers Descartes' finite substance a contradiction in terms; all reality, says Spinoza, is part of the one ultimate substance. The attributes that constitute this one substance he declares to be infinite in number, but of these attributes we know only two: thought and extension. Mind and body are parallel and distinguishable entities, yet in God or Nature ideas and things are identical, since all individual entities are modifications of the one divine substance. Therefore, by refusing to identify God with mind or personality, and insisting rather that thought and extension are but two modes in which divine substance exists, Spinoza, contrary to the spiritualist emphasis that Being is mind or thought or personality, contends that Being has thought and extension.

Leibniz takes exception to the Cartesian view of substance from another direction. Whereas Descartes distinguished between conscious unextended substance (mind) and unconscious extended substance (body), Leibniz asserts the existence only of an infinite number of more or less conscious substances. Reality is composed of myriads of metaphysical monads meshed in a system of preestablished harmony and governed by the all-directing God. On this view only God, the Monad of monads, is pure unembodied spirit. The monads, by contrast, are simple teleological substances; unextended, indivisible and imperishable by natural means, each monad contains its own principles of change. Leibniz characterizes the indivisible

and imperishable monads as percipient souls. Some interpreters think that
his hesitancy to depict the monads as expressly mental sets him apart
from later idealistic traditions; it should be recalled, however, that for
Leibniz and other seventeenth-century writers, consciousness has a somewhat different sense from its twentieth-century meaning. His philosophy
is a prime source of pan-psychic personalism, a view found in Rudolf
Lotze's earlier writings, in James Ward, Mary Whiton Calkins, and Charles
Hartshorne. They consider all reality to be mental; nature is not God's
mental activity, however, but an aggregate of minds or souls. The minutest
units of inorganic matter that most people regard as material substance
they declare to be minds in a phenomenal form or expression.

Between the early modern rationalists partisan to a realistic view and
Hegel and his idealistic followers stand the empiricists Locke, Berkeley
and Hume, as well as Immanuel Kant, who by his Critical philosophy
tried to synthesize rationalism and empiricism. For Locke the so-called
secondary qualities (such as color, taste, smell and sound) that we attribute
to sense objects are actually psychologically subjective; he considers only
primary qualities (figure, extension, mobility, solidity) objective to the
knower. Berkeley denied the reality of physical substance altogether; asserting that primary no less than secondary qualities are in the knowing
subject, he insisted that sensible things are ideas, and that reality consists
only of spirits and their functions. Physical objects he considered nonexistent as a substratum but as mental phenomena imparted to our minds
by the mind of God; nothing is real, he said, except an absolute Spirit
and finite spirits together with their mental content or ideas. Hume extended Berkeley's rejection of substance to psychological subjectivism.
Whereas Berkeley argued from nonsubstantial phenomena (i.e., our ideas
of nature) to God, Hume insisted that we cannot argue from phenomena
to anything. All percepts, Hume maintained, are reducible to sense impressions and to memory images or ideas dependent upon them. The same
denial of any permanent objective substratum Hume applies to the human
soul as well; the soul, he argues, is nothing more than a succession of
consciousness and therefore has no permanent ego.

Kant sought to rescue philosophy from this drift to skepticism fostered
by Hume's theory. The limits of human understanding are such, he held,
that we know only phenomena, although we are required to assert an underlying noumenon or substratum that we do not directly experience. While
Kant ruled out the possibility of cognitive knowledge of God or of the soul,
he nonetheless acknowledged their reality as regulative judgments that
man's total nature is said to require. Kant's defense of a substance view
of reality invited vigorous counterattack by idealists against his advocacy
of an underlying nonmental substratum, since Kant affirmed that reality
is known only in its phenomenal aspect and that no theoretical knowledge
of the *Ding an sich* is possible.

Earlier advocates of realism had insisted that the underlying substratum
is known, at least partially, in and through a knowledge of its attributes
and activity. Locke was later to say only that the substratum or substance

"is something—I know not what." The medieval controversy between nominalism and realism [1] issued in a clear victory for the latter position. Nominalists contended that the attributes we ascribe to God are simply humanly postulated names or concepts that have no objective justification in the nature of God. Realists, on the other hand, held that the very nature of God justifies the different divine properties or attributes that Christian theology affirms. At stake in this conflict is whether or not we possess genuine knowledge of the divine essence. If the attributes defining God's nature are nothing but humanly evolved subjective distinctions and have no justification in the divine nature, then we possess no genuine knowledge of God. The medieval realists were right when they resisted the notion that divine simplicity excludes any and all distinction of attributes in the divine essence, and resisted as well the consequent dismissal of attributive statements as mere human conceptions or names. The realists faced just the opposite danger, however. Some of them discussed the distinction of attributes within the divine nature in a way that seemed to compartmentalize God. Not only was the divine nature virtually bifurcated into the properties of righteousness, love, sovereignty, and so forth, but at times these attributes were also viewed as conflicting with each other and as injecting tension into the divine nature. This approach, which came to be known as extreme realism, required counter-emphasis on divine simplicity. To avoid compartmentalizing the divine nature, moderate realists stressed that even though God's nature lends objective justification for our subjective distinction of attributes, it supplies no basis whatever for forcing a tension of attributes into the divine nature.

Post-Kantian idealism merged the issue of the relationship of divine essence and attributes with that of a substance-versus-mental view of essence. The latter controversy had arisen in modern philosophy not primarily from discussion of the knowledge of God, but rather from debate over our knowledge of cosmic nature. Since an intellectual attack on the substance view in one area was bound to have repercussions elsewhere, both the spiritual and physical worlds were soon swept into the orbit of discussion. Yet it is significant that the issue was first formulated in the context of nature, rather than in respect to God. The realist view that primary and secondary qualities inhere in an underlying substratum was rejected on the ground that all our experience of the world of nature is conscious experience. As the objective source of our conscious experience, realism, it was said, projects an order of being wholly different from our experience; it assumes, that is, that something nonmental is necessary to account for the mental.

The pantheism of Hegel and his followers required extending beyond

---

1. The term realism is here used in a technical sense different from its meaning elsewhere in this chapter. Elsewhere it indicates that reality is not merely mental but has also a substantial nonmental aspect; here, in contrast with conceptualism or nominalism, it stipulates that attributes we distinguish in the nature of God have their actual justification in the divine nature, and are no mere human concepts or names devoid of objective justification.

cosmic nature to divine nature and human nature also, the same philosophical explanation governing essence and activity in the natural world. After all, Hegelianism viewed man and nature as nothing more or less than the divine nature externalized; what holds for the Absolute holds for man and his world, and vice versa, since these are but differentiations of the divine. Hegel, like Fichte, denied objective things-in-themselves. Experience, he said, is without an objective source; the spirit is the source of nature and creates the content of experience. Hence both Hegel and Fichte affirm that reality is thoroughly nonsubstantial, even if Fichte's fundamental principle is Will, and Hegel's is Reason. They differ in another regard, however. For Fichte the empirical ego necessarily assumes the existence of the nonego, that is, the Absolute which underlies experience as its creator and sum total; in other words, while denying a substantial character to the world, Fichte asserts the Absolute to be a subjective *Ding an sich* which becomes self-conscious in individuals. Hegel, on the other hand, dismisses the nonego and rejects any subjective source of experience, any experience underlying the self; for him the Absolute is rather the conscious process of thinking and of experience. For Hegel, in short, the Real is process, not a substance. He considers the individual self not as an expression of the Absolute Ego, but as the very flow of the Absolute. Subject and object prove to be identical in the coincidental experience of the Absolute and the individual. Not physical substance, not even spiritual substance, but divine Reason is for Hegel the essence of reality, and the very law of existence; absolute Reason is the root and flower of the world process.

Hegel consequently progresses beyond Kant's assertion that the *Ding an sich* is an unknowable nonmental substratum. But he does so by a striking reversal. Hegel agrees with Kant that the content of our knowledge is phenomenal, that we know no things-in-themselves. But he denies that finite phenomena are outward appearances of a more basic *Ding an sich*; for Hegel, the phenomenal appearances are themselves reality. Kant's view of the unknowability of things-in-themselves thus supplies the basis for Hegel's denial that such a substratum exists. Hegel objects that Kant postulates the unreal as if it were real, and fails moreover to treat phenomena themselves as the essence of reality. For Hegel, phenomena themselves are reality, the manifestation of the universal divine Idea, the externalizing of the Absolute Spirit which is itself the world process.

During the present century this denial of a substantialist view of reality has won considerable following among both naturalists and idealists. Since modern philosophy first directed the question of substratum and quality to the natural world, it became an issue for those who denied the supernatural no less than for those who affirmed it. Samuel Alexander's notion that reality is a combination of point-instants and John Dewey's theory that reality is active experience in nature, both reflect the naturalistic revolt against the view of an underlying substratum. Ralph Barton Perry's assertion that ultimate reality consists of "neutral entities" suggests, rather, an unqualitized substratum. Rejection of the substance view is not confined to idealists, therefore, but occurs even where theological concerns are not central.

Supernaturalistic views would, of course, be confronted with the need to detail what the implications of stripping the ultimate reality of a substantial substratum are for the doctrine of God. The inherited biblical view distinguished God the transcendent Creator from man and the world and usually insisted upon both spiritual and physical substance endowed with attributes. By contrast, supernaturalist philosophers who reject the realist view of an underlying substratum disagree over an alternative characterization of reality. As already indicated, medieval Scholasticism insisted that ultimate *Being* is *endowed with personality*. Spinoza had denied this; instead of affirming a transcendent spiritual *Being* of which personality is to be predicated, he asserted that *thought* and *extension* are two of an infinite number of *attributes that qualify* the ultimate Substance. Yet he obscured divine personality by developing his philosophy on pantheistic lines. Although also thoroughly pantheistic, Hegelian philosophy, as already noted, identified *Being* as *itself Thought*; in this system the process of thought replaces substance, and is itself reality.

Since Hegel's Absolute comes to consciousness in the cognition of finite selves, its own distinctive personality is problematical. This obscurity results in two schools of thought: one defines ultimate reality impersonally, the other, personally. F. H. Bradley, who influenced A. E. Taylor's early writings, championed the view that ultimate reality is an all-inclusive superpersonality; in the end this leads to the assertion that *Being is impersonal Thought*. The view that *ultimate Reality is personality* won far wider support, however, although its proponents developed it in various ways.

The above-mentioned philosophical alternatives to a substance view of reality hesitated to equate Being with a thinking Subject, or Self, or Personality. Now to be considered are views that expressly make this identification. The distinction, moreover, between these rival conceptions of Being as personal or impersonal is of great importance. Those who espoused an ultimate Self frequently complained that the realist projection of an underlying substratum tends to depreciate the significance of personality. But post-Hegelianism hardly verified the claim that to reject the realistic view automatically ensures a heightened emphasis on personality; such rejection may, in fact, be combined with a depreciation of personality. It could still be argued that the presence or absence of an underlying substratum means little for post-Hegelian views that support an impersonal Ultimate; for views that identify Reality in personal terms, however, the denial of substance is crucial.

Lotze is the fountainhead of post-Hegelian views that identify a spiritualist view of reality with ultimate Selfhood. Hegel had left in doubt the separate personality of the Absolute. Lotze now takes Hegel's thesis that no two totally different kinds of reason and spirit can exist, that is, a divine reason and a human reason, or a divine spirit and a human spirit, and combines this view that all reality is spiritual with the unambiguous affirmation that *all reality is personal spirit.*

Post-Lotzean thinkers develop this approach in three ways. Least popular was J. M. E. McTaggart's view: although he hesitates to affirm God as such and advocates instead a species of idealism without theism, McTaggart holds that *ultimate reality is a society of selves* in which there might be a directing Self. Most post-Lotzean thought holds that *ultimate reality is a Person*; it disagrees, however, over whether finite selves are parts of the Absolute Self, or whether finite selves are divine creations other than the Absolute Self. In the former, the Absolute is the independent, all-inclusive Person; in the latter, the Absolute is the independent, ultimate Person, and is also the creator of other selves that are not parts or differentiations of the divine.

The first of these expositions of divine personal Reality came to be known as absolute idealism, the other as personalism. Both repudiate an underlying nonmental substratum; both insist that selfhood furnishes the best clue to the ultimate nature of things; both assert that all reality is of the nature of consciousness. Absolute idealism is thoroughly pantheistic, since it considers finite selves aspects of the nature of God, whereas personalism compromises the pantheistic principle by distinguishing between finite selves and God. Influential in Germany, Britain and America in the early part of this century, these two traditions tried seriously to work out the implications of the spiritualist view of reality for the doctrines of God, man and nature.

The absolutistic or pantheistic development, which fails to keep finite selves metaphysically independent of the personal Absolute, includes in its ranks A. S. Pringle-Pattison, Josiah Royce, W. Ernest Hocking, Mary Whiton Calkins, and many others. These thinkers insist that *the Absolute is an all-inclusive Self,* or personal agent. Although identifying God as Mind, Hocking, for example, does not develop his system along personalistic lines. Absolute idealists insist that the Absolute is an all-inclusive Self and that individuals exist only as part of the Absolute's own life. This approach creates the insoluble problem of maintaining the reality and responsibility of finite selves.

The personalistic development of Lotzean idealism was promoted in America by Borden P. Bowne. Its distinctive feature is the insistence not only that *ultimate reality is Personality,* but also that *finite selves are dependent creations* of God rather than parts of God. The term personalism,[2] preferred by many expositors over the term personalistic idealism, is intended—in keeping with our knowledge of personality—to stress that the divine essence is as much volitional as ideational. While for personalism selfhood constitutes reality, it considers God the only independent Self; finite selves are created persons with a relative independence. The natural

---

2. Neo-Scholastic personalism, however, in line with Thomism insists on the substantialist view of a "core of being" in things and souls. It views Being as endowed with personality, and denies that the only substance is the experience of personal unity.

world is simply God's thought externalized or, in other words, a part of the experience of the divine Self. This Lotze-Bowne tradition includes in its ranks Albert C. Knudson, Ralph Tyler Flewelling, Edgar S. Brightman and L. Harold DeWolf. Related to this spiritualistic development, in the sense that they also affirm the metaphysical independence of finite selves, are G. H. Howison, F. C. S. Schiller, and James Ward.

Medieval Scholasticism and modern idealism thus arrived at two distinctive views of mind or personality. The earliest modern philosophers, especially Descartes and Locke, accepted the view of Thomistic realism that mind has an independent inner existence and activity alongside an outer nonmental existence. Their successors developed the significance of mind both constructively and destructively. Berkeley considered mind the constituent principle of the universe. But Hume dismissed mind as simply the aggregation of events or constant conjunction of ideas. Criticizing Hume for failing to see the synthetic unity of apperception that exists behind the flux of sensation, Kant combined this emphasis on the unity of mind with belief in an underlying nonmental substratum. Post-Kantian idealists, however, who denied the existence of any underlying substratum, turned against his substance theory Kant's assertion that we have theoretical knowledge of phenomena but not of noumena. Kant had affirmed a "transcendental ego" which, in distinction from the merely subjective ego, he identified only as the categories of thought that all human minds universally employ. His idealistic successors identified this transcendental ego as the Absolute mind, the constitutive principle of existence. In order to stress the importance of volition in the context of the mental, personalism in its several traditions spoke of an ultimate Self or Person; personality, it said, is the only reality.

Whereas naturalism asserted that all reality is ultimately a form of nonmental energy or stuff, and idealism asserted that all reality is of the nature of mind or conscious experience, medieval Scholasticism asserted that the attributes and activity of an entity, whether spiritual or physical, require an underlying substratum or substance that the qualities modify. This realistic, substantialist view elaborated by Roman Catholic theologians in line with Aristotelian metaphysics, Protestant orthodoxy then took over without questioning whether theology based upon special biblical revelation necessarily requires such a view. Protestant theologians frequently championed realism over against idealism. Almost all evangelical Protestant theologians in America, among them A. A. Hodge, Charles Hodge, W. G. T. Shedd, and Louis Berkhof affirmed the realist theory that attributes inhere in an underlying substance. Theologians like Albert C. Knudson and L. Harold DeWolf, who shared the idealistic rejection of orthodox doctrines of the triune God and of miraculous revelation and redemption, generally supported the idealistic emphasis on the conscious nature of all reality.

Although conservative Protestant theology mostly aligned itself with a realistic metaphysics, those relatively few evangelicals who expounded idealistic metaphysics were not on that account inclined toward liberal theology. Augustus H. Strong, the influential American Baptist theologian, gradually moved from a realistic to an idealistic metaphysics; while he modified his theology at numerous points in the interest of larger emphasis on divine immanence, his sympathies remained on the side of conservative theology (cf. C. F. H. Henry, *The Influence of Personalistic Idealism on the Theology of A. H. Strong*). Floyd E. Hamilton combined idealistic metaphysics with conservative theology, avoiding even the compromises of evangelical doctrine made by Strong.

Tensions between proponents of idealistic and realistic views of substance were quickened in recent decades when neoorthodox writers like Barth and Brunner raised the issues in a different context. A theology of revelation, they affirmed, has no basis for distinguishing, in the nature of God, between some aspect which is to be identified as the divine Being in itself and what is revealed or known of God. The view of an underlying substance in the reality of God is thus attacked specifically in the name of the theology of revelation, and not simply on the basis of speculative philosophy.

As already indicated, the problem of substance and its relationship to attributes or qualities has three centers of interest, namely, God, man, nature. In secular philosophy the problem surfaced first with regard to the cosmos, known to us only in conscious experience; the implications of a spiritualist view in this area were later extended to include also God and man. Contemporary theology approaches the problem primarily from the Godward side. Obviously in any comprehensive explanation of existence, the decision to relate being and attributes and activity in a given manner must be applied consistently to every relevant sphere. Secular philosophy arrived at the definition of divine essence and attributes by enlarging conclusions about substance in the natural world. Although our primary concern is the doctrine of God, we must consider these speculations, at least briefly, inasmuch as aspects may surface that relate in one way or another to the doctrine of God.

All recent idealistic traditions agree that the cosmic world is of the nature of conscious experience, is altogether mental, and devoid of any underlying nonmental substratum. This was already the view of Berkeley, who argued that primary and secondary qualities—i.e., all the qualities which we presume to find in external nature—really exist in us as elements of our consciousness. Berkeley regarded the existence of external nature skeptically, and held that phenomena are the infinite Spirit's thought-manifestations made subjectively to us; subsequent idealism, on the other hand, has more firmly insisted on the objective reality of nature, even though like Berkeley it viewed nature as exclusively spiritual. Berkeley espoused a certain kind of objectivity by saying that since God causes the ideas, they have an independent origin and are not in our power; they therefore occur in an orderly way and not chaotically, a fact that distinguishes them from hallucination. Nature, it was said, is a phenomenal activity of the divine will, and not our own activity. From Lotze onward it became popular for idealists to refer to nature as God's thought "externalized" or presented to our sense experience in phenomenal form. The phenomena comprise matter's only reality; their reality is completely mental, the divine thought made known to us. Phenomena have no underlying nonmental substance in which the spiritual or mental inheres. Nature does not involve God's creation of a nonmental substance; nature is itself conscious experience, a part of the divine life.

But to state the matter in this way only nibbles at the problem. To deny an underlying substratum, to exclude a nonmental something in which qualities are said to inhere, seems to lead to one conclusion, namely, that the qualities themselves, or the patterns of nature, constitute the only essence that exists. But does our mental activity then become the ultimate essence of things and even of God? We must avoid the latter conclusions, on the basis of divine self-revelation in which God declares his own existence and that of a real created universe to which we belong. Do divine revelation and logical consistency help us in formulating the nature of God in personalistic or in substantial terms?

Emil Brunner's attitude toward idealism is somewhat confusing. He rejects a substance philosophy in his treatment of the doctrine of God. He repeatedly criticizes the Scholastic doctrine of Being for tending to depersonalize God's love, holiness and sovereignty by viewing these divine attributes as adjectival rather than as substantive. Brunner stresses that "the Being of God as Lord . . . is both metaphysical and ethical" (*ibid.,* p. 150).

Brunner insists, moreover, on what hardly follows from a rejection of divine substance, namely, that God is Absolute Subject, known only as Person and never as object. "God is not an *Ens,* a 'substance', like the Godhead of metaphysical speculation . . . but the Subject who as 'I' addresses us as 'thou'. God is the Personality who speaks, acts, disclosing to us His will" (*The Christian Doctrine of God,* p. 139). "Confusion . . . is created when the doctrine of God, instead of starting from this disclosure of His personal Being as Subject, starts from any kind of neutral definition of being, such as that of the theology determined by Platonism, Aristotelianism, and Neo-Platonism" (*ibid.,* p. 141). Brunner adds: "The Neo-Platonist doctrine of the *anologia entis* . . . based upon a speculative ontological theory of a hierarchy of being . . . lies at the basis of . . . the view that in absolute being, thus in the abstract concept of 'object', in the *'ens',* in that of 'absolute substance', we have grasped what faith calls 'God' " (*ibid.,* p. 178).

God, says Brunner, is "pure Spirit, pure Activity, pure Energy. Only the Subject which is wholly subject and in no way object, has unconditional freedom, unlimited vitality, unlimited independence, purely positing, originally creative Power" (*ibid.,* p. 145).

Brunner further champions "the God whose Nature it is to be the Revealer" (*ibid.,* p. 121), whose nature it is to "communicate Himself" in view of "the indissoluble unity of the nature of God with the revelation." (*ibid.,* p. 127). No distinction is permitted between the Being of God and his self-communication. "Revelation is not something which is *added* to His Nature; it is a part of His very Nature" (*ibid.,* p. 165).

God is "the God of revelation . . . whose very nature it is to be sovereign

Will. . . . The Nature of God is not rightly described if it is not described as *Will* directed towards the sovereignty of God" (*ibid.*, p. 165).

For Brunner, God's holiness and love are not to be developed as attributes distinct from the divine essence nor, in contrast with traditional theology, are they to be "treated after the 'metaphysical attributes'. . . under. . .'ethical attributes'. . . . The Bible really means that Love is God's *Nature,* and not merely His 'temper' (or disposition)" (*ibid.*, p. 191). "The sending of the 'Son of His Love'. . . to the death on the Cross, the act of reconciliation which proceeds from God alone . . . discloses the secret of His being," namely, that God *is* love (*ibid.*, p. 184). We are not to say merely that "God is 'loving'," for "love is not a 'quality' or an 'attribute' of God" but rather "the very Nature of God" (*ibid.*, p. 185). "Love is not a 'quality' of God, but is His Nature, like Holiness" (*ibid.*, p. 188). Brunner considers radium an effective illustration, for we cannot describe its nature "without speaking of radioactivity. . . . Even so the nature of God is. . . communicating activity, personal being, which wills communion. There is nothing 'more metaphysical' in the doctrine of God than this: that God's Nature in Himself is precisely His Being-for-us. If the doctrine of God as He is 'in Himself' is the philosophical formula of 'Being-Subject', then the Christian formula for the Being of God is 'Being-for-us,' or . . .'Being-for-something' (for some purpose) . . . . The Love of God (is) not . . . an 'attribute', but . . . the fundamental Nature of God. . . . In contrast to all other forms of existence, this is the Nature of God: the will to impart Himself. This is Christian ontology, this is the doctrine of the Being of God, and this is fundamentally different from that of speculation" (*ibid.*, p. 192).

Despite such refusal to distinguish between God's being and his activity, Brunner asserts that "God's self-manifestation is the act by which God steps out of the sphere of His own glory and self-sufficiency, in which the One who exists *for Himself alone* becomes the One who exists *for us*" (*ibid.*, p. 124). Here Brunner seems to reverse what he has asserted; he declares God self-sufficient, one for whom creation and revelation are optional. He distinguishes a knowledge of God in himself, therefore, from a divine activity and knowledge dependent upon God in relation to us.

The reason for this distinction is apparent. Brunner's emphasis that God is by nature self-communicating activity that blends holiness and love seems to imply the necessary creation and redemption of the universe; in the Christian approach, by contrast, both creation and redemption are voluntary divine acts. If God's essence is "Being which goes forth from Itself, Being which communicates Itself," if the very nature of God is "communicating activity . . . which wills communion" (*ibid.*, p. 192), if God's nature is revelational love "which goes-out-of-oneself, which stoops to that which is below" because "the idea of self-communication gathers up into one the two elements love and revelation" (*ibid.*, p. 187), then do not the universe and revelation and redemption flow from an inner divine necessity? We are told that "Revelation is not only the means through which God shows us Himself, as He is; but revelation is the flowering of the Divine Nature itself. . . . To go forth from Oneself, to impart Oneself—

this is the Nature of the Living God, in contrast to the self-sufficient Being of the Absolute of thought . . ." (*ibid.*, p. 188). Brunner insists, moreover, upon "an essential and necessary relation between Love and Revelation" and also "between Holiness and Revelation" which, in its development, issues finally in an elimination of their distinction: "Holiness merges into Love, and thus becomes complete" (*ibid.*, p. 190).

The contrast with Protestant orthodoxy is clear at this point. If God's nature is self-communication which goes "out of Himself" to others, then "creation" becomes a necessity, the universe a necessary "emanation," for God's nature can hardly be conceived out of necessary relations to the universe. Moreover, if gracious love is elevated in the nature of God as the very essence of divine self-communication, then the holiness and wrath of God—however much Brunner may emphasize them—are overshadowed. Brunner's theology results quite understandably in a rejection both of propitiatory atonement and of a final everlasting punishment of the wicked.

Brunner tries to avoid the metaphysical necessity for the universe and for redemption. He writes: "At first sight . . . the idea that God's 'metaphysical Being' is not only 'God as He is in Himself' (Subject), but also God as He is 'for-us,' is objectionable, because it seems to suggest that such a relation of God to His creation should be reckoned an integral part of the Nature of God, which, indeed, is unthinkable" (*ibid.*, p. 193). For "it is only from this 'God as He is in Himself' that creatures come into being at all. The first effect of this Being of God 'for us' is the Creation . . ." (*ibid.*, p. 193). "God might, indeed, have existed without creating. He does not need a creation. He is sufficient unto Himself. But He does not will this; He wills to impart Himself; He wills to give Himself to another, 'over against' Himself, to whom He can impart something of Himself" (*ibid.*, p. 193).

Against Hegel and other pantheists, Brunner insists that finite selves are not parts of God. They are finite creations, distinct from the divine nature; God is independent, they are dependent. Brunner's personalistic exposition develops the "I-Thou" relationship not in the context of either the Hegelian or the Lotzean traditions, but rather in that of Ferdinand Ebner, Martin Buber and Friedrich Gogarten, all of whom were influenced by Sören Kierkegaard's philosophy of "existence."

Brunner does not resolve the central difficulty of how to define the intrinsic nature of God as self-communicating sovereign will without acknowledging the necessary existence of other selves. Traditional Christian theology has frequently emphasized that the triunity of God provides an eternal subject-object relationship within the divine nature. In declaring of God that "within Himself, 'before all worlds', He is the Self-Communicating One," Brunner writes of "the mystery of the doctrine of the Trinity. . . . The doctrine of the Triune God contains the truth . . . already perceived to be the decisive element in the Biblical doctrine of God: the unity of God's Nature and of His revelation. . . . The Name in which God reveals to us His Nature . . . is . . . the threefold Name of the Father, the Son, and the Holy Spirit" (*ibid.*, p. 199). Yet Brunner does not assert what is essential for his argument—and what, in fact, he elsewhere denies, that is, the co-existence of persons within the divine nature. For if we appeal to eternal self-communication within the divine nature as an alternative to God's requirement of finite selves as an "other," nothing less will do than an ontological Trinity, or the eternal co-existence of personal distinctions within the divine nature. Brunner opts instead for a view that affirms three persons "one behind the other," and not side by side.

Brunner's revolt against a substance theory of the divine essence therefore involves—supposedly in the name of revelational theology—deriving creation and revelation and redemption inevitably from the very nature of God; in so doing, Brunner sacrifices a biblical view of the triunity, and dwarfs the distinction between God's righteousness and love. Brunner ultimately seeks to give revelation a christocentric foundation. But because he denies an ontological Trinity he must depend on speculation about divine love and holiness to support his view that God is the will to self-disclosure or the will to communicate. Instead of recognizing intelligible divine revelation as the ground of all knowledge of God, he traces revelation to God's nature as pure act and founders on the substance-attribute problem.

Yet unlike all spiritualistic traditions, whether of the post-Hegelian or the Lotze-Bowne schools, Brunner's personalism rejects a pantheistic view of nature. A curious passage in his Gifford Lectures declares the natural world to be "objectively real and subjectively ideal" (*Christianity and Civilization,* Vol. 1, *Foundations,* p. 27). When asked whether he was favorable to idealism of the subjectivistic Berkeleyan type, Brunner insisted only that emphasis fall both on divine will and on divine thought. He did not refer to what was originated as a new energy or substance distinct from the divine nature, but stressed only "the reality of this created world . . . even if it is said that this reality is God's thought and the product of His will" (*Christianity and Civilization,* Vol. 1, p. 160, n. 16). In another passage he says that God is distinguished from nature only in terms of unlimited vitality: "God alone is pure Energy, while all that we otherwise call *energy* also contains the element of indolence, dullness, slackness, in short, that of defective vitality" (*The Christian Doctrine of God,* p. 145).

Brunner's rejection of the doctrine of "pan-en-theism" developed by K. H. Krause and Lotze should also be noted. He objects to it not because it displaces a substantive view of nature and absorbs nature to God as his immediate activity but because the Lotzean view is not activistic enough: "This formula does not adequately express the Biblical idea, because it is too static, and not sufficiently dynamic. God's presence in the world, and His nearness to man, are not correctly described by the formula 'being-in', because God's nature is "actuositas', 'being-in-action' " (*ibid.,* p. 175; at this point Brunner promises to expand his treatment in the second volume of his dogmatics). At the same time Brunner firmly opposes any absorption of nature to God. Emphasizing the transcendence of the divine essence, he asserts that " 'Godhood' is absolutely and irrevocably different from all other forms of being, as the essence of the Creator differs from the essence of the creature; thus God and the world must be kept absolutely distinct" (*ibid.*, p. 175). Refusal to identify nature as a part of God, or as a part of the direct divine activity, is reflected also by Brunner's emphasis that, in contrast with the "I-Thou" relationship involved in interpersonal encounter, man's relationship to nature is to be formulated in terms of "I-it" encounter. Were nature identified as a part of the conscious activity of God and of immediate divine experience, as it is in recent modern absolutistic and personalistic philosophies, then nature would have to be conceived personally rather than impersonally.

It is now time for the present writer to come down either for or against a substance philosophy.

I reject the realistic view that being is a substratum in which attributes inhere, an underlying substance that supports its qualities or predicates. Athanasius, in the fourth century, made an important point about substance. Had Christian philosophers and theologians heeded it, they would have avoided many of the difficulties created by the term's Aristotelian orientation, Scholastic accretions, and modern Lockean modifications. In his *Defense of the Nicene Council* (ch. V. 3 and 8, or para. 19 and 22) (c. 351) and in his epistle *On the Synods of Arminum and Seleucia* (ch. 111, 4, or para. 35) (c. 359), Athanasius declared that the phrase substance of God is simply an emphatic way of saying God. He wrote: "The word God signifies nothing but the substance of Him Who Is." In Greek the term means only reality or existence; it does not mean an element to which qualities are added to make a compound. Moreover, since God's substance is the express reality of God himself, the notion of substance is not to be considered, as does Locke, merely an abstract idea.

For Locke material substance was not a positive concept but simply an obscure notion of "the supposed, but unknown, support of those qualities which we find existing, which we imagine cannot exist *sine re substante*, 'without something to support them'" (Locke's *Essay Concerning Human Understanding*, Book 2, ch. 23, sec. 2, p. 195). Locke affirms simple ideas, abstract ideas, and ideas of relation; substance, either material or spiritual, he considers most abstract of all. Athanasius' comment would make Locke's notion that substance is "an uncertain supposition of we know not what" wholly inapplicable to the nature of God.

Modern discoveries about the energy of the atom, vibration of the atomic nucleus, rapidly revolving electrons surrounding the nucleus, and splitting of atoms to release atomic power, have made untenable the inherited philosophical view that matter is a disparate "stuff" distinct in quality or character from these phenomena. George Berkeley had emphasized that physical reality is reducible to mental qualities. The new energistic view of matter, alongside the modern idealistic and personalistic challenges to the traditional theories of both material substance and soul substance, prompted a demand for reconciliation of theology with modern physics and psychology.

For revelational theism the problem of spiritual substance cannot be fully answered simply by empirical evidence drawn from the natural sciences or even from human psychology, including the psychology of religion.

In view of God's independent existence, the problem of substance may in fact have numerous facets.

There is no necessity that soul substance, if there be such, should require also a material substance in the cosmic world, although if one is possible the other is also possible. Relationships characteristic of the created world need not be predicated of God; unlike God the natural events and objects of the space-time universe have no invariable nature. Probably most scientists consider "laws of nature" to be of this invariable character. But no finite reality can adequately or definitively reflect what is the case in the realm of the supernatural; moreover, the so-called laws of nature are constantly revised. George F. Thomas rightly identifies the tendency to conceive theology anthropocentrically rather than theocentrically as a recurring feature of American philosophy of religion during the first half of this century (in *Protestant Thought in the Twentieth Century*, p. 99). Academic forfeiture of the importance of divine revelation almost inevitably makes human experience rather than God the center of religious interest.

Many problems are created by the realistic Aristotelian-Scholastic notion of a soul substance or spiritual substance that is distinguishable from both the activities of a self and from the unity of its consciousness. If substance of which we have no cognition or experience is simply to be postulated in accord with one's desires, then why may not a number substance or a value substance also exist over and above mathematical entities and ethical virtues? Plato would say that numbers are in fact substances, as are also values—justice, for example.

Edgar S. Brightman stressed that the purpose of all thought about substance is to guarantee (a) permanence and (b) explanation of change. He disavows transcendent divine revelation, and considers experience to be the only reliable way of knowing. Empiricism, he contends, warrants the verdict that personal unity of consciousness is the only verifiable kind of experience that combines permanence and change; anything else, Brightman declares, is either animal faith or abstract mystery (*Person and Reality*. An Introduction to Metaphysics). No experiential evidence whatever, he avers, can validate the soul as an unchanging substantive unity.

Peter A. Bertocci carries forward Brightman's exposition of self-psychology by affirming that the conscious datum-self is not a substantive soul or spirit but a complex unity of conscious experience.

What is God—or divine essence—if not divine mind, will, righteousness, love, power, and so on? Does this emphasis on conscious experience involve us in reducing the conception of divine essence to vagueness? Are we merely restating essence-and-attributes in a circular way, one that clouds the reality of God? Does this conception of divine essence require that God be continually and maximally active in his work of creation or of redemption if he is to be permanent?

A spiritual substance distinct from attributes could not be spirit in the sense of self-consciousness and self-determination, or identifiable in terms of any virtues or perfections whatever, nor be capable of personal revelation or communion. It could at best be spiritual only in the sense of potentiality—that is, essence or substance would consist of faculties or possibilities which, when realized, are conscious and spiritual in nature.

In contrast with finite selves God is the only continuously conscious self or substance. Created finite selves, many personalists emphasize, are not continuously or perpetually conscious in this life, although in the life to come human persons may have continuous consciousness. Berkeley, Lotze, Brightman and Bertocci contend, moreover, that God is also the only uninterrupted self. These scholars reject the notion of soul substance when speaking both of God and of human selves. For this reason they consider any appeal to the subconscious or unconscious as of no use for preserving a perpetually continuous self. Brightman holds that whenever the human person becomes unconscious, he or she literally ceases to exist. During such human unconsciousness God purposes that the created self will exist again, either on awakening or in the life to come.

But this approach weights the discussion of substance and selfhood with unnecessary speculation; Brightman's reliance on empiricism can hardly decide what happens during unconsciousness, beyond consciousness, or beyond death, let alone much else. If we cease to exist, must we then be recreated, and if so, how shall we explain personal identity? Hume contended, on the basis of the limits of empirical knowledge, that we cannot in any case speak of selfhood in terms of an abiding subject. He offered a substitute theory: the human self, said Hume, is only a bundle of sense impressions succeeding each other, of which at any given time only a small proportion of the bundle changes. Kant replied that the self is a synthesizing activity that underlies the categories of understanding and the forms of perceiving.

In some respects reflecting views held by Plato and Kant, F. R. Tennant distinguishes the pure ego as an abiding subject from the empirical self; he insists in his major work, *Philosophical Theology,* that the concept of pure ego is not mere fancy but an indispensable idea. He maintains, however, that activity is one of the pure ego's faculties and capacities, and constitutes its knowable essence. He writes: "Its *known* essence is to function: and though to suppose that its being is exhausted in function, that it must incessantly function in order to be, is perhaps to confound a psychological with an ontological issue, and role with player; still, a substance to which experience is only incidental, is an abstraction from fact, a mere possibility of which psychology can make no use" (*ibid.,* Vol. 1, p. 97).

Theologians and philosophers who reject the notion of a static divine essence distinguishable from God's attributes, and who insist instead that God's essence is known in his activity, are aligned on both sides of the question whether God, or divine essence or nature, is to be wholly identified with God's activity. Personal idealists are not agreed. Brightman, on the one hand, affirms it, and Bertocci rejects Tennant's distinction between the pure ego and the empirical self, holding that "there is no ground to suppose that the self is *anything but* its experiencings" (*The Empirical Argument for God in Late British Thought,* p. 207). Borden P. Bowne, Ralph

Tyler Flewelling and L. Harold DeWolf, on the other hand, deny that God is to be identified simply with his activity, as does also A. H. Strong, who in later years subscribed to a personalistic view of selfhood. Not only biblical theologians, but also existential and/or dialectical theologians contend that we can make no predications about God except on the ground of divine self-revelation. But modern existential theologians also misappropriate Luther's distinction between *deus revelatus* and *deus absconditus* for their own ends. Appealing as it does to personal encounter, existential knowledge-theory cannot affirm a knowledge of God's nature that transcends our inner existential experience. On the other hand, evangelical theologians who insist that divine revelation is propositional and objectively informative, on that basis speak of God's intrinsic nature.

C. A. Campbell has recently reaffirmed Tennant's view, shared also by A. A. Bowman (*A Sacramental Universe*), that the activity of the self implies an active subject and that *"that which is* active in activity cannot possibly be the activity itself" (*On Selfhood and Godhood*, p. 70). Campbell's contentions that knowledge requires a cognitive subject distinguishable from particular cognitions, that psychological performance does not exhaust the subject, and that psychical performance is not the object known in interpersonal relationships, are not in dispute. Many personalists would agree that cognition of any kind implies a subject conscious of its own identity in its different apprehensions, and that especially the experience of remembering requires an identical or abiding subject aware of its identity through a sequence.

Here we may recall Borden P. Bowne's observation that an experience of succession is not a succession of experiences, and that the former and the latter exist only for the person. As Bertocci puts it, "We cannot say that events are in a serial order unless something endures from the beginning to the end of the series. The problem is then: What is it that abides through the succession of unitary moments we have called the person?" (*The Person God Is*, p. 52). In brief, the self, contrary to Hume, is never reducible to relationships or to a flux of content; it is not a sum of atomic and disparate experiences but rather a self-identifying self-consciousness; if this were not the case, cognition would be impossible.

Bertocci takes serious exception, however, when Campbell explains the unity and identity of the self by positing a 'substantival I', that is, a self "over and above" its particular experiences, and infers an 'I' with which we have no acquaintance that 'has' rather than 'is' its experiences. Bertocci grants that Campbell's substantival self is not "a Kantian noumenal self about which we can know nothing," but rather, as Campbell contends, is always a "characterized self . . . manifesting itself in" thinking, desiring and feeling, and disclosing "its real character (in whole or in part) *in and through* these experiences" (*On Selfhood and Godhood*, p. 82).

Although the self is characterized by its activities or experiences, Bertocci protests any intimation of a self that "is always more than they and has them" (*The Person God Is*, p. 54). If the self is not identical with its activities, if it is the same while all of its experiences change, Bertocci remarks, then "no matter how much . . . it manifests *itself* through its changing experiences, how can we say that the sameness is manifested?" According to Campbell the self's sameness includes difference—a point Bertocci does not dispute. But the theory Campbell adduces to account for this sameness in difference—that of "a self not reducible to the totality of activity and experiences should be protested," says Bertocci, "if it proposes relationships which defy either the demands of logical consistency or of experience" (*The Person God Is,* p. 55). Fortunately Bertocci here mounts his criticism on the basis of logic and not experience, for his experience is far less conclusive than he thinks when elsewhere he expounds other facets of his religious views. I agree with Bertocci that logic requires one to accept the view that *"that which is* active in activity cannot be the activity itself" and to reject the view that any basis exists for affirming a self "over and above" its manifestations and distinguishable from them (*ibid.,* pp. 56 ff.).

Here we do well to consider criticisms by John Wild against the voluntaristic view, a view rejected by both those who hold to a substantial theory of the self and many who hold to a personalist theory. In voluntarism the self is synonymous with its acts and no distinctions at all should be made between the psyche and its perfections and activities. Wild sees several negative consequences of the voluntaristic view for human selfhood: (a) instead of remaining the same from infancy to old age and experiencing only accidental changes, the self would be essentially altered by new thoughts and desires; and (b) instead of being living selves even when asleep, human beings would cease to be humans when they are not desiring and thinking.

These criticisms have no relevance for God who is perpetually conscious and neither sleeps nor changes, unless, of course, one holds with process theologians that God's nature is growing. Interestingly enough, this profoundly unbiblical notion has been affirmed occasionally even by some who disown a divine substratum theory.

Wild's first objection should be assessed both in the context of man's creation, fall and regeneration and in that of the final restoration of believers to the full moral image of God. Change of character does not necessarily involve changing one's divinely purposed metaphysical status; man was essentially man in paradise, he is essentially man now despite his fall into sin, and he will be essentially man in heaven or hell. One's thoughts and ethical convictions and spiritual loyalties may change without involving a change in the laws of thought and morality that structure personal reality.

Wild's second objection is also wide of the mark. Even when humans are not desiring and thinking, and even when they sleep, Bertocci contends, their continuity may exist at other than conscious levels, and their identity may well have its ground in the purpose of God, the creator and preserver of the universe. Yet the individual person does not perceive this unity. Descartes and Leibniz, by contrast, hold that man always thinks—a conclusion that they do not, of course, base on experience.

Bertocci affirms that "the self *is* a continuous unity of its activities which are indeed not reducible to the experienced qualities" (*The Person God Is,* p. 54). The problem of how "such a self-identifying agent-knower can be identical from moment to moment and day to day" Bertocci ventures to solve along the lines of Brightman's personalistic self-psychology, namely, that the self—so Brightman affirmed on the ground of radical empiricism—is the unity of activities found in conscious activity and its contents.

Although, as Bertocci stresses, the active self engages in conscious activities of thinking, willing, oughting, remembering, sensing, feeling, desiring, and so on, not any one of these functions can exhaust the total activity of the whole self or person. The continuity of the ontic person is maintained through selective experience; by such experience a person perceives a given unity of activity amid interchange with the world. In short, Bertocci defines the self in terms of essentially conative activities of feeling-emoting-desiring as well as of essentially cognitive abilities.

How then can we explain self-identity even in sleep and unconsciousness? Bertocci disavows any a priori "metaphysics of continuity" and tries to "account for the data" empirically (*ibid.,* p. 60). Identity throughout intermittency, he notes, poses problems no greater for a temporalistic view than for other views, since during lapses from consciousness the conscious activity that characterizes mind does not exist. The self is then no longer a complex of conscious activities, for nonconscious or nonmental mind is "not a mind in any experienced sense" (*ibid.,* p. 60). "Does it actually help," Bertocci asks, "to say that a non-conscious entity (like the physiological organism), or even an infinite Mind, remain as the basis of continuity between intervals? . . . If we tried to allow the continuity of God's being to bridge the gap," he says, the continuity would be "his, not mine" (*ibid.,* p. 60). For Bertocci, "the nature of the individual person" is what best explains the phenomenon of self-identification despite intervening gaps. A person is not only conscious-self-conscious activity, but also a telic or purposive activity. Important as teleology is to this discussion, however, we should note that it is God's purpose, a purpose we do not know.

Before assessing this view, that Bertocci makes determinative, it is well to remember that the question of the relationship between divine essence or nature and personality, bears not only on the question of the nature of divine self-revelation, and on the matter of a substantival versus nonsubstantival essence, and on the ultimacy of the divine attributes; it concerns also the Christian doctrine of the Trinity. Each topic will be considered in sequence.

But first we should observe Bertocci's insistence that human thinking takes the course it does "in good part at least" because it is affected by desire or interest (*ibid.,* p. 61): "telic strivings involved in our feeling-emotive life . . . constitute the world in which . . . intellective activities arise" (*ibid.,* p. 61 f.). "Telic-cognitive processes are broader, though still mental, than the cognitive functions and persist in them" (*ibid.,* p. 62). These telic processes, Bertocci contends, "are neither self-conscious nor conscious" yet "are able to maintain themselves" during intervals in which we lose consciousness (*ibid.*, p. 63). "This *sub*conscious, not non-conscious or non-mental state"—as Bertocci prefers to designate the unconscious—maintains itself as a pole of mentality through all personal interchange.

We agree that man's intellective activity looks not simply to the present or to the past, but looks purposively also to the future and to a goal. But if thinking is as vulnerable to conative considerations as Bertocci suggests, would not his own theory, like its alternatives, be so vulnerable to subjective considerations as to reduce largely to rationalization even the strongly logical and rational appeal characteristic of Bertocci's work? Bertocci does, of course, emphasize the tentative character of his theory, for empirical inferences, as we know, are based on selective data and are subject to revision. Bertocci, however, moves beyond experience in some claims. His acknowledgment that "much more . . . needs to be done to show that this theory can account" for the data overlooks the fact that even herculean efforts will not assure the theory's verification. Asking someone to accept the content of a revisable hypothesis is considerably less than guaranteeing the nonintermittency of human beings.

Having no epistemologically significant doctrine of transcendent divine self-revelation, Bertocci postulates God as "the metaphysical Unity in whose nature and purpose the created orders we know are grounded" (*ibid.*, p. 219). He writes: "I believe that both the existence and attributes of a cosmic Mind can be ascertained by coherently organizing the variegated data which are at hand in the sensory, logical, aesthetic, moral, religious experience of the race. I take it as a basic methodology that no one has a right either to believe or disbelieve in God, or any attributes, unless his hypothesis allows more of the data of experience to become intelligible than any other view" (*ibid.*, p. 189). Surely few evangelical theists would concede that the biblical view of God makes the data of experience less intelligible than does any other view. On the contrary, orthodox Christians contend that the biblical revelation actually broadens experience and even anticipates vistas presently inaccessible to us, or to Christians throughout the centuries; it in fact speaks transcendently to the totality of human experience in the name of God's objective self-disclosure. For Bertocci "no adequate revealed theology is possible" (*ibid.*, p. 190) and the term divine revelation has no place in the index of his book. At one point he equates revelation with intuition (*ibid.*, p. 315); moreover, he allows religious experience and philosophical reasoning to preempt the role of revelation (*ibid.*, p. 338). This approach leads to a view of God that subordinates divine righteousness and judgment to divine love, and implies universalism (*ibid.*, p. 221). Whereas Bertocci cannot establish a fixed morality on the basis of experience, the Bible offers the Ten Commandments as finalities.

Bertocci protests Barthian theology with its denial that "God who reigns over man and the universe does not show himself in them"; this view, to its great disadvantage, shares an "anti-metaphysical scepticism . . . with its arch enemies, positivism and pragmatic naturalism" (*ibid.*, p. 338). But his own effort to construct God's nature from human experience, and to rely on natural theology, natural morality, and aesthetics "to complete the conception of God felt to be revealed in religious experiences" (*ibid.*, p. 338), reroutes us over the inconclusive and confusing paths that prompted Barth to repudiate secular philosophy of religion. Bertocci's appeal to coherence—if he intends to preserve logical consistency at its center (which he fails to do, cf. *ibid.*, p. 207 ff.)—is not in itself objectionable; what is objectionable is his assumption that coherence disallows a biblically grounded faith (*ibid.*, p. 342). Coherence is not a category that philosophers postulate assumption-free, and in these circumstances it can be more restrictively binding than is any appeal to the living God in his self-revelation.

By transferring to the self-identity of God the implications of this nonsubstantival view which Bertocci holds to be empirically licensed, he tenuously retains certain aspects of the inherited view of God on the one hand, but on the other imports changes into the divine nature beyond any biblical propriety (*ibid.*, pp. 217 ff.). How, on the basis of experience, Bertocci can insist on the *eternal* nature of God is less than clear. Nor is it clear why, if God is changing, we must insist on saying that he can never be "other than a Person" and "in this respect is unchanging," or even that "the cosmic Person is unchanging as Person but not in the quality of his experience" (*ibid.*, p. 219). Bertocci writes: "*Since the finite model of personal being exhibits the fact that* change does not defy, nor lie outside of, continuity of unified structure . . . *why not hold, then, that the Ground* of the changing-orderly world keeps its essential structure and norms with it in changing?" (*ibid.*, p. 219, ital. sup.). The italics indicate the principle of God projected in man's image; invoked at colossal risk, this principle leads to a deity somewhat akin to the God of the Bible not because the epistemological procedure requires it, but because the Judeo-Christian heritage leaves an ineradicable stamp even upon Western views that compromise it. The Buddhist considers personal selfhood a liability that ideally empties into nirvana, and projects an atheistic metaphysics. Over against Buddhism, Bertocci's alternative is indeed preferable, and he argues the case for its superiority, although mainly because he volitionally retains an attenuated Christianity. Apart from divine self-revelation neither Bertocci nor you nor I could confidently discriminate what aspects of human nature truly image the nature of God. Since finite persons do not ontologically sustain themselves, how do we arrive through religious experience and coherence alone at the view that God who allegedly changes in the quality of his experience, may not also be enmeshed in some form of ontological dependence? Did not Brightman, insistent empiricist that he was, affirm that God is finite? Only on the basis of God's trancendent self-revelation do we have sufficient ground for speaking of God's self-identity and only on that basis can we confidently challenge all conjectures about a divine substance distinct from God's own active manifestation in and through his perfections.

6.
God's Divine Simplicity and Attributes

STILL TO BE DISCUSSED is God's nature in relation to the panoply of divine attributes and to the persons of the Trinity. All God's attributes known through his self-revelation are to be identified with what theologians properly designate as God's being, essence, nature or substance, and identified with what the Scriptures call the deity or divinity of God who makes himself known. The divine essence is not to be differentiated from the divine attributes, but is constituted by them; the attributes define the essence more precisely. But are all attributes ultimately the same? Or do they differ, and if so, how? Are divine nature and divine personality identical conceptions? Only the *self*-revealed God of the Bible, to be sure, can authorize us to speak definitively of his existence, nature and personal life. But how are the three persons of the Godhead related to divine essence and attributes? This chapter considers essence and attributes; the next, essence and personality.

As already noted, the medieval controversy between nominalists and realists over the relation between divine essence and attributes issued in sharply defined alternatives. William of Occam and the nominalists regarded the usual attributions concerning God as having no objective basis in the divine nature, and hence as being simply names that are subjectively applied to the deity. This view greatly influenced a number of Arabic and Jewish philosophers as well as certain Christian theologians. In his *The Christian Faith,* Schleiermacher in scattered references treats God's attributes as poetic expressions of the universal sense of absolute dependence; he views statements about divine perfections as distinctions in our subjective feelings about God and not as objective information about God's nature.

Realists, on the other hand, spoke of actual divine attributes as irreducible to human postulations and, moreover, as distinguishable or separable even from God's essence. One may recall that ancient polytheism divinized

various energies; Plato deified the Good, Philo personified power, logos
and goodness, and Gnosticism spoke of divine aeons and emanations as
aspects of the divine mind. Somewhat in the same mood medieval realists
distinguished divine attributes from an underlying divine essence.

Outside the Bible God's reality was frequently exposited in terms of abstract "Being." Certain ancient Greek philosophers, particularly Plotinus,
characterized the Ultimate as beyond all limitation and predication, hence
without identifiable attributes. Any ascription of absolutes, it was said,
could only finitize the attributeless Ultimate. For some early Eastern
church fathers, this view was more influential than the Bible in defining
statements of the nature of God. The metaphysics of Plotinus postulates
God as above and beyond all being and thought. No greater contrast can
be imagined than that between the conjectural undefined Being of the
philosophers and the unconditional being of the self-revealed "I Am Who
I Am."

The importance of the discussion of divine attributes is apparent from
the fact that one often alters a subject by applying different predicates
to it. Some philosophers, of course, affirm that God is, in fact, a center of
change and not an unchanging substance. Aristotle's emphasis on potentiality anticipated this possibility long before modern process philosophers
appropriated and developed the notion, although Aristotle's Unmoved
Mover is unchanging. If God is qualified by different characteristics at
different times, however, we can no longer say what God *is* or even that
he *is;* we cannot say what or who is *the subject* of continuing change.
To say anything fixed about God we must abandon the notion of God as
a center of change. The alternative, that no fixed predicates are divine,
leads just as surely to an empty concept of the divine nature as does the
theory of an unknowable divine substratum in which attributes inhere.
When the fourth-century heretic Eunomius (c. 360) held that divine attributes are merely our subjective projections, Basil and Gregory of Nyssa
replied that we use not merely different names for God (conceived subjectively) but rather employ different thoughts about him that signify distinctions based upon the divine nature. Basil and Gregory were right.

Augustine teaches that God's attributes are identical with his divine essence; he views the divine essence as fullness of existence that includes
eternity, goodness, wisdom and other perfections. Much of contemporary
theology, with its subjective and relational emphasis, dilutes the force of
cognitive revelation, and compromises the fact that God, in disclosing his
name and attributes, reveals his very nature, his inmost character, his
essential being.

Thomas Aquinas taught that in this life we can know God's existence
but not his essence, something presumably reserved for beatific vision.
The most extreme form of this medieval theory was held by the French
scholastic Gilbert de La Porrée (1070–1154) who distinguished God's essence
from "God himself." While Aquinas does not deny that God's essence and
existence are identical, he nonetheless holds that we can investigate God's
being and God's activity separately. By philosophical reasoning, and apart

from revelation, Aquinas proposes to establish the existence of God as the *ens realissimum* (the most real being) and reserves investigation of God's works and ways as given in revelation for subsequent consideration. His premise is that, while revelation informs us *what* God is, general reason can establish *that* God is apart from *what* God is. Yet Thomas claims to know the *what* (by natural theology) at least to the extent of God's being a First and Unmoved Mover, cause of the world, and (by natural ethics) presumably moral governor also. In contrast with his silence about the essence of God, however, Aquinas ventures at considerable length to expound divine attributes as given by revelation.

Contrary to Aquinas, Karl Barth insists, and rightly, that we can speak properly of God's existence or of his attributes only on the basis of divine self-disclosure. Barth prefers to speak of the "reality" of God rather than of his "being," on the premise that "reality" implies no separation of being and action, but preserves a unity of essence and revelation. Barth's commendable intention is to avoid a contingent or arbitrary connection between God's inmost being and his works and ways. Yet why is inactive "reality" any less conceivable than static being? Only by his dynamic view of God in his revelation does Barth preserve the "reality" of God from the same ambiguities as the "being" of God, and, moreover, at great cost. Because Barth confines God's revelation to interpersonal encounter devoid of objectively valid information, he precludes man from having any ontological knowledge of God's essence, even by revelation, and forfeits all right to speak objectively of God's attributes. Barth writes: "All we can know of God according to Scripture testimony is His acts. All we can assert of God, all attributes we can assign to God relate to these acts of His. And not to His essence as such. Although the operation of God is the essence of God, it is necessary and important to distinguish His essence from His operation in order to remember that this operation is a grace, a free divine decision. . . . God's operation is, of course, the operation of the whole essence of God. God gives Himself to man entirely in His revelation. But not in such a way as to give Himself a prisoner to man" (*Church Dogmatics,* I/1, p. 426). What Barth apparently cannot bring himself to say is that God reveals theologically objective information, that is, universally sharable truths, about his intrinsic nature. That God remains free in his self-disclosure, and that apart from such disclosure we would not know him at all, is not in debate. But to imply that God remains so intellectually imprisoned within his voluntary self-disclosure that not even inspired prophets and apostles can or do convey objective ontological information about God as he truly is in himself—not only right now but in eternity past and in the eschatological future as well—cannot do justice to what the Bible itself teaches about God as he objectively is. The fact that Barth does indeed devote extensive sections of his *Church Dogmatics* to exposition of God's perfections and expounds some if not all divine attributes largely along evangelical lines is due not to his religious epistemology but rather to the teaching of inspired Scripture on which he leans despite his own faulty view of revelation and inspiration.

What we mean by the essence or nature of God is a living personal unity of properties and activities. Divine essence and attributes are integral to each other. God is not a substance essentially distinguished from his psychic properties or attributes. Such a notion would reduce divine essence to a barren concept, a postulation devoid of content and meaning. God's being is not the bearer of the divine attributes; rather, God's essence and attributes are identical. To know the divine attributes is not the same as knowing what is attributable to an underlying substratum that has a distinct or independent existence but no quality of its own. The God of the Bible is a sovereign will; as such he is a living unity of perfections that coordinately manifests the divine essence. The perfections that constitute the essence of the one living God are what on the basis of divine self-revelation we call God's attributes. To explicate the attributes is to explicate the nature of God. There is therefore no need to preface consideration of God's attributes with a prior inquiry into the divine nature. God is, in short, the living unity of his attributes. The attributes may be thought of as divine activities. God is not an abstract substance but an active spirit, consciousness and will. The activities are God's divine qualities or attributes. God is not the bearer of variable and interchangeable properties. He is the one living God, deity *sui generis,* who in his revelation and relationships prominently displays now one and then another of his superlative virtues; this he does in view of his purposive disclosure and of our divinely intended perception of that disclosure.

The view that divine attributes are completely separate or distinct functions in the nature of God and more or less independent of his essence, reflects the notion of an underlying substance, a notion that influenced even Islamic philosophy. Muhammad stressed divine unity although, due to gross misunderstanding of the Christian view, he denounced the doctrine of the Trinity (the last section of the Koran reads: "they surely are infidels who say, 'God is a third of three,' for there is no God but one God," v. 77). Among Moslems, Mu'tazilite dogma holds that the divine attributes are not eternal; Ash'arites, on the other hand, consider the attributes eternal but distinct from the divine essence.

To explain the multiplication of pagan gods some Hellenic thinkers stressed the similarities between Greek and non-Greek divinities; it was possible, they said, that these many deities are only different names for a commonly shared underlying reality. Sometimes this syncretistic tendency led to the idea that among the numerous deities one supreme deity— Zeus, for example—is to be conceived as a universal deity. Such conceptions do not, of course, fully overcome the fragmentation of divinity and grossly misunderstand the notion of divine unity. Hermann Kleinknecht is wholly right in saying that "neither fusion nor the conjunction of syncretistic and monarchical thinking led to real monotheism in the biblical sense" ("The Greek Concept of God," *TDNT,* 3:76). To promote the metaphysical unity of God neo-Platonism espoused three premises: first, the ancient Orphic notion that "all things have come out of one and back into one all things return"; second, that God is impersonal (strangely in Ennead

VI Plotinus uses masculine, not neuter, pronouns to refer to the One); and third, that God can be defined only in terms of eminence and negation. For all that, neo-Platonism considers the finite world a necessary and eternal emanation and actualization of God.

Evangelical theology insists on the simplicity of God. By this it means that God is not compounded of parts; he is not a collection of perfections, but rather a living center of activity pervasively characterized by all his distinctive perfections. The divine attributes are neither additions to the divine essence nor qualities pieced together to make a compound. Peter Bertocci has well said that God "never was, nor will ever be, ontologically divisible" (*The Person God Is,* p. 219). God's variety of attributes does not conflict with God's simplicity because his simplicity is what comprises the fullness of divine life. Augustine wrote of God's "simple multiplicity" or "multifold simplicity."

For this very reason the statement "God is"—if we know what we are saying—exhausts all that a course in theology can teach concerning him. If we give the subject "God" and the predicate "is" their true and full sense, we must speak of God's essence, names, attributes, and triunity, and do so expressly on the basis of his revelatory self-disclosure addressed to his created and fallen creatures. If we say "God is" on any other basis than God's self-revelation our predications have no sound epistemic ground. Augustine declares that "in God *to be* is the same as *to be strong* or *to be just* or *to be wise."*

Although some Lutheran theologians contend that the divine attributes are really separate in God, the Lutheran dogmatician Johann Baier declares that " 'divine essence' . . . is . . . first in God and . . . according to our mode of conception is the *principium* and *radix* of all perfections which are ascribed to God after the manner of attributes" (*Compendium,* II, 11). Francis Pieper stresses that the attributes are absolutely identical with the divine essence. As an accommodation to man, who cannot comprehend the absolute divine simplicity, Pieper adds, God in his Word "divides Himself, as it were, into a number of attributes which our faith can grasp and to which it can cling," e.g., God's love (Rom. 5:8), God's wrath (Rom. 1:18), God's long-suffering (Rom. 2:4) (*Christian Dogmatics,* p. 428). Yet Pieper also remarks, and without elaboration, that "Scripture distinguishes . . . between God's essence and attributes . . ." (*ibid.,* p. 429). This is disconcerting, since it is from Scripture that we learn whatever Christians properly affirm about God, including the propriety of designating him as the infinite and invisible God. In context Pieper helpfully emphasizes that in reality God's perfections do not differ from the divine essence. But when he writes that "as God is infinite, so also His attributes are infinite and are therefore beyond our comprehension" (*Christian Dogmatics,* p. 431), Pieper seems to place both essence and attributes beyond our knowing. He resorts to the untenable doctrine of analogy to escape skepticism. Pieper confuses univocal knowledge with ontological identity when he contends that if terms like goodness at any point mean the same thing when referring to deity and humanity the essential difference between man and God would be removed and man would be virtually deified. But surely even this term "goodness" has some univocal epistemic overlap when Jesus says "God alone is good" (Luke 18:19) and when Paul writes: "There is none good, no not one" (Rom. 3:10), or no intelligible contrast would be possible.

I. A. Dorner considered it a contradiction to insist on the objective oneness of the divine attributes and yet to distinguish between them (*History of Protestant Theology*). Yet any failure to give the attributes due recognition easily accommodates a compromised view of God; divine righteousness, for example, is not to be transmuted into divine love at the expense of the former.

The Presbyterian theologian Charles Hodge contends that the divine attributes are virtually but not actually separate (*Systematic Theology,* Vol. 1, pp. 369 ff.). What Hodge seems to be saying is that the distinctions we make have a real basis in God's self-revelation. He is to be commended for not dissolving the divine attributes into mere human postulation. The modified realism that he espouses emphasizes that divine simplicity is not to be confused with contentless essence, and also that each attribute is identical with the divine being. If one insists on the unity and simplicity of God, compartmentalization of the divine nature into divergent attributes is precluded. To compartmentalize the attributes within the divine essence would accommodate the notion of tension and contradiction within the nature of God. Our distinction of attributes rests upon the revealed character of God; it reflects not so much man's limited powers of comprehension of the one unified nature of God as the various effects of God's power. All divine attributes are one in God, and are to be differentiated only within the created situation.

If God is noncomposite, and his essence and existence are identical, then all divine attributes are mutually inclusive. Each attribute in the nature of God interpenetrates every other attribute and no conflict or contrast among them is possible. God's wisdom is his omnipotence, God's omnipotence is his justice, God's justice is his love, and so on. God and holiness, and God and love, are mutually exhaustive synonyms; Scripture itself testifies that "God is love" (1 John 4:16), and not simply that love is in God. No divine perfection is therefore inferior or subordinate to another; all God's perfections are equally ultimate in the simplicity of his being. The Bible uses attributes to describe God and to express his essence, e.g., the Holy One, the Gracious One, the Most High. As Bavinck writes: "God's attributes do not differ from his essence nor from one another" (*The Doctrine of God,* p. 120).

The attributes, we have said, are identical with the divine essence and serve more fully and precisely to define God's nature. This view escapes the difficulties posed by the Aristotelian approach of relating substance and attributes. Whether it helps expound the relationship of divine essence and personality, and accommodates a satisfactory doctrine of the Trinity, will be discussed in chapter 9. Evangelical theologians and philosophers must subordinate the question of essence and attributes, along with every other doctrinal concern, to the authority of Scripture and, within biblically revealed principles, to the demands of logical consistency. Not only evangelical Protestants but also Hegelian idealists and nonevangelical personalists reject the notion of a static divine substratum, and view the divine attributes as the active essence of God. But apart from divine revelation any talk about God is speculative and conjectural. Among scholars who affirm special divine revelation and reject a divine spiritual substratum are the dialectical theologians Barth and Brunner (who discard the evangelical insistence on biblical authority) and the evangelical thinkers Gordon Clark, Floyd E. Hamilton and Russell DeLong (who insist upon scriptural inspiration).

Some evangelical theologians devote considerable prefatory attention to the "being" of God before they expound the divine attributes. This preliminary discussion is often really an exposition of the spirituality of God, reflecting the biblical emphasis that "God is Spirit" (John 4:24); it is in actuality, then, an exposition of one of the divine perfections. Insofar, however, as such prefatory discussion of divine being is in principle separate or divorced from an exposition of the divine attributes and considered preliminary to any reference to the attributes of God, it has no valid place in revelational theism. Such discussion is sometimes influenced by natural theology, not least of all by the views of Aquinas, who on the basis of empirical observation alone professed to demonstrate logically *that* God is, in distinction from *what* God is. Here we confront, at least in philosophical terms, the notion of attributeless Being, a notion lurking behind every effort to prove God's *existence* preliminary and preparatory to discussion of his nature or essence. Such argumentation can only issue in skepticism concerning the divine being, since no initial predications are made of God other than his existence, an existence devoid of any attributes or perfections; we are left in the dark concerning the existence of precisely *whom* or *what*. The fact that a philosopher uses the term God, or the term Being, and even politely, devoutly or intuitively capitalizes such words, grants them no meaningful content once we are told that what concerns us is not essence but only existence.

The fact that the being of God is discussed preliminary to the divine attributes—as by Abraham Kuyper, W. G. T. Shedd, and myself—need not however imply an endorsement of natural theology or, worse yet, of the strange notion that we can know God's existence independently of his essence. While Turretin, Bavinck, Hodge and Berkhof consider the being of God in direct connection with the attributes, contemporary philosophical trends may argue for another procedure even by theologians who agree that God's being is identical with his attributes and revealed in them.

To be sure, a further issue is often at stake in the exposition of divine being and attributes, namely, the extent to which a theologian professes to derive the essential nature of God from general revelation or from special revelation. Secular philosophy of religion frequently discusses the being of God in isolation from and exclusive of any specification of divine attributes. But to discuss the divine nature only in connection with the biblically-revealed attributes may also reflect an objectionable dismissal of general revelation. Nonevangelical theologians, moreover, disavow special revelation even though they correlate discussion of divine nature with that of divine activity and deny an ontological substratum distinguishable from the attributes. Brightman, for example, denies that God has any being distinct from his activity. Biblical theism resists this reduction of divine being to divine activity inasmuch as it tends to obscure God the agent whose unchanging identity remains throughout all his activity. The notion that any distinction whatever between the agent and its activities leads toward scholastic substantialism may therefore be questioned. The activities are not products of the self as an ontologically disparate entity; rather, the self retains permanent identity amid its diverse and divergent activities. Brightman rightly stresses the inner difficulties of spirit-substance theory, although his alternative concentrates only on God's general activity at the expense of once-for-all redemptive revelation, and relies on an empirical epistemology that cannot adequately resolve the question of the identity of God in his activity.

Yet the epistemic priority of special revelation is obscured even by some evangelical theologians who avoid the errors of Aristotelian conceptualism and Brightmanian personalism. Hodge, who frequently invokes the common consensus of mankind on philosophical issues, and even more notably A. H. Strong, in view of his later concessions to personalism of the Lotze-Bowne variety, detail the divine attributes by a mixed appeal to general and to scriptural revelation, leaving us unsure whether the nature of God can be adequately expounded through both approaches and whether either has priority in the definitive exposition of the divine nature.

The order in which being and attributes are discussed is therefore less important than the underlying reason for a given arrangement of the presentation and its content. If the attributes have their ground in the nature of God as closer determinations of the divine essence, and if, as Christianity contends, God's attributes are definitively made known in the biblical exposition of God's distinctive activity in Hebrew-Christian redemptive revelation, then any attempt to penetrate God's nature independently of the data of revelation can only issue in theological bankruptcy. When the "existence of God" is presumably established by philosophical reasoning apart from cognitive dependence upon God's self-revelational activity and its inspired biblical interpretation, then the postulated conceptions of "divine Being" easily rely for their content upon creative contributions of secular metaphysicians. Only accidentally, or incidentally and even unwittingly, will such proposed definitions of God coincide with scriptural data, inasmuch as the appeal to biblical revelation comes too late and too half-heartedly; human unregeneracy, moreover, tends to taper general divine revelation to the preferences of a rebellious will.

The Protestant Reformers do not exclude knowledge of the divine essence. While they affirm the incomprehensibility of God, they nonetheless reject both the Scholastic notion that such affirmation rules out all knowledge of God's essential nature, and the rationalistic emphasis on the comprehensibility of the divine apart from man's dependence on divine self-revelation. Calvin stresses the futility of speculating about what God is (*quid sit Deus*) when our actual concern is "rather what kind of a person He is (*qualis sit*) and what is appropriate to His nature" (*Institutes*, I, 2.2); he repeatedly stresses the centrality of revelation for a proper resolution of theological concerns. Calvinists understand Calvin here to be protesting against revelationally unlicensed speculation; surely the Westminster Confession definition of God is a profoundly comprehensive statement of what God is.

In the absence of an appeal to divine revelation, post-Kantians and deists alike evolved their own partisan metaphysical constructions of God. For Kant God is a heuristic idea; for deists he is an honorifically retired creator who engages in no redemptive activity. Here, as in many other mediating secular alternatives, the abstract essence of God is so filled by conjecture that the later collapse of philosophy of religion into theological pluralism and then into atheism should have surprised no one.

Nor could some conservative theologians who distinguish among divine attributes those that are identical with the divine essence, and those that are supposedly not identical with divine being yet are somehow supported by the divine substratum, effectively forestall confusion about the nature of God. Such delineations do not enhance but rather impoverish our conception of the nature of God. To think of certain attributes as merely added to the divine essence, and not present to God in an absolute manner, implies that the created universe somehow partially and outwardly conditions or determines God's nature.

The process philosopher Whitehead distinguishes "the primordial nature of God" from a "consequent nature" that God presumably acquires in response to the process of cosmic becoming (*Process and Reality*). This view is inadequate and objectionable. Any ontological gradation of divine attributes can be carried through only at the expense of God's simplicity and immutability. The notion that some but not all attributes are identical with God's essence has resulted not only in conflicting catalogues of attributes but is in every case predicated on a failure to recognize that God's being is identical with all his perfections. One German theologian, F. A. B. Nitzsch, in proposing a list of fundamental attributes determining the divine nature, even affirmed that love does not belong to God's essence.

A somewhat opposite problem arises when theologians substitute for discussion of the relation of abstract Being and attribute a projection of one attribute over all others as ontologically basic. The fact is that all God's attributes have an absolute divine character; each attribute is involved in every other attribute. When theological exposition of divine attributes subordinates certain attributes to others, instead of acknowledging the equal ultimacy of them all in the nature of God, a quick devaluation of some attributes follows in deference to others. When we ascribe goodness to God properly, we at the same time ascribe justice and omnipotence. If we ascribe love in a way that moderates divine righteousness, or righteousness in a way that cancels mercy, then we depict the totality of God's nature improperly. Each attribute is rightly definable and defined only in relation to every other attribute, since each one reflects the simplicity of God. No doubt an effective discussion of divine attributes requires an orderly arrangement and exposition involving logical priorities. But such exposition does not require certain divine perfections to be submerged to others on the premise that some attributes are ontologically inferior.

Some theologians, trying to determine which attribute supplies a starting point from which all other attributes may best be presented in sequence, have been misled into thinking that one attribute is more basic in the divine nature than others; they have consequently tried to make all other attributes dependent upon one foundational attribute, even if all are considered identical with the divine essence. The equal honor that Scripture bestows on all God's attributes is jeopardized by emphasizing one or a few perfections at the expense of others; some scholars exaggerate or minimize certain attributes even as they stress divine transcendence at the expense of divine immanence, or vice versa.

Logical consistency is a test of the content of revelation in respect to God's attributes no less than other theological concerns; any effort to attain the divine attributes simply by logical reflection and a priori reasoning, however, and without dependence on revelational considerations, can only lead to novel reconstructions of the character of the true and living God. The priority of revelation in no way implies the disjunction of revelation and reason propounded by neoorthodoxy. It does require, however, that the intelligible exposition of the divine attributes follow the requirements of God's own self-disclosure and not the premonitions of human fantasy.

Various basic divine attributes have been proposed: love (Francis of Sales); veracity (Cornelis Jansen); omnipotence (Jean Du Vergier de Hauranne); infinity (Duns Scotus); personality (F. H. Jacobi); reason (Hegel); goodness (Jacques Vincent); moral perfection (Ritschl). Calvinists emphasize the logical priority of God's sovereignty, but avoid making this the fundamental divine attribute. Protestant modernists stress the priority of divine love at the expense of divine righteousness. Neoorthodox scholars exalt divine personality over divine rationality. Evangelicals frequently stress, as did H. C. Thiessen, the priority of God's holiness as the basic divine perfection. That God is holy (separate) because of the attributes which separate him from all creation is, of course, a biblical emphasis. But the historic Christian view is that all God's attributes are identical with his essence, indeed, constitute the divine essence. We are not to exalt preferred attributes in a partisan exposition, but are to exalt God who lives in the unity of all his perfections.

Deists replaced a broad interest in divine attributes with a cold, moralistic conception of God and retained a truncated emphasis on the will of God in unwitting dependence on the biblical view. No other religious or philosophical tradition stresses God's will so prominently as does Judeo-Christian revelation, an emphasis specially preserved by Calvinists. Deistic neglect of special revelation for general revelation, and this in turn for general reason, agnostically siphoned off much about the living God that the Judeo-Christian heritage conveys. With no acknowledgment of inspired scriptural teaching, modern philosophy connected its qualified emphasis on divine will, to which the Bible traces the creation of the universe, with pantheistic and evolutionary conceptions. Such modern reconstructions, while in line with biblical thought that views matter as neither evil nor as independent of God, soon made the universe an essential element in the life of God a speculative option. This option either tries to avoid relapsing into the notion of contentless Being or it reverts to abstract Being in a manner that dispenses with the living God. Barth and Brunner try to escape the notion of abstract Being by stressing God who confrontationally reveals *himself* (albeit in a manner that deprives us of objective ontological information). But Paul Tillich considers the selfhood of God simply a metaphorical device; for him the object of theology is not, strictly speaking, the Ultimate who decisively addresses us, but rather an amorphous and contentless absolute, that is, whatever concerns us ultimately.

Neo-Protestant theologians often make their plea for the unity of God's attributes an excuse for subordinating all divine perfections to love as the major attribute in God's nature. Ritschlian theology rested on a distorted emphasis on divine love, and from love as the determinative category derived all divine activities; it thus did violence to the other attributes, including righteousness and justice, which no less than love are in fact identical with God's essence.

Protestant modernists in the twentieth century carried forward this same promotion of love as the core-attribute through which they channelled all divine activity. W. B. Selbie writes, for example: "The old-fashioned way of playing off the divine attributes one against the other—mercy against justice, and righteousness against love—is no longer thinkable. If God is love, then love is the spring of all His actions" (*The Fatherhood of God*, p. 129). Selbie prejudices the case against evangelical orthodoxy when he says: "It makes all the difference in the world whether we regard God as primarily and by nature a God of love, or as a sovereign judge in the first instance who may on certain terms be moved to act lovingly" (*ibid.*, pp. 163 f.). What Selbie declares "no longer thinkable"—the evangelical view of a just and merciful God who justifies sinners by substitutionary atonement—may be no longer believable to those who demote divine righteousness and elevate divine love; it should be obvious, however, that, under the guise of a unifying view of the divine nature, we are here in fact presented with a profoundly unbiblical reconstruction. It is indeed God who acts, but not God's love, or God's power or justice; it is God in the unity of being who acts. Selbie sees those who do not share his view of the unqualified primacy of divine love as "Christians whose conception of God is more like that of a devil. They base their thinking on the Old Testament rather than on the New and envisage a Deity who is jealous, cruel, vindictive and capricious, from whose righteous wrath they are rescued by the intervention of Jesus Christ" (*ibid.*, p. 163). This comment is an unworthy caricature, except for its admission that the Old Testament at least anticipates the historic evangelical view, and for its reference to the saving intervention of Jesus Christ (which Selbie actually finds repugnant). It is about as correct to assign to Selbie a view of God that embraces the devil, as it is for Selbie to depict evangelical orthodoxy as approximating worship of the demonic.

Karl Barth's insight into atonement doctrine is profounder than Selbie's, but he nonetheless so exaggerates divine love as to make universal salvation virtually inevitable. The objection to Barth's view does not concern his proper insistence that we are not to regard divine love in freedom as a contingent fact separable from the essential nature of God, for God is indeed love, and apart from his love the living God cannot be rightly said to exist. But, as F. W. Camfield summarizes the Barthian perspective, the two words "love" and "freedom" designate for Barth the entire being of God and "express, so far as human words can, the whole essence and reality of God. . . . All else that we may say about Him will be but descriptions of this love and freedom as these unfold . . . and manifest themselves in God's life and action" (*Reformation Old and New*, p. 50). The weakness in this position is its tendential conception of divine love that disallows righteousness an equally ultimate role in God's nature and activity; love, in other words, drowns out aspects of the righteousness of God.

While Scripture emphasizes now one, now another, of the attributes, it nowhere exalts one attribute over another, nor does it represent the divine essence as in a state of tension because of irreconcilable claims of the various attributes within the nature of God. Scripture represents God's attributes as a living unity. Berkhof writes: "The Being of God is characterized by a depth, a fullness, a variety, and a glory far beyond our comprehension, and the Bible represents it as a glorious harmonious whole, without any inherent contradictions" (*Systematic Theology*, p. 42). Bavinck points to the revelation of God in Christ whose earthly life manifested now one divine perfection, and now another; there was no hint of a dominant attribute that cancels all other divine perfections.

Another subject of theological debate is the number of God's attributes. In an earlier volume we noted that the divine names, no less than the divine attributes, are to be listed among God's predicates. Jerome in *Epistola ad Marcellum* and also Luther in the *Treatise on Shem Hamphoras* criticize the Jewish custom of ascribing ten names to God. They point out that Scripture uses even more divine names. But later Lutheran theologians deplored also the opposite tendency of greatly multiplying divine names and attributes as if thereby to glorify the God of the Bible. The work of Roman Catholic scholar Johann Goerres, *Die christliche Mystik* (4 vols., 1836–1842), lists 150 names used by St. Rosa of Lima in addressing God, and Edwin Arnold's *Pearls of the Faith,* or *Islam's Rosary* (1882) enumerates 550 names of Allah. The same tendency to multiply divine names is reflected by J. Blueher's *Die 100 biblischen Namen unsres Herrn Jesu Christi* (1870), which confuses titles with names. Careful theological study must guard against turning every linguistic difference into a difference of meaning.

Moslems hold that God has seven attributes, but disagree over their nature, and over the extent of human knowledge concerning them. Other non-Christians greatly increase rather than reduce the number of divine attributes. Christians consider infinity but one of God's many perfections; Spinoza, on the other hand, declares that God has an infinity of attributes. Pantheist that he was, Spinoza could reach such a judgment only because he identified everything that is as God. At the same time Spinoza declared that we know only two of God's supposed infinity of attributes, that is, thought and extension. If this were actually the case, then the attributes of which we remain ignorant—infinity minus two in number, namely, thought and extension—might then cancel out the ontological significance of the attributes we are said to know.

Nor does the divine simplicity provide any reason to regard all the attributes as our own semantic invention, for the attributes express actual differences in the historical results of God's action. Just as the proper names of God are plural, so the attributive names, the divine perfections, although not infinite in number are plural; this, moreover, is true as well of the personal names of the triune God. Attrition of the attributes is implicit in existential and dialectical theologies, for they disallow objective intellectual revelation and try to characterize God on the basis of interpersonal encounter and responsive truth. In such noncognitive contexts, it is difficult to escape religious subjectivism or skepticism and to avoid reducing the multiplicity of God's attributes to one confrontational denominator. Existential or dialectical theologians tend to speak broadly of the divine in terms of God's lordship, righteousness and love; from these main predications they derive other traditional divine perfections. The fact is, however, that by disallowing intelligible divine revelation existential and dialectical theology can offer no consistent basis for avoiding metaphysical agnosticism. Insofar as such theologies do reflect some or many of the biblically revealed attributes, they do so not because such attributes derive logically from distinctively contemporary religious epistemology, but because these nonevangelical theologians cannot fully rid themselves of Scripture's influence and representations about God.

Even an evangelical doctrine of God predicated on Scripture must avoid semantic proliferation of the divine attributes. Although evangelical Christians honor the Bible as plenarily and verbally inspired, different Hebrew, Aramaic or Greek terms used to depict God's attributes do not always imply distinctive nuances. As the feature of poetic parallelism attests, Scripture is not immune to the use of synonyms. Yet careless scriptural exegesis may dismiss certain significant vocabulary divergences as merely synonymous when in fact they are intended to convey special shades of meaning. In the long run what must decide the adequacy or inadequacy of competing representations of the number and kind of divine perfections is a faithful and consistent handling of the biblical text. The many effects of divine omnipotence are objectively revealed and intellectually intelligible.

In summary, knowledge of the divine attributes, no less than of the divine proper names, involves a knowledge of God's inmost essence. Our knowledge is not exhaustive, to be sure, since God's incomprehensibility, which evangelicals affirm, means that we know no more concerning the divine nature than what God intends and enables us to know by revelation. Although Luther and Calvin speak of the incomprehensibility of God's essence—it is unknowable by a priori speculation concerning divinity—they do not deny authentic knowledge of God's essential nature on the basis of scriptural revelation. Our knowledge of God as scripturally given is genuine, significant and adequate. God reveals all that is necessary for us to know in order to serve him truly and obediently, and to share the blessings of redemption in this life and the next. The Christian view of God is the product of a long history of progressive divine disclosure, a revelation in which both the Old and New Testaments serve an indispensable role, that of informing and revising man's broken, uncertain and fitful notions about God. This fact is as fully evident in God's disclosure of himself as a supernatural triunity, as in God's self-disclosure of his attributes.

7.
Personality in the Godhead

"IS PERSONALITY THE 'KEY to reality,'" asks Edgar S. Brightman, "or is it only one more rusty lock that needs some impersonal key to unlock it?" (*Personalism in Theology*, p. 53).

If it is indeed the key, may not recent modern conceptions so complicate or so oversimplify the nature of personality as to pose as many problems as does the notion of an impersonal divinity?

Attempts by philosophical reasoning to resolve the issue apart from divine revelation have been inconclusive. They appear increasingly unable to resist erosion by naturalistic alternatives.

The philosophical replacement of Spinoza's Substance by Fichte's Self signaled a deliberate effort to identify the Absolute in personal terms. Even Spinoza attributes thought to the system of nature, although he indifferently calls it Nature or God. But without a doctrine of divine creation, and without an articulate doctrine of divine self-revelation of a deity who loves the world and man and with whom personal fellowship is possible, such conjectures merely equate God's being with the being of the universe. Philosophers may speak of ultimate Spirit, but for such a reality the neuter pronoun "It" is more appropriate and natural than any personal pronoun. The choice between Hegel and Spinoza is therefore not as great as it seems; in either case God cannot exist without the universe, that is, the universe supplies the actual content of what we mean by God. For Judeo-Christian religion, on the other hand, God is the self-revealed Creator and Lord of the universe.

Among philosophers who champion the priority of selfhood are absolute idealists, who hold with Josiah Royce that all existence is—or is part of—one Absolute Mind, and personalists, who with Borden P. Bowne consider finite selves to be distinct from the absolute Self. Yet F. H. Bradley, although an idealist, considered the self an inadequate principle of multiplicity in unity. He rejected selfhood as an ultimate category of explanation on the ground that the self requires contradictory relationships; it should therefore not be viewed as reality but be dismissed as appearance.

Existentialists, whose philosophical impact in Europe increasingly influenced theologians, also rejected a substance view of God as did absolute idealists and personalists, but correlated God's personal reality with internal decision and disavowed the objectivity of metaphysical propositions. Process philosophy also rejected a substance metaphysics but substituted the modern categories of activity and becoming; it postulated deity in terms of essential relatedness to and dependence on the world. None of these modern alternatives has stemmed intellectual defection to humanism, however, despite claims by Schubert Ogden that the Aristotelian metaphysics of the Thomists is what has alienated contemporary scientific man from faith in God. In fact, rejection of the supernatural by process theologians in favor of a one-layer view of reality provides no consistent alternative to naturalism.

The self, Bradley stressed, is a construction that transcends immediate experience. For that reason he objected to transferring elements of human experience to the Absolute. "The Absolute is not personal, nor is it moral, nor is it beautiful or true. The Absolute stands above . . . its internal distinctions," he writes (*Appearance and Reality,* p. 472).

Naturalists implemented Bradley's method of analysis more fully. Ralph Barton Perry found only "neutral entities" (whatever they are) where personalists professed to discern consciousness and personality, and where Bradley had professed to find an impersonal Absolute. For Perry mental action is the property of physical organisms. John Dewey likewise objected to locating mind outside of nature, and held that thought bears the same relation to the brain that perception bears to sense organs; in short, Dewey defines mind according to its behavior just as he frames ideas of stars and of digestive tissues according to their behavior.

Pure religion is indeed bound up with the conviction of divine personality. Contrary to Schleiermacher, the pious person cares a great deal whether God is personal or not. Early twentieth-century philosophy of religion and theology both stressed that a worthy conception of God requires the category of personality.

Doubtless all religions and philosophies, even those which view ultimate reality as impersonal, incorporate features that spur their devotees toward belief in a personal divinity. This is true of ancient Buddhism which changed from an atheistic regard for the Way to the personal veneration of Gautama, of Kant's philosophy in Germany which heuristically invoked a personal God while it disallowed cognitive metaphysical knowledge, and of C. E. M. Joad's philosophy in England which forsook humanism for Christian theism. Any ultimately impersonal explanation of the universe requires the self to repudiate its identity. Vestiges of the *imago Dei* in fallen man and the continuing realities of general divine revelation resist any effort to worship a reality inferior to one's conscious selfhood and, moreover, reinforce the conviction that life has authentic spiritual dimensions that embrace a transcendent God and objective truth and values. Universal reference to God by "he" rather than by "it" reflects an intuitive awareness of a personal deity. As Gordon D. Kaufman observes, it "seems unquestionable" that the ordinary English usage of the term "God" and its equivalent in other Western languages designates a transcendent personal being "and this is understood by so-called atheists and believers alike" (*Systematic Theology: A Historical Perspective*).

In *Treatise on the Gods* H. L. Mencken conjectures that primitive man's names for his gods were simply Lightning, Flood, Rain, Fire, and so on; first crudely thought to be volition present in nature, these forces later acquired personality. Naturalistic evolutionary prejudice similarly underlies Knight Dunlap's theory that deity is conceived personally only "in moderately late stages of religious development"; further prejudice underlies his verdict that as religions become older they progress toward impersonalism in their doctrine of God (*Religion: Its Functions in Human Life*, p. 57). While such premises fit neatly into Dunlap's philosophical commitments, neither history nor experience validates them. The pre-Christian Xenophanes argued that if cows and horses were artists they would paint cattle-gods and horse-gods; similarly Dunlap with his presuppositions charts primitive man's successive ascription of supernatural names to certain plants (thallomorphism) and animals (thieromorphism). He seems to be notably unaware that the spiritually backslidden ancient Egyptians had already made and worshiped such gods, and that biblical religion from its beginnings condemned such paganism as an offense to the true and living God. In Dunlap's next evolutionary step man assertedly creates gods in his own image by ascribing human traits to them (anthropomorphism); finally, divinities are reduced once again into abstract powers (*ibid.*, pp. 110 f.). It should surprise no one that Dunlap considers personality unessential to divinity, and God dispensable to vital religion.

Reliance on empiricism or experience to characterize the ultimately real world poses many difficulties, for its verdict always rests on selective data and is therefore tentative. Certainly for investigating nonsensuous personal or mental qualities the method itself is inadequate and even inappropriate. Says A. C. Knudson in commenting on the personality of God, "personality as applied to God must mean more or less of what we understand by the term when applied to ourselves, or it is a misleading symbol" (*The Doctrine of God*, pp. 295 ff.).

Nonevangelical thought based its argument for personality in God so largely on the self-impressive fact of human personality and its implications that philosophical discussions about divine personality often foundered in confusion. A. Maude Royden declares bluntly: "The most real me is my personality: therefore personality exists in God" (*I Believe in God*, p. 23). Knudson argues that communion with others is inherent in the very concept of personality; since God "by his very nature seeks communion with others" then "only in this way can his own true self and his own intrinsic worth . . . come to full expression and realization" (*The Doctrine of God*, pp. 298 ff.). Such formulation obviously jeopardizes God's independence or aseity.

F. H. Bradley exposed the vulnerability of projecting divine personality from man's personality; the superficiality of this approach led him to insist, instead, on the impersonality of the Absolute. "In order to reach the Absolute," he writes, "our finite selves must suffer so much addition and so much subtraction that it becomes a grave question whether the result can be covered by the name of self" (*Appearance and Reality*, p. 497).

Theories of the self are multiple. Metaphysical speculation and psychological study have spawned many diverse opinions about who the "I" really is. There is no philosophical agreement over what the terms person and self imply. To be sure, despite Hume's emphasis on disconnected impressions and William James' stress on a series of psychoses aware of the series, no one has really dispensed with the abiding conscious subject. Some interpreters of personality emphasize conscious intelligence but underestimate volition; others emphasize enduring awareness and underestimate rationality; some neglect conscience and moral capacities. The soul of man—or the conscious person, as our generation prefers to put it—no doubt reflects the nature of reality more profoundly than do the infinitely numerous impersonal things or events around us. But the supports for such a claim are always too obscure, uncertain and evanescent; something more stable and enduring is needed than to suspend upon human personality alone the unquestioned personal existence of God and the fundamental categories to which God's nature is to be conformed.

Karl Barth is right, indeed, in insisting that "we cannot speak of 'personalizing' in reference to God's being, but only in reference to ours. The real person is not man but God" (*Church Dogmatics*, II/1, p. 272). The basic question, says Barth, is not "is God a person?" but rather, "are we" persons? (*Church Dogmatics*, I/1, p. 157). Not God, but man, is person by extension.

The form of neopersonalism represented by Ferdinand Ebner and Martin Buber greatly influenced neoorthodox theologians like Brunner by emphasizing the "I-Thou" relationship. Called by Karl Heim a Copernican turning point in the history of thought, this approach has not, however, fulfilled its early promise to reinstate the priority of God. Ebner insisted that God's personal reality can be grasped only in a personal relationship in which man acknowledges him as "the Thou of his I" (*Das Wort*, p. 108). Brunner, in turn, emphasized divine-human encounter and made "personal correspondence" the basic category of his theory of revelation (*Wahrheit als Begegnung*, p. 17). He distinguishes knowledge of subjects (personal faith-knowledge) from knowledge of objects (objective rational coherence), that is, "I-Thou" knowledge from "I-it" knowledge, by combining Ebnerian personalism and Kierkegaardian existentialism. Brunner's emphasis on "personal correspondence" somewhat balances Barth's on radical divine otherness. Using Ebner's axiom, "without a Thou, no I," Brunner stresses man's likeness to God in order to maintain a role for both general and special revelation. But neither he nor Barth discards the eternity-time dialectic, since they conceive revelation not only as breaking into the world from outside but also as inexpressible in valid propositional truth. Despite its aim to emphasize the personal reality of God, neopersonalism because of existential and/or dialectical commitments soon led to the counteremphasis that human decision is what sustains God's reality.

All the claims made for the Christian religion and for Christian experience stand or fall with the justifiability of the conviction that life has legitimate spiritual dimensions grounded in the reality of the objectively transcendent and personal God. If there is no God, no eternal truth, no divine commandment, then Christianity is a sham, Christian experience an illusion, and human existence but a cosmic accident. Unlike the pseudo-gods of this world, the God of the Bible is neither a tentative working hypothesis awaiting pragmatic validation nor a problematical power that rules the stars. He is the self-revealed God. The problem of coming to terms with God's existence is depicted in the Bible as a problem only for the recalcitrant sinner—not for the wise but for the fool. Controversy over God in the pre-Hellenic biblical books concerns not Yahweh's existence or nonexistence, but rather Hebrew faithfulness or unfaithfulness in the worship and obedience of Yahweh. No disposition toward atheism is found among the Hebrew peoples until many centuries after God's self-revelation (cf. Pss. 14, 94).

As Clement C. J. Webb observes, Christianity more than any other religion has applied personality to deity (*God and Personality,* pp. 61 ff.). Christianity has done so, moreover, on the ground of God's own self-revelation of his nature, and not on the basis of philosophical conjecture, mystical experience, empirical argumentation or psychological experimentation. Indeed, compared with Christianity, ancient nonbiblical religions as well as secular philosophies cloud the very concept of divine personality.

Eastern religions tend to regard as trivial any conception of a personal ultimate reality; neither early Buddhism, nor Taoism, nor Confucianism includes God, and Hinduism affirmed the impersonal principle Brahman. Those religions of the Orient that do speak of divine personality do so more obscurely than does biblical religion.

As for the religious history of Greece, moreover, "neither in the anthropomorphism of Homer," says Hermann Kleinknecht, "nor in the later metaphysics of ideas is there a personal conception of God or even a personal relation of the individual soul to God. The early and later views are merely different but not mutually exclusive forms of the same basic religious attitude in religion, art and philosophy, which as a self-contained unity is absolutely different from the NT concept of God" ("The Greek Concept of God," *TDNT,* 3:79). A. Seth Pringle-Pattison finds "the essential feature of the Christian conception of the world, in contrast to the Hellenic" to be its regard for "the person and the relations of persons to one another as the essence of reality, whereas Greek thought conceived of personality, however spiritual, as a restrictive characteristic of the finite—a transitory product of a life which as a whole is impersonal" (*The Idea of God in the Light of Recent Philosophy,* p. 291). Greek philosophers who define divine essence in categories of being and perfection give notably less prominence to the categories of divine will and personality than do the Hebrews.

Even at its best, moreover, classic Greek philosophy professes to know God only from nature or from society as the developed world of divine activity. There is no emphasis on direct divine personal disclosure mediated through the Logos of God, whether to all humankind in general revelation or to chosen prophets and apostles in special revelation. Homeric literature incorporates the notion of physical intercourse between polytheistic gods and certain mortals, alongside emphasis on the occasional intervention of these gods in the natural events of the world. But this notion merges the realms of spirit and nature and includes nothing about individual communion with God. Even Aristotle's God is not someone to whom one prays. Similarly in Plotinus's system prayer involves no significant relationship between man and God but is ventured only as personal reflection.

The usual habit of religious philosophy is to speak of God abstractly in such terms as Deity, the Divine, Providence, and the like. This characterizes religious perspectives that do not know the living God by his self-disclosed name. Even Judaism suppressed God's revealed name and substituted the term "heaven" and other circumlocutions, although not out of ignorance but supposedly out of excessive reverence.

Christian theology, on the other hand, has always stressed the distinction between persons and things. "The advent of Christianity," J. R. Illingworth notes, "created a new epoch both in the development and recognition of human personality" (*Personality Human and Divine,* p. 8). Christianity so sensitized an awareness of the personal that differentiation between persons and things was taken for granted; it was modern idealism that reduced all reality to Idea, and evolutionism that professed to derive the mental from the physical. Biblical theism found the characteristics of the human person in the *imago Dei,* an entity that tradition-rebellious modern philosophers modified and recast. This dilution, in turn, readily accommodated evolutionary and naturalistic views in which personality becomes but a byproduct of the physical.

However much biblical religion stimulates faith in a personal God and clarifies the conception of divine personality over against crude and vague religious or philosophical misconceptions, it was not the later Jewish prophets who originated the idea of a personal God. Martin Buber persuasively traces Yahweh's relationship to Israel to at least as far back as Moses and the Exodus (*The Prophetic Faith,* p. 27). The primal origin of that relationship is found, in fact, in the earlier patriarchal era, as evidenced by the identification of faith in Yahweh as faith in the "God of our fathers"; Yahweh declares himself, moreover, to be the God of Abraham, Isaac and Jacob (Exod. 3:13, 17). The Bible depicts God as dealing personally with mankind from the very beginnings of the human race.

The notion of the impersonality of God was a later conception spawned by some of the Oriental religions, championed by certain Greek philosophers, and taken up more recently as a refrain by modern naturalists. The term God originally as even now implies personal divinity, even if mutinous man in sin has overlaid that lofty concept with many crass and conflicting notions. The vulgar polytheism of the Greeks encouraged a philosophical reaction that advanced impersonal divinity as a higher concept. Somewhat similarly, modern pantheism that assimilated God to mankind led to an impersonal Absolute, on the one hand, and on the other, to identifying divinity with the impersonal forces of the universe; then finally it led to the elimination of God.

In our century the values of personality have had to compete against reverence for technology. More than ever space science dwarfs mankind in an incredibly vast universe where the human species has existed for but a comparatively short time within the immense age span of the cosmos. Materialistic civilization shapes a world where society is increasingly harassed by impersonal economic forces. Socialist ideologies emphasize collectivism above the individual; in fact they subordinate personal rights and duties to the state's delineation and determination.

According to psychological behaviorism, moreover, man is regulated by impersonal cosmic processes. Earlier in this century William James challenged the positivistic claims still being perpetuated by B. F. Skinner that science has shown personality to be but a passive product of basic physical, chemical, physiological, and psycho-physical forces. James even suggested that "the rigorously impersonal view of science might one day appear as having been a temporarily useful eccentricity rather than the definitively triumphant position which the sectarian scientist at present so confidently announces it to be" (*The Varieties of Religious Experience:* A Study in Human Nature, p. 419, n. 1), although in 1904 he wrote the essay, "Does Consciousness Exist?," and answered, no.

Also rampant is the Western philosophy of "success" that sometimes invades even ecclesiastical enterprises. Earl B. Marlott's claim that some Europeans, rightly or wrongly, trace both Benito Mussolini's devotion to Fascism and the Nazi philosophy of opportunism not to Nietzsche but to James and the American pragmatists should give us pause ("Personalism and Religious Education," p. 236). We often forget how readily the conception of God is replaced in a spiritually insensitive age by such conceptions as industry, science, the state, culture, fortune or fate and how in a sensate environment these preoccupations soon gain the practical status of secular polytheism. By completely immersing the human self in natural or historical processes, contemporary naturalism cancels out any role in the external world for a personal God, and for that matter, for human agency as well. Bultmann talks much of God as a person but does not interpret references to God's inwardly encountered reality as talk about an objectively existing metaphysical being. Although he intends to focus on authentic selfhood, Bultmann by his notion that the Word discloses itself only in encounter as an inner personal event erodes the ontological and epistemological pre-

conditions that make either human or divine personality objectively significant, for he bequeaths the worlds of nature and history to simply impersonal mathematical regularities.

John A. T. Robinson similarly professes a broad commitment to the "personal as the central interpretative category of the whole of reality" (*Exploration into God,* p. 145). He rejects belief in a personal God as "*a* divine
Person," however, holding that such belief originates "not as belief in a
Being but as apprehension of a relational reality." God is properly described
as personal, says Robinson, "not because he is conceived as a Being with
personal attributes" (*ibid.,* p. 74) but because the nearest clue to the nature
of ultimate reality is found in "pure personal relationship."

Despite scriptural data to the contrary, Robinson claims that "the Bible
never directly says God is a father" (*ibid.,* p. 148) and that Jesus' references
to God are simply a vivid way of expressing "personal relationship of trust
and dependence in which his whole life was grounded" (*ibid.,* p. 149).
Jesus spoke the truth too directly, however, to have resorted to circumlocu-
tion; twenty generations of Christian followers have understood his intention. Robinson's view derives not from the biblical writers but from modern
metaphysical agnostics like Hans Vaihinger who wrote: "Christ taught:
God is our father in heaven. He probably meant: You must regard God
. . . *as if* . . . he were your father . . . and constant external observer of
your actions. . . . His disciples . . . took this fictional assertion to be dogma;
and not only religious art but the credulity of the childlike mind took and
still takes that sentence in a literal, concrete and external sense" (*The
Philosophy of 'As If': A System of the Theoretical, Practical and Religious
Fictions of Mankind.* pp. 264 ff.). Both the Old and New Testaments apply
the name Father to the nature of God (Isa. 64:8; cf. Ps. 103:13); it was precisely in his teaching about God as father that Jesus gave new depth to
the prevailing Jewish conception (John 8:41, 54). Jesus used the term Father
over and over, even in the Aramaic form Abba (daddy), which his Jewish
contemporaries seldom if ever applied to God.

Historic Christianity unhesitatingly identifies God as a personal supernatural being, but Robinson strips even the New Testament affirmation "God
is love" of any literal or univocal significance for deity. Yet he expects
us, apparently, to accept as literal truth his assurances that "reality is
reliable . . . in the kind of way in which a person can be trusted" (*op.
cit.,* p. 148). But unless Robinson can supply a theory of knowledge that
vindicates some univocal truth about transcendent reality, his metaphysical claims are doomed to skepticism and subjectivism. A god who is not
love is unlikely to keep his promises.

Robinson is eager to retain the term "God" while depriving it of its historic Judeo-Christian sense. By emphasizing that reality surrounds, sustains and claims us as a cosmic Thou he hopes to avoid a merely
materialistic or humanistic reading of reality (*ibid.,* p. 139). But at the
very point where we need clarity and persuasive argumentation he abandons us to ambiguity, imaginative projection and exhortation: "The trans-
personal character of God is better expressed," says Robinson, "not by

envisaging him as a bigger and better Individual, nor as a sort of Hobbesian Personality incorporating all other persons, but in terms of the interpersonal. . . . The whole of reality . . . must ultimately be seen in terms . . . of a divine 'field' in which the finite *Thous* are constituted what they are in the freedom of a wholly personalizing love" (*ibid.*, pp. 159 f.). Such discourse is too metaphysically imprecise, however, to provide any kind of a significant alternative; it is epistemologically too indefinite to escape philosophical refutation; and it is biblically too revisionary to maintain a reliable tie to the Judeo-Christian heritage. Basic to Robinson's abandonment of biblical theism is his acceptance of definitive aspects of the very secular worldview he is trying to refute, one that removes God as an operative reality who impinges on the whole universe to the very limits and details of man's daily life. When stripped of the element of subjective decision, this view is not unlike that of earlier humanists. Edward Scribner Ames, for example, writes: "We may say that reality is personal" because "there is personality in it. . . . Since man is possessed of personality, the reality which we call nature, or the world, is to that extent personal. Therefore, God conceived as reality is so far personal" (*Religion*, pp. 164 f.). To say that God is personal or that he has personality, declares Henry Nelson Wieman, is philosophically more confusing than clarifying (*American Philosophies of Religion*, p. 305). The notion has suffered continual erosion that the universe, although reducible to impersonal processes and events, can be said to be somehow benevolent or friendly (or that it can be relied upon as "fatherly" if you wish—the last fleeting vestige in a secular evolutionary view of the Christian doctrine of divine providence and of the coming kingdom of God). Man's insignificance in the cosmos is thought to be inferred from the antiquity and immensity of the universe; natural evils that multiply human misery and take a vast toll of human life are thought to confirm the indifference of the cosmos to personal life, and man's own insensitivity to moral values in ravaging and exploiting the cosmos is taken to imply that ethical ideals reduce to self-interest. Apart from a thoroughly theistic view of the world, there is no consistent way to escape the merging of man and nature into indifferent impersonal processes whose monotony is broken only by chance or accident. What Christianity means by God is not simply a different way of looking at the universe, seeing it as a panorama of cosmic harmony and communion, or as a personification of subjectively treasured ideals and values. Christianity means by God an infinite mind and will who transcends the universe as its living creator and preserver.

Will Hordern emphasizes that the concept of God as a person was championed by the Protestant Reformers, and before them by Augustine (*Speaking of God: The Nature and Purpose of Theological Language*, p. 133). Samuel Laeuchli argues that already in the second century Irenaeus spoke of God in personal categories (*The Language of Faith*, pp. 191 ff.). But Tillich considers the notion of "a personal God" confusing, and dismisses it as an outmoded nineteenth-century concept (*Systematic Theology*, Vol. I, pp. 244 f.).

A century ago H. M. Gwatkin recognized, and better than many of his contemporaries, that emphasis on the fatherhood of God in its then increasingly prevalent Unitarian form could not sustain itself unless it articulated a doctrine of God grounded upon biblical claims about the deity. He writes prophetically: "The battle of the next age will be fought round the Nicene doctrine of the Trinity, for the simple reason that it is the only serious theory of religion at present before the world which fully vindicates the social element in human nature, by firmly planting it inside the divine" (*The Knowledge of God and its Historical Development*, p. 298).

Only the biblical revelation of God the personal creator and redeemer of man for life in the new society over which the risen Christ eternally reigns, can effectively counter the factors that put in question the objective value of personality. Where the living God is clouded as the transcendent source of human life and dignity, respect for the meaning and worth of personal existence tends to vanish. Anticonsciousness philosophy, it has been rightly said, leads to anticonscience morality. Nowhere is this more evident than in the callous modern attitude toward abortion. The disregard for the value of fetal life prepares a mood of growing acceptance of euthanasia, and possibly even of infanticide as in the destruction rather than salvaging of malformed infants (cf. C. Everett Koop, in *Whatever Happened to the Human Race?*, pp. 36, 61 ff., 95 ff.). If personality is no longer the unique feature of human existence, humans can with impunity be treated as economic chattel, sex objects, experimental guinea pigs, and much else, for no divine imperative or human necessity exists for treating him as something qualitatively different. When respect for personality is lost the basic values essential to the human family are also readily dissolved. Social compassion, moreover, and missionary urgency as well will soon disappear if so-called humanistic philosophy infects the church, let alone society in general.

In view of its implications for man and the world the question whether God is personal being is therefore of fundamental importance. Judeo-Christian theology does not venture its answer by inference from creaturely life, or by projecting human perfections upon a transcendent realm of being. Biblical religion rests its case for divine personality squarely upon the self-revelation of the Creator and Lord of the universe. It affirms infinite triunal being, God who in his one eternal essence is three persons. More than any other factor in the history of Western thought it is this doctrine of the Trinity that has riveted attention on the fact and nature and importance of human personality.

Before discussing the doctrine of the Trinity, or divine tripersonality in unity, we should note that some religious philosophers consider personality inferior, while others consider it superior to, God's other perfections. Julius Kaftan, for example, declares divine personality superior to divine love (*Dogmatik*, pp. 200 ff.). While personality may indeed hold logical priority, in the sense that only on the ground of divine self-disclosure can we make any authentic predications whatever about God's nature, yet the same divine revelation authorizes us to declare that God is love as surely as that he is triunal personality. Unlike Kaftan, Ritschl considers love more essential than divine personality: "There is no other conception of equal worth . . . which need be taken into account . . . even the recognition of the personality of God" (*Justification and Reconciliation*, pp. 273 f.). Theodore Haering similarly declares that any choice between God as absolute personality and God as love would require us to opt promptly for love (*The Christian Faith, A System of Dogmatics*, Vol. 1, p. 323). Knudson rightly points out, however, that without personality love would be a mere abstraction (*The Doctrine of God*, p. 351). It would be as wrong to say that God is not love as to say that he is impersonal.

Some modern religious philosophers elevated personality as the ultimate divine perfection in order to combat pantheism which equates God with the universe. But isolated from a theology of revelation, their emphasis on divine personality led to conjectural notions about absolute personality that were just as foreign to biblical theism as to pantheism. Such modern theories dismissed the reality of an ontological Trinity and, swayed by idealistic and evolutionary hypotheses, sometimes ascribed growth and development to the nature of God; some religious philosophers combined unipersonality with an unfolding modal trinity of manifestations within the divine life, while others, influenced by process philosophy, expounded a dipolar view of God. When divine personality is postulated in order to account for empirical data that alternative theories seem unable to explain adequately in the absence of revelation, the result does less than justice to the living God's personality, and lacks authority to expound the bearing of that personality on all the divine attributes. This was the weakness, for example, of Borden P. Bowne's application of pantheism to the Godhead in order to account for the organic unity that embraces numerical plurality in the Trinity. Unless God makes himself known personally all Barth's protest against a static, nonacting God, all his rejection of an "'over' or 'outside' to this divine acting," all that he says about "event" or "act" as "the last word" about divine being, about divine revelation being involved in whatever is to be told about the deepest depths of the Godhead (*Church Dogmatics*, II/1, p. 214), becomes simply a morass of impersonal processes and events. God is unknowable, inaccessible, and hypothetical apart from his self-manifestation.

Modern discussion has focused primarily on the nature of selfhood. As Dean Inge contended, because of its modern view that a person is someone who cannot share life with another, personalism rules out the orthodox doctrine of the Trinity (William R. Inge, *Personal Idealism and Mysticism*, pp. 93 ff.). In a passage he reportedly later regretted, A. Seth Pringle-Pattison is once said to have affirmed that the self is "a unique existence which is perfectly impervious to other selves." Yet in his *The Idea of God in the Light of Recent Philosophy* (pp. 258 ff.), he asserts that "the mere individual nowhere exists; he is the creature of a theory. . . . A self can exist only in vital relation to an objective system of reason and an objective world of ethical observance from which it receives its content, and of which it is, as it were, the focus and depository. . . . Historically, the individual is organic to society. . . . He cannot possibly be regarded as self-contained . . . , for such self-containedness would mean sheer emptiness."

At the same time, although insisting that "finite centres may 'overlap' indefinitely in content," Pringle-Pattison says, "they cannot overlap at all in existence; their very *raison d'etre* is to be distinct and, in that sense, separate and exclusive focalizations of a common universe" (*ibid.*, p. 264).

If selfhood is defined in terms of isolated individuality, of hermit solitude, of self-contained enjoyment, then we project a concept of personality that has no known model. If selfhood is an existence impervious to other selves, an existence independent of all social and reciprocal relations, such personality fits neither God nor man. Aristotle's Prime Mover, conceived as self-thinking thought, as a self-conscious individuality directing its activity solely upon itself and incapable of loving the world or communing with others, is seen to be less than personal.

Whereas the term personality in its historical sense came into usage through theological discussion of the Trinity, today's understanding of the word has resulted largely from a century of psychological investigation of man. Rejection of the medieval view of substance led subsequently to the present existential view of personality as merely personal relatedness. To dismiss as marginal everything that falls outside personal reality in relationships could only produce doubt about the ego's transcendence and continuity. Such existential distortion of theology breeds uncertainty about the existence of other selves, divine or human, and even if such selfhood is real, reduces it to little more than a phantom confrontation.

A. C. Knudson insists that trinitarian doctrine and personalism are compatible. Personalists do not espouse the "spiritual atomism" of selves, Knudson emphasizes, since all finite persons both depend on the Supreme Person and share in each other's lives. Yet this argument for metaphysical dependence and separateness, proceeding as it does from the human to the divine, proves at once if it proves anything, both too much and too little. Orthodox trinitarianism does not involve Christ the Son in the same ontological dependence that creatures have upon the Father, nor in the ontological separateness that characterizes human beings.

It is true, of course, that personalism rules out any fusing of nonspiritual substances into the life of the Trinity. Medieval Scholasticism had combined its emphasis on three persons in the Godhead with the notion of an underlying divine essence distinct from personality. To avoid unipersonalism and to preserve instead the doctrine of the ontological Trinity Scholasticism spoke less of God's personality than of his being. God was indeed personal, but not in the essential core of his being; it seemed unfitting to speak of his unity and totality as personal since personality was considered to stand in adjectival relation to the divine essence. But if the essence of personality is selfhood, one cannot define the Trinity in terms of a more ultimate divine essence to which personality is subordinated. The personal threeness of God and the oneness of the Godhead must then be expounded in some other way than by an appeal to quasipersonal or subpersonal substance that supposedly represents a type of being more basic than personality.

Clement C. J. Webb remarks that medieval and early modern Christianity spoke not so much of "the personality of God" as of "personality *in* God"; it avoided the assertion that "God is *a person*" (*God and Personality,* p. 65). The term "person" was not applied to God's unitary being but rather to the trinitarian distinctions within the Godhead. Webb asserts that " 'Personality' was not reckoned among the divine 'attributes' so-called, and was long ascribed to God only in connection with the 'three persons' worshipped by the Christian Church as one God" (*Religion and Theism,* pp. 46 ff.). Thomas Aquinas observes that the Bible nowhere calls God a person (*Summa Theologiae,* I. 29, 4). Not until near the end of the eighteenth century did the phrase "the personality of God" come into frequent use. Only because of the growing impact of modernist theology in the nineteenth and twentieth centuries was God commonly viewed as a person.

Why then do we need to speak at all of the "being of God"? Is it simply to stress his objective metaphysical existence in an age that obscures ontological reality in inner subjectivity? Here one recalls Brunner's insistence that God is not the "Object" of our thought but the absolute Subject, the unconditioned Person. Is it necessary to speak of God's "being," as Bavinck holds, in order "to distinguish between God's nature and its three modes of subsistence" (*The Doctrine of God,* p. 124)? Or is God's nature no less personal than the three persons of the Godhead? If it is true, as Bavinck concedes, that Scripture "nowhere discusses God's being apart from his attributes" (*ibid.,* p. 113), then is it not also true that Scripture nowhere discusses God's being apart from his personal reality as self-revealed, living and active? The notions of God as abstract being, universal substance, absolute causality, the numinous, and so on, belong to conjectural philosophy of religion, and not to the Bible.

Bavinck declares aseity (absolute essence) to be "the primary attribute of God's being" (*The Doctrine of God,* pp. 126 ff.) in the sense of "fulness of essence, the sum-total of all reality and perfection, the totality of essence, to which all other essence owes its origin." In addition to its unintended pantheistic overtone ("sum-total of all reality"; "totality of essence") this statement is objectionable because Bavinck considers "all God's attributes" to be "included" in the conception; he thus makes aseity a designation that, unlike the other perfections, embraces "God in *all* his perfections." Bavinck is not only saying that all perfections are equally ultimate in God, but also that aseity is to be "preferred above . . . love, personality, fatherhood" because of its all inclusiveness. Understood in this way, aseity erroneously implies a divine essence that is not thoroughly personal. The idea of the fullness of divine essence that embraces all attributes is better depicted in terms of the "glory" of God than of his divine aseity; one gains nothing and loses much by exalting the totality of divine essence over personality.

Some writers profess to find in Exodus 3:14 ("I am that I am") and in

John 4:24 ("God is spirit") support for a statement of God's essence in abstract terms of self-existence or self-sufficiency. But biblical representations always reflect the living God who actively reveals himself. To be sure, all terms are abstract in the sense that they are symbols. The insistence that God reveals himself, moreover, need not and ought not be converted into the notion that revelation allows us no ontological definition of God, since divine revelation centers in propositional truth about God's nature and purposes. The notion here in dispute is that the Bible provides a basis for speaking about divine essence in isolation from God's self-revealed names, be they proper, attributive or personal. Polanus erroneously assumed, as Bavinck points out, that such New Testament expressions as "Godhead" (Col. 2:9), "divinity" (Rom. 1:20) and "form of God" (Phil. 2:6) have in view God's nature apart from his attributes (*The Doctrine of God,* p. 113). Another New Testament passage, 2 Peter 1:4, describes believers as "partakers of the divine nature," that is, they share the mind and moral character of Christ.

Today evangelicals routinely depict God as a personal Being; others besides Unitarians speak of "the personality of God" and for non-Unitarian reasons. The motivations for this usage vary according to the underlying religious and philosophical perspectives. There may be emphasis, for example, on a personal supernatural world-ground over against impersonalistic naturalism, or over against post-Hegelian absolutism. Or there may be emphasis on a personalistic metaphysics that regards personality not merely as the key to ultimate reality but as its very essence.

Christianity does, in fact, espouse both the personality *of* God and personality *in* God—or, better stated, espouses both in the same affirmation; trinitarians need not apologize for speaking of the triune God as a personal God. We need not absolutely distinguish between personality *in* God and the personality *of* God, provided we do not insist on the former at the expense of God's unity or on the latter at the expense of his triunity.

Evangelical Christianity rejects the idea of nonpsychic divine substance; it interprets divine personality in terms of understanding and volition, rather than of substantial fusion. It also recognizes, however, the biblical revelation of the Trinity to be something other than a simply unitary self-consciousness with a threefold activity. To say that all reality is mental does not mean that all reality is a single mind, and to say that God is personal need not mean that God is unipersonal. God is transcendent personality, living, speaking, acting, manifesting his nature and will. Those who object to using the term "person" or "personality" in expounding the nature of God have little alternative but to reduce divinity to the impersonal or the unknowable. Those who disavow divine personality on the supposed ground of naive anthropomorphism cannot defend themselves against objections to alternative spiritual conceptions of God; a god who is not spirit is unworthy of the dignity of deity. Since God speaks and acts, and reveals himself to be the supreme I, the most appropriate designation of him is that of divine personality.

William R. Cannon proposes that we consider God's essence as "superpersonal" while at the same time we insist also on the personality of the three distinct persons of the Godhead; this proposal is unnecessary, however, and needlessly complicates the doctrine of the Trinity. Cannon protests Barth's treatment of God as the absolute Person; he argues that Barth so identifies personality with God's essence, rather than with the personal distinctions within the essence, that only a modal concept can safeguard Barth from tritheism. Cannon writes: "If we apply the label 'person' to the essence of God, then we reduce Father, Son and Holy Ghost to mere attributes of that essence, subpersonal relationships, activating or behavioristic characteristics. Karl Barth does precisely this in his reconstruction of the Trinity. He applies personality only to God in his essence, and as a result falls victim to the very modalism which he pretends to avoid" (*The Redeemer. The Work and Person of Jesus Christ*, p. 206). Barth's motivations for insisting on the personality of God are sound, however, and he disavows employing the term "modes" of the Father, Son and Spirit in the interest of a modal trinity. But it is confusing to use the terms "mode" and "person" at two levels of discussion about the Godhead. Cannon perpetuates that confusion in another way by espousing superpersonality alongside personality: "We are much nearer to the meaning of Nicene theology," he writes, "and also the obvious facts of the New Testament if we hold that God in his essence is superpersonal, beyond personality; a triunity of three distinct individuals; a communion of Persons, Father, Son and Holy Ghost, in fellowship with themselves" (*ibid.*, p. 206). Cannon's intention may be only to emphasize divine multipersonality rather than unipersonality, but the notion of a superpersonal essence again raises the spectre of an impersonal essence. Affirmation of personal divine essence need not exclude three personal distinctions in the Godhead and is, in fact, required by their very existence.

Tillich contends that classical theology applied personality to each of the *hypostases* of the Trinity and on this ground he argues against ascribing personality to God himself (*Systematic Theology*, Vol. I, pp. 244 f.). But Will Hordern notes that historically the Western tradition, unlike the Cappadocian, did in fact apply personality to God inasmuch as it stressed that man was created in the image of the triune God, not simply in the image of one person (*Speaking of God*, p. 133). The readiness of some scholars to speak of God as personal but not as "a person" Hordern likens to "the smile of the Cheshire cat after the cat has gone."

One great asset of orthodox trinitarianism, A. C. Knudson concedes, is that contrary to unitarianism it proclaims the living God by emphasizing the eternal activity of the three persons in the inner divine life, and that contrary to deism it emphasizes God's immanent presence and activity in the world (*The Doctrine of God*, pp. 410 ff.). God is continually engaged in intercommunion, in internal self-revelation and holy love. This activity is not an addition to his nature; it is God's essential being in tripersonal activity. That God wills to widen this self-revelation and communion to created persons is, like their creation itself, a decision of sovereign divine freedom.

Knudson rejects the complaint that theological use of "the word 'person'
. . . is an accident, a *damnosa hereditas* which we owe to Tertullian, and
that the word did not originally mean what we understand by it, but, like
the Greek *Hypostasis,* denotes a mode of being midway between a person
and an attribute" (*The Doctrine of God,* pp. 418 ff.). In that event, he says,
the term has no intelligible counterpart in human nature, and we lose
the values that "divine society" has for human community. The deeper
issue that faces us, therefore, is whether God's self-revelation justifies and
requires this term.

One can understand the reluctance to use the word tripersonality because
the prevalent concept of the human person as an isolated, individuated
self would seem to imply tritheism. This objection can be met on its own
ground, however. What is usually forgotten is that the more one hesitates
to speak of divine persons, the less one enters into what love and fellowship
in God really are, and the more one distinguishes them also from what
they are for us. These activities thus tend to acquire an impersonal aura
instead of communicating a significant sense of interpersonal relationship.
Biblical religion is what imparted dimensions and distinctions of love and
fellowship found nowhere else; because these terms gain their meaning
in a context that heightens rather than lessens personal realities, it seems
incredible and it is in fact impossible to ground them in subpersonal or
impersonal relationships or processes.

Supplementary Note: The Feminist Challenge to God-Language

THE FEMINIST MOVEMENT has influenced recent discussions of divine personality by charging that the biblical references to God are sexually prejudiced. Some feminist leaders are demanding a retranslation of Scripture's core symbolism to eliminate masculine gender terminology for the deity.

Many traditional theologians resist this assault on biblical language. Proposed alterations in the direction of a neuter God or of a masculine-feminine God, they say, involve not only semantic changes but a revisionist theology as well. Speaking for Eastern Orthodoxy, A. Kallistos Ware affirms that "if we were to substitute a Mother Goddess for God the Father, we would not simply be altering a piece of incidental imagery, but we would be replacing Christianity with a new kind of religion" ("Man, Woman and the Priesthood of Christ," p. 84). Voicing the view of many conservative Protestants, Donald Bloesch observes that revising biblical language almost always involves also a revision of the biblical sense (*Beyond Feminism and Patriarchalism,* soon to be published).

For some feminist theologians an acceptable alternative to the inherited religious tradition requires totally rejecting the Judeo-Christian emphases on a personal God. They would surmount the controversy over the propriety of male or female pronouns for deity by affirming God's superpersonality or impersonality. Here the controversy over so-called sexist God-language involves at the same time a controversy over God's intrinsic being. Some feminist reconstructionists align themselves with Tillichian theologians who view God as the Ground of all being and declare all personal references to deity to be merely symbolic. Many process philosophers as well prefer to speak of God simply as creativity or creative process and they also, in line with Whitehead's reluctance to affirm divine personality, approve the feminist protest against biblical God-language.

Some radical feminists clearly recognize that their proposals involve replacing the God of Judeo-Christian revelation with foreign gods. Some spokeswomen are drawn to Brahmanism which, like most Hindu religions, views the Supreme God as impersonal and therefore neuter. Naomi Goldenberg regards God as but a vital force in human life and thinks witchcraft best accommodates the divinity she considers latent in women (*Changing*

157

of the Gods). For Germaine Greer the ideal of feminism is sexual freedom (*The Female Eunuch*, pp. 151 f.). The roots of such feminist ideology Krister Stendahl locates not in the Bible but rather "in the Enlightenment or in Hellas or in the cult of Baal" (cf. *Christianity Today*, p. 24).

Some feminist writers promote the androgynous alternative of unisex in which God is the divine hermaphrodite uniting the characteristics of both sexes. They regard masculine and feminine aspects, as did some ancient Greeks and Gnostics, as constitutive of all personality, both divine and human (cf. Sheila D. Collins, "Toward a Feminist Theology," pp. 796–799). When projected upon theology this sometimes leads to a bisexual deity who is addressed as the divine Father-Mother (a terminology anticipated by Mary Baker Eddy) and whose essential nature embraces masculine initiative, determination and power, and feminine receptiveness and loving response. The ancient polytheistic religions, as is known, had both male gods and female goddesses. Mormonism speaks of God as Heavenly Father and Heavenly Mother (Hynum L. Andrus even quotes Joseph Smith as saying that "God, the Father was born of a woman" [*God, Man and the Universe*, Foundations of the Millennial Kingdom of Christ, p. 353]) and in doing so leans away from trinitarianism (cf. Richard A. Purdy, *The Mormon Doctrine Concerning the Nature of God*, pp. 17 ff.) and toward anthropomorphic polytheism. Karl Barth observed, in another connection, that the Christian doctrine of Jesus' birth to a virgin teaches us not only that Jesus had no earthly father but also that he had no heavenly mother (*Church Dogmatics*, I/1, p. 556). Having espoused the androgynous theory in *Beyond God the Father*, Mary Daly later abandoned it, preferring, in *Gyn/Ecology, The Metaethics of Radical Feminism*, to speak of God as impersonal.

Less radical feminists do not propose to eliminate so-called sexist language about God but rather to feminize it. Some would speak of God as our Queen Mother or Heavenly Sister; such terms are not, however, really equivalent to biblical concepts of the Father Almighty or Father-King (or Lord). The scriptural terms involve divine self-subsistence and independency. While a woman-god might be self-subsistent, that is not what feminists emphasize. Some would call Christ not the Son of God but the Child of God; others consider Christ masculine and Jesus feminine; some affirm that Jesus Christ is masculine, but the Holy Spirit feminine.

Both some mainline churches as well as smaller cults have been influenced by the feminist protest against traditional God-language. In 1975 the 187th General Assembly of the United Presbyterian Church adopted a study document that recommended avoiding "personal metaphors" for God and substituting instead designations "like Rock, Fire, the First and the Last, the Holy One, the Eternal One, and Spirit"; noteworthy here is the implicit dismissal of the personality of the Spirit (cf. John 4:24).

A National Council of Churches task force has proposed replacing many biblical designations for deity with neuter or feminine terms, and some ecumenists have urged reissuing the Revised Standard Version in "de-sexed" language. Use of masculine terms for deity, it is said, was due to limitations of the original languages. But does substituting neuter or feminine terms actually overcome semantic limitation?

Many who criticize the predominantly masculine language about God used in Christian circles deny trying to alter the meaning of Judeo-Christian faith. Their objective is only to update biblical language and symbolism; they do not propose to change the sense of the biblical teaching. Some evangelical feminists criticize traditional theology for failing to recognize properly the feminist imagery that the Bible itself employs of God. What they want is not a revision of biblical language, but proper deference to it.

The call to revise gender references to God assumes that the scriptural precedent of masculine terms involves a doctrine of God unacceptable to the modern mind. The biblical view is said to incorporate patriarchalist notions that need to be balanced by feminist emphases. The role of women as depicted by the Bible is declared to be unacceptable. Modern feminism identifies the biblical use of masculine terms for God with male chauvinism and female subjection; it considers the scriptural symbolism incompatible with the Genesis creation account's emphasis that God bestowed his image equally on male and female, despite the fact that the man was first, as the apostle Paul reiterates.

The question that must be asked is what bearing, if any, the linguistic precedents of Scripture have on the teaching of the Bible. The masculine-feminine tensions over biblical nomenclature cannot be satisfactorily resolved without due attention to both scriptural terms and scriptural doctrine. Much theological confusion stems from associating biblical pronouns with an unjustifiable anthropomorphism. Distinctions of gender are taken to imply that God has sexual features that in some respects at least correspond to what male and female signify in the creaturely realm. But the very complaint that the Bible uses sexist language about God rests upon mistaken assumptions. In sharp distinction from the ancient Near Eastern fertility cults and their nature gods, the Bible studiously avoids imputing sexual organs to God even anthropomorphically. Feminine and masculine sexual elements are excluded from both the Old Testament and New Testament doctrine of deity. The God of the Bible is a sexless God. When Scripture speaks of God as "he" the pronoun is primarily personal (generic) rather than masculine (specific); it emphasizes God's personality—and, in turn, that of the Father, Son and Spirit as trinitarian distinctions—in contrast to impersonal entities. Walter Brueggemann stresses that biblical religion is quite disinterested in any discussion of God's sexuality (masculine or feminine) or God's asexuality, but freely uses whatever images are appropriate to advance its central interest in God's personal covenant-relationships with Israel ("Israel's Social Criticism and Yahweh's Sexuality," pp. 739–772). The question of the defense of God's masculinity, or of the promotion of his femininity, is therefore to be detached from any discussion of divine sexuality. Scripture does not depict God either as ontologically masculine or feminine. God is neither male nor female in his being, neither sexually masculine nor feminine. The God of the Bible is pure spirit, incorporeal. The masculine or feminine imagery that the Bible employs of deity carries no androgynous ontological connotation, nor does it imply that God in some or most respects is a male deity and in other respects, a female deity. The irreverent references to "the Man Upstairs" have no precise ontological intention; such profane usage in fact usually has in view only a phantom deity.

What then are we to make of masculine and feminine gender implications in the biblical characterization of God? That masculine gender distinctions predominate in Scripture is unquestionable. Yet feminine imagery appears already in the Pentateuch where God is designated simultaneously as "the Rock who fathered you; and . . . the God who gave you birth" (Deut. 32:18, NIV; cf. also 32:11, where God is depicted as a mother-Eagle guarding her nest). The so-called Wisdom literature depicts Wisdom as the Lord's Co-worker and specifically in Proverbs 8:29 as "the Craftsman" at God's side when he marked out earth's foundations; in Proverbs 7:4, however, Wisdom is depicted as the heavenly Sister. Isaiah portrays Yahweh's concern for Israel in terms of a mother's compassion (Isa. 49:15) and applies to Yahweh the imagery of a woman in childbirth (42:14) and of God's nursing, dandling and comforting his people (66:12). Yet Psalm 103:13 states that God pities his children "like as a father"; here the verb, notably, derives from a stem in which the noun means "a womb," so that the characterization seems applicable to a mother's no less than to a father's response (cf. 1 Kings 3:26, Isa. 66:13). More familiar are the words of Christ's travail over Jerusalem: "O Jerusalem, Jerusalem . . . how often I have longed to gather your children together, as a hen gathers her chicks under her wings, but you were not willing" (Matt. 23:37, NIV).

Church fathers, including Jerome, Augustine, Anselm and Aquinas, therefore had scriptural precedent when they occasionally used feminine imagery to characterize God's activity. Some evangelical theologians would give increased prominence to such references in order to counterbalance the Bible's predominantly masculine imagery. In ancient cultural situations, they imply, an equally balanced masculine-feminine imagery might have seemed odd, even as in our age the preponderance of male imagery is now unacceptable to some people. Others approve some modification of the biblical gender references to deity on the ground that, since sexual distinctions are not in view, gender is a matter of theological indifference.

But the Bible's predominant use of masculine imagery and metaphors is not to be hurriedly dismissed as a matter of indifference. Even as the biblical writers do not indiscriminately employ anthropomorphisms with reference to God, so the gender-uses of the inspired writers involve ontologically important conceptual distinctions, even though they do not convey sexual connotations. The biblical linguistic precedents are to be considered normative for Christian theology. In pointed contrast to the ancient fertility cults the God of the Bible, as Elaine H. Pagels stresses, "shares his power with no female divinity, nor is he the divine Husband or Lover of any. He scarcely can be characterized in any but masculine epithets: King, Lord,

Master, Judge, and Father" ("What Became of God the Mother?", p. 107). While the Old Testament depicts Wisdom in a feminine role, moreover, Wisdom is never depicted as Yahweh's wife.

In respect to trinitarian distinctions, masculine imagery predominates for the Son and the Spirit no less than for the Father. Nor do these personal distinctions imply a subordination of equality or dignity. B. B. Warfield stresses that trinitarian distinctions within the Godhead imply only a subordination of modes of operation, not a superiority and inferiority of essence ("Trinity," pp. 3020 ff.). So too the distinction of persons involves no subordination of masculine or feminine dispositions in the deity, contrary to the contention of some feminist theologians that the Father is masculine and the Son and the Spirit feminine, or that Christ Jesus somehow reflects both masculine and feminine aspects. Christ is the eternal Son. The New Testament identifies Wisdom with Christ (1 Cor. 1:24; cf. Col. 2:3), so that wisdom is depicted in both feminine (Prov. 7:4) and masculine imagery. But the New Testament identification of Jesus Christ as the Wisdom of God clearly is not conditioned by the attachment of sexual significance to the feminine imagery that the Old Testament uses of Wisdom. The church, moreover, is the bride of Christ (2 Cor. 11:2; Eph. 5:23 ff.), not the groom.

Theological debate over the Spirit has focused in this century on the question of the Spirit's personality or impersonality. Quite unbiblical theories have sometimes been drawn from the peculiarities of language. The Greek neuter references to the Spirit provide a case in point. The Greek word *pneuma* is neuter. In some contexts the term "spirit" can in fact be equated with an impersonal force, energy, or influence. But depending on its meaning "Spirit" takes a masculine or neuter article. Christ speaks of the Spirit in masculine gender. The masculine article predominates both in the New Testament and in standard theological references. The New Testament masculine imagery is the more significant because the term spirit is a feminine word in both Hebrew and Aramaic.

Some recent commentators call attention to Jerome's mention of the fact that an earlier apocryphal work (*Gospel According to the Hebrews;* cf. also *The Acts of Thomas*) refers to the Spirit as feminine. There is no indication that mainline Christianity ever shared the notion that the Spirit is a female person. Not even the article of the Apostles' Creed that affirms that Jesus was "conceived by the Holy Spirit" was understood by Christian theologians to imply the Spirit's femininity. Suggestions that the Spirit is to be viewed as masculine in his transcendent activity, as at Pentecost, but as feminine in his immanent presence in the church lack biblical justification and are highly conjectural. The fact that Scripture always refers to the church as feminine does not settle the question of appropriate gender-designations for either Christ or the Spirit. Against contemporary suggestions that the Spirit is "the feminine personal principle in the Godhead," Paul K. Jewett writes: "No matter how one looks at it—whether from the data of comparative religions, the exegetical possibilities of the biblical text, or the erudite implications of trinitarian theologizing—the argument that identifies the Spirit with the female principle is without secure foundation" ("The Holy Spirit as female (?)," p. 12).

The Bible clearly considers male imagery more appropriate than female imagery in respect to God's mighty works of creation, redemption and judgment. Something would be lost by cloaking such doctrines in feminine imagery, or in masculine-feminine imagery. Since the content of the biblical revelation is conveyed in the form of inspired propositional truths and words, the message and meaning of Scripture cannot be confidently formulated apart from due attention to its literary details. The tendency in some church circles to fraternize with God as Divine Brother or Sister conceals something of the authority content of the biblically given name Father. The symbols belong to the revelation, and cognitive considerations are involved in the choice of one symbol over another. Those who say that it is unimportant whether or not Scripture speaks of God as "he" do not tell us why it then becomes important to alter the gender to "she."

Jesus Christ is improperly spoken of as "Child of God" exclusively, since Scripture designates Christ as God's eternal Son (John 1:14, 3:16), prophecy speaks of the Redeemer as both Child and Son (Isa. 9:6), and Christ became incarnate in Jesus of Nazareth who was consecrated in the temple as a firstborn male (Luke 3:21–23). But only in respect to Jesus of Nazareth do masculine pronouns applied to deity imply sexual distinctions, and that solely in view of his incarnation as God-man. It is as necessary to avoid extraneous inferences and to make sound inferences from gender distinctions and scriptural nomenclature as it is to relate other doctrines to the linguistic details of the Bible. Scripture's use of the terms "Father" and "Lord" of God bears an ontological importance beyond merely a description of deity as personal; the personal God is *Father* and *Lord.* This does not mean that he is assertedly like human males in some respect, as feminists often imply; rather, it affirms that God is in these respects intrinsically what creatures reflect only in secondary and often in imperfect ways. Analogical argumentation here helps us little and invariably breaks down. Benedict Ashley's argument that creation *ex nihilo* is more compatible with God the Father, whereas emanation of the universe seems rather to be implied by God the Mother, since the substance of the child is derived from the mother, curiously overlooks the significance of male semen in the conception of life. The conclusion to be drawn is that the significance of biblical nomenclature is not to be projected from human analogy or philosophical conjecture but is to be derived rather from scriptural teaching and the meaning of literary details as they are illumined by the verbal and logical context.

Radical feminist reconstructions of the doctrine of God often employ morally deviant doctrines of human sexual ethics. The view of a bisexual deity is frequently made to imply that homosexuality is as normal as bisexuality. But Karl Barth stresses that the distinction between man and woman is divinely given and fixed, and that no attempt to erode this ontological distinction is justifiable (*Church Dogmatics,* III/1, pp. 186 ff.). Phyllis Trible emphasizes that God made humankind "two creatures, not as one creature with double sex" (*God and the Rhetoric of Sexuality,* p. 18). Elisabeth Elliot shares this stance in *Let Me Be a Woman.* But even evangelical efforts to overcome male-female tensions are now often culturally conditioned either on the right or on the left and do not fully reflect the sense and spirit of the biblical view. If Marabel Morgan's *Total Woman* puts the wife at the disposal of her husband more than it makes her a helpmate, and may in this respect reflect an ancient cultural patriarchalism, the views of Letha Scanzoni and Nancy Hardesty (*All We're Meant to Be*) seem rather to reflect the priorities of contemporary feminism as much if not more than the biblical outlook.

Yet an ideological patriarchalism that correlates the despotic husband with the enslaved wife has, as almost all evangelical feminists acknowledge, no approved place in the biblical view. Any proclamation of the dominantly masculine symbolism of biblical theology in a way that accommodates male chauvinism, or implies superiority of male over female or the lesser dignity and right of the woman, obscures the revealed will of God who, alongside stern moral indictment of homosexuality and of lesbianism, unhesitatingly takes to himself feminine symbolism as well as masculine. In the context of modern masculine-feminist tensions the biblical doctrine of male and female created in the *imago Dei* affirms that neither male nor female is dominant over the other or independent of the other, although it approves a distinction of roles in the orders of creation.

It can hardly be disputed, however, that by the time of Christ not only Oriental society but almost the entire Hellenistic world, Jewish no less than Gentile, mirrored a patriarchal ideology that differs from the Old Testament ideal of male-female relations. Despite the contrary emphasis of the New Testament, moreover, not even the church fathers wholly escaped a prejudicial attitude toward women, nor did some of the most influential medieval theologians.

Karl Barth identifies the biblical view as a modified patriarchalism, and in many respects his exposition is scripturally sound and theologically illuminating (*Church Dogmatics,* III/1, pp. 286 ff.). Both man and woman are created in subordination to God. Man's divinely conferred headship is to be realized by exalting the glory of God even as Jesus Christ was exalted in and through his humiliation. Only where the husband's necessary subordination to God is ignored does the woman's subordination to her husband appear a hard requirement that invites her revolt against subordination to both God and her mate. The wife's primary loyalty is not to her husband but to the Lord, although the Lord calls both to subordination, and within this subordination approves distinctive roles for each. The role of the woman is not that of an independent feminist, any more than the man's role is that of a domineering patriarch or male chauvinist; she is to be man's covenant-partner or helpmate in the service of God. The Almighty Father calls out a new family in Christ, a fellowship of brothers and sisters whose higher loyalties transform sin-warped dispositions and elevate human relationships to a new unity and dignity. Tribal patriarchalism was already known in Old Testament patterns of life: males indulged in prostitution, a sin for which women were stoned, divorce was possible only on male initiative, and parents considered sons more desirable than daughters. It still survives in many parts of the world not yet touched by Judeo-Christian ethics or unaffected by neopagan Western libertarian alternatives. It was Christ who lifted male-female relationships fully to the divine intention by creation, while nonetheless preserving separate roles alongside created equality and dignity. In this context there is no need to minimize the New Testament teaching that as man is the glory of God, woman is the glory of man. The fidelity of God the Father, the sacrificial love of Christ the Son, the holy power of the Spirit, the purity of the virgin Mary, all gain dramatic relevance in a licentious contemporary society in which marital and nonmarital relationships are now more permissive than in any previous pagan environment except perhaps ancient Gomorrah and Sodom. It says something about our age that many of its intellectuals, including some theologs, are more concerned about eliminating supposed aberrations in sexual God-language in the name of feminine libertarianism than about stemming sexual aberrations and licentiousness in human relationships in the name of a holy God.

8.
Muddling the Trinitarian Dispute

Is THE DOCTRINE of the Trinity a futile intellectual effort to resolve inherently contradictory notions of divine unity and divine plurality? Are orthodox evangelicals driven to say that anyone who rejects this doctrine may lose his soul whereas anyone who tries to explain it will lose his mind? Is the doctrine an illogical formulation that depends for its justification upon the notion that God is a mysterious suprarational reality? Was W. T. Stace right in saying that "in the self-contradictory doctrine of the Trinity" the great theologians of the past "threw the Mystery of God uncompromisingly in men's faces. . . . All attempts to make religion a purely rational, logical thing are not only shallow but would, if they could succeed, destroy religion. Either God is mystery or He is nothing" (*Time and Eternity*, p. 8)? In that case, would it matter if Christianity claimed the Godhead embraces two, or four, or six—rather than three—persons, or even that God is sometimes one person and sometimes many persons? Why did Christian scholars insist that affirmation of the triune God rests upon sufficient reason, and that alternative views are less than true to fact? Is the doctrine logically defensible?

Some critics consider orthodox representations of the Trinity a mathematical monstrosity; the doctrine, they contend, is as fallacious in its claim for the three-in-one God as is the formula $3\ x = 1\ x$. But this description patently distorts the doctrine. Christian theology affirms neither that three gods are one God nor that three isolated persons are one God. Rather, it affirms three eternal personal distinctions in the one God, in short, $3\ x$ in $1\ y$. Such a formulation is both intelligible and noncontradictory. It is, moreover, far less complex than most mathematical formulas that engage modern day scientists. In scientific research the presence of unresolved problems is no reason for rejecting rationality or relevant data; such problems become a challenge, rather, for further clarification and complex explanation. By contrast, neo-Protestant theologians all too readily consider complexity an evidence of ultimate contradiction and a sign of irrationality. But historic Christian theology does not even invoke notions of complementarity, as does modern science, for example, to explain light on the basis of wave and particle theories where some data are considered true on only one level and other data on only another.

The reason for rejecting the doctrine of the Trinity cannot then be its illogicality. That approach would only rationalize personal unbelief, or reflect one's profound misunderstanding of a basic Christian doctrine. Muhammad thought that the Christian Trinity is comprised of God, Mary and Jesus, and that the Holy Spirit is Gabriel. Upton Sinclair spoke of Christianity's "three-headed God" (*The Profits of Religion,* p. 42) and Knight Dunlap dismissed the Trinity as a departure from genuine monotheism. "Christianity," says Dunlap, "deviates from strict monotheism, in its orthodox sects, by postulating a trinity; a postulation that theologians have endeavored to harmonize with monotheism. . . . To many Roman Catholics, in fact, the trinity that is designated as J M J (Joseph, Mary, Jesus) is more real and more venerated than the official trinity of the church" (*Religion: Its Functions in Human Life,* pp. 56 ff.). Both non-Christian Jewish scholars and modern universalists declare the doctrine to involve three gods and therefore to constitute a form of tritheism. Yet no world religion more than Christianity has deplored polytheism as paganism; none has as aggressively channeled missionaries around the world to divert masses of humanity from polytheistic misconceptions of God.

New Testament writers nowhere suggest that the Trinity is veiled in incomprehensibility, but associate what they say about the Father, Son and Spirit with intelligible divine self-disclosure. Thomas Aquinas later placed the doctrine not simply in the sphere of revelation but beyond reason; by so doing he gave needless comfort to secular philosophers and to mediating theologians who consider the doctrine mystical or conjectural rather than rational.

Dialectical theology in the recent past has characterized the Trinity and the incarnation as paradoxical beliefs. But this prognosis has been more confusing than helpful. When the early church fathers spoke of these tenets as paradoxical, they did not mean that the doctrines convey no rational information about objective realities. They were insisting rather that because God is so much greater than man our knowledge of him does not exhaust all that can be said about him. Neoorthodoxy, however, was much more radical and, in fact, antiintellectual. Addicted to a theory of dialectical divine revelation and human response, it held that not even Christians have objectifiable knowledge of God in himself. By rejecting the possibility of revealed truths about the existence and nature of God as he eternally is, neoorthodoxy makes of all theological propositions but fallible pointers to internal divine confrontation.

Only a unipersonal God, insisted critics of trinitarian doctrine, can escape the charge of polytheism. But why should human beings necessarily conceive the one God as a human personality inflated to infinity—a colossal projection of even so exalted a religious figure as Hegel or Schleiermacher or Harnack? Why should God be conceived as a reflection on an infinite scale of your being or mine? Scripture declares not that God properly or actually exists in man's image, but that man was specially made in God's image. Let it be emphasized, moreover, that we bear God's image only in certain and not in all respects (or even in most); we are neither infinite, unchanging, omnipotent nor omniscient and, as creaturely persons, we are embodied, independent selves. Even though as persons we bear the divine image, personality in God is far more complex and intricate than that of created life.

Trinitarianism does not require belief in rational contradiction; if it did, neither sound Christian faith nor reason could commend it. Belief in the Trinity should be assessed on the basis of its own claims and not dismissed out of hand because of crude misunderstandings. The difficulty with the doctrine issues from attempts to conceive divine personality within the limits of human personality, an error to which modern liberal thought became prone because of the speculative idealistic correlation of the divine and the human. If divine personality were indeed only an expansion of human personality, and if God were but a more complex image of the human person, then the assertion of tripersonality must in any form involve a numerical plurality of isolated beings and therefore the existence of three gods.

Brightman, for example, makes the human self determinative for the nature of the divine: "The personalist of today must say that the . . . ousia, the godhead, is person in the modern sense." Then he proceeds to "reconcile" personalism and trinitarianism by espousing a merely modal trinity: "But a person is a *unitas multiplex*. . . . The *ousia* may well have three *hypostases,* that is, three essential modes of acting. . . . 'Person' as used in some formulations of trinitarianism," he writes, does not "mean what 'person' means to a personalist" or that would mean "pure polytheism." Knudson likewise holds that "so long as each Person, or Hypostasis, is regarded as 'having self-consciousness and making self-decision,' it is difficult to see" how the objection that the doctrine is tritheistic "can be completely met." Real self-decision means independence, he argues, and independence is impossible in the framework of a necessitated underlying unity (*The Doctrine of God,* pp. 415 ff.).

But divine personality is the archetype of human personality, not the reverse. God and man have ontological differences as well as ontological likenesses; the *imago Dei* does not imply total metaphysical identity. God and man are personal beings, but divine personal reality involving a plurality of persons with a unitary essence is more intricate and complex. The conjectural argument from the human self as a *unitas multiplex* would of course be as compatible with a hundred *hypostases* in the Godhead as with three, while at the same time it would prejudicially preclude all but one divine person. The objection that tripersonality necessarily involves tritheism rises from the misconception that personality in man is archetypal. Since human personality involves individuated being, divine tripersonality would in that event indeed involve three separate individual divinities. But whereas modern theology seeks to postulate the nature of ultimate reality from human nature, biblical theology takes its rise in divine self-disclosure and, because of human finitude and fallenness, protests every effort to establish the nature of God by ballooning the human self to infinity.

Instead of obfuscation of meaning, the doctrine of the Trinity contributes significantly to resolving the vexing problem of the one and the many, a problem that troubled Greek philosophy from its beginnings. Anaximander, Anaximenes, Parmenides, Xenophanes and the Eleatics all coped with the question of an ultimate ground of the vast multiplicity of things and arrived at differing explanations. Monism that denies multiplicity and pluralism that overrides unity are alternatives that turn philosopher against philosopher in successive but unsatisfactory efforts to reconcile the one and the many (cf. Werner Jaeger, *The Theology of the Early Greek Philosophers,* pp. 136 ff., 153). Those who stressed the One tended to dismiss the Many as mere appearance; those who emphasized the Many lost the eternal One. Small wonder that Christianity found Greek philosophy unserviceable as a prime resource for delineating the inner nature of God, the doctrines of creation and incarnation, and the relationship of God to man and the cosmos. By emphasizing the eternal Logos as the creative source of all the substance and structures of reality, Christianity metaphysically guaranteed the general possibility of the correspondence of divine and human thought about God, the world, and other selves, and did so by avoiding pantheism.

Plotinus in the Christian era and later early modern rationalists from Leibniz to Spinoza and Hegel sought a nonbiblical solution of the problem of the One and the Many. In the twentieth century personal idealists proposed that consciousness be taken as the ultimate model of complex unity. Resisting Hegel's pantheistic reduction of reality to the Absolute, and insisting instead on the created individuality of human selves, personal idealism nonetheless routinely conceived the divine Self in a manner that tapered the divine *hypostases* to modes of acting at the expense of an ontological Trinity. In view of the modern multiplication of psychological conceptions of the invisible world it becomes apparent why philosophers determined to rid the world of thought of superfluous conceptions. But the history of philosophy succeeded only in replacing some objectionable theories by other objectionable theories. Secular philosophy lacked adequate resources to identify the trinitarian alternative as valid because it arbitrarily ruled out transcendent revelation and hence ignored revelational monotheism.

Already at Pentecost the apostles preached openly in trinitarian terms. The New Testament is uniformly trinitarian, although the systematic philosophical exposition of the primitive Christian doctrine came later. Peter speaks at Pentecost not only of sin and salvation, but also of the Father, the Son, and the Spirit as coexisting persons. The essential difference between the person of the Father and the person of the Spirit, on the one hand, and the person of the Son, on the other, is that the eternal Christ was sent by the Father as incarnate; as crucified and alive from the dead, the glorified Lord then poured out the Spirit upon the church. At the same time apostolic preaching insists upon and unfalteringly declares throughout the Book of Acts the truth of divine monotheism. Paul's vivid confrontation of the unknown God in Athens (Acts 17:23) and of the cult of Artemis in Ephesus (19:27; cf. 26:37) mirrors the clash between this living monotheism and polytheistic religion. After the apostles' miraculous works, crowds hailed them with idolatrous acclamation. At Lystra the people shouted: "The gods have come down to us in human form" and called Barnabas Jupiter, and Paul, Mercury (Acts 14:11 f., NEB); at Malta Paul was considered a god because he was unharmed by a venomous snake (28:3–6). The apostles rebuked "these follies," however, in the name of "the living God who made heaven and earth and sea and everything in them" (14:15, NEB). No more sweeping indictment of the religious debility of the Gentile world can be found than in the introduction of Paul's letter to the Romans where the apostle decries man's idolatrous defection from the one true God.

The Bible is monotheistic from core to circumference. From its beginnings Christianity is no less irreducibly monotheistic than Judaism. It unwaveringly joins the Old Testament in insisting that the living God reveals himself as the one and only God. The Bible nowhere presents monotheism as the product of a prior religious history of polytheism, nor as the prelude to a later supposedly quasi-monotheistic or supermonotheistic Christian view. Monotheism is the first and only religion of revelation and thoroughly negates polytheism. Nor does Scripture perceive the one living God as a more satisfactory conception of divine unity achieved by a gradual process of demythologizing and depopulating the realm of supernatural beings. Nor does biblical monotheism emerge through philosophical conjecture to complicate the hidden mysteries of God's inner life. The one living God is known only through his self-revelation, first to Adam and Eve as forerunners of a race divinely intended for spiritual fellowship with their mighty Maker, then to the patriarchs and Moses and the prophets. Doubts cast by documentary hypotheses of the Old Testament on the uniqueness and antiquity of Israel's faith in the one God become increasingly insignificant as the speculative historical foundations of those theories continue to weaken.

This passionate monotheism penetrates the New Testament as deeply as the Old; if anything, the Christian age surpassed Judaism in abhorring the worship of false gods. Throughout its history the Christian missionary cause has purposed worldwide deliverance of mankind from the grip of false gods and its restoration to the true and living God. Peter Green writes: "The Christian can say, 'I believe in God' not less truly, but really more truly, than the Jew or the Mohammedan" (*The Holy Ghost: The Comforter. A Study of the Nature and Work of God the Holy Spirit*, p. 12). Ethelbert Stauffer reinforces the point that Christology in no way signalled for Christians the slightest deviation from monotheism: "Early Christian monotheism is confirmed rather than shattered by the Christology of the NT" ("The Uniqueness of God," *TDNT*, 3:102). Every attack on Christology that professes to defend monotheism against polytheism, whether issuing from Jewish or Muslim sources, either grossly fails to understand the Christian doctrine of God or is motivated polemically more than rationally. Christianity proclaimed three divine persons, but it never proclaimed three gods. Christianity has never held a brief—only abhorrence—for polydemonism and polytheism, for the pluralism of Greek religion, and even for the complex doctrine of Godhead found in Hinduism and Buddhism.

Despite Greek philosophical influences that stressed the unity of the divine and rejected the rampant anthropomorphism of polytheistic religion, the Greeks retained interest in a divine world of many gods. While Homer at times does call Zeus simply God, when Zeus initiates or decides the course of action, he applies the same term also to Apollos, Eros and others of the panoply of divinities. Monotheism even came to be widely regarded as an objectionable depopulation of the invisible realm. So deeply entrenched was polytheism in some circles that Apollonius in the first century B.C. charged the Jews with atheism because they repudiated polytheism and thereby emptied the spiritual world of its gods. In affirming trinitarian monotheism, the early Christians had to contend not simply with the misunderstandings and misrepresentations of non-Christian Jewish spokesmen who imputed blasphemy to Jesus and his followers; they contended also with the pagan religionists who, once Christians rejected the imperial Roman cult, revived the charge of atheism earlier leveled at the Jews.

In reporting the monotheism of some ancient Greeks, modern scholars are sometimes tempted to read more into the earlier references to God than is warranted; from the standpoint of later thought, they presume to see a clear conception of unity where the use of *theos* may have reflected mainly an intuitive recognition of Supreme Being or a *genus divinum,* just as we often speak of man without articulate reference to the unity of the race. To be sure, some classic philosophers expound and insist on one God, and a few do so at considerable length, for all Plato's vacillation between the eternal Ideas and the Idea of the Good. Plato's emphasis on the eternity and intractability of matter, and on the Demiurge, alongside the Ideas, introduces three independent principles, and not just one. Kenneth Hamilton remarks that the dominance of abstract monotheism "was never absolute. Its purest form was probably in Stoic and neo-Platonic philosophers, of the late classical and early Christian centuries, and later in the rationalist-agnostic scientists of the nineteenth century. . . . Many if not most of the great scientists since the seventeenth century were able to combine the scientific dogma of universal causality with a faith in the living God (earth's Creator and man's Redeemer). But just as polytheism continued in an underground form through the Middle Ages and lives on today in modern cults of witchcraft and Satanism, the imagination of Western man was never fully Christianized or even convinced by abstract monotheism's picture of a universe of law" (*To Turn from Idols,* p. 40). Hamilton adds that "An abstract monotheism was no nearer to Christian faith than a naïve polytheism had been, for it delivered men from bondage to nonexistent gods only to turn them over to the tyranny of abstract powers and invisible forces" (*To Turn from Idols*, p. 28). The early modern Unitarians—among them Belsham, Priestley and Channing—constructed their doctrine of God largely along the lines of deism even if at the same time they inconsistently preserved more Christian content than do their successors.

Oriental religion is not characteristically monotheistic, nor does it depict the deity as does Hebrew revelation as God internally alive and active, and as independent creator of the world. The Vedanta, in the books of Shankara, calls for knowing and understanding the metaphysical entity Brahma who has no determinate moral qualities and imposes none; in Judaism, by contrast, the God of Israel is righteousness and justice, lovingkindness and mercy (Num. 14:18; Hos. 2:21; Jer. 9:23) and the truly religious man emulates these perfections (Micah 6:9). While a few religious and philosophical theories in India and Persia correlate monotheism and morality, they lack the pervasive unity of the Hebrew revelation that brings all areas of life, without exception, under control of the one living God. In the post-Christian era, Muhammad gave fresh impetus to the lost abstract monotheism of the non-Hebrew world. To be sure, his emphasis that there is no God but Allah leans heavily on the Mosaic revelation. But an obscure doctrine of revelation crowds out the living monotheism of the Old Testament and allows Muhammad to emerge as Allah's prophet; moreover it clouds the dynamic monotheism of the New Testament by displacing the revelation of the supremacy and deity of Jesus Christ.

William F. Albright observes that "much of the onslaught on early Israelite monotheism comes from scholars who represent certain theological points of view with reference to monotheism, i.e., who deny that orthodox trinitarian Christianity . . . is monotheistic, or that orthodox Judaism and orthodox Islam are monotheistic. . . . Neither of the last two religions can be called 'monotheistic' by a theologian who insists that this term applies only to Unitarian Christianity or to liberal Judaism. But no 'dictionary' definition of monotheism was ever intended to exclude orthodox Christianity" (*History, Archaeology and Christian Humanism*, p. 155).

What routinely passes for popular faith in one supreme God today often reflects—as in Gallup Poll reports that 99 percent of the American people "believe in God"—some modern version of the phantom monotheism of pagan philosophy and religion. We deceive ourselves if we think that the pagan monotheisms of the past were all alike and that no divergence of monotheisms exists today. The doubts concerning God among young intellectuals today often rest on their secular misunderstandings of monotheism whose survival value is more emotional than intellectual. Hamilton is right when he observes that "The recent explosion of odd and often archaic religious beliefs, especially among the young, points to a break-up—or at the very least a severe questioning—of abstract monotheism" (*To Turn from Idols*, p. 40).

Even Christians have been misled too often by the propaganda projections of unitarian theists who consider the doctrine of the Trinity an embarrassment to rational faith. When God is depicted by world religions as rigidly and aloofly unipersonal, as a divinity not incarnate in Jesus and not manifest by the Holy Spirit, then the notion of deity soon blurs into the Nebulous or into the All. By stressing psychological analogues that view God as a unitary self, modern interpreters have tended to replace the conventional doctrine of social love that is found in God's eternal nature and is based on an interpenetration of persons. This fallback to a psychological view of the Trinity, combined with an emphasis on modal manifestations, sacrifices not only many of the Christian view's religious values but also its ontological claims. W. G. T. Shedd characterized ancient Sabellianism, which has been revived in modern modal theories of the Godhead, as "the most subtle and also the most elevated of all the forms of spurious trinitarianism" (*History of Christian Doctrine,* Vol. 1, p. 252). Also known as modalistic monarchianism, Sabellianism was named for Sabellius of the third century who contended that the Father, Son and Holy Spirit are not three distinct personalities, but only three different modes of divine manifestation. Driven by a rigid monotheism, and in order to escape any suspicion of ditheism, Sabellius designated the one God as the "Son Father"; he held, however, that God is not simultaneously Father and Son but manifested himself in three successive personal energies as creator (Father), redeemer (Son), and giver of new life (Holy Ghost).

Claiming that the doctrine of three persons requires tritheism, Protestant modernism rejected the doctrine of the Trinity. Some modernists approved the ancient notion of three successive modes of God, setting it in the context of Hegelian pantheism. For others, however, the three names were but symbols for the inexhaustible richness of the divine nature. Many identified the significant idea in trinitarianism to be the Christlikeness of God. The doctrine of the Trinity developed, suggested Francis J. McConnell, in order to preserve a continuity of divine moral character with the historical revelation in Jesus of Nazareth (*The Christlike God,* p. 70). Such emphasis rested metaphysical identity completely on the ethical unity of the Son with the Father. Knudson considers this emphasis on divine love and grace fundamental and indispensable, but declares it "uncertain" whether three eternal persons are "essential" to the absoluteness of God's love and ethical character (*The Doctrine of God,* p. 428).

Yet the eternal interchange of holy love between the persons of the self-revealed Godhead provides in the inner divine life a stronger basis for holy love than does trying to preserve the moral values of Christianity by merely postulating them retroactively from the incarnation. The fact of God's perfect revelation mediated through Jesus Christ cannot be divorced from but logically requires a doctrine of essential metaphysical unity. Bare monism tries to lend living content to the conception of God by viewing him as the Whole of which man and the cosmos are essential parts; God thus ceases to be the Other, and in the course of time is easily regarded as nothing distinct from the world and man. In this way a bare theism easily degenerates from monotheism to nontheism. Buddhism exhibits this rivalry between personal and impersonal conceptions of divinity, a tension that eventuates in the prejudice that personality is an inferior characterization of the ultimate.

Most early modern Western philosophers presupposed divine personality as an inheritance from Judeo-Christian thought, but some discounted and even denied trinitarian theism. Reflecting a broken interest in Christian motifs, modalistic trinitarian speculations subjected the biblical view to rationalistic attack.

In its New Testament representations, God's triunity cannot be reduced to either a divine triad or a threefold movement in the life of the Godhead. The notion of a triad is found in Oriental religion and is expounded in terms of three gods. Modern pantheists espoused the modal view, and under Hegelian influence, depicted the Infinite in a threefold impulse: articulating itself to itself, differentiating itself into the finite, and then returning to the Infinite again; to this process Hegel assigned familiar trinitarian names. That God stands in different relationships to the world and man as creator, redeemer and judge, and that the divine persons engage in distinctive functions in a variety of creative ways, is apparent from Scripture. But this fact gives no license, however tempting, to transform these relationships into essential modes of God's being. Into the chasm that separates the eternal God from the changing universe some theorists have inserted a variety of intermediary beings; others have postulated in place of God an Absolute who has no relations with the world. Added to this confusion are the conjectural notions of mediating theologians and philosophers that promote a functional rather than ontological Trinity.

In his Gifford lectures Viscount Haldane, for example, reduced New Testament trinitarianism to "the recognition of the three moments on which metaphysics lays such stress . . . first of all, . . . the aspect which belongs to what Hegel calls 'Logic.' . . . Mind in itself may be said to represent what in theological language is described as the Father. In the element of the Son you have mind gone into otherness, hetereity, finite mind . . . God, in other words, imposing on Himself the limits of man's finitude. . . . Then there is the third moment in the movement, the return of the Absolute Mind into itself in the fullness of its self-consciousness, the Holy Spirit, the aspect in the Trinity which is in reality the logical prius of the two other aspects, aspects which are separable only in abstraction" (*The Pathway to Reality,* pp. 484 f.). Haldane here presents not three eternal personal distinctions in one divine essence, but three different aspects or movements in one personal center of consciousness.

In the very first series of Gifford lectures James H. Stirling had lamented the rationalistic reconstruction of the doctrine of the Godhead already underway among early church fathers; this deviation took hold long before medieval writers of a mystical bent nurtured speculative rather than revelational elaboration of trinitarianism. Stirling writes: "In them, for example, as in more modern philosophical writers, it is quite usual for Christ to stand as the existent world. Now, I am not at all a foe to a warranted religious philosophizing; I am not at all a foe even to the carrying of trin-

ity—trinity is unity—into the very heart of the universe in constitution
of it. But it strikes me that . . . so to attempt to philosophize the Christian
Godhead would only repugn. I, for my part, cannot feel at home in it"
(*Philosophy and Theology,* pp. 27 f.).

While Barth avoids the term persons and speaks instead of "modes,"
he rejects Unitarianism and insists on an eternal divine Trinity of Father,
Son and Spirit. Evangelical Christians have not hesitated to use the term
"person"—on the ground that each person of the Trinity is a center of
self-consciousness and self-determination—but deny that three separate
and independent individuals are intended; evangelicals therefore speak
just as unhesitatingly of "the personality of the Holy Spirit" as of the Father
and of the Son.

Hendrikus Berkhof charges that "this concept must inevitably lead to
some kind of tritheism" and commends modernists for rejecting the "per-
son-concept in pneumatology" (*The Doctrine of the Holy Spirit,* p. 115).
Berkhof insists on a unipersonal God and considers Father, Son and Spirit
as names for distinctive divine activities of the Person of God in relation
to us. Yet Berkhof argues that the Old Testament "does not preach a God
who is numerically one" (*ibid.,* p. 117), a statement that on the surface
seems clearly to contradict the Shema. But by this he means only that
"God in the Old Testament is a communion within himself, an organism,
a unity in diversity" (*ibid.,* p. 117). Berkhof believes in modes of divine
being, as well as modes of revelation; that is, there are distinctive activities
in the eternal nature of God no less than in God's relations to the cosmos
and man.

That verdict falls considerably short, however, of what Scripture implies
by distinctions of self-consciousness existing side by side in the one Godhead. As Lorenz Wunderlich reminds us, "with one exception, exactly the
same basis which Scripture affords for judging that Jesus Christ is a person
is offered to us in speaking of the personality or person of the Holy Spirit—
and that exception is the incarnation of the Son of God. A person is usually
associated with the essentials of intellect, sensibility and will" (*The Half-
Known God,* p. 28). If we mean by sensibility a capacity for perception,
that capacity would of course characterize only conscious bodily existence;
it need not be thus limited, however, when applied to a broader sense of
capacity for moral emotion. But, Wunderlich contends, if Scripture allows
speaking of the Father as person, and not simply as mode, why should
not the Son and the Spirit also be thus conceived? The point of difficulty
lies in the contrast between separate individuals—(God conceived in man's
image, a projection involving the possibility of polytheism)—and a union
of three eternal persons in one eternal essence. The latter view requires
careful attention to the selective aspects of divine personality involved
in man's creation in God's image.

Jürgen Moltmann considers "the death of Jesus on the cross . . . the
centre of all Christian theology. . . . Anyone who really talks of the Trinity
talks of the cross of Jesus, and does not speculate in heavenly riddles"
(*The Crucified God,* pp. 204, 207). Jesus' death involves inner trinitarian

tensions and relationships that require, Moltmann holds, our speaking of the Father, the Son and the Spirit. Moltmann deplores the modern reduction of the doctrine of the Trinity "to an empty, orthodox formula." Moltmann claims that the trinitarian theology of early Christianity correlated the doctrine, much as he does, with the "incarnation and death" of Jesus (*ibid.*, p. 215). He criticizes Barth's dogmatics as insufficiently trinitarian and too theological (*ibid.*, p. 203). If we exchange a "simple concept of God" for an adequately trinitarian alternative, says Moltmann, we must emphasize that the Father "suffers with" the Son on the cross, although "not in the same way" (*ibid.*, p. 203). When we say "God in Christ" the phrase refers not only to the Father who abandons, but also to the Son who is abandoned (*ibid.*, p. 204).

For Moltmann there is a trinitarian solution to the paradox that "God is 'dead' on the cross and yet is not dead." He rejects "only a dialectical relationship between the divine being and human being" and insists on divine self-emptying (*ibid.*, p. 205). But he abandons the traditional doctrine of Christ's two natures in favor of a view of "God's being in process" (*ibid.*, p. 206).

The trinity of crucifixion disputes "the theory of the immutability of God and with it the axiom of the impassibility of the divine nature" and requires a new trinitarian conception of kenosis, says Moltmann. Whereas the Eastern Church declared the entire incarnate work of the Son to be the work of "the entire most holy Trinity," Moltmann specially calls the Son's death on the cross "a God-event in trinitarian terms" (*ibid.*, p. 206). What sense Moltmann makes of the cry of desolation ("My God, my God, why hast thou forsaken me?", Matt. 27:46) is unclear.

On the basis of crucifixion-trinitarianism Moltmann rejects metaphysical theism or rational monotheism because for it "the being of the Godhead . . . as the zone of the impossibility of death, stands in juxtaposition to human being as the zone of the necessity of death" (*ibid.*, p. 214). "But Christian theology," says Moltmann, "must think of God's being in suffering and dying and finally in the death of Jesus, if it is not to surrender itself and lose its identity" (*ibid.*, p. 214). Jesus' death, Moltmann adds, "cannot be understood 'as the death of God,' but only as death *in* God" (*ibid.*, p. 207). The life of the three persons has in it the death of Jesus. Christian faith cannot be understood metaphysically as radical monotheism whose God cannot die, but must understand God from the event of the death of Jesus (*ibid.*, p. 215). "God died on the cross of Christ" (*ibid.*, p. 216).

If in all this Moltmann would have Christians die a tranquil death in the confidence that Christ has triumphed over death, he seems in actuality to assure us, rather, that death has overtaken God. He emphasizes nonetheless that because God died on the cross death cannot separate us from God (*ibid.*, p. 217). He rejects diluting Christ's resurrection (in the context of God's death), moreover, to a bare existential extension; appealing to Romans 8:20, he reminds us that God who died on the cross of Christ also made "the crucified Christ the ground of his new creation, in which death is swallowed up in the victory of life." On the surface this appeal exudes an evangelical confidence in the propositional truth of the text. Yet Moltmann's broken approach to the Bible allows him to appropriate only what he prefers; like the divine Spirit, but without divine license, he blows where he lists (John 3:8). What he selects, moreover, he readily deploys to support a view foreign to Scripture.

The theology of the cross involves a presuppositional faith-eschatological metaphysics, says Moltmann, so that "metaphysical theism is inapplicable" to it (*ibid.*, pp. 218 ff.). "For this theology, God and suffering are no longer contradictions, as in theism and atheism, but God's being is in suffering and the suffering is in God's being itself, because God is love" (*ibid.*, p. 277).

We need not stop to dispute the colossal assumption that because God is love he suffers internally and can be holden of death. Moltmann in any case assures us that "we cannot say of God who he is of himself and in himself; we can only say who he is for us in the history of Christ which reaches us in our history" (*ibid.*, p. 238). God's omnipotence nonetheless implies for Moltmann that he can voluntarily open himself to suffering and death (*ibid.*, pp. 223, 230)—and, we may suppose, also to such incongruities as lying (cf. Heb. 6:18), contorting himself into some alien deity (perhaps even the Devil), or perchance even defecting from divinity and later recovering it again.

Moltmann's theory accommodates and requires his rejection of two natures in Jesus Christ and the insistence that God himself suffers in the suffering of Jesus. Yet Moltmann rejects the notion that the Father suffers and dies "in patripassion terms." Rather, the Father's suffering in the death of the Son "is a different kind of suffering" from the suffering and dying of the Son forsaken by the Father (*ibid.*, p. 243). But if such suffering differs *in kind,* and is not simply a different personal experience of a suffering that is qualitatively the same, does Moltmann not sacrifice all that he hopes to gain by insisting on the Father's suffering? Moltmann explains that the Father "suffers the death of his Fatherhood in the death of his Son." But where does the New Testament teach that Calvary extinguished the fatherhood of God? And, since Moltmann speaks constantly of a trinitarian view of the cross, on what biblical basis does he involve the Spirit who seems barely to gain honorable mention? Since Jesus "gave up the ghost" (John 19:30) are we—in view of the fact that Moltmann abandons a two-nature Christology—to assume that the Son expelled the Spirit, as well as that the Father expelled the Son?

The question whether the predicates of divine nature can be transferred to the human, and those of the human nature to the divine, still demands fuller discussion than Moltmann accords it. The one-layer theory of reality on which Moltmann relies multiplies rather than resolves basic christological problems. To imply that on Calvary the first person of the Trinity expels and destroys the second person is to introduce into Christian theology mythological nuances that the New Testament nowhere sanctions.

Moltmann connects a nebulous religious epistemology with an equally nebulous ontology and dignifies the whole as a devout trinitarianism that preserves the God of suffering love. For his theory of eschatological trinitarianism he offers no objective supports in the form of inspired biblical doctrine or rational divine revelation, nor can he do so, since he disowns these epistemic principles. His assertions reduce to private phenomenological faith-constructs rather than public ontological claims about God. Such views of themselves carry no more validity than contrary faith-constructs. Since Moltmann does not clarify where faith and reason intersect, his view lacks the force of logical argument that would propel either atheists or antitrinitarian theists toward trinitarianism. His exposition has the character of ingenious reflection on isolated elements of the New Testament. Moltmann's theory is vulnerable moreover to the same counterattack that he deploys against the God of the philosophers, since not even the conception of a suffering and dying God can forever escape rational appraisal and criticism. If Moltmann can give no logical reasons to distinguish his theological claims from naked faith then the divine "forsakeness" of Jesus reduces to transcendent mythology.

In the subsequent volume *The Trinity and the Kingdom* (tr. from the German *Trinität und Reich Gottes* by Margaret Kohl, London, SCM Press Ltd., San Francisco, Harper and Row, 1981), Moltmann rejects "monadic monotheism" which conceives God not as three personal subjects but as one absolute subject manifested in three modes of being or in three self-relationships. Although he at times speaks of his view as "not monotheistic, but trinitarian" (*ibid.*, p. 71; cf. pp. 69, 74), what he actually promotes is a Christian version of monotheism. For Moltmann three co-active personal subjects, namely, Father, Son, and Spirit who exist simultaneously in the one divine essence are manifested in "the history of God." For him, moreover, the Trinity is not merely economic but immanent in the Godhead as well: "Statements about the economic Trinity must correspond to doxological statements about the immanent Trinity" (*ibid.*, p. 154). This cautiously worded formula would indicate that Moltmann regards statements about the immanent Trinity to be more vulnerable than those about the economic Trinity. Indeed, he rejects "objectivistic orthodoxy" (*ibid.*, p. 5); ideas and concepts with which we presently conceive and know God, he insists, must "suffer *a transformation of meaning*" if they are to be applied to the mystery of the immanent Trinity. In short, our knowledge of the transcendent God is only doxological (*ibid.*, p. 162). Such caveats undermine the universal validity of Moltmann's largely orthodox statements about the immanent Trinity and lead us to ask how he can then confidently affirm anything about transcendent deity. Yet when Moltmann insists on suffering and pain in the eternal Godhead, and on God's panentheistic relation to the universe, he clearly expects us to treat such claims as something more than doxological. But such postulations about the suffering God have the ring more of post-Christian mythology than of biblical truth.

More and more contemporary theologians contemplate the metaphysical status of the Godhead not through the medieval substance-theory of reality but through the modern view that reality is a complex of processes and events. Assailing the radically secular concept that all biblical references to a divine person or persons and to a supernatural power and presence are mythical, these theologians resist reducing religious symbols to internal experience that lacks objective cognitive importance. But instead of expounding the Trinity in terms of substance or essence, which they disavow as antiquated philosophy, they probe modern alternatives offered by recent trends in philosophy and psychology.

Process philosophy rejects supernaturalism as well as substance-metaphysics and proposes instead a dipolar conception of God that requires extensive reconstruction of the biblical view. Some proponents welcome Alfred North Whitehead's thought as supplying a contemporary metaphysics that retains at least some role for God; others reject or modify Whitehead's view in order to reflect Christian theism more fully. Schubert M. Ogden's *The Reality of God* (1967) utilizes Whitehead's approach to vindicate numerous Christian beliefs; Charles Hartshorne, on the other hand, in pursuing the content of religious faith appeals to process philosophy on merely secular terms.

Whitehead's philosophy rules out orthodox trinitarianism since it excludes distinct subjectivities within the Godhead. Some process thinkers propound a trinity comprised by creativity as the divine ground of being; for them the primordial nature is the divine Logos, and the consequent nature, the Holy Spirit. But such proposals reveal the inability of secular metaphysicians to free themselves wholly from the influence of Christian motifs, more than they reflect a doctrinal necessity inherent in process metaphysics. Lewis Ford expounds the Logos not as the preexistent Christ, the second person of the Trinity, but rather as the totality of divine aims (*The Lure of God*, p. 100). "The risen Christ is more transhuman than divine," he writes (*ibid.*, p. 101). "Logos and Spirit . . . reflect . . . two distinct natures of God, the primordial and the consequent" (*ibid.*, p. 105). Ford consequently adduces "an ultimate triunity of principles defining the divine life" (*ibid.*, p. 110). Rather than to evaluate process theory through scriptural principles such exposition accommodates the biblical data to Whiteheadian premises.

For process theologians the Logos does not become the God-man; instead, God becomes ideal humanity (cf. J. E. Barnhart, "Incarnation and Process Philosophizing," pp. 225–232). No specific actual event is understood by process theorists as either wholly God's work or wholly man's work; every creaturely activity incarnates God's aims to a higher or lesser degree. What shall we say then of Jesus' uniqueness? Norman Pittinger, Peter Hamilton and Ronald Williams emphasize Jesus' total obedience to God. But this criterion, Lewis Ford grants, cannot by itself establish an absolute Christ-event (*The Lure of God*, p. 52); moreover, as David R. Griffin observes, the criterion traces Jesus' specialness solely to his own initiative (*A Process Christology*, p. 218). According to Griffin, Jesus, in fulfilling God's particular aims for himself, also actualizes God's general aims for the whole creation (*ibid.*, p. 220). This is doubtless true, but the statement is too indefinite. Ford develops God's decisive action in Jesus of Nazareth. In an evolutionary context that implies "myriads of planets sustaining life" the Logos as a symbol for divine activity sustains all God's creative aims and the possibilities of complex actualization (*The Lure of God*, p. 54, 63 f.). "To affirm that Jesus is the Christ is to confess that in Jesus of Nazareth we behold the embodiment of the divine intent addressed to mankind" (*ibid.*, p. 64). But what then becomes of the eternal personal Logos who as God-man added human nature to intrinsic deity?

John B. Cobb, Jr. in *Christ in a Pluralistic Age* similarly refers "incarnation" to the embodiment of divine aims in people's lives rather than to an exclusive and accomplished actualization. Yet he holds that in relation to the Logos Jesus somehow possesses a unique psychic structure of experience, a divinely constituted center of subjectivity. But does this differ essentially from the unique experience that each individual has, and which, on process premises, is also divinely co-constituted? If it does, asks Ford, how could we possibly recognize its uniquely different features (*The Lure of God*, p. 67)—except of course through special revelation that process theologians, Ford included, disallow? Ford proposes to identify Jesus as the Christ on the basis of his resurrection—not a bodily resurrection assured by apostolic testimony but a spiritual resurrection vouchsafed by the believing church's testimony to Jesus' presence and activity (*ibid.*, pp. 72 ff.). "The body of Christ's resurrection," says Ford, "is none other than the body of Christ which is the Church" (*ibid.*, p. 78). But then could not Marxists similarly contend that Marx, too, is alive in the community that believes him to be personally present in the dynamic ideals of revolutionary social change?

Process theologians who somewhat reflect Christian influences by expounding a doctrine of the Trinity in relation to nature, history and conscience, emphasize that Christianity assigns to the Holy Spirit not only an internal significance but also a vital external role. But a doctrine of inner distinctions in the activity of God that relates the Spirit aggressively to the cosmic world and to man while it at the same time obscures the essential divinity of Jesus Christ as the eternal Son, does little for the orthodox view of the Trinity. Process theology tends to concentrate on a dipolar activity in God in relation to the cosmic world and focuses more readily on a lively doctrine of the Spirit than on christological concerns.

Robert Neville attempts, on the basis of process philosophy, to vindicate a doctrine of the Holy Spirit that retains certain biblical functions and traditional orthodox language. We are to contemplate reality, Neville emphasizes, not in terms of enduring substances, but rather in terms of events in process. At the same time he disavows Whitehead's doctrine of God as inadequate and unacceptable, and proposes to modify it. Every event, Neville tells us, has double causation. The ground of all events is past events together with the spontaneously creative transcendent God; but God as immanent, he says, is the ground of each particular event. God's active presence in the world—which Neville declares a basic proposition of all reality and life—he characterizes as the Holy Spirit.

Such metaphysical representations of the Holy Spirit, observes Gordon Kaufman, are vague, general and abstract. Neville provides so little ontological information that the Spirit barely escapes being mythical. With scant effort one could superimpose upon the same cosmic data quite different conceptions having no biblical content. How can such vague predications based on factors that readily accommodate rival expositions be turned into truth-claims that disallow conflicting views? If Neville offers only a tentative theory, adaptable to competing views of processes and events—e.g., Marxist, humanist and religious—between which we must necessarily and indefinitely postpone a final decision, are we not then dealing simply with a choice between myths? Christian theology has historically professed to make ontological truth-claims about the supernatural and to speak definitively concerning the being, nature and work of the triune God. Neville, on the other hand, accents the Spirit's *that*ness but ignores the *what* and *who*.

To be sure, Neville considers God's existence and character to be present in all his creation, present in the *what* of both antecedent events and of present spontaneous creation. But where in this process does one infer the Spirit's character from past and new events in respect to the origin and role of each event? Is a valid conclusion possible the morning after the Hebrew exile? The afternoon of Jesus' crucifixion? In the midst of Auschwitz? If God is an aspect of all experience, and cannot be causally and creatively absent from any, can we any longer invoke his causation and creativity to distinguish between experiences? If the Holy Spirit is causally involved in all creative changes, what objective distinction any longer obtains between the divine and the demonic? Pantheism, which relates the Holy Spirit to vice no less than to virtue, and makes God the cause of both good and evil, is dealt a death blow by the problem of evil. How in pantheism can a malevolent Satan confront the Holy Spirit or the Holy Spirit confront demonic spirits, since both the Spirit of Jesus and the demons he exorcises would need to be aspects of the same Spirit?

If one is unwilling to wait for all relevant data and to hold one's breath until the final triumph either of good or evil, one may venture an empirical appeal to flesh out one's postulations or conjectures. It is something quite different, however, to perceive both good and evil as the Holy Spirit's work—so different in fact, as to exclude being in any sense Christian.

Scripture, moreover, presents another hallmark of the Holy Spirit. The spirits, we are told, are to be tested by appropriate criteria. In Christian revelation the christological thoroughly infuses the character of the Holy Spirit, that is, the Spirit is revealed in Jesus. Far from being an indeterminate ontological reality the Holy Spirit is clearly identifiable in Christian exposition. The Spirit's witness to Christ, and the ethical fruit that the Spirit nurtures in life, are what distinguish the Holy Spirit from alien spirits. Scripture delineates the Spirit in relation to God's creative activity, his redemptive activity, and his eschatological goal. While Neville at times relates the Spirit to God's intentionality, such references do not become epistemologically decisive for him.

In summary, Neville's attempts to expound a doctrine of the Holy Spirit on the basis of modified process theology gain Christian overtones only because Neville selectively borrows biblical language and develops his theory in correlation with preferred biblical emphases. The central features of his process philosophy could just as readily be expounded in terms of philosophical alternatives that dispense with the biblical Creator-Redeemer God. The selective use of biblical categories serves to commend process philosophy by focusing on the Holy Spirit as a traditional Christian motif familiar to those whose language and thought are scripturally conditioned. To state the theory abstractly on its own terms would quickly forfeit this potential religious interest. Here and there to supplement the conjectural and merely speculative with borrowed biblical features without allowing scriptural revelation at the same time to criticize the speculative, however, does violence to the biblical data by accommodating it to alien alternatives. If we presume to speak for biblical theology, we have no right to hypothesize a Creator *ex nihilo* who created some other world than the biblical cosmos, or who created no world at all; the world of which Elohim is creator has as determinate a character as Elohim himself. To depict the God of creation as less determinate than Scripture indicates only prepares the way for a merely conjectural deity spuriously clad in the royal robes of the living Lord, and hardly undergirds a plausible reflection of the Christian revelation of the Holy Spirit.

Indeed, if Whitehead's conception of God is unsatisfactory, no less so are the alternatives proposed by an adjusted process theology. Process theology adduces no persuasive considerations for requiring that God be personal; in the absence of divine self-revelation, it cannot effectively refute Buddhist and other nontheistic claims that personal characterization of the absolute falsifies the nature of reality.

When professedly Christian theological circles venture to expound a view of the Holy Spirit on the basis of process philosophy and not on the basis of supernatural revelation, their efforts usually betray several doubts— about a transcendent supernatural realm, about the reality of cognitive revelation, and in particular about the serviceability of Scripture as a source of authoritative doctrine. Yet they make no clean break with Christianity since process theology borrows an indispensable role for the Holy Spirit from revealed theology. The current trend that makes natural theology a starting point for discussion of the divine Spirit leads in other directions, however, none in firm contact with the biblical data and none sufficiently substantive to avoid a relapse to skepticism.

Robert W. Jenson thinks that spirit is a universal historical religious phenomenon, one which he proposes to particularize and refine into the Holy Spirit of the believing Christian community. The boldness of Jenson's proposal is evident when one recalls that even Thomas Aquinas grounded trinitarian discussion in special revelation rather than in natural theology and professed to derive from natural theology not *what* God is but only *that* he is. The difficulties of Jenson's proposals are also apparent. How does one get from the presence of spirit-in-every-community to the presence of "a spirit"? How can Jenson's easy transition from phenomenological language to statements of biblical language be justified? How are we to

leap from analysis of experience to transcendent ontology? Jenson sometimes speaks of the Holy Spirit adjectivally, sometimes as creative vitality,
sometimes substantially as a power or thing, and sometimes vaguely even
as person. He does not consider the Spirit an eternal personal entity, however, and projects a merely functional trinity. What is noteworthy is that
while Jenson touches base with scriptural elements, at many points un-
steadily, however, he thinks philosophical reasoning independent of revelation can arrive at a valid conception of the Spirit. It is not surprising that
Jenson's effort vacillates between human spirit, holy spirit and the Holy
Spirit; least satisfactory is his exposition of the Holy Spirit which lacks
firm ties to the biblical data and smacks of Hegel and Pannenberg.

According to apostolic testimony, the New Testament church would not
exist were it not for the Holy Spirit whose creative work and presence
among believers contrast markedly with the Spirit's involvement elsewhere. While the New Testament assuredly sets out with a view of the
Spirit essentially like that of the Old Testament, that is, with forefront
emphasis on the Spirit as God's special powerful activity, yet the Spirit's
relationship to Jesus Christ—no less than to God the Father—requires his
personal reality. The Bible, moreover, sharply contrasts the Holy Spirit
with evil spirits, especially with Satan. On what basis does Jenson propose
to handle this distinction other than by doubts about the existence of evil
spirits? If one spirit is a delusion, why not the other? Jenson's epistemology
cannot safeguard against this further extension. The New Testament declares the Holy Spirit to be "the Spirit of truth" whose authenticity is evident from the Spirit's testimony to Jesus Christ. The choice between spirits
made by the Christian community is therefore one that the Holy Spirit
desires all communities to make. The Bible nowhere depicts the Holy Spirit's redemptive ministry as an automatic universal phenomenon; excite-
ment in the New Testament about the Spirit's presence would vanish were
the Spirit's absence not in some sense also a very real possibility.

Cyril C. Richardson's *The Doctrine of the Trinity* illustrates the intellectual confusion and poverty that besets modernist efforts to salvage remnants of a trinitarian faith. On the one hand, Richardson unjustifiably
criticizes the traditional trinitarian formulation as being riddled with contradiction; on the other he boldly defends his own contemporary alternative
(Godhead not as three persons in one essence but as Absolute and Related,
that is, as the One and the One related to the Many) on the premise that
thinking about God necessarily involves paradox and logical contradiction.
Richardson unhesitatingly promotes the doctrine that Jesus is God on the
ground that this affirmation is a self-contradictory paradox, one that calls
nonetheless for faith and commitment (*ibid.,* pp. 15 ff.).

The Christian doctrine of the Trinity, however, intends nothing less than
three persons—Father, Son and Holy Spirit—existing eternally and co-
equally within the one divine essence. To this doctrine objections have
been voiced from three standpoints:

(1. That the doctrine is self-contradictory, since it assertedly involves

the conflicting notions that God is one but that God is also three. We have already indicated the fallacy of this argument, and have noted that some modern theologians consider logical contradiction the special merit of their alternatives.

(2. That the doctrine presupposes the Aristotelian definition of substance, and therefore depends for its exposition upon the debatable philosophy of metaphysical realism. But, as already shown, biblical trinitarianism by no means necessarily depends on a realistic philosophy of spiritual substance; in any event no religious epistemology has anything to gain from the notion of an underlying essence totally beyond human comprehension. There is, in fact, good reason to question the notions that an impersonal spirit substance underlies the divine persons and attributes, and that an impersonal soul substance underlies the nature of man. We shall more fully discuss tripersonality and personal essence in the following chapter.

(3. That the doctrine of the Trinity belongs to the history of dogma rather than to biblical theology. We must therefore ask whether this fundamental Christian tenet takes its rise only from the history of ecclesiastical thought, or is rooted in the history of special divine self-revelation.

Trinitarianism unquestionably belongs to the best theological traditions spanning almost two millennia of Christian thought. Emil Brunner, who carries forward the nineteenth-century modernist bias against locating trinitarian theology in the Bible, readily acknowledges that the Reformers affirm it, as well as Augustine and other medieval theologians. For that reason Brunner himself gives special emphasis to the doctrine, not indeed as a "biblical doctrine" (let alone as "revealed doctrine"!) but as the most respected theological framework for comprehending the self-revelation of God (*The Christian Doctrine of God,* pp. 205–240).

"The history of Christian theology and of dogma," Brunner writes, "teaches us to regard the dogma of the Trinity as the distinctive element in the Christian Idea of God . . . which distinguishes it from the Idea of God in Judaism and in Islam, and . . . in all forms of rational Theism" (*ibid.,* p. 205). Instead of emphasizing three eternal persons in one essence, Brunner emphasizes "*three* Names—Father, Son and the Holy Spirit" in which "the *One* God makes *His* Name known to us" (*ibid.,* p. 209). Declaring that the "deepest content" of the doctrine of the Trinity is its identification of the self-revealing God as Father, Son and Spirit, Brunner nonetheless insists that even in his revelation God is clothed in mystery, so that we are forbidden to think of God as he is in himself (*Revelation and Reason,* p. 47). The trinitarian statements are meant, says Brunner, to assure us that in Jesus we encounter the self of the holy and merciful Lord (*ibid.,* p. 114).

Unlike Barth, Brunner refuses to begin the doctrine of God by expositing the doctrine of the Trinity; the holiness and love of God, says Brunner, are known by divine revelation whereas the doctrine of the Trinity "springs from reflection upon this process" (*ibid.,* p. 237). We need not stop here to ask how Brunner knows the doctrine of divine holiness and love without

reflection; indeed, we might even add that a little more reflection upon
the biblical revelation would preclude the objectionable neoorthodox subordination of divine holiness to love.

Although Brunner has no sympathy for the doctrine of three eternal
persons existing "side by side" he denies espousing only a modal doctrine
of triunity. Indifferent to biblical representations such as John 1:1 and
Matthew 28:19, Brunner defines the Christian doctrine of the Trinity as
that of persons one "behind" the other. He therefore shifts emphasis from
the immanent ontological Trinity, interior to the nature of God, to an economic Trinity of functional manifestation.

There is no doubt that the terms essence and person, which early Christianity employed in formulating the doctrine of the Trinity, are not used
in the Bible itself. But that does not cancel the doctrine's origin in the
Scriptures or make it the product of church history. If evangelical theology
consisted only of a rearrangement of the Bible's original words there could
be no exposition of Scripture. The basic issue is not whether theologians
confine themselves to the vocabulary of Scripture, but whether the biblical
revelation of God logically involves the doctrine of the ontological Trinity.

Barth's treatment is in some ways remarkably different from Brunner's,
although the difference is not as absolute as might at first appear. Whereas
Brunner discusses trinitarianism as a supplement to the doctrine of God,
Barth discusses it as preliminary and introductory to the doctrine. Trinitarianism supplies, in fact, the structure and substance of Barth's religious
epistemology. Barth considers the Trinity the very movement of divine
self-revelation, the form and content of the knowledge of God. Perhaps it
would be as accurate to say that for Barth religious epistemology and trinitarian doctrines are one, as to say that his exposition of the doctrine of
God concentrates first and foremost on the Trinity.

Barth's theology of dynamic revelation allows us to speak only of God-
in-disclosure, and not of God-in-himself. Because he admits no objectively
valid theological assertions, Barth obscures the ontological or essential
Trinity and turns interest instead on a trinity of manifestation. Barth disavows a merely modal trinity, however, and insists that God's self-revelation as Father, Son and Spirit unveils the eternal Trinity. But he compromises this exposition by the fact that in principle his dynamic view of
revelation disowns knowledge of God in his transcendent being and speaks
only of God in relations to man. Discussion of the ontological Trinity is
ruled out by the metaphysical agnosticism of an antiintellectualist theology
of decision.

Barth's reluctance to speak of three persons in the Godhead follows from
the fact that the modern term "person" suggests discrete individuality or
three juxtaposed beings and hence tritheism. This avoidance of a descriptive term especially preferred by historic Christian theology flows therefore
from philosophical considerations rather than from theological prejudices;
the motivation for avoiding the term is not antitrinitarian. Barth prefers
to speak of three modes of existence, but repudiates modalism. Yet what
prevents both Barth and Brunner from expounding the doctrine of the

Trinity in historic biblical dimensions is their shared exclusion of objective cognitive revelation by which God conveys valid information about his nature and personhood.

For Barth divine self-revelation is triune in content and form, and God's being should therefore not be discussed apart from God's triunity. Barth is right in resisting a divine being or essence ontologically distinguishable from divine personality and knowable apart from God's selfhood; only non-biblical motives would require us to speak of God's existence before we discuss his nature disclosed in divine revelation. But when Barth identifies revelation as interpersonal redemptive confrontation he deprives divine disclosure of both its form of general or universal revelation, and its content of valid objective information about God's attributes. To be sure, all discussion of God, insofar as it has revelational license, centers in God's disclosure of himself—his names and activities; his larger self-revelation, moreover, leaves no doubt that it is the triune God with whom we have had to do in all divine disclosure. But Barth's refusal to discuss the nature of God apart from the Trinity stems in part from an inadequate view of what is meant by divine revelation as personal, and from an epistemology which if consistently applied would demand metaphysical agnosticism concerning God's objective perfections. Divine revelation, while it is indeed revelation of the triune God, may also convey objective information; it may manifest God's "eternal power and divine nature" (Rom. 1:20, NIV) or his righteous judgment (Rom. 1:32) as in the case of general revelation. As special revelation it may focus at times mainly on the incarnation (Matt. 1:22 ff.) or on the work of the Spirit (Acts 2) or of the Father (Matt. 6:9 ff.). Yet this expanded revelational content does not justify postponing discussion of the Trinity until after exposition of the being of God has been completed, or discounting the Trinity as integral to divine self-disclosure.

Brunner treats the doctrine as only a theological appendage to biblical revelation; he consigns it to postbiblical reflection rather than to New Testament teaching or to the very nature of God known in his self-disclosure. So too, in keeping with the antipathy of many personal idealists toward an ontological Trinity, Knudson considers the theme of tripersonality in only a marginal way. But if the doctrine of divine incarnation in Jesus Christ is truly regarded as the high point of divine self-revelation, then it is difficult to postpone the question of a plurality of persons in the one God until after discussion about the divine essence. If systematic theology, moreover, closely follows the example of biblical theology in expounding progressive divine self-disclosure in the revelation of God's personal names, then it least of all can afford to forego the gospel narrative emphasis on the name of the "Father, Son, and Holy Spirit" (Matt. 28:19).

There is good reason within the evangelical exposition of the doctrine of God, however, to postpone full discussion of the triune God in terms of the personal names, or of distinctive centers of divine consciousness and volition, until after the proper names and attributive names of God have been examined. The generic name of God, and his attributive names (or attributes), are common to the entire Godhead, and hence pertain to all three divine persons; the personal distinctions, on the other hand, are made within the unity of the Godhead. In discussing God's being, it is therefore proper to proceed first to the generic and proper names, and attributive names, and then finally to the personal names of God. The attributes are perfections without which the living God would cease to be God; they are not predicates of God, such as creator, preserver, ruler, which concern his divine relationship to the created universe. Nor are the attributes properties, applicable only to one or another person of the Trinity; the divine perfections apply equally to the Father, the Son, and the Spirit.

Over against those who contend that the doctrine of the Trinity is a speculative doctrine not essential to the Christian message, and that it arose after the New Testament was written, Arthur W. Wainwright contends that the doctrine emerges in the New Testament and has its roots "in the worship, experience, and thought of first-century Christianity" (*The Trinity in the New Testament,* p. vii). "It would be misleading," Wainwright insists, "to say that trinitarian theology is entirely post-biblical" (*ibid.,* p. 5). The problem of the Trinity "did not first occur when later generations of thinkers reflected on the scriptures" (*ibid.,* p. 265).

The clear impress of the threefold formula appears even in Paul's earlier letters (1 Cor. 12:4–6; 2 Cor. 13:14). Passages naming the three divine persons occur in the non-Pauline literature as well (cf. 1 Pet. 1:2; Titus 3:4–6). Yet, Wainwright contends, while "a strong body of evidence . . . shows that the writers of the New Testament were influenced in thought and expression by the triad 'Father, Son, and Holy Spirit' " neither the above passages nor similar ones that reflect the triadic pattern in Paul's letters or in Hebrews, Peter, Jude and Revelation conveys "any clear doctrinal implications about the relationship between Father, Son and Spirit" (*ibid.,* pp. 245 ff.). Wainwright contends that despite Matthew's attribution of it to Jesus (Matt. 28:19), the threefold baptismal formula was probably "developed in the early Church and was later ascribed to Jesus" (*ibid.,* p. 240).

Oscar Cullmann holds that the New Testament contains triadic liturgical formulas but not confessions of trinitarian faith (*Earliest Christian Confessions,* p. 36). The New Testament confessions of faith, he contends, have in view either Christ or God and Christ (e.g., 1 Cor. 8:6). Yet formal credal confession or not, the New Testament data leaves no doubt that the early Christians believed in the Father, the Son and the Spirit (1 Cor. 12:4–6; Rom 15:30; Eph. 3:14 ff.; Phil. 3:3). The writers take for granted, moreover, that their Christian readers will grasp the meaning of the juxtaposed names Father, Son and Spirit.

C. K. Barrett declares that "more than any other New Testament writer" John "lays the foundation for a doctrine of a co-equal Trinity" (*The Gospel according to St. John,* p. 78). Wainwright emphasizes that no formal statement of the doctrine of the Trinity appears in the New Testament, yet that aspects of the doctrine emerge as a problem in the Pauline and Johannine writings and in Hebrews. Only the Fourth Gospel has a deliberately conscious trinitarian doctrine: "Paul and the author of Hebrews did not see the problem as threefold. They concentrated on the relationship between Christ and God. . . . The Fourth Evangelist . . . was conscious of a threefold problem of the mutual relationships of Father, Son and Spirit" (*ibid.,* pp. 266 f.). The Fourth Gospel, Wainwright observes, carefully differentiates the Father and the Son while insisting that Jesus is God, and moreover differentiates the Father, the Son and the Spirit in a manner that indicates an awareness of "the trinitarian problem" of divine interpersonal relationships (*The Trinity in the New Testament,* pp. 248 f.). Other New Testament writers "show trends in the direction of a threefold pattern of thought," but the Fourth Gospel alone goes beyond mention of a threefold formula only as "the background of worship and thought" and beyond deliberate emphasis on the triad "Father, Son and Spirit" to a further recognition of "the problem of their relationship" and an attempted explanation (*ibid.,* p. 250).

Wainwright asserts that, although Jesus "is deeply conscious of his relationship to the Father and speaks occasionally about the Spirit," nowhere in the synoptic gospels except in Matthew 28:19 whose authenticity Wainwright questions "is the close association of Father, Son and Spirit . . . prominent in his thinking." The "threefold pattern" is indeed present in the synoptic narratives, but no articulation of trinitarianism is found that involves the divinity of Son and Spirit and a special interaction between Father and Spirit and Son and Spirit. The apostle Paul attempts an answer, says Wainwright, "to the Christological core of the trinitarian problem" in 1 Corinthians 8:6 and 15:24 f. and in Philippians 2:5–11, but "he has not clarified the relation of the Father and the Son" (*ibid.,* p. 260). Wainwright suggests that Paul may have thought about this aspect more than he wrote about it, but his epistles show no awareness of "a threefold problem."

But says Wainwright, the Fourth Evangelist, by contrast, sees the "nature of the triadic problem" and supplies "the supreme biblical pattern of trinitarian thought. . . . His answer does not cope with all complexities. . . . There was much room for development and explanation" (*ibid.,* p. 260). The Johannine passages that mention the Father, Son and Holy Spirit side by side are well known: 1:33 f., 14:16, 14:26, 16:15, 20:21 f. (cf. also 1 John 4:2, 4:13 f.). Additional passages refer to the Son and the Spirit: 7:39, 16:7. "There is sufficient consecutiveness," says Wainwright, to consider the relationship of the Father, Son and Spirit as "one of the major themes of the gospel." The Fourth Gospel, he adds, "approached more nearly to the trinitarian position than any other writing of the New Testament" (*ibid.,* p. 263). "The Fourth Evangelist goes further than any other New Testament writer in stressing the fact that Jesus is God, and that the Spirit is a person whose functions are not wholly identical with those of Father and Son. Moreover he works out more fully than any other New Testament writer the relationship between Father and Son. All these matters lay the foundation of trinitarian theology. . . . There is no doctrine of a co-equal Trinity in the gospel but only the foundations" (*ibid.,* pp. 264 ff.).

Yet "a biblical doctrine of God can begin with an account of the names and title of Father, Son and Spirit, and their divine functions and mutual relationships," Wainwright comments. "Such an account of the Three in One cannot be summarized in a pithy formula, but its lack of rigid technical vocabulary and the absence of the word 'Trinity' do not rob it of the status of doctrine" (*ibid.*, p. 266).

The triadic references in Matthew, while not a dominating theme, Wainwright concedes, "occur at crucial moments in the gospel story, from the initial baptism of Jesus to the closing climactic baptismal formula" (*ibid.*, p. 252). We would note, moreover, that since John prominently reports Jesus' teaching that the Spirit's activity must await his crucifixion and resurrection (John 16:7), a basis exists in the larger teaching of Jesus for the content of the final great commission. While Matthew reflects no awareness of "trinitarian problems" involving Father-Son relationships, does it follow that he uses the triadic formula with implications of worship and practice but without a deeper theological intention? Luke's Gospel closes with the Son's anticipation of his sending of the Spirit in fulfillment of the Father's promise (Luke 24:49) and is compatible with the emphasis of Matthew's postresurrection commission. If in the Great Commission attributed to the crucified and risen Jesus we have an apostolic or postapostolic intrusion of beliefs that Jesus did not share, and the ascription to him of a statement alien to his teaching, why should we take as authentic other teaching that the narrative attributes to the Nazarene? The fact that the writers do not expressly and systematically articulate detailed relationships between the three persons need not indicate that they have less than a trinitarian theological commitment. Presuppositions and incidental references can be as important in identifying beliefs as is didactic teaching.

We credit Wainwright for recognizing that the progressive nature of New Testament revelation required a gradual articulation of trinitarian faith, even as the historical revelation of God in Old Testament times. We commend him, moreover, for patient probing of the biblical data, for insisting that trinitarian doctrine has an explicit basis in the Fourth Gospel, and not simply in postbiblical teaching. Wainwright correctly emphasizes that while John uses none of the technical metaphysical terms of later trinitarian discussion, he nevertheless states the essentials of the doctrine of the Trinity, namely, that the Father and the Son both are God, that they are one, and that the Father has priority over the Son, even though in discussing the Spirit in relation to the Son, John does not expressly say that the Spirit is God (*The Trinity in the New Testament,* p. 265). Absence from all New Testament sources of the term "trinity" does indeed indicate that the task remained of fully organizing and explaining the biblical teaching. But Wainwright rests New Testament grounding for trinitarian doctrine onesidedly on the Fourth Gospel and achieves this view too much at the expense of Pauline representations.

Furthermore, in examining John's trinitarian views he stresses John's inner experience and reflection and the devotional practices of the Christian community more than revelation: "The main reason for John's distinctive contribution to trinitarian thought is his own genius, which led him to investigate the nature of God" (*ibid.,* p. 265). In that event, although Wainwright carries back to Scripture the essentials of the later doctrine, its limitation to the Fourth Gospel can only raise questions, while the clouding of the role of divine self-revelation in respect to the doctrine would tend to anchor its features in John's private ruminations.

Christian experience and reflection will commend the doctrine of the Trinity, but religious experience—Christian or otherwise—is not its source. Leonard Hodgson notes that Clement C. J. Webb (*God and Personality*) and H. Wheeler Robinson (*The Christian Experience of the Holy Spirit*) both base their theology of the divine persons on an analysis of religious experience, yet reach very different conclusions. This divergence, Hodgson observes and rightly, follows from differing philosophical assumptions that scholars bring to experience. Hodgson, moreover, renders the intellectual validity of the doctrine of the Trinity unsure by identifying revelation only with divine acts repeated in successive generations; he derives the doctrine, in turn, from an interpretation of the biblical representations that has the character of inner certainty but not of obligatory revealed truth (*The Doctrine of the Trinity,* pp. 25 ff.).

Even so, John's supposed nonmention of the deity of the Spirit would involve binitarian doctrine rather than trinitarianism. Wainwright concludes his study on the disappointing note that "it is a matter of private taste whether to use the description 'Doctrine of the Trinity' for the teaching combined in certain parts of the New Testament or to reserve this description for later writings" (*ibid.,* p. 266).

Yet J. N. D. Kelley insists that even "if trinitarian creeds are rare, the trinitarian pattern which was to dominate all later creeds was already part and parcel of the Christian tradition of doctrine" (*Early Christian Creeds,* p. 23).

The fact that the Fourth Gospel, for all its clarity and precision in formulating the doctrine of the Spirit, does not reflect the Pauline emphasis on life in the Spirit but only intimates and anticipates it (14:7, 23–27), suggests that Johannine hints of the divinity of the Spirit (cf. John 14:26, concerning the one whom the Father is to send in Jesus' name) would likewise gain fuller clarity through postresurrection realities. If God is to be present in the Spirit no less than he was manifest in the Nazarene, the Spirit's divinity is clearly implied.

For the New Testament the decisive triad is indubitably God the Father, Christ and the Spirit. All other Old Testament *hypostases* alongside God— particularly Word and Wisdom—channel into Christ. Wainwright criticizes what he conceives to be Paul's failure to distinguish clearly between the indwelling Christ and the indwelling Spirit (*The Trinity in the New Testament,* p. 260). But Paul actually reflects a special correlation and interchangeability already taught by the Gospels. Not only was Jesus conceived of the Spirit (Matt. 1:18; Luke 12:10), but blasphemy against Jesus is also the sin against the Holy Spirit (Mark 3:29 ff.). Even in his independence the Spirit is therefore linked with Christ (cf. Ethelbert Stauffer, *"Theos:* The Uniqueness of God," *TDNT,* 3:107 ff.). Not only Paul but John too (1

John 2:1; John 14:16) reflects this interchangeability. In fact, Paul not only takes cognizance of this interchangeability but, as Stauffer notes, leaves no doubt that the Father, Son and Holy Spirit are all "linked in an indissoluble threefold relation" (*ibid.*, p. 108).

If in its concentration on incarnational revelation John's Gospel does not specifically affirm the Holy Spirit's divinity, Matthew 12:31, Mark 3:28 ff. and Luke 12:10 all record Jesus' statement that blasphemy against the Son of Man can be forgiven, but not blasphemy against the Holy Spirit. And the apostle Paul implies nothing less than the Spirit's divine personality when he emphasizes to the Jews in Rome (Acts 28:25) that the One who revealed to Isaiah the divine warning against the spiritual callousness of the Hebrews was none other than the Holy Spirit.

9.
The Doctrine of the Trinity

ANCIENT JUDAISM KNEW that God is one, is spirit, is eternal and unchanging. The Old Testament revelation of God exalts the oneness of the living personal God and disdains the polytheism of pagan religions. That "The Lord our God is one Lord" (Deut. 6:4) is the first truth the Bible declares about the nature of God. The early Christians were Jews who without exception and without compromise shared this revealed faith in monotheism and its horror of polytheism.

At the heart of Christianity's revelation of God is a trinitarian form of monotheism. That the living God is triune—that three eternal persons coexist within the one divine essence—is the distinctive Christian affirmation about deity. Alongside the proper names of God and his perfectional names the Bible arrays the personal names Father, Son and Holy Spirit. The doctrine of the Trinity is Christianity's unique declaration concerning the divine being and is definitive for Christian theism.

Modern philosophy, in the main, has opposed the doctrine of divine personality. To be sure, Descartes, Leibniz, Locke, Berkeley, not to mention Malebranche, Pascal, and later Catholic and Protestant philosophers, are exceptions. But philosophers debating the personality of God have shown a preference either for divine impersonality or superpersonality. At most they have allowed the unipersonality of God. Ascription of personality has been thought to limit or degrade the Infinite. This notion of the incompatibility of divine infinity and divine personality is not confined to early Greek philosophy; modern philosophers including Spinoza and many post-Hegelians and more recently Paul Tillich have shared it, and, wittingly or unwittingly, have prepared the way for a naturalistic alternative to biblical theism.

The life and ministry of Jesus Christ, the events of Pentecost and the inspired apostolic interpretation of this revelational history pressed the

191

early church irresistibly to a supreme affirmation about God. The resurrection of the crucified Jesus that vindicated his claim to be the messianic Son of God posed the live options either of affirming personal distinctions in the Godhead, revising bare Judaic theism in a new modal form, or, and this was absolutely unthinkable, sponsoring a new version of pagan polytheism.

The New Testament offers no retreat from affirming the deity of Jesus Christ. The inspired apostolic writings give us the narrative of the historical self-revelation of the Logos, only Son of God and the Messiah of the Old Testament prophecy. Explicitly or implicitly, the Gospels in their entirety teach the supernaturalness of Jesus Christ.

In the conversation where Jesus quotes the Shema he queries the scribes about the person of whom David spoke when, "inspired by the Holy Spirit," he declared, "The Lord said to my Lord, sit at my right hand, till I put thy enemies under my feet" (Mark 12:36, RSV; cf. Ps. 110:1). As Charles F. D. Moule comments, "David calls the Messiah 'my lord'; how, then, can that Messiah be David's junior, his son? The answer intended by Jesus would seem to be, 'Because, although he is his son by descent . . . he is also, in some mysterious way, superior to David and therefore his senior in rank.' It was a way of saying that the Messiah is more than an ordinary human descendant of a Jewish royal house . . ." (*The Gospel According to Mark*, p. 99). While Jesus instructs the disciples to address God in prayer as "our Father," he himself by way of contrast speaks to God only as "my Father" to whom as "the Son" he stands in an absolutely unique relationship (cf. Matt. 6:9; John 20:17, "I ascend unto my Father, and your Father; and to my God, and your God"). Jesus claims divine power and authority, even to forgive sin (Mark 2:7), and affirms that he will sit upon God's throne to judge the world (Rom. 14:10; 2 Cor. 5:10). Although he fulfills divine functions and is very God come in the flesh, he does not, however, replace God; the title, Son of God, makes this plain. He is at once both God's representative in human history, and himself God.

In John 5:17–41 we sense the dramatic atmosphere of destiny-laden decision that confronted Jesus' contemporaries. Yet for Christianity the conviction of the deity of Jesus Christ is not merely an inference drawn by his contemporaries from his remarkable claims and works; nor does it rest ultimately on the believer's present-day internal spiritual encounter with the living Christ. The supreme basis for affirming Christ's deity lies in divine revelation, especially in the propositional content recorded in the inspired New Testament writings; earlier the promise of Messiah to come had been conveyed in the inspired Old Testament writings.

The Word become flesh (John 1:14) was the Word who, in his preexistence, was "with God" and veritably "was God" (John 1:1). In a religious heritage that banned creaturely images of God the Word is declared the Father's "very image" (2 Cor. 4:4; Col. 1:15; Heb. 1:3). He is to be honored equally with the Father (John 5:23); refusal to honor him therefore dishonors the Father also (John 5:24). Although Christ's adversaries considered his overt claim to deity (Matt. 26:63; John 5:18, 10:36) blasphemous, Christ's followers heralded the resurrection as vindication of his claim to be the promised Messiah and veritable Son of God (Rom. 1:4; Phil. 2:8 ff.); they accordingly worshiped him as Lord and God (Titus 2:13).

Because of its irrefutable conviction of Christ's deity, the Christian community was impelled either to affirm polytheism, to affirm a modal view of the self-revealing God, or to affirm coexisting personal distinctions in the Godhead.

For a brief time the question of a plurality of persons seemed to make binitarianism the alternative to unitarianism. The problem of divine personality soon expanded beyond this alternative, however. Since the question of Jesus Christ was inseparable from that of the Holy Spirit, the early church was almost immediately called upon to face the question of trinitarianism. In the progress of special revelation, even before the Spirit was fully given (Acts 2; cf. John 7:39), the Son was manifested as God's historical gift (John 3:16). Launching his earthly ministry in his own fullness of the Spirit (Luke 4:1), Jesus prepared his followers for the Spirit's dramatic manifestation to them at Pentecost (Acts 1:5). Jesus' own teaching (cf. John 14:28) and the Spirit-breathed apostolic proclamation and writings (cf. 2 Tim. 3:16) fix the issue in larger than binitarian dimensions.

Yet the decision that first faced our Lord's contemporaries was clearly one for or against the truth of his messiahship and deity. The Christian believers were convinced that rejection of the deity of Christ requires also repudiating the sending God of Old Testament promise (cf. John 5:23 ff., 9:7). Anyone indifferent to fulfillment of the ancient prophecies in Jesus of Nazareth must sooner or later be embarrassed by the Old Testament promises of messianic redemption. For this reason Judaism, having rejected Jesus as the Christ, easily exchanges its orthodox heritage for a bare ethical theism that espouses essentially a works-salvation and repudiates substitutionary atonement. The Jews' earlier emphasis that their survival through many historical hostilities evidenced God's special providence gave way after Auschwitz; many succumbed to ethical humanism and even to atheism, although the later regathering of Israel reinforced orthodox Jews in their original conviction of Yahweh's covenantal care. Jewry's deliberate rejection of Christianity has isolated and preserved the race but has also exposed the Jews to ready persecution. The New Testament writers insist, however, that the gospel of Christ fulfills the Hebrew prophetic promises and is intended first of all for the Jew; a revived Jewry, they declare, will one day participate in the benefits of Christ the Messiah. Many evangelicals see a token of eschatological development in the fact that today the United States alone has about 10,000 Christian Jews.

For those who lived contemporaneously with Jesus the initial decision may have seemed at first to involve a choice between abstract monotheism and binitarianism, and not yet trinitarianism. Unlike the early Christians, we who live this side of the first century have the complete scriptural record which as a unit presents the progressive drama of divine revelation; here we see God unveiled in the public ministry, crucifixion, and resurrection of his eternal Son who then poured out the Holy Spirit upon the church. By intimations in the teaching of Jesus, by the events of Pentecost, and then by the inspired teaching of the apostles, the early Christians were left no consistent option but to affirm that three eternal centers of consciousness coexist in the Godhead.

Old Testament revelation ruled out for the Christian movement any commitment to the polytheistic doctrine of two or more gods. Hebrew devotion to the one God and its horror of polytheism permeate both the Old and the New Testaments. That God is one is the foundational theme of both Testaments. Jesus himself unreservedly approved and quoted the Shema, the prayer spoken morning and evening by every pious Jew and the opening call to temple worship (Mark 12:29 ff.). He sharpened the monotheistic stance of the Jews by making obedience to the living God crucial for the good life and by himself depending upon God in every personal decision and action. He even turns aside the address "Good Master" with the retort that "no one is good—except God alone" (Mark 10:18, NIV). The Christian apostles condemned polytheism with all their might, and as the divine alternative to it proclaimed the religion of Christ as the pristine fulfillment of Hebrew monotheism. Christian choice was therefore not between monotheism and polytheism, but between two kinds of monotheism. The texts which the Sabellians and Arians later invoked against trinitarianism were in fact long-favored Christian verses for the one true and living God.

In confessing Jesus Christ's essential deity, the Christian community did more than just affirm the reality of the one God against pagan polytheism. It also opposed representing the one God in terms of a skeletal theism implied by the Judaism of that day, and anticipatively also by Mohammedanism, and modern philosophical theism and religious Unitarianism. As Arthur W. Wainwright observes, ". . . Christ was not regarded as a Second God in the New Testament, he was regarded as God" (*The Trinity in the New Testament,* p. 7). He was worshiped as Lord and God by monotheists who lauded him in doxologies and considered him the divine agent in creation, salvation and judgment.

Abstract monotheism denies a plurality of persons in the Godhead, and tends to reject the deity of Jesus Christ because it insists that God's unity permits only one center of divine consciousness. Its advocates in predominantly Christian lands often say complimentary things about Jesus; sometimes they even convey a surface impression that Jesus is ontologically something special (early Unitarians argued that Christ is supernatural in his works although not in nature). But for the early Christian community, to deny the deity of Jesus Christ was tantamount to repudiating the one true and living God in his consummatory salvific activity. First-century Jewry knew that to reject Christ's claims required also, to be consistent, repudiating him as a blasphemer.

Jesus warned his hearers, however, that their choice was not between monotheism and blasphemy; it was between salvific monotheism and practical atheism: "He who does not honor the Son does not honor the Father, who sent him" (John 5:23, NIV). The alternative to dishonoring the Father was confessing Jesus Christ the divine Son as Savior and Lord. The Roman centurion's exclamation, "Surely he was the Son of God!" (Matt. 27:54, NIV), is the verdict of the entire New Testament.

The options that remained for early Christians were two: either regard the incarnate Son as some kind of modal manifestation of one ultimate Person, or contend for the existence of a plurality of divine persons in the one God. Addressing these concerns, the Nicene and Athanasian creeds delineated what biblical revelation requires us to say over against inadequate and false statements of Christian doctrine. The creeds left no doubt that the personal distinctions in God's nature in no way annul or threaten the unity of the divine essence. Just as in the great creation passage we find the plural Elohim with a singular verb used of the one God, so in the great commission passage we find "the name of the Father, and of the Son, and of the Holy Spirit."

Adolf Harnack and others have noted that the phrase "in the name" is a Jewish phrase with no equivalents in familiar Greek expressions. According to Charles W. Lowry, the Evangelist must have been aware both of "the sharp break with Judaism represented by including under a singular name not simply the Father, with the Jewish as well as Christian associations of such a term, but also the Son and the Holy Spirit"; he must have known also "the associations for all Jews of the 'Name' of the ancient *Shema:* 'Hear, O Israel: Jehovah our God is one Jehovah' " (*The Trinity and Christian Devotion,* p. 53).

The biblical doctrine of the Trinity carries no implication whatever of three gods, or even of a plurality of personal subdivisions or independent individuals within the one God. To be sure, the biblical writers did not use the terms that are commonplace in modern psychology, e.g. person, individual, personality, but they nonetheless employed the conceptions and Christian theology first articulated them. The Christian doctrine of the Trinity—whatever else is to be said about it—is a way of emphasizing the complex personal unity of the one living God. God is not one despite being tripersonal; he is essentially one God in whose inviolable unity three persons eternally coexist.

The Bible exhibits the progressive self-revelation of God. From the Genesis record onward, early anticipations gain increasing clarity in the course of an enlarging scriptural disclosure. The tendency of liberal theologians to assume that the doctrine of the Trinity is postbiblical has worked against a probing of trinitarian intimations in the Old Testament. But a number of studies—among them the monographs by A. R. Johnson (*The One and The Many in the Israelite Conception of God*) and G. A. F. Knight (*A Biblical Approach to the Doctrine of the Trinity*) have given new impetus to such investigation. Neither Johnson nor Knight finds in the Old Testament a veiled trinitarianism. But both nonetheless find that Old Testament conceptions of God are consummated in the New. Johnson argues rather imaginatively that the social extension of personality prevailing in the Hebrew conception of collective responsibility together with that of individual personality has its parallel in the name Elohim which while plural in form is singular in meaning. No less fancifully Knight contends that the Father-

Son principle operative in the Hebrew conception of covenant is an extension of an underlying fact of divine personality. Quite aside from the fact that Knight's discussion involves an artificial contrast of Hebrew and Greek thought-forms, the major obstacle to accepting his position is that the Old Testament nowhere views the nation Israel under the imagery of divine personality. Old Testament religion gives a basic role in faith and practice to the one God in the context of Elohim, the creator of all worlds and of man in his image; of Yahweh's redemptive revelation to be consummated in the messianic Son; and of the Spirit who renews and enlivens the people of God. The Old Testament nowhere considers angels and other created beings divine; a number of passages assign divine dignity to the Son of man, however, even if the prophetic word allows us to decipher little more than broad outlines of the incarnation of the Logos.

Only rudimentary intimations of trinitarian truth seem to appear in the Pentateuch, such as the first person plural pronouns ("Let us make . . ." Gen. 1:26); the plural form of the name of God, Elohim, used with a singular verb; and the threefold form of the divine benediction (Num. 6:24). Those who approach the Bible with other scriptural presuppositions can always view such intimations as remnants of an abandoned polytheism or as inconsistencies within an emerging monotheism. But these conclusions do not accord with the manner in which the Bible itself presents God in his self-disclosure, and depend upon critical premises alien to the Bible. Scripture provides no sanction whatever for the notion, for example, that the name Elohim is a remnant of polytheism and that Eloah is the only acceptable singular form. Wainwright surveys the passages in which God speaks of himself as plural (Gen. 1:26, 3:22, 11:7 and Isa. 6:8) and makes some striking observations. Written in the second century before Christ, the apocryphal Book of Jubilees, in telling the creation story (Jub. 2:14), deletes all reference to "let us make man in our image" and conforms the passage to rigid monotheism. Likewise its account of the expulsion from Eden deletes reference to man "become as one of us." These narratives as well as that of the tower of Babel passage are restated so as to eliminate any plural dimension in the Godhead. In the Targum, or Aramaic translation of the Old Testament used by Jews in the centuries before Christ, the plural pronoun is deleted from Isaiah 6:8. In short, Jewish postcanonical theology betrays a tendency to reconstruct these passages in the interest of a barren monotheism. While it would be anachronous to exegete the sublime "I am" (Exod. 3:6) into an exposition of trinitarian distinctions and all the divine attributes, its content became progressively manifest in the course of biblical history; finally in the incarnation of the Nazarene, the "I am" found appropriate and climactic embodiment in Jesus Christ.

The earliest books of the Old Testament identify both Yahweh and the angel of Yahweh, and distinguish between them; they also ascribe divine titles to them and enjoin worship (cf. Exod. 23:21, "my name is in him"). Isaiah 61:1 f. speaks at one and the same time of Yahweh and of his anointed messenger of salvation upon whom Yahweh's Spirit abides; in Mark 1:9 f. after the Holy Spirit descends upon Jesus at his baptism a heavenly voice confirms Jesus' divine sonship. God's messianic messenger is revealed step by step as a distinct divine personality being variously designated as the Word, the Wisdom and the Son of God. While he is said to be "of old," the Mighty God, the Adonai, the Lord of David, Jehovah our righteousness, yet he is to be born of a virgin and to bear the sins of many. Barth writes that "practically the whole of the attributes significant of the *Yahweh* of Israel"—righteousness, lovingkindness, faithfulness, glory, Word, Spirit, wisdom, "and also the 'countenance'. . . His 'arm,' His 'hand,' His 'right hand' . . . are from time to time given expression in such a way as though they were not only in or of *Yahweh* but simply *Yahweh* Himself in another way a second time" (*Church Dogmatics,* I/1, p. 363). The Bible requires a distinction between anthropomorphic passages that speak of God's "hand," "arm," "eyes," and so on, and ontological teaching that depicts personal distinctions in the nature of God. Those who consider the latter just as figurative as the former do so on interpretative principles that erode the reality of God. Scripture itself authorizes and requires a distinction between what we may say literally or figuratively about God.

The Hebrew revelation, moreover, not only uses the terms Elohim/*Theos* (God) and Yahweh/*Kurios* (Lord), but also refers the hypostases *logos*/Word, *sophia*/Wisdom and *pneuma*/Spirit to God. It presents them not as independent beings, yet nonetheless as *hypostases* alongside the living God and as subordinate deputies active in the creation and history of the universe. Over against created beings who have wills of their own and may even resist God, the *hypostases* are not simply divine representatives but personal realities whose being and that of the loving God are somehow integrated. In the Old Testament they do not appear in triune juxtaposition, however, and therefore only isolated questions arise over the relationship of Spirit to Yahweh, of Word to Yahweh, and of Wisdom to Yahweh. What is in view is plurality in the one Godhead, but not yet specifically trinitarian distinctions.

Without the fuller light of the New Testament, the Old Testament use of terms such as Word, Wisdom, Spirit, Son, would of itself leave us unsure whether two, three or more centers of consciousness exist within the one God. This question does not arise decisively until the incarnation of Christ, the promised Messiah, who then confronts the community of faith with a life-or-death decision. Any student of the parables can see how often Jesus applies metaphors to himself that the Old Testament conspicuously applies to God. In many instances Jesus claims to exercise functions that the Old Testament prophets ascribe only to God.

Both in early and late epistles the apostle Paul declares Jesus Christ to be God. Whether Romans 9:5 teaches that Christ is God has long been disputed; already in 1904 F. C. Burkitt commented that "the punctuation has probably been more discussed than that of any other sentence in literature" (*Journal of Theological Studies,* Vol. V, April, 1904, pp. 451–455). After a survey of Greek manuscripts, early translations, and the grammar and structure of the passage, Bruce M. Metzger concludes that "if one confines one's attention to the verse itself, the balance of probabilities favors refer-

ring *theos* to Christ" ("The Punctuation of Rom. 9:5," p. 109). Those who
argue that Paul nowhere in "genuine" Pauline letters calls Christ God,
resist this view, and then declare Titus 2:13 to be deutero-Pauline. But
even on this assumption, Raymond E. Brown holds, if the Pastoral Epistles
are "a homogeneous development . . . the usage in Tit. 2:13 *may* be interpreted as a continuation of Paul's own way of speaking already instanced
in Rom. 9:5" ("Does the New Testament Call Jesus God?", p. 560, n. 35).
As Metzger points out Paul does not hesitate to call Christ Lord of the
living and the dead (Rom. 14:9), the Lord of glory (1 Cor. 2:8), the one
through whom all things hold together (Col. 1:17), to whom all creatures
are to bow (Phil. 2:10); he is, moreover, the veritable image of God (2 Cor.
4:4, Col. 1:15) and the power and wisdom of God (1 Cor. 1:24). Paul represents
Christ as preexistent (Gal. 4:14; 2 Cor. 8:9), as being in the form of God
and having equality with God (Phil. 2:6). To this we may add that while
the Old and New Testaments alike find the basis of all moral obligation
in God himself, Paul depicts Christ who perfectly exhibits and fulfills God's
will; Christ is not only teacher and revealer, but also the very life of God
who is the source of our life; conformity to the image of Christ is conformity
to God.

Juxtaposition of the names of the Father and the Son and the Spirit in
the baptismal formula (Matt. 28:19) and in the apostolic benediction (2
Cor. 13:13) keeps the three personal names prominent before the people.
The passages that mention the divine persons imply personal equality,
voluntary subjection and dependence as well as other relationships unintelligible apart from personal distinctions in the divine nature. By addressing
three persons of the Godhead the apostolic benediction implies their distinct personality and common divinity. The threefold personal character
of God is indicated also in such passages as 2 Thessalonians 2:13, Romans
1:1–4 and 11–33, and 1 Peter 1:2.

This threefold emphasis that shaped the mind and experience of the
early Christians led to a view of God at once different from that of Judaism
and of paganism, yet which in many of its popular statements frequently
lacked precision in content and exposition. Unitarianism survives on the
misconception that, as Jack Mendelsohn puts it, "early Christianity was
neither Trinitarian nor Unitarian" (*Why I Am a Unitarian*, p. 43). But
to say that the New Testament makes no metaphysical claims about Jesus
Christ usually serves only to accommodate briefs for an antitrinitarian
ontology that appeals to Arius and Sabellius rather than to Paul and the
other apostles. Richard M. Vaughan writes, for example: "In the New Testament we find a Trinity of experience. It is later theological speculation
which gives us technical, metaphysical Trinitarianism" (*The Significance
of Personality*, pp. 143 f.). Vaughan then proceeds to a metaphysical restatement in which "the precise nature of Jesus' ontological relation to God
is impossible to define" yet in which Vaughan redefines the divinity of
Jesus in terms of "the realized moral values of his personality" (*ibid.*, p.
147). The remarkable fact is that as humanism more and more engulfed
this thinly christianized monotheism, modern Western theology snared

in rebellion against trinitarian theism soon nullified any case even for a transcendent personal God.

The church in the early centuries had double reason, therefore, to publish sound doctrine. It had need to avoid contradiction in its own expositions to guard the truth from being falsely and inadequately expounded. And equally important the church had to avoid misunderstanding of its doctrine by outsiders, misunderstanding that stemmed from a diverse and confusing Christian use of terms by those who readily correlated them with alien philosophical notions.

Even today the new convert who had found regenerate life in Christ and attends a confessional church will soon find himself asking questions about the larger implications of faith. Why does Christianity insist, for example, that the second person of the Godhead—and not the Father, or the Spirit—became incarnate in Jesus of Nazareth? Would it matter if these claims were exchanged? The issue at stake—as the early church councils pondered the sending Father, the sent Son, the incarnate Logos, the outpoured and now indwelling Holy Spirit, and much else—was fidelity to the biblical teaching, and fidelity to God's authoritative, scripturally conveyed self-revelation.

Before the ecumenical creeds were adopted, Gnostic and Platonic concepts had been invading aspects of trinitarian teaching as this was being formulated not only by opponents of the doctrine but even by its defenders.

The Gnostics taught that a series of emanations of graded ranks or orders proceeded from the primal Being. Converts to Christianity from such a background therefore tended to represent Christ as emanating from the lowest of these eons or emanations. This view, while it allowed a consubstantiality of Christ with the Father, and derived all things from him as personal Creator, nonetheless depicted Christ as a dependent being, and moreover denied his true identity. Hence while this Gnostic view retained some biblical elements it definitely sacrificed others, and led to heretical views of the Trinity.

Carrying forward Philo's understanding of the Hebrew-Christian scriptures, some neo-Platonists tried to find fuller points of contact between the Christian revelation and philosophical theology. Philo, although more influenced by Stoicism than by Platonism, identified the biblical Logos with the Ideas that Plato had considered the formative principles of all existence. He then projected these Ideas as the Son or Image of God, indeed as a second God. When applied to Christ, as by Justin Martyr, Tatian and Theophilus, this view made of Christ a subordinate divinity, preexistent but not eternal. It conceived the Logos not theistically in the dimensions of biblical revelation but pantheistically in terms of conjectural philosophy. By representing the Demiurge as architect and not creator of the world, Platonism led to views of Christ that subordinated his divinity. The Bible uses the term Logos of the Son primarily to exhibit his personal divine relationship to the Father (John 1:1-3) and secondarily to express a relationship to the space-time universe (cf. Col. 1:16 f. where Christ exercises a logos-function even if the term Logos is not expressly used).

Origen gave the Platonic doctrine a higher level of meaning by insisting on the eternality of the Son, as well as on his distinct personality. But by referring the generation of the Son to the will of the Father, Origen reduced Christ to creatureliness even though Christ was held to be created from eternity. Origen therefore repeated the essential error of the Logos-speculations, that is, he failed to vindicate the deity of Christ and made of the Son simply a creature. The Logos-speculations, moreover, could not save genuine significance for the Holy Spirit. In short, they led toward a diadic, but not triune, conception of God.

For that reason, the doctrine of a modal trinity (c. A.D.. 250) gained influence. Named after Sabellius, the theory acknowledged the true divinity of the Father, Son and Spirit but affirmed that God is one person who expresses himself in three different relations to the world and the church. Since God is regarded as one person, the terms Father, Son and Holy Spirit suggest only *ad extra* relations, not internal, necessary and eternal relations. Sabellianism's strength lay in upholding the true divinity of Christ and of the Spirit, its weakness, in denying personal distinctions in the Godhead and therefore the distinct personalities of the Father, Son and Holy Spirit. While Sabellianism combines the fact of the incarnation with Hebrew monotheism, it does so by excluding a personal interrelatedness within the interior life of the Godhead. On the one hand it attempted to add a dynamic historical redemption to bare static theism; on the other, it sought to drive a wedge between the ontological Godhead and Jesus and the Spirit. The Christian community could not yield to this view, because it denied Christ's distinct eternal personality. By negating personal plurality in the Godhead modalism contradicted both biblical teaching and Christian experience.

The Bible represents the persons of the Trinity as coexisting and not as having merely a successive or alternating existence. The Father who constantly addresses the Son as "Thou," is depicted as sending, loving, and exalting him. The Son constantly addresses the Father in personal terms, and refers to his own activity as being consistent with the Father's will. Scripture places the personal coexistence of the divine persons beyond doubt by juxtaposing the terms Father, Son, and Spirit. By representing Christ as the express image of God, Scripture implies his uncreated personal distinctness; man, on the other hand, shares personality as an endowed perfection and as a creature bears God's image in only a limited way.

Through worship and prayer Christian religious experience enters into relationships that presuppose the personal coexistence, as well as the divinity, of each member of the Trinity. Apart from the guidance of biblical revelation the Christian community cannot, of course, discriminate infallibly in spiritual experience between the persons of the Trinity. But a modal trinity would introduce vast confusion, and would require far-reaching revision of the highly specific religious experience shaped by biblical theology. It was experiential as well as biblical motivation, therefore, that explains why the Christian consciousness quickly, and almost universally, rejected Sabellianism.

The Arian alternative affirmed Christ's distinct personality but denied his essential divinity. Had the church followed this direction, a new triumph of pagan polytheism would have resulted, viz., the worship not only of God, but also of a creature alongside him. According to Arius the Son became unchangeable by ongoingly and uninterruptedly following the good. Having attained absolute perfection by effort, the Son was therefore designated "only begotten God," and given other divine titles. Because of his exalted nature, including his relation to all other creatures as their creator and governor, Christ was worthy of their worship. The idea of worshiping one who was not intrinsically divine was no less incongruous, however, than the idea of a creature that evolves progressively into divinity even if only in some metaphorical sense.

Origen had earlier led the way in designating Christ as God even though he disallowed Christ's equality with God and denied a unity of essence. But Arius, also of Alexandria, took a more radical step. He regarded the Son as preexistent but not as eternal, not even by creation. In other words, he regarded the Son as the first creature who, in turn, became the creator of all other finite persons and things.

This is the doctrine that was sweeping the Christian churches when the first ecumenical councils were summoned. The dispute among belivers had become so debased that Jews publicly scoffed at the controversy and ridiculed the church's sacred doctrine of the deity of Christ. Christian families divided over it as some declared the Logos to be a creature.

Favorite Arian texts were Deuteronomy 6:4, 32:39; Proverbs 8:22; Psalm 45:8; Matthew 12:28, 26:39, 41, 27:46, 28:18; Mark 13:32; Luke 2:52, 18:19; John 11:34, 12:27, 13:21, 14:28, 17:3; Acts 2:36; 1 Corinthians 1:24, 15:28; Philippians 2:6 f.; Colossians 1:15; Hebrews 1:4, 3:2. But non-Arians did not reject or ignore these texts. At stake rather were antecedent assumptions— e.g., whether the texts place Christ on a par with creatures, or depict his earthly life as that of only a human being, or whether they affirm Christ's ontological subordination to the Father. Arianism like Sabellianism believed that Christian monotheism teaches the unipersonality of God and that the predicate "underived" belongs to but a single divine person, a thesis supported more readily by Aristotelian philosophy than by the Old and New Testaments. But it would be inaccurate to suggest that Aristotelian philosophy dominated exposition of the biblical passages. Aristotle was not admired in the third, fourth or fifth centuries. Arius himself appealed to Scripture, or explained it away, and Athanasius used virtually no philosophy at all. Arianism taught that the unipersonal God alone is unbegotten, without beginning, eternal; no other person is equal in dignity. If the Son had the same substance, nature and constitution as the Father, there would be two Gods. Wisdom and Logos, moreover, are not persons but powers coincident with the divine substance. The one personal God created an independent person, namely, the preexistent Son, by whom, in turn, the world was to be created. As regards his substance, the Son is unrelated to the Godhead. This preexistent creature, said Arius, became incarnate. The Holy Spirit, moreover, is a second, independent substance and created by the Son. Arius thus committed Christianity to separate persons worthy of worship, even though he himself denied the essential deity of the Son and the Spirit.

The confusion in Christian circles was more a feature of the intellectual life of some presbyters and of other clergy than of ordinary worshipers whose simple faith was stimulated by the Scriptures. Even at the Nicene Council most participants were at first completely disinterested in the debate. But widening doctrinal disagreements led inevitably to ecclesiastical confrontation in which the respective merits of competitive views were tested by biblical revelation.

Nonevangelical scholars often scorn the early ecumenical creeds as a translation of Christianity into Greek metaphysics. But the decisive question is whether the creeds affirm what is true. The fact is that early Christianity opposed much of Greek metaphysics, including its notions about God, evil, matter and the body. Syriac christology, moreover, in no way relies on Greek categories, yet its intellectual affirmations about Jesus Christ's ontological status parallel the Chalcedonian creed. What decided the formulation of the ecumenical creeds was not Greek philosophy or Christian consciousness but rather and only the biblical data. The creeds resist reducing New Testament statements about the persons of the Trinity to merely functional significance, a disposition later revived by Ritschl and other neo-Protestant theologians. Paul M. van Buren, for example, tells us that the apostolic and the Nicene statements about the Trinity are simply an affirmation that God is to be trusted; as for the Chalcedonian statements about Jesus, their real concern is said to be the character of Jesus' earthly life and its effects upon us (*The Secular Meaning of the Gospel*, pp. 158 ff.). Such reinterpretation of credal intention prompts Langdon Gilkey to observe that "while an Episcopalian can dispense with God, he has a harder time relieving himself of ecclesiastical tradition" (*Naming the Whirlwind: The Renewal of God Language*, p. 126).

The first ecumenical council, the Nicene Council, was summoned in A.D. 325 by Emperor Constantine. Its task was etymological, polemical and theological.

The first problem to be solved grew out of confusion in the use of terms bearing on the doctrine of the Trinity. These expressions had not yet acquired a fixed and technical use, and were sometimes employed even in opposite and contradictory senses. If Christian doctrine was to be made intelligible to the world of its day, it was necessary to state it in the Greek and Latin vocabulary already in use but with an awareness that certain philosophical shades of meaning infused this vocabulary. The effort to combat Sabellianism, or modal monarchianism, with its notion of three successive manifestations of one divine person, or any other theory, for that matter, required agreement on technical meanings to be assigned to relevant theological terms.

The terms then in popular use carried more than one meaning, and both the Greek and Latin churches inherited this semantic confusion. The fact that the ancient pagan world lacked clear and distinct words for personality pays its own striking tribute to the genius of Hebrew-Christian revealed religion. Not until the acceptance of biblical monotheism with its supernatural disclosure of divine triunity did the world first inherit a distinct conception of personal reality, both divine and human. To be sure, the Stoic notion of *to hegemonikon* included a somewhat vague conception of personality, the term being used for both the world-Soul or Reason and for man's reason and seat of emotion. But full awareness of the uniqueness of the human person is a debt that the Western world owes ultimately to Christian trinitarianism. At the same time use of an already prevailing vocabulary, to which alien connotations were often quite automatically attached, threatened Christian statements about the divine essence with future controversy over realistic and idealistic alternatives.

The Greek word *hypostasis* bore the ordinary sense of "substance." Greek churchmen translated the Latin *persona* by *hypostasis* rather than by another Greek word *prosōpon* because the latter meant not only personal reality but also outward facial features and could therefore support merely phenomenal or modal rather than essential trinitarianism. The Nicene Council affirmed three *hypostases* and one *ousia*. *Hypostasis* therefore held the dual meaning of "substance" and "person."

The Latin terms *substantia* and *subsistentia* were often used as synonyms, each word conveying the dual notions of substance and of subsistence. Facing up to this confusion Christian theologians subsequently fixed the standard usage by affirming three subsistences in one divine substance.

The Greek term *prosōpon,* and the Latin word *persona,* raised similar problems. As already noted, *prosōpon* was used of a self-conscious agent, although it also properly denoted a face or outward aspect and hence served the Sabellian modalists as readily as nonmodalists. In its primary meaning the Latin word *persona* referred to the mask worn by an actor, and only secondarily to his essential character or role; for that reason it, too, was serviceable to modalism. Something of the same ambiguity attached to the Greek term *homoousios* meaning sameness of substance. It left unsure, however, whether that sameness is specific or numeric, and its use provoked accusations of tritheism while it also promoted monotheism. The Nicene Council stipulated the sense these and other terms were to bear in Christian theology.

A second task of the Nicene Council was to repudiate errors that had crept into the church wherever Arian and semi-Arian speculation had gained prominence alongside the orthodox view. The Arians denied the eternity, self-subsistence, essential deity and immutability of Christ; the semi-Arians, including partisans of Origen's Christology, while they acknowledged Christ's eternity, conditioned his existence on the Father's will,

denied that he was of the Father's essence, and subordinated him both
in the nature and mode of his subsistence or rank. For all that, both Arians
and semi-Arians regarded Christ as creator of every other created reality,
identifying the Holy Spirit as the first and highest of these creations.

Alongside the etymological and polemical task of the Nicene Council
stood its theological task. The Nicene Creed,[1] adoption of which climaxed
the Council's work, succinctly expresses the orthodox doctrine: (1) one God;
(2) three persons; (3) the Son begotten (not made) of the essence of the
Father; (4) the Son consubstantial with the Father; (5) the Son very God
of very God; (6) the eternity of the Son. These affirmations were the strength
of the Nicene Creed.

Because theological controversy centered around the doctrine of the Son
and his relation to the Father, the Nicene Creed developed no statement
concerning the Holy Spirit. Only the bare confession appears: "And we
believe in the Holy Ghost." This lack was the Creed's weakness. But the
expounders and defenders of the Nicene Creed affirmed as the view of
the Council that the Spirit is consubstantial with the Father and the Son,
a doctrine that was set forth in several provincial councils (e.g., Alexandria,
A.D. 362; Rome, A.D. 375).

Disputes occasioned by these declarations led to the second ecumenical
council, that of Constantinople in A.D. 381. It supplemented [2] the Nicene
Creed and made further statements concerning the Holy Spirit: (1) the
Spirit is the lord and giver of life; (2) the Spirit proceeds from the Father;[3]
(3) the Spirit is worshiped and glorified equally with the Father and Son;
(4) the Spirit spoke by the prophets.

Orthodox trinitarianism, especially its implications for the person of
Christ, was amplified more fully by the so-called Athanasian Creed. Formulated as late as the fifth or sixth century, the creed bore the authority
of no council, nor was it authored by Athanasius. Generally adopted in
the West, the Athanasian Creed was universally regarded as an ecumeni-

---

1. The Nicene Creed reads: "We believe in one God, the Father almighty, the
maker of all things visible and invisible; and in the one Lord Jesus Christ, the
Son of God, only begotten, begotten of the Father, that is, of the essence of the
Father, God of God, Light of Light, very God of Very God, begotten and not made,
consubstantial with the Father, by whom all things were made whether in heaven
or on earth; who for us men and our salvation came down from heaven, and was
incarnate and became man, suffered and rose again on the third day; ascended
into heaven, and will come to judge the living and the dead. And we believe in
the Holy Ghost. But those who say, that there was a time when He (the Son) was
not, that He was not before He was made, or was made out of nothing, or of another
or different essence or substance, that He was a creature, or mutable, or susceptible
of change, the Holy Catholic Church anathematizes."

2. The Council of Constantinople added to the words "We believe in the Holy
Ghost" the following: "Who is the Lord and giver of life, who proceedeth from the
Father, who with the Father and the Son together is worshiped and glorified, who
spoke by the prophets."

3. The addition of the *filioque* clause to this creed by the Synod of Toledo in
A.D. 589 contributed to the separation of the Eastern and Western Churches in A.D.
1054, when the papacy sought to justify the interpolation.

cal symbol.[4] It affirms: (1) the unity of God; (2) the distinct personality of the Father, Son, and Spirit; (3) the unity of the divine substance; (4) the equal divinity, glory, and majesty of the persons; (5) the uncreatedness, infinity, eternity, omnipotence of each of the persons; (6) the begottenness of the Son from the Father alone, but not made or created; (7) the procession of the Holy Spirit, but not creation or begottenness; (8) the coeternality and coequality of the three persons.

Against Sabellianism the several ecumenical creeds declare that the three personal distinctions are internal, necessary and eternal, and not simply modal; against Arianism and the followers of Origen they declare that the three persons are essentially divine, being identical in substance and equal in power and glory. At the same time the Councils state that the same numerically indivisible essence subsists in the three divine persons.

The ecumenical symbols were content to simply affirm the statements of Scripture and their successors who went beyond the creed to discuss the mutual relation of the persons of the Trinity.

The creeds speak of the subordination, distinction, and union of the three persons without implying an inferiority of any; since all three persons have a common divine essence, they affirm the Son's subordination to the Father, and the Spirit's subordination to the Father and the Son. This subordination pertains to mode of subsistence and to mode of operation. Consistent with the biblical data concerning mode of subsistence, the Son is of the Father and the Spirit is of the Father and the Son; as to mode of operation, the Father works through the Son, and the Father and the Son work

---

4. The Athanasian Creed states: "Whoever would be saved, must first of all take care that he hold the Catholic faith, which, except a man preserve whole and inviolate, he shall without doubt perish eternally. But this is the Catholic faith, that we worship one God in trinity, and trinity in unity, neither confounding the persons nor dividing the substance. For the person of the Father is one; of the Son, another; of the Holy Spirit, another. But the divinity of the Father, and of the Son, and of the Holy Spirit, is one, the glory equal, the majesty equal. Such as is the Father, such also is the Son, and such the Holy Spirit. The Father is uncreated, the Son is uncreated, the Holy Spirit is uncreated. The Father is infinite, the Son is infinite, the Holy Spirit is infinite. The Father is eternal, the Son is eternal, the Holy Spirit is eternal. And yet there are not three eternal Beings, but one eternal Being. In like manner, the Father is omnipotent, the Son is omnipotent, and the Holy Spirit is omnipotent. And yet, there are not three omnipotent Beings, but one omnipotent Being. Thus the Father is God, the Son, God, and the Holy Spirit, God. And yet there are not three Gods, but one God only. The Father is Lord, the Son, Lord, and the Holy Spirit, Lord. And yet there are not three Lords, but one Lord only. For as we are compelled by Christian faith to confess each person distinctively to be both God and Lord, we are prohibited by the Catholic religion to say that there are three Gods, or three Lords. The Father is made by none, nor created, nor begotten. The Son is from the Father alone, not made, not created, but begotten. The Holy Spirit is not created by the Father and the Son, nor begotten, but proceeds. Therefore, there is one Father, not three Fathers; one Son, not three Sons; one Spirit, not three Holy Spirits. And in this Trinity there is nothing prior or posterior, nothing greater or less, but all three persons are coeternal, and coequal to themselves. So that through all, as was said above, both unity and trinity, and trinity in unity is to be adored. Whoever would be saved, let him thus think concerning the Trinity."

through the Spirit. Each of the three persons of the Trinity is distinguished by its unique characteristic as expressed by the personal names. The first person is Father, in relation to the second; the second is Son, in relation to the first; the third is Spirit, in relation to the first and second. The property of the Father is paternity; of the Son, filiation; of the Spirit, procession. The three persons have a common intelligence, will and power since the essence of the Godhead is common to them, an intimacy of union expressed by the Greek term *perichōrēsis* and the Latin terms *inexistentia, inhabitatio* and *intercommunio.* The purpose of these terms was simply to express that the Father is in the Son and the Son in the Father, that where the Father is, there the Son and Spirit are, and that what one person of the Trinity is doing, all are doing.

Venturing beyond the biblical statements and attempting explanations beyond what the creeds affirmed, the Nicene fathers set off a wave of later medieval speculation concerning subordination and eternal generation. The Reformers showed little interest in the scholastics' ecclesiastical theorizing about the inner life of the ontological Trinity. They, in fact, found distasteful the detailed intimacy with the interior life of the Godhead implied by medieval thinkers.

Both Luther and Calvin preferred to abide by the simple statements of the Bible. In fact, because Calvin refrained from speculative statements about the ontological Trinity he was suspected of both Sabellianism and Arianism, suspicions that were wholly unfounded. Calvin noted the apparent confusion introduced into the Christian doctrine by God by the themes of generation and procession. Although Scripture affirms the generation of the Son and uses the verb *gennaō,* the difficulty of drawing valid inferences may have evoked Calvin's disapproval of "curiosity." He also expounded the essential divinity of the three persons more cautiously than the others. Like Augustine he emphasized that the personal names refer to reciprocal relations, not to the one essence. Each person, considered in himself, is God; in relation to each other, the persons are Father, Son and Spirit. Each person of the Trinity considered as God may be called the sole first cause. But the peculiar properties of the persons considered in themselves produce a certain order in which the original cause is the Father. In this way the unity of the essence is preserved and the order of the persons is retained. "The first book of Augustine on the Trinity is entirely occupied with the explication of this subject," Calvin writes, "and it is far more safe to rest satisfied with that relation which he states, than by curiously penetrating into the sublime mystery, to wander through a multitude of vain speculations" (*Institutes,* I, 136). Calvin urges that the vocabulary and concepts of Scripture be kept at the center of every Christian statement of the doctrine of the Trinity: "On this, indeed, if on any of the secret mysteries of the Scripture, we ought to philosophize with great sobriety and moderation; and also with extreme caution, lest either our ideas or our language should proceed beyond the limits of the Divine word" (*Institutes,* I, 137).

Calvin's hesitancy was not, as sometimes represented, due to an uncertainty about the ontological status of the three persons, or to any limitation of legitimate theological belief to simply the economical Trinity of redemptive manifestation. Like Calvin, Luther emphatically rejected both tritheism and unipersonalism: "Although there are three persons," he said, "God the Father, God the Son, and God the Holy Ghost, yet the Being is not divided or distinguished; since there is but one God in one single, undivided, divine substance" (*Works*, Walch ed., XIII, 1510).

The biblical data put beyond doubt the subordination of the Son and the Spirit to the Father, and the eternal generation of the Son. Neither Scripture nor the ancient creeds explains these terms, however. The Nicene fathers expand these statements. They affirm the Father's communication of the essence of the Godhead to the Son, so that the two have this essence in common, but avoided any derivation of the essence of the Son from the Father.

That our Lord is eternally the Son of God, and that the term Son designates not merely his office but his nature as well, and moreover designates sameness of nature and hence equality with God, was affirmed already by the Nicene Council. That is what the Bible teaches. The personal names used of the Trinity, Father, Son and Spirit, are terms of relation, not simply a relation to creatures and the world, not in consequence of development in time (e.g., the incarnation), but terms for a mutual eternal relationship between the persons of the Trinity in the Godhead.

The biblical passages that bear on the sonship of Christ do not stop simply with designations of his supernatural conception, his exaltation, and the Father's unique affection for him; they also involve the teaching that Christ is the express image of God. They designate Christ "only Son of God" (John 1:18) who in an ultimate and proper sense called the Father "his own" (John 5:18). Some passages explicitly apply the term Son to the Logos, that is, to Christ in his divine nature prior to incarnation (Rom. 1:3 f., Gal. 4:4, John 1:18); others use the term Son to ascribe divinity to Christ and to indicate his equality with God (John 5:18–25, 10:30–38; Hebrews 1:3–12, cf. 3:6, 5:8, 7:28).

Objections to the doctrine of eternal sonship are usually pressed by an appeal to a select number of Scripture passages. The phrase in Psalm 2:7, for example, "Thou art my Son; this day have I begotten thee," is held to imply that Christ's sonship has a temporal beginning. It is also argued that Acts 13:32 ff. applies the Psalm to our Lord's resurrection, thus indicating that Christ became the Son of God when he rose from the dead. While often used of raising up (e.g., the dead), the fact is that the term *anistēmi* also bears the sense of instituting or installing someone in a special role or function, and hence may be used in certain Acts passages of the God-man's exaltation to messianic glory. Because certain verses indicate that the God-man was in a particular sense constituted Son of God need not, however, prejudice the interpretation of those verses which in a higher sense present the Logos as the eternal Son of God. The fact that Luke 1:35 ("The Holy Ghost shall come upon thee, and the power of the Highest shall overshadow thee; therefore also that holy thing which shall be born of thee, shall be called the Son of God") makes Jesus' miraculous conception one reason why the God-man was called Son of God is not inconsistent with the doctrine of eternal Sonship taught by other passages. According to Charles Hodge even Psalm 2:7 teaches that the day of resurrection unveils Christ's eternal sonship; translation of Acts passages goes beyond the original text, he asserts, when it defines the "raising up" of Christ in terms of resurrection (cf. Acts 2:30, 3:22, 26, 7:37).

Despite Bultmann's efforts to perpetuate it, the "history of religions" theory that Greek and Hellenic influences accounted for Christian representations of Jesus as "Son of God," has virtually collapsed. Evidence has grown that New Testament vocabulary and concepts are grounded not in a Hellenistic milieu but in an Old Testament and Hebrew environment (cf. Martin Hengel, *The Son of God: The Origin of Christology and the History of Jewish-Hellenistic Religion*). Bultmann's interpretation of the Fourth Gospel in the context of Gnostic mythology (*The Gospel of John*, pp. 42 ff.) is conjectural. The emphasis that God "sent" the Son into the world (Gal. 4:4) and passages about the Son's preexistence (John 1:1, 17) work against Bultmann's notion of a Gnostic redeemer-myth correlated with ascension or exaltation. The absolute reference to "the Son" in Paul's earliest letters (1 Cor. 15:28; cf. Rom. 1:3, 9) coincides in principle with what the Gospel of John affirms on the basis of historical incarnation.

The doctrine of the Trinity organizes the teaching and language of the New Testament in a comprehensively consistent way. To understand the New Testament doctrine of God in any other framework oversimplifies the biblical data, impoverishes the scriptural revelation, and leads to inadequate and heretical views of the one true and living God.

The objection to a personalistic view of the divine essence is often formulated as follows: if the divine essence is personal, then trinitarianism must necessarily speak of three persons in one person, something that is manifestly absurd. The personalistic view, we are told, suggests four personal centers of divine consciousness.

Gregory of Nyssa had already suggested the possibility of conceiving the divine essence as personal while yet maintaining the three personal distinctions. Although Gregory appealed to the analogy of human society, he conceived personal unity in terms of (Platonic) Idea, not of a social organization. In view of the discrete character of human selves, the usual rejoinder is that Gregory's analogy does less than justice to the living unity of the Godhead; the theory, it is argued, implies tritheism. Yet, as A. Seth Pringle-Pattison remarks, "society, taken by itself, is an abstraction hypostatized, but the idea of a divine *Socius* has been one of the most abiding inspirations of religious experience" (*The Idea of God in the Light of Recent Philosophy*, p. 297).

Early in the twentieth century the British metaphysician J. M. E. McTaggart propounded the theory that ultimate reality is a society of selves, a pluralism of spiritual beings without one divine being. In many respects, this view was a revision of a form of Hegelian idealism that eliminated the Absolute. In his book *Some Dogmas of Religion* McTaggart both disavows an overarching divine mind that includes within it all human minds, and criticizes belief in a personal God.

The contrasting views of Gregory of Nyssa and of McTaggart are noteworthy because they both emphasize the metaphysical priority of the personal over against a realistic substance theory of reality (although Gregory's view was realistic in the Platonic sense). But McTaggart, living under the long shadow of Hegelian pantheism, dismisses God and retains only finite selves; Gregory, on the other hand, in keeping with biblical theism considers the Godhead to be thoroughly personal and creative of human selves. He conceives divine essence as the personal living unity of three persons, and differentiates the eternal Trinity from created finite persons.

W. G. T. Shedd, by distinguishing "the personality of the Essence or Godhead from that of a Person in the Essence or Godhead" (*Dogmatic Theology*, Vol. 1, p. 193), implies that it is proper to speak of personality as a quality of the Godhead as well as of the three persons. By no means does Shedd suggest, however, that four divine persons are involved, the three persons of the Trinity and, as it were, a divine "overperson." Rather, "the existence of the three divine persons in the divine essence results in the self-consciousness of the essence. The general self-consciousness of the triune Godhead must not be confounded with the particular individual consciousness of the Father as Father, of the Son as Son, of the Spirit as Spirit. The personality of the trinity is not the same as that of one of its persons" but is "the *result*" of the personality of the three persons; "the three hypostatical consciousnesses make one self-consciousness, as the three persons constitute one essence" (*ibid.*, p. 193). Shedd declares that "it is preferable to speak of the *personality* of the essence, rather than of the *person* of the essence; because the essence is not one person, but three persons" (*ibid.*, p. 194). The personality of the divine essence, therefore, is the divine self-consciousness that results from the trinal consciousness of the three persons subsisting as one essence.

But is Shedd implying that, while each of the three persons has consciousness, none has self-consciousness? To be sure, none has self-consciousness in isolation since none of the persons exists in isolation; each has self-consciousness only within the self-consciousness of the complete essence of God. But what is "individual consciousness" if there is only one intellect and one will? And can the Godhead be the "result" of the three persons? If each person had independent self-consciousness then the three persons would constitute not simply three integrated and coordinated centers of personal consciousness, but three independent centers of self-consciousness; tritheism would be the result. But the Godhead, in biblical dimensions, is not three persons in one person; it is three persons in one personal essence.

We are doubtless right in believing that absence of consciousness and absence of volition means absence of personality. Yet in expounding the doctrine of God, his intellectual, moral, and volitional perfections are discussed not simply under the personal names of God but as attributes, since they qualify his entire essence and are not peculiar to but one of the persons.

Although his personal distinctions are three, God acts with unity of mind and will. On the ground that the divine essence is common to the several persons Charles Hodge therefore emphasizes that God may be addressed as a Person consistently with divine tripersonality.

While revelation supplies hints for solving philosophical difficulties, it does not provide a fully developed metaphysical system to which we can accord revelational status. Christians must therefore avoid claiming supernatural authority for one or another interpretation that seems to resolve the problem of persons and essence in the Trinity. Even regenerate believers are vulnerable to false inference from revelation, especially since not all philosophical alternatives may be apparent to us. It is nonetheless helpful to see just where the implications of our inferences lead, and to set aside whatever tenets issue in logical contradictions.

Gregory of Nyssa considered the Trinity a Platonic Idea, that is, the three persons are subsumed under the one idea of God just as three men are subsumed under the one idea of Man. To be sure, the three persons of the Godhead are much more intimately unified than three men in the genus Man. But the Trinity might for all that be less unified than a Platonic Idea. Although Augustine thought that the doctrine of the Trinity requires a doctrine of Ideas, others dispute this. To speak of a common essence among the three persons need imply nothing more, they say, than a common quality among any group of things. Unlike Platonic realism, nominalism deals with particulars rather than universals, that is, with particular persons, trees and chairs. It allows no common qualities. When we speak of the biblical Trinity we do not of course have in view one of a variety of trinities. By the self-revealed Trinity of three persons in one essence we mean the one and only member of this genus.

There is little doubt that the formula "one essence, three persons" creates problems, but any alternative formulation only multiplies the difficulties. Augustine was dissatisfied with the term *persona* but found no preferable alternative: "We say . . . three persons, not that we would say this, but that we would not be silent" (*De Trinitate,* V, 9); ". . . not because Scripture does so, but because Scripture does not forbid" (VII, 4). But Western Latin theology has used the formula "one substance, three persons" ever since Tertullian. Eastern or Greek theology had translation problems with the Latin formula (in Greek, the Latin *persona* becomes *prosōpon* which means "mask" and thus seems to deny essential identity) so Basil the Great and the Cappadocians, distinguishing two terms that until then had also been used confusedly, spoke of three *hypostases* in one *ousia.* The Latin translation, however, was *una essentia, tres substantiae* ("one essence, three substances") which implied tritheism. Apprehensive lest three "persons" might imply three "substances," Anselm affirms "three I do not know what" (*Monologium,* c, 78). Aquinas equates "person" with a relation that is "its own mode of being" (*Summa Theologiae,* I, W. 29, Art. 4). Calvin defines person as "a 'subsistence' in the Divine essence . . . distinguished . . . by an incommunicable quality" (*Institutes,* Book I, XIII, 6). To this day Eastern theologians (cf. for example Vladimir Lossky, *The Mystical*

Theology of the Eastern Church) insist that the Greek term *hypostasis* best fits the meaning of "person"; Roman Catholic theologians, on the other hand, find it unserviceable as a clear alternative to pagan polytheism and to bare monotheism. Nevertheless their mutual recognition of theological intention serves to override semantic differences.

The real difficulty in trinitarian formulation may lie not where many theologians find it, in the definition of *person*, but rather in the definition of *substance*.

We must not assume that Christian exegesis has exhausted all the implications of Scripture concerning trinitarian theism, nor can we be wholly sure of what is not found in the Bible. Yet evangelical theology best serves the living God in his revelation by speaking boldly only where the Scriptures do so, and by speaking cautiously where Scripture requires caution. Instead of trying to clarify what God has not even chosen to reveal we do well in expounding the doctrine of the Trinity to stay as close as possible to the clear statements of Scripture and to exhibit their teaching and meaning. Modern theology has compounded the error of church fathers who went beyond the license of Scripture and propounded ontological novelties.

Mental or personal reality can exist in multiple forms and, whether infinite or finite, such personal existence may be constitutive of diverse kinds of life. In the eighteenth century deism supplied an incentive toward unipersonal theism; in the nineteenth century Hegelian pantheism provided a framework for modern theories of modalism; in the present century personalism and neoorthodoxy prefer modal constructs to an ontologically eternal Trinity, process philosophy encourages dipolar views of divinity, and Moltmann's doctrine of God's self-revelation is a new version of modalism with the manifestation of God as Father coming last as the climactic eschatological unveiling. Century by century such conjecture empties into channels of contradiction that foment other and even less desirable theological oddities. The realities of revelation are not to be appropriated piecemeal or to be combined with conjectural god-concepts. The God of the Bible, the one sovereign and triune God, is the God of creation and redemption and judgment to come—the God and Father of Jesus Christ who renews us by the Spirit. Loss of the eternal triune God means increasingly a loss also of the realities of creation, of redemption and regeneration, and of personal hope and objective meaning.

Knudson assured Christians that there is "no serious discord" between personalism and biblical theism, and that the personalist attitude toward "the unique and characteristic elements in Christianity is favorable" (*The Philosophy of Personalism*, p. 328), but brushed aside the ontological Trinity as less than unique and characteristic. Brightman insisted that God is both finite and unipersonal. McTaggart, for whom God at best would be but one finite person among others, even if more powerful and good, saw no reason to even postulate such an entity, and held the equally groundless notion that reality is a spiritual unity of eternal individual spirits. However distorted, one or another aspect of the Bible returns to haunt us as the penalty for neglecting the triune God who reveals himself.

Despite modernism's mediating landslide to Unitarianism, and in fact largely because of it, modernist theology is in disarray, whereas trinitarian theology once again mounts an impressive initiative. Reemphasizing the evangelical view of the tripersonality of the one God, John B. Champion stresses that both the reality of the three persons and their absolute unity are essential to the biblical teaching (*Personality and the Trinity*, p. 48). While Karl Barth's dialectical repudiation of modal theology, Leonard Hodgson's correlation of the three eternal personal distinctions in the one God mainly with the practical aspects of our religious life, and other halting defenses of trinitarian theism may leave much to be desired, their common premise is that the modernist doctrine of God is false. Charles W. Lowry affirms that "within the unity of one God there are three real and distinct Persons, three centers of consciousness, will, and activity" (*The Trinity and Christian Devotion*, p. 107). Louis Berkhof, Cornelius Van Til, J. Oliver Buswell, Jr., Gordon H. Clark, and Samuel Mikolaski support the orthodox view in their theological writings. But American evangelical theology has not on the whole contributed significant literature to the current revival of trinitarian interest. Evangelical publishers meet some of the rising interest by reprinting last-century volumes, and sometimes without even indicating an original publication date. The doctrine of the Trinity is seldom preached in evangelical churches; even its practical values are neglected, except for occasional emphases on the role of the economic Trinity in the church's world missionary mission ("As my Father hath sent me, even so send I you," John 20:21).

In his Croall Lectures (1942–1943) on *The Doctrine of the Trinity,* Hodgson observes that the practice of trinitarian religion is as important as its philosophical exposition for opening man's minds to trinitarian theology (*ibid.,* pp. 175 ff.). To live as those adopted into the sonship of Christ, to live in the power and fruit of the Spirit, and to be one in the body of Christ as Christ is one with the Father, will bring a spiritual pattern to evangelical life that reflects the realities of trinitarian truth. Evangelical Christians do indeed cling to an orthodox Christology in a generation of modernist and humanist defection from the deity of Christ, and do indeed champion the charisma of the Spirit in an age of sensate priorities; they do not, however, sufficiently allow the realities of the Trinity to elicit comprehensive adoration of and obedience to the majestic triune God. The doctrine of the Trinity does not concern only man's mind, but has implications also for his whole being. Although in *The Trinity and Christian Devotion* Lowry speaks to the intellectual demands of the doctrine, he obviously is more concerned with its practical implications. Our adoption by the Father as sons in Christ, our life in the Spirit manifested in spiritual devotion and ethical endeavor in fulfilling the Father's will and purpose, must indeed project into history the era of more profound privileges opened by the New Testament. To avoid falling into the pit of a merely modal trinity we need not fall instead into the pit of denying economic or functional activities reserved for each member of the trinity in relation to the cosmos and mankind. The mighty divine activities—creation, incarnation, and the giving of the Holy Spirit—truly correspond to modes of spiritual experience that memorialize the historical revelation of the Trinity and appropriate its vitalities. The affirmations about the Trinity are not abstractions irrelevant to life and thought. They affect Christian worship which is not only of the Father, but also of the Son and the Spirit.

Nor is that all. The doctrine is important not simply for salvation-historical relationships but also for concerns of creation and preservation and judgment as well. Moreover, the very doctrine which of all Christian beliefs might seem at first sight remote and dry "to the ordinary man" turns out instead, as Mark Pontifex remarks, to supply the very foundations of Christian ethics (*Belief in the Trinity*). Trinitarian religion involves all man's relations to God and to society; the social relationships within the Trinity call out against any antisocial interpretation of personal religion.

However practical the interests of the New Testament writers may be, we are not to assume, however, cautions Arthur W. Wainwright, that they are completely disinterested in the nature of God (*The Trinity in the New Testament*, p. 6). The history of Christian doctrine leaves no doubt that neglect of the ontological aspects of trinitarianism soon erodes the practical values of the doctrine as well, and that the philosophical attempt to preserve a semi-Christian God divested of inner personal distinctions soon yields to humanistic disbelief. Karl Rahner notes that Protestant theology speaks much of God becoming man but not enough about the Word become flesh, a condition that focuses on incarnational verities at the expense of trinitarian realities (*Theological Investigations*, IV, p. 79). By its disbelief a large segment of Protestant theology severed the doctrine of the Trinity from the realm of devotion and socio-ethical and spiritual implications, and pigeonholed it as speculation and conjecture. For all that, the central issue of Protestant theology continues to be the nature of God as he truly is. Schleiermacher, who deferred discussion of the doctrine of the Trinity to the very closing pages of his dogmatics, and who had an affinity for Sabellianism, may nonetheless have unwittingly spoken better than he knew: "there must still be in store for it (the doctrine of the trinity) a transformation which will go back to its very beginnings" (*The Christian Faith*, 172, p. 747). Moltmann and others rush through this door to propose novel alternatives. The revelation of true beginnings, however, only God can reveal (cf. John 1:1, 2). Since no doctrine of the trinity of any kind can be deduced simply from experience, mediating efforts to evolve a trinitarian doctrine more compatible with current philosophical theory often rely on logical fallacies. It is God who makes himself known in self-revelation, who authorizes us to speak of what neither the nonbiblical religions nor secular philosophy discerned, namely, that three eternal personal distinctions coexist in the one living Godhead.

10.
God the Ultimate Spirit

BY AFFIRMING THAT "God is spirit" (John 4:24) Christianity asserts that God is primordial personal being, invisible and immaterial. He is both self-conscious and self-determinate.

To speak of God as spirit involves more than identifying personality as a divine attribute. Clement C. J. Webb notes that early Christianity did not in fact reckon personality among the attributes of God, but connected it rather with worship of the three persons in the one God (*Religion and Theism*, pp. 46 f.). In other words, affirmation of "personality in God" took priority over any exposition of divine attributes, since the attributes define the essence fully shared by the persons. For that reason discussion of at least certain aspects of the doctrine of the Trinity properly precedes discussion of the divine attributes.

Self-consciousness is the power of making one's selfhood an object of rational thought, and of knowing that one does so. Among human beings rational self-consciousness is considered a condition of human responsibility. Humans are conscious of their identity through time, that is, they are aware of their continuing duration, of being the same entity today as they were yesterday. Unlike general consciousness of objects around us, self-consciousness comprises one's own self-awareness of those objects. Consciousness is dual, for it requires a subject mentally aware of an object. But that is not all. Self-consciousness is trinal, involving in addition the subject's consciousness of being itself the subject aware of the object.

The eternal God is his own object of contemplation and ever conscious that he is subject and object of this contemplation. He is self-contemplative, self-cognitive, and self-communing.

By self-determination we mean free agency or spontaneous voluntariness. God has free will, a will that is self-moved. His thoughts and acts are shaped neither by external necessity nor by internal limitation except as he is self-determined in what he thinks and does. Only God alone, moreover, is a totally free agent. He sustains himself in voluntary self-determination. He has liberty to create or not to create. He has supreme moral freedom; he cannot be tempted (James 1:13). The attributes or perfections of God are virtues that he himself wills in sovereign freedom. They are not external constraints to which God's nature and will must conform. God would not be the living God of the Bible if some external agency or force set the ground rules to which deity must be subject as a condition of either existence or activity. God alone establishes truth and the good; they have no existence independently of his will.

W. G. T. Shedd writes that "the doctrine of the trinity . . . pours a flood of light upon the mystery of the Divine self-consciousness" (*Dogmatic Theology*, Vol. 1, p. 183). In the Christian Trinity "the media to self-consciousness are all *within the divine essence*, and are wholly separate from, and independent of the finite universe" (*ibid.*, p. 186). God is therefore not dependent upon the universe for his personality, as in the case of Hegelian pantheism; rather, the universe is dependent upon God's prior personal existence. "The Biblical doctrine of three distinctions in one essence, each of which possesses the whole undivided essence, shows how God's self-consciousness is independent of the universe. God makes himself his own object" (*ibid.*, p. 189). God finds the object of consciousness in the eternal personal distinctions within the Godhead and through them maintains reflective self-consciousness.

The religious and philosophical identifications of God as spirit often differ with the biblical representations and may, indeed, stray far from them. Contrasting sharply with the unqualified biblical distinction between Creator and creation (cf. Gen. 1:1, 26; Exod. 20:4) animistic conceptions view natural entities as manifestations of ultimate spirit. And Aristotle, while declaring God to be Spirit (*nous*), does so with connotations quite different from Jesus' affirmation of God as *pneuma*. Aristotle's spirit does not love the world like God the creator and preserver of the universe and redeemer of the penitent loves the world (John 3:16; 1 John 4:19).

Biblical religion declares that God is Spirit, that the Holy Spirit is one of the persons of the Godhead, that there is a spirit in man, and that when properly qualified this human spirit constitutes man a son of God. This may seem to be highly confusing, and the difficulties may seem hopelessly worsened when compounded with modern misconceptions and superstitions that connect the notion of spirit with ghosts, goblins and fairy tales.

Randall and Randall, who themselves give the term "spiritual" a merely humanistic sense, complain that the word has been used in religion to mean so many things it may no longer be serviceable. But "in its best significance," they suggest, "the word *spiritual* points to a quality of human experience too precious to be disregarded, a quality, moreover, for which there exists no other term half so satisfactory" (*Religion and the Modern World*, p. 192). In naturalistic fashion they suggest divorcing the term from any association with "a supposed supernatural" which, we are assured, psychologists have "explained . . . in purely natural terms, often as patho-

logical abnormalities; many have grown sceptical as to whether there is
any such thing as 'the spiritual' outside the domain of psychiatry. . . .
Spirit can have a meaning only if it be applied to certain qualities of human
experience as lived in its natural setting in the universe whose secrets
scientific inquiry seeks to penetrate" (*ibid.*, pp. 193 ff.). No discerning
reader can fail to see that naturalistic prejudices here exclude in advance
any objective status for supernatural spiritual entities; empirical or observational science and not revelational considerations are made the final
arbiter of all that passes for truth and reality. In keeping with this restrictive verdict, spiritual life is said to be "a certain level of human experience,
a certain quality of man's action" not to be coordinated with what is prejudicially labeled "the myths" and "superstitious encumbrances"—that is,
with the idea of a soul or spirit that endures forever and that by divine
grace has a quality of life fit for eternity. Instead, we are informed, one
"has a soul" or is "a great soul" if one "has in marked degree qualities
of sensitive, rich and coordinated participation in all the situations of life,"
an approach in keeping with John Dewey's purely naturalistic redefinition
of the psyche (*Experience and Nature,* pp. 183–191). What is good for the
spirit, we are told, varies from religion to religion, but modern science
has determined, presumably with finality, that by soul or spirit we mean
simply certain activities that characterize our bodies.

Interestingly enough, such views are not the crowning discovery of contemporary scientific investigation and learning, but are in fact not only
hundreds but thousands of years old. They were promulgated by the ancient
Greek naturalists Democritus and Leucippus, who considered all spiritual
reality to be a manifestation of the physical, but who did not rationalize
their claims as experimental scientific discoveries. Not even the classical
pagan philosophers of antiquity, however, found such theories either an
adequate or logical explanation of psychic phenomena.

The methodology of laboratory science lacks competence to resolve the
pertinent issues. To think that man's dignity and nature are enhanced
by deflating into myth representations of the divine Spirit and of man as
the created bearer of God's image shows vast insensitivity to the human
condition; an environment reduced to only impersonal cosmic processes
and events drains the personal existence of multitudes of meaning and
worth. By contrast, wherever belief remains in God the triunal Spirit who
enters into personal relations with all who love and serve him, there the
human spirit finds true dignity and independence, and a quality of life
fit for both the present life and the life to come.

God is immaterial and invisible Spirit, self-conscious and self-determinate. This immateriality and invisibility of God are fundamental emphases
of revealed religion. The Decalogue prohibits the making of graven or
sculptured images of God: "Thou shalt not make unto thee any graven
image, or any likeness (of any thing) that (is) in heaven above, or that
(is) in the earth beneath, or that (is) in the water under the earth: Thou
shalt not bow down thyself to them . . ." (Exod. 20:4, 5). In view of Exodus
20:23 ("Ye shall not make with me gods of silver, neither . . . gods of gold")

and of Exodus 34:17 ("Thou shalt make thee no molten gods") the prohibition extends also to molten images (cf. Isa. 30:22, 40:19, 44:10; Jer. 10:4); no images whatever are countenanced.

Since God is the creator of the space-time universe, any aspect of the created universe becomes idolatrous if taken to represent deity. Pagan worship of the sun, moon or stars, or of human or animal or other creaturely forms, creations which the Hebrews knew by revelation to be of divine origin, could be nothing other than worship of the creature in the Creator's stead (Rom. 1:25). Such worship implied the essential entanglement of divinity in the processes of nature, a feature of the pagan religious cults, and hence spatialized, temporalized and fragmented deity. Modern process philosophy is in part a revival of such views; while purged of their polytheism it retains their notion that aspects of divinity are time-bound and that the cosmos is a necessary aspect of divine life and activity. Nowhere does the Bible suggest that the universe is necessary to God's being.

Both Old and New Testaments affirm the invisibility of God. No image or human representation of God appeared in the "holy of holies" since Yahweh provided his own presence. John Wisdom writes that a God made visible as a numinously authenticated sovereign would thereby be revealed as non-God (*Paradox and Discovery*).

Comparative religion is replete with notions of sudden, fleeting appearances of deity conveying private revelation. Scripture has theophanies in which God reveals himself in perceptual manifestations; these are not essentially epiphanies, however, and center around audible or verbal revelation that contains a message intended for the larger community. When we are told that the Lord "spake unto Moses face to face, as a man speaketh unto his friend" (Exod. 33:11) the context informs us that Moses did not see God's face but rather saw his glory (Exod. 33:20–22). Yahweh says: "Thou canst not see my face: for there shall no man see me, and live" (Exod. 33:20). Beatific vision awaits the life to come.

Yet, as the New Testament emphasizes, the immaterial and invisible God has manifested himself in flesh in the exclusive divine incarnation of the Logos in Jesus Christ. "No man hath seen God at any time; the only begotten Son, which is in the bosom of the Father, he hath declared him" (John 1:18). The Greek term *exēgeomai* here means to present or to expound, in short, to reveal. Jesus Christ is "the image of the invisible God" (Col. 1:15) and "it pleased the Father that in him should all fulness dwell" (Col. 1:19). Jesus reminds unbelieving Jews: "Ye have neither heard his voice at any time, nor seen his shape" (John 5:37); "Not . . . any man hath seen the Father, save he which is of God, he hath seen the Father" (John 6:46).

The author of Hebrews refers to God as "the Father of spirits" (Heb. 12:9), a designation that recalls references in the Book of Numbers to "the God of the spirits of all flesh" (Num. 16:22, 27:16). The eternal Spirit is the creator and preserver of all to whom he gives life, both unembodied spirits and embodied spirits. Attempts to read into the passage in Hebrews a specific theory of the generation of the human psyche, whether by cre-

ationism or traducianism, have no solid basis in the text. What the passage
in Hebrews emphasizes, rather, is that in order to enjoy fullness of life
we must be subject to God who disciplines those whom he loves.

Although God is immaterial and invisible Spirit, his personal presence
can become just as vivid in the experience of the devout and dedicated
believer as is the cosmic world. As John Hick puts it: "The biblical writers
were (sometimes, although doubtless not at all times) as vividly conscious
of being in God's presence as they were of living in a material environment.
Their pages resound and vibrate with the sense of God's presence, as a
building might resound and vibrate from the tread of some great being
walking through it" (*The Many-Faced Argument,* p. 344).

But what lifted the sense of the personal presence of the invisible God
to new heights was the incarnation of the Logos, and later the presence
of the Holy Spirit in the very body of believers as the temple of God. These
vitalities will be discussed at length in connection with the persons of
the Trinity. Here it is sufficient to note that John's Gospel frequently associates knowledge of God with the vision or seeing of God, but in no sense
in terms of Greek notions of epiphany. John rejects the claim of Hellenistic
mystics to immediate vision of God, and does so on the premise that such
vision is anticipatively mediated by Christ (John 1:45, 14:9). John neither
denies the Old Testament's insistence of the invisibility of the Eternal
nor alters the fact that both the Old and New Testaments say very little
about the vision of God as a form of religious experience. Yet, as C. H.
Dodd remarks, "The Fourth Evangelist can speak of men as knowing and
seeing God, without actually contradicting the fundamental assumptions
of Judaism, just because it is the presupposition of his whole view of religion that the Age to come has come; eternal life is here" (*The Interpretation
of the Fourth Gospel,* p. 167). The emphasis remains that "no man hath
seen God at any time" (1:18); direct vision of God is predicated only of
Christ (6:46). Jesus Christ is the person in whose historic life the glory of
God is seen (1:14); its divine quality discloses a knowledge of God that
constitutes vision of God. The vision of God is here embodied in a particular
historical person who speaks the words of the Father (14:24).

11.
God the Self-Revealed Infinite

RELIGIOUS PHILOSOPHY has often considered infinity an attribute essential to any ideal conception of deity. Yet the word infinite has a wide range of nuances and is significant in logic and mathematics as well as in metaphysics and theology. In modern pantheism the term implies that God is ontologically dispersed in the universe, a view diametrically opposed to the Hebrew-Christian concept of God as infinite Creator of a finite universe. Taken by itself, therefore, and without more precise definition, the notion of infinity is too vague to be serviceable.

Ancient Zarathustrianism depicted "the Good and the Bad Spirit, Aûharmazd and Aharman," as "both limited and unlimited" (*Sacred Books of the East*, Vol. 5, pp. 4 f.). The first Greek philosopher to speculate on the concept of infinity, Anaximander, meant by the infinite (*to apeiron*) a limitless or inexhaustible substance that fuses nature's basic elements, a substance eternal, internally undivided, but having no definite quality; from this substance Anaximander derived all limited things that constitute the world. The Pythagoreans somewhat modified this conception by postulating a limit (*peras*) that gives structure to the infinite (Anaximenes identified the infinite with air).

Plato in his *Philebus* regards infinity (in the sense of *to apeiron*, the formless) as evil, and its opposite (*peras*, definite form) as good. H. P. Owen comments that in classical Greek philosophy "infinity represents a substratum which is formless, characterless, indeterminate. It is a pejorative word. An entity is good to the extent that it is limited by form" ("Infinity in Theology and Metaphysics," Vol. 4, p. 190). The important consequence is that Plato therefore could not depict God as infinite since the world in turn would then be a cosmic chaos, formless and unintelligible. Aristotle reviews the various senses that Greek philosophy and science attach to the idea of infinity (*Physics*, Book III), and focuses specially on ideas of the indeterminate and of perfection as aspects of the problem of measurement.

For the Greek skeptic Carneades (ca. 214–129 B.C.) the idea of divine infinity is inevitably contradictory. Since an infinite God is everywhere and therefore has no place to move, he comments, an infinite God would be limited and restricted. This argument is more a verbal ploy than an intelligent objection, however. God need not move where he already is; he can withdraw, moreover, or even intensify his presence. Carneades also held that the idea of divine infinity conflicts with that of personality (the problem of reconciling divine sovereignty or omnipotence with divine personality is discussed in a supplementary note to chapter 14). By his approach Carneades anticipates Hume's argument in which the norm or essence of personality is equated with its human mode. We have previously rebutted this view (chapter 7: "Personality in the Godhead"). As H. Maldwyn Hughes remarks: "Christian thought does not conceive of God as one personality among many, any more than it thinks of Him as the all-including Personality. It regards Him as the personal Creator of all being, in and through whom all that is lives and moves" (*The Christian Idea of God,* p. 150).

In the interim between Greek philosophy and later Christian theology something happens to the use of language that emboldens Christians to envisage the God of the Bible as infinite. A change of meaning was already underway in later Greek philosophy, for we find Plotinus ranking infinity first among the divine attributes. The divine mind, the One, he contends, is *apeiron* (or *aoriston*), that is, unbounded—a complete unity, self-sufficient, and of unending power. Yet because of reluctance to apply positive predications Plotinus refuses to affirm that the One is infinite. According to L. Sweeney infinity was not explicitly ascribed even to the being of the Christian God until 1250 ("Divine Infinity: 1150–1250," *The Modern Schoolman,* Vol. 35, pp. 38–51).

William Newton Clarke asserts that "the idea of infinity, strictly speaking, is an abstract idea that belongs rather to philosophy than to religion" and that "religion does not concern itself with the distinction between the infinite and the finite, but it does impel the soul to stand in awe before a Being who impresses it as infinite" (*The Christian Doctrine of God,* p. 300). Although Clarke professes to speak for revealed religion, his representations here seem to me to be wrong or misleading at almost every turn. Christian assertions about God cannot reduce merely to expressions of feeling. Any religion that fails to preserve some objective distinction between the finite and the Infinite will soon find itself violating the Second Commandment. Moreover, all ideas, strictly speaking, are abstract; what Christian theology affirms dogmatically on the basis of revelation is not to be considered philosophically untrue simply because of its abstract statement.

Although the Hebrew language has no word for infinity, the term infinite occurs in the King James translation of Job 22:5, Psalm 147:5 and Nahum

3:9. Here the translation represents two Hebrew words meaning "very great." Job 22:5 concerns Eliphaz's declaration that Job is a great sinner; the Revised Standard Version translates it, "Is not your wickedness great" (KJV: "infinite")? Nahum 3:9 refers to the strength of Egypt (RSV: "without limit"). In Psalm 147:5, which deals with God's understanding, the Revised Standard Version replaces the term "infinite" with "beyond measure."

Are Christians then to say that Scripture stops short of the conception of divine infinity, just as empirical argument from the finite universe can arrive only at a very great but not infinite divinity? Or is the vocabulary of the Bible even in metaphysical and scientific matters cast in everyday language rather than in technical terms whose use is often limited to a particular period? The simplicity of Jesus' vocabulary puts us on guard against thinking that the biblical writers avoided elaborate metaphysical terms because they lacked philosophical understanding. The basic issue is therefore whether the Bible, whatever its vocabulary and once we clarify the sense of the relevant terms, requires a conception of God's infinity, or whether a scripturally controlled theology must affirm that God is finite.

No sooner does the classic definition of God in the Westminster Shorter Catechism mention the existence and spirituality of God than it affirms infinity first among the divine perfections: "God is a Spirit, infinite in his being. . . ." and so forth. Although some have argued that the confession limits God's infinity to certain expressly stipulated perfections, the statement that God is infinite in being seems to affirm that God is infinite in the totality of his nature and hence in all his perfections. So too J. Gresham Machen, contributing to a symposium on *My Idea of God*, expresses the orthodox evangelical view by saying: "I for my part cling with all my heart to what are called the metaphysical attributes of God—His infinity and omnipotence and creatorhood," and professes to do so on the basis of "the really distinctive revelation that the Bible contains" (*ibid.*, pp. 46, 48). The discussion of infinity—so frequently connected in recent modern times only with problems of space and time—here finds its rightful context in the doctrine of God.

Christian theology rejects restricting the exploration of the theme of infinity to a discussion of the theory of limits (such as infinitesimals and infinite series in mathematics). As Charles Hartshorne remarks, "the mathematical infinite is not the theological infinite" (*The Logic of Perfection*, p. 107). Yet the theological and mathematical conceptions of infinity have sometimes been strangely confused. Here one recalls the mathematical symbolism of the medieval Roman Catholic cardinal Nicolas of Cues (1401–1464) who proposed contemplating the infinity of God by taking a clue from mathematics and geometry, and then proceeding analogically to the infinite being of God. Cusanus did this by analyzing the conception of the infinite straight line as a maximal limit, and then transcending the idea of a purely quantitative limit in order to arrive at the Absolute Maximum (cf. Nicolas Cusanus, *Of Learned Ignorance*, I, xii). But this dialectic of limits can yield neither demonstrative knowledge nor revealed knowledge of the Infinite. Wherever God stands merely as the "limit-concept" of human imagination there can be no shared knowledge of the infinite God, for the divine remains clouded in mystery.

In Christian theology God is infinite in an objectively perfect and not a privative or indefinite sense. When applied to the God of the Bible infinity means that the attributes comprising the divine character are unlimited by external restriction and are limited only by God's own nature that is constituted of these very attributes. God is incapable of increase or diminution. His being is not restricted by nonbeing or by any being other than himself since all other being is dependent for its powers upon the Creator and is therefore finite. God is infinite in the totality of his being, and he alone is infinite—infinite in power, knowledge, wisdom, justice, righteousness, love and kindness. Each of his attributes is perfect and unlimited; he is infinitely powerful, infinitely wise, infinitely righteous, infinitely loving, and so on.

God's infinitude is known, moreover, not by soaring metaphysical speculation, but on God's own terms through his own modes of manifestation. On the basis of God's universal revelation in nature and reason all humans have some irreducible knowledge of the infinite God ("His invisible attributes, that is to say his everlasting power and deity, have been visible, ever since the world began, to the eye of reason . . . ," Rom. 1:20, NEB). God's infinity is also declared in his redemptive scriptural revelation.

Rightly understood, infinity must be predicated of the self-revealing God even though neither the Old Testament nor the New uses the precise term. The affirmation of divine infinitude exemplifies the proper contribution that philosophical reflection can make to the history of theology; secular philosophy sometimes discusses the nature of God in terms for which the Bible has no exact equivalents, but which biblical revelation nonetheless illumines through its teaching about God's perfections. This fact requires that a choice be made from among the various meanings that secular metaphysics attaches to its terms.

In wrestling the claims for or against divine infinity, Christian theists reject all notions of the infinity of the universe and hold instead that the universe is limited and is in fact the creation of a transcendent Creator. That God is infinite does not require the notion that he is everything, e.g., Nature in Spinozistic terms or the Absolute in Hegelian terms. A proper conception of God's infinity, including infinity of power, can accommodate a view of absolute creation so that God need not be identified as temporal or spatial. The fact that the cosmos is contingent argues conclusively against an unlimited universe. God the self-revealed Creator is free of such limitation and in him preexist all ontological perfections reflected in the universe. God is the self-revealed Creator of the world and of man out of nothing (Gen. 1:1). He is the source of the substance and of the structures that at creation he declares to be good (Gen. 1:3 ff.) or, in man's case, very good (Gen. 1:31).

Scholastic theology sought to establish God's infinity on the ground that the creaturely is limited to a specific genus whereas God is existence *simpli-*

citer, a view reaffirmed by E. L. Mascall (*He Who Is. A Study in Traditional Theism,* pp. 8 f.). In response we must ask why God may not in fact be subsumed under a genus of which he exhausts all instances. Scholastics argued additionally that, whereas the creaturely derives its being from a source other than itself, God exists by his own power; in him essence and existence are identical. But this empirical argument from dependent effects to an independent and self-sufficient cause rests on concealed assumptions of God's reality and therefore lacks logical compulsion. Scholastic theology further complicated its discussion of God's infinity by declaring that divine infinity is an incomprehensible perfection that can be predicated only analogically but not univocally. This view leads to epistemological skepticism. The fact that man is made for the knowledge and service of God; that not even man's fall into sin destroys his rational and moral categories; that God reveals himself objectively so that man even in sin has responsible knowledge of his maker, provides biblical writers and evangelical theology a basis on which finite creatures can speak positively of the infinite God.

Reflecting upon divine revelation is a fully proper role for philosophical reasoning. By stating the claims of both the theological and secular philosophical traditions in terms that promote mutual understanding, it allows each tradition to cast light on the other by its questions and proposed solutions; it also assesses metaphysical alternatives in the light of the biblical view and appraises the latter by the former as well.

But the effort to establish God's perfections only by analyzing the creaturely world, particularly in its present sinful condition, leads to inconclusive and diverse results. As both Descartes and Calvin observed, the finite does not give rise to notions of the infinite; instead, the Infinite gives rise to the reality and conception of the finite. No amount of negating the finite will lead to the infinite; unlimited negation leads, rather, to nothingness—to the notion that all divine qualities differ so extensively from whatever we know of finite being that we can form no positive idea of them.

The Infinite can comprehend the finite without active relationships between the two. But the finite comprehends the Infinite only because the infinite Creator has fashioned the finite and relates himself to it. Nor will any postulation of different degrees of finiteness lead us, by way of affirmation rather than of negation, to the Infinite. The dynamism by which the human mind passes from finite reality to the infinite God is always, contrary to Thomas Aquinas, something other than logical demonstration based on empirical observation. There has probably appeared no more thorough modern presentation than Austin Farrer's attempt to rise to the infinite God by philosophical reasoning from an apprehension of "the universal aspects of finite existence or of human existence" (*Finite and Infinite,* p. 299). But argumentation that leads from finite to infinite without any appeal to the Creator's self-revelation, hardly seems to justify Farrer's confidence that "all finites, in being themselves and expressing their natures in their acts, are expressing also the creativity of God who creates through them" (*ibid.,* p. 299). Much the same criticism may be directed at Mascall's view; he holds that the Thomistic fivefold proof, in persuading us to apprehend finite beings in their radical finitude, leads us to apprehend God their creator but without giving us any knowledge of God in his inner essence (*He Who Is. A Study in Traditional Theism,* chapters V and VI).

Giordano Bruno (1548–1600) who left the Roman Catholic Church to espouse religion without revelation, stood the Thomistic fivefold proof on its head. Bruno contended that if God's power is infinite, the results of that power must also be infinite. To deny the infinity of the universe, he argued, is to deny the infinity of God. With the rise of modern secular philosophy, the infinite universe increasingly emerges to replace the God of the Bible as the hope of human happiness and salvation (cf. James Collins, *God in Modern Philosophy,* p. 22). Yet simply to enlarge our conceptions of the physical universe neither justifies the notion of its divinity nor makes the affirmation of God as its creator logically inconsistent. The eagerness of recent modern scientists to expand the age and size of the universe was recently challenged by three American astronomers who in 1979 declared that the usually accepted figures rest upon an erroneous computation of spatial distances and should be halved. The universe, they contend, instead of being 15 to 18 billion years old, is only half that age, and, moreover, is only half as large as currently thought. An error of such magnitude in projections confidently accepted by the scientific community indicates how extensively recent theories of the evolution of the universe and of the age of stars rest on philosophical premises rather than on conclusive empirical data. But the age and size of the universe has no bearing on the question of divine infinity.

Descartes rejected the theory that the conception of the infinite is arrived at merely by "the negation of the finite. . . . On the contrary, I clearly perceive that there is more reality in the infinite substance than in the finite," so much so that my consciousness of the infinite, he added, is in some sense prior to my consciousness of the finite—or, in other words, that consciousness of God takes priority over consciousness of the self (*The Method, Meditations and Philosophy of Descartes, Meditations* III, p. 243). The finite self can know itself only in relation to God as infinite; the conception of the infinite is innately given as a prius of human thought. Descartes, like Augustine and Anselm and Calvin, develops this emphasis in the context of God's creation of mankind. "It is not to be wondered at," declares Descartes, "that God, at my creation, implanted this idea in me, that it might serve, as it were, for the mark of the workman, impressed on his work" (*ibid.,* p. 248). Many philosophers failed to connect the conception of divine infinity with an intuitive awareness grounded in man's primal creation, however, and thus opened the door to growing doubt that humans innately possess this positive idea of an absolutely perfect Being; consequently there arose alternative explanations of the origin of the conception of infinity.

Christian theists firmly rejected the absolutely infinite God of Spinoza, who identified God with Nature and ascribed to this merged reality an infinity of essence and an infinity of attributes. They also rejected Hegel's view that the infinity of the Absolute requires the infinity of the universe, the universe being for Hegel a rational development of the Absolute. Hegel nonetheless exerted great influence on many mediating Christian scholars. While John Caird, for example, rejected the unscriptural notion that the universe is necessary to God's perfection, as if God would be "only a potential God" were there not a universe to call forth divine power and knowledge and love (*The Fundamental Ideas of Christianity*, Vol. 1, pp. 72 f.), and rejected the attempt to mount a ladder from the finite to the infinite. "That which is finite can never exhaustively express or reveal that which is infinite," he writes; "if the finite world were the only medium of divine self-revelation, it would follow that the nature of God is a progressive one, and that we can think of a past time when He was less, of a future when He will be more and greater than now" (*ibid.*, pp. 74 ff.). Yet he toys with the neo-Hegelian notion that "the existence of the world is involved in the very nature of God" (*ibid.*, p. 155); this involvement, says Caird, is not simply by divine decree but in view of "the all-embracing being . . . of the Infinite" (*ibid.*, p. 140). A pantheistic frame of mind misconstrues God's infinity as the All or the Absolute; the infinite must of necessity include the finite, it is said, or the infinite is simply another finite and belies its name. But the finite need not be subsumed under the infinite as part of the infinite; indeed, Judeo-Christian revelation knows God the personal Infinite to be creator of the finite. The Infinite known to biblical religion is not a totality embracing all finitudes, a Whole including all that is. It knows God, rather, as alone infinite in thought and will. All finite relations have their ground in him, and neither human power nor reason nor love can surpass him. He is, says Scripture, the first and the last, the alpha and omega, the beginning and the ending (Rev. 1:8, 21:6, 22:13), the God of eternity and of creation who sustains all that is.

Locke held that we have no direct experience of supernatural realities and that the idea of God is empirically formed; he professed to derive the idea of divine infinity from reflection that removes from sensation all finite limits. But if the entire content of our understanding of infinity is drawn from finite realities—albeit not by deifying the finite as in the case of Hegel and Spinoza, but rather by negating the finite—then we have no positive understanding of God's infinite mode of being. Locke nowhere indicates how the human idea of infinity in mathematical quantification can lead to a conception of the nonquantitative nature of illimitable deity.

Hume failed as conspicuously as did Locke in explaining how ideas drawn from the temporal and material world lead to concepts of divine infinitude. He writes: "The idea of God, as meaning an infinitely intelligent, wise, and good Being, arises from reflecting on the operations of our own mind, and augmenting, without limit, those qualities of goodness and wisdom" (*An Enquiry concerning Human Understanding*, p. 19). But how does one rise from the mathematical paradoxes of indefinite divisibility, on which Hume focuses, to the predication of what infinity means in God?

Voltaire forges links in the chain of empirical reasoning that Hume did not foresee. Both writers—if indeed Hume believed in any god at all—consider God benevolent and infinite in durational existence, yet finite in power and presence. For Voltaire God is finite in knowledge as well as in power, a verdict based, supposedly, on the restricted order and design of the world whose limitations Voltaire ascribes to God as cause.

For Kant inference from empirical things to an unconditioned transcendent beyond our experience does not lead to an actual determinate existent; it leads rather to an indefinite concept devoid of any real content and existential significance. For Kant God is only an infinitely perfect logical ground that determines an ideal existence. But to speak of God's real existence as the infinitely perfect being involves for Kant a confusion of the ideal and the real. Man has no intellectual intuition for grasping God's reality, Kant contends, so that God as infinite being is outside the scope of speculative knowledge.

While Hegel protests Kant's division of reason into theoretical and practical, he recaptures man's knowledge of the infinite by a daring merger of human reason with the rational Absolute. He encloses finite reason within the Absolute not only epistemologically but also ontologically. In doing so Hegel espouses the infinitely perfect Absolute but sacrifices the God of biblical theism; this he does by demoting the infinitely perfect Judeo-Christian God into merely a pictorial equivalent of the philosophically proper absolute Spirit. To welcome Hegel's reassertion of divine infinitude requires doing violence, therefore, to the God of Moses and Isaiah and of Jesus and Paul. Nor is that all. Hegel also surrenders the reality of the finite as a creation other than God. For Hegel the finite becomes the Absolute in a state of negativity, that is, an external manifestation and development of the Absolute separated from its original infinite state. Hegel writes: "The finite has no truth; the truth of the finite spirit is the absolute Spirit. The finite is no veritable being. There is in it the dialectic to sublate itself, to deny itself" (*Lectures on the Philosophy of Religion*, Vol. 3, p. 352). In other words the finite reduces to merely a dialectical aspect of the infinite mind. Thus Hegel's notion of divine infinitude sacrifices both the transcendence of God and the created character of the universe. The Bible, by contrast, depicts finite existence as distinct in being from God, and yet as totally dependent upon him for its existence. To preserve a proper doctrine of divine infinitude one need neither smuggle in a pantheistic Absolute nor camouflage the finite universe as a dialectical movement in the life of the divine.

Two lessons are to be learned from these speculative developments: first, no analysis of finite beings, however thorough, will securely support a ladder that reaches to the Infinite, and second, to reject a demarcation between the infinite and the finite, even while such rejection seeks to preserve the finite within the life cycle of the Infinite, actually sacrifices the living God of the Bible. Valid knowledge of infinite being is possible only on an alternative model of the relationship between God and the universe.

Feuerbach rejects Hegel's dialectical identification of human beings with the life of the Absolute, but does so, no less erroneously, by absolutizing the human essence. To be sure, Hegel had manufactured the Absolute in his own image, but that could not justify Feuerbach's rejection of the transcendent infinite God of biblical theism. Instead of viewing finitude as a euphemism for nothingness—as the Hegelian dialectic in principle maintained by depicting the finite as canceling itself—Feuerbach considers man himself to be "infinite" in nature, and not deduced from a higher principle as the reflex of an all-encompassing Spirit. In his system man is himself the Absolute. Feuerbach protests—and rightly—against idealistic monism, a denial that in principle is shared, strengthened, and authorized by a biblical view of infinite and finite. Feuerbach is wrong, however, in thinking that the Hegelian confusion is implicit in all theistic religion and philosophy. He is even more wrong in thinking that human awareness of the infinite is only an awareness of man's own "infinite" nature—a turn of thought that strips infinitude of those very qualities that distinguish it from finitude.

The intellectual background of Karl Marx's atheism assumes that Feuerbach's demolition of Hegelian idealism is a refutation also of biblical theism. Marx's counsel not to preempt energies in combatting God and religion presumes that Feuerbach's assault on Hegelian pantheism has completely undermined theism.

In order to overturn Hegelian misconceptions, said Feuerbach, one must affirm finite being as the only reality. Revelational theism, of course, inverts Hegel, Feuerbach and also Marx on quite other premises, premises that reject not only Hegel's infinite Absolute but also Feuerbach's "infinite" mankind.

Some scholars who struggled to avoid both the dialectical monism of Hegel and the atheism of Feuerbach, but who had also blurred biblical theism into Hegelian pantheism, proposed the notion of a finite God as an alternative to the infinitude of the Absolute or of man. Since the problem of evil emerges as a crucial concern, for certain philosophers the question of divine infinity centers around the attribute of infinite power. Here Hume (*Dialogues concerning Natural Religion*, Pt. XI) and then John Stuart Mill (*Three Essays on Religion*, pp. 242 ff.) led the way. Although the theory of a finite, growing God was motivated by other considerations as well, the difficulty of reconciling divine omnipotence with the problem of evil preoccupies some philosophers we discuss in Volume 6. For Samuel Alexander (*Space, Time and Deity*), Alfred North Whitehead (*Process and Reality*), Charles Hartshorne (*The Divine Relativity*) and Edgar S. Brightman (*The Problem of God*) the doctrine of a finite god professedly arises independently of religious considerations. For Alexander "Deity is a nisus and not an accomplishment" (*Space, Time and Deity*, p. 364), that is, God is the striving universe that emerges at each stage of evolutionary development.

William James grounded the discussion of God's nature not on philosophical argumentation but on personal pragmatism. God's moral attributes, he declares, have a determinate significance for human behavior, whereas divine infinity and other traditionally indicated metaphysical attributes make no observable difference in conduct and are therefore meaningless. James disjoins the question of divine perfections from transcendent metaphysical claims and concludes that no philosophical doctrine of God can give valid knowledge. Yet he holds that informal pragmatic inferences of a tentative nature are indeed possible. But even technical philosophers disagree widely over what inferences can be derived from experience. James opted finally for pluralistic pantheism involving a finite God. In *A Pluralistic Universe* he stresses the multiplicity and finitude of beings, and thinks of God as "having an environment, being in time and working out a history just like ourselves" (*ibid.,* p. 318). An infinite God, says James, would threaten (rather than create and preserve, as in biblical theism) finite realities. In the background of James' objection to God's infinity lurks Hegel's logically coercive Absolute; James thinks that the best way to distinguish deity from the all-encompassing Absolute is to finitize God.

Over against the forfeiture by Kant and James of theologically objectifying knowledge, and their restriction of interest in divinity to the moral sphere, Whitehead reemphasizes the importance of the metaphysical aspects of God's nature. His comprehensive exposition has been more influential than any other modern theory of theistic finitism. He expressly rejects "the Semitic concept of God" (*Religion in the Making,* pp. 68 ff.)—by which (in distinction from the religion of Jesus and of John the Evangelist) he designates Old Testament teaching and Christian and Mohammedan theologies. The Judeo-Christian and Moslem perspectives Whitehead categorizes as extreme transcendentalism that disallows any relationship of mutual dependence between the divine and actual entities in the universe.

Whitehead's alternative doctrine of God provides a religious framework that compromises the infinity of God and declares deity to have a dipolar nature. Whitehead considers God as both permanent and fluent; not only does God create the world, but as Whitehead sees it, "the World creates God" (*Process and Reality,* p. 528). He writes: "Neither God, nor the World, reaches static completion. Both are in the grip of the ultimate metaphysical ground, the creative advance into novelty" (*ibid.,* p. 529). Strictly speaking, as Collins observes, Whitehead disowns the doctrine "that God is the creative first cause of the world. The Whiteheadian God does not create the world but saves it by presenting it with persuasive ideals. This position is admittedly closer to the Platonic demiurge, the Aristotelian first mover, and the evolutionary vital nisus than to the Creator of the Christian tradition" (*God in Modern Philosophy,* p. 316). John B. Cobb, Jr. points out the contrast of the implications of Whitehead's philosophy "with the traditional doctrines that have insisted only on the permanence, unity, eminent actuality, transcendence, and creative power of God" (*A Christian Natural Theology.* Based on the Thought of Alfred North Whitehead, p. 166).

A remarkable feature of much recent process theology is that it borrows and revises elements of Judeo-Christian theology while disavowing the epistemological foundations on which these biblical emphases depend. Although Whitehead "thought of God as *an* actual entity rather than as a living person," Cobb proposes instead "to assimilate God more closely to the conception of a living person" (*ibid.,* p. 188). Then, departing from a Judeo-Christian doctrine of divine revelation, he ventures "clarification and illumination by the use of Whiteheadian concepts" of such fundamental biblical motifs as "the presence of God in Jesus Christ, the way in which the Christian is bound to him in faith, the nature of the new being in him, the sacraments, the present working of the Holy Spirit" (*ibid.*, pp. 280 ff.). In other words, while the infinitude and other perfections of the God of the Bible are disowned, certain elements are retained willy-nilly as if Christian theology easily accommodates itself to independent philosophical expositions of pick-and-choose revelatory aspects.

Albert C. Knudson, who appeals to personalistic philosophy in selecting preferred facets of the biblical view of God and the universe, retains insistence on the infinitude of God. A finite God, he says, is both religiously and metaphysically unsatisfactory; religiously a finite God leaves us with "a truncated and disintegrating faith," and metaphysically such "a growing and struggling God would himself need a God in much the same way that we do" (*The Doctrine of God*, p. 259). It is noteworthy that Knudson shifts the emphasis from divine infinity to divine absoluteness, and comments that "no matter . . . what limitations may be ascribed to God, he is absolute so long as he is regarded as the independent and self-existent source or ground of the universe" (*ibid.*, p. 263). While Brightman, Knudson's colleague, affirmed the latter role for God, he declared God to be finite and viewed him as incorporating a "given" or retarding factor that results in the presence of irrational evil in the universe (*The Problem of God*, chapters V and VII). Eugene W. Lyman emphasizes the infinity of God, yet says that the conception should not be understood to imply "that for him there is no achievement, nor that his achievement is free from striving"; rather, the idea "should be employed only as an expression of the faith that his triumph is sure" (*Theology and Human Problems*, p. 149).

Neither personalism nor process theology has a doctrine of transcendent intelligible divine revelation. For that reason they cannot effectively defend claims about God against charges by naturalists that secular metaphysicians simply project upon the outer world their own individually preferred aspects of man's psychic nature and experience.

Kierkegaard and later existential thinkers placed fundamental emphasis on the infinite qualitative distinction between man and God, time and eternity, finite and infinite. "The absolute difference between God and man," Kierkegaard writes, "consists precisely in this, that man is a particular existing being . . . while God is infinite and eternal" (*Concluding Unscientific Postscript*, p. 195). Arthur C. Cochrane wonders whether Kierkegaard "simply took over this ontological framework from Greek and modern philosophical tradition . . . without seeking proofs for it" (to seek proofs would have contradicted his whole approach) or whether his ontology is "just the thought form in which he gave expression to the individual's relation to God who is revealed in Jesus Christ" (*The Existentialists and God*, p. 25). Whatever the case may be, Kierkegaard's notion of truth as paradoxical rules out any objective knowledge of the infinite or even of the infinite-finite disjunction; the infinite God exists only for passionate inwardness.

Translated into German in the 1920s, Kierkegaard's works greatly influenced the theological thought of Barth, Gogarten, Bultmann and others, and must be largely credited for the dialectical-existential revolt against Hegelian rationalism. Barth writes in the preface to the second German edition (1921) of his *The Epistle to the Romans,* "if I have a system, it is limited to a recognition of what Kierkegaard called the 'infinite qualitative distinction' between time and eternity, and to my regarding this as having negative as well as positive significance" (cited from the translation of the sixth edition by Edwyn C. Hoskyns, London, Oxford University Press, 1933, 1950, p. 10, which includes Barth's earlier prefaces together with one specially prepared for Hoskyns' translation). But Barth later dramatically qualifies this thesis by stressing that in Jesus Christ the paradox is a unity of infinite and finite.

Although Kierkegaard equates the infinite with the timeless transcendent, his concentration on the inner dialectic precludes him from stating anything positive about God other than God's qualitative difference from man. In this way, Cochrane points out, Kierkegaard "fathered modern existential ontology which speaks in various ways" of man in relation to the transcendent—or to "the comprehensive" as Jaspers called it, or to "being" (Heidegger) or to "the nothing" (both Heidegger and Sartre) (*The Existentialists and God,* p. 40).

The vagueness of the term infinite in recent modern philosophy and theology therefore calls for critical comment. Surely the nonbiblical views cannot be invoked to challenge the biblical representation of divine infinity if their use of the term is meaningless or obscure.

Barth lifts the discussion of infinite and finite to a different context, namely, that of God's self-revelational activity. Infinity for Barth is not an infinite number of finitudes, nor is it nonfinitude: infinity is God himself. Barth finds neither an empty conception of infinity nor high-sounding sentences about pure being, the unconditioned, being-itself, or whatever, to be a proper basis for expositing God's nature. Barth rejects discussion of God's infinity based only upon philosophical speculation. The term infinity notably has virtually no place in the index of his *Church Dogmatics.* For Barth God's infinity is the plenitude of the divine perfections.

It is God the Infinite who alone preserves the finite from vanishing into the nothingness of pre-creation. This nothingness or *nihil,* moreover, is not an ontological category that constantly competes against God as a second ultimate principle and is discernible by metaphysical analysis of the structure of being; rather, nothingness is known only by the revelation of God the Creator and Redeemer who alone is free to create or not to create out of nothing.

In Paul Tillich's view, "Being-itself is beyond finitude and infinity," whereas, by contrast, "everything finite participates in being-itself and in its infinity" (*Systematic Theology,* Vol. I, p. 237. Tillich contends that "nonbeing belongs to being; it cannot be separated from it" [*The Courage to Be,* p. 179]). The presence of nonbeing, Tillich holds, spurs being-itself to actualize itself. "Nonbeing makes God a living God" (*ibid.,* p. 180). If true, Tillich's ontology would make any claim that God is infinite meaning-less except in polarity to finiteness; in any event all predications about Being-itself lose objective significance because Tillich views them as meta-phorical or symbolic.

Cochrane calls attention to the similarity of Tillich's view to that of Heidegger, who likewise considers the nothing or nonbeing as integral to being. "Unless nonbeing is a relatively harmless thing," Cochrane pro-tests, "it would seem to be monstrous to say that it is in God," worse yet, that "it makes God to be a living, loving God" (*The Existentialists and God,* p. 87). The fact is that a doctrine of God known in his self-revelation provides no basis whatever for including nonbeing in God. As Collins re-marks, "There is no need to seek" with Tillich "for a god beyond the God of theism but only for a philosophical theism for which God is known to be other than all finite existents and conceptions" (*God in Modern Philoso-phy,* p. 402).

Barth tries to eliminate the ontic paradox of infinite and finite in Jesus Christ by insisting that Jesus Christ reveals both divine and human nature in a distinctive way, that is, God becomes man and in this servant-form reveals his glory (*Church Dogmatics,* IV/1). Yet since Barth rejects objec-tive intellectual revelation, he remains as opposed to Christian possession of valid truths about God as was Kierkegaard. Cochrane's verdict on Barth is therefore justified: "We do not perceive any *fundamental* opposition between Barth and Kierkegaard, though we acknowledge the necessity of the Christological corrective Barth has given to Kierkegaard" (*The Existen-tialists and God,* p. 47), a corrective, we would add, that requires still fur-ther correction. Barth derives from God's infinity the assertion that "hiddenness" is one of God's divine perfections, and that because of this hiddenness the knowledge of God comes only by revelation. Barth goes beyond evangelical orthodoxy, however, by maintaining that this revela-tion—whether special revelation or general (which Barth disallows)—does not confront reason in the form of objectively cognizable truths. Barth, for whom revelation is addressed to faith, that is, to the obedient will, and continues sporadically in the present, does not consider God to be theo-logically objectifiable. The Infinite, in Barth's view, is therefore only indi-rectly the scripturally revealed God.

The shadow of Heidegger, who presumes to transfer the debate into a sphere beyond the conflict of theism and atheism, falls over much of recent existentialist discussion about God. Heidegger's concern is with Being, said to be present in various modes that both reveal and conceal it. The infinite God cannot be grasped by philosophical thought, says Heidegger, but is grasped rather by poetic and religious minds in symbol and myth. While we cannot rest in the notion of God's nonbeing, we have no access in this view to philosophical theism or to revelational theism for valid conceptual information concerning God. It was disagreement with Heidegger's notion that transcendence holds no meaning for contemporary man that spurred Tillich to seek an intellectually viable and religiously adequate metaphys-ical alternative. But in displacing supernatural theism by an infinite

Ground of all being Tillich created as many difficulties as did Heidegger's phenomenological analysis.

This survey of the fortunes of the conception of divine infinity in the history of philosophy clearly shows that in order to speak significantly of the infinitude of God we must speak not only of God but specifically of God in his revelation; we must speak of God who has made himself intelligibly known both as creator of the cosmos and man and as lord of the universe. In so doing we speak not of some conjectural infinite, postulated from an impressive galaxy of finitudes, or even of an emanating infinite that needs the finite as much as the finite needs the infinite; we speak, rather, of the living Infinite who declares both our creatureliness and sinfulness, and who depicts us as creatures endowed with rational categories adequate to the knowledge of God and also with ethical categories that we violate in our present plight as moral rebels.

The Bible gives us no basis for applying to God an empty conception of infinity which, taken by itself, says nothing definitive. In view of the many notions of "the Infinite" projected by secular philosophers the Christian theologian is on safe ground if he insists first of all that the infinite of secular metaphysics is not the God of the Bible; the term "infinite," in short, is not self-interpreting. If we designate the God of the Bible as infinite, we must append the term to his specific perfections, and not use it as a synonym for such generalities as being or substance, terms that in turn call for yet further clarification. That God is infinite Spirit in distinction from finite spirits is indeed the case. But the biblical God, as the Westminster Shorter Catechism proceeds to state, is "infinite, eternal and unchangeable" in respect to specific attributes. D. W. D. Shaw remarks that the unfortunate connotations of the word infinite can be avoided by using the term "not to denote some attribute . . . but to qualify another adjective; by using it adverbially, in other words, rather than adjectivally. We shall not say, then, that God is infinite. But we shall say that God is 'infinitely' this or that, loving, for example, or gracious" (*Who Is God?*, pp. 60 f.). What infinity means in respect to God's perfections is to be learned therefore from God's own revelation of his nature and ways.

Gerhard Kittel comments on the striking departure of the Septuagint, and of the New Testament in turn, from the accepted Greek meanings of *doxa* (from *dokeo,* to think, to seem) in translating the Hebrew term *kabod* when applied to God ("Doxa," *TDNT* 3:242 ff.). The Hebrew *kabod* has a variety of senses, including 'good repute' and 'honor'; it is used also of man's inner spirit (Ps. 16:9, 108:1) and, moreover, A. M. Ramsey comments, of "the revealed being or character of God" (*The Glory of God and the Transfiguration of Christ,* pp. 9 f.). In respect to God the Bible routinely and impressively translates *kabod* by *doxa* to convey the meaning of glory, honor, excellency, majesty, splendor, power and beauty, as well as holiness and mercy. Yahweh is the God of glory (Ps. 28:3) and the King of glory (Ps. 23:7).

Everett F. Harrison presents a strong case for understanding the glory of God in its biblical intention to mean the totality of God's revealed perfections. The glory of God may be comprehended, says Harrison, as the absolute uniqueness of his person in view of the completeness and perfection of his attributes ("The Use of DOXA in Greek Literature with Special Reference to the New Testament"). The New Testament not only uses the term glory of one or another of God's perfections (Rom. 1:23, 3:23, 6:4; Col. 1:11) but also declares God to be "the Father of glory" (Eph. 1:17). When it refers to the panoply of God's attributes, we may consider the term glory to be the preferred biblical equivalent for the term infinitude or infinity in respect to the divine nature.

The dramatic doctrine of the New Testament is that the glory of God is supremely revealed in the God-man Jesus Christ. Christ is the effulgence of divine glory (Heb. 1:3), that is, his life and work make known the divine perfections. He is the Lord of glory (James 2:1). That glory, disowned by rebellious sinners, was discerned and heralded by the disciples who in Jesus beheld the glory of the Father's one and only Son (John 1:14; cf. 2:11, 13:13, 17:1, 5).

On the surface the doctrine of divine incarnation might seem to relativize the conception of divine infinity. Yet the doctrine affirms that the infinite Logos stepped into history in one Jesus of Nazareth who bears both divine and human natures. The infinite is no less infinite because of its distinctive infinite-finite disclosure.

So centrally is the glory of God connected with the accomplishment of the divine will that, as Harrison observes ("Glory," pp. 236 f.), the apostle John views the substitutionary death of the Son of man in terms of divine glorification: "The hour is come that the Son of man should be glorified" (John 12:33). Heaven is not the only arena for displaying God's glory but, as Sverre Aalen remarks, God discloses his glory in the history of mankind, and supremely in the sufferings, death and resurrection of Jesus Christ (John 12:23–28) ("Glory/Honour/*Doxa,*" p. 48).

No philosopher has affirmed divine love to be an attribute of the Infinite except through the influence of Christianity. Christianity declares that the Infinite meets us in the Gospels, that the divine agent in creation, redemption and judgment is none other than the incarnate, crucified and risen Nazarene. Secular philosophy, by contrast, could even champion a God of "infinite indifference." F. J. Sheed comments appropriately: "Aristotle's concept of God as Pure Act is one of the most splendid achievements of the human intellect; but if it dims our vision of the God who is Christ's Father and ours, then Aristotle has not served us. . . . It was without Aristotle's consent that Aquinas baptized him: and one cannot feel that the baptism wholly 'took'" (*God and the Human Condition,* p. 196).

That it is the God of infinite righteousness and love who goes to Calvary to salvage penitent humans is made manifest in word and life by the incarnate Christ. If Jesus does not overtly expound divine infinity in propositional form, he nonetheless exhibits divine infinity, as the Scripture affirms, in his own life by his servanthood. Jesus in no way revised the Old Testament's teaching about God, but openly displayed God's nature in action. His life and work are commentaries on a comprehensive worldview and lifeview. The Kingdom of God is central in his teaching and mission. God clothes the grass of the field and without him no sparrow falls. The prayer "thy will be done" sums up Christ's entire view of human fortunes and of the world. The declaration "All things are delivered unto me of my Father: and no man knoweth the Son, but the Father; neither knoweth any man the Father, save the Son, and he to whomsoever the Son will reveal him" (Matt. 11:25; cf. Luke 10:21) states the supreme principle of the universe. The New Testament confession "Jesus is Lord" (1 Cor. 12:2) mirrors this majestic truth. The messianic, moral and metaphysical implications are staggering.

Yahweh alone, declares the Old Testament, governs all of human existence; there is no room for other gods. Many New Testament passages (cf. Acts 17:24; 1 Tim. 6:15) state and reflect the same truth. But the New Testament focuses specially on the incarnate Son who is Lord of the human harvest and hence of global history (Matt. 9:38). New Testament statements on infinity underscore the sovereign authority of God and his Christ. To the Son, God the Father himself gives the name Lord (Phil. 2:9 ff.). He alone is worthy to receive and to open the record at the climactic end of world history (Rev. 5:12). Wielding all power and authority in heaven and earth (Matt. 28:18), the Risen Jesus in his session at the Father's right hand (Acts 2:36; cf. Ps. 110) rules jointly with the Father; by redemption, reconciliation and judgment he exercises divine sovereignty in the moral subordination of humanity and of the cosmos (Col. 1:20). When Christ the Lord has overcome hostility and rebellion, he will restore all things to God's direct rule by presenting the world and himself to the Father (1 Cor. 15:28). Thus as God the living Infinite strips away the last vestiges of creaturely revolt infinity will pervade the finite.

12.
Divine Timelessness
or Unlimited Duration?

OUR CENTURY FOCUSES far less attention on the nature and eternity of God, than on the nature of the temporal universe, or on the frenetic character of daily life in a technological society. Until very recently most contemporary astronomers accepted the scientifically espoused view that the universe is 15 to 18 billion years old. In 1979, however, three American astronomers controverted these calculations by insisting that a major error had been made in Hubble's Constant, the yardstick used to decipher the distance between objects in space; the universe is therefore now said to be only half as big as the experts had held and not more than half as old, that is, not more than 9 billion years (cf. Beverly Karplus Hartline, "Double Hubble, Age in Trouble," *Science,* Jan. 11, 1980, pp. 167–169). For a time-primed generation little interested in eternity, the charge of a 9-billion-year error quite understandably shocked a scientific community proud of spectacular successes in outer space. The difference between Ussher's much ridiculed creation date of 4004 B.C. and the presently indicated date of 9 billion B.C. is not much different from the reformulated calculations of 18 billion years B.C. to 9 billion years B.C.

Frontier twentieth-century theologians, on the other hand, have referred very little to time and history in their discussion of eternity. In the 1930s dialectical and existential theology promoted divine revelation in the context of a vertical "moment" in which eternity bisects time. Inherent in this approach is the problem of the relation between the timeless and the temporal and at stake is not only the revelatory worth and meaning of time, but also the connection between revelation and history. While influential religionists were compressing the eternal into an inner confrontational moment, influential astronomers were coping with an alleged computational error of 9 billion years.

The fulcrum in the conflict between theology and current secular reduc-

tions of reality to only temporal processes is the eternity of God. As Gerhard
Ebeling puts it, "the thought of eternity signalizes most visibly—so one
might think—the place where theology's concern clashes with the modern
understanding of reality" ("Time and Word," p. 251). Ebeling speaks of
"eternity as an epitome of the perfections of God and the sustaining ground
of all theological statements about the eternal Word, which creates time
and everything temporal and toward the end of time enters temporality
by becoming man in order to give men a part in eternal life. . . . All this
is now placed into question, from root to crown," he adds, "by the fact
that time itself takes the place of God and declares the creator of time to
be a product of time" (*ibid.*, pp. 251 f.).

The controversy over time and eternity rages disconcertingly even among
theologians; while they refuse to concede that God's time is past, more
and more mediating scholars nonetheless temporalize aspects of God's being and life.

Dialectical postulations of an infinite qualitative difference between eternity and time that accommodated a mere momentary intrusion of the eternal by way of inner existential encounter did not effectively confront
secular repudiations of eternity and atheistic efforts to annihilate the transcendent. Nor could the biblical understanding of eternity and time prevail
where, in reaction to dialectical misconceptions, critics espoused Hebrew
over Greek views but covertly added the biases, presumably supported by
Scripture, of recent German philosophy. Not only ontological propositional
revelation but also and even divine cognitive disclosure was hastily dismissed as a vestigial remnant of Greek rationalism. All emphasis on God's
timeless eternity was said to be Platonic speculation; the terms eternal
and eternity were said to designate not divine timelessness but fullness
of time found in God, the inwardly experienced Lord of time.

But precisely because it tried to eliminate metaphysical overtones and
historical importance from the conception of eternity, and tried to transfer
the reality of the transcendent to the sphere of internal personal decision,
this existential-eschatological alternative could not make God's eternity
powerfully and permanently significant. The "presence" of God as mere
existential encounter or as the "presence of the future" now displaced
two distinct levels of ontological reality, the supernatural and natural; in
the context of mythical views of eschatology this "presence," moreover,
brought confusion to evangelical orthodox concepts of the transcendent.
Modern alternatives to biblical teaching concerning God and time did not
take seriously either divine creation or final divine judgment of the universe, doctrines that involve inescapable questions of datable chronology
and of salvation-history as a time-continuum.

Kierkegaard's infinite qualitative distinction between eternity and time,
as the Danish philosopher worked it out, disadvantaged both revelation
in history and rational revelation. Yet Kierkegaard perceived that no infinity of instants could be confused with eternity. He writes: "In vain would
the temporal assume an air of importance, count the instants, and add

them all together—if eternity has any say in the matter, the temporal . . . never comes to more than the 'once.' For eternity is the opposite . . . not . . . to a single instant (this is meaningless), it is the opposite to the temporal as a whole, and it opposes itself with the power of eternity against the temporal amounting to more than that" (*Christian Discourses,* pp. 103 f.). Kierkegaard sweepingly identifies God with pure being or eternity and, as Arthur Cochrane observes, does not develop a doctrine of the being of God (*The Existentialists and God,* p. 30). Kierkegaard discerns full well, however, that no combination or recombination of the temporal can yield the eternal.

For Barth the being of God in eternity is anything but an abstract being-itself; he ventures to give christological or trinitarian content to the Godhead. But while Barth strives to preserve intelligible ontological transcendence, on the one hand, he constantly focuses on confrontational revelation, on the other, in the context of a dialectical theology. Modifying his earlier commitment to the radical discontinuity of eternity and time, he views eternity neither as timeless nor as endless, but as a preform of time. In the triune Godhead past, present and future are one, yet there is also beginning, succession and end. Says Barth, "While time is not eternity, neither is eternity timeless for it is togetherness and interrelation of past, present and future" (*Church Dogmatics,* III/2, pp. 529 f., 536). Howard A. Slatte interprets such comments as a "shift away from an earlier transcendental view of eternity itself" (*Time and Its End,* p. 135). Barth considers eternity "not the negation of time but the boundary of time"; it can embrace a past, present and future, although it does so as a past and future also present (*Church Dogmatics,* II/2, pp. 183 ff.). The wording here is cautious, and might in fact be compatible with divine timelessness no less than with infinite duration. Yet for Barth the eternal and the temporal constitute a dialectical duality that only subjective personal faith can bridge.

Emil Brunner declares that "God stands above Time because He is its Creator and Lord. The God who creates Time, who makes a beginning, who 'allows' time and who will one day say: 'Now it is ended!'—this God is not Himself involved in the Time-process" (*The Christian Doctrine of God,* pp. 269 f.). But, with an ambivalence not uncharacteristic of dialectical theology, Brunner adds that, because God wishes to fulfill the temporal, "This Eternity . . . is something quite different from timelessness. . . . God's Being is not timeless. . . . The Eternity of God is concerned wholly and entirely with His relation to *created* Time" (*ibid.,* p. 270). The implication seems to be that time was divinely created from eternity, and for that reason God is continually involved in time. One wonders how God's being can be at once "not timeless" and yet "uninvolved in the time-process."

To its credit the salvation history school paced by Oscar Cullmann at least showed clearly that the biblical understanding of revelation and redemption involves external sequential history, and not merely internal confrontation; it once again correlated God's eternity with external salvific history. The modern historicist emphasis, however, that each person creatively sees history from his own perspective soon began to challenge the hesitant gains made by redemptive history theologians.

Edgar S. Brightman, speaking for many personalists, argues for a temporalistic view of God, as did Cullmann. "The divine eternity means God's endless duration," he writes (*The Finding of God*, p. 131). Brightman finds the notion of an "absolute end or beginning of time . . . rationally impossible" and, professing to take time seriously, he ascribes memory and limited knowledge to God.

In Wolfhart Pannenberg's view, eternity is not the antithesis of time but the unity of time. In his essay on "Der Gott der Hoffnung" (1965) he reformulates time and eternity in eschatological context and grounds divine eternity in the future of God ("The God of Hope," pp. 234–249). By contrast with Jürgen Moltmann, in whose view the future is radically discontinuous with the past and the present, Pannenberg's construction postulates the flow of historical time from the future toward the present and the past, and then toward the future. This is philosophical assertion; it is neither self-evident nor free of ambiguity.

Tillich rejects the idea that eternity nullifies time in God, but promotes a dialectic of eternity and time in ontological categories. Eternity he defines as "the transcendent unity of the dissected moments of existential time" (*Systematic Theology*, Vol. I, p. 271). By keeping the temporal within the eternal without sacrificing the differences of each he hopes to avoid an antitemporal eternal (cf. *The Eternal Now*).

For John Macquarrie ". . . time and history are not just forms under which we perceive a timeless and non-historical Being. They really belong to Being," he says, "and without them Being could not be dynamic, it could not manifest itself, it could not be God or holy Being, it could be only an inert static Being. . . . But Being is not in time and history, as if these were more ultimate than Being. Rather, the expansion and expression of Being creates time and being" (*Principles of Christian Theology*, p. 191). But, we must ask, if Being would be inert without time, how could such Being (through expansion and expression) create time? Macquarrie deprives theology of any say as to whether the cosmos is eternal or whether it began at the first moment of time; he looks for answers, instead, to radio telescopes and other scientific investigative techniques (*ibid.*, p. 199). By formulating the doctrine of creation existentially in terms of responsive creaturely dependence upon grace, he makes external causal factors irrelevant. According to Macquarrie the "beginning" of creation is "not some moment of past time" but simply God as permanent *archē*, that is, the ground that he is "at any time and at all times" (*ibid.*, p. 200). Macquarrie considers God a reality beyond existence (*ibid.*, p. 108). Like his predecessors Basilides, Kierkegaard, Brunner, Bultmann and Tillich, Macquarrie nonetheless pleads the case for temporally structured being. He is vulnerable on both fronts, whether he says that finite beings inhere in God, or that time does also (cf. Tillich, *Systematic Theology*, Vol. I, pp. 263 f.). In the former case God alone is responsible for whatever happens in the universe; in the latter, God cannot foreknow the future and, in fact, cannot be sure of his own future, since he does not transcend time.

But pervasive secularism, aggressively and radically naturalistic, categorically declared all reality to be simply impersonal temporal processes and events. As Harry Blamires observes, "secularism is, by definition, time-locked; it accepts time as a determinative dimension" (*Tyranny of Time: A Defense of Dogmatism,* p. 11). Under the influence of empirical science, secular scholars forego the reality of the transcendent and dismiss divine timelessness or duration as irrelevant. Paul M. van Buren comments, for example, that to say that Jesus is eternal is merely to say that his perspective has always been and always will be needed (*The Secular Meaning of the Gospel,* p. 162). The day is long gone when hesitant naturalists, like Samuel Alexander and Henry Nelson Wieman in an earlier age, any longer apply the term "God" to the emerging tip of space-time evolution; in his day even John Dewey had spoken deferentially of divinity as creative interaction between the real and the ideal. The notion of temporary or perishable deities belongs to crude and primitive stages of religious thought. Homer and Hesiod alike, although they viewed the gods as eternal, as "the immortals" who neither age nor die, held that the gods came into being and are not preexistent. Serious theology views divine existence as eternal, as neither created nor temporary.

The way humans conceive divine eternity has great significance for human belief and action not only in Christianity but also in nonbiblical religions like Buddhism and Hinduism. The word eternal carries various nuances such as everlasting and unending, unchanging and unalterable, perfect and unbetterable. A verdict on the character of divine eternity therefore affects both the destiny of man and the nature of God.

Almost invariably the popular notion of God's eternity is synonymous with endlessness of temporal existence. On first impression this notion of the deity's infinite duration in time is plausible enough. Yet, as Lewis R. Farnell notes, both classic and modern religious philosophy show marked preference for the alternative view that God is a Being who transcends time or is outside time (*The Attributes of God,* p. 255).

The God of Christian orthodoxy is timelessly eternal as mainstream theologians like Augustine, Anselm, Aquinas, the Protestant Reformers, and in fact, most Christian theologians affirm. They assert that God's perfections, including wisdom, righteousness, omnipotence and omniscience, characterize the divine nature even before he created the universe; such predications they consider timelessly true of God. Even Schleiermacher, for all his modernism, contrasted the nontemporal life of God with the life of the universe which, he said, extends backward and forward infinitely in time (*The Christian Faith,* Para. 52, Sec. 1). Since God is timeless, Schleiermacher emphasizes, he has neither temporal limits nor temporal location; his being has no time span, nor does it involve "temporal opposition of before and after" (*ibid.,* Para. 52, Secs. 1 and 2).

Augustine affirms in the *Confessions* (Book XI, ch. 13): "Thy present day does not give way to tomorrow, nor indeed, does it take the place of yesterday. Thy present day is eternity" (*Fathers of the Church,* p. 343). While Boethius writes of God as existing in the "eternal-present" (*De Consolatione Philosophiae,* Part V), he does not mean by this, Nelson Pike reminds us (*God and Timelessness*), that God has a location in time; rather, like Augustine, and later, Anselm, Boethius intends to declare—as he elsewhere expressly states—that God has "always an eternal and present state" (*Consolation of Philosophy,* 11. 61 f., p. 403). Anselm states in the *Proslogion* (Ch. XIX): ". . . Neither yesterday, nor today nor tomorrow thou art; but simply, thou art, outside all time" (*St. Anselm,* p. 25). And in the *Monologium* (Ch. XXII) he asserts: "In no place or time . . . is this being properly said to exist . . . neither then, nor now nor at any time; nor does it exist in terms of the fleeting present in which we live, nor has it existed, nor will it exist in terms of the past or future, since these are restricted to things finite and mutable, which it is not" (*St. Anselm,* p. 81).

Pike calls special attention to Boethius's acknowledged dependence on Plato for his conception of eternity (*Consolation of Philosophy,* line 36). Expressly contrasting the timeless eternal with the temporal creation, Plato writes: ". . . 'was' and 'will be' are created species of time which we in our carelessness mistakenly apply to eternal being" (*Timaeus,* 37E6–38Ab). The view of a timeless God is routinely disparaged by its critics as an unfortunate legacy of Greek philosophy, one that they consider incompatible with the biblical view of God; the Greeks, it is often said, were disinterested in time, whereas the God of the Bible is vitally concerned with both time and history. But Aristotle's extended discussion (*Physics,* Book IV, 218a–224a) shows that he was, indeed, interested in time. What the Greeks lacked was a metaphysical interest in the course of time; they perceived no comprehensive purpose in history, and failed to connect human destiny with personal decision and a specific historical event. Augustine, Anselm, and the Protestant Reformers insisted on God's timelessness, but insisted, as well, on the great importance of God's relationship to the temporal universe and to human history.

Besides the views that God is timeless or that God has unlimited temporal duration, a third alternative has sometimes been suggested: that divine cognition of all things is an "everlasting now" in which there are no distinctions of past and future. This proposal actually attempts to blend the conceptions of timelessness and of unlimited duration. Although this view does not expressly temporalize God's nature its attribution of time to the mode of divine consciousness and cognition involves deity in a mode of time-determination. Charles Hodge, for one, seems to waver between divine timelessness and this insistence that all things are "ever present to [God's] view" (*Systematic Theology,* Vol. 1, pp. 385 ff., 390).

The rejection of divine timelessness need not imply that God is *in* time, as though time were a reality that antedates and perhaps postdates God. Those who say that God has infinite duration hold that God's existence has no temporal *location,* that is, his existence is not confined to a *limited* time; his existence, moreover, has no temporal *extension,* that is, God does not exist only in an interval between two times. In short, God does not exist in time; rather, time is in God.

No generation in Christian history has debated like ours about whether God is timeless or whether he has unending duration, that is, whether temporal existence extends interminably forward and backward. In recent decades even some evangelical theologians have abandoned the inherited emphasis of God's timelessness. J. Oliver Buswell, Jr., for example, denies that God's consciousness is timeless, and contends, instead, that God like us has a sense of time involving past, present and future (*A Systematic Theology of the Christian Religion*, pp. 45 ff.). Clark Pinnock is another who disavows the timelessness of God. Donald Bloesch's brief treatment of divine eternity is less clear: "Eternity is not timelessness nor the endless duration of time; it is rather 'the fulfillment of time' " (*Essentials of Evangelical Theology*, Vol. 1, p. 30). What he means by "the fulfillment of time"— a phrase that now often has existentialist overtones—Bloesch does not specifically tell us. He does add, however, that "the eternity of God signifies his sovereign rule over time" (*ibid.*, p. 30), but emphasis on divine sovereignty hardly clarifies the nature of divine eternity. Ronald Nash suggests that we should perhaps view time much like Augustine viewed the *rationes aeternae*—the eternal ideas—as eternal and yet in some manner dependent upon God. But that would not of itself decide between timelessness and duration.

Among evangelicals, Nicholas Wolterstorff voices perhaps the most forthright rejection of the inherited doctrine of timeless divine eternity. He insists that "a theology which opts for God as eternal cannot be a theology faithful to the biblical witness" and "cannot avoid being in conflict with the confession of God as redeemer" ("God Everlasting," p. 182, in *God and the Good*, Essays in Honor of Henry Stob. Clifton J. Orlebeke and Lewis B. Smedes, ed., William B. Eerdmans, pp. 181–203). In "Time and Eternity in Theology," Wolterstorff approves William Kneale's contention that the influence of classical Greek philosophers on early Christian theologians accounts for the tradition of God's timelessness though he acknowledges that Plato (*Timaeus,* 37–38) did not connect eternity and divinity. Wolterstorff calls for "dehellenization" and repudiation of "the God eternal tradition" ("God Everlasting," pp. 182 f.).

The motivation for modifying the traditional doctrine of divine timelessness derives from many influences: hurried ascription of the medieval view to Greek sources; larger preoccupation with time in modern philosophy and contemporary technology; writings of process theologians and of salvation history theologians, particularly Oscar Cullmann; and certain philosophical problems thought to be associated with the inherited view of God's eternity. Nash attributes most of the current unrest over divine timelessness to the supposed philosophical difficulties of correlating this view with other divine attributes and with biblical descriptions of God's activities.

What light does Scripture throw upon the question of God's timelessness?

Do the inspired biblical writings come down firmly on one side or the other of the issue? Does biblical language or biblical teaching require the view of God's unending duration or, alternatively, of God's supratemporality? Does the scriptural doctrine require us to reject any of the several views of divine eternity?

The relevant biblical passages are disappointingly few, and philological resources for resolving the issue may seem too meager to be of help. The main Old Testament terms for time are *'et*, which bears quite ordinary meanings about time, *'olam*, which refers to remote time or perpetuity, and *mo'ed*, which carries the sense of "appointment" and is used not only of humanly appointed meetings but also of divinely appointed festivals and seasons and of allotted times.

Genesis 21:33 reads: "Abraham planted a grove in Beer-sheba, and called there on the name of the Lord, the everlasting God" (RSV; NIV: "the Eternal God"). Psalm 89:2 declares that Yahweh's love "was established for ever" (RSV; KJV: "from everlasting to everlasting"). Psalm 90:2 reads, "Before the mountains were brought forth, or ever thou hadst formed the earth and the world, from everlasting to everlasting thou art God" (RSV). Isaiah 26:4 states: "The Lord God is an everlasting rock" (RSV; "is the Rock eternal," NIV); and Isaiah 40:28 reads, "Have you not known? Have you not heard? The Lord is the everlasting God, the Creator of the ends of the earth . . ." (RSV).

The Old Testament term most frequently used in this context is *'olam* and is generally applied to a temporal period of indefinite duration, as when it characterizes the "everlasting hills" (Gen. 49:26). Something more is apparently intended, however, when *'olam* is used as a title for God (El Olam, Gen. 21:33), when God alone is declared to be everlasting King (Jer. 10:10) and his kingdom called everlasting (Ps. 145:13; Dan. 4:3, 34), or when God's attributes are pronounced everlasting (mercy, Ps. 100:5; righteousness, Ps. 119:42, 44; strength, Isa. 26:4; love, Isa. 54:8, Jer. 31:3).

According to Hermann Sasse the older Old Testament writings reflect "a very simple concept of eternity. The being of God reaches back into times past computation" (*"Aiōn," TDNT* 1:201). But Sasse holds that this "primitive idea of eternity" changes in the Old Testament; moving from the conception of an incomputable remote past to the more expansive idea of unending time (Isa. 4:28) it incorporates the emphasis "I am the First and the Last" (Isa. 44:6). Although the heavens will perish (Ps. 102:24–27), God is "from everlasting to everlasting" (Ps. 90:2), the One "whose years endure throughout all generations" and "have no end." Resting upon a debatable dating of the Psalms and Isaiah passages, this developmental theory also assumes that the Hebrews found the idea of a timeless eternity mentally inconceivable. Sasse writes: "Eternity is thought of as an unending time—for how else can the human mind picture it?—and the eternal being of God is represented as preexistence and postexistence. . . . In the New Testament, too, eternity is thought of as the opposite of . . . cosmic time which is limited by creation and conclusion" (*ibid.,* p. 202).

The view of eternity as the antithesis of time—a view that Sasse finds only in "later Judaism" (e.g., Slavonic Enoch 65)—he dismisses as a philosophical intrusion into Judeo-Christian theology of "timelessness as in Plato" (cf. *Timaeus,* 37e).

The Septuagint translates *'olam* by the Greek equivalent *aiōn.* In the New Testament, Romans 16:28 designates God as "the eternal God." "Never in the New Testament," remarks F. H. Brabant, "are the words Aion or Aionion used of limited periods of time" (*Time and Eternity in Christian Thought,* p. 42). While Schleiermacher grants that Psalm 90 does not conclusively prove God's timelessness, he nonetheless cites 2 Peter 3:8 (". . . one day is with the Lord as a thousand years, and a thousand years as one day") in support of it; the passage may be taken equally well, however, in the sense of unending duration. The New Testament designates God (and Christ in Revelation 1:4, 8, RSV) as the One "who is and who was and who is to come." Although neo-Protestant interpreters refer the "who is" to God's present revelation in time, the phrase sequence is important; both Origen and Augustine interpreted the priority of "is" as meaning God's eternal being. Farnell finds "a dim reflex of the concept of timelessness" not only in the Old Testament formula 'I am that I am,' but also "in the eschatological belief that after the final judgment of the world 'there should be time no longer' " (Rev. 10:6) (*The Attributes of God,* p. 255). When recent interpreters translate the latter verse to mean only that "time runs out" before the inbreaking of impending eschatological events, they overturn a longstanding exegetical tradition.

Two comprehensive efforts made in recent decades to expound the biblical view of the nature of divine eternity reach very different conclusions. One is by the French New Testament scholar Oscar Cullmann and the other by the English theologian John Marsh. Both appeal to the scriptural data as normative. Both reject as unbiblical the "Greek cyclical view" of time—although to speak of a Greek cyclical view of time is to confuse history with time; Aristotle considered time to be endless in both directions. Both Cullmann and Marsh disown Rudolf Bultmann's emphasis on sporadic existential revelation and insist that the God of the Bible reveals himself on a horizontal time line. Both agree that Jesus Christ is the midpoint of the biblical two ages (the present from creation to parousia, and the future from parousia onward) and as such has already inaugurated the coming future age. They disagree dramatically, however, over the character of divine eternity.

Cullmann conceives God's eternity in terms of infinitely extended time (*Christus und die Zeit*), an emphasis now shared by many biblical scholars. Ernst Jenni, for example, insists that the Old and New Testaments are "not acquainted" with the conception of a timeless God ("Time," *The Interpreters' Dictionary of the Bible,* 4:643). Cullmann interprets the Old Testament view of God's "everlastingness" as endless duration, and holds that the New Testament term *aiōn* similarly expresses an indefinite period of time, at least one of whose terminals is uncertain. Cullmann views eternity not as timelessness or without time but as "endless time"; eternity is a continuum into which time runs. The series of aeons or ages comprising history he regards as limited parts of the unlimited temporal extension that comprises God's eternity.

Marsh, by contrast, insists that the biblical revelation of God's nature and ways implies a very different conception of divine eternity and its relations to time. In *The Fulness of Time* he proposes "on the basis of the religious insights of the Hebrew-Christian tradition to formulate a sound philosophy of time, eternity and history" (*ibid.,* p. 17). His verdict is that the Bible sees divine eternity as qualitatively different from infinite temporal duration. Marsh declares: "However right we may be to reject Platonic notions of eternity as a 'nunc stans' we cannot, consistently with the New Testament, ascribe the limitations of successiveness to God's time; and that means we cannot think of God's 'time' or his 'eternity' as endless duration" (*ibid.,* p. 181). While Marsh empties the eternal of temporal succession, he does not entirely negate its relation to time, and insists that the incarnation evidences the eternal's ingression into time (*ibid.,* pp. 139 ff.). Marsh contends, however, that the Old Testament writers stretched the term *'olam,* the only term available to them meaning an extended timespan, beyond its usual sense of unlimited duration in order to convey the idea of timeless eternity. This they did by using the term in the plural as a double superlative ("from everlasting to everlasting") (*ibid.,* p. 30); they thus relied on the only means available to them within the limitations of language to say that God's eternity is not simply infinitely extended time but is other than temporal. The plural use thus becomes an expression for transcending temporal limits and conveys the idea of the timeless eternal.

Cullmann contends, however, that examination of the New Testament use of *aiōn* shows that eternity does not differ from time, but is the totality of time, that is, unlimited or endless time. *Aiōn,* he stresses, is used both for a precisely limited timespan or age, and for an unlimited, incalculable duration. When eternity is in view, says Cullmann, the biblical writers prefer the plural *aiōnes.* He comments: "The fact that one can speak of eternity in the plural proves that it does not signify cessation of time or timelessness" but rather "the linking of an unlimited series of limited world periods, whose succession only God is able to survey" (*Christ and Time,* p. 46). Hermann Sasse reflects a similar view (*"Aiōn," TDNT* 1:199).

James Barr has strenuously criticized both Cullmann and Marsh for manipulating the lexical data of the Bible to support their preferred expositions of the nature of divine eternity (*Biblical Words for Time*).

Before detailing Barr's complaints, however, we should note that even if Cullmann and Marsh had based the conclusions they profess to draw from biblical key words on a sound exegetical methodology, they nonetheless allow damaging philosophical concessions to undermine the transcendent ontological validity of their positions. From the fact that all human experience, even of the eternal, is in time, Marsh draws the unfortunate conclusion that "all we can do is to stretch our temporal terminology to point to what lies beyond time" (*The Fulness of Time,* p. 144). He thus weakens his study by failing to insist that man, however timebound, can indeed have valid knowledge of God who is ontologically transcendent. While he insists upon historical divine revelation (*ibid.,* pp. 145 ff.), Marsh seems nonetheless to imply that we can know nothing of God's eternal nature; such a claim contravenes the historic evangelical insistence that even in sin man can perceive God's "eternal power and deity" (Rom. 1:20, RSV) since by creation man was endowed with categories for knowing the Creator. The inspired biblical writers, moreover, convey theologically objectifiable information about God. Marsh stresses the inadequacy of human language "fully to describe the eternal nature of God" (*ibid.,* p. 145), yet he apparently finds that same "human temporal speech" fully adequate to establish his own definitions and descriptions. If, as Marsh contends, human words are indeed inadequate to express the transcendent eternity of God, then the question arises whether they are adequate to express anything at all about the transcendent except in poetic form; if God's eternity permits only poetic representation, must not all biblical representations of divine perfections that differ qualitatively from human characteristics be tapered to mere poetic or doxological formulations?

Cullmann weakens his position in much the same way by insisting that talk of God's transcendent ontological being is rationalistic conjecture. He writes: "The New Testament never speculates about God's eternal being, and . . . is concerned primarily with God's redemptive activity" (*ibid.,* 3rd ed. rev., p. xxvi). While he qualifies this verdict somewhat in view of the prologue of John's Gospel and the opening chapters of Hebrews and Colossians which refer to the eternal Christ, he curiously insists that the New Testament exegete must "avoid philosophical categories" and philosophical verdicts on God's eternal being. The fact is, that philosophical assumptions of one type or another are unavoidable; even if Cullmann professes personally to escape them, his own handling of the biblical data reflects assumptions that Cullmann brings to rather than derives from the scriptural writers. Rejection of ontological theology would rule out the claim that God's own transcendent eternity is time infinitely extended, and would thus frustrate Cullmann's central tenet that in the Bible "eternity is conceived as different from time only with respect to its unlimited character" (*ibid.,* p. 69).

Barr impressively analyzes the terms which both Marsh and Cullmann use to establish their rival views of temporality and divine timelessness. He criticizes their practice of attaching specific theological meanings to semantic units divorced from their syntactical context, and of translating key words into fixed theological concepts. Barr shows that the appeals that Marsh and Cullmann make to biblical vocabulary often depend upon a selective or tendential appropriation of linguistic data. The biblical terms, he stresses, designate a duration relative to the objects they qualify; a simple appeal to isolated Hebrew or Greek words is therefore not decisive for the nature of divine eternity: "The question of the extent of time involved by relating an object to 'olam," says Barr, "is . . . relative to what the object is. . . . Where the being of God is so related, nothing less than the totality of time would be meant; but this does not settle a question

whether it would also involve some other kind of time or some kind of
supertemporality, and such questions can probably not be answered by
an appeal to the word 'olam itself at all" (*Biblical Words for Time*, p.
74).

To Cullmann Barr points out that the plural use of *aiōn* supplies "no
general reason why we should accept Cullmann's argument that the use
of the plural demonstrates that timelessness or cessation of time is not
intended" (*Biblical Words for Time*, p. 68). The plural form, suggests Barr,
may be only a linguistic phenomenon to indicate extension rather than
unlimited multiplication of time. In any event, Barr affirms, "We may assert
with assurance that Cullmann's argument that the use of the plural demonstrates the existence of a series of world periods, or demonstrates that
eternity is not an absence of time, is entirely without validity" (*ibid.*, p.
69).

The debatability of Cullmann's thesis, namely, that the New Testament
does not contrast time and eternity qualitatively, Barr supports in part
by a detailed examination of linguistic specifics to which Cullmann appeals. The evidence cited by Cullmann, claims Barr, does not demonstrate
"that eternity differs from time only in being the unlimited entirety of
time" (*ibid.*, pp. 72 f.). As Barr sees it, Cullmann exchanges the biblical
framework of meaning for a conjectural one which the biblical vocabulary
is then made to serve; what Cullmann consequently depicts as biblical
teaching is a speculative conceptualization and not what the New Testament expressly affirms. This danger besets all biblical interpretation, of
course; no theologian, whether evangelical in intention or not, is exempt
from its perils.

Cullmann relies for his notion that time precedes creation on a prejudiced
reading of *ek tou aiōnos* ("from the ages"), says Barr. Actually the New
Testament context requires no reference to a time period before the creation of the world (*ibid.*, p. 78). Barr insists that the New Testament phrase
eis ton aiōna does not mean only unlimited time or "the whole of time,"
but bears also an alternative sense of "eternally." In the biblical uses of
aiōn in the sense both of a limited temporal period and of a timeless eternity (*ibid.*, p. 76) Barr finds parallels not unlike Plato's uses of the term.

Marsh believes that the doubling of 'olam, to depict a timeless eternity,
is a poetic device that transcends man's temporal categories of speech.
This view also draws Barr's sharp countercomment. He finds this interpretation "quite as improbable" as Cullmann's translation of the plural into
illimitable time. Marsh's argument (which Barr indicates was anticipated
by C. von Orelli, *Die hebräischen Synonyma der Zeit und Ewigkeit genetisch und sprachvergleichend dargestellt*, p. 81), Barr considers "remote
from a realistic explanation of the linguistic facts" (*Biblical Words for
Time*, p. 69, n. 4). Since the Hebrew Old Testament uses the plural of
'olam with relative infrequency, Barr considers its use a stylistic rather
than linguistic device to express the transcendent (*ibid.*, p. 70, n. 1). He
indicates that Qumran documents employ the stylistic plural (*ibid.*, p. 70,
n. 2).

Barr does not try to disprove Marsh's claim that divine eternity differs qualitatively from temporality, or to invalidate Cullmann's contrary claim that eternity and time are qualitatively the same. What he does, rather, is fault the exegetical supports invoked by both scholars to accredit their views as biblical. Barr's complaint is that in expounding the biblical understanding of time many recent expositors rely on an appeal to biblical vocabulary that does not actually support their theological claims. Interpreters err if they think, says Barr, that simple analysis of the Bible's lexical stock produces theological principles; meaning stems not from words seen as isolated linguistic phenomena but from their combination in meaningful statements. Biblical as well as other writers use the words for eternity and time in diverse syntactical contexts. Barr decries a logical method that hypostatizes words into concepts and theological statements, all the more so if the linguistic context of the words is obscured or distorted. Declares Barr: "the hypostatization of vocabulary items is one of the principal ways in which modern biblical theology has forced dogmatic and philosophical schemata upon biblical material, while at the same time professing on the one hand to be nonphilosophical and nondogmatic, and on the other to be exact and scientific linguistically" (*Biblical Words for Time*, p. 140).

Even where dogmaticians presume to rely on usage, tendential interpretation often nullifies the dependability of their claims. Some process theologians, for example, try to exhibit a semblance of biblical support for their emphasis on the temporality of certain aspects of the divine nature. But when they adapt the sense of supposedly relevant scriptural passages to contemporary philosophical theory, such effort becomes a matter of theological double-talk. Schubert Ogden asserts that the supposition of God's essential temporality is "not an invention of Heidegger and certain other modern philosophers" but "it is, rather, the central discovery implicit in the witness of Holy Scripture, and its *locus classicus* is the Old and the New Testaments" (*The Reality of God and other essays*, p. 161). We have every right to require biblical verification of this lofty claim. Ogden offers us the following: "One thinks, for example, of Jesus' summary of the law in Mark 12:28–34, where the God who is witnessed to is so intimately related to the self and the neighbor that a proper love of them is implicitly contained in the whole and unreserved love of them. Or, as an equally striking expression, there is the portrayal of the Last Judgment in Matt. 15:31–46. . . . Therefore, when Heidegger asserts God's temporality, there is no mere concession to the modern temper, but the restatement in formal ontological terms of the understanding of God implicit in Holy Scripture" (*ibid.*, pp. 161 f.). But to derive the temporality of God from an exposition prejudiced by process theology departs both from what the biblical writers intended and from what these scriptural statements expressly affirm.

Numerous thinkers consider eternity a much more obscure category than time, although philosophers have disagreed sharply throughout the centuries over time's elements and nature (cf. *The Philosophy of Time*, Richard M. Gale, ed.). This disagreement prevails even though time, while less accessible to sense perception than space, is a part of everyone's daily experience. Interestingly enough, linguistic scholars observed a century or more ago that Hebrew has more words for eternity than do Arabic and Greek, a circumstance that Orelli attributes to the influence of the revelatory conception of God upon Hebrew thought and language (*Die hebräischen Synonyma der Zeit und Ewigkeit*, p. 105). Orelli, unfortunately, sought to find the meaning even of the biblical terms for eternity and time in their supposed etymological origin, rather than from their scriptural usage. In a penetrating analysis of his approach (*Biblical Words for Time*, pp. 86–101), James Barr calls attention to Orelli's sensory view of the origin of language. According to Orelli humans have an intuitive awareness of the infinite, and even before thought clarifies infinity man ongoingly struggles by the way of negation and eminence to find language appropriate to infinite realities. On this view, the words for eternity stem from terms previously applied to temporal reality; as a result both finite and infinite time are seen as qualitatively continuous. Here the verdict that eternity is not above or beyond time is already assured through the prior assumptions that philology defines its objects by projecting the finite upon the infinite and that human reason is limited to knowledge of time-structured being. Since Orelli maintains that extratemporal being is foreign "to human ways of conceiving things," we should not be at all surprised by his dogmatic claim that the concept of an extratemporal being is foreign to Old Testament thought (*Die hebräischen Synonyma der Zeit und Ewigkeit*, pp. 102 ff.).

Marsh stresses the inadequacy of human language to depict the eternal. But in contrast to Orelli he emphasizes that Christianity did not derive its conception of the eternal, as did neo-Platonism, by abstracting a world of unchanging reality from sensible particulars that are subject to time and change. For the Christian "the historical order is that within which the eternal has revealed itself and in which it may be entered." Neo-Platonism held, on the other hand, that "the world of eternal objects would not be attained without complete abstraction from the world of sense" (*ibid.*, p. 145). Although "the order of knowing certainly is from the historical to the eternal, . . . the order of reality is from the eternal to the temporal and historical" (*ibid.*, p. 147). "The eternal gives shape and character to the historical" as a directive "nontemporal, eternal, living mind and will" (*ibid.*, p. 148). Marsh therefore tries to derive the character of divine eternity from God's revelatory initiative rather than from inference and projection from creaturely realities. But his strange subjection of the priority of divine revelation to limitations imposed on theological language and conception by the finite space-time realm cancels the objective intellectual significance of divine discharge.

To Barr's criticism that he rests his view of divine temporalness upon tendentially interpreted scriptural vocabulary, Cullmann replies that his view of time rests solidly on New Testament conceptions of eschatology, and not onesidedly on the lexical stock of Scripture (*Christ and Time*, pp. xxxi ff.). But it is as difficult to translate the biblical teaching on last things into the view that time pervades the essential nature of God as to derive that view from linguistic specifics. In a passing footnote Cullmann himself curiously remarks that the adjective *aiōnios* "has the tendency to lose its time sense and is used in the qualitative sense of the divine-immortal" (*Christ and Time,* p. 48, n. 21). In response to this concession Cullmann's critics claim he mitigates his own contention that divine eternity and the temporal are not qualitatively different. Cullmann has also said that he views "linear time" as merely the framework of New Testament thought and not as a central idea in the minds of the authors. But to make linear time the biblical framework for temporalizing the transcendent nature of God requires presuppositions that the interpreter imparts into the meaning of *aiōn* and *aiōnes* and imposes an interpretation not called for by the lexical data.

We had better freely acknowledge that the Bible contains no express declaration about God's timeless eternity or about time's pervading the nature of God. Barr is right that "a valid biblical theology can be built only upon the *statements* of the Bible, and not on the *words* of the Bible. . . . Theologically, it is the communications made in the Bible, and not the lexical stock used in them, that 'teach us' the truth about God or about sin or about redemption" (*Biblical Words for Time,* pp. 154, 161). While the inspired writers may presuppose a distinctive view of time and of eternity they do not systematically expound or expressly formulate such a view. Without such specific statements, we can only discern the writer's intention and test our inferences by the biblical context as a whole. Even a devout interpreter runs the risk of addressing to the Bible questions that the text does not presume to answer, or of plundering the biblical materials to unearth possible intimations that support preconceived philosophical-theological predilections. Consciously or unconsciously held, tendential assumptions can decisively weight doctrinal interpretation. Not even theologians who avoid drawing conclusions from vocabulary fragments of the Bible, who escape overdependence on etymology, who shun invoking key concepts supposedly inspirited by special meanings, are therefore assured of an authentically biblical outcome. Even defensible and quite commendable positions sometimes rest on a religious epistemology that cannot sustain them, and that accordingly makes theological discussion vulnerable, even powerless.

Actually the biblical materials from which we derive a conclusion about the nature of divine eternity need not be confined to the specific scriptural passages about God's relationship to time. As long as we do not violate the express biblical teaching where the inspired writers touch on the themes of time and eternity, we may draw doctrinal inferences from what they affirm about other divine perfections, and thus bring to light and formulate what is inherent in the scriptural data. Valid theological-philosophical considerations may be present even where the fragmentary linguistic elements are inconclusive. The Bible may supply at least certain theological principles for evaluating secular alternatives. Whether it be the deification of time by ancient Indian religion, for example, or the Western reduction of time to illusion by modern idealists like F. H. Bradley and J. M. E. McTaggart, neither can be reconciled with the biblical teaching (cf. S. G. F. Brandon, "Time as God and Devil," pp. 12–31).

It is important to note, however, that specific biblical statements on such basic doctrines as God's spirituality and sovereignty, Christ's virgin birth and incarnation, his substitutionary death and atonement, his bodily resurrection and exaltation, his second coming in power and glory, lend a direct kind of didactic support that other important theological dogmas do not have. Biblically responsible Christian philosophy, for all that, has a proper and indispensable proof of its own; while it may not supply the content of theological truth, it can at least clarify that content by a demand for consistency and coherency, and by exhibiting its implications for contemporary alternatives.

There are, however, several scriptural starting points for contemplating the nature of God's eternity. Barr thinks it highly probable that the Genesis creation narrative affirms time to have originated with the origin of the universe; he finds it difficult or even impossible to produce biblical evidence that time—or some other kind of time—existed prior to the cosmic creation (*Biblical Words for Time*, p. 152). The early Christians, he feels, very likely found in Genesis an implication that time began simultaneously with creation. Augustine contends that God created the world *with* time, not *in* time (*De Civitate*, XI, vi.), and that the Creator energizes the universe under space-time forms. For both Karl Barth (*Church Dogmatics*, III/2, p. 438) and Walther Eichrodt ("Heilsfahrung und Zeitverständnis im Alten Testament," *Theologische Zeitschrift*, Vol. 12, 1956, pp. 103–125) the natural sense of the creation narrative implies that time arises with the first acts of creation. Ernst Jenni observes: "God's dominion over time is most clearly revealed by the fact that he created time along with the universe as its creature form of existence. Time has its beginning, from which point the days can be numbered" ("Time," op. cit., p. 647). Yahweh's time, remarks Kornelis H. Miskotte, is "qualitatively different from human time. The 'Name' includes not only Lordship over times and seasons (*kairoi*), but also the ground of all time and the root of redemptive history" (*When the Gods are Silent*, p. 168).

Cullmann's effort to extract everlasting duration from the term *aiōn*, Barr indicates, overlooks certain references to God himself and to the eternal world where *aiōn* is used to contrast the eternal nature or condition with that of the present temporal status; these particular uses do not readily accommodate the notion that eternity is coterminous with the total span of time (*Biblical Words for Time*, p. 153). The phrase *eis ton aiōna*, Barr stresses, need not carry the sense of eternal divine duration.

We need not yield, however, to Barr's own expanding doubt whether the Bible contains any unitary and distinctive view of time or for that matter of any other doctrine; he doubts that one can any longer consider the Bible as a literary unit that contains a unified theology devoid of divergent and at times actually contradictory content (*Biblical Words for Time*, p. 172; cf. his later *Fundamentalism*). Many critical scholars prejudiced by the presuppositions of comparative religions studies perceive the Bible to contain only later adaptations of extraneously derived views. They should be reminded that the world of religion has borrowed and perverted many elements that constitute the biblical doctrine of God. In the course of progressive revelation the biblical writers themselves no doubt had a deepening awareness of the implications of divine eternity and of its nature. But it never occurred to them to dismiss timelessness as simply an impersonal abstraction or, as the pagans at Alexandria did two centuries before Christ, to worship *Aiōn* as a god, or, as have modern secular philosophers, to capitalize and deify such abstractions as Infinity and Space-Time. The biblical writers could not have emptied timelessness into such abstractions as mathematical truth or logical validity because they knew that the laws of reason and the course of nature depend upon the nature and will of the eternally active God, the self-revealed source of scriptural conceptions concerning him.

The modern theological contrast of Greek philosophical abstractions with concrete biblical truths is, however, often prejudiced by an encounter-theory of truth. When critics deplore Aristotle's view of time as Greek abstraction they seem to ignore his specific definition of time as the numerical aspect of motion. One may, of course, call this abstraction, but so is all science; so, for that matter, is justification by faith, if one's philosophy admits of any abstraction. The fact is that Plato and Aristotle had no abstract ideas.

13.
The Modern Attack
on the Timeless God

MANY CONTEMPORARY RELIGIOUS philosophers consider the idea of a timeless God full of problems, and more and more Christian theologians declare it at odds with biblical representations about God.

The view of a timeless God, some theologians argue, conflicts with belief in divine creation and preservation of the universe, with divine incarnation in Jesus Christ, and with the doctrine of divine omniscience (see chapter 14). Charles Hartshorne even declares boldly: "The entire notion of deity as outside of time is unethical" (*Man's Vision of God and the Logic of Theism*, p. 159).

The Bible depicts God as loving, responsive to human need, approachable in prayer, and purposeful. "If God is timeless," asserts Nelson Pike, it is not at all clear that any of these themes can be retained" (*God and Timelessness*, p. 176). While Schleiermacher emphasized God's timelessness, a timeless being, he said, could not act purposefully; this notion has been frequently repeated, in recent times by William Kneale ("Time and Eternity in Theology," p. 99) and by Robert Coburn ("Professor Malcolm on God"). L. R. Farnell finds the doctrine of timeless eternity partly responsible for Arian views that, in wrestling the sonship and divinity of Jesus Christ, denied his coeternity with the Father (*The Attributes of God*, pp. 257 f.). Pike sees a fundamental contradiction between God's timelessness and the incarnation of the Logos; he exaggerates this claim by depicting the incarnation as God becoming a man, and by saying that most Christian theologians consider the incarnation an intellectual paradox.

Other modern critics declare divine timelessness incompatible with the historic Christian creeds. The Nicene Creed, they stress, speaks of Christ as begotten of the Father "before the aeons"; other creeds declare Christ's eternal existence—when as yet there was no temporal universe—in words that seem to have temporal overtones. Such terminology, they therefore contend, suggests Christ's existence in time infinitely extended into the past; were that not so, some commentators add, the question of how long Christ existed would have erupted as a major theological concern.

Neo-Protestant theologians now routinely contend that the traditional evangelical view of divine timelessness not only nullifies significant divine-human relationships but also reduces the incarnational ministry of Christ to a docetic sham activity. They emphasize that in creating the universe God fashioned new possibilities of experience for himself; that in divine relationships with the cosmos and mankind something happens not only through, but also in God; and that the cross added a still further dimension of experience to the Godhead. Some scholars who reject nontemporal theism and insist that God's nature is pervaded by time, at least in some respects, identify their emphasis as neoclassical theism; the theory's many alterations of classic theism make such piggybacking quite inappropriate, however. Schubert Ogden writes that "those who represent the position of classical theism can explicate Christian faith's reference to a transcendent God only by denying or seriously obscuring the reality and significance of temporality" and they allow us no option but "the sacrifice of time and man to God's eternity" (*The Reality of God*, p. 160).

Some proponents of process theory, Ogden among them, distinguish between time-transcending and time-structured aspects of God's life. But this approach suggests a schizophrenic divinity; instead of successfully blending what they consider the best of the biblical tradition with features of contemporary thought, the process theologians compromise both. It should be obvious that a timeless being cannot also be a temporal being.

One point is all too seldom recognized: when professional philosophers and systematic theologians project modern theories that eliminate timelessness from the nature of God they do more than simply reconstruct a particular perfection of the biblical God; what they do is substitute a deity very different from the God of orthodox theism. This is true even if sponsors of such mediating views appeal on occasion to biblical teaching. Not only has Whitehead's God, as Mascall reminds us, a function in relation to the world very different from that of the biblical Creator, but his metaphysical status also departs profoundly from that represented by classical theism (*The Openness of Being*, p. 169). While Whitehead represents God as nontemporal in his "primordial" nature, he means by primordial "not *before* all creation, but *with* all creation" (*Process and Reality: An Essay in Cosmology*, p. 521); God's "consequent" nature, says Whitehead, is not nontemporal. Creativity plays a more fundamental role in Whitehead's metaphysics than does what he calls "God"; this fact has led critics to complain that his introduction of "God" confuses rather than clarifies his exposition. We should recall that, while both Platonic and Christian thought lay stress on the creatureliness of time, the naturalistic exponent of emergent evolution, Samuel Alexander, "emphasizes," as Alfred P. Stiernotte states, "the creativity of Time" (*God and Space-Time*, Deity in The Philosophy of Samuel Alexander, p. 48).

Some later process theologians expound their theories with no interest whatever in the God of Judeo-Christian revelation; others correlate their theories to some extent with biblical representations. Yet in pleading their case for subjecting God, at least in certain aspects of his being, to temporal process and development, they depart from the God of evangelical theism and alter much more than his divine timelessness. Mascall therefore alerts Christians to the dangers of thus modifying God's nature. "Admit the tiniest element of time into God's timelessness," he warns, "admit the tiniest element of dependence into God's self-existence, and the very existence of the temporal, finite and dependent world becomes altogether inexplicable and unintelligible" (*The Openness of Being,* p. 173).

Pike observes that a theologian's position on the issue of divine eternity significantly influences "the general shape and texture of his broad theological view about the nature of God. . . . If a theologian holds that God is timeless (rather than everlasting) he is committed to a very specific interpretation of the negative modal predicates used in theological discourse . . . such as 'immutable' and 'incorruptible.' . . . In similar fashion, the interpretation one assigns to the predicate 'eternal' has an important bearing on the doctrine of divine omniscience" (*God and Timelessness,* pp. 14 ff.). "The predicate 'eternal' occupies something of a pivotal position within the logical-geography of traditional Christian thinking about God" (*ibid.,* p. x).

Pike insists that no champion of divine timelessness has vindicated the doctrine's adequacy, either in terms of the biblical data or of philosophical considerations (*God and Timelessness,* p. 187). The doctrine derives from Plato, he contends, and was introduced into Christian theology because Platonic thought was stylish at the time and because the doctrine appeared to have considerable advantage "from the point of view of systematic elegance" (*ibid.,* pp. 189 ff.). Yet he feels the view offers little in the way of "systematic advantage." Pike concludes that "if the doctrine of timelessness could be justified by reference to the basic Christian concept of God (i.e., God as an absolutely perfect being—a being than which no greater can be conceived), or if it could be supported by reference to biblical or confessional materials, then it might have to be retained in theology even if its systematic effect were that of chaos" (*ibid.,* p. 190). But historic Christianity combined its belief in divine timelessness neither with paradox nor with chaos. Its motivation for affirming God's timeless eternity lay not in Platonism—a philosophy that was not uncritically welcomed—but rather in avoiding conflicting and chaotic representations of the living God known by Christianity to be attested in Scripture and depicted in the classic creeds. Pike seems not to have reconciled his statements about the doctrine's apparent "systematic elegance" and its lack of "systematic advantage." Elsewhere he states that the doctrine of divine timelessness "is not only coherent with, but actually 'points toward' . . . other elements in the traditional concept of God," among them immutability, incorruptibility, ungenerability, and incorporeality (*ibid.,* p. 176).

The limited contribution of process philosophy—one supported by evangelical theism but which process thinkers inexcusably combine with costly misconceptions about the supernatural—lies in emphasizing the reality of the temporal world and its changing and developing character; some idealistic views, by contrast, dismiss time and even the finite universe as mere appearance. Although it did not lead the way, process philosophy also commendably protests the European neoorthodox and existential emphasis on God's radical transcendence. Dialectical and existential theology depicted God as accessible only outside all external relations to nature and history, that is, only in an inner "moment" in which eternity confrontationally bisects time; except for such sporadic encounters, it was said, God's revelational activity was isolated from history and time. Kierkegaard contended not simply that God has no temporal duration, but also that he is unrevealed and unknowable except by periodic divine inner confrontation that calls for private response. In his *Epistle to the Romans* (1919) Barth applauded the "infinite qualitative difference" between eternity and time. Rejection of radical transcendence by process theology was essential for recovering divine relationships to the cosmos and to universal history. But the flaw of process theory no less than of scientific humanism was its imposition of time upon all categories of ontological existence, and its failure to do justice to redemptive history and the incarnation of God in Jesus of Nazareth.

In a footnote in *Sein und Zeit* Martin Heidegger indicates the changes he would like to see in the doctrine of God; he proposes reinterpreting the eternity of God in terms of infinite temporality. Heidegger insists that his formal "ontological" use of concepts should be distinguished from material "ontic" assertions of theologians, but, observes Schubert Ogden, this footnote passage indicates an "ontologizing" of the understanding of God in terms of phenomenological analysis (*The Reality of God*, pp. 145 f.). Heidegger writes: ". . . The traditional concept of eternity, in the sense of the 'stationary now' (nunc stans) is drawn from the vulgar understanding of time and is limited by an orientation to the idea of 'constant' presence-on-hand. If the eternity of God would admit of being 'construed' philosophically, it would be understood only as a more primal and 'infinite' temporality. Whether the *via negationis et eminentiae* could offer a possible way to this goal would remain uncertain" (*Being and Time*, p. 499, n. xiii). But Heidegger overcomes the speculative Greek alternative to the biblical view by an equally novel alternative to scriptural theology: he asserts, in effect, that God is structurally related to beings other than himself (that is, to all beings, past and present, that are distinguishable from God himself). According to Heidegger, God's being, like man's, is a "being-in-the-world," and God must be understood as essentially related to others in whose being he shares through a similar basic structure of care. Contrary to the teaching of evangelical orthodox theology, Heidegger believes that the concepts of eternity and temporality imply each other.

For Schubert Ogden, a timeless God would lack both divine volition and divine purpose. He writes: "God is conventionally conceived as having a will or purpose and still other perfections that imply temporal distinctions. . . . Such analogical speaking is completely emptied of meaning by the nonanalogical denial that the being of God is in any sense temporal being. The concept of his eternity is so understood that it can only mean the literal negation or exclusion of the distinctions that the concept of temporality entails" (*The Reality of God*, p. 152). The fact is that while classic Christian theism denied that eternity and time imply each other, it did not deny that God's nontemporal eternity precludes the possibility of a created temporal order. Why must divine will and purpose exist only under conditions analogous to human will and purpose? For it is not God who bears man's image but man who bears God's image, and that only in certain respects. Ogden arrives at God's temporalness in advance; indeed, he assumes rather than demonstrates his premise that God is timeless. Why may not purpose and volition coexist with God's timelessness? Can God's fixed purpose and invariable volitions, in fact, be consistently maintained unless the divine purpose and will transcend time?

According to Daniel Day Williams God shares in the temporality and becoming of the temporal world he creates. "The true contrast between God and the world," he writes, "is not that between timeless eternity and the temporality of the creatures. It is the contrast between the supremely creative temporal life of God and the fragmentary limited creativity of the creatures" (*The Spirit and the Forms of Love*, p. 139). Williams emphasizes that creatures are not less perfect than God because they are temporal, but "only because their creativity is fragmented, distorted and partial." But would not God's dependence upon time also fragment divine creativity? And in that event, would not God's creativity also be partial? And by what norm are we to measure perfection once we reject the absolutely timeless? If God shares the becoming of the temporal world, can he escape its imperfections?

The philosophies of Alexander, Whitehead, Cobb and Ogden attest the fact that process philosophy substitutes a variety of conceptions for that of the timeless God of Christian orthodoxy. The process philosophers' efforts to coordinate the eternal and the temporal more securely by making time an aspect of God's being has not won its way. The imposition of divergent notions of temporally grounded theism on biblical revelation lacks scriptural support and philosophical stability. Not even most neo-Protestant theologians who try to recast the traditional view of divine eternity find process theology's time-invaded deity tenable.

The Christian Reformed philosopher Nicholas Wolterstorff is another who promotes the thesis that "God is fundamentally noneternal" ("God Everlasting," p. 187). He insists that God must indeed exist in time if we are to affirm that he acts as Scripture says he does, that is, as a being active in creation, in providence and in the renewal of mankind, an agent acting in human history, a redeeming God acting "centrally and decisively in the life, death and resurrection of Jesus Christ" ("God Everlasting," p. 181). Such affirmations, Wolterstorff contends, require us to reject the doctrine of divine timelessness. One would think that these activities require divine intelligence, sovereignty and mercy, rather than divine noneternity. Wolterstorff maintains that "at least some" aspects of God "stand in temporal order-relations to each other. . . . God, too, has a timestrand. His life and existence is itself temporal. . . . The events to be found on God's timestrand belong within the same temporal array as that which contains our timestrands" ("God Everlasting," p. 202). Other writers earlier in this century have made similar claims, but the argument remains unpersuasive.

Bertrand R. Brasnett contends that "time . . . always has been real for God," that "there never was a time when time was not" (*The Suffering of the Impassible God,* p. 81). While he grants that God's reality does not depend upon the reality of time, he considers it "extremely difficult" to combine the idea of creation with a God essentially timeless: "How can a God himself out of time produce that which is new, and therefore in time?" he asks (*ibid.,* p. 81). Brasnett stresses, moreover, that "if the Incarnation is . . . a real incarnation (and Christianity is wrecked at its center if it is not), it is an emergence of God in a world where time is real," and he then asks: "What reality could such an Incarnation in time have for the Timeless?" (*ibid.,* pp. 81 f.).

I insist, of course, that the eternal Logos of God stepped into history as God-man; this is a central emphasis of the New Testament. The New Testament emphasizes no less that the incarnate God-man does not in this dramatic act therefore cease to be God. Precisely because the Word incarnate has both human and divine natures does the incarnation hold its central temporal and timeless importance for the Eternal God. As to God's original creation the Genesis creation narrative tells us how the eternal God created the universe; that he was able to do so is a consequence of his sovereignty. God can bring about changes external to himself without himself changing or being in time.

Finally, Brasnett asks, "If the Incarnation is true, and God is timeless, we have to face in connection with the Incarnation just the same difficulty that met us in connection with creation, why should a timeless God create. . . . Why should a timeless God desire to enmesh himself . . . in the trammels of time by Incarnation?" (*ibid.,* p. 82). The New Testament answers the question unambiguously: it was for the salvation of sinners that the Word became flesh in dramatic manifestation of the grace of God.

Brasnett is mistaken if he thinks his questions are best answered by insisting that time has always been real for God. While this theory may on the surface seem to relieve some problems, it creates and multiplies others. Time need not structure the being of God in order for man's life to be of divine concern; we need not put God in time or time in God to assure the meaning and worth of either profane or redemptive history. The fact is that God created a space-time universe in which man was made in his image for purposes of intimate fellowship and in which fallen man is an object of divine compassion. The created cosmos is a vast theatre in which every human decision gains eternal import. In this context God becomes what he previously was not, the incarnate God-man. It may be difficult, as Brasnett says, to reconcile the fact of the incarnate Son's presence in the eternal Trinity. But while this presence involves a distinctive mode of the Son's being, it does not involve a new mode of the divine nature. The incarnation of the Logos in which divine nature adds human nature dramatically exhibits the fact that God cares intimately about human life and destiny; the ascension, moreover, confirms that this divine concern is not temporary but permanent. For all that, neither the incarnation nor ascension temporalizes the intrinsic life of the Godhead.

Religious barrenness followed hard upon rationalistic philosophies that postulated vague forms of theism that ignored divine self-revelation, obscured divine personality and lacked supernatural vitality. One can readily see why some writers tried to revitalize secular conceptions of a cold, distant deity. But to think that temporalizing the divine essence and experience is what best assures God's free creative and redemptive activity snares deity in time and is therefore self-defeating. Brasnett is aware of some of these consequences, but he minimizes them. He writes: "It may be true in a sense to say that to make time real for Deity, to bring Deity within time, is to limit him. It may be so, but our contention is that the Deity by being in time could, and did, and does, achieve results otherwise unattainable . . ." (*The Suffering of the Impassible God,* p. 86). Brasnett himself concedes that a God who copes constantly with time may be unassured of complete and final triumph in the future: "We do not know whether the will of God will completely triumph at some point in the distant future, or whether through unending ages it will be ceaselessly striving for its fulfillment" (*ibid.,* p. 87). To temporalize eternity compromises the religious power of biblical theism and lends no additional power to spiritual experience. A deity whose knowledge is timebound cannot give unqualified assurance about the future or, for that matter, about the present.

God's timeless eternity as Christians affirm it does not rule out all that properly characterizes the biblical representations of creation and preservation, revelation and redemption, incarnation and atonement. Judeo-Christian religion is irreducibly a religion of historical revelation and redemption; it locates God's supreme disclosure in the Word become flesh in the history of the world. The Christian doctrine of God and his relation to the universe must be fully reconcilable with the Christian experience of God. God's own timelessness does not imply, of course, that space-time processes and human events have no meaning for him. No view of God can be biblical if it deprives human history and personal life of its high importance. Scripture teaches that man's religious consciousness knows that God is concerned over human defeats and triumphs, and that temporal events have meaning for him. While God is essentially independent of time, he is not on that account ignorant of or indifferent to it. He is, after all, its living creator. Christian teaching rules out any notion that the temporal is ultimate or, as Bergson would have it, that duration (*durée*) is the ultimate real while the eternal and unchanging are but intellectual fantasies. It also denies that God is an unchanging and timeless Absolute who inwardly commutes all time, change and even evil into mere appearance. But no less does Christian doctrine exclude the notion that temporal succession characterizes God's inner life and experience.

Is God's timelessness—the traditional orthodox understanding of divine eternity—then a necessary truth? Is it a predication logically implicit in the very idea of God? Is it known to man intuitively, independently of and prior to special Judeo-Christian revelation? Augustine and Anselm apparently thought so; man, they said, has innate knowledge of God by creation. God is identical with each of his attributes, they taught, and since each attribute entails every other, to forfeit any one divine perfection would logically erase God. In this view, God's timeless eternity is not a contingent attribute; God cannot have temporal duration and yet be God. For Augustine and Anselm God's timeless eternity is an essential perfection of what it means to be God. In keeping with the ontological argument, namely, that the reality of God is implied in the very idea of him, some theologians therefore contend that God is eternal, omnipotent, immutable and incorporeal as a matter of logical necessity.

Thomas Aquinas's formulation of the cosmological argument on the basis of natural theology spurred philosophical debate over whether he makes divine being logically necessary or ontologically necessary. Alvin Plantinga considers the Thomistic argument ineffective on either score (*God and Other Minds,* A Study of the Rational Justification of Belief in God, p. 25).

The Bible allows philosophers to ponder, as a mark of man's alienated spiritual relationship, whether God is logically inconceivable, logically impossible, or logically necessary. The Bible itself, instead of asking whether God is logically necessary, grounds the very necessity even of logic in God's own intellect. Viewing God as *ontologically* necessary, the Bible thus implies a specific view of logical necessity and of the nature of logic; that is, God is necessary to explain the world—a declaration far different from the speculative question of logical necessity. Expounding this theological emphasis on God as necessary being (*Proslogion,* III), Anselm does not debate whether the idea of "God exists" is logically inconceivable, self-contradictory or logically necessary; he emphasizes, instead, that God upon whom all else depends is the incomparable One known a priori through the Creator's preservation of his creatures and exists necessarily from himself and is not an ontologically contingent being (*Monologion,* VI). From God's ontic independence Anselm derives divine eternity, indestructibility, and incorruptibility.

Recent modern philosophers frequently confuse logical and ontological necessity. Norman Malcom and Charles Hartshorne argue from God's ontological to his logical necessity by basing the surety of God's actual existence not in revelation as does Anselm but in speculative philosophy. In his *God, Freedom and Evil* Plantinga, who defends a sophisticated form of the ontological argument, maintains that to say God's existence is logically contingent does not require the conclusion that God has "duration rather than eternity" (*God and Other Minds,* p. 93).

Pike finds Anselm's contention unpersuasive that the concept of God as unsurpassable being must logically entail divine timelessness (*God and Timelessness,* p. 130), and thus reveals his basic rejection of the ontological argument. He writes: "I have been unable to discover any clear logical connection between the idea that God is a being a greater than which cannot be conceived and the idea that God is timeless" (*ibid.*, p. 165). He does not consider what is timeless per se "an appropriate object of my respect or loyalty"—for example, "the number two" as a timeless entity (*ibid.*, p. 165). Anselm is speaking of Number One, however, of God whose timelessness cannot be isolated from other divine perfections. Pike also has doubts about other divine perfections; immutability, or logical inability to change, he thinks, has no necessary connection with a being's worthiness of worship (*ibid.*, p. 164). He does not clarify, however, what necessary worthiness of worship attaches to notions of divine transiency and change. Not even the ancient Greeks found any basis for hope in ultimate ontological change.

Historic evangelical theism stresses and insists upon divine timelessness. It disavows, however, any immobile divine being or condition that, as espoused by some Greek philosophers, precludes divine creation and preservation of the universe, divine purposive activity in human history, and divine incarnation in Christ. Evangelical orthodoxy affirms that God has vital and stable personal relationships with the entire space-time universe; it repudiates the idea that time is an illusion, and declares time, rather, a divine creation correlative with God's fashioning, ordering and sustaining of the universe. Over against Greek notions, as F. H. Brabant observes, Hebrew-Christian thought combined its insistence on divine eternity with the sense of divine purpose in history (*Time and Eternity in Christian Thought*, p. 35). Because Greek and medieval speculative notions of static divine Being cancel the reality and significance of time does not justify identifying Reformation and post-Reformation evangelical doctrine with such conjecture. The neo-Protestant charge that historic evangelical theism does not take time seriously is more propagandistic than academic.

Judeo-Christian religion has never supported the idealistic tenet that time is unreal. Calling it the "monstrous proposition," G. E. Moore confronted Bradley and McTaggart by saying: "If time is unreal, then plainly nothing ever happens before or after anything else; nothing is ever simultaneous with anything else; it is never true that anything is past; never true that anything will happen in the future; never true that anything is happening now, and so on" (*Philosophical Studies,* p. 209). Biblical religion insists on a specific Old Testament era of redemptive promise and on a specific New Testament era of redemptive fulfillment. This fulfillment the apostles identified with Christ's incarnation, crucifixion and resurrection in their recent past; the present age they declared to be a season for repentance while awaiting the future triumph of Christ in great power and glory.

Yet Christian belief in time's created reality does not warrant belief in the temporalness of divine eternity. As already noted the Genesis creation account makes time coterminus with the created universe. God's timelessness poses fewer problems for the doctrine of creation. If Deity exists in time, and at some remote point in time creates the world, then the question inevitably arises as to what God was doing before he created the world and what motivated him to create. But if time, like space, is finite, and belongs to creation itself, then the Creator of the space-time universe cannot be regarded as himself in time, nor can time be viewed as an aspect of God's essential nature.

The doctrine of the Trinity exhibits in the eternal nature of God a life of intimate love, communion and self-giving that in principle cancels the complaint that a timeless deity must be loveless and introvert. In creation God affirms himself as the living ontological source and continuing support of every finite reality. The doctrine of the incarnation, the center of the primitive church's Christian affirmation, controverts any implication that a timeless God must be as self-preoccupied and remote as the Aristotelian prime mover.

Mascall elaborates the superior relation to the world that is possible to the timeless God of Judeo-Christian faith, but not to a time-bound deity. He writes: "A God in whom, in his timelessness, the whole spatio-temporal fabric of the world is eternally present is not less but more concerned with the world and its affairs than would be a God who was entangled in it. For the latter kind of deity would be limited in his experience at each moment to the particular stage in its development that the world reached at that moment, while the former, in his extratemporal and extraspatial vision and activity, embraces in one timeless act every one of his creatures, whatever its time and place may be. . . . A God to whom every instant is present at once has a vastly greater scope for compassion and his power than one would have who could attend to only one moment at a time" (*The Openness of Being,* p. 172). Mascall thus demolishes not only the prejudice that a timeless God is necessarily remote from history, but also process theology's claim that the doctrine of a transcendent timeless God cancels any consolation and warmth provided by religion. The eternal God has within himself all the necessary elements for perpetual activity and involvement in his created universe, even though this relation of the eternal to the temporal and historical does not import succession into God's eternality. As perpetual creator and sustainer of the finite temporal world, God stands in intimate relation to each of all created beings or things and to every phase of their history. But does God's creative relation to temporal events and his knowledge of them, Mascall asks, constitute "a genuine experience of change and development on the level of his activity and consciousness?" (*The Openness of Being,* p. 163). God's acts, which from our standpoint are temporal, Mascall replies, are timeless from God's perspective. While God raised Jesus from the dead on what he knew to be a particular day, God "timelessly exerts a creative activity towards and upon the whole spatio-temporal fabric of the created universe . . . experienced as temporal by each creature . . . from his own spatio-temporal standpoint" (*ibid.,* p. 166).

"The fact that we can experience and speak of God only in temporal terms," Mascall emphasizes, "does not mean that we cannot speak of him accurately; it means that even when we speak of him accurately we have to speak of him in temporal terms" (*ibid.,* p. 167). This appropriate comment preludes a remark in which Mascall unfortunately barters away much that he has commendably preserved. Our limitation to "temporal language," he observes, means that "there is a great deal about God that we cannot know or about which we cannot speak, except perhaps in the most distant and obscure way" (*ibid.*, p. 167). Such "distant and obscure" theologizing he depicts as "mystery but not absurdity" (*ibid.*, p. 168).

Mascall's frail epistemology seems in effect to jeopardize any and all valid knowledge of God. The difficulty is not that Mascall carefully ponders the possibility of time-conditioned creatures conceiving and comprehending timeless being, but that Mascall appeals to analogy to span the gulf between the temporal and the timeless. The continuing weakness of such an appeal is that, in the absence of univocal truth, epistemic claims splash into a "no mind's land" that breeds agnosticism. The difficulty of erecting an analogical bridge between human temporality and divine timelessness is evident when Mascall writes: "If it is asserted that . . . there must be asserted in God's own existence something analogous to time, we can only reply that this must in fact be God's eternity and that what differentiates it from time is the absence of change and succession" (*ibid.*, p. 168). This is not, however, the "only reply" possible when argumentation is predicated on analogy; equally possible is the conjectural alternative that historic Christian theism rejects, namely, that God ontologically includes time.

No less confusing and prone to skepticism is Mascall's emphasis on the limitations of temporal language and temporal concepts. From one point of view, human language and concepts are temporal like everything else that is human. But the fundamental issue is whether language and concepts can and do carry universally valid and hence enduring truth about God and anything else. If they do not, it is futile for Mascall or anyone else to try to persuade others of an alternative view; to do so would merely verbalize metaphysical constructs that carry no claim to belief by others. The question of knowing God's timelessness—in human concepts and language—does not differ essentially, therefore, from knowing other divine attributes. We need not be sovereign to know God's sovereignty, nor need we be timeless to know God's timelessness. What we need is not infinite language or infinite concepts or even infinite knowledge. All that is necessary is God's intelligible self-revelation, and divinely gifted creational categories that enable us to know God as he truly is. Although time is the universal form of man's experience, the fact is that even human consciousness is supertemporal or time-transcending in nature; so are valid distinctions of truth. Hence we need not join Mascall in resigning outselves to mystery because God's finite creatures "can experience his timeless relations to time only under the forms of their own temporal existence" and because they "have only their temporal concepts and speech in which to envisage and describe his timelessness" (*ibid.*, p. 168).

The shift in the defense of divine timelessness from revelational and scriptural considerations to philosophical rationalism was in fact a key element, a century ago, in reformulating the time-eternity debate in terms of idealistic metaphysics. Idealist Bradley contended that time is an illusion, being unreal for God and unreal in human experience. He emphasized, as do also post-Einstein scientists, that even human beings incorporate various time series, and what is past in one person may be future in another. The events in one work of fiction are not temporally related to those in another work of fiction, and in either case what is past for one reader need not be so for another. But in dealing with God's eternity we are not concerned only with his conscious relationship to a variety of relative time series; at stake, rather, are time-transcending existence and knowledge. Like Bradley other secular philosophers denied that time has ontological and even creational status. For some metaphysical monists who believed that God's will immediately actualizes all existence apart from any causal reality, the ideality of time and space represented a devastating argument against mechanism. Borden P. Bowne, for one, declared time ideal rather than real. Albert C. Knudson insisted that temporal terms do not apply to God himself, yet urged "against ascribing too much exclusive a timelessness to the divine consciousness" (*The Doctrine of Redemption*, p. 44).

A number of philosophers viewed creation as a timeless essential activity of the divine nature, and therefore regarded the universe, or some world, at any rate, as coeternal with God (A. Seth Pringle-Pattison, *The Idea of God in the Light of Recent Philosophy*, p. 303). Pringle-Pattison champions continuous creation, over against Origen's notion of repeated creations. Origen had held that God has always been creator and had created an indefinite series of worlds before creating the present universe (*De Principiis*, I, 2.10; III, 5.31), and even presumed to find scriptural support for his theory (Eccl. 1:9; Isa. 66:22). Aquinas had concluded that, while revelation requires our belief in a temporal creation, philosophical reasoning can provide no rational ground for rejecting the Aristotelian view of the eternity of the world; revelation, he added, warns us of our philosophical blunders. The eternity of God does not imply the eternity of the world, he said, unless one views the world as a necessary or inevitable divine emanation.

Farnell notes that "no ancient or recent writer has succeeded in showing how the idea of creation is compatible with the idea of timelessness. To maintain is not to create; for to create is necessarily to make something new, something which at least in that shape does not exist before; and 'new' and 'before' are time-determinations. If therefore by the constraining essence of his nature God is eternally creative, an activity that demands a time-determination is part of his essence, and this clashes with the concept of his timelessness" (*The Attributes of God*, pp. 256 f.). Immutability and a once-for-all act are indeed difficult but not impossible to synthesize. God can have ordained from eternity an effect that was not present from eternity (cf. Aquinas, *Summa contra Gentiles*, II.35; cf. II.36, 4). Since God acts voluntarily in actualizing effects, the effects need not be eternal; and the temporality of the events need not temporalize the nature of God.

Knudson ranged personalism on the side of the eternity of the created universe. Although he conceded that "there is no logical contradiction in the idea of a temporal creation" (*The Doctrine of Redemption*, pp. 40 ff.), he also declared that "there is nothing in the notion of first cause that is inconsistent with the idea of eternal creation" (*The Philosophy of Personalism*, p. 286). "So long as we do not hold to the infallibility of Scripture," Knudson adds, "it does not from the religious point of view matter much which answer we give" concerning eternal or temporal creation. Taking the next step, Edgar S. Brightman not only refers creation to the essential and eternal nature of God but also rejects divine timelessness ("A Temporalist View of God," pp. 544–555). The eternity of the world thus became a dogma both of secular philosophers who insisted on divine temporality and of those who affirmed divine timelessness.

The notion of God's coeternality with the world, or that God cannot be imagined without the world, consequently led by way of speculative reaction to asserting God's temporality as the hypothesis that best guards the significance of space-time realities. This transition was facilitated by misconceptions of the Christian view, a view often confused with secular expositions of divine eternity that eclipsed biblical indications of the creational reality of time. Nonbiblical philosophy of religion combined God's timelessness with the dismissal of all time as illusion; its view of God's aloofness from all external relations virtually canceled meaningful divine involvement in earthly history and nullified the transcendent significance of human activities. Orthodox Christian theism, on the other hand, views time as a concomitant of the divine creation of the universe and affirms God's intimate relationship to space-time realities as creator, preserver, redeemer and judge. For modern philosophers to insist that God is nontemporal or supertemporal involves also a denial that God can initiate change.

The motives for assigning a revised role to time were numerous; the method for determining that role shunned revelatory scripture and relied instead on philosophical reasoning or on scientific empiricism. Kant had regarded time as merely a form of conscious experience. It is indeed difficult to define time other than in terms of sensory intuition. To insist that time is a created form of mental knowledge that involves the succession of ideas is hardly to reduce it to an illusion. Personalists, for example, consider the Kantian doctrine of the ideality of time to imply not its metaphysical unreality, but rather its non-dependence of mind.

By contrast, twentieth-century evolutionary thought elevated time as the creative principle that displaces God. Time becomes a central theme for twentieth-century literature, moves on to become an obsession and finally a problem.

Dominant in the forepart of the century, the secular belief in progress shifted solution of humanity's problems and utopian provision for mankind's needs to the near future. The past, in which Christianity located the great historic redemptive events, was passed over as irrelevant; hope no longer centered in the eternal God but in impending evolutionary scientific breakthrough. Awareness of what Christianity declares to be continuously available on the ground of already provided redemption was replaced by disdain for the past and depreciation of the present in prospect of a utopian future. This faith in tomorrow blended into the radical social activism of the Sixties to produce revolutionary expectations and demands. Annulling the supertemporal resulted in isolation of the present from the past and in loss of present durable meaning. Time enthroned became time the tyrant. As Blamires observes, "Aldous Huxley's *Brave New World* and George Orwell's *1984* present Time the great Healer as finally dethroned, and Time the Despoiler in control" (*Tyranny of Time: A Defense of Dogmatism*, p. 12). "No one familiarly acquainted with the work of Proust, Joyce, Eliot, Camus, Beckett and their peers, could imagine that the modern mind, at the cultural level, thinks of the human situation as offering . . . progress, security, and confidence. . . . Life is an emergency . . . perhaps an absurdity" (*ibid.*, p. 18).

Man will recover his proper role in time only by acknowledging the Creator who dwells in a dimension beyond temporal boundaries, and by acknowledging time as a divinely created sphere for destiny-laden human decision and dedication. The significance of time is not grasped by simply exaggerating it to ontological ultimacy, nor is it exhausted by insisting, as did Einstein, on its relativity. Modern physical science, in contrast with the Newtonian view, considers the space-time matrix a systematic network of relationships between specific physical point-instants. Nelson Pike implies that all finite beings have the same time-process in common, a time-process that logically antedates them. Mascall considers this view gratuitous (*The Openness of Being*, p. 165). In keeping with modern biological science Mascall emphasizes that "each individual physical or mental subject has its own individual spatio-temporal frame of reference, which is distinct from, although systematically related to the spatio-temporal frame of others" (*ibid.*, p. 168).

For Mascall time "is neither a kind of *Ungrund* or *Urgrund*, antecedent to God himself, nor a medium created by God in which, having created it, he then finds himself to be immersed and into which he subsequently launches his creatures" (*The Openness of Being*, p. 168). "God's transcendence of the finite world necessarily includes transcendence of temporality and of becoming," he adds (*ibid.*, p. 163); "in his own ontological depth he is entirely timeless and changeless." Thomas F. Torrance points out the needless difficulties created for theology by accepting a receptacle view of time and space that makes them an antecedently existing continuum (*Space, Time and Incarnation*). Mascall considers "temporality . . . a characteristic of the finite world," or at least of its material aspects; time, he says, is "a derivative from, or an aspect of, the existence of finite beings and is not an antecedently existing medium into which they are launched" (*The Openness of Being*, pp. 164 ff.).

Since man experiences time in a variety of relationships one level of experience does not cancel out another. While striking differences mark the Hebrew and Greek views of time, these contrasts must not be exaggerated into totally exclusive perspectives. Both share the conception of the "24 hour day" and of calendar years composed of such days. To say that the Old Testament has no conception of the Greek *chronos*, or mere chronological time, is wrong. The Bible speaks of time concretely, in terms of supernatural and theological referents; the Greeks also speak of time concretely, although not in relation to Yahweh. While the Old Testament, particularly Ecclesiastes, is aware of a cyclical conception of history, it does not teach that view as truth. In the Bible, days and years exist through God's prior ordination and providential purpose. *Yom* is strikingly correlated with a theological content beyond mere chronological location (e.g., the day of God's vengeance; the day of God's power; the day of the Lord; the year of redemption; the year of visitation; the acceptable year of the Lord). The Old Testament *'eth* and New Testament *kairos* are used not simply of chronological time but of spiritual opportunity, e.g., the time of sowing, of ripening, of reaping. The Greeks used *kairos* of special opportunities also, albeit in different contexts. The Hebrews reckoned time differently than did the Greeks; day began at sunset; a specific event constituted the "first day" of a sequence (e.g., the death of Christ climaxed by Christ's "third day" resurrection).

As G. B. Caird observes, certain New Testament passages use *chronos* and *kairos* interchangeably in key passages that disallow the comprehensive contrast between impersonal chronological time and a season of personal opportunity (*The Apostolic Age,* p. 184, n. 2) proposed by both John Marsh and Alan Richardson (on "Time," in his *A Theological Word Book of the Bible*; cf. also Gerhard Delling on *"Kairos," TDNT* 3:461). Marsh holds that there is no biblical view of time other than a regard for decisive moments (*The Fulness of Time,* pp. 175 ff.); such "realistic" biblical time he distinguishes from so-called Greek chronological time. James Barr considers the texts cited by Caird (Mark 1:15/Gal. 4:4; Acts 3:20/3:21; 1 Pet. 1:5/1 Pet. 1:20/Jude 18) merely representative of other passages that indicate simply the general New Testament usage; he does not see them as supporting Marsh's distinction between "chronological time" and "realistic time" (*Biblical Words for Time,* p. 23). Barr contends further that Marsh and Richardson crisscross and interchange the content of supposedly contrasting terms, and in so doing lessen the importance of biblical chronology (*ibid.,* pp. 25 ff.). He therefore rejects Marsh's claim that Scripture typically locates events by their content and not by chronology (cf. also the illuminating essay by A. L. Burns, "Two Words for 'Time' in the New Testament," pp. 7–22). In short, Marsh and Richardson marshal selective linguistic support for preconceived notions about biblical usage.

Barr does not completely equate *chronos* and *kairos,* however; he only insists that they do not stand for contrasting conceptions of time. In the fact that the New Testament writers were persuaded about the critical decisiveness of certain historical events occurring at a particular time, and that at times they distinguish a critical or opportune time from time in general, Barr sees no basis for Marsh's fuller distinction between 'realistic' and chronological time as a biblical category.

Cullmann contends that the New Testament use of *kairos* and *aiōn* expresses a distinctive conception of time, the former to define time by its content, and the latter to depict a limited or unlimited duration or span of time (*Christ and Time,* p. 39). Barr agrees that in some usages *kairos* does indeed mean a period or extent of time (e.g., Mark 18:30/Luke 19:30 and Heb. 9:9). While *aiōn* is indeed used more frequently than *kairos* for a great epoch of world duration, the distinction between *kairos* and *aiōn*, Barr insists, cannot be stated as "that between 'moment' and 'age' or 'period' " (*Biblical Words for Time*, p. 51).

Although biblical word studies of the past generation tried to establish a distinctive biblical view of time that was totally dissimilar from the Greek view, that emphasis seems to have been short-lived. It is dangerous to treat isolated words as concepts and to press upon them some preferred theological meaning; sound exegesis reinforces the fact that a word seldom has only one sense. Moreover, wild biblical and nonbiblical views of time and history do indeed show striking differences; those differences do not inhere in the use of a peculiar vocabulary. They lie rather in certain truths about history that can be translated from Hebrew and Greek words into the languages of the world. Among such truths are that God is the creator and lord of time; that he works out his specific purposes in time and is in sovereign control of history; that he revealed his redemptive plan to Hebrew prophets and fulfilled his messianic promise in Jesus of Nazareth; that history is moving toward a climax when the risen Christ will judge men and nations and will fully vindicate righteousness.

14.
Divine Timelessness
and Divine Omniscience

THE BIBLE'S EXPLICIT teaching about the nature of divine eternity, we have said, is inconclusive. We are left to reach conclusions, as we must do for every doctrine, on the basis of all the scriptural statements about God. The most relevant texts are the passages that affirm divine omniscience.

By divine omniscience we mean, as A. H. Strong states, "God's perfect and eternal knowledge of all things which are objects of knowledge, whether they are actual or possible, past, present or future" (*Systematic Theology,* Vol. 1, p. 282).

While the Bible does not apply to God the specific terms "omniscient" or "omniscience," it does everywhere depict him as all-knowing. God's understanding is very great (Ps. 147:5). First of all, God thoroughly knows himself; in the divine nature there are no dark and hidden recesses. God also thoroughly knows his created universe. "Known unto God are all his works from the beginning of the world" (Acts 15:18). He comprehensively knows both his inanimate creation (Ps. 147:4) and also the creaturely world (Matt. 10:29). No aspect of our vast universe, which some space-age observers are prone to consider infinite, is concealed from God. When they accurately disclose secrets of outer space, computer scientists identify only fragments of what God comprehensively knows about his creation. God knows all processes and events of the universe not simply as unrelated facts but in their interrelationship with one another, and to all of reality.

God knows the motives, thoughts and purposes of all created minds. He knows the human will (Ps. 33:13 ff.) and the human heart (Ps. 139:2; Acts 15:8). Psychologists and psychoanalysts speak of deep areas of subconscious experience of which human beings are hardly aware. But God knows all men thoroughgoingly, psychologists and psychoanalysts and theologians included.

God intuitively possesses truth because he has self-consciousness of his own nature and of what he can and will do. In knowing himself he eternally and exhaustively knows all objects of knowledge. His knowledge of man and the world has its source in his self-knowledge, because God knew what he would make. God's knowledge of what will be is grounded in his knowledge of his eternal purpose. Within the realm of God's knowledge we are all as accessible to him as he is to himself. In his knowledge as in all other aspects of his being he is sovereign and self-sufficient. "He . . . calls the things that are not as though they were" (Rom. 4:17, NIV).

God's knowledge is declared to be humanly incomprehensible (Ps. 139:6; Rom. 11:33; Eph. 3:10) because it simultaneously embraces knowledge of the past, the present and the future (Job 14:17; Ps. 56:8; Isa. 41:22–24, 44:6–8; Jer. 1:5; Hos. 13:12). His knowledge of the past (Mal. 3:16) and of the future (Isa. 46:9 f.), including future human acts (Isa. 44:22), is both comprehensive and detailed.

But God's knowledge is more than comprehensive; it is also eternal. God knows from eternity (Acts 15:18). Without sense experience, without conjectural imagination, without such mental processes as reasoning and generalization, he knows the reason for all things and the logical relationships between axioms and theorems; he foreknows even the acts of his creatures and the complex purposes that motivate their decisions and deeds (Acts 2:23). Neither God's mode of existence nor his mode of knowledge involves passing from one time to another.

Only God has perfect knowledge. His knowledge is unerringly correct; it involves no mistaken assumptions or false beliefs. Human knowledge is but partial and, unless grounded in divine revelation, is also imperfect and subject to correction. Apart from a priori or innate knowledge, the knowledge gained by humans comes only gradually, and both its quality and extent are variable. Megalomaniacs may be tempted to claim omniscience for themselves, but only God has perfect, complete and eternal knowledge.

Those who dismiss *omni*-predications in respect to God as "mere overbelief" and as "extrapolating to the skies," as did Episcopal Bishop James Pike (*Time* magazine, Nov. 11, 1966), comments D. W. D. Shaw, "do violence to the biblical evidence and to the evidence of individual and collective experience" (*Who Is God?* p. 103). Although Judeo-Christian doctrine has traditionally emphasized divine omniscience, Christian churchmen intimidated by modern antimetaphysical theories tend to devalue such claims. As Methodist Bishop Francis John McConnell puts it, Jesus' reference to the Father's awareness of the sparrow's fall is not intended to show "the grasp of the Divine Mind on detail but to reveal the spirit of the Father of all." He adds, "God's approach to men can be conceived of not as through an overpowering intellectual omniscience, but as through moral insight" (*The Christlike God,* pp. 114, 116). But could we speak so confidently even of the Father's spiritual and moral insight if God's knowledge is, in fact, limited and if we have no knowledge of the transcendent? The false disjunction of intellectual omniscience and of moral insight should be clear to every student of the many biblical passages that bear on the knowledge of God who calls the innumerable stars by name (Isa. 40:26) and knows all the fowls and the beasts (Ps. 50:11). To be sure, God's omniscience has moral implications. God's unitary nature implies not merely knowledge by a perfect mind, but also his ethical probing of human rebellion. As the Psalmist acknowledges: "There is not a word in my tongue, but, lo, O Lord, thou knowest it altogether" (Ps. 139:4). What we mean by divine omniscience is neither divine righteousness nor moral authority nor compassion; what we mean concerns unlimited knowledge.

The practical consequences of divine omniscience are far-reaching. Where human intentions and ways are thought to escape God's knowledge the result is devious and libertine conduct. Unlike the mythical polytheistic gods who were sometimes unaware of what was happening and were overtaken by surprise, the living God of the Bible knows all things (cf. Ps. 10:11 f., 94:7 ff.; Isa. 29:15; Jer. 23:23; Ezek. 8:12, 9:9). That fact helps to deter secret sin, religious hypocrisy, and the temptation to hide from God (Job 31:4, 34:21; Ps. 56:18; 1 Cor. 4:5; Heb. 4:13). God's omniscience challenges false concepts of security and rectifies man's warped self-knowledge (Ps. 19:2 ff., 51:6, 94:11, 139:23 f.). When the wicked misunderstand and misrepresent them it supports and sustains the godly (Ps. 142:5 ff., 143:9 ff.). God's omniscience topples finite man's search for infinite knowledge apart from biblical truth; it attests God as the source and ground of all truth, and underscores divine revelation as the only sure access to what is otherwise unknowable.

Both divine omniscience and divine sovereignty imply that divine knowledge is timeless and rule out temporal succession in the activity of divine knowledge. Time involves a succession of ideas and learning and forgetting. But God's knowledge is independent of all limitations (Isa. 41:22 f.). If divine knowledge requires a succession of ideas, then God is not omniscient. It is futile, therefore, to try to preserve God's omniscience if his timelessness is denied. Some theists redefine divine eternity in terms of everlasting temporality and thus try to preserve divine omniscience. Divine omniscience, they assert, does not depend upon timeless eternity. But if God is a being to whom temporal predicates apply, then he has time-location. Even if God is said to be located in all time or times, how can this claim isolate God's knowledge or other aspects of his deity from temporal implication? If God's knowledge is temporally conditioned, he cannot then have simultaneous knowledge or complete knowledge of all objects and events as omniscience requires.

Addison H. Leitch remarks, "God's nature is not subject to the law of time. . . . There is no *chronological succession* . . . in God's thoughts" ("Omniscience," p. 532). God's knowledge cannot be dated or positioned in time. It is a direct spiritual comprehension, a single act of cognition, independent of insight conditioned on space-time realities. Extension and succession are not to be predicated of divine thought.

"If there are no universals which transcend the time-process," then, as W. R. Matthews observes, "we can have no knowledge of reality. . . . In the same way, it would be difficult to justify absolute moral judgments. There could be no absolute value and no permanent principles of good" (*God in Christian Experience,* p. 253). The eternity of "abstract" universals is identical with the eternity of God for they are God thinking; the universals of logic and mathematics are grounded in the eternity and constancy of the living God. Matthews, unfortunately, allows time to pervade some aspects of God's nature; the conception of divine will would be meaningless, he avers, if God were absolutely timeless (*ibid.,* p. 262). He insists only that "God cannot be 'in time,' if we mean by that phrase that His whole Being is subject to succession and change" (*ibid.,* p. 261). But surely a god internally divided in respect to succession and nonsuccession can only be a deity at odds with himself.

Evangelical theism affirms that God's knowledge is timelessly eternal; we should not therefore infer, however, that Christianity approves all formulations of divine timelessness. Both Greek philosophy and modern nonbiblical theism have periodically encouraged unacceptable expositions of time and eternity.

Boethius's exposition of God's knowledge in terms of an "eternal now," for example, seems to preclude any distinction in God's mind between events occurring yesterday, today and tomorrow. Borden P. Bowne like some modern idealists held that time is unreal; he affirms that God knows all things as a comprehensive present, as "an eternal now" that excludes temporal distinctions (*Philosophy of Theism,* p. 159). Certain Christian mystics expound God's eternity in a way that disparages his intelligible spatio-temporal revelation, and declare that the divine is experienced only outside spatio-temporal relationships. Thus they postulate an ontological tension between eternity and time.

Charles Hartshorne holds the notion that God transcends past, present and future as an Eternal Now to be contradictory, on the ground that it annihilates the meaning of the term "now" (*Man's Vision of God and the Logic of Theism*). That God knows all things in a single act does not imply a temporal Now, however; it implies, rather, a timeless intellectual vision whereby he eternally knows all things. "Now" may be metaphysical. An Eternal Now need not be self-contradictory, for a *Now* is not a division of time any more than a *point* is the end of a line.

Bishop McConnell contended that to make time ideal rather than real for God, as did Bowne, so contrasts the processes of the divine mind and the human mind as to "narrow extremely the likeness of the human person to the Divine person" (in *Personalism in Theology,* pp. 30 f.). Brightman likewise contends that God's consciousness is "an eternal time movement" (*The Finding of God,* p. 132); "to be a person is to be a time movement," he says, "as well as to transcend time" in certain ways (*ibid.,* p. 133). But this argument involves serious misunderstanding. All that is necessary to question the thesis that temporal experience is inseparable from personality is to insist that divine personality involves more complex and more profound selfhood than human personality, and that man bears God's image only in some respects—rationality in particular—and not in all. While

McConnell and others argue for divine temporality on the basis of the *imago Dei,* others insist that this divine image in man in no way undermines the Creator's superhuman and supertemporal nature. Some scholars try to preserve divine transcendence over time by inexcusably making God superpersonal or impersonal.

Neo-Protestant process philosophers react against the speculative exclusion of time-distinctions from God's range of knowledge by unjustifiably importing time into God's very nature and making it an essential aspect of divine life. Protesting that the orthodox view of divine omniscience destroys the meaning of time in that it supposedly yields an all-knowing God who does not know things in their concrete changing actuality, Hartshorne ventures a drastic revision of the inherited doctrine of God. He affirms that God knows everything for what it is—the past in terms of memory, the future as possibility, and the present as contemporary with his experience. He contends, as Edward Farley observes, that "if future is really future, God too has a future and is not Pure Act in which all potentialities are actualized" (*The Transcendence of God,* p. 153). Such involvement of God in temporal processes compromises his divine transcendence and portrays him as becoming progressively enriched in experience with the passing of time. The result of Hartshorne's panpsychism is loss of the omniscient and immutable God of the Bible; God becomes so meshed with historical processes that he internally experiences the quality of evil and is steeped in inner conflict (*Man's Vision of God,* p. 196; cf. *The Logic of Perfection and Other Essays in Neoclassical Metaphysics*). We are told that "God must suffer all things, for he must participate in all things to know them" (*ibid.,* p. 197). This comment calls to mind an observation by W. R. Matthews in another connection. "The Christian conception of God certainly compels us to assume," he says, that the evil thoughts and imaginations of wicked men are "not entirely unrelated" to God upon whom all things finally depend. But are we therefore to conclude, asks Matthews, that they "form part of the divine Experience" (*God in Christian Experience,* p. 239)? What really underlies Hartshorne's view is an incorrect identification of the object of knowledge, which consists of propositions.

The reactionary alteration of the doctrine of divine timelessness found in process theology has no biblical basis, introduces division and confusion into the nature of God, and in the end leads to a conception of theism that rivals rather than merely revises the Judeo-Christian view. Its projection gains interest mainly through the unfortunate intrusion into orthodox Christian circles of inadequate alternative statements of God's relation to the temporal world. But the attempt to preserve both the essential nature of God and his vital relationships to the temporal realm by importing time into his very being is just as unsuccessful and unacceptable as was the earlier idealism that stressed an all-inclusive Absolute and dismissed the reality of time. Both conjectural hypotheses compromise and sacrifice essential aspects of the biblical revelation.

Insistence on divine duration and succession depends largely on empirical argumentation for God. While F. R. Tennant affirms the timelessness of truths and ideas, he holds that divine eternity is not nontemporal. God is "out of time," he writes, only in the sense that all time is in him (*Philosophical Theology,* Vol. 2, pp. 135, 139). God, then, is not the supratemporal source or creator of time, but like humans is involved in succession which is the essence of time. As Peter A. Bertocci writes: "If we are to reason empirically about God's attributes, time, as duration and succession, must be applicable to God's experience, even though his time-span be much greater and his tempo different from ours" (*The Empirical Argument for God in Late British Thought,* p. 287).

Pannenberg likewise rejects God's timeless eternity and insists rather on God's "powerful simultaneity with every time" ("The Philosophical Concept of God," Vol. 2, p. 174). For Pannenberg the futurity of God implies his eternity; God as the power of the future determines the historical past and the present. In Pannenberg's view God's essence implies time. Whereas some would infer from a time-pervaded God the nondurability of God, Pannenberg holds that the movement of time continually contributes to determining the essence of God. Unlike process theologians, however, who espouse a growing God, Pannenberg contends that the future will reveal what has been true of God all along.

Arthur Prior argues that a timeless God cannot be omniscient ("The Formalities of Omniscience," p. 116). Robert Coburn pursues much the same line of argument. A timeless being might know the eternally valid principles of logic and mathematics which involve no necessary temporal relations, but knowledge of temporal facts, holds Coburn, requires temporally qualified knowledge and not a God who grasps all in a single act of cognition. He asserts: "A necessary condition of being able to use temporal indicator words is being an occupant of time. Hence, God's alleged eternity is logically incompatible with his alleged omniscience" ("Professor Malcolm on God," pp. 156 f.).

Nelson Pike rightly questions this assumption that a timeless being cannot know a given historical fact to be factual because it has no essential location in time (*God and Timelessness,* New York, 1970, p. 89). Unlike Coburn, he sees no reason "why a timeless being could not make use of sentences utilizing temporal indexical expressions such as 'today' or 'now' " (*ibid.,* p. 92).

But would such expressions—if spoken by a being lacking temporal position—be false assertions, since they would involve a speaker's temporal position relative to the occurrence? Pike recalls Norman Kretzmann's emphasis that "an omniscient being must know not only the entire scheme of contingent events from beginning to end at once, but also *at which stage of realization that scheme now is*" ("Omniscience and Immutability," pp. 409–421).

Kretzmann contends that divine omniscience is incompatible with divine immutability and, for that matter, with also the personal God of theism. His arguments are intricate and rest heavily on the supposed irreconcilability of divine self-referential or indexical statements with omniscience. A being that always knows what time it is, says Kretzmann, is subject to change. The fact is, however, that a change in the object of knowledge does not require a change in the knower, nor does it require a change of knowledge. God's knowledge, as Aquinas emphasizes, is "altogether invariable" (*Summa Theologiae*, I, 3.6, p. 364). Aquinas writes: "As it is without alteration in the divine knowledge that God knows one and the same thing sometimes to be, and sometimes not, so it is without variation in the divine knowledge that God knows that an enunciation is sometimes true, and sometimes false" (*ibid.*, p. 365). Aquinas cites as illustration the enunciations "Christ will be born," "Christ is born" and "Christ was born." God invariably knows that each enunciation is true at a given time. In Kretzmann's view, for a person to know the time at a given time, that person must make self-references that put him into the stream of a changing world, and this precludes immutability.

His argument is unpersuasive, however. In replying to Kretzmann, Hector-Neri Castañeda declares that "neither theism nor immutability is incompatible with God on account of indexical references' being personal, untransferable, and ephemeral" ("Omniscience and Indexical Reference," in *The Journal of Philosophy*, pp. 209 f.). An omniscient and immutable being, says Castañeda, "knows the contents of other minds on grounds other than behavior and circumstances."

Pike finds no reason to think that a timeless individual and a human being may not know or report the same events; the sentences they use involving indexical language may have "different meanings," but they could nonetheless designate the same facts (*God and Timelessness*, pp. 93 f.). But a timeless individual, Pike holds, could not formulate a true proposition involving words like "now" or "today" which identify the speaker's temporal position (*ibid.*, pp. 94 f.). Yet such statements may be translated into sentences having "equivalent meanings but which are free of temporal indexical expressions" (*ibid.*, p. 95). Pike might have added that Hegel showed that "now" and "today" do not identify the speaker's temporal position. In opposition to Coburn and Kretzmann, Pike argues that while they have established that a timeless being could not use "certain *forms of words* . . . when formulating or reporting his knowledge," they have not established "a range of facts that a timeless individual could not know" (*ibid.*, p. 95). A timeless God could surely know, says Pike, and we would agree, that Christ ascended at the very time the disciples considered the fortieth day after his resurrection from the dead.

This whole line of argument nonetheless has a speculative character far removed from biblical revelation of the God who daily publishes his divine glory (Ps. 19:1) and who continually exhibits his "eternal power and divine nature" (Rom. 1:20, NIV) in a universe divinely created on successive "days" (Gen. 1). Although a timeless God grasps all things in a single cognitive act, to speak significantly of external events he must also know the temporal successions of both calendrical time and of all other varieties of temporal relationship that prevail throughout the created universe. There is no logical basis whatever for insisting that God's own experience and knowledge must be temporal in nature for him to know and voice true propositions about temporal processes and events. The meaning of temporal "facts" may vary greatly between one beholder and another, and a good case can be made for saying that unless there is someone to interpret such facts they do not even exist. But if the divine and the human propositions about historic facts are true there must be some overlap between what God means and what humans mean. Moreover, it is the meaning God attaches to temporal events that is normative. That the Logos became incarnate on a particular day and in a particular place, and that Christ died for our sins and on the third day rose for our justification are historical realities whose truth we could know only because the timeless omniscient God reveals it.

Coburn insists that a timeless being cannot be personal, since among other activities, as he sees it, a person must be logically capable of remembering, anticipating, reflecting, deliberating, deciding, intending and acting intentionally ("Professor Malcolm on God," p. 155). Pike agrees that such activities take time or require a temporal location (*God and Timelessness,* p. 122). But Pike considers the notion premature that a timeless being cannot be personal because in principle he is prohibited from these activities (*ibid.,* p. 123). The inability of a timeless omniscient person to perform some of the stipulated mental activities would not negate its personhood (*ibid.,* p. 123). Pike emphasizes that knowledge does not require deliberation or other temporal activities adduced by Coburn (*ibid.,* p. 124); knowing need not take time nor involve a temporal relationship between the knower and the content of his knowledge.

Yet the eternity of the God of the Bible does not preclude him from relationships to his created order that are properly identified as familiar mental activities. It may be true, as Pike says, that an immutable timeless being that "could not be affected or prompted by another" and whose actions therefore could not be regarded as "a response" to another, and whose knowledge or awareness is beyond our understanding, "could not be counted as a person" (*ibid.,* p. 128). "How much of a person would a timeless person be?" Pike asks (*ibid.,* p. 129) since, so he comments, one could not consider such a person friend or foe. But the Bible disallows such inferences; one might with equal propriety ask, how much of a person could a temporal person be? The triune God not only has eternal personal relationships within his own timeless being, but also engages in interpersonal patterns with creatures to whom he manifests himself in righteousness and wrath and love and mercy.

Wolterstorff suspends some of God's actions upon human decisions and acts. He assumes that God cannot stand in relations of precedence and succession unless succession characterizes his own knowledge ("God Everlasting," pp. 185 ff.). If God were timelessly eternal, he contends, God could not know that any temporal event is or was or will be occurring; instead, he postulates a God whose actions are in part "a response to the free actions of human beings" (*ibid.,* p. 197) and who "remembers" what has occurred (*ibid.,* p. 200). Such notions are precisely what theologians who affirm God's timeless eternity deny. God's knowledge is a knowledge of propositions eternally constituting the divine mind and is not dependent upon temporal order relationships. The fact that the three modes of past, present and future characterize all temporality is not decisive for the nature of God who transcends time.

The biblical view, it seems to me, implies that God is not in time; that there is no succession of ideas in the divine mind; that time is a divine creation concomitant with the origin of the universe; that God internally knows all things, including all space-time contingencies; that this knowledge includes knowledge of the temporal succession prevalent in the created universe. Although God's nature, including his knowledge, is not in time, nonetheless because he is omniscient he cognitively distinguishes between what I did in the past, what I am now doing, and what I shall do tomorrow. God includes time not as a constituent aspect of his being or knowing, but as a conceptual aspect of his knowledge of created realities. God's time-transcending knowledge in himself does not cancel out distinctive space-time relationships to his created universe. God is not limited to simply one track of relationships to the temporal order; he knows all historical factualities and contingencies through his eternal decree, and he knows them in personal presence in the historical order.

It is therefore one thing to say that God simultaneously knows all things— past, present and future—and quite another to insist that he knows them only in an eternal "now" that makes all time distinctions wholly irrelevant. As G. Galloway puts it, "a God who could not know the time-changes in finite minds could not be reverenced as God" (*A Philosophy of Religion,* p. 479). But God's nature need not itself be time-structured in order for him to know simultaneously all events and also to know them in the way that his creatures know them. Divine omniscience comprehends all experience. God's omniscience involves both simultaneous knowledge of all that is past, present and future, and an awareness of the succession of events in the created temporal order. There is nothing contradictory in saying that God knows all things simultaneously, and that within this comprehensive knowledge he distinguishes between what is forever true and factual and what is temporally contingent. He eternally knew that I would write these sentences yesterday and give them a final editing this morning.

In the knowledge of his own nature and will God knows all his purposes with respect to as yet nonexistent objects and events. He eternally knows them as they will be, are now, and have been. God has knowledge of the universe through his own thoughts and purposes. Though it was fashioned with and in time, God knew the created universe conceptually and eternally through his decree to create. His plan of a finite creation, present in the divine mind from eternity, became an accomplished fact by an exercise of divine volition. God purposed a temporal creation; time became a creaturely reality only with the actuality of creation.

In creating the universe God related himself to conditions of space and time that had not prevailed until the creation, inasmuch as extension and succession are not predicable of divine ideas. Although God's knowledge is not knowledge in succession, he has knowledge of succession. Here one might take a cue from Augustine and show how ridiculous it would be to contend that God is spatial because he knows space.

Knudson questioned Bowne's readiness to speak of the ideality and unreality of time, and wrote instead of time's relativity: "All that we can say is that God may have an intuitive grasp of the future that transcends our human way of knowing. Future, past and present may for him constitute a kind of 'eternal now,' but, if he thus knows the future, he must nevertheless know it as future and not as present" (*The Doctrine of God,* p. 322). While Knudson's retention of an "eternal now" is unhelpful, his emphasis that God knows the future as future is valid. God knows all things at once, and has knowledge of succession as part of his omniscience; he not only knows events as they become actual in time and space, but he also knows them as certain from eternity. What creaturely minds grasp in their time sequences God knows immediately as a comprehensive totality; his decree to create a specific universe involves knowledge of all its eventualities and possibilities.

God has knowledge of the universe as a created reality. He knows it now not simply as something purposed from eternity, but as a creaturely reality preserved and judged by him and in which he manifests his grace. The God of the Bible fully knows that in human experience and in the created universe yesterday, today and tomorrow are not simultaneous, and that creaturely decisions and deeds lead to further events in the external world. Some passages of Scripture pointedly connect God's knowledge with his omnipresence in the created universe (Ps. 139; cf. Ps. 33:15, 97:9; Isa. 29:15). Although the phrase is hardly adequate, since divine ideas are not qualified by extension, omniscience has been called "the omnipresence of cognition." The fact of divine omniscience does not imply that God's knowledge is dependent upon his creation. But God does know human decision and human activity in its dramatic day-to-day and age-to-age occurrences. He distinguishes the presently actual in the space-time realm from the yet future and from the irrecoverable past.

Yahweh emphasizes his past mercies to the Hebrews, particularly their divine deliverance from Egypt, as a basis for continuing trust in him (Joshua 24:2–15). He declares himself "well pleased" with the incarnate Son manifest once-for-all for the redemption of contrite sinners (Matt. 3:17; cf. Heb. 3:8). He pleads for decision and commitment in the present hour (Heb. 3:7). He warns of future judgment that awaits mankind after death (Heb. 9:27). The time sequences of human history are crucially important both in God's sight and in man's. The space-time universe owes its very existence and continuance to God, and is the cosmic setting for the divine incarnation in Jesus Christ, the final triumph of righteousness, and the doom of injustice.

Yet we need not therefore contend, as Edwin Lewis does, that the living God of the Scriptures can be preserved only if we insist that for God no less than for ourselves much that happens must be "a *novelty*" (*The Creator and the Adversary,* p. 161). To be sure, all that happens to any and every human being happens, in a sense, once-for-all-time. In any case the biblical redemptive acts centering in the crucifixion of Jesus Christ and his bodily resurrection are once-for-all events. But we seriously question the premise that God's purpose and omniscience in no way can and do anticipate the "novelty" of events, if by that we mean they are unknown. The more one stresses the possibility of divine surprise by novelty as significant evidence that God is personal and living, the less predictable will be the final outcome of history and, for that matter, the manifest purpose of God in the course of human history itself.

Besides the Bible's specific teaching that God is all-knowing, the main argument in support of divine foreknowledge of future acts comes from the predictive element in Scripture. Yahweh is the God of prophecy as well as of history; he announces "from of old the things to come" (Isa. 44:7, RSV). Whether this passage refers to the protevangelium or to Noah, or to Abraham, it emphasizes divine foreknowledge. The New Testament speaks in many passages of God's prior disclosure of the future. Acts 3:15 and Acts 7:52 use the term *prokataggellō* ("to declare or announce beforehand"). Stephen asserts that the prophets "previously announced the coming of the Righteous One" (Acts 7:52, NAS) and Peter states that "God announced beforehand by the mouth of all the prophets, that His Christ should suffer" (Acts 3:18, NAS).

Modern biblical criticism circumvents major biblical prophecies by redating books that contain dramatic examples of divine foreknowledge and by insisting that the supposed predictions are actually post-event fabrications. The critics, asserts Albert C. Knudson, have "greatly weakened, if not completely undermined" the case for predictive prophecy. He writes: "There is hardly a specific prediction in the Bible that requires divine foreknowledge of free acts for its explanation" (*The Doctrine of God*, p. 321). Knudson's comment is both ambiguous and erroneous. The validation of a single specific prediction, such as that concerning Israel's rejection of the promised Messiah, would invert the covert assumption that the doctrine of divine foreknowledge is an apologetic invention. Many of Scripture's predictive passages can be annulled only if we superimpose questionable redatings. But even granted the latest critical datings, the predictions of the Messiah were all written before 50 B.C. If no predictive basis exists in the Old Testament for the life, character, ministry, crucifixion and resurrection of Jesus Christ, then not only the apostles (Acts 2:22 f., 30 f.; 1 Cor. 15:3 f.) but also Jesus himself (Luke 24:25 f.) were deeply mistaken, and the very continuity of Old and New Testament theism is impaired.

Both the Old and New Testaments teach that God foreknows the future, that he is prescient of the events and circumstances of the created temporal world. This foreknowledge of the future distinguishes the living God from idols and false gods: "Who then is like me? . . . let him foretell what will come. . . . Did I not proclaim this and foretell it long ago?" (Isa. 44:7 f., NIV). The Old and New Testaments alike speak of God's foreknowledge (*proginōskō*, from which derives the medical term prognosis or "advance knowledge" that physicians have used since Hippocrates). Daniel tells Belteshazzar: "There is a God in heaven who reveals mysteries, and he has made known to King Nebuchadnezzar what will be in the latter days" (Dan. 2:28, RSV). The apostle James speaks of "the Lord, who has made these things known from of old" (Acts 15:18, RSV).

That Scripture affirms God's prescience is recognized by the historic creeds of Christendom. Here we need mention only The Formula of Concord (Art. XI, sec. 2–5) and the Westminster Confession (Chapter 5, sections 1 and 2).

The usual objection to foreordination as the ground of divine foreknowledge is that any decisive predetermination of the acts of creatures necessarily erodes their freedom. Some theologians therefore distinguish between God's foreordination of his own plan and acts and his knowledge of so-called "contingent" events. They depict God's knowledge of human affairs in terms of the foreordination of only such divine acts as creation, preservation, and eschatology, in distinction from free human choices. But this approach truncates divine omniscience; it unacceptably postulates in God both intuitive knowledge and an a posteriori knowledge somehow derived through his observation of the universe, even if that knowledge is said somehow to transcend time.

Augustine's early view terminates free will at Adam's fall and rules out free will in heaven; his later views are even more anticipative of Calvin. He denies that God's knowledge that man will sin eliminates voluntary choice ("On Free Will," pp. 175 f.). Augustine observes that even humans sometimes foreknow the decisions and acts of others; these activities do not therefore become necessary or involuntary.

The sixth-century philosopher Boethius, on the other hand, held that unqualified divine omniscience does not leave room for voluntary human agency; he consequently disallows divine foreknowledge of human actions.

Aquinas and most medieval theologians, however, insist that God does indeed know all events, and that his omniscience is not incompatible with human freedom. Whether Aquinas really affirms that God foreknows future contingent events is questionable, however. Arthur Kenny observes (*Aquinas: A Collection of Critical Essays*) that according to Aquinas God knows all because his eternity overlaps the whole span of time; hence for God all events occur simultaneously. For Aquinas contingent events are consequently always present and never future to God's knowledge (*Summa Theologiae*, Ia. 14, 13; cf. *De Veritate*, 2:12 ad 7). Kenny, who defends the view that divine foreknowledge and human freedom are compatible, considers a timeless eternity simultaneous with every part of time as something radically incoherent, for it makes every moment also simultaneous with the whole of eternity. But this involves confusions resulting from an absence of definition; so does Jonathan Edwards' earlier argument that divine foreknowledge necessitates human decision and events and is inconsistent with contingency, but that such necessity is consistent with man's liberty as a moral agent (*Freedom of the Will*, 1754, Sec. 12).

Whether humanistic or existential, modern atheism declares not only divine foreknowledge to be incompatible with human freedom, but the very reality of God himself. The rejection of all supernatural, transcendent, universal authority is made the presupposition of human autonomy. Not only Friedrich Nietzsche but also Nicolai Hartmann and Jean-Paul Sartre reject the existence of God presumably to preserve the freedom of man. Biblical theism affirms, on the contrary, that everything that can be predicated of man, whether his existence and continuance, or his responsible decisions and deeds and final destiny, finds its necessary presupposition in a divine reality beyond himself. The God of the Bible is the source and not the adversary of responsible human choice and agency.

The atheistic views, in this debate over human freedom, recognize that a significant conception of God involves his eternity, sovereignty and omniscience; for theism nothing happens in time that God does not foreknow and foreordain. Yet they leap from this acknowledgment to the questionable inference that God's reality would exclude voluntary human choice, and that responsible human action requires the nonexistence of God. Those Christian theists who regard divine foreknowledge and foreordination as antithetical to voluntary human choice, and confuse the latter with arbitrary choice or liberty of indifference, unwittingly encourage this misconception.

Wolfhart Pannenberg thinks that the only way to confront the attack upon God's reality by the atheism of freedom is to modify the inherited Christian view so that divine eternity is conditioned by human history. He contends that "an *existent* being acting with omnipotence and omniscience would make freedom impossible" ("Speaking About God in the Face of Atheistic Criticism," p. 109). Pannenberg proposes a radical alteration of the reality of God, and conceives God not as existing as an eternally perfect and omniscient being, but as a God whose omniscience should be understood only from the standpoint of eschatological futurity. Hence no significant doctrine or divine foreknowledge of foreordination remains.

Donald Bloesch connects divine omniscience not with specific events but only with an "overarching providence" (*Essentials of Evangelical Theology,* Vol. 1, p. 30). "Although God knows the future before it happens, he does not literally know the concrete even until it happens," Bloesch writes, for the latter would require "a closed or static universe in which real history and freedom become illusions" (*ibid.,* pp. 29 f.). But obviously Old Testament predictions fulfilled in the New are not only general but also highly specific. Such explicit biblical teaching (e.g., Ps. 139:4, 16) contravenes the notion that God does not and cannot foreknow particular future events. If real history and freedom require that God does not know the concrete until it happens, can we any longer declare that eternal bliss awaits every individual who trusts Christ or that condemnation awaits every sinner who rejects him?

Donald Mackay also seems to imply that the doctrine of divine omniscience nullifies personal freedom. He does not deny that God is sovereign over every detail of the past, present and future. But he does contend that we would be incorrect to believe that God has foreknowledge of an event

involving our own free action since for us, unlike for God, such foreknowledge would involve a contradiction (*The Clock Work Image*, pp.
110 f.). Are we to say then that we can have correct knowledge of the inevita-
bility of events only if God does not foreknow them? Would it be incorrect
for humans to accept as inevitable a free decision and deed that God has
disclosed to be inevitable? Mackay seems to imply, Gordon Clark protests,
that "God can have no foreknowledge that a man would be unable to falsify,
if only he knew it" (*Behaviorism and Christianity*, p. 171). Critics have
noted that on this basis Jesus of Nazareth could not have known the inevita-
bility of his own death (cf. William Hasker, "Mackay on Being a Responsible Mechanism," and "Reply to Donald Mackay").

Nelson Pike holds, gratuitously I believe, that God's timelessness and
his foreknowledge of voluntary actions are incompatible emphases (*God
and Timelessness*, p. 86, n. 29). For Pike "no action is voluntary if it is
not within the power of the agent at the time of action to refrain from
its performance" (*ibid.*, p. 57). He rejects as inadequate the expositions
by Augustine and Leibniz, and more recently by Arthur Prior, all of whom
hold that divine foreknowledge does not necessitate the future.

For Prior, God's omniscience comprehends only what is true at the time
and not what is indeterminate; in brief, he assumes that there are indeterminate events and that God does not have divine foreknowledge of all
human acts (*Past, Present and Future*, Chapter 7, Section 1). Only on the
basis of divine determinism, he insists, can propositions concerning future
actions be assuredly true. Prior asserts that no voluntary act can be decisively foreknown before its actual performance: "I cannot see in what way
the alleged knowledge, even if it were God's, could be more than correct
guessing. For there would be, *ex hypothesis*, nothing that could *make* it
knowledge, no present *ground* for the guess's correctness which a specially
penetrating person might perceive" ("The Formalities of Omniscience,"
pp. 124).

Critics of Prior's view find his temporal dating of the truth value of
propositions highly questionable (cf. Rogers Albritton, "Present Truth and
Future Contingency"; cf. also Richard Taylor, "The Problem of Future Contingency"), all the more so in the case of God's knowledge. Wolterstorff
also rejects the constancy of the truth-value of propositions ("God Everlasting," p. 192). Pike considers "obscuristic and strange the whole idea of
dating the truth-value of a statement in which a date is already assigned
to a given event or action" (*God and Timelessness*, p. 71). Propositions
concerning something one does are *true* when one does it, but they are
not contingently true before the act occurs, even though they may be foreknown; to append "temporal qualifiers on the truth-values of the propositions that God believes is likely to cause confusion" (*ibid.*, p. 71).

Prior would in any case have to concede the antecedent truth of propositions, says Pike, if the future action anticipated by foreknowledge actually
occurs. However, Pike observes, Prior's exclusion of divine foreknowledge
proceeds moreover on principles that would also exclude the phenomenon
of human foreknowledge; the fact is that by knowing the character and

dispositions of others we can to a considerable extent foretell specific choices they will freely make (*God and Timelessness*, p. 86, n. 28). Prior's way of relating God's foreknowledge to temporal events also bypasses the classic Christian emphasis that God knows exhaustively by immediate vision what transcends created spatio-temporal limits.

Boethius stressed that God knows, not in terms of past or future but only in an eternal present, and thereby completely disconnected God's knowledge from the time of performance (*Consolation of Philosophy*, Book V, Section 6). But, comments Pike, although a timeless God beholds all in his eternal present, "there is no way of formulating the problem of divine foreknowledge that does not involve locating God's cognitions in the *past* relative to the actions cognized" (*God and Timelessness*, p. 75).

Pike argues that essential divine omniscience would necessarily exclude free human agency ("Divine Omniscience and Voluntary Action"). If God is intrinsically omniscient and has advance knowledge of all human acts so that those acts are certain, then, says Pike, it is "not within one's power to do other than he does" and no human action can therefore be voluntary (*ibid.*, p. 45).

Voluntary action does not, however, depend upon intellectual doubt or divine ignorance, or upon arbitrary subjective power to reverse our each and every decision and deed. It depends rather upon voluntary choice. If humans voluntarily choose to do what God foreknows to be certain, then the conditions of voluntary human agency are fulfilled. Human actions are not causally determined by God's prior beliefs, even if God foreknows them and if in view of this foreknowledge they are certain; we do not choose because God has determined our choices. John Turk Saunders writes: "Our freedom is no more infringed by God's previously believing that we will act in a certain manner than it is by His later believing that we did act in a certain manner; we will never perform an act which conflicts with His beliefs, no matter what the dates of those beliefs" ("Of God and Freedom," pp. 220 f.). Saunders contends, however, that we have power to act so that "the past would be other than in fact it is" (*ibid.*, p. 224). He illustrates this claim by citing as example that, had he not written his rejoinder to Pike in 1965, Caesar's assassination would not have preceded by 2009 years the writing of Saunders' paper. To this Pike replies that Saunders confuses causal laws with questions of fact and truth. Saunders' paper written in 1965 is the "logically necessary and sufficient condition of its being the case" that Caesar died 2009 years earlier, but the later event, says Pike, stands in no necessary relation to the earlier. Marilyn McCord Adams insists nonetheless that Pike's claim "that the existence of an essentially omniscient and everlasting God is inconsistent with the voluntary character of some human actions has yet to be made out" ("Is the Existence of God a 'Hard' Fact?," in *Philosophical Review*, Vol. 76, 1967, p. 503).

Some scholars contend that divine "foreknowledge" is a viable option only if God's knowledge is in time. If God exists wholly "outside time," they stress, then foreknowledge becomes a mere figure of speech. To be sure, God's relation to time, whether on the theory of divine timelessness or that of divine temporalness, differs from man's relation to time; God's knowledge of the created universe, moreover, differs quantitatively and in many respects also qualitatively from man's. But this fact does not of itself settle the propriety of speaking of divine "foreknowledge." If God is in time, and his knowledge is temporally conditioned, then divine foreknowledge of all events is actually precluded. From our perspective, God's knowledge of any and all temporal events appears as a divine "foreknowledge." But in his own omniscience God knows all things simultaneously; his knowledge does not, like ours, arise in temporal succession.

Arminian theologians contend that there are innumerable future events that God does not purpose, and that to make God's purpose the only ground of his foreknowledge is to destroy human freedom and to constitute God the efficient cause and author of sin (cf. Randolph S. Foster, *God—Nature and Attributes,* p. 147).

Difficulties posed by the fact of sin and evil in the world are examined at some length in Volume 6. Augustine writes that "God compels no man to sin though he sees beforehand those who are going to sin by their own free will" (*De Libero Arbitrio,* in *Augustine's Earlier Writings*). Yet even in this early stage he held that man after the fall could not choose not to sin. In context Augustine finds in divine foreknowledge no more determinism of future sinful actions than he does in human foreknowledge of another's sinning, and here emphasizes, moreover, that man has voluntary choice (cf. also *The City of God,* chapters 9–10). God's foreknowledge does not involve determination that cancels voluntary action, but God knows what man will voluntarily choose.

To say that God wills sin and redemption as factors in the universe he purposes to create is not at all to say that God sins, or that he has a light view of sin. He is the holy God who publishes his righteousness in the declaration of man's need of redemption and in the costly gift of his Son as the Savior of sinners. The purpose of God in creation is fully grounded in his wisdom, power and goodness. The alternative view is that the creature incurs sin by his own voluntary misdeeds totally outside the purposes of God for his creation; this view involves a conception of the universe so open-ended that it nullifies the relevance and significance of God's purposes in the eschatological future as well. God does not force man to sin, since sin is man's deliberate action contrary to the precepts of God. Through man's responsible decision and choice sin enters a universe in which sin and redemption are integral elements in God's purpose.

The argument that God foreknows what he does not purpose, and which shifts the ground of divine knowledge to something other than God's purpose, raises many difficulties. The speculative rationale that is sometimes introduced to sustain foreknowledge, namely, that God's relationship to all specific times is that of an everlasting now, is both beyond reason and contrary to it. There can be no other ground of divine foreknowledge of nonexistent processes, events and creatures if they were not divinely purposed. God's purposes are eternal, and effectuate all futurities.

The effort to limit divine foreknowledge only to events that do not involve creaturely decision and action, that is, to God's own acts in distinction from so-called "contingent" events, is conjectural and without biblical basis. In Scripture divine omniscience embraces even what is contingent from a human perspective (1 Sam. 23:9 ff.; Matt. 11:22 f.). Scripture contravenes the claim that divine nondetermination is necessary for human freedom and responsibility, for God's foreordination includes even such events as fallen man's rejection and crucifixion of Jesus Christ, events for which mankind is held responsible (Acts 2:23).

Because divine omniscience seems to require the certainty of events, it would appear to exclude voluntary choice. But actually it is the purposing will of God, and not omniscience, that governs the certainty of events (cf. Ps. 65:4). Divine foreknowledge involves essentially the same divine relationship to the human thinker and doer as does foreordination. Foreknowledge of a "psychologically undetermined and indeterminable" decision suspended on man's free will is, as Geerhardus Vos notes, difficult to imagine ("Omniscience," p. 2192). Yet if God can foreknow human decisions and acts before their psychological self-determination, and can do this compatibly with man's free will, then why should divine foreordination be considered any less compatible? After all, the essential point is already granted in regard to foreknowledge, namely, that divine certainty of the event prior to man's inner decision is compatible with free agency. To say that, despite man's voluntary choices, those choices also include an element of divine foreordination to which divine omniscience attaches itself, avoids a host of inconsistencies and has biblical support. This is especially the case in regard to that most heinous of human acts for which humans are held fully accountable, namely, the crucifixion of Jesus Christ; Scripture depicts it both as divinely foreordained and as responsibly ventured by sinful mankind (Acts 2:23). Jesus' crucifixion is portrayed not simply as a matter of divine foreknowledge in distinction from divine foreordination, but as God's "determinate counsel" (KJV), "definite plan" (RSV), "predetermined plan" (PHILLIPS), "deliberate will and plan" (NEB), and "set purpose" (NIV). Yet human responsibility is not one whit minimized: Jesus Christ was slain "by wicked hands" (KJV), "by the hands of lawless men" (RSV), by "heathen men" (NEB).

Given the view of God's timeless eternity, the distinction between divine foreknowledge and divine foreordination falls away. Nelson Pike tries to eclipse that distinction by depicting God's decrees as having complementary consequences for each possible human decision; the nature of man's volition or response, Pike holds, affects the decree pertaining to that particular decision. This view jeopardizes a meaningful doctrine of divine decrees. There is a much sounder basis for correlating divine foreknowledge and divine foreordination that preserves the significance of the decrees.

The effort to preserve divine foreknowledge apart from foreordination runs counter to biblical teaching. A connection appears between God's knowledge and his will and election already in the Old Testament conception of divine knowledge. The usage in Numbers 16:5 ("him whom he will choose he will cause to come near to him," RSV) and in Psalm 65:4 ("Blessed is he whom thou dost choose and bring near," RSV) is far from exceptional; the correlation of divine knowledge and election is quite characteristic of the Old Testament. Similarly in the New Testament, as Rudolf Bultmann comments, God's foreknowledge is not merely prior knowledge but "an election or foreordination," whether of his people (Rom. 8:29, 11:2) or of Jesus Christ (1 Pet. 1:20) (on *proginōskō,* p. 715). God's foreknowledge is a predeterminative knowledge.

John Knox acknowledges the apostle Paul's correlation of divine foreknowledge with divine predestination ("for those whom he foreknew he also predestined," Rom. 8:29, RSV). He remarks that the Old Testament use of the verb "to know" in regard to divine knowledge of human beings (cf. Amos 3:2; Matt. 7:23) disallows reducing the meaning of foreknowledge simply to prevision of those whose faith would qualify them for justification ("Epistle to the Romans," p. 525).

Discussions of foreordination and foreknowledge all too often ignore the fact that these terms are two of three that pertain to God and the human future; the most neglected of these is the term "providence." Twice the apostle Paul uses the noun *prothesis* (a previously made divine resolve or purpose); in Romans 9:11 he declares this *prothesis* to be the foundation of the election of Jacob, and in Romans 8:28, the foundation of the "call" of Christians. Paul ascribes both the existence of the church (Eph. 1:11) and the plan of salvation in Christ (Eph. 3:8 ff.) to God's purpose. The theme of divine knowledge therefore necessarily involves consideration also of divine sovereignty, divine decree and election. Long ago the prophet Amos wrote: "Surely the Sovereign LORD does nothing without revealing his plan to his servants the prophets. . . . The Sovereign LORD has spoken—who can but prophesy?" (Amos 3:7 f., NIV).

15.
The Unchanging Immutable God

THE LIVING GOD is the immutable God who can neither increase nor decrease; he is not subject to development or decline. "I am the Lord, I change not" (Mal. 3:6a). In him is "no variableness" (James 1:17, KJV; "variation," RSV, NEB). He "does not change like shifting shadows" (NIV). The Psalmist declares in contrasting the enduring and unchanging Creator with the ever-changing and perishing components of the space-time universe: "They will perish, but thou dost endure. . . . Thou changest them like raiment, and they pass away; but thou art the same, and thy years have no end" (Ps. 102:26; cf. Heb. 1:10 f.).

According to Norman Kretzmann the orthodox Christian principle of divine immutability was "drawn from Greek philosophy" and later supported by certain biblical passages ("Omniscience and Immutability," p. 409, n. 1). Nicholas Wolterstorff likewise contends that "the theological tradition of God's ontological immutability has no explicit biblical foundation" ("God Everlasting," p. 202). Wolterstorff, in fact, considers the ascription of immutability to God an extraneous imposition on the biblical text.

It is true that medieval theologians were aware of the teaching of certain Greek philosophers in discussing God's immutability (cf. Aquinas, *Summa Theologica*, I, Q. 9, art. 1). They noted Plato's argument that change in a supremely perfect being constitutes corruption, deterioration and loss of perfection (*Republic*, II, 381B). They referred to Aristotle who considered a being subject to change as not fully developed and therefore less than perfect (*Metaphysics*, 1074b, 26). The fact is, however, that the Hebrew-Christian belief in God's immutability arose independently of Greek philosophy; it stemmed from revelational sources rather than from speculative conjecture.

286

The biblical revelation attests a living active God who differs remarkably from Greek projections in his interior life and in his relations to man and the world. It affirms that God is unchanging, and yet that he is sovereign creator of the universe, preserver of man and the worlds, active in secular and in redemptive history, and incarnate in Jesus Christ.

Shailer Matthews is therefore wrong when he asserts that Plato's influence accounts for the Christian conviction of God's immutability (*The Growth of the Idea of God*, p. 98). It would be more accurate to say that even some Greek philosophers—notably the Pythagoreans and Plato—were constrained to acknowledge that the ultimate explanatory principle is immutable, than to derive the biblical view from secular philosophy. Charles Hartshorne is alert to the influence of the Bible upon the medieval outlook although he laments that "when the Scriptures say God is perfect or unchanging, this was taken to mean, in every respect and sense perfect and unchanging, as though the Bible had been written for the express purpose of guiding philosophers as such" (*Man's Vision of God and the Logic of Theism*, p. 71). Hartshorne's comment about the Bible and philosophers is gratuitous, of course, for the Bible was written for all people, philosophers included.

Some scholars have attributed the Christian commitment to the immutability of God to the use by medieval theology of the philosophical category of substance. Christopher Steed has shown from ancient philosophers, however, that to describe God as substance did not necessarily require identifying him as unchanging substance, that is, as immutable (*Divine Substance*, pp. 106, 171).

In teaching God's metaphysical immutability, Scripture stresses especially God's moral constancy or ethical stability. It underscores God's faithfulness to his holy will and to his promises more than the larger theme of God's unsusceptibility to ontological change; in popular thinking God's changelessness is usually associated more with his moral character than with other metaphysical aspects. Passages affirming that God's counsel stands forever (e.g., Ps. 19:21, 33:11; Isa. 46:10) and that deny that God repents (e.g., Num. 23:19) illumine this important facet of his nature.

Yet it would be wrong to imply, as does H. Maldwyn Hughes, that biblical interest in God's changelessness ignores so-called metaphysical attributes, and concentrates only on God's moral nature and purpose, that is, on holiness, righteousness and love (*The Christian Idea of God*, p. 36). At one point Hughes does speak broadly in terms of "constancy and consistency in His nature and in His purposes," but he elsewhere shuns claims for objective metaphysical knowledge (*ibid.*, p. 152). Francis J. McConnell similarly allows interest in God's moral constancy to crowd out other aspects of divine immutability (*The Christlike God*, p. 73). Concerning Charles Hartshorne's comments on "the essentially ethical meaning of the divine constancy as posited by Hebrew writers" (*Man's Vision of God*, p. 159), Edward Farley observes that Hartshorne uses terms like "absolute" and "independent" in an unorthodox way; Hartshorne's reinterpretation of "absolute" in the context of religious adequacy, says Farley, substitutes a functional approach for the traditional doctrine (*The Transcendence of God*, p. 149).

But, as William Newton Clarke reminds us, it is God's all-embracing changelessness that constitutes the ground "of his own consistency, intellectual, moral and practical, and of the consistency of his perpetual and abiding operation" (*The Christian Doctrine of God*, pp. 309 ff.). A god subject to alteration in some aspects of his being is not the self-revealed God of the Bible. A creator and sustainer of the world who is vulnerable to mutability, a redeemer and judge of mankind whose essential nature might waver and whose purpose may vacillate, is not a deity in whom we can ever be religiously at rest. The gods of change and caprice belong to the world of paganism. A deity of shifting whims and moods is too much like mere mortals to merit worship.

Christian theology has affirmed both God's essential timelessness and his essential changelessness. For Augustine genuine eternity involves unchangeability: "One and the same thing is . . . said, whether God is called eternal or immortal, or incorruptible, or unchangeable" (*De Trinitate*, Book XV, Ch. 5, Sec. 7). Scholars who deny divine timelessness and divine omniscience understandably also reject divine immutability, for, as Stephen Charnock comments, "if God did not know all future things he would be mutable in his knowledge" (*Discourses upon the Existence and Attributes of God*, Vol. 1, p. 492). William Newton Clarke writes: "His [God's] independent, self-existent being is beyond the reach of alteration, and from eternity to eternity he is the same. So the best Hebrew faith discerned, and so the Christian doctrine has always set him forth" (*The Christian Doctrine of God*, p. 309).

The changelessness predicated of an eternal being, E. L. Mascall observes, differs greatly from the changelessness that would be predicated of a being existing in time yet undergoing no change (*The Openness of Being*, p. 159). Nelson Pike remarks: "If an object changes, that object is different at a given time from what it was at an earlier time. This is what it is to change. Thus, in order to change, an object must exist at two moments in time. It follows that if an object is timeless . . . it does not change" (*God and Timelessness*, p. 39). In brief, timelessness logically entails changelessness and unchangeableness, or immutability. Even Schleiermacher granted this in his exposition of God's timelessness (*The Christian Faith*, Para. 52, postscript). Change is predicable only of subjects existing in time. If we affirm that God is timeless we must also affirm that he is unchanging.

Pike doubts that an immutable or changeless being must necessarily be timeless (*God and Timelessness*, p. 42). "Before it can be claimed that the doctrine of timelessness has 'scientific' value by virtue of its logical connection with the predicate 'immutable,' " he writes, "it must be shown that the sense of 'immutable' that connects with 'timeless' can be identified with the sense of 'immutable' intended in the Christian dogma of immutability" (*ibid.*, p. 179). "If there is a discrepancy here, we could no longer claim that the doctrine of timelessness entails and is entailed by the *Christian* claim that God is immutable."

Pike raises questions also about the thesis that God's immutability involves the logical impossibility for God "to change in any way whatsoever" (*ibid.*, p. 176). When Christianity affirms that Yahweh cannot change, does it mean, he asks, that (1) "He cannot change *in any way whatsoever*" and that (2) the term "cannot" expresses *"logical* impossibility" (*ibid.*, p. 177)? For Pike divine immutability means only that God's character will not change in respect to his attributes, that is, God "cannot bring Himself to behave" contrary to them (*ibid.*, p. 178). Alvin Plantinga suggests that "incorruptible" be understood materially and causally rather than logically; for nothing could cause God to cease to exist. The predicate "ingenerable" reflects the same emphasis, for nothing can cause God to exist ("Necessary Being," pp. 97 ff.).

This approach detaches interpretation of these predicates from the context of divine timelessness. To emphasize character-stability avoids the concept of "logical impossibility," notes Pike; it leaves open the door to God's response to others, and to divine knowledge that changes as the objects of God's knowledge change. Moreover, Pike considers it "closer to the intentions of the biblical and confessional authors than the analysis of 'immutable' that goes with the doctrine of timelessness" and more compatible with "a being that is worthy of worship" (*ibid.*, p. 179). His argument not only denies omniscience, but it is also a non sequitur.

The biblical view is that the living God, alone worthy of worship, is timelessly eternal and that immutability characterizes all his perfections. He does not change either for better or for worse for he possesses all perfections from eternity. Malachi 3 emphasizes the unchangeableness of God's counsel (cf. Prov. 19:21; Heb. 6:17); James 1:17 the unchangeableness of his righteousness; Hebrews 4:13 the immutability of his knowledge (cf. 1 Tim. 1:17, the "only wise" God; Acts 15:18); Ephesians 1:11 the immutability of his purpose (cf. Isa. 46:10). At the same time Scripture also exhibits God as active in the creation and preservation of the world, as purposively involved in profane and redemptive history, as incarnate in Jesus Christ the crucified and risen Messiah of promise. Scripture emphasizes not only God's immutability but also his active relationships to the space-time world and to mankind.

The doctrine of divine immutability entails many practical consequences. Directing our adoration and reverence from the transient world of creaturely change and uncertainty to the reality of the unchanging God, it shows us to be but perishable creatures except as the Creator preserves us from nonbeing. Our confidence rests in God whose decrees are unchanging and whose promises are unfailing. Yahweh is an "everlasting rock" (Isa. 26:4, RSV) whose enduring support is pledged to all who trust him. His changelessness spurs us to greater constancy in worship, fellowship and service. God's immutability allows us no hope that God will change his holy intention for the universe; to escape doom sinners must change their ways.

Pantheistic philosophers who consider the universe to be God's developing thought and life; personal idealists who hold that nature is a part of God; process theologians who affirm that time pervades certain aspects of the divine nature, all deny the essential changelessness of God. Brightman depicts God as a finite deity who "achieves his aims through wrestling and suffering and loving" (*The Finding of God*, p. 122). God is a God vexed by "the given"—an alien principle—within his own eternal nature (*ibid.*, p. 13). God is an "unfinished deity," a deity for whom "growth" remains possible; he is "a being who has not yet realized all that he is to become" (*ibid.*, pp. 130 f.).

For Knudson, however, metaphysical immutability implies more than simply God's independence from external being or beings that can alter his nature or character. It implies also that no internal causes can alter or condition the being of God. As even Emil Brunner asserts, "The God of the Bible is eternally Unchangeable. . . . He is the Same from everlasting to everlasting, the First and the Last, the Alpha and the Omega" (*The Christian Doctrine of God*, p. 269).

W. R. Matthews, however, considers "the conception of the self-sufficiency of God in and for himself . . . an abstract conception which cannot be allowed to dominate our theology without disastrous results" (*The Purpose of God*, p. 173). But, we would ask, are not all conceptions (e.g., gravity, vertebrate, conic) abstract? If so it cannot be the abstractness of the evangelical orthodox conception to which Matthews objects; what he apparently dislikes is its assertion of the unchanging nature of the God of the Bible.

In contemplating Whiteheadian notions of God and change, we need to remember that Whitehead's basic metaphysical principle is not God but creativity. What Whitehead designates as God is a postulated reality very different from the God of biblical revelation. The "primordial nature" of Whitehead's God has no tangible actuality; it is completely abstract. Only by interacting with the real world of actual occasions does this God acquire a "consequent nature" and thereby become both conscious and concrete. Whitehead moreover sacrifices the doctrine of transcendent creation. He achieves the emergence of consciousness through "prehension" and "feeling," say his critics, by turning mere words into metaphysical realities. Mascall finds in Whitehead's approach no justification for Whitehead to endow "God" with personal attributes or to depict his consequent nature in terms of compassion and understanding (*The Openness of Being*, p. 162).

Hartshorne, also, tries to combine immutability with change, a feat as difficult as riding two horses moving in opposite directions. He writes: "To attribute change to God, so far from conflicting with permanence or stability in his being, means rather that nothing positive that ever belongs to God can change but only the negative aspect of the *not yet* being this or that. Except in his negative determinations, his not-being, God is utterly immutable. Yet since negative determinations are inherent in positive, God is really mutable" (*Man's Vision of God*, p. 130). Hartshorne therefore speaks of possible but not-yet actual states of God (*ibid.*, p. 133). "Unchangeably right and adequate is his manner of changing in and with all things, and unchangeably immortal are all changes, once they have occurred, in the never darkened expanse of his memory. . . ." (*ibid.*, p. 298). Hartshorne rejects the orthodox doctrine of the Trinity, and speaks instead of "the temporal series of self-states in God" as "immutable" (though not eternal or ungenerated) because "once they occur they are immortally there in the life of God" (*ibid.*, pp. 351 f.). Hartshorne has clearly substituted a conjectural deity for the biblical God who reveals himself. A doctrine of divine "immutability" based on such tortuous exposition is more confusing than true or useful.

Schubert Ogden likewise speaks of a contingent and growing God; he claims, moreover, that such a God is the God taught by the prophets and apostles: "The scriptural witness to God can be appropriately interpreted only if his nature is conceived neoclassically as having a contingent as well as necessary aspect" (*The Reality of God*, pp. 122 f.; cf. pp. 59 f.). Ogden rejects John Macquarrie's suggestion that a growing God—such as the God of Whitehead and Hartshorne (and Ogden)—cannot be "satisfying religiously" (*Twentieth Century Religious Thought: The Frontiers of Philosophy and Theology, 1900–1960*, p. 277). But the notion of what is personally "satisfying" is in any event highly subjective. Like Hartshorne, Ogden represents God's supposed development as "a wholly positive conception . . . of which . . . God is the eminent or perfect exemplification" (*ibid.*, p. 60, note 97). Ogden is but playing word games with the term "perfect."

Pannenberg thinks that in view of the attack upon God's reality made by the atheism of freedom we must reject the inherited Judeo-Christian emphasis on God's changelessness. Where the being of God is conceived "as already perfect and complete in itself at every point in past time and therefore at the beginning of all temporal processes," Pannenberg writes, there God necessarily appears as the foe of human freedom ("Speaking About God in the Face of Atheistic Criticism," p. 108). "If Christian theology is nowadays to think of God as the origin of human freedom, then it can no longer think of him as an existent being" (*ibid.*, pp. 110). To preserve man's free agency, we must concentrate instead, says Pannenberg, on God's eschatological activity and on the *future* of the good whose fullness is still to be realized in the world. As E. Frank Tupper observes, Pannenberg "considers the protest of the atheism of freedom against the traditional concept of God as an eternally existing essence eminently valid" (*The Theology of Wolfhart Pannenberg*, p. 200). Pannenberg's alternative of panentheism—the doctrine that all reality is in God—raises multiple problems, not least in its tendencies to blur the radically sinful aspects of fallen human history, its confusion of voluntary choice with indeterminate free agency, and its emphasis on the future at the expense of the past and the present.

Moltmann repudiates the theistic view of "an all-powerful, perfect and infinite being" as idolatry (*The Crucified God*, pp. 249 f.); for him such predications project the image of imperial world rulers upon the conception of God. Like Pannenberg he would dethrone the evangelical orthodox

God in order to preserve human freedom. He promotes, instead, the priority of a self-humbling God of love. To transcend the dispute between theism and atheism, he holds, one must emphasize the God who is also man and who as the crucified God suffers and leads to life (*ibid.*, p. 252). By considering it a sign of the poverty of orthodox theism that its God cannot suffer (*ibid.*, p. 253), Moltmann inverts the lessons to be learned from the history of Christian doctrine. His notion of the Trinity as a dialectical event centering in the Cross and facing an eschatologically open history is obscure (*ibid.*, p. 255). God conceived primarily as our "fellow sufferer" is not the immutable God of the Bible. All talk of the final liberation of man—psychological, moral, spiritual, political—must end in a question mark if God himself is a struggling, suffering deity.

God's immutability in no way implies powerlessness, however. Unlike the immutable deity of Plato, or the speculative neuter Absolute of Fichte and some other modern idealists, the unchanging and unchangeable God of Scripture who creates the universe, is active in temporal processes and historical events, and in the incarnation steps personally into history. The God of the Bible is not the God of Aristotle who is limited in knowledge, who does not hear prayer and who is disinterested in man and the world.

The fact that the biblical God answers prayer; that he fulfills his promises contingently in view of man's response; that he offers mankind the options of repentance or judgment, constitutes no basis for modern notions of a changing and growing deity; in no way is he trapped by a "becoming" of his essential nature.

To insist that ontological change is predicable only of the world, and not of God, in no way eclipses the fact that creation adds to the realm of reality and existence along with God a space-time universe created and continually preserved by him. Creation of the world in time did not involve a change in God; he had planned creation from eternity so that formation of the universe was not the product of an unwilling deity who suddenly became willing to create. Nor was creation the result of new powers in God. Nor did creation involve new divine perfections; God is infinite and embraces the totality of all possible perfections. God is sovereign from eternity and from eternity is personally active in self-giving holy love.

That God is timeless and immutable makes a great difference in respect to the world's origin and nature, preservation and power, duration and destiny. But the world does not alter God ontologically. That is hardly to say that God is indifferent to the created universe. Not only are man and the world totally dependent upon God in every moment of their existence, but God is also fully involved and active in nature and history. Nor does God's immutability dwarf the fact that the incarnation of the Logos conjoins human nature enduringly to the Son of God. Theological representations of something new "added to the Godhead" by the incarnation have often been misleading; the fact remains that Christ did not become *man* in lieu of his divinity, but that the divine person and nature added human nature and carried that nature in glorified form into eternity. The permanent inclusion even of this glorified human nature in the experience of the Godhead did not involve a new mode of deity, however, even though it brings into profound and intimate interrelationships the timeless experience of God and the context of time-structured experience in which the exalted Christ rules as head of the Church.

We need to read with skepticism, therefore, Wolterstorff's declaration that "God the Redeemer is a God who changes" and that although God is "steadfast in his redeeming intent . . . *ontologically,* God cannot be a redeeming God without there being changeful variation in his states" ("God Everlasting," p. 182). The Calvin College professor insists that neither Malachi 3:6 nor Psalm 102:37 makes any ontological claim for God's immutability; theologians have grossly misinterpreted and ontologized these passages, he avers, whereas in actuality they speak only of God's "unswerving fidelity."

Malachi 3:6 ("I am the Lord, I change not") does indeed emphasize constancy of nature—God's righteous nature in contrast to the sinful nature of the sons of Jacob. Remarkably, Kittel's massive *Theological Dictionary of the New Testament* wholly ignores this verse. Wolterstorff contends that only deep misunderstanding can locate in this passage an emphasis on ontological immutability; the prophet "on the contrary" states rather that "God is faithful to his people Israel—that he is unchanging in his fidelity to the covenant he has made with them" ("God Everlasting," p. 201). But several comments are here in order. The prophet could surely have found, as Old Testament writers do elsewhere, a less circuitous way of stressing God's unswerving fidelity, had that been his exclusive concern; the Hebrew vocabulary customarily uses *aman* or *emunah* for fidelity, whereas Malachi uses the term *shanah.* Furthermore, Wolterstorff's insistence that "no ontological claim whatever is being made," prompts the question whether divine moral constancy is to be considered a nonontological predication; constancy of nature is what immutability is all about. The term *shanah* ("change"), moreover, raises questions of immutability as readily as questions of stability and steadfastness.

The second text cited by Wolterstorff is Psalm 102:37, which the author of Hebrews applies to the exalted Christ (Heb. 1:10 f.). Wolterstorff declares it "gross misinterpretation" to regard the Psalmist as teaching that God is "ontologically immutable" ("God Everlasting," p. 202). He concedes that "the Psalmist is making an ontological point of sorts," namely, that God, in contrast with the universe, is unending, since the Psalmist expressly declares that God's years "shall have no end" and that God "endures." But, we should note, unlike perishing and changeable things and creatures, God, adds the Psalmist, is unchanging: "Thou art the same." The declaration that God remains "the same" would be an odd and curiously indirect way of saying merely that God has unending existence. Wolterstorff's interpretation rests on his antecedent bias against divine immutability. Stephen Charnock observes on the passage in Psalm 102, "The essence of God, with all the perfections of his nature, are pronounced the same, without any variation, from eternity to eternity: so that the text does not only assert the eternal duration of God, but his immutability in that duration: his eternity is signified in that expression 'thou shalt endure,' his immutability in this, 'thou art the same.' . . . He could not be the same if he could be changed into any other thing than what he is" (*Discourses Upon the Existence of God,* Vol. 1, pp. 352 f.). Wolterstorff entirely ignores James 1:17 where the apostle's statement about "the Father of lights" focuses not on fidelity but on God's ınvariable nature or ontological changelessness.

The affirmation that "Jesus Christ is the same yesterday and today and forever" (Heb. 13:8, RSV) is, Philip Hughes contends, a declaration of the Savior's "unfailing reliability. . . rather than. . . an ontological definition" (*A Commentary on the Epistle to the Hebrews,* p. 570). Jesus Christ who had "yesterday" been the source and object of the triumphant faith of the early Christians remains their all-sufficient Savior and Lord, and will forever continue thus. The text has even greater significance, however. Christ has an unchangeable and imperishable priesthood because he endures for eternity, declares Hebrews 7:24, and Hebrews 13:9 indicates that Christ himself and the truth concerning him are both unchanging. The expression *'o autos* ("the same") applied to Christ refers not simply to faithfulness but also to changelessness. Thayer declares that, when used without a noun, the sense is that of "immutable," and he refers to Hebrews 1:12 (*A Greek English Lexicon of the New Testament,* p. 85). The New Testament writers used *pistos* of God's faithfulness. The writer in Hebrews 1:12 was not contrasting divine faithfulness and the "faithfulness" of the cosmos; he was stressing rather the immutability of God and of his Christ. At the beginning of Hebrews its writer applies to Christ the Son the Psalmist's (Ps. 102:37) contrast between the ever-changing universe and the immutability of the Creator. At its conclusion he speaks of the immutability of the crucified and exalted Christ. Athanasius found in Hebrews 13:8 and other New Testament passages a reflection of both the immutability of the Son and his consubstantiality with the Father (*Letters to Bishop Serapion,* ii. 3; *Deposition of Arius* 3). Because Christ is ontologically changeless his salvation is permanently reliable; a changing Christ is no sure ground of hope.

Modern existential and dialectical philosophies have stripped the classic passage "I am that I am" (Exod. 3:13) of much of its traditional ontological significance. But the words imply both eternity and changelessness; if God were mutable and datable, he could not truly say "I am that I am."

Supplementary Note: Anthropomorphism and Divine Repentance

WHAT DOES GOD'S CHANGELESS BEING imply about his relationships to the changing universe and to humanity? Donald Mackinnon writes: "The image of the eternal changelessness of God, whether we conceive it in terms of immediate and synoptic comprehension at once of himself, and of his creation, or in terms of unshaken, unchallengeable, all-determining will, is one which besets every theist, and sets him on edge in the presence of the contingent. . . . Christianity faces men with the paradox that certain events which could have been otherwise are of ultimate, transcendent import; and this without losing their character as contingent events" (*Borderlands of Theology*, p. 87).

Does the very notion of "events which could have been otherwise" violate divine omnipotence and omniscience?

What do predications of God's unchanging nature imply, moreover, about apparently contradictive anthropomorphic representations in Scripture, and especially about statements that speak of a divine change of mind and purpose, that is, of divine "repentance"?

Scripture does not accommodate an inner ontological or epistemological change forced by external limits on God's power or presence.

Process theology rejects absolute divine immutability, infinity and omniscience; God is said to grow with the universe and with the times. While Schubert Ogden contends that God does not foreknow the future on the ground that future events would otherwise not be free, an argument of which we have already disposed, process theologians must also cope with far-reaching consequences of abandoning divine omniscience. If God is a growing God, as process theologians aver, he cannot foreknow the future; he cannot, in fact, then fully know himself. (For a recent contrast of biblical theism with process theology see Colin Gunton's *Becoming and Being*). A God whose identity in some respects is in the making, and who copes with finitude in his own nature, is a god whose full reality is unassured and whose deity is largely a matter of semantics. It mocks the biblical view to claim that the self-revealing God can be rescued from disinterest in man and the world only if the divine nature is itself both involved in change and also changes in some respects. Even if one does not consider sovereignty the fundamental divine attribute, without it all other attributes of God lose their efficacy.

Karl Barth occasionally makes unnecessarily open-ended comments about divine ontological change. This he does as a consequence of loose representations of the Christian doctrine of divine incarnation in Christ in terms of God's becoming "a creature" (*Church Dogmatics,* IV/1, p. 181) instead of the technically more accurate emphasis on the Logos's becoming God-man: "The incarnation . . . means . . . God's becoming a creature, becoming a man—and how this is possible to God without an alteration of His being is not self-evident . . ." (*ibid.,* p. 185). Assuredly, none of the content of special divine revelation is "self-evident." But neither revelation nor self-evidentiality commends the doctrine of God that changes ontologically. Surely God realizes values in and through the world; he ascribes worth to the created universe (Gen. 1:9 ff.). But to hold that this requires change in God, or implies that he is personally incomplete, as does process philosophy, is gratuitous and unjustifiable.

Elsewhere (Vol. IV, pp. 110 ff.) we have noted that biblical representations of God, although often anthropomorphic or anthropopathic, avoid zoomorphic motifs so common to pagan Semitic religion. The biblical doctrine that, in distinction from the lower animals, man is God's created image, implies that we can appropriately affirm some divine-human similarities. Yet the image refers primarily to rational and moral capabilities, whereas the debate over anthropomorphism concerns physical referents to God's eyes, ears, mouth and hands, and passions such as jealousy and revenge and the act of repenting. We shall deal with divine "repentance" separately after preliminary comments on biblical anthropomorphism in general.

Anthropomorphism is common also to early Greek depiction of deity. But Greek poetic excesses and misconceptions provoked the subsequent philosophical repudiation of anthropomorphism and even of the later Stoic defense of God as Father. Each of these three Greek perspectives is, however, to be distinguished from the biblical outlook. Greek polytheism portrays the gods as actually having human qualities, emotions and customs, and, moreover, human form. H. F. von Arnim notes (*Stoicorum veterum fragmenta*) certain Stoic writers who sought to vindicate this ascription of human form to deity. But the Bible views the attribution of human form to God as idolatry; such emphasis, as Hermann Kleinknecht observes, runs contrary to the second commandment in Hebrew doctrine ("The Greek Concept of God, *TDNT* 3:71). Greek classical thought was therefore constrained to attack anthropological misconceptions both on ontological and on ethical grounds. But to dehumanize the humanized God leads by way of overreaction to an absolute repudiation of anthropomorphism, and by no means necessarily in the interest of a spiritualistic view of God. Xenophanes conceived God instead as cosmomorphic; the loss of anthropomorphism here involves a forfeiture also of divine personality. Plato criticizes anthropomorphic distortions of God, but does so in order to promote God's spirituality. Yet in his advocacy of the reality of supernatural mind Plato at the same time accommodates an emphasis on divine presence, participation and copy.

In repudiating polytheism and mythology the Hellenic philosophical counterthrust viewed anthropomorphism as a needless concession to degenerate conceptions of religion. Scholars have noted that presumably under Hellenic influence the Septuagint translation moderates Old Testament anthropomorphism in order to advance a "pure" conception of God. So, for example, in Joshua 4:24 the hand of God becomes the power of the Lord. Massoretic textual references to occasions when God was seen are revised to preserve divine invisibility (cf. Job. 19:27; Isa. 38:11); Exodus 24:10 f. is altered so that Moses and the elders, instead of seeing God, see only the place where God "stands." Septuagint translators considered references to God's "repentance" similarly objectionable and softened them to indicate only God's anger (Gen. 6:6 f.; cf. Exod. 32:12).

But Hebrew religion, which repudiated religious polytheism and myth long before the Greek sages, and more powerfully so in the name of the self-revealing God, did not exclude all anthropomorphic usage. Old Testament anthropomorphism in no way dulled the distinction between the living God and polytheistic or other conjectural misconceptions of deity. Prophetic religion does not consider anthropomorphic references totally unsuitable to the living God and a defilement of pure theism. Every strand of Old Testament revelation not only contains a certain anthropomorphic range of expression but even grounds this in God's way of speaking about himself.

While anthropomorphism may pose problems for certain philosophical misconceptions of God—especially for theories that stumble equally over all representations of God as personal—Hebrew revelation unhesitatingly correlated belief in the living God with a restricted range of anthropomorphic terms; it contrasts therefore both with Greek polytheistic myths which were insensitive to inappropriate referents, and with elements of Greek philosophical tradition that overreacted by discarding both a personal God and anthropomorphism. Yet the prophets leave no doubt that, unlike the impotent pagan gods who are unable to will or do anything, and in distinction from the conjectural religious constructs of pagan Gentiles, the God of revelation to whom they apply anthropomorphic referents exercises his commanding will in nature, history and the life of mankind. As Ethelbert Stauffer comments, "in the Greek world the idea of a personal God was regarded as the final relic of the anthropomorphic thinking which had to be overcome. In the Jewish world the distinction between anthropomorphic conceptions and faith in the personal God was not only maintained but grasped with increasing clarity. God is not as a man. But He is a God who wills and speaks and hears" ("The Uniqueness of God," *TDNT*, 3:94).

Not even the emerging theism of the Stoics, with the deference to God as Father, nor Plotinus's use of the masculine pronoun for the neuter *to en* (the One), signaled a decisive reversal of the Greek antipathy for anthropomorphism.

Old Testament anthropomorphism carries clear reminders that no ontological correspondence is intended between God and man. So in the Book of Job, for example, God asks Job: "Hast thou an arm like God?" (Job 40:9). Students of Near Eastern fertility cults often note, moreover, that despite

its emphatic insistence on God's love, the Bible refuses, in striking contrast
to surrounding pagan religions, to ascribe sexual features to God—a point
too seldom grasped in today's feminist clamor to desex biblical language.
Nor do the New Testament writings labor under any burden to avoid whatever anthropomorphism the Old Testament revelation authorizes. The
larger revelation of God in Christ is presented without a deliberate evasion
of anthropomorphic elements. Old Testament usages reappear in the cita-
tion of Old Testament references, and the New Testament writers even
add certain anthropomorphic elements in expounding the revelation of
God in Christ Jesus. In the New Testament no less than the Old, therefore,
certain anthropomorphic representations go hand in hand with emphasis
on the spirituality and personality of God. There is no sharing of either
the Greek philosophical hostility to anthropomorphism or the Hellenized
Hebrew effort to soften or minimize anthropomorphism in the inspired
canon.

The New Testament preservation of anthropomorphic referents to God
dates from the very beginnings of the Christian church. The Gospels retain
Old Testament anthropomorphisms in depicting God's works. In portraying
the birth and early life of John the Baptist, Luke writes: ". . . the hand
of the Lord was with him" (Luke 1:66), and in the Magnificat Mary declares
that God "hath shewed strength with his arm" (Luke 1:51; cf. Ps. 98:1).
In belaboring the Sanhedrin for the unbelief of Israel, Stephen recalls
that some of Moses's contemporaries lacked spiritual understanding that
"God by his hand" would deliver the children of Israel (Acts 7:25). Paul
declares that God rescued the Israelites from Egypt "with an high arm"
(Acts 13:17) and recalls that in Solomon's time Yahweh asked: "Hath not
my hand made all these things?" (Acts 7:50). Elsewhere in the Acts of
the Apostles we read that when Christians preaching the Lord Jesus came
to Antioch "the hand of the Lord was with them" (Acts 11:21). Voicing
judgment on the sorcerer Bar-jesus (Elymas), the apostle Paul declares:
"And now, behold, the hand of the Lord is upon thee, and thou shalt be
blind . . ." (Acts 13:11). Peter exhorts Christian believers: "Humble your-
selves . . . under the mighty hand of God . . ." (1 Pet. 5:6).

In respect to the incarnate God-man, human referents gain literal rather
than merely figurative propriety, in view of the divine assumption of human nature. But even apart from this consideration, however, the New
Testament retains anthropomorphic references to deity per se. Speaking
prophetically of his anticipated exaltation Jesus invokes the striking reference to God's "right hand" (Mark 14:62/Luke 22:69), and Peter also, quoting
David (Acts 2:25, 33; cf. 5:31). Stephen claims to see Jesus "standing on
the right hand of God" (Acts 7:55 f.). The disputed ending of Mark likewise
uses this phrase in connection with the ascension (Mark 16:19), and the
epistles do so as well (Rom. 8:34; Eph. 1:20; Col. 3:1; Heb. 1:3; etc.).

But the reality of the incarnate and risen Christ confers upon some Old
Testament anthropomorphic statements about deity a literal rather than
merely figurative appropriateness. The bodily incarnation and bodily ascension turn what in the Old Testament was merely figurative affirmation
into metaphysical actuality. The fact that the Word became flesh and that

the risen Christ retains human nature even in his exaltation lends ontological validity to some once merely anthropomorphic representations. Since as its climax Judeo-Christian revelation anticipated the incarnation of God in the flesh, some anthropomorphic usage is uniquely and dramatically appropriate to biblical theology. Paul writes of the revelation of "the glory of God in the face of Jesus Christ" (2 Cor. 4:6, NEB). Of the risen Christ Peter writes: "For the eyes of the Lord are over the righteous, and his ears are open unto their prayers: but the face of the Lord is against them that do evil" (1 Pet. 3:12). When the Risen Lord returns, says the Apostle John, "every eye shall see him" (Rev. 1:7). The apostle Paul writes that in eternity our knowledge of God will be "face to face" (1 Cor. 13:12). Writing of the new paradise where believers live in the presence of God and the Lamb, the Apocalyptist says: "The throne of God and of the Lamb shall be in it; and his servants shall serve him: And they shall see his face . . ." (Rev. 22:3 f.). In interpreting such passages it is important to recall that sense experience is dependent, as far as we know, upon the present type of body which must be distinguished from the resurrection body, and that in the life to come knowledge will be intuitive and direct; even in this life, moreover, sense experience is not as such a source of truth.

Of special note, then, is the fact that the New Testament is not embarrassed by appropriate anthropomorphisms; it considers them no threat whatever to a pure doctrine of monotheism or to an insistent affirmation of God's incarnation in Jesus Christ and the Redeemer's retention in eternity of human nature in a glorified form. Among some modern philosophers as among some ancient Greeks an antimetaphysical mentality tends to view all assertions about God as merely anthropomorphic; the question it swiftly prejudges is whether any anthropomorphism is appropriate to God. It does this by declaring all personal divine predications, nonanthropomorphic and anthropomorphic alike, to be cognitively illegitimate. On other speculative grounds, Tillich also states that "most of the so-called anthropomorphisms of the biblical concept of God are expressions of his character as living" and then rejects divine personality for a preferred impersonal Ground of all being (*Systematic Theology*, Vol. 1, p. 242). Biblical religion, however, emphasizes that God is living, personal Spirit; and its carefully chosen anthropomorphism, moreover, neither dissolves personality nor demotes the living God to an impersonal Ground.

Christian use of anthropomorphic terms about God involves no relapse to naive "primitive" beliefs in the supernatural or to "precritical" ways of discussing the divine. Some evolutionary philosophers disparage and demean all anthropomorphic language as a reflection of primitive piety and religion; instead they champion a theory of an impersonal ultimate reality as the intellectual achievement of modernity. But linguistic specialists know full well that anthropomorphic terms to describe the activities of God are not peculiar to a primitive stage of communication. As an integral part of any linguistic communication such conceptions are found at all levels of culture (cf. Hermann Güntert, *Grundfragen der Sprachwissenschaft,* pp. 63 ff.).

If the choice of literary figures has no cognitive significance and validity, then the nature and extent of anthropomorphic representation of God would be a matter of complete indifference. But when the Genesis writer, for example, affirms that God "rested" on the seventh day, he intends by the term to convey a specific cognitive content. The inspired writer is telling us that, in contrast to his original fiat-creation, now complete, God's rest is integrated into the universe that he now preserves. Even Psalm 78:65 that depicts God as a drunken man, is, as Calvin comments, an anthropomorphism that by shocking and penetrating statement accommodates the stupidity of the people.

Some interpreters have sought to impose upon Calvin's doctrine of revelation a doctrine of divine accommodation to error not actually found in the Reformer's writings. Calvin does indeed speak of God accommodating man's capacity for knowledge by the use of such anthropomorphisms as God's mouth, ears, eyes, hands and feet (*Institutes,* I, 13, 1) and by representations of divine repentance (*Institutes,* I, 17, 13). Calvin emphasizes that God's plan proceeds unchangeably from all eternity, but in order to accommodate our weak capacity, God depicts himself in the repentance passages to reflect how he seems to us and not as he is in himself. But this need not imply either that God discloses nothing of his essential nature or that he misrepresents the facts, since in that case accommodation would become distortion or evasion rather than knowledge.

"God is certainly the immutable," declares Karl Barth; he is the God of constancy, "consistently one and the same." Yet Barth qualifies this verdict to stress "a holy mutability of God" over against "the unholy mutability of man" (*Church Dogmatics,* II/1, p. 496). God's consistency, Barth emphasizes, is "not the consistency of a supreme natural law of mechanism," "not as it were mathematical." "Biblical thinking about God would rather submit to the grossest anthropomorphism" than to a confusion that would imply that God lacks life and sovereign decision. The freedom of God in his revelation differs from necessity and from chance or accident; it does not have the routine orderliness of impersonal mathematical continuities. Nor does God occupy, as Barth puts it, "an indeterminate middle point . . . in a dialectic which is eternally incomprehensible," so that at any moment he can indifferently act one way or its opposite (*ibid.,* II/1, p. 498), for "the first and last word" must be the declaration that "the gifts and calling of God are without repentance" (Rom. 11:29; RSV, "are irrevocable").

Barth therefore thinks it "most unwise . . . to try to understand what the Bible says about God's repentance as if it were merely figurative" and implies only an alteration in man's ways but no change in God's attitude and relations to man, albeit consistent with his revealed nature as the living and acting God (*ibid.,* II/1, p. 498).

Our discussion of anthropomorphic referents brings us therefore to a special consideration of the biblical passages relating to divine repentance.

In a clear statement of the changeless character of God, Numbers 23:19 affirms that God is not a man that he should repent. But other biblical passages declare that God repents of certain promises, threats or acts, and thereby cancels his earlier intentions. Genesis 6:6 affirms that because of the great wickedness of mankind "it repented the Lord that he had made man. . . . And the Lord said, I will destroy man whom I have created from the face of the earth; both man, and beast, and the creeping thing, and the fowls of the air; for it repenteth me that I have made them." In Genesis 8:21, after the Noahic flood, God declares: ". . . Neither will I again smite any more every living thing, as I have done." Are such statements reconcilable with the emphasis that the unchanging God has an unchanging eternal plan? How can the sovereign will of an immutable God be compatible with a divine change of mind and purpose?

The Hebrew term *nāham*, in some uses translated "repent," occurs in almost all Old Testament references to God's repentance, whereas *sub* is most frequently used to denote human repentance. The term *nāham* need not carry any implication of personal transgression and culpability, and surely does not do so when used of God. The Septuagint renders the Hebrew term some 35 times either as *metamelomai* or as *metanoeō*, terms that in classical Greek are not clearly distinct. The Septuagint uses the verbs not only of humans repenting of their sins (Jer. 8:16, 31:19) but of God who "repents." These texts do not as such draw a clear line between what is metaphysical or metaphorical. But if certain texts teach divine infinitude, then references to divine repentance cannot consistently be interpreted metaphysically.

The terms *metanoeō/metanoia* can signify a change of mind (*nous*); if such a reversal is premised on the conviction that an earlier view was unjustifiable or wrong, then this "after-mind" can imply regret or remorse. Although the term is seldom found in classical Greek, *metanoia* is common in koine where it usually refers to a change not of mind only but of the will and the emotions also. Even in extrabiblical Greek *metanoia* can signify a change of moral judgment, thereby carrying an ethical sense. The New Testament, notably, connects *metanoia* with personal spiritual conversion and hence with enduring moral change. God requires a deep sorrow for sin that issues in new relations to him and a consequent change of character.

The Septuagint translators found Old Testament references to God's repentance fully as unacceptable as anthropomorphic terms generally. Consequently they altered texts that speak of God's repentance. As Ethelbert Stauffer notes: "In Gn. 6:6, 7 God is angry that He has made man, but he does not repent. In Ex. 32:12 the prayer is not that God should repent, but that He should be gracious. In many cases the LXX traces back events to man's sin rather than to God's wrath. It does violence to Nu. 1:53 . . . and also to Job 42:7" (on *"Theos," TDNT,* 3:109).

The scriptural teaching is best summarized in two main tracks of biblical passages which, on the one hand, deny that God repents as humans do, and which, on the other, speak of his repenting.

In the former category we may include Numbers 23:19 ("God is not a man . . . that He should repent. Has He said, and will He not do it? Or has He spoken, and will He not make it good?" NAS); 1 Samuel 15:29 ("The

Glory of Israel will not lie or change His mind; for He is not a man that He should change His mind" NAS); and Malachi 3:6 ("For I, the Lord, do not change; therefore you, O sons of Jacob, are not consumed." NAS). When God is said not to repent (Ps. 110:4; Jer. 4:28, 20:16) he stresses his constancy and faithfulness and guarantees that he will undeviatingly carry through his plan. Hebrews 7:21, quoting Psalm 110:4, speaks of the oath that God will never regret (in both verses the RSV translation is "change His mind"). God is not a vacillating human who backtracks on his word (Num. 23:9; 1 Sam. 15:24; Zech. 8:4).

In the latter category are statements that God repents of a promised good (Jer. 18:10) or alters his purpose to punish (1 Sam. 15:11, 29, 35; 2 Sam. 24:16; Jer. 18:8, 26:19, cf. 4:28; Amos 7:3, 6; Joel 2:13 f.; Jonah 4:2; Zech. 8:14). As representative passages we may cite Genesis 6:6 f. ("And the Lord was sorry that He had made man on the earth, and He was grieved in His heart" NAS); Exodus 32:14 ("So the Lord changed His mind about the harm which He said He would do to His people" NAS); Psalm 106:45 ("And He remembered His covenant for their sake, and relented according to the greatness of His lovingkindness" NAS); and Jonah 3:10 ("When God saw their deeds, that they turned from their wicked way, then God relented concerning the calamity which He had declared He would bring upon them. And He did not do it" NAS).

James Barr summarizes the biblical data this way: "In the Bible God . . . can regret what he has done, he can be argued out of positions he has already taken up, he operates in a narrative sequence and not out of static perfection" (*Fundamentalism*, p. 277). Such sweeping overstatements create the misimpression of a vacillating and indecisive deity whose fallible and faltering actions are suspended on the course of human events.

The focus of some passages on God's determination to punish covenant-enclosed humans for their sins, and his announced abstention from threatened judgment, nonetheless suggests that God alters his intentions by a divine deviation expressed in certain words and deeds. The theological issue must therefore be faced whether such a variation of course or stay of execution is truly compatible with God's unchanging purpose and reconcilable with the steadfastness of his divine intention.

The question whether God's eternal purpose is compatible with subsequent changes of previously announced intentions need not, of course, imply an acceptance of Helmut Thielicke's discovery in references to God's repentance not only of "the *heart* of *God* confronted with a *choice*, a *decision*," but beyond that also with "a question of *self-overcoming*" (*The Evangelical Faith*, Vol. 1, p. 170). The Bible's distinctive view of God's relation to man does not lend itself to such fragmenting analysis of supposedly competitive and conflicting divine experience.

L. Berkhof considers expressions of divine repentance "only an anthropopathic way of speaking. In reality the change is not in God, but in man and in man's relations to God" (*Systematic Theology*, p. 59). But when Scripture declares that God repents, is evangelical theology on any firmer basis than are the anti-metaphysical theologians if statements about God are translated into statements about human attitudes? Charles Hodge declares that the references to God's repentance have no more literal significance than "those in which He is said to ride upon the wings of the wind" (*Systematic Theology,* Vol. 1, p. 391). Is this interpretation wholly adequate?

God's specific responses and actions in specific situations do indeed attest and confirm his eternal purpose. His rejection of some persons despite a prior proffer of grace and his mercy to some despite a prior declaration of judgment, are not in principle incompatible or irreconcilable with his eternal decision and purpose. Even divine "repentance" can be viewed as the temporal fulfillment of a possibility eternally present to God and foreknown and foreordained by him. The sequence in 1 Samuel 15:11, 29, 35 is instructive. God's rejection of Saul is depicted as divine repentance (vv. 11, 35). Yet God's refusal to reinstate Saul, that is, to repent or change his mind, is ascribed to unchanging divine purpose (v. 29). Since God is free to "repent" or not, his action is never imprudent or unjust. Moreover, God achieves his goal (Rom. 11:29) despite man's disobedience and hardness of heart.

The tension between righteousness and grace, election and judgment, arises in view of God's determination to punish evil while yet he proffers mercy to a fallen humanity. Only in view of Christ's substitutionary salvation, as stated most comprehensively in Romans 3:23–26, does God justly forgive sinners and justify any of the unrighteous. In the "repentance" passages God notably withdraws a promised blessing because of crass moral rebellion or retracts a warning of impending doom because of evident moral renewal. The passages thus focus on the ethical sensitivity of God's salvific work and concern the moral orientation of God's redemptive economy. They reflect the fact that God himself would be unrighteous by his own standards if his dealings with humanity were indifferent to human iniquity. God is not a vague universal cosmic love but is wrathful toward fallen humanity and needs to be placated. Fallen man's one acceptable course is repentance and turning to God from his wicked ways. The Old Testament prophets repeatedly warn of factors that invite God's wrath (Joel 1:13, 2:15, 18; Jonah 3:7 f.). The prophets protest that the people's penitence is external and superficial and not firmly anchored in personal relationships with Yahweh (Hos. 6:1–6). Although their relationships to God and fellow humans are unaltered the people think that ritual will stay God's hand (Zech. 7:5, 6). But real renewal requires turning to faith in Yahweh and away from apostasy and everything ungodly.

God correlates his "repentance" with the season for repentance (Rom. 2:4) that he mercifully allots to rebellious man (Rom. 2:4). He holds before us the fact that our opportunity for repentance is limited, and that God has provided even our temporally limited human opportunity at great personal sacrifice. Scripture does not say that God "repented" of his demand for moral atonement and godliness. God's immutability does not conflict with his life, freedom, love or wrath; indeed, his immutability confers awesome importance upon all his perfections.

The divine "repentance" passages remind us, moreover, that God is the sovereign lord of history to whom at every juncture alternatives remain open. Even amid human contingencies it is God's determination and action that is decisive for outcomes. Donald Bloesch accordingly takes references to divine repentance as indicating "God's freedom to change his mind or the ways in which he deals with his people, though he remains inflexible in his ultimate purpose for them" (*Essentials of Evangelical Theology,* Vol. 1, p. 28). A valid emphasis in Barth's comments on immutability is his insistence that God "advances from each to-day posited in His freedom into a to-morrow which in its turn will be posited in His freedom. It is in this way that the eternal God lives in His relationship to time, in His relationship and covenant with the man loved and created by Him" (*Church Dogmatics,* II/2, p. 218).

But none of these considerations implies that God changes either in his eternal being or his eternal purpose. When all due allowance is made for the literal and objective truth conveyed by figurative statements, divine repentance is itself an anthropomorphic representation. The notion that such representation implies a "static" deity rests on semantic obfuscation. One might as readily say that the modern alternative is a vacillating God. God is perfect and, if perfect, can only change for the worse, and hence he will not change himself nor can he be compelled to change by anything outside himself. This emphasis not only excludes polytheistic myths about God's assuming the form of humans and animals, but it also assigns a fixed and consistent character to God.

For all that, remarks George F. Thomas, the exclusion of all change from God "has created difficulties for Christian theology, since it has been interpreted in a static manner" (*Religious Philosophies of the West,* p. 3). Thomas's complaint apparently is not against static interpretation, although he protests a static view of God; he dislikes static divine immutability, which he considers irreconcilable with the biblical emphasis on God as creator and on his purposive activity in the cosmos and in the lives of man (*ibid.,* p. 15). But such blanket disavowals of a "static deity" do not clarify why a God active in creation, preservation, redemption and judgment must be a changing God. The term "static" today shelters a great deal of theological ambiguity; it is given pejorative connotations. Even the alternative emphasis on divine constancy makes little sense unless that constancy is stable, that is, static.

We may complain of other persons that they are no longer the persons they claim to be, because of advancing age or altered character. But no such complaint can be made about the persons of the Godhead, who maintain their personal identity forever. Even the dramatic assumption of human nature by the incarnate Logos involves no change in the identity of the person. In respect to the Godhead, the whole divine essence belongs to each of the persons, and their identity is unchanging. Among human beings we frequently say that bodily alterations due to calamity, or failure of memory or mind, suggest that the person no longer is what he or she was or appears to be. The validity of such observations cannot be decided apart from a discussion of the nature of selfhood.

In human experience, assuredly, occasions occur when human bodies lack personal identity—e.g., corpses, or corpses that are medically alive but mentally dead. Terence Penelhum holds that even when the body is lifeless bodily identity will serve to reidentify persons ("Personal Identity," Vol. 6, p. 101). If, as Christians insist, there is personal life after death, not even dismemberment or being devoured by the emperor's lions will transform one into a different person. Even if the self may be in a condition of incompleteness in the interim period between physical death and bodily resurrection, since man is normatively an embodied spirit, Christians deny that the dead are partial persons. Personality is not divisible. We do not know the full role of bodily continuity in the future bodily resurrection of mankind. The New Testament insists on some continuity of our memory with past and present experience in eternity and on a continuity and glorification of body in the case of the Risen Jesus who is "the same yesterday, and to day and for ever" (Heb. 13:8).

Some philosophers contend that bodily criteria have no bearing on personal identity. Would that judgment make the incarnation—God coming in human flesh—irrelevant to the present identity of the Logos of God? To dismiss the incarnation as wholly insignificant to the identity of the Logos would involve the heresy of Docetism. But the incarnation does not involve new personhood, although it is not merely a bodily consideration; the eternal Christ assumed human nature, psyche and flesh, in his role as God-man. Christ was a divine person and bodily criteria were inapplicable to him; humans also are identifiable persons although our bodies are constantly changing and being replaced.

Some recent discussion of divine immutability and divine incarnation seems motivated by a desire to formulate doctrine dialectically in terms of logical contradiction or paradox, and then to appeal to naked faith and inner decision for Christian affirmation. Some theologians propose a new theory of kenosis framed in terms of divine hiddenness and not in terms of the ontological emptying of the eternal Logos. Paul Althaus holds that "the full and undiminished deity of God is to be found in the complete helplessness, in the final agony of the crucified Jesus, at the point where no divine nature is to be seen" but this in turn is viewed "as a law of the life of God himself." As Althaus recognizes, this emphasis collides head-on with "the old idea of the immutability of God." Christology, says Althaus, "must take seriously the fact that God himself really enters into the suffering of the Son. . . . This divine miracle cannot be rationalized by a theory which makes God present and active in Christ Jesus only so long as the limits of being human are not crossed. Yet on the other hand the Godhead may not be located ontologically in the humanity of Jesus. The Godhead is there hidden under the manhood, open only to faith but not to sight. It is therefore beyond any possibility of a theory" ("Kenosis," cited by Moltmann, *The Crucified God,* p. 206). What Althaus cannot formulate intelligibly or rationally cannot of course be rationally examined, disputed or commended. What is "open to faith," by contrast, is as wide as human incredulity; apart from cognitive considerations Althaus's preferred private option exerts no claim whatever that calls for universal subscription.

In contrast with modern notions that God is changing and growing, Calvin warns against the idea that God is changeable. Calvin would have been astounded by G. A. F. Knight's emphasis that "God has gained something throughout the centuries as a result of what has happened in the sequence of time; God has himself grown in experience as a result of his gracious love for man" ("A Biblical Approach to the Doctrine of the Trinity").

Advocacy of a changing God is but a confusing declaration that Change is god. Christopher Derrick laments that contemporaneity obsessively focused on the mythological Now (*Trimming the Ark: Catholic Attitudes and the Cult of Change*, pp. 23 ff.) and Kenneth Hamilton derides the worship of the Great God Change (*To Turn from Idols*, p. 94). Renegade modern man in flight from the eternal and fascinated by the temporal and novel exalts change to the level of divinity. "The Great God Change seems to be the controlling power most favored today. . . . The Great God Change . . . is invested with the supreme power which is understood in the Judeo-Christian tradition to belong to the living God" (*ibid.*, p. 95). But divinity whose name is Change cannot be the guarantor even of the continually changing.

Supposedly on biblical grounds this altered conception of God dooms all conceptions of "static" divinity, emphasizes instead a "dynamic" deity, and connects all life with change. Process philosophy projects a bipolar God in whom one aspect changes, another does not; thus conceived, God can only be in some respects beside himself, since change becomes a second or secondary god. More radical theories view the absolute as evolutionary process, no longer seen, as by Hegel, in terms of a logical unfolding by orderly patterns, but as a revolutionary force that shatters the status quo and promotes utopia by radical mutation. The god of Change is here nothing less than the true God *exchanged* for an intellectual idol; in the apostle Paul's words, it is a mental projection by those who have "exchanged the truth about God for a lie" (Rom. 1:25, RSV).

Speaking for contemporary biblical critics, James Barr moves beyond the modern emphasis on a mind-changing God and demands an altered conception of God; this he does in view of "massive changes in the way Christians understand the Bible, God and Jesus Christ" (*Fundamentalism*, pp. 185 ff.). "The concept of heresy has ceased to be functionally useful for the evaluation of present-day theological opinions," writes Barr (*ibid.*, p. 197). One gains the impression that Barr does not wish to demote his own perspective to simply one of three billion prejudices, and implies for it a certain normativity over against Judaism, Roman Catholicism, Greek Orthodoxy, and Reformation Christianity, all of which he places outside the pale (*ibid.*, p. 182). Change, in other words, becomes an obsession for the critical scholar. Instead of drawing a skeptical conclusion from it, Barr attaches to it an implicit claim to the objective validity of his own private a priori.

16.
The Sovereignty
of the Omnipotent God

THE SOVEREIGNTY OF GOD has become for twentieth-century thought one of the most troublesome aspects of the Christian view of deity. The difficulty arises not primarily from the incredible immensity and complexity of the universe, but rather from the problem of evil (see Volume VI). Constantly focusing on the world's natural, social and political calamities, global communications media bring to instant view the staggering sufferings and afflictions of large masses of people.

Today modern technological power represents a kind of human omnipotence that replaces the universal sense of absolute dependence upon deity that had so impressed Schleiermacher in the last century. Varied uses of atomic energy, astronauts circling in space and walking on the moon, and brilliant medical conquests of many once fatal diseases, all suggest man's ability to cope with matters long relegated to the disposition of the gods. Modern secular humanism, moreover, by renouncing many moral distinctions stipulated in the Bible, eliminates divine sovereignty as a viable practical consideration for human behavior. If God's commands involve a stringent view of marriage and divorce, and of much else that Christians once associated with the good life, then many people would declare God to be neither sovereign nor loving.

In an earlier work I noted that the nonbiblical religions and secular philosophy tend to polarize the personality of God and his sovereignty by opting for either one or the other but not for both (*Notes on the Doctrine of God*, pp. 92–102). When the Apostles' Creed so confidently affirms "God the Father almighty" at its outset it gives no hint of the problems that this predication raises outside the biblical heritage. In the earliest Christian creeds, in fact, the personality and omnipotence of God decisively shape all the other divine perfections.

With little reservation nineteenth-century scholars conceded that the Bi-

ble teaches divine sovereignty, and even made this doctrine the occasion
for rejecting the Bible, especially the Old Testament. But some twentieth-
century theologians question whether the Bible does, in fact, teach God's
omnipotence.

The actual term "omnipotence" nowhere occurs in the Bible and the
designation "the Almighty" (*pantokratōr*) is found only in Revelation 1:8.
But from its very outset the Genesis creation narrative focuses on Elohim
as the sovereign creator of man and the world (Gen. 1:1 ff.; cf. John 1:3 f.).
And El Shaddai, the patriarchal name for God (Gen. 17:1; etc.) refers to
God's might. J. A. McHugh reminds us that the Old Testament contains
"more than seventy passages in which God is called Shaddai, i.e., omnipotent" (*Catholic Encyclopedia*, New York, Robert Appleton, 1911). The Book
of Job, the book that might seem most prone to question divine sovereignty,
actually uses the term "almighty" of God more frequently than any other
Old Testament book. Yahweh is Lord of lords who does what he wills (Ps.
115:3). Many biblical passages speak of God's incomparable power manifest
in his acts. God's creation of the universe and the exodus deliverance of
the Hebrews for covenant-community are permanent reminders in the
Old Testament of the divine power; in the New Testament forefront re-
minder of this power attaches to the resurrection of the crucified Jesus
(Rom. 1:4; cf. Eph. 3:20 f.; Phil. 3:21). God's power is as complete as the
potter's to whom the clay belongs (Jer. 18:6; Rom. 8:29). Paul writes,
"Whether we live, we live unto the Lord; whether we die, we die unto
the Lord: . . . we are the Lord's" (Rom. 14:8, KJV). God is the one and only
Lord (1 Tim. 6:15). In his parable on the goodness of God, Jesus quotes
the householder: "Am I not allowed to do what I choose with what belongs
to me?" (Matt. 20:15). Prominent in numerous passages in the Book of Revelation, which depicts the end-time consummation of history, is the almightiness of God.

God's power is revealed to man by his divine creation and preservation
of the cosmos (Ps. 19; Rom. 1:20). The fact that the universe is revealed
to be the work of the sovereign Creator *ex nihilo* unmasks as hollow all
secular speculation about an intangible omnipotent divinity, a merely abstract God-concept to which one is free to assign whatever content one
wishes. God is sovereign not only as the creator and preserver of all life,
but also sovereign over creaturely death and/or afterlife.

Many references to God's great power are connected, moreover, with
his redemptive work. He displays his sovereignty in the miraculous redemption of humanity as well as its creation. There is no doubt that the
inspired Hebrew writers affirm God's omnipotence. Their strong emphasis
on divine sovereignty has in fact encouraged some critics like Lewis R.
Farnell to misrepresent the Old Testament writers as being "more interested in the attribute of omnipotence than of beneficence" (*The Attributes
of God*, p. 267). The Old Testament unqualifiedly affirms the Hebrew profession: "Yahweh, your God, is your King" (1 Sam. 12:12). Yahweh's universal
and eternal sovereignty is proclaimed in the Pentateuch (Exod. 15:18), the
Psalms (22:28, 59:13, 103:19) and the Prophets (Isa. 40:25–31, 52:7, 10).

Writing of Yahweh's assertion of sovereignty over the life and activities of Israel, Martin Buber says: "The unconditioned claim of the divine Kingship is recognized at the point when the people proclaim JHWH Himself as King, Him alone and directly (Exodus 15:18), and JHWH Himself enters upon the Kingly reign (19:6)." Yahweh is not content to be "God" only in the religious sense, Buber stresses, but lays claim to and exercises rule over all of life. Yahweh makes his will known by constituting not only cult and custom, but also economy and society (*Kingship of God*, p. 119).

Buber contrasts this Israelite submission even of public political concerns to Yahweh, ruler over all life and history, with the generalized conceptions of divine kingship found in other ancient religions. "All sorts of communities in the world acknowledge a 'lord' without on that account thinking seriously of conceding to him also the actual lordship over the actual community. . . . The prophetic . . . even early-prophetic . . . rejection of a politically indeterminate belief concerning divine lordship, seems to me to be fundamental for Israel. To be sure, Varuna of the Vedas is also a 'king,' and indeed one who protects 'holy law,' but to wish to subordinate the political actuality of the world of men to him would be contrary to his image. To be sure, Ahura Mazda also has his 'lordship,' which is one day to attain completion in his victory, but this is not the realm in which political decisions are found. More concretely . . . Egypt and, still more, Babylon conceived of divine kingship, but here it is well nigh exhausted in the task of protecting human authority" (*Kingship of God*, pp. 21 f.). The ancient Hebrew prophets who stress the sovereignty of Yahweh as mirrored in the theocracy and its political and historical concerns, view their earthly kings as God's representatives, but never as divine incarnations who wield ultimate power.

Yet the kingdom of God, as John Marsh emphasizes, connotes not simply a geographically localized political realm exhausted in the Hebrew theocracy, but a kingly rule, a universal spiritual-moral sovereignty (*The Fulness of Time*, p. 163). "That kingly rule belongs to God as creator, and has been exercised over his creation from the beginning" is "a factor in history even though man rebelled against it. . ." (*ibid.*, p. 164). The world has "never seen in its history any example of the perfect obedience that would in fact exhibit the glory of God's reign. The great men of the Old Testament . . . treasured the hope that one day the Kingdom of God would come" (*ibid.*, p. 164). The kingdom of God, Marsh adds, has both present and future dimensions; it is "not the end-term of an historical series, nor yet the 'absolutely other' realm that will supervene upon the destruction of the present order" (*ibid.*, p. 165).

According to A. W. Argyle, the New Testament conception of God's sovereignty builds on the Old Testament view that while God's reign, eternal in heaven, operated within Israel, it is also universal and will consummate in a future messianic reign (*God in the New Testament*, p. 35). The kingdom of God, or God's kingly rule, is a central theme of Jesus' ministry. With the declaration, "The time is fulfilled, and the kingdom of God is at hand" (Mark 1:15; cf. Luke 4:21) Jesus inaugurates his public ministry.

In the person and work of Christ the Old Testament hope was anticipatively fulfilled in the kingdom's coming. The Gospels depict the kingdom as present already in an anticipatory sense in the life and mighty acts of Jesus. God's reign is present in Jesus who conquers sin and Satan, defeats sickness with its proclivity to death, and then defeats death itself. Sinners who receive Christ enter into a transforming divine power that restores them to God's fellowship and service. The Fourth Gospel focuses on God's reign as an eternal reality in which believers already share anticipatively (John 5:24). Although the kingdom of God is "full and complete in him," it is still partial and incomplete in history and in mankind, even in the regenerate church over which Christ reigns. Jesus spoke of the future consummation of the kingdom (Mark 14:25/Luke 22:15, 29), and taught his disciples to pray for its coming (Matt. 6:10/Luke 11:3). Christ himself will reign over the eschatological kingdom, a reign that involves a judgment of all nations (Matt. 24:14, 28:19; Mark 13:10; Luke 24:47), and the consummation of history in the final advent of Christ (Matt. 24:31, 26:64; Mark 13:27, 14:62). The risen and ascended Jesus stands therefore at the center of apostolic preaching concerning the kingdom, a kingdom that is both a present reality and a future expectation (Acts 1:6, 14:22; 2 Thess. 1:5; 1 Tim. 4:1, 18; James 2:5).

All the Greek and Latin church fathers declare God to be omnipotent and all creeds bearing on the nature of God, Catholic or Protestant, affirm God to be omnipotent creator and preserver of the universe. We should not uncritically assume, however, that in passing through Greek, Latin, and then German and English thought, theological discussion of God's sovereignty may not have added semantic obfuscation. And secular philosophy has accommodated the idea of divine omnipotence to rationalistic deductions unwarranted by Scripture. What do we properly mean, then, when we declare the God of Judeo-Christian revelation to be omnipotent?

Brunner tells us that revelation "teaches nothing about *omnipotentia*" in the sense that God "can do everything"; this secular conception, he says, grafts unto the biblical view the neo-Platonic and Dionysian notions of "all-Being and all-existence, of the All-One" (*The Christian Doctrine of God,* p. 248). If we confuse divine omnipotence with *potentia absoluta,* Brunner cautions, we end up in pantheism ("the sole reality of God") and with the correlative notion of "the sole working of God" at the expense of all finite causality (*ibid.,* pp. 250 f.). Aquinas distinguished *potentia ordinata,* power that God voluntarily exercises, from *potentia absoluta,* power he can but has chosen not to exercise. According to the Bible, God's absolute power is revealed in and through creation, redemption and judgment. Because later philosophy suspended the universe on immanent causal sequences, it associated *potentia absoluta* with only divine miraculous intervention.

Medieval and post-Reformation theology, Brunner says, listed omnipotence "not . . . first, as we might have expected, but . . . usually near the end of the list of Divine Attributes," and adds that "teaching on the subject is very meagre" (*The Christian Doctrine of God,* p. 248). He attributes this situation to an essentially rationalistic approach that, influenced by secular philosophy, refused to "test all doctrine by the touchstone of revelation."

The biblical conception of divine omnipotence, says Brunner, means specifically "God's power over the universe," that is, his divine power over all that God has created (*The Christian Doctrine of God,* p. 248). In the Bible God's omnipotence "always means exercising power over *something"* that God has freely created; God is therefore free to preserve the course and causality of nature, to work miracles, or even to do away with nature entirely if he wills. Yet over against the metaphysical determinism inherent in secular notions of absolute divine power, the biblical doctrine of God's omnipotence preserves the relative independence and responsible freedom of the creation.

But by viewing divine power only in relational terms Brunner denies that God is by nature inherently omnipotent. "God is not, in Himself, 'the Almighty' " says Brunner (*ibid.,* p. 250). He justifies this strange verdict on the ground that in contrast to abstract speculation about "Omnipotence in itself" the revelational alternative depicts God as actively manifesting himself as he wills in relation to the created universe. However, this contrast hardly requires a denial that God is intrinsically almighty. What actually precludes Brunner from affirming God's inherent omnipotence is an anti-intellectual doctrine of revelation that disallows objective metaphysical knowledge.

Secular metaphysicians indifferent to the biblical data, and mediating Christian philosophers and theologians embarrassed by that data, have indeed grotesquely compromised the notion of divine omnipotence. Any method that speculatively appeals to God as an unlimited cosmic potentate in order to generate a metaphysical system independent of divine revelation runs the risk of invalid deductions. The history of modern philosophy exemplifies only too well this conjectural extension of the doctrine of divine omnipotence.

Descartes, who gives two inconsistent accounts of the will, appeals to the infinite intensity of man's free will as providing a glimmer of God's self-positing power. From God's immutability he draws the inference, moreover, that mathematical regularities can wholly explain the external world inasmuch as God has willed inviolable physical laws. Descartes seems to turn divine omnipotence into a rationale for theological deduction, and grants a universally demonstrative force. The English Anglican fideist Joseph Glanville rejected absolute certainty in physics, and rightly so. Declaring the laws of physics hypothetical and pragmatic, yet beyond reasonable doubt, he protested the tendency "to set bounds to Omnipotence and to confine infinite power and wisdom to our shallow models" (*The Vanity of Dogmatizing,* pp. 211 f.).

Whereas Descartes considered the omnipotent Creator the noetic ground of human knowledge, Spinoza held that we can have certainty only if God is the all, and if man is a modal part of Nature. Spinoza viewed extension not as a predicate of finite substance but as an attribute of divine substance of which he declares all finite reality to be a part. Spinoza stipulated the attribute of thought but not of will (unless he included will in thought) to be the corollary of extension. Spinoza theorizes that the universe arises only as a logical development and not by voluntary purposive divine creation. God or Nature, he said, is self-asserting power divorced from personality and purposive divine intelligence. Modern naturalists not given to semantic equivocation substituted simply a self-generating universe untroubled by veiled notions of divine omnipotence.

The Enlightenment dispensed with special revelation in formulating its case for philosophical theism. It not only shared Descartes' neglect of biblical revelation but also ignored the Cartesian insistence on innate and immediately known truths, and emphasized that empirical investigation—from which Descartes presumed to derive mathematical certainties—yields at most only metaphysical probabilities. Pierre Bayle, who contributed to the Enlightenment mood, projected the alternatives of either an omnipotent God who is malevolent, or a benevolent God who is limited in power. He then escaped both options by espousing moral claims that were outside the realm of both philosophical theism and revealed theology.

The global presence of natural and moral evil lifted the discussion of divine omnipotence to a special context. One possible approach was to declare evil a necessary consequence of God's action in creating the finite universe, a view that biblical theologians unqualifiedly reject. Calvinists insist that God sovereignly defines both good and evil, and hold that he is the source of evil in the sense that everything results from his creative act. To exculpate God from such moral responsibility for evil, modern philosophers resort to an ingenious array of explanations. Voltaire, for example, supposedly on the basis of empirical data, speculates about a god who gave form to possibly eternal matter; he thus stands near the beginning of a philosophical development that later broke with the Christian metaphysics of creation and affirms instead the contingency of all of reality. Hume holds that limited order in our observable world allows at most a "finitely perfect" god, whereas Mill thinks that induction leads at best to a divine demiurge instead of to a creator; Mill sacrifices not only divine omnipotence but also human freedom and immortality. In his rationalistic effort to resolve the problem of evil Mill speculates that cosmic matter contains an initial "given" not imparted by divine creation; a century later Brightman projects this "given" upon the very nature of God.

James Collins notes how Mill and others who restrict God to limited power at the same time completely isolate this divine power from God's other attributes. "He does not concern himself with the nature of the distinction . . . between the divine essence and its perfections," says Collins. "He is in no way disconcerted about holding that God is infinite in some of His attributes and finite in others. The divine simplicity is not a real problem for Mill, and therefore he can isolate power and adjudge it to be finite without having to reckon with any metaphysical consequences" (*God in Modern Philosophy*, p. 294).

What began as the problem of evil in a theistic view of God soon ends, because of philosophical conjecture, in demolishing God's objective morality and in confusing God with the universe. Kant does not even derive the experienced world from the power of God, and in fact considers the very idea of God merely regulative. For Hegel evil is merely a finite distinction that has no validity for the Absolute.

Schleiermacher criticizes the distinction made between what God is *able* to do and what he actually *does;* for him, God has no ability that he does not activate (*The Christian Faith,* Para. 54, Sec. 3). God sustains the universe as a whole, says Schleiermacher, and the universe, in turn, is absolutely dependent on him. But the underlying theological implication is clear, namely, that God's omnipotence is no greater than his sustaining power. God's transcendent being and power are therefore eclipsed, and the cause of every process or event is found solely within the temporal matrix. While God timelessly produces the world, "the divine omnipotence can never in any way enter as a supplement (so to speak) to the natural causes in their sphere; for then it must like them work temporarily and spatially; and . . . would be neither eternal nor omnipotent" (*ibid.,* Para. 54, Sec. 4).

Schleiermacher is here prejudiced, Nelson Pike contends, by a lurking assumption that God's timelessness precludes the traditional doctrine of omnipotence, namely, that divine creative ability is distinct from the exercise of that ability in the creation of a temporal universe (*God and Timelessness,* p. 110). God's timelessness means that he cannot produce objects in a specific time; "it is inadmissible," therefore, "to suppose that at any time anything should begin to be through omnipotence" (*ibid.,* Para. 54, Sec. 1). In short, as Pike remarks, Schleiermacher holds that God is unable to "create, produce, or bring about a temporal state of affairs" (*God and Timelessness,* p. 107).

Since Schleiermacher believes that God, as timeless, cannot produce objects or conditions in time, and hence could not create the universe in time, he repudiates as speculative myth the Mosaic representation that God's creation of the world has a temporal focus. The orthodox evangelical doctrine of creation *ex nihilo* of a temporal universe Schleiermacher transmutes into a doctrine of divine preservation (*The Christian Faith,* Para. 38), a term from which, as Pike observes, he deletes the temporal implications associated with the biblical view of creation. God's preservation of the whole universe is thus now dissociated from the concept that creation had a "beginning" (*ibid.,* Para. 36, Sec. 1).

Christians have traditionally insisted that God's power is not exhausted in the universe he sustains, and that his cosmic activity is not reducible simply to his preservation of the universe. For Schleiermacher God's divine sustaining activity is continuous, without beginning or ending.

Over against pantheistic and idealistic misconceptions that translate divine will directly into divine activity and view the universe as a necessary and exhaustive divine manifestation, Gordon Clark, Cornelius Van Til and other evangelical theologians insist that God's omnipotence is by no means completely manifest simply in and by his works. They reject any implication that God becomes omnipotent only as he creates, and that apart from the universe he is less than omnipotent if not impotent. The living interrelationships of the persons of the Trinity prior to creation in the eternal nature of the Godhead already manifest divine omnipotency. The credal distinction of begetting and proceeding (or generation and procession) from creation and preservation leaves no doubt that God freely and eternally preserves himself in triune personal distinctions. God has absolute power to be himself internally and eternally as Father, Son and Holy Spirit. His omnipotence does not exhaust itself either in his supernatural creative or redemptive work. For this reason are not only his continuing preservation of the universe and protracted reconciliation of sinners possible, but also his coming eschatological consummation of all things. He in himself—*intra se,* as the Latin theologians put it—is the omnipotent God who freely wills to create, to preserve, to redeem, to judge. However much we glory, and rightly, in the mighty or almighty God of incarnation and atonement and resurrection, we have no license to impose upon divine omnipotence a limitation that restricts God's omnipotence to even these stupendous works. Neither the reality and orderliness of the finite universe nor once-for-all works of supernatural redemption can singly, or together, express or exhaust the totality of divine omnipotency. Far less should the impression of divine almightiness that lurks in man's religious consciousness or behind his sense of dependence be viewed as corresponding fully to the omnipotence of the Creator-Redeemer God. Not merely what God does and will do, but also what he can do defines his omnipotence.

We nonetheless have no evangelical liberty to ascribe to God all manner of possibilities and unknowable activities over and above what revelation authorizes. To impose upon God's nature some general conception of power unlimited in and of itself, and having no other defining characteristics, could only elicit the perverse notion that Power is God, and that every manifestation of power is therefore divine. Power in the abstract, power for power's sake, can only be arbitrary power, the more unlimited the more arbitrary; such power has more in common with satanic energy than with the character of God. Aquinas presumed to derive the content of divine omnipotence not from God in his revelation but from the concept of Being. Therefore he insisted that God's power implies absolute possibility, or rather, that God's power is to be interpreted in terms of a general conception of absolute possibility. Speculative discussion led Aquinas to ask "whether God could make the Past not to have existed," whether God "can make that which He does not make," or make "still better" what he does make (*Summa Theologiae,* I, 25, 4 ff.). Concerning things self-contradictory or inconsistent with God's nature, Aquinas thinks it better to say these "cannot be done than that God cannot do them" (*ibid.,* I, xxv, 3c).

Descartes remarked that, had God so willed, he might have populated the universe with an infinity of forms and species other than those presently existing (*Discourse on Method,* Vol. 6, p. 41). God might even "have made creatures not to be dependent on him" (cf. *Philosophical Writings,* p. 292). Christian Wolff went beyond Leibniz by affirming not only that God created the best of all possible worlds, but that God could also freely bring other worlds into existence, and even actualize all these possible worlds simultaneously (*Theologia Naturalis methodo scientifica pertractata*, I, 175). One can readily understand why Erasmus mocks some fanciful postulations of divine possibility (*Epistolae virorum obscurorum*, in *Opus Epistolarum*).

Such conjectural notions of possibility entertained by secular philosophers who imagine the possibility of other and better worlds, or who remold the present universe to fit pantheistic, idealistic or naturalistic patterns, attest fallen man's propensity for endowing himself with epistemological sovereignty. The history of nonbiblical religions and secular philosophies shows how founders of worldviews project their own preferences and prejudices upon the real world, and play the pretentious role of cosmic creator. If, moreover, rationality is denied as a divine attribute, then God's power can be correlated with the most ludicrous contradictions; indeed, the more ridiculous, the more supposedly is his glory enhanced. But Nelson Pike assures us that "nothing an incorporeal being could do would count as swimming the English Channel, . . . jumping a fence, riding a bike, etc." (*God and Timelessness*, p. 98).

The question whether God can create a stone too heavy for him to lift still stimulates debate. Both George Mavrodes ("Some Puzzles Concerning Omnipotence," pp. 221–223) and C. Wade Savage ("The Paradox of Stone," *The Philosophical Review*, LXXVI, No. 1, 1967, p. 74 ff.) argue that an agent's inability to create such a stone entails no limitation of his power. Mavrodes sees in the question a self-contradictory task, while Savage believes that God can indeed lift any stone that he creates.

Pike argues that God's inability to sin (cf. James 1:13) should be regarded as a necessary truth that concerns a general concept of deity, and that it is true of Yahweh only because he has the status of God ("Omnipotence and God's Ability to Sin," p. 208). To say that deity sins is logically contradictory (*ibid.*, 209). But James has in view the living God, and no deity in general. This living God has the creative power necessary to bring about a morally reprehensible state of affairs, for he determined and prophesied that Judas would betray Christ. But the foreordination of an evil act is not itself evil, since God need not will what he wills for the reasons others may will them.

In his essay "Can God Do Evil?" Samuel Clarke affirms that although God acts voluntarily and not necessarily, "it . . . is absolutely impossible for God not to do (or to do anything contrary to) what his moral attributes require him to do, as if he was really not a free but a necessary agent" (in *Discourse Concerning the Being and Attributes of God, the Obligations of Natural Religion, and the Truth and Certainty of the Christian Revelation*). Here the character of God is not defined by his will, but determines God's will.

It should surprise no one that rationalistic notions of divine possibility have stimulated, by way of reaction, a complete dismissal of divine volition in terms both of its actual or possible effects. Scott Buchanan distinguishes three kinds of possibility—imaginative, scientific, and absolute. Genuine possibility, he holds, is found only in scientific investigation and naturalistic explanation; as for absolute possibility, it is the kind "written about in books by philosophers and theologians" (*Possibility,* pp. 4 ff.). Buchanan treats divine possibility as a regulative idea (*ibid.,* p. 81) serviceable only for scientific explanation (*ibid.,* p. 84). The notion of divine presence is simply a "desperate metaphor" (*ibid.,* p. 93).

The self-disclosed God of the Bible is indeed omnipotent, not because divinity qualifies a neutral contentless conception of Power, but because power is itself a defining divine attribute. Nor does God in his revelation authorize us to impute to him some privately formulated conception of power. *His* power, rather, he discloses to be almighty. That God constitutes "all real power," as Barth says, does not mean that all power conceived by humans as real power is therefore God's power, since on that score we could blindly deify nature or history or fate (*Church Dogmatics,* II/1, p. 531). It is of "God the father almighty" that the Apostles' Creed speaks. It is this omnipotence of the living God that is normative over against all merely conjectural notions of infinite power that explicitly or implicitly claim to reflect an actual rather than merely imagined power. Barth stresses that "we depart from Scripture in any statement [about omnipotence] which either openly or secretly has any other subject than God the Father, the Maker and Lord of the covenant with Abraham, the Father of Jesus Christ, and with Him His Son and His Holy Spirit, or in which we fail to understand the predicates 'mighty' and 'almighty' as wholly filled out and defined by this subject" (*Church Dogmatics,* II/1, p. 526). If we transfer awe and praise and trust that belong only to the power of God to lesser powers, be they stars in their courses, assumed patterns of history, the supposed causal network of nature, or mighty earthly führers and rulers, we prepare the way to reverence the devil.

Basil may be right in saying that the Creator's power is adequate not only to create this present world, but also to fashion an infinite number of worlds (*Hexaemeron,* Homily I). But the Bible does not require us to honor the self-revealing God by imputing to him all manner of conceivable possibilities when in fact God has chosen not to actualize them by creation and preservation, any more than it allows us to replace the living God with postulated strange gods as the source and support of the present universe. Secular philosophy and world religions abound in imaginative constructs of divine agency in the universe. But just because Scripture expressly reveals the possibilities and nature of God's omnipotence we may speak meaningfully and confidently about God's power. To speculate about whether God, as evidence of his omnipotence, can wholly contradict himself, is therefore ridiculous, because such proposals are self-contradictory and would, in principle, destroy God no less than the patterns he freely imposes on his creation. It dishonors rather than honors God to question his omnipotence if he does not conform to our creaturely notions of a hypothetical unrevealed divinity who operates in conjectural ways in an imaginary universe. Scientists and philosophers are never so unprepared for sweeping changes of theory as when they confuse sheer possibility with actuality. The nature and limits of divine omnipotence are expressly defined by the fact that the omnipotence of which we speak is that of the self-manifested omnipotent God. Biblical theism thus elucidates the doctrine of possibility. God's power is not "blind" power, nor, in fact, does "blind" power even exist, since all power is subject to the Omnipotent's judgment.

Scholars who think that science is best served and the riddle of the universe most readily solved by devotion to mathematics and logic while God is exiled and considered replaceable, actually serve neither logic nor mathematics very well. Where unlimited possibility prevails, there the wildest alternatives are possible, no matter how intrinsically contradictory they may be. Historians may smile, but, as Scott Buchanan reminds us, "Kepler . . . wrote an astrological almanac for a living. Faraday transferred a religious symbol to the magnetic field, Newton shot cannon balls around the earth to rival the moon, and the carbon ring came out of the lurid imagery of a morning after party" (*Possibility*, p. 187). Even today the writings of some philosophers of science seem to welcome symbolism and to accommodate reconstituted Homeric divinities no less than did the most imaginative metaphysics of the past. The fact that space science has successfully put men on the moon is compatible with theories of reality quite different from those currently reigning today. If mathematical formulas apply throughout our incredibly vast universe, only a prior intelligence constitutes their symbolic approximations of intellectual form. Nor can all phenomena, whether human or divine, be caught in this net of algebraic symbols. The mind of God accounts for the intrinsic possibility of all things, and the power of God accounts for their extrinsic possibility; the creation of actual existents involves decision of divine intellect, power and volition to produce the world we know. God actualizes his power in many forms, upholding planets in their courses, birds and beasts, humans, and angels and a heavenly host of which we are but dimly aware.

Barth uses God's freedom as a synonym for his power (*Church Dogmatics,* I/1, p. 112)—the freedom to be himself, to create, to redeem, to judge, to reveal himself, the freedom to choose or to bypass Israel, to choose another or to choose no one; the freedom to choose Israel as the preferred people of special revelation and also the freedom to terminate her history, the freedom to incarnate himself or not to do so. "God is the lord, above whom there is no other person or thing conditioning him. . . . God is *a se.* . . . But the aseity of God is not empty freedom. In God all potentiality is included in his actuality, and so all freedom is His decision" (*ibid.*, pp. 78 ff.). God's revelation is the revelation of his lordship; lordship means freedom, that is, ontic and noetic independence (*ibid.*, p. 352). God's own activity is a free divine activity, grounded in, yet not necessitated by, his nature.

God is King of the universe by his creation of it. He has power over all creatures as their Creator and Judge. The freedom he bestows on human creatures is determined by considerations that we ourselves neither create nor control; among them are the capacity to hear God's Word, the perilous alternatives of either faith or unbelief and of life either as God's servant or as mutinous rebel, and the high penalties of disobedience. Human self-determination is limited: we are free even as sinners to hear God's Word, but we are no longer free to do the good, and least of all to save ourselves.

To be sure, Barth translates many of these formally commendable premises into questionable and indeed highly objectionable specific positions. He holds, for example, that God's freedom in his revelation requires sporadic nonpropositional personal encounter, that it requires his conceptual hiddenness, and that God reveals himself only in a superhistory that is inaccessible to historians.

God's omnipotence, the Bible tells us, is power over all other power and powers. Unlike God's power, all other power is created and creaturely; God is sovereign over and in and through all other power. God's power, moreover, and even more fundamentally, is power over powerlessness, over the powerlessness of nothingness that obtained before he called the creaturely universe into being, and over the redemptive powerlessness of the sinner alienated from God. All hostile powers are powers created originally from powerless nothingness and subsequently become rebellious. Yet God maintains sovereignty over them even amid their hostility in order to remind them of his lordship, of their nothingness apart from his creation and preservation, and of inescapable judgment to come. No one can frustrate God's will; no one can force God to go against his will. God in his omnipotence unmasks throughout eternity the illusions and imagined possibilities ascribed to false gods; they are, in fact, no gods at all. He will finally bring proud man and Satan as well to acknowledge that only the sovereign Lord governs all realities and possibilities.

In relation to man made in his image, the God of the Bible attests himself not in sheer overpowering power but in powerful majestic presence and deeds. But the power of the living God pertains not only to physical possibility (*potentia*) but also to moral and legal possibility (*potestas*). God's might and right, as Barth observes, are always related, so that divine power is "in itself and from the beginning legitimate power, the power of the holiness, righteousness and wisdom which is grounded in itself, in the love and freedom of the divine person" (*Church Dogmatics*, II/1, p. 526). The power of God is therefore a highly specific moral conception.

Some scholars oppose the idea that divine omnipotence is a Christian doctrine; they note that by the terms *pantokratōr* and *omnipotens* the early Greek and Latin creeds do not expressly mean "almighty" in the sense that God can do anything whatever but affirm only that God powerfully rules over all. It would be wholly unjustifiable to infer from this, however, that the early church believed God's power to be limited. As E. L. Mascall remarks, "If God is in any absolute sense the Ruler of all things and powerful in all matters, if creatures depend upon God's incessant creative action for all that they have and all that they are, if he is the very source of their existence and nature, then it is absurd to suppose that his power over them is limited by anything outside himself" (*He Who*

Is, p. 120). But what limits, if any, does God's own nature impose upon the exercise of his power?

"God is able . . . to do everything," writes Barth, "everything, that is, which as His possibility is real possibility. God has possibilities—all the possibilities which, as the confirmation and manifestation of His being, are true possibilities" (*Church Dogmatics,* II/1, p. 522). "God is the criterion of all genuine possibilities and in the actualization of all genuine possibilities, God is the criterion of all genuine actualities" (II/1, p. 532). "It can be said that God can 'do everything' only if the 'can' is understood to mean that He Himself in His capacity to be Himself is the standard of what is possible, and if the 'everything' is understood as the sum of what is possible for Him and therefore genuinely possible, and not simply the sum of what is 'possible' in general" (II/1, pp. 532 f.). God alone decisively governs and determines the limits of possibility and of impossibility both for himself and in the created universe. "There is nothing outside Him which is possible in itself" (II/1, p. 536).

God's will or nature implies certain limitations on his actions and normatively defines the very conception of omnipotence in terms of his own omnipotence. That God will not alter his own nature, that he cannot deny himself, that he cannot lie and cannot sin, that he cannot be deceived, and that, moreover, he cannot die, are affirmations which historic Christian theology has always properly associated with divine omnipotence and not with divine limitation or divine impotency, because the "possibility" as stated is a logical impossibility. Any conception of omnipotence that requires God to contradict himself reflects a conjectural and ridiculous notion of absolute power. It remained for recent modern theology to project change in God as a philosophical asset, and the death of God as an historical actuality.

Having willed moral and mathematical distinctions in the creation of the universe, God will not affirm vice to be virtue or two times two to be three; he is faithful to himself and to the relative unity and continuity he wills for his creation. This constancy does not imply an ontological or logical or moral order independent of God to which God must conform his omnipotence. At stake, rather, is the constancy of God's free and orderly expression of his power. The law of contradiction does not set limits to which God must conform; God himself wills the law of contradiction as integral to both divine and human meaning. The nature of God is logical. God could indeed have willed that two times two equals five, but he could not have so willed if we are to retain the usual meanings of two and five. The laws of logic are the way God thinks; they are the organization of the divine mind. God's omnipotence does not imply the possibility of the impossible, once we understand that God himself is the ground of all possibility. To postulate contradictions constitutes nonsense; logically impossible projections can hardly impose actual limits on divine sovereignty.

The ultimate outcome of human disavowal of divine omnipotence is rejection of the supernatural and assertion instead of human omnicompetence. David Ehrenfeld calls humanism "the dominant religion of our time," particularly in "the 'developed' world" whose bounty the developing countries now envy (*The Arrogance of Humanism,* p. 3). "Humanism is at the heart of our present world culture," he writes; "its unseen assumptions . . . make a mockery of the more superficial differences among communist, liberal, conservative, and fascist, among the managers and the managed, the exploiters and the preservers . . ." (*ibid.,* p. 20). "Its assumptions are incorporated in communism and capitalism alike," he observes; "public communications media . . . , business, economic theory, politics and technology" take its doctrine for granted (*ibid.,* p. 4).

Ehrenfeld considers "some of humanism's religious assumptions . . . among the most destructive ideas in common currency" (*ibid.,* p. 4), particularly its "irrational faith in our own limitless power" and its "supreme faith in human reason . . . to rearrange both the world of Nature and the affairs of men and women so that human life will prosper" (*ibid.,* p. 5). Humanism rejects "the power of God"; displacing "the power of supernatural forces," it affirms man's own power over "the undirected power of Nature" (*ibid.,* p. 5).

Implicit in humanism are the notions that humanity should seek its own goals; that man has unqualified ability to shape and control his destiny; that no inherent limits circumscribe scientific manipulation of the environment; that behavioral engineering of one's fellows is justifiable whenever it promotes the common good.

Once the biblical emphasis on man as a responsible steward of nature is set aside, technology becomes the means of achieving human dominion over nature on the premise that man has sovereign freedom to manipulate the cosmos for his own preferences. What becomes the final purpose of the universe, in short, is the increased comfort and convenience of man. "We *must* worship the machine," explains Ehrenfeld, "if we wish to maintain the fiction that the myth of control is true. . . . Technology is our major godly output, our flow of miracles" (*ibid.,* p. 102).

Man's illicit desire ever since Eden to preempt the role of God has issued in our time in his bold enthronement of himself as sovereign. Between the alternatives of obedience or mutiny emerges a vast assortment of intermediary positions; here mankind debates or tries to define God's limits, may disown God and his Word as normative for what is possible or permissible, may declare God impotent in the face of certain eventualities, or even now dead and hence powerless to perform the possible let alone the impossible.

Such unquestioning faith in man's own omnipotence, such unbridled confidence in his reasoning and power, contrasts so sharply with "the living reality of the human condition" that Ehrenfeld calls for "humane alternatives to the arrogance of humanism" (*ibid.,* p. viii). He declares it impossible to expect a humanistic future in which we can "prevent our intentions from betraying us" (*ibid.,* p. 225).

Science fiction nonetheless revels in charting the still unexplored paths to human omnipotence. The greater the human contrivance, the more utopian society will be. Genetic engineering will not only produce new plant and animal species in the service of man, but will also hopefully enable us to incorporate in man himself all desirable traits found in other species. Now viewed as inherently defective, the human body is considered remarkable by medical construction. Environmental control, we are told, will conquer all natural evils. In this approaching technological Eden science will clone a species better than *homo sapiens.* Contemporary man purposes to be god, proposes to decide his own behavioral destiny and to make outer space his dwelling place; he ventures even to transmute the human species into a superspecies that makes the divine preservation and salvation of man as we know him retrogressive and irrelevant. "If one sees humanism for what it is, a religion without God," Ehrenfeld comments, "then the idea is not so strange: space with its space stations and space inhabitants is just a replacement for heaven with its angels. Even the idea of immortality is there," he notes, for futurologists make "hazy reference to relativity and time warps, ways of making immense journeys of many light years' distance without aging. . . . Space is nothing more than a watered-down heaven for modern unbelievers. Only now we have located heaven more precisely in the solar system than in the days when Dante wrote about paradise" (*ibid.,* pp. 120 f.).

This imaginative projection of a modern utopia borrows from the paradise of Scripture only those elements it fancies. "We have been reading the old biblical story of the expulsion from the Garden of Eden too carelessly of late," Ehrenfeld remarks. "For was not the Garden of Eden described as a *better* place than the world outside after the fall? And was not the clear implication of Genesis that all the new-found skills and knowledge that the fateful apple could provide were imperfect? The serpent was lying when he said, 'Ye shall be as gods'. . ." (*ibid.,* pp. 124 f.).

A more profound difficulty than the unwanted byproducts of technology is the overlooked question of who decides what the "better" race would be and, indeed, who defines "better." Technology provides only the means; it can serve either of two contrary principles.

The limits of human knowledge and power, Ehrenfeld stresses, are attested in various ways: by man's inability to discern the long-range future due to the complexity and uncertainty of contributory events; by the fact that new technologies tend to worsen our problems in the very course of confronting them; by inadequate assumptions that complicate our efforts at control; by the resistance of some ecological factors to human interference; and by the perverse human use of control technologies for evil ends (*ibid.,* p. 127).

The last of these limits, of course, concerns man's inability to control himself. Despite the academic cult of professional humanists, modern civilization keeps moving toward ever more violent societies, toward ever more horrendous weapons of destruction and techniques for human suppression. In efforts to escape death or entrapment in moral evil, man is powerless to control the forces that besiege him. The dread possibility of global destruction by nuclear weaponry or nuclear accident is no longer an idle fantasy. "Modern weapons can vaporize much of the human environment, and seem likely to vaporize all of our money even if they are not used," Ehrenfeld comments (*ibid.*, p. 237). "Population pushes toward five billion, and millions starve while economists debate whether Malthus was right. Communism—Soviet, Chinese, and Cambodian varieties—is a humanist fraud. . . . As our computers and communications get better and better, the less responsive, decent or even coherent become the institutions that use them," Ehrenfeld writes. "All this is denied, ignored, or excused—anything to keep us from questioning our own ability to engineer a wise future" (*ibid.*, p. 237).

Ehrenfeld's personal appeal to emotion rather than to reason and logic to refute humanism (*ibid.*, pp. 144 ff.) provides no adequate basis of countercriticism. It helps little to confront the "irrational" (*ibid.*, p. 163) by emotion only in obscure interaction with reason or by a role for the "a-rational" (*ibid.*, p. 154). While Ehrenfeld rightly deplores rationalization, or specious reasoning, he exaggerates the "internal weakness and limitations" of reason. Reason, he affirms, functions most superbly when it grasps "all essential elements" (*ibid.*, p. 163) but he does not stipulate divine revelation as an essential. Ehrenfeld considers it "one of the main functions of reason . . . to help sort out useful emotions" (*ibid.*, p. 163). But even if emotion may sometimes be "useful," utility is hardly the criterion of morality or truth; however wicked, some tyrant may consider the unleashing of a nuclear missile useful.

We need to confront the humanist implication that evangelical questioning of naturalistic assumptions reduces inevitably to a counsel of despair, to life's reversion to a prescientific level, to a bleak redirection of human destiny, and to wretched resignation in a world of stifling impersonal forces. To candidly admit the limitations of human wisdom and power by no means implies the notion of human impotence and insignificance. Rather, it involves realistic assessment of what humans can and cannot do, and recognition that human felicity, in defining and confronting the catastrophic problems of our age, finds its context in the reality and will of God. Ehrenfeld, to the contrary, thinks we ought to welcome the "growing adulation of the rational mode of thought" (*ibid.*, p. 168); regard for the rational and reasonable would be a welcome turn in modern life. Astrology hardly serves Ehrenfeld well as an example of the rational, for its roots are more volitional and emotive than cognitive. That feeling and reason need to be reconciled is true enough (*ibid.*, p. 173). But the flaw in humanism is not, as Ehrenfeld suggests, "its fear of emotion and crazy worship of reason" (*ibid.*, p. 170); rather, its error centers in a perverse worship of presuppositions that compromise the truly real world and the nature of personal life. In the Torah, Ehrenfeld confusedly tells us, Judaism embraces the emotional represented by the Pentateuch and the rational represented by the oral tradition of laws and rituals; Christianity, he says, embraces the same synthesis (*ibid.*, p. 173). Discerning as his criticism of humanism may be, Ehrenfeld's proposed alternative is far from satisfactory. He affirms belief to be "always something of a mystery to reason.

. . . Reason alone is a very poor guide to matters of value and judgment" (*ibid.*, p. 223). Indeed, he considers "emotion . . . the seat of judgment" (*ibid.*, p. 224). That multitudes of people confuse the rational with their feelings we do not question, but this is part of the plight of modern man, and not an ideal to be commended as normative.

The Bible declares man to be not Nature's origination but the crown of God's creation, and bearer of the divine image. Were man Nature's crowning creation he might be forgiven the lunacy of considering himself the final cause of the universe. One might then understand why proud humanism bans Christian eschatology and projects its magical utopian myths upon the future. Given the strong economic motivation of contemporary man, moreover, it need surprise no one that all lower forms of nature are regarded humanly dispensable unless they have economic value or potential. The coming judgment of man's stewardship of nature becomes all the more awesome therefore because the universe exhibits the cumulative scars of human abuse and exploitation. Of this deliberately ravaged and despoiled cosmos Charles Babbage writes (in *The Ninth Bridgewater Treatise*): "There exists, not alone in the human conscience or in the omniscience of the Creator, but in external material nature, an ineffaceable, imperishable record . . . of every act done, . . . of every wish and purpose and thought conceived by mortal man, from the birth of our first parent to the final extinction of our race, so that the physical traces of our most secret sins shall last until time shall be merged in that eternity of which not science, but religion alone, assumes to take cognizance" (quoted by Ehrenfeld, *The Arrogance of Humanism*, p. 191). In view of modern efforts to eliminate insects deleterious to agriculture and to preserve only those of economic value, Ehrenfeld warns that our interference with the biological richness and cycle of nature may have unforeseen and serious consequences. In the account of the Noahic flood, he observes, not a single living species was locked out of the ark (Gen. 7:8, 9). Commending this "excellent precedent" to a humanistic age, Ehrenfeld argues that the existing species and communities should be conserved "because they 'exist' and because 'this existence' is itself but the present expression of a continuing historical process of immense antiquity and majesty" (*ibid.*, pp. 207 f.). Yet Ehrenfeld's emphasis that "long-standing existence in Nature" carries with it "the unimpeachable right to continued existence" (*ibid.*, p. 208), is itself less than adequate; this emphasis smacks of a humanistic justification for preserving the species, even if it reaches a conclusion contrary to that espoused by those who readily sacrifice certain species as expendable. It is God who is the giver of life, and whose will is paramount; he can dispense even with human survival as in the biblical mandate for capital punishment. Existence per se is too nebulous a criterion of the value of created entities. Popular emphasis to the contrary, human beings have no "infinite" value; the fact of God's creation, preservation and redemption of his dignity-endowed creatures is what gives enduring value to human life. The Creator wills that his created kinds of life should reproduce until creation has run its intended course. To be sure, creation exists under the sign of the fall and its curse, and fallen nature must be contained wherever it turns against fallen man, the capstone of creation. The notion that forests and rivers have "rights" (cf. C. D. Stone, *Should Trees Have Standing?*) is, however, overdrawn; but the insistence that man has responsibilities to the cosmos willed by his Maker is not. Containment of fallen nature is not the equivalent of extinction or overkill.

Humanism gratifies the ego by its promise of man's control of nature and history and even of human destiny. Its rejection, therefore, is not easy, once it infects the human spirit. Mediating alternatives that speak of the supposed "inherent rights" of other species of life simply perpetuate unchallenged the notion of man's own invincibility and illimitable dignity. Humanists addicted to this colossal fantasy and bent on mind-altering drugs to restore normative perspective, may yet seek to erode belief in the supernatural; this they may attempt through frontier medication to effect personality change and by imposing naturalistic dogma. Signposts already on the way are the communist requirement of naturalistic belief by the political élite, and compulsory academic suppression of a theistic alternative.

The alienation of mind, conscience and will promoted by humanism is best met both by emphasizing its inadequacies and inconsistencies, in view of its approval of interpersonal relationships of unselfishness that humanism itself cannot sustain, and by calling for finite and sinful man's repentance and redemptive restoration to the living God. "To understand that we are not steering this planet in its orbit . . . means new freedom and a great relief," Ehrenfeld observes (*ibid.,* p. 261). "Those who understand the limitations of humanity can partake more than others of the creation of God, and in this there is both satisfaction and a different kind of power" (*ibid.,* p. 269). In quest of a significant alternative to humanism, which he calls "a stubborn philosophy," Ehrenfeld comments that "Even if the breakdown of arrogance comes early and not too abruptly, much has already been lost. . . . I doubt that there is any way short of the supernatural or divine for world society to undergo such a massive transition without experiencing much suffering in the process" (*ibid.,* p. 259).

To be sure, man can somewhat manipulate nature, but he can neither establish nor ultimately control its behavior. The reliability of nature is a matter of God's will, not of human imposition nor of mechanical causation. Nor are the so-called laws of logic and mathematics independent realities to which God must necessarily conform; God wills them as presuppositions of the created universe, and as divinely willed, they gain not only creaturely reliability but have ontological status as well. The created world is not straitjacketed by mathematical equations, however, for God freely purposes both once-for-all events and recurring processes. The laws of nature are coextensive with the will and purpose of the self-revealed God who is alone unqualifiedly trustworthy. In no case does our trust repose finally in cosmic nature, but in the Creator of all. "The limit of the possible," Barth remarks, "is not self-contradiction, but contradiction of God" (*Church*

Dogmatics, II/1, p. 536). Only what has its basis in God cannot be contradicted.

But when Barth on this ground demeans the law of contradiction in order to promote a theology of paradox we may properly demur. He writes: "The law of contradiction, as the limit of the possible imposed by the creature itself, is so far from being tenable in all circumstances that sooner or later it will inevitably be directed against itself and without the slightest doubt will render impossible all certainty and every certain advance in the realm of creation" (*Church Dogmatics,* II/1, p. 537). Barth appeals instead to certainty or security guaranteed by God's Word in our response to his grace. But Barth must in fact rely on the law of contradiction to clarify even his tenuous and subbiblical theory of religious knowledge. It would be illuminating had Barth indicated circumstances in which the law of contradiction is or will be untenable, and had he showed how by demeaning the laws of logic "certain advance in the realm of creation" would be facilitated.

While the logical law of contradiction indeed has no independent reality, it does have its ground in the mind and will of God, and through God's omnipotence is expressed throughout the created universe. In Chapter 5 we distinguished God's essence and his activities not in terms of an underlying substance but in terms of his personal identity that pervades all his perfections, or, as we have stated it here, in terms of his free will that is grounded in his nature yet not necessitated by it. God discloses in his omnipotence that he is able to perform whatever he wills.

The earliest creeds, Barth observes, considered it sufficient to ascribe to God only the one attribute of omnipotence, even as the so-called Apostles' Creed affirms belief in "God the father Almighty. . . ." Barth comments: "Clearly they saw in this attribute that which embraced all the others; what might be called a compendium of them" (*Church Dogmatics,* II/1, p. 522). All God's perfections are "perfections of His omnipotence. Otherwise they would not be divine attributes. . . . God really is the One who knows and wills to be gracious and holy, merciful and righteous, patient and wise, these being the real determinations of His knowledge and will and therefore of His power" (*Church Dogmatics,* II/1, p. 545).

It is indeed divine sovereignty that permeates the Bible narrative, whether one turns to the creation, incarnation or final judgment. If one considers the omnipotence of God as foundational, then all other divine attributes or activities express that omnipotence as applied to different historical situations. In a statement profounder than his own subsequent exposition of it, Barth declares that "truth, righteousness, holiness, mercy, deserve to be called what their names declare, because they really are so in the freedom of God" (*Church Dogmatics,* I/1, p. 352). God is "the ground without grounds, with whose word and will man can but begin without asking Why, in order therein and thereby to receive everything worthy the name of true and good" (*ibid.,* p. 353).

Recent African theology has tended to moderate the sovereignty of the

God of the Bible by exaggerating the importance of African traditional religion. Many nonevangelical African theologians consider their religious tradition to stand in the same relationship to the New Testament as the Old Testament did for Asian Jews. Quite apart from problems of definition posed by the extensive diversity of the traditional religions, by the difficulty of arriving at adequate written representations of them, and moreover of formulating precisely what one is to understand by the term "African," the fact is that some interpreters, Byang Kato, for example, insist that traditional religion is basically "opposed to the new religions . . . such as Islam and Christianity" (*Theological Pitfalls in Africa*, p. 24). Kwesi A. Dickson achieves a continuity between tribal religion and the religion of the Bible by superimposing an evolutionary theory on the history of religion ("Continuity and Discontinuity Between the Old Testament and African Life and Thought"). But then why should African "preparatory" religion be viewed in the perspective of Christianity rather than of Buddhism or Islam or religious humanism or atheistic communism? From the standpoint of the Bible, African traditional religion is retrogressive; when magic and witchcraft occasionally intrude into the life of the Hebrews, it is denounced in the name of Yahweh.

Those who, like John S. Mbiti ("Christianity and Traditional Religions in Africa," pp. 430–440), regard traditional religion as a positive preparation for the gospel of Christ, are exasperatingly obscure when it comes to specifics. If the relation of African traditional religion to biblical theism is to be discussed, it must be done not in terms of a continuity of special revelation, not even in a preliminary form, but rather in terms of general revelation and human rebellion. Does not the God of the Bible claim to be sovereign and exclusive? Does not the sovereignty of Yahweh, his final revelation in Jesus Christ and the risen Lord's universal mediatorship, underlie the Great Commission? Omnipotence is no generalized conception for revealed religion; the Old Testament conjoins it specifically with the sovereignty of Yahweh, and the New Testament with the lordship of Jesus Christ.

According to Gottfried Quell the name Yahweh displaced other designations of God in the Old Testament because the Hebrews experienced Yahweh to be "Lord of All" (on *"Kurios:* The Old Testament Name for God," *TDNT*, 3:1062). The question to be asked, however, is whether human experience, past or present, can by itself conclusively demonstrate that God is sovereign over the future, or over those phases of earthly life and history that await a future vindication of righteousness, or demonstrate that the origin of the universe was a creation *ex nihilo*. The name Yahweh does indeed integrate into the conception of God the whole content of Hebrew redemptive revelation, including those specific experiences of divine authority and power that go back as far as Abraham's migration from Chaldea to Canaan (Gen. 12:1–8). Hebrew redemptive revelation includes also the rise of "the people of Yahweh" (Judg. 5:11) whose special story the Old Testament canon sets forth in acknowledging Yahweh as the only lord over human life and history. Historical revelation is surely the ground of Old Testament belief, and the continuing contact of the Israelites with their special history progressively enlarges the conceptual content of that belief. But that does not require grounding belief in Yahweh's lordship, as Quell does, in "historical experience." The fact is that the transcendent initiative of the sovereign self-disclosed Lord of Israel himself who vindicates his purposes and promises in the life and experience of God's chosen people, is what establishes Hebrew faith in the omnipotent Lord. Hebrew faith in Yahweh is faith in the self-revealed Sovereign of the universe and Master of mankind.

The New Testament term Lord (*kurios*) is the exact equivalent of the Old Testament divine name Yahweh. As in the Old, so in the New, it designates God's sovereign relationship to his creation (Matt. 1:20, 11:25; Luke 4:18). But the New Testament uses the title especially of Jesus Christ. The Christian church's earliest credal formulation was probably "Jesus is Lord" (Acts 8:16, 19:5). In his discussion of *"Kurios* in the New Testament" (*TDNT,* 3:1086 ff.), Werner Foerster notes that Paul contrasts the alternatives of believing affirmation of "the Lord Jesus" and blasphemous denial of Jesus' lordship (1 Cor. 12:3). It is "to the glory of God," Paul declares, that the risen Jesus is designated Lord or *kurios* (Phil. 2:9 ff.). The New Testament pervasively affirms that the risen Jesus is Lord (cf. Matt. 28:18; Acts 2:36; Rom. 10:9; Heb. 2:6 ff., etc.). And the connection between Jesus' resurrection and his divine coregency is anticipated in Psalm 110:1 by relating divine lordship to Messiah's exaltation and session at God's right hand (Matt. 22:44; Mark 12:36; Acts 2:34; Heb. 10:12 ff.).

Christ's lordship was affirmed already prior to the resurrection both in prophecy and during his incarnational history. Besides the title *kurios* in personal address, thirteen references to "the Lord" occur in Luke's Gospel and five in John's Gospel.

Hindus affirm many *avataras,* or descents of God, and many Hindus acclaim Jesus as one such *avatara* among many. Those who accept Jesus as an *avatara* of God, perhaps as even the supreme *avatara,* but who refuse to acknowledge him as the only *avatara* of the living God, see him in Arian rather than in truly trinitarian terms. Since Hinduism pays little attention to historical manifestations of *avataras,* however, to attach this term to the historical manifestations of *avataras* is hardly meaningful. Many Hindus do view Sri Krishna as an historical figure, but others simply allegorize the ancient accounts. The decisive objection to Christian use of the term is the fact that Hindu writers speak both of complete *avataras* (e.g., Krishna) and also of partial *avataras* (e.g., Rama and Laksmana) and give the term a prevalently docetic connotation. A. J. Appaswamy uses the term only in regard to Christ's descent (*The Gospel and India's Heritage*), whereas others base their entire christology upon it. V. Chakkarai uses the term in this larger way, but stresses that, in contrast to many *avataras* coming for limited manifestations, Jesus is the continuing Godman (*Jesus the Avatar,* pp. 138 ff.). Chakkarai avoids the question of the metaphysical implications of divine incarnation, however (*ibid.,* p. 218). According to his strange exposition of divine kenosis Jesus' human selfhood was extinguished on the cross; Jesus becomes divine, says Chakkarai, through moral union in obedience and suffering (*ibid.*, p. 89), an emphasis that denies his personality is eternally in the Godhead.

The concept of *avatar* raises serious difficulties when applied to Jesus Christ in full explanation of the incarnation, for the Hindu mind considers the manifest *avatars* to be on a lower level than the unmanifest Absolute; Christianity, on the other hand, declares Jesus Christ who came in the flesh to be at once very God of very God and the supreme manifestation of God. In sharp contrast to the impersonal *nirguna Brahman,* the unqualified Absolute of Hinduism, the Bible unhesitatingly and insistently speaks of the Godhead in personal terms, and declares the fullness of the Godhead to be manifest in Christ. The final objection to applying the term *avatara* to Jesus Christ is the fact that the Hindu doctrine of reincarnation, as Robin H. S. Boyd reminds us, views every man's soul not simply as eternal, but also as passing "through a long series of incarnations (*avatara*) until at last, somehow or other, it attains to unity with *Brahman,* the supreme Soul" (*Khristavaita,* A Theology for India, p. 335).

The term Lord was not applied preponderantly to Jesus Christ during his earthly ministry because the disciples came to recognize his messianity only gradually in consequence of Jesus' progressive self-disclosure. His lordship was fully exhibited, moreover, only through his resurrection from the dead. The designation occurs frequently enough, however, to override any suggestion that Jesus' disciples did not discern his lordship until the resurrection (cf. references in Acts 11:16 and 20:35 attributing earthly teaching to the Lord Jesus, and a reference in Hebrews 2:3 to the historical Jesus).

If we allow ourselves to be intimidated by critics who hold that the theological faith of the New Testament writers precludes certainty about any words or acts ascribed to Jesus, then consistency requires us also to forego any preferred stratum in the Gospels thought to be historically reliable. In remarkable fashion Gustaf Aulén, for example, rescues Jesus' "central message" and "pattern of behavior" from documents considered untrustworthy where they report specifics of Jesus' ministry (*Jesus in Contemporary Historical Research*). Such analysts take pride in the fact that the message they retain reflects the relative consensus or critical minimum of contemporary critical interpretation. Their analysis lacks an objective basis of religious knowledge, however, and by disavowing the reliable particular sayings and deeds of Jesus they deflect the central significance of christological titles and claims that rest on such specifics.

The notion that all references in the Gospels to Jesus as Lord must be understood merely as titles of respect ("sir," "master" or "rabbi") is confuted by the fact that Jesus clearly applies the title to himself and in a far more profound sense (Matt. 7:21; Mark 12:35 ff.). Stephen Neill reminds us that "The things that he says about God are not the same as the sayings of any other religious teacher" (*Christian Faith and Other Faiths,* p. 231). There is no evidence whatever that the New Testament writers tried to give supernatural status to an exceptional healer or extraordinary rabbi.

Nowhere do the Gospels or Epistles present Jesus as inferior to or merely on a par with any other man; the emphasis everywhere falls, rather, on his vast superiority even over the most prominent leaders.

It is curious that while mediating theologians attach "general" reliability to their skepticism about specifics, some higher critical Jesus-research proceeds on very different premises; on the other hand, it either forfeits general along with specific reliability, or, on the other, insists on or presupposes the reliability of specifics, at least within a particular vista of special interest. Without the assumption that the specifics are reliable, a great deal of contemporary biblical study would collapse into confusion. Leslie L. Kline, for example, focuses on express words and sayings of Jesus in the canonical gospels in order to compare them with Jesus' sayings as reflected in the gospel tradition of the early church in the Pseudo-Clementine homilies (*The Sayings of Jesus in the Pseudo-Clementine Homilies*).

But had Jesus not risen, and had the crucifixion terminated the disciples' personal relation with Jesus their Lord, the disciples could at best have proclaimed their knowledge of him as Lord only in the recent past, but no longer in terms of an intimate present relationship. This is unthinkable. The resurrection lifted the followers of Jesus to unquestioning faith in his lordship (John 20:28). Peter spoke of "the Lord Jesus" before (Acts 1:21) as well as after Pentecost (Acts 2:36). Contrary to modernist views Paul did not originate the conception of the lordship of Christ; it was part of the "received tradition" that he heard in the primitive missionary churches while still an enemy of Christians; in connection with the Lord's Supper Paul refers to "the Lord Jesus" in the context of what he had "received from the Lord" (1 Cor. 11:23). The phrase *marana tha* (1 Cor. 16:22: "our Lord, come"?) shows that the early Aramaic-speaking believers worshiped Jesus as Lord. If, as many think, Philippians 2:6–11 is a primitive Christian hymn, then the title Lord obviously had wide currency in the earliest churches.

In the Great Commission the risen Lord himself stressed his universal and endless lordship: "All authority in heaven and on earth has been given to me" (Matt. 28:18, RSV). The New Testament Epistles expound the details. Christ is Lord over the cosmos (1 Cor. 15:28) and Lord over mankind (Rom. 14:29); he is the coming King (1 Cor. 4:5, 11:26; Phil. 4:5; 1 Thess. 4:15 ff.; Rev. 19:16) and future judge of all (Acts 17:31; 1 Cor. 4:4, 11:32; 2 Cor. 5:11, 10:18; 1 Thess. 4:6; 2 Thess. 1:9). As Foerster emphasizes, Paul makes no distinction between *theos* and *kurios,* as though *kurios* were an intermediary God; "there are no instances of any such usage in the world contemporary with primitive Christianity" (*"Kurios in the New Testament," TDNT,* 3:1091). The New Testament emphasizes not only that Jesus Christ shares God's sovereign rule, and implements it, but that he also fully shares God's nature; it unhesitatingly applies to the risen and exalted Christ references that the Old Testament applies to Yahweh (Rom. 10:13; Heb. 1:10; 1 Pet. 2:3, 3:15). The New Testament concentrates supreme divine authority in God's messianic Son, Jesus Christ, by and in whom the Father makes himself known. Had it not been for the incarnation and resurrection of the crucified Jesus the Spirit would still remain "ungiven" (John 7:39), for it is Jesus Christ who pours out the Holy Spirit and from the eternal order bestows upon the regenerate church powers and virtues that anticipate the coming age.

The modern church's failure to let Jesus Christ function fully in its midst as Lord is the worst scandal of the twentieth-century ecclesiology. Roman Catholicism with its supposedly infallible papacy and teaching hierarchy and its doctrine of partial works-justification; neo-Protestant ecumenism with its revolutionary politicization of Christianity, theological pluralism and evangelistic listlessness; evangelical Protestantism with its neglect of the very world and lifeview concerns it trumpets as religious distinctives; charismatic internalism with its indifference to controlling theological concerns—each and all frustrate the lordship of Christ in his Body, the Church. Much of today's religiosity is an affront to Christ Jesus in a world deluged by secular humanism and in dire need of biblical vitalities to overturn its dilemmas.

It is Jesus, moreover, who declares that "with God all things are possible" (Matt. 19:26). While the immediate context of the passage is the difficulty of salvific entrance of the rich into God's kingdom, its application is much wider. "Is anything too hard for the Lord?" God asks Abraham when aged Sarah laughs at the prospect of a son (Gen. 18:14). "I know that thou canst do every thing" troubled Job affirms of God (Job 42:2). "It is thou," declares Jeremiah, "who hast made the heavens and the earth by thy great power and by thy outstretched arm!" "Nothing is too hard for thee . . . , O great and mighty God whose name is the Lord of hosts, great in counsel and mighty in deed. . . ." (Jer. 32:17 ff., RSV). "For with God nothing will be impossible," the angel tells Mary, the virgin, in regard to the Messiah's impending birth (Luke 1:37, RSV). "God is able from these stones to raise up children to Abraham," declares John the Baptist (Matt. 3:9, RSV). Succinctly and comprehensively stated: "Our God is in the heavens; he does whatever he pleases" (Ps. 115:3, RSV).

God's purposes and Christ's kingdom are therefore invincible. God has sovereignly so disposed the course of the universe and of history that even the severest hostility to his will instrumentally displays and promotes his sovereignly redemptive plan. "And we know that all things work together for good to them that love God, to them who are the called according to his purpose" (Rom. 8:28). As the apostle Paul affirmed and experienced while in the Mamertine prison, God achieves his purposes in the lives of his followers through prayer and the supply of the Spirit (Phil. 1:19). God himself guarantees that eternal hell will subordinate the powers of evil and subjugate the impenitent wicked, that unreconciled freedom will not forever frustrate love, and that ultimately the created universe will be totally in the service of righteousness.

Supplementary Note: Sovereignty and Personality

WHY DO SOME THINKERS reject personality and sovereignty as simultaneous perfections of divinity? Why do they insist instead that divine infinity and divine personality are logically exclusive?

The infinite, they say, is unlimited, while the personal, on the other hand, is limited; for them, personality naturally and almost inevitably implies a kind of human limitation. We are told, therefore, to avoid transferring anthropomorphic features to the divine.

For some post-Hegelian idealists the Absolute spirit embraces all that is of value in personality yet is not itself personal but rather "superpersonal." They arrive at the "logical" Absolute by subordinating the individual to the universal and assuming that while the highest universal (ultimate reality) embraces all finite modes of being it nonetheless transcends them all (e.g., Plotinus's all-inclusive *unity,* Spinoza's all-inclusive *substance,* Hegel's all-inclusive *spirit*); the transcendent Absolute can therefore not be identified with any specific mode of being. While it expresses itself in and through the finite, nothing finite expresses the essential nature of the transcendent. Consciousness or personality are not to be attributed to the transcendent Absolute, since to do so presumably limits it to one mode of being. The Absolute is projected as a logical universal whose existence is arrived at by a process of logical subordination that empties the ultimate universal of concrete content even while it is identified as all-inclusive being. This universal consequently lacks specific character and is therefore nonpersonal. More important, however, is the fact that this universal is but a fiction of conceptual thought. Other post-Hegelian idealists assert the necessary finitude of divine personality on the ground that since consciousness implies a distinction between subject and object, or between ego and nonego, an absolute Being embracing all reality must transcend such distinctions. But surely, we would reply, God can know himself as object as well as subject, and, as biblically depicted, knows the universe as other than himself.

The term "Absolute" has diverse meanings in non-Christian representations of God, a fact that contributes little to philosophical lucidity. Sometimes "Absolute" simply means to stand in total nonrelation to anything else. Hegel's Absolute was the culmination of the universe; man becoming self-conscious exhibited more and more of the Absolute. Over against the

Christian God who is alone infinite in contrast to the finite universe, Spinoza's god (Substance) is infinite absolutely; the divine Substance, says Spinoza, is both unextended (thinking) and extended (spatial) and, moreover, has an infinite number of other attributes, all unknown to us. Gordon Clark observes how unintelligible this latter notion of God's absoluteness is, in contrast with the definite, positive representations of Scripture about the self-revealed God (*Thales to Dewey*, pp. 333 ff.).

A. C. Knudson emphasizes, and rightly, that there is no inconsistency between absoluteness and the essence of personality (*The Doctrine of God*, pp. 299 ff.) as conjectural conceptions of the Absolute would have us believe. If by claims that deity is superpersonal philosophers mean only that God represents a higher type of consciousness and will than does human personality, then, remarks Knudson, they are stating "what has not only been conceded, but maintained by all theistic personalists" (*ibid.*, p. 300). What personality stands opposed to is not a higher type of intelligence, but nonintelligence. The real question is whether the Absolute is self-consciousness and self-directing; to deny personality to the Absolute is to deny both its intelligence and freedom. In that case the Absolute becomes pure will without intellect (Schopenhauer), or unconscious intelligence (Hartmann), or even blind force.

Christian doctrine, as William Newton Clarke insists, "does not yield to this suggestion" that "personality fades out in infinity"; rather, "it makes bold to affirm the infinite Personal" (*The Christian Doctrine of God*, p. 303). In its biblical sense of being the sovereign causal Creator of all, the metaphysical Absolute is not inherently incompatible with personality; the Absolute is the independent personal cause of the universe. For the Christian theist God is both omnipotent and personal; divine infinite being represents personality in its most perfect form, and, moreover, God's sovereignty and other perfections can be affirmed solely on the basis of his personal self-revelation. Instead of declaring personality to be inconsistent with absoluteness, Christian scholars emphasize the perfect personality of the Absolute. The God of Christianity is the self-existent Absolute who personally makes himself known as the free sovereign Creator and Redeemer.

Clarke needlessly confuses matters, however, when he depicts the Christian representation of God as "both personal and infinite," as "the great paradox," but he quickly insists that this paradox involves "no absurdity" (*ibid.*, pp. 303 ff.). In view of emphases by certain Greek philosophers no less than by some post-Hegelian idealists, intellectual absurdity might indeed seem to be the case. The historian of ideas Arthur O. Lovejoy thinks Greek philosophy confused Western European theology by compounding two essentially different and incompatible deities into one. He points to Plato who in the *Timaeus* portrays the Demiurge as an intermediary good being that wishes the world to lack nothing. Aristotle, on the other hand, posits an unmoved mover of the universe, an immutable, eternal self-sufficient God who shows no interest in the physical universe which in some sense he ultimately authors. Thus an inevitable tension arises concerning

God's nature, one that subsequent Western thought fails to resolve. Lovejoy considers the very idea of an infinite-personal God to be contradictory (*The Great Chain of Being*). Obviously to accept this prejudice makes Christianity's emphasis on the sovereign personal God of the Bible absurd and paradoxical. Aristotle's aloof and disinterested divinity is not the God of Christianity, the sovereign personal Creator of a providential cosmos and of man in his image. Nor can Edgar S. Brightman's "finite-infinite God," as a conscious personal Spirit infinite in duration but limited by his own nature (*Personality and Religion,* pp. 97 ff.), overcome the onus of paradox and absurdity. One can no more have a God at once infinite and finite, than a God at once personal and impersonal.

Christian thought stands under no antecedent necessity to compromise the sovereignty of God because he is personal, nor to demean his personality because he is sovereign. That God is sovereign and personal must be evident if the living God of the Bible exists. In one and the same self-disclosure the God of revelation discloses his sovereign personality. Only on the basis of his revelation do we know that if man as the bearer of the Creator's personal image worships an infinite that lacks personality he worships something inferior to himself. Secular conceptions of ultimate sovereignty or of ultimate personality have little in common with the living Sovereign who reveals himself personally and redemptively.

By affirming that God is personal, Christianity declares that the fundamental power of creation, the cause of existence, is capable not only of interaction but also of communication and fellowship. The living bridge between the infinite invisible world and the finite visible world is therefore God's revelation. Here the sovereign Creator unveils himself as the personal source of all goodness and values. Apart from a personal God there is no grace, and apart from grace there is no salvation; apart from a sovereign God there is no assurance that divine grace will endure or can prevail.

Jesus' emphasis on the fatherhood of God reinforces what is already plain in the Old Testament, namely, that not every monarchical conception, or for that matter, not every conception of love can be superimposed upon the God of Scripture. The Bible's dual emphasis on sovereignty and personality guards us from hastily inferring that divine grace implies rejection of propitiatory and substitutionary atonement (contrary to Georgia Harkness, "Divine Sovereignty and Human Freedom," p. 150), or that the inherent value of human personality implies democratic rights and opinions unanswerable to transcendent duties and truth. The present struggle between totalitarian and democratic societies over the proper place of human beings vacillates between exalting arbitrary power on the one hand and pretentious individuality on the other. Arbitrary and unstable conceptions of man in society are inevitable when emphasis on the ultimacy of moral personality disregards Creator-creature distinctions, or when emphasis on the ultimacy of omnipotent power disregards the justice and morality that God affirms.

17.
God's Intellectual Attributes

GOD'S TRUTH DISTINGUISHES him as true in himself, veracious in all his words and deeds, author of all truth in the creaturely world, and foreign to all falsehood and pretense.

God is the source and ground of all rational distinction. As Robert Flint says, "Intelligence *per se* is an element of the Divine personality" (*On Theological, Biblical, and Other Subjects,* pp. 377 ff.). The laws of logic are the "architecture" or organization of the divine mind. They are the systematic arrangement of God's mind or the way God thinks. The laws of logic, therefore, have an ultimate ontological reality. God is the author of all meaning, the foundation of all facts; his thought is ultimately decisive for all predication. Without the very God who in revelation speaks in Christ through the Bible, nothing has eternally durable meaning. To say that divine intelligence violates the laws of logic deals a deathblow to rational divine revelation and to the whole enterprise of systematic theology. Those who argue that God is illogical and then presume to say anything ontologically significant about him, indulge in religious babbling.

God's sovereignty requires the confession that all existence and all knowledge have their ultimate source in the divine Logos. Truth is truth because God thinks and wills it; in other words, truth depends on the sovereignty of God. God sovereignly upholds the truth; he establishes and preserves whatever is true. As creative, the Word of God is the ground of all existence; as revelatory, it is the ground of all human knowledge.

By contrast, some, but not most, Greek philosophers consider eternal reason a realm independent of deity and objective to it. Hebrew-Christian theology, on the other hand, affirms that rationality is one of the intrinsic perfections of God. Plato's World of Ideas was a living Mind, although it was not the Maker of the cosmos; for Plotinus, the World of Ideas is explicitly subordinate to the Supreme One. The Bible refuses to hold God accountable to an idea of goodness or truth superior to himself. In the Christian view, the ultimate world of ideas is not a "given" to which God is himself subject; it is, rather, the very mind or thought of God. Reason is a divine attribute and the laws of reason are definitive of God's nature and descriptive of his will. God is sovereign in the sphere of logic and truth; had he wished, he could have thought other thoughts and decreed a different logic.

E. S. Brightman championed the law of reason as an eternal and uncreated divine attribute. Yet he claimed that the attribute of reason is independent of God's will, and held that God cannot do what is logically absurd because the structure of reality precludes doing so (*Philosophy of Religion,* pp. 285, 303). Gordon Clark rejects this assertion of God's finiteness, and insists that God can do anything. But the logically absurd, says Clark, is nothing, is a contradiction. Contradictions cannot have ontological existence, and an inability to do nothing is not an inability at all. The laws of reason, Clark affirms, are not independent of God's will nor do they limit God's power. "The laws of reason may be taken as descriptive of the activity of God's will, and hence dependent on it though not created as the world has been created" (*A Christian View of Men and Things,* p. 268).

The divine Logos is creative and revelatory. The ontic articulation (creation and preservation of the universe) and the noetic articulation of the cosmos (that is, its intelligible meaning and purpose) have their common source and ground in the divine Logos. The divine Word both absolutely originates what he voluntarily articulates and normatively articulates what he voluntarily originates.

That the divine Word is absolutely creative and originative means that the cosmos owes not only its origin but also its present forms and substance to the Word of God. As Vincent Bruemmer reminds us, "The Word of God is not without categorical content. It is an articulate Word and therefore it calls into existence an *articulate* cosmos. . . . The created cosmos exhibits an articulate *Logos*-structure because it is called into existence by the *Logos* of God" (*Transcendental Criticism and Christian Philosophy,* p. 167). In other words, the creative Logos is at one and the same time the sole originating principle of the cosmos and the ultimate foundation of the logical form of the cosmos and of its coherent content.

Since God's Word, unlike our human words, is creative, we must distinguish between articulation by the divine Logos and articulation by the mind of man. The activity of the divine Logos is what gives the cosmos its present concrete actuality, its existence and structure.

But the divine Logos is not only creative; it is also revelatory: the Word of God is the revelation of God. Revelation is divine self-disclosure, the manifestation of the divine Logos. The Logos communicates revelation in God's works universally, but especially in Jesus of Nazareth and in the Scriptures.

Man's knowledge of God, of himself and of the world around him takes place within prearticulated Logos patterns. The creative and revelatory Logos is what makes possible the logos of human knowledge by divine creation of the universe, and of man in the divine image to know and to serve the Creator. Since God is the source and ground of all truth, all truth is in some sense dependent upon divine disclosure and therefore "revelational." Truth consists of cognitively meaningful propositions; the totality of these propositions constitutes the mind of God. What puts Augustine over against both Plato and Hegel is, among other things, his emphasis that truth consists of propositions, in contrast to the notion that reality consists of ideas or concepts. God's omniscience consists essentially in his knowledge of all propositions in all their relationships. God is not merely an abstract principle of rationality; he is a living mind and will who as Creator of all is the ground of the meaning of the spatiotemporal universe. To be sure, mind and will are not two antithetical entities; God's knowing is an act of will, as Augustine emphasized. Augustine insists, moreover, that God's presence in the human mind enables it to recognize eternal truth. Truth is the conformity of our propositions to what God knows to be the case; insofar as we know anything we know God's mind, that is, we think God's thoughts after him. Without the antecedent activity of the Logos neither human knowledge of God nor human knowledge of cosmic reality would be possible. All human experience presupposes the divine Logos and involves intuitive reception of divine revelation. As the Light "which lighteth every man" (John 1:9), the eternal Logos is the source of all intellectual, moral and spiritual illumination.

It is noteworthy that, over against the frequent biblical anthropomorphic use of "hand," "arm," "eye" and "face" in describing God's activity, the Bible shows great restraint in using the term "head" in regard to God. The Old Testament does not specifically use the Hebrew word *ros* to designate the "seat of thought." The word *ros* does occur metaphorically for the rationality of the wise man ("The wise man's eyes are in his head," Eccl. 2:14). The term "head" is used in the New Testament of Christ, the exalted Lord, in relation to the church (Eph. 1:22 ff., 4:15 ff., 5:23 ff.; Col. 1:18, 2:10, 2:19). Colossians 1:18 relates Christ's headship to his preexistence and to his primeval creation of all created things, a conception not far removed from that of the Johannine prologue; the Logos of God is the source of all the substance and structures of reality. Only this divine activity by the creative and revelatory Logos is what makes human knowledge possible.

Despite their common emphasis with Christianity on God as living Mind, neither Platonic nor Hegelian idealism espouses the biblical emphasis on God as *transcendent* Reason. Judeo-Christian religion asserts the reality of supernatural revelation and of the divine communication of truth to finite and sinful men. The Logos of God is the standard of truth for the logos of man. Christian theology therefore not only rejects all self-sufficient modes of existence for the cosmos, but it also rejects equally all self-sufficient modes of attaining cosmic meaning and of humanly interpreting the cosmos. The entire space-time creation depends upon the sovereign Creator for its actuality, its meaning, and its purpose. In confessing that

Jesus is not only the incarnate Christ but also the very Logos of reality, the Christian church affirms that the truth that Christ is, does not differ essentially from any truth that is known anywhere.

The creative and revelatory Word accounts for both the particularity of created existence and the universality of its structural categories. Noetic articulation by the human logos does not originate or create; it merely reconstructs or reproduces. Man's articulation of the cosmos depends upon the prior divine ontic and noetic articulation by the Logos. Human noetic *logos*-articulation in knowledge-experience at best simply repeats the divine ontic *Logos*-articulation of the cosmos and depends on the divine noetic *Logos*-articulation of the cosmos.

Because Genesis depicts God as creating by his Word, some scholars distinguish between God's "non-addressive" and his "addressive" speech. Since, we are told, the creation fiat "let there be . . ." antedated the existence of creatures and was not addressed to them, the word of creation is therefore considered "non-addressive." This distinction seems somewhat artificial. Some creation-declarations may in fact have been "addressed" to unformed elements of the primal creation, although not as person-to-person communication since inanimate objects lack understanding. In any event, divine person-to-person address need not have been delayed until the creation of either angels or men. Whether the words "let us make man in our image" merely express divine majesty or eminence, or carry an anticipative attestation of interpersonal relationships within the Godhead that the Christian doctrine of the triunity makes explicit, the triune God may in eternity past have spoken intelligibly in and to himself, even if that address lacked the vocabulary and syntax of a specific human language. Why should it be thought that before the creation of the world and man the Father, Son and Holy Spirit were not on speaking terms? To be sure, if language consists in audible sounds, the Trinity has neither larynx nor language. If this precreation divine speech is said to imply that God does not reveal himself in any particular language, then revelation under any and all circumstances must be only conceptual. But the divine speech of eternity may have had significant implications for human language as an aspect of the *imago Dei,* and for God's use of human language as well in accommodating his revelation to his creatures.

God's living mind consists of rational propositions. When used epistemologically, the verb "to know" means to have in mind a number of self-consistent truths. God is rational and the source of all rationality. And because he is the originator and sustainer of truth, all truth is one and self-consistent. God is the God of intelligible order, not of irrationality, self-contradiction or paradox. Scripture speaks of him as *Logos* or *Wisdom,* not as the Irrational or the Paradoxical.

Among the vexing problems in the history of Western thought is that of the nature of ideas. What shall we say about the world of ideas? Are ideas simply psychological reflexes of our sense experience? Are they basically an activity of supernatural mind of which man *immediately* partakes as a spiritual being? Or are ideas, as Christianity affirms, a rational activity gifted by the Logos to humans who bear the divine image by creation, and who are thus enabled to think God's thoughts after him?

W. J. Sparrow-Simpson is certainly right in emphasizing the superiority of the Christian view that God is personal, over notions that identify ultimate reality simply with abstract eternal forms. Eternal truth and the divine mind and personality stand or fall together. As Sparrow-Simpson maintains: "The conception of eternal truth involves the conception of an eternal God" (*The Christian Doctrine of God,* p. 97). Yet the human mind is not to be considered identical with the divine mind. Even Plato avoids making man's mind a part of the world of ideas. In the *Timaeus* Plato assigned distinct existences to the Demiurge and the Ideas, regarding the latter as external and independent realities which the Divine Mind knows. The Demiurge is not the Divine Mind. Plato was no pantheist, nor was Aristotle, who, albeit somewhat vaguely, claimed that the active intellect came to man from without. Averroës later tried to identify the active intellect with the Unmoved Mover by insisting on only one active intellect for all men, and thus anticipated modern pantheism.

Philosophers have depicted the divine Logos variously as the Supreme Idea, the totality of Divine Ideas, a world of Ideas existing externally to God's mind, and as Logos immanent in the sensible world. The first century Jewish philosopher Philo at times portrayed the Logos as the faculty of reason in God although in some passages he depicts the Logos as external to God's mind (cf. H. A. Wolfson, *Philo*). In contrast to Plato who taught in the *Parmenides* that the Ideas must exist independently of and prior to God's knowledge of them, Philo taught that God created the Ideational world; by assigning mental activity to God prior to the Ideas, Philo asserts God's superiority to the Ideas. But it is unclear whether, alongside his view that Ideas have an objective created existence, Philo asserts that Ideas are eternally subjective in the Divine Mind, and that the world of Ideas must be related to the supremacy of God the Creator.

Although the New Testament and neo-Platonic writers espouse different doctrines of reason, Plotinus's identification of the world of Ideas with the Divine Mind is formally quite acceptable. The Divine Mind is not to be assigned an independent priority over the Ideas, as if it were at any time a mental vacuum in which the Ideas were later actualized or created. In one very explicit passage in the *Sophist* Plato had actually anticipated Plotinus's later identification of the world of Ideas as a supernatural Mind; the argument of the *Timaeus* and that of the *Republic* seem also to require this conclusion.

The influence of Greek thought misled certain medieval Christian thinkers in formulating their doctrine of biblical Logos. Nonetheless even Justin Martyr, who mistakenly held that as a personal being Christ is not eternal but rather was created in time by an act of the Father's will, identified the Logos with Christ, and taught that the substance of the Logos (the reason of God) is eternal.

With Augustine a Christian doctrine of Ideas begins to take more comprehensive shape. For him Ideas are not superior to God (Ideas higher than himself in which God participates) but are identical with the divine essence. The human use of reason involves divine revelation, Augustine avers, since Christ "the true Light . . . lighteth every man." All knowledge, he maintains, involves men in knowledge of God (not in the sense of automatic saving knowledge, but rather in that all are illumined by God's light), as well as in knowledge of the self.

On what basis or presupposition, we might ask, do our ideas pass from the order of thought to the order of reality? Can the human mind make any judgment at all about what is real simply by analyzing its own subjective ideas? Or must the mind somehow be related to what lies beyond it, gaining confidence in external reality from beyond its own conceptions?

Recent revival of interest in Anselm's ontological argument has brought this problem to the fore once again, particularly as it bears on our knowledge of God. For Anselm, the human mind has from the outset a direct understanding of God's essence. Therefore the mind does not face the problem of breaking out of a closed circle of mere subjective thought into the extra-mental realm of divine reality (cf. Arthur C. McGill, "Recent Discussions of Anselm's Argument," p. 72). The idea of God is not simply a subjective conception. There is in man a coincidence of intuitive awareness with transcendent reality; he could neither create an idea adequate to the reality of God, nor move toward God and speak truly of him, unless the idea of God in some way came from God's reality and not simply from human ingenuity. Anselm nowhere assumes that the human mind can directly grasp ultimate reality through *nous* in the manner of Plato and Plotinus. Although he explicitly divorces his argument from scriptural revelation, he implies that man's knowledge of God's existence presupposes general divine revelation to the mind of man who is created for the knowledge and service of God.

Anselm likewise insists, as does Duns Scotus, that God's essence does not participate in a superior Idea-realm. But William of Occam, an empiricist and Aristotelian of sorts, and in fact a nominalist, reduced ideas from an aspect of God's eternal essence to simply divine knowledge of individual things and events, and thereby implied that God's knowledge is contingent on his relation to external created realities. In Occam's view there are no Ideas at all.

With the rise of modern philosophy the role of the rational Creator is gradually attenuated and obscured. Spinoza the pantheist ascribes to God the attributes of thought and extension, and represents God as the source both of matter and of mind in the world, and as possessing infinite knowledge. But by God Spinoza means merely to designate the ultimate structure of the world, impersonal mathematical structure that necessitates all events. The relationship of infinite divine knowledge to human knowledge is therefore that of a mathematical whole to its determinate parts. Spinoza rejects the historic Judeo-Christian view that divine thought is identical with a supernatural personal deity; instead, he applies the term God to the all-embracing world-substance. Between the two views of thought and meaning, expressed by Philo the Jew and Spinoza the Jew, the Hebrew doctrine of creation loses all significance. Yet from the ancient Hebrew religion that Spinoza disowns, he nonetheless retains the conception that thought is as basic as extension and motion in the structure of the universe. Spinoza's philosophical heirs were to extend his rejection of transcendent Reason to much broader consequences. First they would demote human intelligence in relation to the physical universe as well as to the supernatural; then they would abandon the scientific quest for a rational comprehension of nature.

With the rise of modern empiricism John Locke reduced the ontological significance of ideas even further. Ideas now become simply a product of reflection on man's sensory experience. Whether human ideas about God conform to God's essential reality becomes doubtful. David Hume's skepticism widens this theological uncertainty into agnosticism. Because of their supposed empirical origin, ideas now no longer have valid reference to the essence or reality of the supernatural.

Hume's philosophy is striking evidence that efforts to base human knowledge on experience alone lead to skepticism. Yet the very possibility of knowledge requires admission that ideas are more than just reflexes of sensation. Indirectly, then, Hume renews interest in the question of what makes knowledge possible, and in the neglected emphasis on man's relationship to transcendent Reason.

For Kant human reason is significant only because of transcendental Reason. Stressing that skepticism results from a regard for experience as the ground of knowledge, Kant restores the converse thesis, that it is knowledge that makes experience possible. Although he derives the whole *content* of knowledge from sensation—a fatal concession to empiricism—Kant bases the very *possibility* of knowledge on innate forms of reason. But his exposition of the innate forms of human reason compromised the Hebrew-Christian doctrine, as promulgated by Augustine and Calvin, of a divine creation of innate categories as aspects of the *imago Dei*, one that involves also an intuitive knowledge of God.

Kant's reintroduction of an attenuated a priori factor fell prey to nineteenth-century empirical and evolutionary onslaughts on his theory of knowledge. Kant's premise that sensation alone supplies the content of knowledge undermined a genuinely theistic epistemology. His emphasis on the transcendental unity of apperception is less a pale shadow of the transcendent Reason that historic Christianity knows as the mind of the living God than a shadow of the human mind functioning to unify sensations into meaningful experience. Critical philosophy, therefore, was but a halfway house to theism, and an unstable one at that. Kant insists that by virtue of their rationality human beings belong uniquely to the intelligible world. But his knowledge-theory includes God only as a regulative principle, and not as an objectively existing transcendent rational Deity. While Kant acknowledges God to be an indispensable idea of human reason, he nonetheless fails to recognize that the necessary presupposition and ground of human rationality is the reason of the one true God.

Hegel perceives that to contain reason within Kantian limits offers no secure alternative to skepticism. He, therefore, boldly identifies reason with the Absolute. He does so, however, in a manner highly contrary to the revealed theology of Judeo-Christian religion, and in the profoundly unbiblical form of pantheistic idealism, whose broad antecedents in turn lay in Platonic rationalism. Hegel indeed makes all reason to be revelation, which need not of itself be theologically objectionable. But he does this by denying divine transcendence, and by considering man's mind an actual part of the Absolute Mind and not created in the image of the divine. For Hegel the Absolute is the universal mind of which all finite minds are differentiations.

In order to deliver truth from dependence on individual judgment, Kant linked its content to a comprehensive finite mind, that is, to the transcendental ego. Hegel's thinking Subject, likewise, is not merely an individual human being. But neither is Hegel's Absolute or universal mind the personal God of biblical theism. Although Hegel considers Being as Reason, he depicts divine-human rationality as an immanent dialectical process.

By directly identifying all finite minds with the Divine Spirit, Hegel stirred up against his rationalism a spirited counterthrust whose radical excesses unfortunately struck hard against aspects of Judeo-Christian theology as well. Hegel had discounted the finiteness and sinfulness of the human mind by exaggerating the *imago Dei* into man's immediate participation in the divine life and mind. Post-Hegelians reacted in the opposite direction, overturning Hegel's thesis that "the real is the rational," and championing instead the premise that "the real is the irrational." For Schopenhauer the universe is a manifestation of incomprehensible will; neither this universal will nor the universe it sustains is rational. Søren Kierkegaard declares that Reality cannot be comprehended by reason. To rescue the individual from subordination to Hegel's all-encompassing Absolute, Kierkegaard relates the individual to Ultimate Reality through passionate personal decision. Reality is not the rational Creator who communicates rationally with his creatures, it follows, nor do they rationally comprehend him. While Kierkegaard indeed maintains that God is "truth," he also insists that he exists for me as such not in intellectual comprehension but in subjective decision. Kierkegaard's theory of paradox, subjectivity, and inward appropriation waves aside all interest in objective religious truth and in theoretical discussions of God's existence. What Kierkegaard means by religious "knowledge" and by God as "truth" is inexpressible in universally valid propositions; it can only be grasped, he tells us, in the subjective moment of intense personal decision. Spiritual truth may in fact even seem logically invalid as it confronts the human mind. "An objective uncertainty held fast in an appropriation process of the most passionate inwardness is the truth, the highest truth attainable for an existing individual." Hence "the individual is in [subjective] truth, even though he is . . . related to [objective] untruth" (*Concluding Unscientific Postscript*, words in brackets supplied to emphasize Kierkegaard's subjectivism).

Recent personalism, or personalistic idealism, stresses that a personal

God is the ground of intelligibility. Thought, therefore, has a transcendent role, not merely a transcendental basis as Kant said. Whereas Kant loosed the laws of thought from dependence on a supernatural mind, and from knowledge of objective reality, except as the ego constructs objective reality, personalism revives the classic Western tradition that associates laws of thought with the law of existence. Personalism once again so relates human thought to a creative divine intelligence that ideation becomes possible because man's reason reflects an antecedent Divine Mind. Personalism, moreover, avoids a pantheistic view of man; finite persons are not parts of God but distinct creations. Human reason is not completely creative in the process of intellection; our ideas are true only when and as an individual thinks God's thoughts after him. L. Harold DeWolf accordingly applies the term revelation to any divine activity whereby truth is disclosed to human beings, and stresses that without such revelation we would have no knowledge whatever (*A Theology of the Living Church,* p. 63). DeWolf affirms that "the belief in a Supreme Mind undergirding our own experience seems best to commend itself as the solution of the problem of abstract truths," that is, truths of logic and mathematics (*ibid.,* p. 49). But Edgar S. Brightman exaggerates the primacy of the forms of reason. He sets them above the divine nature as a "given" to which God himself is subject. Most discussions of Brightman's "finite god" theory concentrate on his ascription to the divine nature of an "irrational given" over which God lacks full control. But Brightman insists also on a "rational given" in God's nature. Brightman's theory is a striking example of how personalism, which rejected the authority of biblical revelation, reverted to secular idealistic speculation from certain selective attachments to Christian theology.

The biblical emphasis on a rational Creator, whose image man bears by creation, elevates the role of reason and the laws of logic to timeless significance, since it grounds intelligibility not in this world but in the supernatural. Hebrew-Christian religion exalts divine reason as transcendently superior to human reason because the divine mind is archetypal and creative and because the human mind is finite and is deflected by sin from its proper knowledge and service of God. Yet neither God's rationality nor human rationality necessitates the opposition that dialectical theologians and existential philosophers establish between revelation and reason and between faith and reason. The alienation of the human mind from God's truth reflects man's predicament in sin, a condition that violates God's intended purpose for man and that redemptive revelation aims to overcome.

Christian theology traces the origin of universal meaning and the possibility of human cognition to the Creator. Divine creation has adapted the horizons of human experience to the knowledge of personal beings (the divine self, the finite knower himself, and other finite selves). Man was creatively constituted to know God and divinely revealed truths, and to know the variable individuality of events and things. These dimensions of knowledge and experience are not arbitrarily related to the human knower. Rather, as the Dutch philosopher Herman Dooyeweerd reminds us, they are integrated "into a perspective coherence in accordance with the Divine order of creation" (*A New Critique of Theoretical Thought,* p. 560). According to Dooyeweerd, only the knowing self knows the universal, and the self knows its own selfness only in relation to God and to other selves. "The religious meaning of the created world binds the true knowledge of the cosmos to true self-knowledge, and the latter to the true knowledge of God. . . . Every spiritualistic view which wants to separate self-knowledge and the knowledge of God from all that is temporal, runs counter to the Divine order of creation" (*ibid.,* p. 561). The human creature cannot experience self-knowledge except in simultaneous relationship to God and to the created world.

In every age the many schools of philosophy have had to consider on what basis, if any, individual thought gains universal significance and validity. Does an objective, invisible thought-world supply the ground of the validity of thought? In stressing the universal validity of truth, Aristotle, Kant, and Hegel all discuss the fundamental importance of the categories of thought. But whereas Aristctle derives his categories empirically from the rules of grammar (not wholly fantastic, if one considers the connection between language and thought), Kant formulates his categories analytically from the table of judgments supplied by transcendental logic.

Kant properly recognizes that without immanent mental principles no articulate experience would be possible. He therefore attempts an exhaustive exposition of the law of mental activity inherent in the mind of man. All human thought involves the self's creative activity. Even the simplest sensation involves more than just sensory qualities; it also includes judgment and interpretation. Bowne rightly remarks that "since the time of Kant sensationalism has been kept alive only by ignorance of the fact that it is dead" (*The Theory of Thought and Knowledge,* p. 274). Both Christian and non-Christian philosophers have criticized noetic particulars of Kant's exposition, especially the number and relations of his categories. Bowne adopted Kant's general framework, although he considered space and time as categories of thought, whereas Kant regarded them only as forms of sensation. Orienting his knowledge-theory more empirically than does Bowne, Brightman views time as the fundamental nature of the experience of all personality. Personality, Brightman dogmatizes, cannot exist without the experience of time. Brightman therefore elevates time into an experience for God as well as for man, whereas Bowne grants time only phenomenological and not ontological reality. For Bowne the fundamental category is purpose; for Hegel, it is Being; and for Whitehead, creativity. Whitehead's plea for a fresh approach to the question of basic categories complicates the inquiry, since he invented fifty or more new categories or terms to deal with the persistent problems of philosophy.

Any complete theory of knowledge requires profound investigation of the immanent structure of thought and of the universal conditions that make valid thought possible. Dooyeweerd has taken a neglected initiative among evangelical Christian scholars by proposing a new schema, but it has received a mixed reception. In expounding a Christian alternative to

Kant's *Critique* of knowledge, Dooyeweerd attacks Kant's dogma that theoretical thought is autonomous. Instead, he projects a searching analysis of the categories of thought from a religious-revelational point of view. Shaping all human experience, he contends, are fifteen irreducible structural modes, including "a numerical aspect, a spatial aspect, an aspect of extensive movement . . . followed by the economic, aesthetic, juridical, and moral aspects, and finally by the aspect of faith or belief" (*In the Twilight of Western Thought,* pp. 7, 122). To account for the divergent secular systems of philosophy he cites a speculative tendency to absolutize one or another of these modes.

Like Kant, Dooyeweerd approaches epistemology as a problem of synthesis that we attain through self-reflection that discerns a transcendental Ground Idea. But the Dutch philosopher contends that Kant misinterprets cosmic meaning-coherence, the cosmic-meaning totality, and the ultimate origin of all meaning. He assails Kant's *Critique* for failing to grasp the cosmological basis for epistemology. By reducing the primary datum of experience to chaotic conceptless impressions and, by isolating sensation from the complex but coherent cosmic meaning-structure found even in naive experience, Kant made human understanding the lawgiver of the cosmos.

No less significant, Dooyeweerd complains, is the fact that Kant limits the transcendental thinking ego to what is logical and identifies the knowing self only with its abstracted logical function. Kant failed to provide a satisfactory account of epistemological synthesis, says Dooyeweerd, because cosmic meaning-coherence cannot be reduced simply to logical coherence.

According to Dooyeweerd, Greek philosophy was dominated by the *form-matter* motive; medieval scholasticism by that of *nature-grace* (an attempted synthesis of the Greek and Christian); modern humanistic philosophy, by Kant's *nature-freedom* motive. Such central ground-*motives* are not mere philosophical *motifs* or theoretical themes. They are fundamental religious presuppositions that underlie each and every philosophy. Dooyeweerd calls them supratheoretical religious motives that transcend theoretical thought; they cannot be conceptually comprehended. They can only be approximated in the transcendental ideas which various philosophies express theoretically in divergent hypotheses.

Kant assigned a supratheoretical role to his three transcendental ideals of the universe, selfhood, and absolute origin. But he failed to consider these ideals the religious presuppositions whose content supplies the ultimate hypothesis of the critique of knowledge. Like other apostate motives espoused by secular philosophy (which in principle rejects or compromises the Christian motive of *creation-fall-redemption*), Kant's *nature-freedom* motive has actually a religious character, albeit one that is plagued by unresolvable dialectical tension.

Whether one accepts the religious unity of one Arche as the root of the modal aspects, or asserts two principles of origin in opposition to each other, notes Dooyeweerd, determines how one understands the mutual relation or coherence of meaning of these modal aspects. Basic to the transcendental ideas therefore is the transcendental *ground-Idea*, or, as Dooyeweerd calls it, the Cosmonomic Idea. This Arche, or absolute and integral origin of all meaning, the Scriptures identify as the sovereign holy will of the Creator-God whom Christ has revealed. Man's fall and its marring of the *imago Dei* issues in the diverse content of the Cosmoganic Idea and explains the spirit of apostasy manifest in the variety of religious ground-motives.

An incisive evaluation of Dooyeweerd's position is found in Vincent Bruemmer's *Transcendental Criticism and Christian Philosophy,* a dissertation completed at Utrecht. Bruemmer complains that divine cosmic law (Nomos) rather than the divine Logos supplies the content of Dooyeweerd's philosophic ground-Idea. Dooyeweerd finds the unity of the cosmogonic order in a transcendent divine harmony in the will of God. But because Greek philosophy attributed prime significance to the intellect and tried to forge a rational harmony immanent in the cosmos, Dooyeweerd seems by contrast to affirm the sovereignty of divine creative will in independence of the rational nature of God (*ibid.,* pp. 143 ff.). Sovereign law stands as an absolute boundary between divine and human reason as well as between divine and human will (*ibid.,* p. 149).

Even if the knower is *theoretically* able to isolate or separate the various modal functions of the concrete act of knowledge, says Dooyeweerd, the concrete act of knowledge nonetheless involves the mutual inter-coherence of the corresponding modal aspects of the cosmic meaning-structure. Dooyeweerd contends that whereas theoretical thought because of its problematic character breaks up experience into various abstracted modal aspects, the naive "pre-theoretical" attitude leaves intact the cosmic meaning-coherence and directs itself to concrete things and events.

Bruemmer declares this antithetical representation unsatisfactory and inadequate to deal with the epistemological problem of synthesis: "Like Kant . . . Dooyeweerd initiates his philosophy by *isolating* the logical and non-logical 'modalities': Kant does this through abstraction, Dooyeweerd through the principle of sphere-sovereignty. From the start the intrinsic coherence between the logical and the non-logical appears to be problematic in the philosophies of both Kant and Dooyeweerd. It is hardly surprising to find both of them faced with the epistemological problem of synthesis between the various law-spheres, a problem which is central in the transcendental critique of both" (*ibid.,* p. 160).

Dooyeweerd may even be considered less rationally affirmative than Kant. While both men consider the cosmos to be an order of meaning, Dooyeweerd does not identify meaning, as does Kant, with *logical* meaning (*ibid.,* p. 164). Whereas Kant's theory of antinomy presupposes the law of noncontradiction, Dooyeweerd rejects the universal cosmological relevance of this logical principle. Kant denies that the divine Logos furnishes the ontic and noetic articulation of the cosmos, and emphasizes that man's logical consciousness produces the meaning-structure of the phenomenal world. Dooyeweerd by contrast restricts the logical modality to one law-sphere in isolation from the others, and denies that the ultimate cosmological principle is logical. Instead of insisting that the cosmic meaning-structure gains its logical character from the divine creative Logos, Dooyeweerd explains cosmic meaning as a structure of divine laws.

Dooyeweerd therefore asserts his cosmo*nomic* Idea not only against Kant, but also against Abraham Kuyper and other evangelical theologians who insist that the cosmos has logical structure (*ibid.,* pp. 175 ff.). Evangelicals do not criticize Dooyeweerd's insistence that the relation between God and creation is that of purposive will. What some do criticize is his failure to stress the rational nature of the divine sovereign will and to ascribe the origin of the cosmos to the divine creative Logos. Both the Mosaic creation account and the Johannine prologue refer the concrete realization of God's purposive will to the creative rational Word of God. If we properly ground all creation in the divine will, we must assign the creation and preservation of the universe and its cosmic meaning to the Logos.

Gordon Clark complains, moreover, that "the fifteen irreducible structural molds" of human experience, on which Dooyeweerd insists, are in some respects quite arbitrary. Clark criticizes the sequence in which Dooyeweerd ranks the 15 different sciences or law-spheres by which he declares the universe to be governed (*New Critique of Theoretical Thought; In the Twilight of Western Thought*). Since the lowest law-sphere, the numerical, is preceded by the spatial as a higher sphere, Clark notes that geometry cannot then be reduced to arithmetic. Dooyeweerd gives precedence to the physical aspect over the movement aspect; Clark questions whether the movement aspect can be thus separated from the physical. But Clark's main objection is that Dooyeweerd lists logic or thought in a way that dissociates the laws of logic from number, space and motion ("Several Implications," in *The Philosophy of Gordon Clark. A Festschrift,* pp. 95 ff.; cf. also, Clark, "Cosmic Time," pp. 94 ff.; and Nash, "Dooyeweerd and the Amsterdam Philosophy").

We should recall here that although Christian philosophers have assailed Kant's epistemology in more than just its details, Kant did detect the necessity of an a priori theory. Kant recognized that by its imposition of innate categories the mind organizes otherwise chaotic sense experience into knowledge. For all his emphasis on the applicability of the forms of reason to existential subject matter, Kant was fully aware that neither the bare rules of logic nor sensory content can yield truth. He was mistaken, however, in invoking sense experience alone to supply the content of knowledge, and even more profoundly mistaken in ruling out the *imago Dei* as the basis of man's logical rationality. Evangelical critics repudiate Kant's limitation of the content of our knowledge to the sense world, his consequent denial of knowledge of the transcendent spiritual world, and his failure to derive the forms of reason from the creative activity of God.

In the *Critique* Kant hurriedly brushes aside the view that our thought categories are subjective aptitudes that the Creator has implanted to insure the harmony of human reason with the laws of nature that regulate experience (*Critique of Pure Reason,* pp. 174 f.). To this supernaturalistic view, Kant registers two objections—objections that, as Gordon Clark acutely notes, may be turned with full force also against Kant's postulation of nonsupernaturally derived a priori categories (*A Christian View of Men and Things*, pp. 314 f.). We have detailed elsewhere (*God, Revelation and Authority*, Vol 1, pp. 356 ff.) the defects of Kant's objections and of his own alternative.

On Christian premises the categories of thought may indeed be viewed as innate, but only in the larger context of divine creation. The rational God fashioned both the mind of man and the intelligible world to harmonize with each other. Kant's failure to adopt this preformation theory results in the self-destructive features of his own epistemology, namely, skepticism about the real world, incoherent and meaningless sense data, and the ascription of orderly experience solely to the activity of the human mind.

The question of the identity and number of categories remains a proper theme of Christian philosophy. Although Kant sensed the danger that their number might be exaggerated (and attached this danger to the preformation view), his twelve categories (derived from twelve types of judgment) have been widely criticized. Most students of the axiomatization of logic today would argue for no more than seven types of judgment, and some for less. At any rate, a complete index of categories is now complicated by disagreements among the exponents of symbolic logic. The fact that modern physics disputes some of Kant's categories (causality and substance, for example) may suggest only that Kant's exposition of the categories was somewhat rationalistic (because he allowed himself to be influenced by the leading scientific theories of his day!), but it does not of itself destroy the case for a priori elements in the mind of man. Bella K. Milmed doubts that post-Kantian science establishes the empirical irrelevance of Kant's categorial structure (*Kant and Current Philosophical Issues:* Some Modern Developments of His Theory of Knowledge, p. 146). The absolute necessity of our present categories of thought cannot in any event be established empirically. The thoroughgoing evolutionist must contend that other forms might serve a comparable purpose. But if alternative forms of reason do exist, we are ignorant of them, and wholly lack any experience of them. Were they to become presuppositions of experience, and were the logical structure of experience to be lost, our present experience would be not simply transformed but completely unthinkable.

Because recent modern thought detached the categories of knowledge from their supernatural source and significance, and referred them exclusively to the sense world, it has increasingly questioned consistency and coherence as criteria of truth. In pursuing "the whole truth" about nature by the empirical method only, modern explanation needs repeatedly to revise itself. Kant ruled out the ontic reality of a preexistent transcendent rational deity, and tried to preserve universally valid knowledge—that is, truth—by emphasizing the a priori character of "mind" in the transcendental sense. Kant's "transcendental deduction" was presumably an early attempt, which was later replaced by his deductions from the forms of transcendental logic.

Naturalistic philosophy rejects a transcendental deduction of the categories no less than their derivation from a transcendent divine mind. C. I. Lewis, for example, attacks Kant's theory from within; denying that the structure of mind must be of a specific character, he repudiates any metaphysical deduction of the categories whatever, and justifies their significance only in terms of systematic consistency (or utility) in defining special areas of experience (*Mind and the World-Order,* pp. 231 f.). Along with postevolutionary naturalism generally, Lewis substitutes a genetic psychological origin for a transcendent theological or a philosophical derivation of categories. While Lewis stresses the inherence of the same categorical structure in all human minds (a premise necessary to meaningful communication about a common world), his explanation can guarantee the permanent identity neither of the categories nor of human nature; the theory, in fact, erodes all basis for its own validity. Lewis's abandonment of a "universal pattern of human reason" (*ibid.,* p. 20) and of "an initial community of categories, as a psychologically identical and miraculous endowment" (*ibid.,* 96) is intellectually suicidal. On the one hand, Lewis tells us that the nonconceptual becomes intelligible only through the categories; on the other, that the categories spring from the preconceptual as a pragmatic social development.

Lewis theorizes that the categories may be "given up and replaced by new ones" for empirical reasons (*ibid.,* p. 268). In contrast to Kant, as Milmed reminds us, Lewis believes that "the categories are not bound by their extremely fundamental and general character to be forever unchangeable," but some of them might even be so changed in adaptation as to be ultimately "irrelevant or inadequate (though not actually false)" (*Kant and Current Philosophical Issues,* p. 100). Here the categories obviously no longer so structure the nature of consciousness that they determine experience, but rather are determined and revised by experience. This pragmatic notion of the formation and selection of concepts for empirical application recalls Émile Durkheim's view that the categories evolve from social adjustment.

Like all empirical theories, this one too is unable to show how a blank mind—that is, a mind lacking all a priori equipment—can arrive at knowledge. To view the categorical structure of consciousness as a product (rather than as the presupposition) of human knowing, as pragmatically evolving in experience rather than as making possible meaningful experience, leads to the dogma that sense experience alone defines what knowledge we have. Such a theory inherits all the other ills of empiricism, not least among them the surrender of truth in the sense of universally valid propositions. It cannot show that "all dogs are mammals" or that "no fowl are fish." Durkheim and Lewis destroy their own conclusions about anything.

Hans Reichenbach's explanation of our "habits of belief" as a successful evolutionary adjustment (*Experience and Prediction,* p. 402) likewise undermines the conceptual goal of knowledge, since there is no finality of truth in the "regulative validity" he ascribes to the tentative conceptual ordering of probabilities. This view, moreover, does not readily accommodate Reichenbach's emphasis that human beings continue to experience "a common world." The attempt to base all knowledge on experience dissolves knowledge itself; empiricism inevitably ends in ontological nihilism and epistemological skepticism, because it is impossible for the sense flux to intellectualize itself. Reichenbach may deplore the rationalism of philosophical assertions unsupported by "the facts of the empirical world" (*The Rise of Scientific Philosophy,* p. 73), but the naturalistic dogma that sense experience is the source of all knowledge is no less arbitrary, since the underlying dogma that knowledge arises only from sensation is not supplied by sensation. Why the content of consciousness should be conceptually organized, and how we can have common experience and communication concerning a common world, cannot be adequately explained except on theistic premises. Once we loosely conceive mental structure as subject to change, both the "standard human mind" and "universal meaning" become mere postulations.

All "absolutes" that modern empirical science predicates as "valid" for universal experience—like the notions of absolute uniformity or universal causality—are always vulnerable to disconcerting revision. But neither the fallibility nor the pretensions of scientism justifies tentativeness over the categories of thought. One may tolerate much flexibility in the postulates of empirical science—indeed, the intrinsic revisability of scientific theory should be continually stressed—without on that account assigning flexibility to the basic categories that structure the human mind. The fact that empirical science has a propensity for obsolescence need not imply that logic shares this same propensity. Kant properly recognized that the forms of logic are part of the very structure of human consciousness. The universal and necessary factors in knowledge, particularly the law of contradiction and the validity of implication, required some sort of apriorism.

If Kant's own theory harbored the inconsistency (in the context of his epistemology) of occasional references to the world of experience as objective reality, Lewis and other naturalists, by acknowledging the possibility of replacing the categories, deprive them no less than did Kant of any capacity actually to define reality as such. Lewis's categories yield us merely an "if . . . then" world. The cost of eliminating all a priori elements from the nature of consciousness is that the "comprehension of reality" reduces to systematic empirical postulations for which one can claim neither universal validity nor permanence.

To explain the conceptual structure of human reason as a pragmatic-genetic byproduct of our common activity and quest for communication relativizes human nature. Milmed notes "awkward implications" of the view that "logic itself . . . evolves with . . . consciousness and ultimately changes with the content of our common world" (*Kant and Current Philosophical Issues,* p. 120). She acutely detects the dilemma that results from Lewis's assignment of only a half-significance to logic. For "Some logic is true," Lewis insists, "and hence some logical principles are necessary." Yet, he asserts, "the stamp of mind's creation is . . . the absence of impulsion and the presence of at least conceivable alternatives" (*Mind and the World-Order,* pp. 210–213). But by "what logic" other than the selfsame logic that Lewis apparently compromises, Milmed asks, are we to discriminate valid from invalid logic (*Mind and the World-Order*, p. 121)? We can hardly maintain the importance of the conceptual element in knowledge if speculations about the genetic and pragmatic origin of human concepts dissolve the objective significance of mind. While Lewis struggles against the view that logic has only a subjective character that varies with the individual mind, nevertheless his alternative—a common human 'mind' subject to continual empirical revision—deprives man of any universally valid knowledge.

The task of properly formulating the categories of thought remains to be completed. To delineate a sound theory of knowledge within the framework of revelation is a major constructive assignment facing Christian philosophy. Modern philosophy's controversy over the rational molds through which human experience flows is of utmost importance. But no less important is the analysis of concepts and mental procedures inherent in human knowledge analysis that leads properly and necessarily to reflection on the mind of God as the hinterland of man's knowledge. The coincidence of the categories of reason with sense data, indeed, their applicability to all experience, and their indispensability to organized or meaningful experience, Christian philosophy explains not simply by an epistemological deduction from the conceptual structure or framework of human knowledge, but rather by the metaphysical deduction of the forms of reason. The categories of reason are related not only to the nature of human consciousness, but are also derived ultimately from God's intelligible attributes and his purpose in creation; they exist through the fact that man bears the *imago Dei,* and beyond that, through the eternal relationship between consciousness and logic. The intelligible character of the world of experience is due to selective definition made possible by the formal connection of human reason with the *imago Dei;* it is not due to our own subjective exclusion of intrinsically unintelligible aspects of the objective world. The structure of human consciousness is explained by its inherent logical structure, and this structure of logic in turn is explained by the mind of God.

By the creative element in human reason, Christian theology does not mean, as Kant does, that the human mind originally contributes the organizing conceptual element to experience; nor does Christian theology mean, like the pragmatists, that the knower has an active role in creating the object of knowledge itself; nor does it mean, as do the extreme empiricists, that concepts are the revisable instruments whereby we connect and order our sense impressions. Christian theology denies that experience *originates* our knowledge, denies even that knowledge arises out of experience as its source and ground, and also that the mind of man legislates meaning upon reality. While our knowledge arises on the *occasion* of experience, the forms of reason are given to man on the basis of divine creation.

Insofar as we have valid knowledge, the content of reason is correlated with divine revelation, and mirrors the thoughts of God. God's rationality is the ultimate explanation of the primacy and ubiquity of rational structure in the created world of men and things, and supplies also the formal possibility of completely coherent experience. We comprehend the universe through categories not derived from sense experience; the fact that it is a rational creation explains not only why our experience of the sense world is intelligible, but also why the subjective conditions of thought are universally valid. If it is true that logic is objective rather than subjective; that there can ultimately be only one set of "rules of the understanding"; that all persons in all times and places have the same criteria of truth, then the Christian doctrine of creation provides the best explanation of the objectivity of logic and of the fact that human beings as such share a minimal conceptual structure.

Christian theologians need not be intimidated by the fact that existential irrationalists and even subevangelical dogmaticians today brand every intimation of a priori psychology as specious rationalism. The existentialists must themselves recognize that logical procedures exist within the field of experience. Without some common mental apparatus humans could neither experience a common world nor communicate their experiences intelligibly; without logical coherence no universally valid knowledge is possible. As Milmed notes, while "we can and often do think irrationally . . . we cannot understand irrationally" (*Mind and the World-Order*, p. 47). The obvious collapse of one secular theory of logic after another (Milmed thinks "we may probably assume without too much arbitrariness that both the Platonic rationalist conception of logic as existentially self-validating and the empiricist conception of logic as derived from sense experience may be regarded as discredited") should encourage bold discussion of the Christian alternative to the speculative problem-beset theories of human rationality. We are repeatedly thrown back on Aristotelian logic or laws of thought, systematically formulated (but surely not invented!) by Aristotle, and of which even Bertrand Russell's theory is basically a subdivision. Neither Nietzsche nor Durkheim nor Dewey who asserted that there would be new logics ever illustrated or formulated such.

Unless modern scholars are ready to concede (and no scientist is) that no more progress in scientific theory is possible, it seems likely that the currently fashionable scientific, mathematical and logical theories, oriented one-sidedly to empirical considerations, will in time be viewed as obsolete as scientific, mathematical and logical theories of several centuries ago. Empiricism assures no enduring status to the so-called existential logic now current. Recent attempts to justify the role of deductive logic in empirical scientific procedures indicate that so-called existential logic is being driven beyond its own presuppositions. If, moreover, over and above pragmatic control of environment, contemporary scientists once more revive the quest for truth, they must inevitably reraise the question of the relationship of the rational to an independent objective realm, as well as to man's common knowledge. The very existence and possibility of truth demands the indispensability of logic not simply for purposes of shared knowledge, but for valid constructions about reality as well. The biblical declaration, "God is truth," affirms that truth has ontological status and it therefore retains driving relevance to the persistent problems that confront current philosophical inquiry in this area.

Consider, for example, the pressing problem of the empirical applicability of logic. To assume that all existential experience is inchoate (that is, that the actual world is unstructured by logical forms), and that conceptual knowledge is simply a process of human abstraction (that logical forms are pragmatic inventions), implies that the real world and logic are essentially unrelated. Yet, as Milmed reminds us, "scientific knowledge of the very foundations of the existent world is expressed more and more in mathematical symbols. . . . Whatever fails to fit into a deductive system is nevertheless treated mathematically, in terms of probability" (*ibid.*, pp. 235 ff.). This increasing readiness to understand physics in mathematical terms, and mathematics in logical categories, immediately poses the questions of how mathematical physics itself is possible, how conceptual reasoning about the world of reality is possible, and how logic is applicable to existential experience.

The existentialist revolt against an intelligible universe presents a still deeper problem. By arbitrarily disjoining experience and reality, existentialism grants intellectual significance (in view of man's cognitive abilities) only to the conceptually organized world, and demotes independent reality to an enigmatic or uncertain existence. But to equate the real world either with our abstractions or with existential experience autocratically restricts the role of reason at great cost to philosophical science. Reason, moreover, thereby loses its touch with that "bare" objective independent reality which scientific philosophers assert in order to escape subjectivism. Failure to apply logic to independent reality inevitably jeopardizes any confident application of reason to the world of human concerns, and to the logical integration of life's experiences.

Beyond these considerations stands the larger concern of the unity of knowledge. As long as the tentative and revisable nature of empirical studies is held in view, scientific acceptance of mutually contradictory theories poses no fundamental challenge to the goal of a comprehensively explanatory view of life and the world. But growing distrust of any and all attempts to formulate a logically consistent and coherent overview of reality and experience is undermining the search for a proper Weltanschauung. Such disdain for logical consistency springs partly from a fear of "rationalism" (empiricists are apparently impervious to such transgression!), and more fully from the postevolutionary revolt against the larger significance of reason. Curiously enough, while they disown any desire to formulate a comprehensive world-life view, some scholars nonetheless now increasingly try to delineate understanding of our cosmic environment in ever more inclusive theories. In so doing they are compelled to face the underlying problem of the nature of explanation itself. Milmed's verdict is doubtless right, therefore, that Kant's *Critique of Pure Reason* with its inquiry into the preconditions of human understanding is not to be dismissed as "a dead classic of the rationalistic and idealistic past" (*Kant and Current Philosophical Issues,* p. 233) and Kant's lingering influence even on current naturalistic philosophy is not to be overlooked.

The massive problem of the primary and enduring relationship between logic and mind and reality therefore continues to call for attention. Milmed observes that contemporary philosophy lacks any adequate explanation of "the nature and justification of logic" itself (*ibid.,* p. 237). If logic is simply a man-made invention for supplying mere "rules for the game" of thought, then it shipwrecks both logic and experience. The only adequate alternative is that logic is a fact about the structure of the human mind. Even so, only some explanation beyond that of genetic development and empirical derivation of the conceptual structure of human minds can preserve the self-validating character of reason by which human beings communicate with each other about a common world.

The problem of the ultimate meaning of logic consequently pushes us also to a thorough reconsideration of epistemological concerns. Modern thought may neglect the Christian option but its relevancy becomes apparent. It affirms that meaning has a supernatural foundation, and that the forms of logic belong to the human mind because man bears the *imago Dei.* Christianity supplies, in fact, although unrecognized, the indispensable preconditions without which even arbitrary rival theories could neither be formulated nor be made intelligible to those who hear and dispute them. A Christian theory of knowledge therefore illumines such enigmas of scientific philosophy as the conceptual element in experience, the deductive element in science, and the relationship of human thought to an independently real world. Only the Christian explanation of meaning securely reinstates existence without stumbling into bare existentialism, and securely reinstates logic without conjectural rationalism.

The problems that modern antirational theories pose in relation to knowledge of the supernatural realm are not dissimilar to those bearing on the physical world. If reason has no ontological status, if the intelligible ordering of experience is merely a human achievement, and if our (spiritual or sensory) conceptions are to be referred to an unknown and unknowable independent reality, then the obvious problem becomes that of avoiding, in the one case, the reduction of theology to inner "religious experience," and in the other, the reduction of science to mere phenomenalism. Theology must inevitably be embarrassed by any emphasis *that* God is if it indicates no knowledge of *what* he is. Likewise the premise of scientific philosophy inevitably reaps confusion and contradiction when it states that our sensory perceptions and conceptual structures imply a real world about which no valid affirmations are possible. Completely indeterminate thought of "something in general" has no significance whatever for either theological or scientific knowledge; it is, in fact, not thought at all but merely sentiment. When empirical philosophers like Reichenbach and Lewis appeal to "a hypothetical observer" in order to escape the net of subjectivism and to establish an independent reality (since its independence cannot be established *within* the arena of experience alone), one detects an unwitting appeal to some "unknown God" to avoid skepticism.

The validity of our knowledge-claims arises immediately and becomes an issue when the scientist, for example, insists that there is more than just the phenomenal world, that an independently real world is "given" as an object of phenomenal experience; or when the theologian insists that there is more than just religious experience, that a divine reality is accessible in religious experience. If the theologian or the scientist contends only that our rational processes confer intellectual significance on otherwise unintelligible perceptions, then neither the existence of the independent object nor any qualities we attribute to the object can be regarded as valid knowledge. That something beyond our sensory precepts and rational constructs is indeed real—a conviction that misled Kant into asserting his highly controversial *Ding an sich*—is assured by the prior reality of God and the biblical doctrine of creation. The only sound alternative to skepticism in philosophy no less than in theology is to recognize the ontological significance of reason. Only when human reason coincides with the intrinsic rationality of the objective world do our affirmations about independent reality gain the status of knowledge. The coincidence of our concepts and perceptions in a coherent structure does not of itself provide valid knowledge, inasmuch as our conceptual constructs do not themselves constitute truth. Merely to assert the independent reality or existence of an object does not of itself hold any status as knowledge, since existential subject matter supplied by our perceptions and structurally organized by our concepts does not necessarily carry us beyond subjective experience. The validity of knowledge and experience is assured only if its content includes a relationship to the all-embracing rationale constituted by God's mind and plan and purpose. The rational Creator who exists and reveals himself in cosmic nature and in and to the mind of man, has also shaped intelligible scriptural revelation. Within this framework we may best comprehend the significance of perception, the conceptual ordering of our experience, and valid knowledge of independently real spiritual and physical worlds. Christianity premises that existential content of experience, when it becomes our experience, is conceptually structured not alone by our individual sensory and rational apparatus, but also in terms of an antecedently rational world order, including man and nature, and beyond that through the ontological significance of reason. Our mental capacities and activities supply the formal possibility of knowledge, but they do not constitute either the existence of the object of knowledge or its intelligible nature.

Christianity rests its case for the ontological status of reason not simply on idealistic or rationalistic conjecture, but on the self-revelation of the rational Creator-God. Divine creation—both of man and of the planetary universe—involves a realm independent of our sense data and logical constructions. The world of nature as a created reality preexisted human life and knowledge. Reason was already significant prior to man's creation and prior to all creation, since truth is the very character of God. Human experience comprehends the world and its meaning not as an act of postulation but because of divine meaning and revelation. The Creator not only knows what is unknown or unknowable to man, but also imparts the true meaning of what man does and can know.

Prior to the neoorthodox revolt against reason, evangelical theologians routinely stressed the logical relationship between divine and human intelligence and the intelligibility of the universe. W. T. Conner, for example, asserts that "God as the creator and sustainer of man and of the world constitutes the bond of union between man's mind and the world as an object of man's knowledge. . . . A rational God, who constitutes the ground of man's existence and of the existence of the world, by his immanence in both man and the world constitutes the possibility of man's knowledge of the world." Such a God desires to bring man into "intelligent communion with himself" (*Revelation and God: An Introduction to Christian Doctrine*, p. 62). More than most liberal theologians evangelicals like Charles Hodge, A. H. Strong, L. Berkhof, and H. C. Thiessen insisted on the rationality of God.

While Christianity approves antirationalism, it cannot accept the antirationality of existentialism. The rational universe is not an ultimate cosmic given, nor is reason as such an independent lawgiver of cosmic reality. But the rejection of secular rationalism gives no license for making either subjectivism or subjectivity the criterion of experience. The modern attack on the truth and rationality of God soon deteriorates, and understandably so, into an attack on his very existence. The rejection of rational metaphysical knowledge and of God's objective existence characteristic of Martin Heidegger and existential philosophers, is philosophically interrelated. Revolt against a rational God leads inevitably to rejection of the intelligibility of the universe and of human experience.

Christian theology insists that God maintains the logical rationality of his creation and rules the universe as an intelligible order. The divine Logos is the norm and measure of reality and of truth (J. M. Spier, *Christianity and Existentialism*, p. 125).

Only an ontological structure that is implicitly rational, that asserts the rationality of God and vindicates the ontological significance of reason, can be considered sound Christian philosophy. Unless a rational God and his rational revelation are reinstated, the points of departure from the modernism of Kant, Schleiermacher and Ritschl announced by contemporary theologians cannot qualify their theology as truly biblical. Like the earlier modernistic movements, the theology of the recent past often regrettably lends itself, wittingly or unwittingly, not only to rejection of divine truth but also to a modification of truth as an attribute of God.

So strong was the influence of Christian thought on the Middle Ages that from the time of Augustine until the rise of modern philosophy no one doubted that the Creator God is the ultimate ground and source of reason and wisdom. Until modern times standard texts on the doctrine of God affirmed God's omniscience and wisdom, and honored God's truth as the only authoritative guide to human welfare and destiny.

Recent scholars tend to expound God's intellectual attributes less fully and less precisely than his divine moral and volitional attributes. Sometimes this diffidence in delineating God's rational nature reflects an emphasis on divine mystery that first passed into early Christian theology from neo-Platonism. Since the time of Aquinas, moreover, Roman Catholic philosophy has disclaimed univocal knowledge of God. After 1600, speculative thinkers exalted the creative role of human reason over that of divine revelation (cf. Gerald R. Cragg, *The Church and the Age of Reason—1648–1789*). Modern thought soon affirmed the all-sufficiency of man's autonomous reason and stressed the authority of empirical observation. In view of the supposed limits of human reason Kant rejected the very possibility of conceptual knowledge of the supernatural. In our time logical positivism caricatures statements about God as meaningless nonsense.

In contrast to these developments evangelical Christianity maintains a metaphysically affirmative stance. On the basis of God's intelligible self-revelation attested in Scripture it affirms God's being and defines his nature. Such definition, if legitimate in respect to other divine attributes, is no less proper and necessary in respect to the divine intelligence. In some respects the truth of God is the divine attribute most fiercely under attack today, and hence most urgently in need of exposition. Evangelical neglect of this aspect of theology unwittingly accommodates alien theories that promote divine irrationality or compromise the revelation of the Logos. Donald Bloesch, James Daane and Jack Rogers, among others, assail as rationalism theological convictions long affirmed by evangelical orthodoxy, including revelationally based claims about the transcendent nature of God, the propositional nature of revelation, and the insistence that the object of faith be rationally credible.

Many churchmen fail to realize that the present dissociation of truth from the nature of God and from divine revelation confronts the Christian church with a decision fully as serious as the Arian controversy of the third century. Both crises are christological; both involve ontological and epistemological considerations. The judgment one passes on the relation of truth to the nature of God and to the revelation of the Logos involves a verdict both on the character of God and on the status of truth. As churchmen who stripped the incarnate Logos of the status of divine being once wielded ecclesiastical leadership, so influential ecumenical spokesmen today deprive the incarnate Logos and the inscripturated logos of the status of final truths. Even dialectical theology that professedly aims to exalt Christ the incarnate Logos strips his self-disclosure of propositional intelligibility and validity.

Strange indeed was the twentieth-century Christian forfeiture of worldview concerns and of an appeal to reason precisely at a time when the communist movement (deliberately antichrist) presented its naturalistic alternative not simply as a call for existential response but as a coherent and consistent materialistic philosophy. Edwin A. Burtt notes that, in contrast to the nondogmatic mood of both Oriental religions and Western science, communism has appropriated the Christian missionary's motif: "Ours is the saving truth, and the only saving truth." This emphasis, Burtt reminds us, is "radically alien" to Eastern religions; "even Buddhism, the great missionary faith of the East, spread through Asia not by any dogmatic claim to final truth . . ." (*Man Seeks the Divine*, p. 471). To a vacillating Christian generation in which speculative forces have weakened belief in the Christian realities, the communist claim provided a rallying point for faith in some kind of an absolute. Secular undermining of faith in a supernatural plan and purpose had shaped a vacuum that readily absorbed the communist contention that an invisible power—not the biblical Creator-Redeemer but the principle of economic determinism—governs the course of history. The Marxist rejection of objective truth as mere superstition, however, enabled communist leaders to subvert truth and morality for Marxist ends, and to employ deception to gain disciples. Burtt comments relevantly that "the civilized religions (including the earlier Western faiths) have not, in basic conviction, at least, been led into any such self-deception and ruthlessness. . . . In general these religions have committed themselves to the freedom of reason to seek the truth . . ." (*ibid.,* p. 473). No less important is the emphasis of revealed religion—so widely overlooked and even repudiated by many twentieth-century theologians—on the objectivity of truth and the good as identical with God's will and nature, and its reference of untruth and evil to the demonic. Communism's "saving truth" is the antithesis of the eternal and revealed truth declared in Jesus Christ; it retains only the form and urgency, while it falsifies and perverts the essential content of gospel proclamation.

Beneath the current disposition to renounce metaphysical "absolute truth" lurks the Western "scientific" quest for empirical truth and the pursuit of practical "saving truth." Communism lifts dialectical materialism (with its exclusion of changeless truth and morality) above the status of theory to one of absolute dogma. The modern attempt to confine truth within the limits of "scientific" methodology seldom resigns itself as it ought to tolerant skepticism. By arbitrarily excluding supernatural realities and changeless revelational truth—and hence truth in the larger sense—the scientific mentality becomes vulnerable to its own false absolutes. The Christian emphasis not only on the Logos-Creator but also on a logos-image in nature and man, bears importantly on both the secular philosophies and the scientific theories of our time. If scientific thought and practice can wholly ignore the truth of God, it can, of course, by manipulating nature and the human species, likewise wholly ignore the question of what is divinely declared to be good and evil.

Modern liberal learning is now widely regarded as intellectually chaotic because of its lack of comprehensive integrative principles. The study of ontology (the science of reality), of epistemology (the science of knowledge) and of axiology (the science of values), proceeds on competitive and even contradictory principles of explanation that reflect the many divergent theories of modern proponents. Even the most prestigious professional societies reflect extensive theoretical disagreements among scientists, philosophers and theologians. Since university learning no longer begins with God as its first principle, the horizons of human experience are subdivided into separate themes of metaphysics, cosmology, epistemology, anthropology, and so on. Independent investigation of these themes frustrates any effort to unify their diverse and divergent content. A prime factor in the failure of modern philosophy to convincingly and coherently integrate reality is the modern loss of the ontological significance of reason, that is, of the ultimate role of reason in all realms of being and life. Secular education simply overlooks the fact that Christianity offers a comprehensive explanatory principle that correlates the great concerns of life and reality.

To some extent the Christian community itself is responsible for the secular eclipse of its perspectives. For one thing evangelical institutions tend to announce or pronounce Christian world-life view more than they elaborate its principles in a way that comprehensively engages all vistas of modern university learning. What Christianity taught the world of ancient thought, namely, that all truth is identical with the living mind of God, is forfeited in an age that assigns God and mystery to one realm, and man and rationality to another. At the outset of modern philosophy, no idea was so clear to Descartes as the idea of God, an idea he held to be divinely implanted in man and hence, innate. Arrogating to itself the prerogative of implanting whatever ideas humans are to live and die with, twentieth-century learning has been more resigned to the death of God than to a significant doctrine of his living reality.

According to three leaders of the California Institute of Technology's Advance Projects for Tracking and Data Acquisition Planning (Jet Propulsion Laboratory), "The question 'Are we alone?' . . . will challenge science until positive evidence of extraterrestrial intelligence is encountered by design or serendipity, or until a dominant negative view is built up incrementally from diverse, observational tests. Either outcome will be one of the greatest scientific achievements imaginable, with profound philosophical and theological significance" (Bruce Murray, Samuel Gulkis, and Robert E. Edelson, "Extraterrestrial Intelligence: An Observational Approach," p. 491). Here the key word is "observational," and behind it lie the haughty assumptions that in order to be acknowledged by the scientific community God must transform himself into an object of sense perception and, moreover, must do so in a space-time appointment scheduled by the contemporary experimentor. Contemporary scientific probing of extraterrestrial intelligence proceeds usually on the assumption that a number of life-favoring planets exist on which manlike intelligence has developed, and that telescope-radar astronomy, given the correct frequency, modulation and direction, can detect signals of extraterrestrial origin thousands of light years distant. Such experiments, conducted with highly sophisticated technology in low-noise reception and data processing, are appropriate, to be sure, for detecting orderly interstellar sounds in deep space; none, it should be mentioned, has yet been discerned. But even if they were to be detected, such sounds are not signals identifiable self-evidently in terms of interpersonal communication. They are, in fact, of a different order than the rational-verbal communication of God—the God who speaks universally of his transcendent power and righteousness in the cosmos and in man's consciousness but whose revelation eludes the empirically addicted observer, however much he cannot wholly escape it.

18.
Shadows of the Irrational

INTERPRETERS OF THE history of thought increasingly identify the characteristic element of contemporary philosophy as pervasive irrationalism. While earlier Western philosophers—ancient, medieval and modern—had disagreed about the nature of Reality, they nonetheless agreed and insisted that the ultimate world is intelligible and capable of rational definition. Classic Greek idealism, mechanism and empiricism, medieval theism, and even early modern naturalism viewed the real world as objectively ordered and coherent. The dominant view from 1600 to 1900, as Dirk Jellema observes, is that nature is a patterned reality of intelligible laws discoverable by human reason ("The Rise of the Post-Modern Mind," p. 13).

It is the revolt against Hegelian rationalism, however, that changes man's perception of Reality and inaugurates a basic commitment to nonrational or irrational world perspectives. Assault since 1850 on Hegel's premise, "the real is the Rational," which he unfortunately expounded pantheistically, has helped support the contrary premise that Ultimate Reality is nonrational. Among intermediate thinkers who stressed irrationalism were Marx, Nietzsche, and Freud.

Displacing both the triune God and patterned reality, the emerging coterie of philosophical irrationalists in Western philosophy emphasized impenetrable unpatterned reality to which man alone supplies values and meanings. This view denies that a rational and moral reality exists independently of human beings, and rejects universal rational and moral principles. If this outlook retains the concept of deity at all, it identifies God as ultimate Unpattern or postulates him creatively in an individual commitment to personal meaning. A world externally beyond values, beyond truth, beyond structure, upon which the self imposes its own meaning and values, is foreign to the worldview even of pagan antiquity. For classic thinkers the cosmic role of reason as a formative principle of the universe had not yet become merely a late evolutionary emergent having only temporary passing significance. Even though modern thought came to view nature as ultimately real, it did not at first detect the inherent antirationalist and antireason implications of this approach. Nature was viewed as something that evolved into mind and would ideally be comprehended by reason, man's distinctive glory. Truth and morality were seen as the apex of the evolutionary process. The eventual affirmation of Unpattern by Western philosophers was not widely foreseen before the twentieth century. But reaction against Hegelian rationalism—itself a devastating deviation from biblical theism—plummeted contemporary philosophy into a culminating revolt against reason itself.

Recent modern man consequently probes the dimensions of reality more and more in the extrarational, indeed, in the irrational. Given Divine Unpattern and the creative self as governing premises, man's incurably religious spirit autonomously fashions novel concepts of deity; the idolatrous self seeks to express its creative freedom by patterning the Unpattern. Jean-Paul Sartre finds value for the self in its creative freedom from the Unpattern (the blind world of unfree Being). Martin Heidegger seeks value for the self in contemplation or intuition of the mysterious and wonderful world of Unpattern. Others contemplate the Unpattern simply as glorious and mysterious, deserving of worship. Many observers note certain similarities to Oriental religions, to Zen, for example, with its passive openness to unstructured reality, or to Hinduism with its emphasis on divine reality as "beyond" meaning and nonmeaning, good and evil, love and hate. Huston Smith identifies the distinctive feature of new frontier thinking, whether in science, philosophy, theology or the arts, as a philosophical acceptance of reality "as unordered in any objective way that man's mind can discern" ("Revolution in Western Thought," p. 61). This change from "the vision of reality as ordered to unordered," he adds, "has brought Western man to as sharp a fork in history as he has [ever] faced." Emerging not simply as a detour or diversion in the history of Western thought, this philosophical development constitutes a frontal attack on biblical religion in which the intelligibility of reality is a major premise. For the first time in its long struggle against pagan philosophy, notes Dirk Jellema, the Christian Church is obliged to proclaim the Truth not merely against rationalism but against irrationalism as well ("Christianity and the 'New Faith,'" p. 11).

Even more astonishing is the fact that recent expositors of Christianity have borrowed leading features of this irrationalism in order to expound the Christian view of God in an antirational way. That many Christian scholars affirm God to be irrational is an exclusively twentieth-century phenomenon and is a byproduct of existential and dialectical fashions in modern philosophy.

Now and then in previous centuries Christian thinkers had insisted that God's essence is unknowable. While an irrationalistic tendency emerged periodically among the church fathers, their comments were mainly in the nature of *ad hominem* apologetic thrusts or pious formulations of God's incomprehensibility. Even the principle often attributed to Tertullian, *Credo quia absurdum* ("I believe what is absurd"), appears nowhere in his extant works. And the Protestant Reformers, despite their deep distrust of fallen human nature and unregenerate reasoning, like Augustine before them, emphasized that faith seeks understanding and that reason is an indispensable instrument of faith.

It remained for a cluster of modern neoorthodox theologians to propound irrationalism as a theory of Ultimate Reality and also as a theory of knowledge. To be sure, when they invoke the limits of human reason to neglect the ontological aspects of Christian theology, dialectical theologians tend more to ambiguity than to overt irrationalism in metaphysics. Yet their nonconceptual theory of divine disclosure and consequent rejection of revealed truths (or propositional revelation) leaves dialectical theology, I noted at midcentury, with but "a stuttering deity, a transcendental self who roams about in a super-rational sphere not fully subject to the categories of thought" (*The Protestant Dilemma*, p. 117). Writing at about the same time, L. Harold DeWolf insisted that no living theologian can be unqualifiedly called an irrationalist. He deplores, however, the "frequently recurrent and profound distrust of reason" that the neoorthodox questioning and dismissal of human reason in all its forms implies in regard to the living divine center of theology (*The Religious Revolt Against Reason*, pp. 19 f.). Such dispositions "to doubt the right of reason to judge between truth and error in affirmations of Christian belief" DeWolf describes as "developments of theological irrationalism . . . peculiar to the present age and . . . largely due to the critical work of Søren Kierkegaard" (*ibid.*, p. 21).

It was Kierkegaard with his religious epistemology explicitly devoted to the internal criticism of reason who set in motion an irrationalistic trend in Christian theology. Says Emil Brunner, "if anyone has ever used the slogan *credo quia absurdum*, it was Kierkegaard" (*Revelation and Reason*, p. 376), and ascribes first to Kierkegaard, and then to the dialectical theology influenced by him, the "solution" of the tension between reason and revelation by emphasizing their radical antithesis (*ibid.*, p. 310). It was Kierkegaard who fostered the existential rejection of rational and objective method in philosophy.

Kierkegaard depicts God as so totally other that no human concept or analogy appropriately represents him; he repeatedly assumes that man would have to be a part of God in order to know him rationally. Kierkegaard thus rules out both univocal and analogical knowledge of the self-revealed God. ". . . If man is to receive any true knowledge about the Unknown (God) he must be made to know that it is unlike him, absolutely unlike him. This knowledge the Reason cannot possibly obtain of itself. . . . It will therefore have to obtain this knowledge from God. But even if it obtains such knowledge it cannot understand it. . . . How should the Reason be able to understand what is absolutely different from itself?" (*Philosophical Fragments*, p. 37).

Kierkegaard nowhere affirms the irrationality of God, however. In some passages he even insists on God's complete (even if complex supra-human) rationality: "An existential system cannot be formulated. Does this mean that no such system exists? By no means. . . . Reality itself is a system—for God; but it cannot be a system for any existing spirit" (*Concluding Unscientific Postscript*, p. 107). Here Kierkegaard repudiates the rationalism of Hegel who by declaring that the Real is the rational, resolved all antinomies or paradoxes of divine-human thought pantheistically in an ultimate intellectual synthesis. But Kierkegaard, who rejects rational synthesis, demands total commitment even in the face of God's confrontation of human thought with paradoxes and logical contradictions.

Yet Kierkegaard considers only God truly rational and only God's work completely rational. But because even the best reason or man is skewed by finitude and perverted by sin, God's steadfast purpose seems irrational to him. In Kierkegaard's words, "the eternal essential truth is by no means in itself a paradox; but it becomes paradoxical by virtue of its relationship to an existing individual" (*ibid.*, p. 183). "By virtue of the relationship subsisting between the eternal truth and the existing individual, the paradox came into being. . . . Let us suppose that the eternal essential truth is itself a paradox. How does the paradox come into being? By putting the eternal essential truth into juxtaposition with existence. Hence when we posit such a conjunction within the truth itself, the truth becomes a paradox. The eternal truth has come into being in time: this is the paradox. . . . If the individual does not existentially and in existence lay hold of the truth, he will never lay hold of it" (*ibid.*, p. 187).

H. V. Martin is correct, therefore, in noting that for Kierkegaard man's existence in time precludes valid rational knowledge of God. Martin summarizes Kierkegaard as follows: "Eternal truth, as the conformity of thought and being, is not in itself paradoxical; for in God it is a unity. But in relation to an existing individual eternal truth must always become paradoxical, because for man in this world, thought and being are radically divided. His thought is one thing; his existing being is another. Therefore, it is existence in time which necessitates that eternal truth becomes paradoxical to man. It arises from the inevitable collision between thought and being in the existing individual. God alone can see all things *sub specie aeternitatis*. We as existing beings in this world can only view reality *sub specie temporis*. This means that in relation to eternal truth, logical thinking is useless, and that we must resort to existential thinking . . . ; eternal truth can never be objectivized by human thought. If ever man is to know eternal truth it can only be by a special Divine revelation, and even then, only in the form of an absolute paradox. Christianity proclaims such a revelation of God to man. . . . It is not a communication of knowledge in an intellectual sense which has to be apprehended by man through his thought and reason; it is a communication of existence or reality, to be apprehended by the act of faith" (*Kierkegaard: The Melancholy Dane*, pp. 64 f.).

"At the bottom of Kierkegaard's theological terminology," notes Michael

Wyschogrod, "lies an ontology, a distinction between pure Being and existence" (*Kierkegaard and Heidegger: The Ontology of Existence,* p. 82 f.). According to Kierkegaard, human reason cannot go beyond the apprehension of God as the great Unknown without colliding with the Paradox. The Unknown is known as existing, but as existing in such a way that reason has no capacity to apprehend it. As Kierkegaard would have it, "The Reason cannot advance beyond this point, and yet it cannot refrain in its paradoxicalness from arriving at this limit and occupying itself therewith" (*Philosophical Fragments,* p. 35). As H. V. Martin observes, in interpreting Kierkegaard, "The Unknown is the absolutely different and therefore to man the absolute Paradox; for reason cannot conceive an absolute unlikeness to itself. If man still tries to go farther, he can only attempt to conceive the unlikeness of the Unknown by means of categories of likeness extended to infinity. In other words, he conceives God in a human image, or in images of things comprehensible to him, adding to such comprehensible qualities the category of the infinite" (*The Melancholy Dane,* pp. 40 f.).

We have in Kierkegaard, then, a redefinition of the norm of rationality, one which excludes logical self-consistency and coherency and is abbreviated to God's own purpose; this purpose cannot be considered irrational, however, unless it were changing or simultaneously self-conflicting. But if, as Kierkegaard contends, no discoverable kinship exists between the rationality of man's mind and the truth as it is in God, then how can Kierkegaard offer any assurances whatever about God's purpose? If man can have no rational knowledge of the supernatural, then affirmation of God's rationality would seem to express simply human desire or volition rather than an authentic verdict of the intellect. If, as Kierkegaard tells us, no one can experience the Eternal except as paradox, on what basis can Kierkegaard himself affirm that God is rational and that eternal truth itself is not paradoxical? In view of his theory of knowledge Kierkegaard nowhere explains how he can speak of God, that is, of pure Being or eternity, without attributing paradox to this ontological realm also. By asserting God's complete rationality does not Kierkegaard fall into the contradiction of somehow "rationalizing" what is assertedly beyond the limits of reason, since man, he says, cannot experience the Beyond except in nonrational encounter?

Writers on the history of Western thought are only now elucidating the far-reaching import of this decisive revolt against reason in the name of Christian theology. Although professedly writing as a Christian scholar, Kierkegaard inaugurated a movement more deeply antirationalistic than anything to be found in theology or philosophy since the earliest Christian centuries. His support of antireason extended far beyond hostility to Hegelian rationalism and to the qualified rationalism of Kant; it is, in fact, irrationalistic in principle. Since Hegel's pantheism equated human minds with the Divine Mind, the result of his dialectic was rational synthesis. Kant, on the other hand, because of the supposed limits of human understanding, denied both divine revelation and metaphysical statements about the supernatural. But Kant was not an irrationalist. He based his disavowal that human reason grasps the supernatural not on the premise that ultimate reality or that knowledge as such is inherently contradictory, but rather on the human knower's inability to attain genuine knowledge of the metaphysical world. Despite his emphasis on the limits of human reason, Kant saw the categories of thought as structural elements in a knowledge-situation that is identical for all experiencing subjects; that is, all knowledge is universally valid, and truth is not suspended upon individual judgment or subjective response. But Kierkegaard, by asserting both divine revelation and irrationalism, inaugurated an epoch of theological irrationalism. The ultimately real world, says Kierkegaard, cannot be grasped by reason, cannot be comprehended intellectually, but must be grasped in passionate decision.

Behind these views, as D. C. Macintosh observes, are the assumptions that "the real is irrational and the irrational is the real," and that "neither experience nor rational reflection can serve to give us either real religious knowledge or positive religious truth. . . . The same irrationalistic prepossession determines the interpretation of revelation" (*The Problem of Religious Knowledge*, p. 330).

Kierkegaard's driving antirationalism even requires that God be "wholly other" and "absolutely unlike" man (*Philosophical Fragments*, p. 37). Since the total otherness of God in Kierkegaard's view is deliberately intended to affirm God's complete unlikeness to any qualities predictable of humanity, he seems to disallow every scriptural affirmation about God including the declaration that God is our Father. The outcome of such theological negation can only be not simply the total otherness of God but his complete unknowability.

Voicing the possibility that man's nature does involve a religious a priori (Kierkegaard discarded this possibility), Rudolf Otto referred spiritual experience not to a rational a priori, but to irrational intuition. Man has a nonrational capacity, says Otto, for intuitively feeling the presence of a transcendent, mysterious, "wholly other" reality: a *mysterium tremendum et fascinosum* (cf. *Das Heilige*). Otto's view could not resist the rising tide of dialectical and existential theology that inundated Europe after World War I because like it he also minimized the rational aspects of the *imago Dei* in man and basically identified religious experience as mystery. Commenting on Otto's premise that the religious reality is thus "wholly other," Macintosh observes that the Divine may therefore be defined "only in negative terms, and it tends to become an object of superstitious dread, divested of all ideal spiritual qualities" (*The Problem of Religious Knowledge*, p. 302).

Swedish theologians influenced by Kierkegaard included Gustaf Aulén, who expounds the idea of *Deus absconditus*, the hidden God, along antiintellectual lines. Aulén characterized God as the Unfathomable. He asserts that "If you would try to say what revelation may add to the knowledge of God reached through reason, you would be speaking of another God than the God of the Christian faith" (in *Revelation*, John Baillie, ed., pp.

275 ff.). Aulén contends that God is hidden, in the sense that we must not interpret his nature and ways according to our own imaginings and apart from his self-revelation. Furthermore, he states that we must distinguish our faith-view from any kind of rational world-view; the latter he deplores as "unwarranted human intrusion into the divine mystery." For Aulén divine revelation is itself unfathomable; as God's disclosure progresses, mystery not only remains but increases (cf. Edgar M. Carlson, *The Reinterpretation of Luther,* pp. 147 ff.). "The idea of 'the hidden God,' " writes Aulén, "does not mean merely that the understanding of faith has its insurmountable limitations. . . . That which faith comprehends is likewise unfathomable, and the revelation itself is inscrutable. . . . The unfathomable . . . which faith perceives is by its nature incomprehensible even to faith" (*The Faith of the Christian Church,* pp. 98 ff.). "The divine revelation is a revelation of God's 'essence,' " says Aulén, "but at the same time it confronts faith with the Unfathomable . . . . Faith beholds the revealed God as the Unfathomable, the 'hidden' God . . . . The more God reveals himself and the deeper faith looks into the mystery of his divine heart, the more He appears as the Unfathomable" (*ibid.,* pp. 46 f.).

As European and American Protestantism succumbed to Liberalism (widely encouraged by Hegelian pantheism), twentieth-century reaction against theological rationalism fed on Kierkegaard's irrationalism. What resulted was the theology of paradox, or dialectical theology, which Karl Barth fostered on the Continent. Rejecting Hegel's misrepresentation that man and the world are the rational externalization of the Absolute mind, dialectical theologians revolted against reason itself, considering it less important than personal decision for grasping ultimate reality. Barth's early writings deprecated the role of reason and widened the inroads of irrationalism. Emil Brunner, Rudolf Bultmann and others followed suit. In various ways, these theologians reflected the philosophical influence also of Martin Heidegger, whose perspective Barth later actually repudiated. In some passages Brunner disowns Kierkegaard's total antithesis between revelation and reason as well as his complete rejection of reason as an instrument of theological knowledge (*Revelation and Reason,* p. 58). In *The Divine-Human Encounter* Brunner tells us, nonetheless, that the knowledge of God derived from revelation does not require true ideas and propositions. Indeed, in Brunner's words, "God can . . . speak his Word to a man even through false doctrine" (cf. *Wahrheit als Begegnung,* p. 88). Elsewhere he tells us that God is incomparable and cannot be known (*The Christian Doctrine of God,* p. 117). "The God of thought *must* differ from the God of revelation" (*ibid.,* p. 136). "This one who is Free can never be known by way of thought—for only the Necessary can be known thus, but never the Free" (*ibid.,* p. 144).

Although Karl Barth expounded the notion of *Deus absconditus* more cautiously than many later neoorthodox scholars, and modified his views in a futile effort to counteract theological existentialism, Barth more than any other theologian was responsible for encouraging the notion of irrational revelation in Euro-American thought. While in his exposition of

God as naturally inconceivable and unknowable the role of irrationalism is less metaphysical than epistemological, Barth nonetheless frustrates his dogmatics by insisting that God's revelation involves no valid truths about God as he objectively is.

Barth's early writings rule out all ontic statements on the premise that nondialectical propositions belong only to abstract or speculative metaphysics. We must never identify God "with anything which we. . . conceive . . . as God" (*The Epistle to the Romans,* p. 331). By maintaining that "even after the revelation man cannot know God, for He is always the unknown God" (p. 53), Barth emphasizes not only divine transcendence, but also the very inconceivability of God. In the first edition of *The Doctrine of the Word of God* (1927) Barth deplores all theological ontology as illicit objectification of God and rules out all transphenomenal religious knowledge or knowledge of God-in-himself. He declares God to be not only unknowable but even unthinkable (*Church Dogmatics,* I/1, pp. 206 f.). Barth criticizes Schleiermacher for claiming direct experience of the inmost center of God's act; this he does on the ground that dogmatic theology, as Barth then asserted, does not deal with God himself. Even Barth's revised *Church Dogmatics* (1932, Eng. tr. 1936) explicitly affirms not only "the inadequacy of knowledge of the revealed God" but also "the inconceivability of God" (I/1, p. 426).

In his later writings Barth is less irrationalistic, however. God is affirmed to be an object of knowledge. God's revelation in Christ the Word, says Barth, provides a basis for genuine ontological statements.

Barth's dialectical epistemology (which disallowed valid truths about God) had kept him from deriving the content of special divine revelation from Scripture. By what alternative would Barth then escape the predicament of paradox and profess genuinely to comprehend God's very being? Barth's work *Anselm: Fides Quaerens Intellectum* (1931) is now often regarded as "the bridge" between the earlier and later editions of his *Dogmatik.* Here Barth views faith as a call to cognitive understanding.

Although this did not dominate his theology, even Barth's earlier writings incorporate an interest in genuine knowledge of God. He clearly asserts that, as he sees it, the Word of God is not irrational. He scorns Rudolf Otto's 'Idea of the Holy' as a spurious rival: "Whatever else it may be, (it) is at all events *not* to be regarded as the Word of God, for the simple and patent reason that it is the numinous, and the numinous is the irrational. . . ." (*Church Dogmatics,* I/1, p. 153). In some passages Barth not only concedes but even stresses that the experience of God's Word is a personal communication that includes the reason (*Church Dogmatics,* I/1, p. 234); that God speaks in intelligible language (I/1, pp. 152 f.); and that divine revelation conveys information (I/2, pp. 29 f.). Faith does not suspend the subject-object relationship, Barth insists, nor does it attain unity with God at some irrational interior level of human consciousness (II/1, p. 57). "The Word of God . . . is a rational and not an irrational event" (I/1, p. 153). "The form in which reason communicates with reason, person with person, is language. . . ." (II/1, p. 57). "Language or speaking stands in correlation to hearing, understanding, and obeying" (I/1, p. 154). Barth even writes that "God reveals himself in propositions by means of language and human language at that . . . . Thus the personality of the Word of God is not to be played off against its verbal character. . ." (I/1, p. 156).

Barth ranges himself also against modern efforts to exclude and to discredit the intellect as a center of possible experience of the Word of God (I/1, pp. 231 f.). He speaks of "the extraordinary polemic which it has been the fashion in recent years to wage against the so-called 'intellect' of man, his powers of comprehension and thought, as a center of possible religious experience of the Word of God" (I/1, p. 231). Barth thinks it notorious that "on the retreat before modern agnosticism" Christian faith should "hit upon this extraordinary judgment" that man is guilty of perverse self-determination particularly in the act of thought. Precisely because the Word of God "is quite literally language, not ultimately but primarily and predominantly so," Barth insists, the communication of the Word of God to man "must at least also involve a claim upon the intellect, and the experience of it must at least involve the co-option of the intellect." Barth even warns that "the anti-intellectualism of modern theology . . . must inevitably end in disillusionments" and suggests that it involves "a restriction of possible experience of the Word of God at its most crucial point which might very soon mean complete denial of it" (I/1, pp. 231 f.).

Barth cautions, however, that this polemic is not intended to establish the special competency of reason in religious experience; its purpose, rather, is to assure a place for reason alongside other anthropological centers that the Word of God addresses. "Determination of a man's existence by the Word of God . . . may equally well be regarded as a determination of feeling, as of will or of intellect; psychologically considered in the concrete instance," says Barth, "it may even actually be more the one than the other. But in substance, it is definitely a determination of the whole self-determining man" (ibid., p. 233). The Word of God, Barth concedes, is "communication from person to person, from mind to mind, spirit, a rational event, the Word of truth, because it is directed to man's ratio, by which, of course, we are not to understand the intellect alone, but the intellect at least also and not last of all" (ibid., p. 234). Indeed, insofar as so-called special centers of possible religious experience "are claimed at all as human possibilities, they are, in the comprehensive sense of the concept, rational possibilities" (ibid., p. 232).

For Barth, moreover, true faith includes also the actuality of cognition of God; faith, in fact, makes knowledge possible (ibid., p. 261). Faith expresses more than knowledge but it includes knowledge (ibid., p. 262). Christ the Word gives himself as object to faith (ibid., p. 263).

Barth then notes that in Anselm's Proslogion the hiddenness of God is due not to the metaphysical inconceivability of God but to man's sin (ibid., p. 264). To say that faith and God are correlative can be easily misunderstood (Barth approvingly quotes Luther: "Whoso hath faith and hath not the Word, believeth like Turks and Jews. . . . Word and faith are given together in wedlock . . . " [*ibid.*, pp. 266 f.]). Barth agrees with Luther that faith "has its ground and its truth and its measure . . . beyond itself in its object in Christ or in the Word of God" (*ibid.*, p. 268). By interpreting faith as *fiducia* (trust, confidence), he asserts, the Reformers and the Old Protestants did not push the reality of faith "out of the object of faith into the believing subject." Against some modern interpreters Barth declares "with certainty" that "even in the early period of the Reformation none of its responsible leaders took . . . seriously for a single minute" any proposal "to exclude from faith the element of *notitia* or *assensus*, i.e., the element of knowledge, to conceive of faith as pure trust, which is intellectually without form, or, in view of its intellectual form, indifferent, as any kind of trust in any kind of thing to make the object of faith problematic and to transfer the reality of faith to the believing subject. . . ." In brief, *fiducia* is trust in God's mercy which meets us in the objectivity of the Word only when it is also *notitia* and *assensus*, although the latter by themselves would not be faith at all but merely *"opinio historica* which even the godless may have" (*ibid.*, p. 269). In connection with its object, faith is not to be regarded (contrary to G. Wobbermin, *Wort Gottes*, p. 10) as " 'subordinately' also *notitia* and *assensus*," for *fiducia* presupposes grounds for relying on its object, and signifies the connection of faith with its object no less than do *notitia* and *assensus* (*ibid.*, pp. 269 f.).

For all that, Barth moves only part way from critical to positive theology. Although he now grants that the "logico-grammatical configuration of meaning" is present both to belief and to unbelief, he nonetheless insists that the religious Reality itself is present only to belief. Barth distinguishes this logical configuration from knowledge of God. Theological theses, he insists, are so inadequate to their object that no identity can be affirmed between the propositional form and its object; that is, we have concepts only of objects that are not identical with God (*Church Dogmatics*, II/1, p. 17). Despite the later Barth's greater emphasis on analogy than on dialectic, Barth still sidesteps conceptual knowledge of God. In the last resort, he refuses to regard revelation and reason as correlative in any primary sense.

Barth asks: "Where do we find the veracity in which we apply to God human words which as such are inadequate to describe him? . . . Does there exist a simple parity of content and meaning when we apply the same word to the creature on the one hand and to God's revelation and to God on the other?" (II/1, p. 224). Barth denies a simple parity not because God's revelation stipulates which concepts or concepts and words definitively apply to him, but rather because God's "hiddenness" precludes any such identity. Nor is this gulf to be overcome by a Thomistic doctrine of analogy which projects divine "similarity, partial correspondence and agreement" with the creaturely (II/1, p. 225). "God is not an object comparable to other objects" (II/1, p. 226). Yet God's own revelation, Barth adds, can posit himself as a comparable object and thereby make use of analogy as an instrument to express not parity or disparity but similarity, a similarity that revelation authorizes as God participates in our thought and language. "Between our views, concepts and words, and God as their object," says Barth, "there exists, on the basis of the revelation of God, the relationship of analogy, of similarity, of partial correspondence and agreement" (II/1, p. 227).

But how does this partial correspondence and agreement arise? Barth disallows any doctrine of the divine image that on the basis of creation endows man with categories of reason and morality by which he can know God. He likewise disallows general divine revelation, with its orthodox emphasis that God reveals himself universally to the mind of man through external nature and history. When Barth insists that partial correspondence and agreement arise only on the basis of God's revelatory activity, so that our "concepts and words . . . for all their unsuitability . . . can still be correct and true" (II/1, p. 227), it is highly important to note that the creative act establishing this appropriateness (II/1, p. 228) is an internal, individual, sporadic act, an act that involves no divine communication of valid, universally sharable propositions, but exists only in personal obedient response to God's inner confrontation. In his self-revelation God "causes the miracle to happen by which we come to participate in the veracity of His revelation, and by which our words become true descriptions of Himself" (II/1, p. 229). Barth can therefore reconcile all that he says about the veracity of knowledge of God with his continuing insistence on God's incomprehensibility (II/1, p. 233). The sporadic creative act whereby God enables our concepts to become adequate for knowing him is none other than the sporadic internal act of divine grace on the occasion of penitent response; it is bounded fore and aft by the hiddenness of God (II/1, p. 244). In this way Barth subsumes his whole discussion of the veracity of God under the correlation of revelation and grace defined in dialectical context.

Despite his verbal assurance therefore that theological theses and propositions are finally "adequate" to their object, Barth does not assign reason an adequate role in the knowledge of God. Correspondence and congruity between our theological predications and the self-revealed religious object do not, after all, turn out to be a matter of universally valid truths. The correspondence and congruity emerge only in subjective decision, assertedly as an internal miracle of divine grace. But evangelical orthodoxy does not depict truth about God as first created in the mind of the believer by the gift of saving faith. Regeneration itself involves a response to previously known truth about God, truth against which the sinner in his unregenerate state had maintained an attitude of revolt.

In asserting correspondence and congruity Barth explicitly excludes epistemological identity between God's revelation to our minds and our knowledge of God as he objectively is in himself. God is still represented as standing in cognition "between" positive and negative attribution and judgment. Parity is not univocity. Barth's denial of univocal knowledge of God therefore remains; not even by the miracle of faith does the believer possess such univocal knowledge. Nor, if a miracle is required to assure correspondence between our ideas and the religious object, is it clear why this miracle needs to be a recurring sporadic phenomenon, instead of one original divine act that equips man by creation for a rational knowledge of the Creator. Despite all of Barth's verbal stress that revelation involves the miracle of understanding, his theology does not convincingly transcend the gulf that isolates human reason from knowledge of God-in-himself.

F. W. Camfield also denies the objectivity of divine revelation. He is motivated not simply by a pious avoidance of rationalism, as he professes, but rather by an unjustifiable bias against reason as a medium of revelation. "Speak of revelation in the most objective way conceivable," Camfield tells us, "we are yet unable to regard it from any purely objective point of view." "It is not a body of truth which we can, as it were, sit down before, and proceed from our side to examine and assimilate, so that the two acts, the giving and the receiving, might be considered entirely apart from one another. The conception of revelation as purely objective in this sense, leads to orthodoxy where a body of statement purporting to be the truth of God is accepted on the authority of Church or Bible and defended on more or less rationalistic grounds. Orthodoxy is constantly driven to come to terms with rationalism, because it is itself an intellectualist thing; it is addressed to the rational understanding and demands the assent of the reason as such. . . . But orthodoxy can never be on comfortable terms with reason, because its subject-matter is transcendent and miraculous. . . ." In these circumstances the Holy Spirit is "not, as such, the truth," Camfield continues, but "some supernatural power which enables a man to accept a body of doctrine whose nature is intellectual and rational" (*Revelation and the Holy Spirit,* pp. 227 f.). Why the Holy Spirit cannot be "the Spirit of Truth" Camfield does not make clear; indeed, on Camfield's premises, Christian theology runs the risk of losing not only revealed doctrines but the Spirit of God as well.

We do not insist that orthodoxy has no dangers, but they are hardly the dangers that Camfield imagines. That faith may degenerate into assent to propositions about God, or that less importance may be assigned to a living relationship between God and man than to doctrinal purity, is always a present danger. The cure for such danger is not, however, as Robert McAfee Brown thinks along with Camfield, in fleeing to an unorthodox view that no longer conceives of revelation in propositional terms (*P. T. Forsyth: Prophet for Today,* p. 48). The cure, rather, is orthodoxy (that is, to realize that such deviations are themselves condemned by the biblical view of faith; sound doctrine prescribes the requirement of sound behavior).

While he refuses to speak of revelation "with pure objectivity," Camfield at the same time hesitates to speak of it "with pure subjectivity." Revelation, he tells us, is "not simply an experience within the soul which finds intellectual and rational expression as a body of truth. . . . If revelation be identical with experience, the truth element is always secondary and relative. . . . But revelation is truth. The Spirit is not a mere experience from which truth may be deduced—der Geist ist die Wahrheit (Barth)" (Camfield, *Revelation and the Holy Spirit,* p. 228). If Camfield intends simply to avoid confusing revelation with inner spiritual experiences which we rationalize, then this is commendable indeed. But his intention is much wider. He rules out even the possibility that rational divine disclosure can be addressed to man through the intellect even to chosen prophets and apostles. "What is given to us in revelation is neither belief as such, nor experience as such, but God Himself in personal action, that is, as we have seen God Himself in address to us. . . . We cannot take revelation as a datum, a fact of history or a truth of reason, or a state of experience, and then give it a value which we call revelation. We are ourselves personally involved and wholly involved, and involved in constant crisis and decision. We do not postulate, and we do not evaluate, and we do not rationalize, we respond" (*ibid.*, p. 231). Revelation is therefore addressed to the will, but not to or through the mind of man.

Many other scholars have made major concessions to the irrationalistic trend in twentieth-century theology.

Although Edgar S. Brightman allows a far greater role to reason as an instrument of religious truth than did Kierkegaard, the Boston personalist assigns to the nature of God a nonrational "given" as well as a rational structure. L. Harold DeWolf remarks, "Brightman sacrifices the complete rationality of God in order to defend the adequacy of human reason," whereas "Kierkegaard defends the complete rationality of God by admitting the inadequacy of human reason" (*The Religious Revolt Against Reason*, p. 96). Neither Kierkegaard's nor Brightman's formulation is acceptable.

Alfred North Whitehead's metaphysics also embraces elements of ultimate irrationality. For Whitehead God is indeed the Principle of Concretion, the ultimate reason why each thing is what it is. Yet he thinks "no reason can be given" for the particular limitation that God imposes on reality. "God is not concrete, but He is the ground for concrete actuality" (*Science and the Modern World*, pp. 249 f.). Despite his emphasis, therefore, on God's nature as the ground of rationality, Whitehead's distinction between God's "primordial nature" and his "consequent nature" compromises God's complete rationality. Whitehead's metaphysics is more Platonic than Christian in orientation (cf. A. W. Levi, *Philosophy and the Modern World*, pp. 525, 529).

More rationalistic in his theology than Barth and many mediating modern scholars, however, is Paul Tillich. In his early writings Tillich designated God as "the Unconditioned-Transcendent," "the Abyss of Truth" (cf. *The Interpretation of History* and *Religiose Verwirklichung*). In an abrupt departure from the traditional exposition of the Christian doctrine of God, he asserts "there is no special ontology which we have to accept in the name of Biblical message" (*Biblical Religion and the Search for Ultimate Reality*, p. 85). Yet Tillich correlates his theological method with philosophical-ontological affirmations about ultimate Being more than do many dialectical philosophers. In his exposition of Being as transcending all differentiation and all categories, interpreters discern a kinship to the ontological tradition of Parmenides, Plotinus, Eckhart, Boehme, and Schelling, and particularly to neo-Platonic mysticism (cf. Daniel D. Williams, "Tillich's Doctrine of God," p. 41, 50). Tillich professedly resists "metaphysically constructive" expositions and disowns any rational attempt to discern the structure of Being (*Systematic Theology*, Vol. I, p. 247). He therefore rejects the theistic view of God. He contends nonetheless that ontology points to Being itself, and in view of this ontological vision Tillich promotes a mystical encounter with the divine.

Reinhold Niebuhr, in *The Nature and Destiny of Man*, initially stresses the importance of reason, but then goes on to deny reason any role as the arbiter of religious truth. "The religious faith through which God is apprehended cannot be in contradiction to reason in the sense that the ultimate principle of meaning cannot be in contradiction to the subordinate principle of meaning which is found in rational coherence," he first assures us. But then he says, "Religious faith cannot be simply subordinated to reason or made to stand under its judgment. When this is done the reason which asks the question . . . has made itself God" (Vol. 1, pp. 165 f.). While Niebuhr's first statement properly implies the invalidity of faith that contradicts reason, the second statement implies, as L. Harold DeWolf notes, that faith is unanswerable to rational evaluation (*The Religious Revolt Against Reason*, p. 30).

For Karl Jaspers "the old proposition that God is the Truth . . . is empty and can only be felt by me historically. Here, where I cannot penetrate, truth can retain no thinkable sense" (*Reason and Existenz*, p. 105). Jaspers declares that "all communication must be thought of as canceled in Transcendence," and likewise "all conceivability in general." For Jaspers Christian faith represents the triumph of nonreason over reason, the transmutation of the nonrational into Providence, the expression of fundamental beliefs in irrational antinomies (*ibid.*, p. 21). While he thinks philosophy's proper task is to strive to change the nonrational and counterrational into a form of reason, he holds that "both the defiant will and honest mind . . . recognize and assert the unconquerable non-rational" (*ibid.*, p. 19). Through reason man sights "something which is only communicable in the form of contradiction and paradox. Here a rational alogic arises, a true reason which reaches its goal through the shattering of the logic of the understanding" (*ibid.*, pp. 111 f.).

For Jaspers man's reason lacks "assured stability" and is "constantly on the move." No sooner does reason gain a position but reason "presses on to criticize it" (*Reason and Anti-Reason in Our Time*, p. 39). "The incompleteness . . . of truth disappears in the presence of Transcendence" (*ibid.*, p. 43). Jaspers does not expound this larger transcendent world in terms of divine rationality and meaning. However, by depriving man of fixed ideas, Jaspers in effect denies man's created rationality (*ibid.*, pp. 50 ff.). Despite an existential emphasis on personal decision, Jaspers declares that as men we are "again and again . . . faced with the possibility of becoming ourselves through Reason" (*ibid.*, p. 69), and that "reason dares to rely upon itself in a world of Un-Reason and in the face of its constant perversion into Anti-Reason" (*ibid.*, p. 65). He even laments the fact that "it looks

today as if Reason . . . is, paradoxically enough, being pushed into isolation.
. . . It is as though, without any prearranged plan, all the powers of the
mind were instinctively allied, because they have only one thing in common, the urge to make Reason disappear and to put some grand absurdity
in its place" (*ibid.*, pp. 76 f.).

That its derogators seem at times to plead the cause of reason, at least
on the surface, is one of the curious features of contemporary irrationalism.
Antirationalism currently champions a "new understanding" of "the significance of reason based on existential rather than intellectual validation,"
Jaspers comments. But Jaspers and other dialectical and existential philosophers consider any commitment of antireason to fixed intellectual constructions a betrayal of truth. Jaspers pleads the cause of reason, not in
behalf of intellectual truth, but in behalf of existential commitment; indeed, he deplores "the collapse of the breadth of Reason" into "mere intel-
lectualism" (*ibid.*, p. 86). "Myth is the indispensable language of
transcendent truth" (*ibid.*, p. 70), he tells us. The faith of Reason is "different in character from all the other faiths which are determined by denomi-
national creeds, objective certainties and guarantees. . . . It has nothing
tangible to offer" (*ibid.*, p. 79).

The inner development of both twentieth-century philosophy and theology attests that loss of the rational God and of the rational facets of the
imago Dei in man leads to the surrender of reason as a criterion of reality.
Having substituted speculative rationalism for rational revelation, modern
Western philosophy, despite its initial optimistic reliance on unaided human reason, swiftly declined to skepticism. Many tendencies supply evidence of this dismal outcome: Nietzsche's exposition of world evolution
in terms of irrationalism; Marx's denial of objective truth; William James's
reduction of truth to whatever "works"; the commitment of many pragmatists to successful biological adjustment; John Dewey's claim that neither
empirical science nor any alternative provides data about the "real nature"
of things. The main tenet of naturalistic evolution, namely, that evolution
explains intellect (rather than that intellect accounts for evolution), won
over even some idealist philosophers and some theologians of professed
supernaturalist loyalties. Neither modernist nor neoorthodox expositors
of Christian theology resisted such evolutionary speculations; indeed, many
eagerly promoted theories of the late emergence of reason. Even professedly biblical theologians joined openly anti-Christian scholars to champion irrationalism in the name of piety. To avoid a completely naturalistic
outcome, the former appealed to "paradoxical" or "dialectical" revelation,
and brashly advertised such theories as a return to the theology of the
Protestant Reformers.

The antireason philosophy and theology of the recent past made still
another boldly unscriptural concession, one that Augustine, Anselm and
Calvin would have deplored. By dismissing the categories of reason and
the forms of logic as mere accidents of historical evolution, the antireason
crusaders implied that human ways of thinking could as readily have taken
a fundamentally different direction. If this is the case then human thought

can no longer be confidently said to grasp "the real world," or to be universally valid (in all time and space). Surrendered was the ontological significance of reason, that is, the conviction that reason is the essential foundation of ultimate reality. Dismissal of the rationality of God therefore not only engendered the retreat of reason's role in religious experience, but also discouraged the coherent integration of experience in general in terms of world-and-life view, and called off the search for a comprehensive explanatory principle. The factor that inevitably decides the significance of reason in human experience is whether the role of reason is ontological or whether it is merely conventional—in short, whether ultimate reality is intrinsically rational or not.

Max Horkheimer answers with a resounding "yes," the question whether contemporary industrial culture contains defects that vitiate the notion of rationality (*Eclipse of Reason,* p. 4). To reduce the reasonable simply to the useful and subjective, he says, signals the profound loss of "a diametrically opposite view of reason as a force not only in the individual mind but also in the objective world." Horkheimer attributes the present crisis of reason to the fact that modern thinking either regards such rational objectivity as inconceivable or simply negates it as a delusion (*ibid.,* p. 7). Western man has debased reason into merely an instrument for promoting efficiency, and not for comprehending reality (*ibid.,* p. 9). "The weak modern view of reason readily surrenders the concept of religious truth, and is therefore constantly in danger of surrendering to the 'irrational'" (*ibid.,* p. 13). It is not surprising that in our generation theology has conferred Christian respectability on the category of myth. Although all five New Testament uses of the term myth are derogatory, myth is inoffensive to the theologian who dismisses the ultimacy of rational truth.

19.
The Knowability of God

THE GREAT CREEDS OF CHRISTENDOM, Orthodox, Catholic and Protestant, all affirm the incomprehensibility of God. Finite man cannot fully fathom the mysteries of creaturely life let alone exhaustively define the nature and activity of the infinite God. Only God totally knows his own being.

God's incomprehensibility in no way implies God's unknowability, however. An unsound theological premise underlies mystical speculations about God's ineffability and pervades also Kant's critical philosophy, Herbert Spencer's agnosticism, and dialectical and existential theories. All these speculations locate the supernatural outside the categories of cognitive reason.

The scriptural view of God's incomprehensibility contradicts all such speculative jargon about divine unknowability. To say that we can have no knowledge whatever of God's essence, or that we can know God only in his relations to us (but not as he is in himself), or that our knowledge of God is merely regulatory or practical, exaggerates the limits of religious knowledge. As Robert Flint cautions, "We are apt to conceive of the Divine incomprehensibility as if it were an attribute of the Divine nature itself" (*On Theological, Biblical and Other Subjects,* pp. 377 ff.).

We must not, of course, ignore the antecedent importance of God's self-knowability, that is, his knowledge of himself. But our knowledge of God is, as Barth observes, "in consequence of God knowing himself—the Father knowing the Son and the Son the Father by the Holy Spirit of the Father and the Son" (*Church Dogmatics,* II/1, p. 67). Yet we may question Barth's further comment: "Because He is first and foremost knowable to Himself as the triune God, He is knowable to us as well." The foundation of knowledge of God exists in God's own being, but in principle there is no contradiction between saying man cannot know God and God can know himself.

Whether or not God is knowable by man is solely a matter of God's sovereign revelation.

By God's incomprehensibility, says Hodge, we mean not that God is unknowable, but that we do not have "complete and exhaustive knowledge." Nevertheless, Hodge stresses, "our knowledge, as far as it goes, is true knowledge" (*Systematic Theology*, I/337 ff.).

We do not speak of the knowability of God as only an abstract possibility, however, nor are we left to metaphysical speculation to defend the possibility of truly knowing God; in and through divine revelation God himself actualizes the possibility of knowing him. Mankind is divinely made for the knowledge and service of God. God has therefore allayed all reticence and all fear of impropriety in man's seeking to know the Creator-Redeemer. All Scripture supports and encourages our expectation of truly knowing God and his will and purpose. Too timid, we think, was Arminius's assertion that man can know the nature of God "in some slight measure," or only in a degree "infinitely below what it is (in) itself" ("Disputation on 'The Nature of God,'" p. 434). Donald Bloesch even asserts that "the true God lies beyond the confines of man's conception" (*Essentials of Evangelical Theology*, Vol. 1, p. 26) and completely ignores any exposition of God's intellectual attributes. Although we cannot know God exhaustively, we can know him truly and adequately. Although we cannot know him apart from our finitude, we can know him as creatures divinely intended to apprehend their Creator. Although we can know him only through the forms of our understanding, these divinely created forms convey reliable knowledge about God.

To be sure, both theology and philosophy are exasperatingly full of expositions of God's nature that can hardly be dignified as genuine or trustworthy. Secular thought may even be seen as a succession of running attacks by energetic thinkers on views of Ultimate Reality alternative to their own. From this perspective one can understand Feuerbach's negative judgment that theologians and philosophers simply construct gods in their own image. The emergence of heretical ideas of God even in Christian circles (Barth unhesitatingly applies the term "heresy" to Protestant modernism, and Van Til decries even Barth's early alternative as *The New Modernism*) warns us against the everpresent danger of distorting the divine. Not even invoking Scripture guarantees proper conclusions about the self-revealed God; Hobbes the philosophical materialist, for example, and Hegel the philosophical idealist, both quote the Bible to support profoundly unbiblical views. Not even well-intentioned evangelical theologians necessarily and always enter into the mind of Scripture even though they may begin with the proper premise that the Bible normatively defines the content of faith. The Gospel according to Carl Henry is sure to be less precise than the Gospel according to Paul; only God's inspired biblical exposition is authoritative. It is sheer delusion for any contemporary theologian, however devout or gifted, to think that he or she has fully mastered God's truth as God knows it. The competitive character of systematic theology even between the major branches of Christendom, and between and within particular denominations, constantly calls us back not to the commentaries of dedicated men and women, but to the authority of *the revealed Word of God.* Between supernatural revelation and inspired Scripture on the one hand and fallible interpretation on the other, remains a gulf that not even the Church of Rome actually bridges with its supposedly infallible popes and its assignment of an authoritative teaching role to the priestly hierarchy. The Spirit of God alone definitively communicates the propositional sense of the written Word through its grammatico-linguistic form, for the Spirit is both the author and interpreter of the Scriptures.

In adopting the Greek word *mustērion,* which in the mystery religions referred to secret rites of their initiates, the New Testament writers applied the term instead to God's once-hidden purpose *now disclosed* by special revelation (Matt. 13:11; Rom. 11:25; 1 Cor. 4:1, 15:51; Eph. 3:3–6; Col. 1:20).

A striking and unjustifiable transformation of the biblical idea of revealed mystery took place, however, when the classic theological sense of divine incomprehensibility was adjusted to eighteenth-century deistic, nineteenth-century agnostic, and twentieth-century dialectical and existential views. The Deists denied divine immanence; the post-Kantians stressed the inaccessibility of the supernatural to human reason; and numerous dialectical-existential theologians simply abandoned the quest for objective knowledge of reality. After Kantian Criticism substituted "practical" for "metaphysical" knowledge of God a number of liberal Protestant theologians made much of divine mystery. For recent philosophy the incomprehensibility of God implies that ultimate reality is not rational, and that prerational, subrational, nonrational, or irrational factors are most significant for experiencing the divine. In the mid-twentieth century, Rudolf Bultmann and his followers, while maintaining the inaccessibility of God, merged Heidegger's atheistic philosophy with a form of "existential revelation" in an effort to overcome agnosticism by relying on inner nonrational revelatory divine action. Although it stresses dialectical rather than existential revelation, much neoorthodox theology nonetheless deviates from Christian orthodoxy because it does not correlate God's incomprehensibility with universally sharable revelatory truths.

Neoorthodoxy inherited its bias against rational revelation from Protestant liberalism no less than from Kierkegaard. For Schleiermacher, the father of Protestant modernism, the religious ideas of Christianity were not a product of divine revelation but a byproduct of devout feeling. He thus isolated discussion of divine disclosure from the traditional Christian confidence that scriptural conceptions of God's nature and works are integral to God's self-revelation. Ritschl, no less then Schleiermacher, emphasized that we misconceive the nature of revelation if we suppose it to involve the supernatural communication of theoretical knowledge. In the period between Schleiermacher and Barth many influential liberal theologians followed suit in revolting against rational revelation. Julius W. H. Kaftan, for example, pontificated that revelation "cannot consist in a communication of doctrine" (*Dogmatik,* p. 14). The loss of rational revelation led promptly and logically to the loss of the self-revealing God.

Religious humanism soon characterized the early twentieth century, especially in America. Sentimental naturalists interpreted religious truth as
poetic myth. To think that one's religion is literally true George Santayana
considered a fanatic illusion, one that the Jews arrogantly invented and
bequeathed to the Christians and Moslems (*The Life of Reason,* pp. 214 f.).
Santayana's theory depends, of course, on his private claim to possess "the
truth" about religion, a claim he conceals beneath the notion that religious
affirmations are essentially poetic. He considers religious truth-claims an
illicit conversion of mythology into wisdom (*ibid.,* p. 208), claims which
biblical religion then reinforced by the double myth of special revelation
(p. 217).

It is now widely conceded that the twentieth-century emphasis on revelation as dynamic, ongoing, and nonintellectual first became prominent not
through a renewed study of biblical Christianity but rather through a venture into comparative religion led by Nathan Söderblom (*Uppenbarelsreligion*). Swedish theologian Ragnar Bring then applied this approach to
primitive Christianity. Reinforcement of the dynamic-dramatic theory of
revelation was then sought by relating it to the study of the New Testament
and to Luther's writings. To Luther's *The Bondage of the Will,* for example,
Bring ascribes his notion that the hidden God must be believed rather
than understood, and that reason is important to provide a rationally consistent account of God's activity (*Dualismen hos Luther,* p. 295). The God
of reason, he says, is directly opposed to the God of faith (*ibid.,* p. 137).

Swedish Luther-research scholars defined Christian revelation as God's
dynamic, ongoing, redemptive self-disclosure, and attributed this definition
to the Protestant Reformers. These expositors, including Einar Billing, and
more comprehensively and influentially Gustaf Aulén, wrongly burdened
Luther's theology with a view of God and revelation that was essentially
neo-Kierkegaardian. Luther's prominent emphasis on divine transcendence and revelation was made to accommodate a dynamic and nonintellectual view of God's nature and disclosure.

Edgar M. Carlson's volume on *The Reinterpretation of Luther* examines
the main aspect of this Swedish transformation of Luther's theology. Generally speaking, modern researchers disowned all efforts to find a rational
theological system in Luther's writings. While Luther's writings are obviously not orderly dogmatic expositions, they are hardly the work of an
irrationalistic dialectician as Friedrich Gogarten and others have unsuc-
cessfully tried to portray him. Those few passages in which Luther considers his theology valid although it lacks logical consistency, and in which
he views the absence of logical support as a further opportunity to exercise
faith (cf. *W.A.,* 18,633, 1.15 f.; 18,708, 1.1 f.), are hardly normative for the
entirety of his dogmatics. By first tagging the Reformer's dogmatics as
dynamic and nonsystematic and denying the coherence of his theology,
contemporary interpreters were then free to rearrange and restructure Luther's views in keeping with neoorthodox motifs, and to reorient his emphases around a supposedly nonintellectualist thrust. For "logical
coherence" the Swedish researchers substituted "existential coherence"

and thus subjected faith to an underlying spiritual reality devoid of rational system. For them "the unity and truth of faith excluded any possibility of rational systematization." As Carlson declared, faith now embraced what "can be stated only in terms that are logically exclusive, if not contradictory" (*The Reinterpretation of Luther,* pp. 169 f.). The antithesis between God and revelation on the one hand and reason on the other was ranged like the conflict between God and the devil.

Even Ragnar Bring was forced to concede that Luther's criticisms of reason pertain to man in a state of sin in which reason is perverted from an instrument of truth into an instrument of inordinate self-interest. In that case, as Carlson comments, statements of faith do not necessarily involve theoretical contradictions; the movement of divine revelation *toward man as sinner* explains its apparently paradoxical relation to human reason (*The Reinterpretation of Luther,* pp. 126 f.). Bring also contrasts Luther's understanding of paradox with that of Emil Brunner and Karl Heim.

Luther and Calvin objected only to the abuses of reason in religion, to its arrogance and distortion in the service of a hostile mentality. In this same sense the apostle Paul opposed secular philosophy (Col. 2:8) and knowledge falsely so-called (1 Tim. 6:20). Human reason cannot sit in judgment upon God's revelation, said Luther. Nonetheless he praised reason as a gift of God and honored it as the differentiating factor between man and beast. He approved Melancthon's *Erotemata Dialectices* (1547) which outlines the use of logic in approaching and reading the Scriptures.

Motivated more by devotional than by epistemological considerations some evangelical pietists have so exaggerated God's transcendence that they unwittingly jeopardize a genuine knowledge of God. A. W. Tozer, for example, finds a barrier to the knowledge of God not alone in man's finitude and sinfulness, but in God's ineffability as well. This ineffability, he writes, places "a great strain on both thought and language in the Holy Scriptures" (*The Knowledge of the Holy,* p. 14). Tozer approvingly quotes mystical and skeptical philosophers who affirm not simply the natural incomprehensibility of God, but also God's intrinsic inconceivability. While Tozer says that we know certain divine attributes by revelation, he asserts that these theological distinctions gained by "intellectual response to God's self-revelation" are "as far as the reasoning mind can go. . . . Exactly what He is He cannot tell us." Tozer certainly does not affirm the irrationality of God. But on the basis of Tozer's limiting premises, the Christian, even given special revelation, can make only inexact and inaccurate statements about God's nature and will.

Even though Claude Beaufort Moss insists that reason is God's gift to man for understanding divine revelation, he contends that the profoundest religious truths are antinomies that cannot be fully reconciled by reason. Quite in accord with historic Christian doctrine he affirms: "Reason is always to be treated with the greatest respect, because it is the possession of reason that makes us human beings; God has given us reason that we may understand His truth" (*The Christian Faith: An Introduction to Dogmatic Theology,* pp. 47 ff.). But Moss then reflects the alien influence of modern theories of language and knowledge by asserting that Christian mysteries "can only be stated symbolically," that dogmas must not be used as premises in a logical process.

The possibility of human knowledge of God himself and of his revealed purposes follows from God's rationality and from man's creation in the divine image. As Gordon Clark observes, "On the assumption that God created man in his own image, it cannot further be asserted that God is totally other and unlike. Though God is infinite and man finite, and even in spite of the intellectual blindness due to sin, a revealed religion must assert that man can know God" (*Thales to Dewey*, p. 207).

Barth in his early writings holds that God is *sui generis* (*Church Dogmatics*, II/1, p. 376), and implies a denial of any relevant similarity to man. To subsume God under a common genus would eliminate the self-revealing God of the Bible. But the fact that God cannot be subsumed under a higher category of being that he shares with other beings, does not mean, as Barth insisted, that no rational conception of God is possible. Barth employs the fact that we cannot subsume God under a more general concept to argue that no concept of God is more than a "pointer." For dialectical theologians all conceptions of God are rationalizations of a nonlogical, paradoxical communication of revelation. Their antipathy to propositional knowledge of God is rooted in a false dismissal of the possibility of metaphysical knowledge; it is not derived from the account that the biblical writers give of God's revelation to them, but represents the imposition of an extraneous and alien philosophy of religion upon the structure of Scripture. This alien philosophy asserts that God is logically inaccessible and consequently renounces the right to communicate coherent knowledge about him. To say that God is totally other leads consistently to the notion of God's unknowability. In later writings Barth rejects this premise of God's total otherness (cf. *The Humanity of God*, p. 42), but stops short of a satisfactory alternative view.

Skepticism about God's nature is inimical to the doctrine of the *imago Dei* unless one speculates, contrary to biblical theology, that man's fall into sin totally eradicated the divine image. In Calvin's words, "Now if the end for which all men are born and live, be to know God,—and unless the knowledge of God have reached this point, it is uncertain and vain,— it is evident, that all who direct not every thought and action to this end, are degenerated from the law of their creation" (*Institutes*, I, iii, 3).

The crucial issue is not simply finite man's capacity for forming concepts about a Supreme Being. Such conceptions, in fact, are found everywhere throughout the history of human thought. The real question, rather, is whether certain of man's conceptions of the supernatural accommodate trustworthy information about God and his purposes. The answer determines the validity and value of our rational concepts of the divine nature. If man bears the image of a rational God, and by creation is made for the knowledge and obedience of his Maker, then the scriptural representations of God, however tapered they may be to man's finite faculties, nonetheless provide human consciousness with truths that adequately depict the Creator.

Nineteenth-century theologian George Christian Knapp reminds us of the necessary centrality of reason in the service of God. Reason, he says, constitutes "the peculiar characteristic of humanity, and is that by which alone we are capable of religion. Reason alone can acknowledge and receive the truths of either natural and revealed religion and give them an influence upon the human will. It is therefore always mentioned with respect in the Bible; and the use of it, in the study and examination of religious truth, always recommended. Cf. Rom. 1:20; Psalm 19; Isaiah 40, 41" (*Lectures on Christian Theology*, p. 38).

Communication between God and man, insofar as it is intelligible, must be rational. God's self-revelation has a logically consistent character. So, too, if we are to know God and his will for us, we must use human concepts and words. No doubt a personal Spirit can relate himself to creatures in other ways than by the communication of words and thoughts. But if God desires to reveal truths to man, that revelation must take intelligible form. Christianity affirms that divine revelation, inspiration and illumination are rational activities; God uses thought and language to convey information about his nature and work and about man and his destiny. God's thought and language do not rest on wholly different principles than ours, or we could not confidently interpret anything he says, since what he says might then mean contrary or contradictory things. In that case Scripture loses all value as an intelligible verbal revelation.

Over against the widening disposition of contemporary liberal theologians to contrast redemptive revelation with rational disclosure, it is noteworthy that even Adolph Harnack conceded that rational disclosure is deeply identified with Christian theology. Harnack reminds us that Christianity correlates eternal life not only with forgiveness, but also with truth. Yet he considers the emphasis that the Lord of life is also the Father of truth to be a Hellenic theme which penetrated Palestinian Jewish theology (*History of Dogma*, Vol. 1, p. 170, n. 1). This verdict cannot be justified, however, for the theme is found not only in the early theology of the Apologists, but also in the earlier Didache (9:10), and in John's Gospel, as well as in the New Testament generally. "This is life eternal, that they might know thee the only true God, and Jesus Christ, whom thou hast sent" (John 17:3) is a fundamental postulate of the Christian religion; that he must be known aright for life abundant and life eternal is an emphasis integral to the Gospels. That God can be known, that divine revelation is rationally given and is to be rationally understood, is a basic presupposition of biblical theology.

20.
Man's Mind and God's Mind

KNOWLEDGE OF GOD is not a possibility that rests simply in man as an ingenious creature. Finite intelligence is not divine intuition; man's own intelligence is not an originating source of divine revelation. Man's intelligence is, however, as much a divine revelation as is nature in general—and more so. Man is a specially created rational-moral-spiritual creature made in the divine image, a responsible creature uniquely lighted by the Logos (John 1:9a). He is to think God's thoughts after him and is morally accountable for his knowledge of the truth and of the good.

As William Newton Clarke observes, "the differences between God and man are differences between beings that are essentially resemblant." Having made full allowance for the fact that God knows all truth intuitively and originally, that man is finite and bears the image of God only in certain respects, we must still affirm that sin introduces no metaphysical or epistemological changes that destroy the categories of human reason. It is not too much to say, as Clarke does, that "in having personality man must be the finite counterpart of the mind that conceived him" (*Can I Believe in God the Father?*, pp. 81, 105).

The Old Testament asserts that "In thy light shall we see light" (Ps. 36:9). It is only because of this hinterland relationship to the divine mind that humans know the truth about anything. The *nous* of God is not a mental faculty wholly different in kind from the *nous* of mankind in its content. Man not merely has the image of God but *is* the image of God.

To be sure, the renegade will rails against the truth of God and distorts truth about mankind and about the cosmos, especially in matters of morality. A distinction becomes necessary therefore between the manifestations of human reason as originally created when it fully reflected the content of divine revelation, reason as it is presumptuously and rebelliously used after the fall, and reason in the life of the regenerate Christian obediently dedicated to his Creator and Lord. The New Testament says of believers, ". . . we have the mind of Christ" (1 Cor. 2:16). Children of the Risen Lord know more propositional content about certain relationships and realities than do unregenerate persons, and seek to live in and by God's light. William Temple remarks: "The truth of things is what they are in the mind of God, and it is only when we act according to the mind of God that we are acting in accordance with reality" (*Basic Convictions,* p. 54).

The fact that human minds and God's mind—or that Christian minds and the mind of Christ—coincide in the knowledge of certain propositions does not, of course, equate God and mankind either pantheistically or existentially. To be "in the truth" is to appropriate the teaching of Scripture, Scripture given by the Spirit of Truth who recalled Jesus' earthly instruction to his disciples, who inspired the definitive apostolic exposition of Christ's atonement, resurrection and ascension (John 14:26), and who illuminates believers in their comprehension of biblical teaching.

The Supreme Reason makes human reason possible. Christian theology therefore connects the human faculty of reason not merely with our sense experience of the outer world, or with our subjective knowledge of an inner psychological world. Rather, it correlates man's reason also and above all else with the Divine intelligence. The Logos of God has endowed man with the logical forms of the mind. Secular philosophy, sociology and psychology give the impression that man's special glory is to unravel the intricacies of nature, to decipher complex human interrelationships, or to penetrate secrets of the inner conscious and subconscious life. But the Bible affirms that man's distinctive characteristic is his endowment with logical and moral categories, his responsible knowledge of God, and the spiritual union with God that is therefore a human possibility.

The rational-moral image that man bears by creation distinguishes him from all other earthly creatures. Although man is finite, human reason is metaphysically competent to know God and to comprehend supernatural revelation. Man's relationship with God does not bypass the anthropological center of reason, nor does it occur "beyond" or "outside reason." Reason involves man's necessary epistemological relationship to God and dependence on him. Our knowledge of God is not immediate but is mediated. Man is limited in knowledge and lacks intrinsic competence to acquire a proper understanding of the meaning and end of life. This obstacle is not absolute but conditional, however, since supernatural revelation can offset man's limitations.

The fall of man into sin does not wholly destroy the mind's objective competence. The fall surrenders man's reason to the service of an inordinate will, however, and greatly enlarges man's necessary dependence upon special divine revelation for reliable exposition of the nature and will of the living God.

The Supreme Reason has established human reason for the proximate goal of shared truth and for the ultimate goal of spiritual obedience. Man's supreme end is not merely to know God but to love, serve and enjoy him. Only in the obedient appropriation of revealed knowledge does man rise to his true and full dignity. The Protestant Reformers, like Augustine before them, in view of what the Bible teaches (cf. Rom. 1:20 f.; 2:14 f.) emphasize the divine constitution of the human mind for comprehending God's nature and will, and for communicating and communing with God.

Given the Christian concept that all truth is revelational, valid knowledge becomes possible only in view of man's relationship to the Divine Mind. W. P. Paterson states this fact succinctly: "Reason is an instrument for recognizing not for creating truth" (*The Rule of Faith,* p. 117).

The Logos of God is the source of all the substance and structures of created reality (John 1:3). To deny that the divine Logos originates the structural relations of the cosmos is to dispute the Creator's sovereignty. Modern philosophy improperly views the meaning-structure of the cosmos as merely a conventional human articulation; it regards this meaning-structure as simply the product of human thought. But the New Testament declares of Christ: "By him are all things (the universe) organized" (Col. 1:17, CFH).

Human knowledge as human activity has its ultimate ground in God. Such knowledge involves at once a knowledge of God, of the universe, and of human selves. Since man is by creation a psychosomatic entity, his knowledge involves intuition, religious faith, psycho-introspection and -extrospection, as well as sense perception. But what makes human knowledge ultimately possible is God's revelation of himself and of the universe he orders and in and through which he also makes himself known. God the creator and sustainer of all gives the cosmos its intelligibility and meaning and hence its human knowability. In Hendrik G. Stoker's words, "God reveals himself in his Word and works (our created universe); . . . he has created our universe or cosmos knowable; . . . he has endowed man with the acts and functions to know; . . . and he *sets man his calling* to know and to act upon it" ("Van Til's Theory of Knowledge," p. 30).

Man's knowledge is derivative and dependent. Without a revelatory consciousness of God, human self-consciousness would not be possible, nor would consciousness of the finite world of finite selves or of the divinely patterned finite universe.

Kant dissociated his defense of logic from the transcendent supernatural mind of God and held that man's own transcendental logical consciousness originates and produces the meaning-structure of the phenomenal world. The "creative human logos" thus replaces the Creator-Logos and becomes the *arche* or formative principle of the phenomenal world. Man's logical faculty supposedly furnishes all the universal principles necessary for conforming sense impressions into objects of knowledge. The origin and totality of meaning Kant considers immanent in the transcendental consciousness of man. Kant's loss of the Logos and hence of Logos-articulation of the source and ground of knowledge, involved his loss also of revelatory cosmic meaning. His denial of cognitive knowledge of an independently real world, his loss of logical connection between concepts, perceptions and independent reality, and his restriction of knowledge merely to the world as we perceive it, left Kant no justification for referring to any independent reality beyond sensory existence. In place of an independently real world he ended up with an unknowable and conjectural *Ding an sich.*·

The modern depreciation of reason found great encouragement in Kant's contention that man has no valid ontological knowledge of external reality. Despite this negation of ontological knowledge, Kant felt it necessary to account for the applicability of logic to experience and to the experienced world. But because he had already dismissed the significance of rationality for existence, it was difficult to retain the significance of rationality for knowledge. Kant's ill-conceived effort to avoid Humean skepticism actually enthroned man as the positer and determiner of truth and led indirectly to existentialism and positivism, views that reflect Kant's wedge between pure reason (cognition) and practical reason (postulation). Kant was unable to repair the growing cleft in the then current philosophy between reason and reality, being and value. The modern perpetuation and extension of that divide led finally to the rise of the apparently rival schools of existentialism and positivism. As William Barrett says, "Positivist Man and Existentialist Man are no doubt offspring of the same parent epoch, but, somewhat as Cain and Abel were, the brothers are divided unalterably by temperament and the initial choice they make of their being" (*Irrational Man*). These schools exchanged Kant's rationalism for antirationalism.

Naturalists like Hans Reichenbach deplored Kant's formalistic conception of logic and by asserting merely the "scientific validity" of "probability logic" endeavored to answer Hume's attack on the scientific validity of induction. Consequently he abandoned the universally valid assertions on which Kant insisted, and that are required by any theory of fixed truth. According to Reichenbach's doctrine of "frequency probability," only events or propositions that can be included in a "similar class" may be regarded as at all probable or "true." This arbitrary predefinition excludes in advance the possibility and intelligibility of "once-for-all" divine events and supernaturally revealed final truths. Reichenbach disclaims not only "classless" events and propositions, but also laws that state universal and necessary relationships. Yet the antimiraculous bias of his own theory presupposes the universal, necessary nonreality of the supernatural. At the same time Reichenbach's confidence in "scientific validity" rests simply on unique subjective decision. He confesses that on an empirical basis "the system of Knowledge, as a whole, is a blind posit. . . . The uncertainty of knowledge as a whole . . . penetrates to the simplest posits we can make" (*Experience and Prediction*, p. 401).

C. I. Lewis considers our recognition of an objective world of orderly experience to be "an achievement of intelligence expressed in our categorial distinctions" (*Mind and the World-Order*, p. 114). But does this mental ordering of experience originate the intelligibility of reality? Has reality no intelligibility other than that contributed by the subjective knower? The forms of meaningful experience belong to the structure of human knowledge (as an endowment at creation, says the Christian) and it is this mental structure that makes possible our personal intellection.

Evolutionary theory asserts the arbitrary and accidental character of the categories of human thought. Naturalism contends that we know only the conceptually ordered world postulated and continually revised by science. Its claims fluctuate helplessly between the notion that our sense experience is somehow elicited by a "given" reality of which we are ignorant, and a total reduction of reality to phenomenalism, that is, to mere sensory experience, organized by human cognition. While naturalistic philosophers like Reichenbach and Lewis reject existential dilution of objects to sense data only, and attack logical positivist reductions of knowledge to mere sense validation, they escape these alternatives only at a great price. Probing reality only in terms of empiricism and of man's conceptualization of experience, they declare any (supposed) object of sense experience unknown and unknowable. Thus naturalism deprives us of knowledge of any real world, or at least has a very different notion of reality, since it reduces knowledge to merely revisable tentativities.

Kant's doctrine of an unknowable *Ding an sich* at least avoided reducing noumenal reality to simply our own rational constructs or to the sensory world. Kant, moreover, insisted on universal and enduring validity as the criterion of truth. Logic in any case cannot be conventional.

But much of the contemporary quest for an externally real world is frustrated by the insistence that concepts have existential meaning only in relation to sensory data, and that sensory data become objective only in terms of our concepts. If the world is either wholly conceptual or wholly sensory, or partly conceptual and partly sensory, and thus depends entirely upon man's categorial and sensory equipment, then it is not independently real. It would of course be very hard to prove that there are sensory *data,* a conception more Aristotelian than Augustinian; not all contemporary science, or philosophy, asserts such *data.* Insofar as contemporary philosophy equates the real world with scientifically conceptualized experience that is modified progressively by empirically required revision, it excludes a world existing independently of human experience, and makes the phenomenal world (our sense experiences) all that is "given."

Bella K. Milmed reminds us that while Einstein located the basis of all natural science in "the belief in an external world independent of the believing subject," he nevertheless viewed reality at times not only as *known by means of* our conceptual constructs but as *constituted by* them (*Kant and Current Philosophical Issues,* pp. 175 f.). Milmed insists that neither Reichenbach nor Lewis consistently escapes the phenomenalism implicit in the positivist approach. Reichenbach leaves in doubt whether any reality exists independently of the observer's sense perceptions and intellectual constructs (*ibid.,* pp. 180 ff.). Likewise the knowledge of independent reality stressed by Lewis reduces to our own conceptual organization of sense data (*ibid.,* pp. 185 ff.).

John Dewey applied the underlying premise, namely, that successful evolutionary adjustment and not transcendent reason guides our rational construction of sensory perceptions (cf. Reichenbach, *Experience and Prediction,* p. 402) in a way that deliberately forfeits what Reichenbach and Lewis try to preserve, that is, present truth about a present independently real world. Dewey is not at all interested in antecedent truth, and in any reality other than human experience. He denies sensory data, and replaces "the given" by "the taken." He invokes the evolutionary origin of concepts and the evolutionary progression of the universe in order to destroy all "truth" (including that of advance probabilities) except that of successful adjustment (*Logic: The Theory of Inquiry*, p. 154). If taken seriously, Dewey's evolutionary view of reality and life means that there is no fixed antecedent reality, and consequently no understanding of its properties. Once naturalistic philosophers like Lewis and Reichenbach concede the pragmatic formation of all concepts, they are helpless to refute Dewey's extension of pragmatism to the whole realm of consciousness, cognition and truth.

Recent empirical philosophy, therefore, not only loses an adequate definition of *knowledge,* but also the ontic *reality*—whether natural or supernatural—of all being external to the human knower. To avoid phenomenalism some empirical philosophers imply an objectively independent world by appealing to a "hypothetical observer" for whom the object would exist in the absence of all human minds. Thus "the unknown god" is unwittingly projected to guard against the subjectivism latent in empiricism's controlling principles. An implicit skepticism haunts every attempt to derive a real world from an analysis only of subjective conceptual reconstructions of sensory experience. Any scholar who decides the question of independent reality entirely by empirical considerations must either locate the independent reality *within* the realm of his knowledge (the world *as conceptualized*)—in which case he cannot distinguish it from conceptualized experience—or he must locate independent reality *outside* the realm of his knowledge—in which case he can say nothing about it. By restricting himself to phenomenal reality and conceptualized experience, the empiricist loses the created world that exists antecedently to and independently of all human consciousness.

The skeptical implications of naturalistic theories are avoided by the theological connection of man's reason with the *imago Dei.* The rational image of God in man explains the permanent logical structure of the human mind, and supplies a solid alternative to the naturalistic notions that basic categories of thought are transitory and culture-contingent.

Yet it may be questioned whether the biblical view requires an *independent* world that can be *known.* Reality, to be sure, is what God preserves and knows. But how and what does God preserve? Augustine's philosophy got along very well without an objectively independent given, and without adding to perception a distinct activity of sensation and a sensory world. The rational structure of the real world—insofar as we truly know it—is not a product of our way of understanding, but of God's way of willing and knowing. The relevance of the mind's rational structure is not constituted, as Kant thought, simply by appropriate sensory matter. Its relevance lies, rather, in the fact that the mind enables us within limits to know reality as God preserves and knows it. The formal conditions of all scientific judgments, that is, the underlying logical foundation or system of categorical principles that make possible even our tentative affirmations, presuppose a transcendent supernatural ground. Our own understanding as constituted may indeed be the creative source of so-called scientific "laws of nature," and of nature's formal unity conceived in these terms. But the orderly character of the universe, its ultimate plan and rationale, are the Creator's work and thought. Scripture does not tell us the plan and order of the universe. That order need not therefore be considered mathematical rather than teleological. The specific system of physical laws affirmed by scientists in any given generation or decade on the basis of empirical observation is not identifiable, per se, as the objective order of nature. Nor do these changing interpretations of nature imply that the categories constituting the human mind are dynamic and changing. The revisable formulas whereby scientists presume to understand the sensory world and to which they can ascribe only regulative validity, are not necessarily broken fragments of a comprehensive divinely given rationale; the claims legitimately made for them are more utilitarian than ontically objective.

The possibility of unifying all sciences into one organic system of human knowledge exists only on the broad postulate that the actual constitution of nature is consonant with reason. Any denial of the logical structuring of the empirical world must sooner or later surrender this possibility. The fact that secular science projects more and more inclusive hypotheses to account for empirical observations and thus must constantly resystematize its verdicts, is easily taken to imply that no ultimate explanation exists. Christian philosophy, on the other hand, sees the unifying principle of the cosmos to be the divinely revealed Logos (Col. 1:17).

By correlating the mind of God, the mind of man, and the rationality of nature, classical objective idealists and philosophical theists had a firmer philosophical foundation than do modern scientific naturalists. Rationalism insists, and rightly, that the certainty and universality of logic and mathematics establish a priority for insight into the nature of ultimate reality. Philosophical naturalism, on the other hand, by emphasizing the abstract, nonexistential character of logic, tends to reinstate the empirically experienced world as the primary and sole reality. Reichenbach reinforces this naturalistic tendency by resolving principles once considered logically necessary laws of the finite world into revisable analytic constructs of probability logic (*The Rise of Scientific Philosophy*, p. 125). Rationalism insists that experience involves an indispensable conceptual element; human knowledge cannot be reduced simply to experienced factors, for not even the rules of logic that determine the relationships between concepts or propositions can be thus explained. Logical positivists who press for a verifiability theory of meaning cannot verify even their own controlling thesis on the premise that only what is susceptible to sense verification has meaning. Revealed religion confronts the revolt against reason in the name of the rational Creator who is the source of meaningful existence and of extant meaning. It affirms the self-revealed God whose rational image man bears as an instrument for spiritual obedience and for the rational integration of life's experiences. Revealed religion ascribes the scientific eclipse of the rational Creator not to lack of evidence but to a methodological limitation that cannot get beyond provisional explanation.

Yet to say that God's mind is rational and logical, and to refer all things to God, does not define "things." The fact that mathematics comes from God is no help in solving equations. God created both tigers and tarantulas, but this of itself supplies no hint of the distinction between them. The sensations of various human beings professing to observe the same reality often diverge over precise color and much else. Objective reality is found only in the propositions in God's mind. The unification of "data" by mathematical formulas is of no sure significance in defining the nature of reality. Any random scattering of data can be unified by some mathematical formula or other, and in many ways, just as historians also selectively manipulate "events" in their writing of history. Nor will an appeal to the divine Logos help us in seeking to establish a mathematical index to the universe. How, for example, will one get from an appeal to the Logos as the source of the structures of reality, to a statement of the divine rationale for the fact that Jupiter has seven moons and the earth only one?

Both the metaphysical status and the moral status of scientific knowledge are today in vigorous debate. Early scientists like Kepler and Newton held that scientific knowledge of the universe reflects the mind of the Creator whose creating and preserving activity structures man and the cosmos and grounds the rationality of the universe. But today only a minority of scientists insist that science seeks accurate, comprehensive knowledge. Even scientists who reject this goal nonetheless accept research grants supposedly to validate conclusions on which corporations and governments predicate huge military or financial commitments. Mounting controversy over man's cosmic duties also presupposes that human beings as rational agents have a special role in regard to the subrational creation. Others insist that science yields objective knowledge that the human mind can employ for human good, although they do not work out its coherence with comprehensive truth or universal good nor do they inform us how they identify the good. Some insist that science corrects a false understanding of the world and leads to more accurate understanding. But since empirical conclusions are always tentative, and major scientific progress involves the overturn of comprehensive assumptions, these views, too, are vulnerable.

But many contemporary scientists forthrightly insist that their knowledge has nothing whatever to do with God. As they see it, science is simply a detailing of observable mathematical continuities in the external world which man is free to deploy to whatever uses he desires. The same equation can be used equally well for good or bad purposes. Science has no interest in the purpose and goal of human life, they contend; it knows no superior source that can impart direction to the human-natural scheme of things. Operationalism holds that physical entities, processes and properties have no independent existence that transcends the operations through which we observe them; empirical science deals only with what is useful, and does not provide us with what should be regarded as truth (cf. Percy W. Bridgman, *The Logic of Modern Physics*).

It was one thing for scientists to insist that an empirically limited methodology provides no tools for coping with questions of truth and the good; it was quite another when, on the ground of scientific investigation, some presumed to redefine truth and the good in terms of mere chemical or physical changes. The most notorious offenders were the behaviorists, whose views were influentially articulated by B. F. Skinner. Earlier in this century John B. Watson reduced soul, mind and thinking to chemical processes. "No one has ever touched a soul, or seen one in a test tube," he wrote (*Behaviorism*, p. 3). Watson proposes social reeducation directed by behaviorists, and envisions the dawn of a behavioristic political utopia. Reflecting the same prejudices, Gilbert Ryle held that "overt intelligent performances are not clues to the workings of minds; they are those workings" (*The Concept of Mind*, p. 58). Ryle tries to rescue human agents from mechanical determinism, but his argument is more verbal than logical.

For Skinner mental behavior is to be explained in physical categories. His representation of truth, moreover, is remarkably vacuous. He writes: "A proposition is 'true' to the extent that with its help the listener responds effectively to the situation it describes" (*About Behaviorism*, p. 201). Since "every chemical and physical action is effective" and "every action produces its effect," observes Gordon Clark, the distinction Skinner proposes regarding truth has no meaning whatever (*Behaviorism and Christianity*, unpublished manuscript, p. 82). Clark notes that Skinner's emphasis—that "the environment preforms the functions previously assigned to feelings and introspectively observed inner states of the organism" (*About Behaviorism*, pp. 248 f.)—offers no basis for exempting anyone, including Skinner, from computerized behavior (*Behaviorism and Christianity*, p. 83). Skinner rejects as invalid the rejoinder that if one is conditioned to say what he says, this must be the case with the behavioral scientist himself, since his assertion, therefore, cannot be true. The argument stands firm, however; Skinner's theory disallows its own objective truth. Beyond the fact that empiricism cannot justify universal propositions, Clark adds, behaviorists do not identify the precise chemical reactions that they equate with thoughts, and empirical supports are in principle therefore unavailable for their theory.

Clark notes that Calvin in effect repudiated a behavioristic view that reduces the soul of man to a bodily function and insisted instead that the soul has independent reality (*Institutes*, I, xv, 2). If one says that man can be exhaustively understood in causal terms, whether of chemistry or of physiology, he then breaks with the biblical view of man in which the soul, while embodied, is carefully distinguished from the body (Gen. 2:7). The mind of man, not the brain as a physical organism, is what produces thought. At physical death, and even before he receives a resurrection body, the believer is consciously gathered into Christ's presence. To say that thinking can be equated with a physico-chemical function of the brain and that human behavior can be charted by mathematical laws contradicts the biblical view.

Whatever may be the disputed knowledge status of scientific formulas, the fact is that interest in objectively valid truth has yielded before the contemporary obsession with workable hypotheses and spectacular results. The realm of ontology has been virtually forsaken because of preoccupation with observable sequences; interest has waned in the Christian doctrine of God, man and nature. The mystery fringe of science replaces the supernatural, nature becomes merely a mechanism of predictable continuities and man loses his soul.

One is more and more hearing the emphasis, however, by Carl Friedrich von Weizsacker and others, that scientific knowledge is ambivalent, and that its further exploration should be suspended on an examination of its larger social and spiritual implications. Appeal to scientific reason has put humanists on opposite sides of major issues such as the feasibility of solar energy, for example, the effective disposal of nuclear waste, or the anticipated side effects of personality-changing drugs. Not only is scientific-technological reason incapable of organizing its data in a way that gives unambiguous ethical verdicts; it also lacks any basis for validating as good any policy whatever on which it might achieve unanimity. The metaphysical question keeps being raised, therefore, concerning the comprehensive relationship of man, nature and ultimate right, that is, concerning the possibility and basis of values. Science has marched mankind to the brink of destruction; now lest it destroy itself and the technological civilization it nurtured, it must face the question of truth and the good. Spokesmen are reaching once again for gods and ideals—for example E. F. Schumacher along Buddhist lines (*Small Is Beautiful*), some to the process philosophies of Whitehead and Hartshorne, some to neo-Thomism, still others to the reexamination of biblical theism.

As Charles C. West observes, most scientists pursuing one or another of these rival world views as the most preferable post-Newtonian theology of the relation of God to the world, are searching for a metaphysical justification of preferred personal values, one reaching for a larger constellation of ideals in which to set the task of science. Consequently neither the reality of divine revelation nor the fact of sin surfaces in a significant way ("God—Man/Woman—Creation").

All such speculation grinds to a quick halt, however, where scholars accept Jacques Monod's "first commandment" that requires strict adherence to scientific method and the disavowal of final causes (*Chance and Necessity*). From the perspective of scientific objectivity Jacques Ellul shares Monod's depiction of the external world as one determinate system, but he then leaps into the transcendent by means of existential decision and eschatological hope. But no amount of dialectical critique can avail to lift Ellul or anyone else from human and world processes to transcendent ontological reality. While the existential and the dialectical appeals to divine calling, covenant, promise, judgment and mercy lend themselves to an emphasis on interpersonal divine-human relations affirmed in faith, they do not correlate divine revelation with questions of ontological structure, worldview, and the universal validity of faith-claims. Despite all the god-talk in this approach, the physical world here still gains its meaning from the deciding self; it has no objectively given meaning accessible to and sharable by all persons.

Permeated as it is by naturalistic evolutionary assumptions, the modern scientific view has lost all assured conviction of the goodness of the cosmos and of man at their beginnings, and hence of their continuing objective value. Where there is no fixed doctrine of man and nature, where all is subject to change, no Archimedean lever exists against the presumptive sovereignty of science and technology. That is one reason why Marx, whose doctrine of nature seems on the surface to provide a theoretical context for expounding the problem and solution of the social crisis, still attracts followers, especially among those who, although they delete God from the God-mankind-nature framework, nonetheless look for the continuity of man and nature in a coming social utopia.

When empirical scientism eclipsed God and the supernatural it created an intellectual climate that comprehended the human only in terms of the nonhuman. By deleting everything from the universe except the structure and development of nature, the rebellious secular mind clouds the fact of human "lostness"; this it does by synthesizing man into nature either in Marxian or some other naturalistic terms. Not only are these secular alternatives hostile to the supernatural, to God and his Christ, and to revealed truths and divine commandments, but they also lack any basis for validating ideals. Apart from a recovery of transcendent divine revelation the effort to place science in the service of the good is unavailing.

Although Marxists are preoccupied with their own world-life view, their own metaphysics and epistemology, they more than all others have been vocal in deploring the awakening interest in God and in sound rational and moral criteria. Liberation theologians like Rubem Alves stigmatize all theistic interest as a diversion by retrogressive intellectuals committed to the status quo and who seek to deflect interest from the burning need for social revolution. At the World Conference on Faith, Science and the Future (Massachusetts Institute of Technology, 1980), Alves pressed the point that alleviating the miseries of the poor and oppressed is the absolute priority and exclusive purpose of science; theoretical issues like the relation of science and faith, he protested, are merely pseudo-issues whose discussion is an idle luxury. Alves apparently considers his own faith-stance off limits to debate, even though social critics increasingly consider Marxism one of the miseries from which the poor now need to be rescued. The hard economic truth that Marxism chooses to ignore, except to dismiss it as a capitalistic hangup, is that in a finite world the limits of growth may require not only the affluent to embrace a simpler lifestyle, but also many of the poor to be satisfied with a life that escapes destitution. Marxists are in fact abandoning their own demands for swift utopian realization, in view of the conspicuous failure of communist and socialist nations to carry out their glittering socio-economic promises to the masses.

It was Pierre Gassendi (1592–1655) who first called atheists intellectual monstrosities or sports of nature. The fact that powerful nations are officially committed to atheism and that the masses are indoctrinated against theism does not disprove Gassendi's point. Humans are not born atheists. Man's ability to conceive God is a propensity of the human mind in view of the created divine image, and is a product of universal divine revelation. As such it precedes any reflective case for theism that might be projected on the basis of empirical observation, philosophical reasoning, or even of special biblical revelation. Theistic reasoning exhibits the congruity of the external universe with implanted human knowledge that God exists. Scriptural revelation corrects fallen man's misconceptions about God and his relation to the universe. But preceding such scriptural illumination and correction, and preceding theological reflection as well, is some universal limited knowledge that God exists.

Loss of the transcendent rational God has involved also the sacrifice of enduring and objective truth. In his historic 1978 commencement address to Harvard students, Alexander Solzhenitsyn spoke of the modern tendency to value ideas in terms of what is fashionable rather than in terms of what is permanently true, and linked this tendency with Western culture's loss of its Christian heritage. The humanist emphasis that all reality is temporal and changing implies that no fixed truths or moral norms exist. If all is in change, then truth also is trapped in and by change.

"The notion of absolute truth is hard for Americans to take," comments Arthur Schlesinger, Jr. "Knowing the crimes committed in the name of a single Truth, Americans prefer to keep their ears open to a multitude of competing lower-case truths" ("The Solzhenitsyn We Refuse to See"). To be sure, false truth-claims have exacted a heavy toll, from the Nazi myth of Nordic superiority to the humanist myths of technocratic utopia and of an impersonal evolutionary or accidental origin of the universe. But the humanist has in fact no methodology for arriving at anything more than revisable truth-claims, whereas biblical theism can at least make out a credible case for durable and permanent truth. When Schlesinger declares that "Americans" prefer relativism to objective truth he is universalizing his own prejudices, and seems, moreover, to imply national or cultural determinism. The difference between truths, furthermore, is not shown by contrasting upper- and lower-case truths, for if absolute truth is ruled out, we are left with only lower-case tentativities, and in no case with valid truth. Schlesinger's veiled dogmatism is the more evident when, for all his promotion of pluralism, he is sure that Solzhenitsyn's adverse judgment on Western culture is absolutely wrong.

William H. McNeill ridicules "the straitjacket of one Truth and one Duty to defend that truth" ("The Decline of the West," p. 125). Yet McNeill promotes his own single line of conviction that allows no contradiction. To be sure, he does "not see how to impose my own or anyone else's standard of taste upon the rest of society without becoming . . . tyrannous" (*ibid.,* p. 126). But tyrannical imposition is not what biblical theism is all about, nor is it about matters of personal taste.

McNeill at least senses the futility of intermediary positions; he cites Sidney Hook's effort, for example, to separate truth and morality from theology while trying to vindicate moral validity on the basis both of an "enlightened majority" and of the intrinsic character and consequences of conflicting ethical proposals ("On Western Freedom," p. 93). Once we forfeit transcendently revealed truth and right, the speculative efforts to avoid their mutation into private standards of taste become futile. McNeill speaks not of conserving moral validity but, in contrast to Hook, of unifying ideals or myths, although among these myths he seeks to elevate rationalistic humanism to special significance. "Individualism," McNeill concedes, is the critical deficiency of modern culture, yet he knows of "no sure answer" to promote social groupings (and, we presume, shared values).

The fact is that those who deplore as intellectual chauvinism any claim to the finality of certain truths and to the superiority of certain values have no logical option but to concede that rape, terrorism and murder may be as right as their opposites, or that the value of a camel may be as great as that of a man. Critics may call it coercive or arrogant to hold to final truths and fixed moral norms; the skeptic who by excluding such finality and fixity professes to find a polished mirror of the real world is even more arrogant or coercive, however, for both his methodology and the ultimate nature of the universe disallow such a verdict. It is indeed true that no universally shared system of truth or morality has survived since man's fall into sin. That does not mean, however, that no divine revelation of truth and the good therefore exists; indeed, despite man's rebellious will, God's universal revelation continually penetrates every human mind and conscience. Human beings may either declare all morality relative and thereby reinforce their condition of moral revolt or propose conjectural supports for shared ethical claims and thereby perpetuate the confusion of rival traditions. Or they may recognize God's revealed commands objectively published and exposited to a rebellious claim-torn world.

21.
Reflections
on the Revelation-and-Culture Debate

THE RELATIONSHIP OF biblical revelation and human culture is stated very differently today than it was by evangelicals at the beginning of our century or by modernists in the 1920s and 1930s. Since the manner in which we relate revelation and culture impacts importantly upon the fortunes of religion and upon the character of culture, it is my purpose to trace and assess this development, to indicate the problems it poses for revealed religion, and to note some of its inherent difficulties.

By culture we mean those beliefs, norms and practices that distinguish the lifeview and lifestyle of a particular society. While religion as such is more difficult to define, Judeo-Christian religion, our main concern, can be readily characterized as the biblical system of faith centering in worship of the self-revealing God.

When our century began many Christian missionaries seemed to require a dual decision, that is, decision for Western culture along with decision for Christ. This encouragement of a two-fold conversion was both unwitting and understandable. Western culture, unlike that of Asia and Africa, contained many Christian elements; it was therefore easier to identify Christianity with American and European than with Asian and African cultures.

But missionary leaders soon realized the dangers of diluting the transcultural uniqueness of God's revelation whenever they project Jesus as a kind of Euro-American model. Maintaining the transcultural message of revealed religion therefore became a desideratum of missionary proclamation.

Missionaries were no less concerned that receptor communities not assimilate the incarnate Christ to their entrenched cultural norms and inherited misconceptions of the invisible world. In India, for example, where Hindus regarded Jesus as but one of many divine manifestations in the flesh, missionaries found it necessary to insist that Christ is no mere *avatar.*

Because Christianity claims to be a transcultural religion of miraculous once-for-all incarnation and redemption, its tenets were not to be conformed to the speculative cosmology and anthropology of nonbiblical religions and secular philosophies. As transcendent revelation the Bible fearlessly thrusts its message into the world culture of both its own time and ours. Nothing less than a full confrontation of all ages is involved, in fact, when the writer of Hebrews declares that "in these last days" God has spoken his consummatory Word in his Son (1:2), and that Christ "has appeared once and for all at the climax of history to abolish sin by the sacrifice of himself . . . and will appear a second time . . . to bring salvation" (9:26, 28, NEB). Equally inflexible is the apostle Paul's proclamation to the Greeks that God "has fixed the day on which he will have the world judged, and justly judged, by a man of his own choosing," namely, the crucified and risen Nazarene (Acts 17:31, NEB). The danger of geographically or culturally limiting or localizing this transcultural revelation became a necessary concern of all evangelicals worldwide.

Today the revelation-and-culture debate reverberates with much deeper and more distressing problems. Almost every discussion of biblical doctrine and interpretation must wrestle now with the contention that all religious claims, even those of the Christian religion, are inevitably and inescapably culture-conditioned.

It should be said at once that Christians have never considered their religion to be superhistorical and supercultural in all respects. Some mystical Asian religions, both ancient and modern, argue as does Zen that human reason distorts divine truth, and that human language corrupts it. Muslims depict the Koran as a direct transcript of God's *ipsissima verba* eternally written in Arabic and preexisting in heaven. Mormons affirm that an angel messenger delivered their books in the form of now long-missing gold tablets. Such claims appear bizarre to Christians who insist that biblical revelation has profounder connections with human reason and language and history.

Christianity traces the very possibility of culture to the Creator's gifts of human reason, language and dominion. Cultural development is both divinely intended and humanly necessary. Only the dreadful intrusion of sin altered human allegiance to Elohim, sweeping man's social patterns into the service of alien gods and engendering bleak misconceptions of the supernatural. Not even at its best is culture therefore the revelation of God, for human resistance to God's purposive will has corrupted it. For all that, culture remains the universal human context within which God addresses his own transcultural revelation to mankind.

Language is the primary means of cultural expression. Without language, no generation of mankind could convey its conceptual distinctives to succeeding generations. In the period between 1400 B.C. and A.D. 100 God used the specific cultural forms of Hebrew, Aramaic and Greek language to convey his inscripturated Word to certain Mediterannean peoples. These biblical languages are not noncultural means of communication.

God's communication of redemptive revelation in the Hebrew and Greek languages does not imply, however, that He approved and applauded Hebrew and Greek cultures per se. The inspired writers bring under divine judgment rebellious foreign cultures no less than the culture of backslidden ancient Jews who invited exile, and retrograde Christian societies like that of Corinth.

Not only are the biblical languages culturally contingent, but scriptural communication also employs the various literary forms existing in their day. Genres like poetry, proverb, parable, and historical narrative, among others, are common both to the Bible and to the overall literary milieu of its time. While Gospels as theological biography may be a unique form, Plutarch's *Parallel Lives* bears some resemblances.

The meaning-criteria for identifying the sense of Scripture, moreover, do not differ from the tests that apply to language, speech and writing in general. To be sure, the Bible finds in the Logos of God the ultimate source of all meaning and truth. Christianity holds that divine creation imparts certain common structures to all human thought and language and that mankind is divinely intended for knowledge of both God and human duty. But the principles for understanding Scripture do not differ from those for understanding other writings. The functions of understanding are universal; human culture itself is possible only because humans are creationally endowed with common rational and moral capacities. Although there are cultural prejudices and culturally shared beliefs, there is no universally fixed "cultural understanding" that determines one's outlook. Understanding pertains to clarifying words and concepts that may involve a diversity of meaning. Which particular content one assigns to a word or concept depends upon a critical judgment. Prevailing cultural beliefs can of course deeply influence critical judgment, but culture does not actually necessitate or dictate one's judgment and views.

To hurriedly reduce thought and language to a mere byproduct of man's sociological development arbitrarily rules out a theistic explanation. In fact, it rules out any and all significant explanation, theistic or not. Not even the world's great diversity of languages and cultures can fully relativize the meaning-content or the truth of linguistic expression. To deny this fact is to reduce even one's own denial to senseless prattle.

The biblical prophets leave no doubt that Yahweh addressed them in intelligible sentences. Divine revelation, evangelical Christianity emphasizes, consists not of unrelated word-units but of semantically related word-constellations, that is, of propositions. Revelational truth can therefore lift the recipient above transitory cultural perspectives by conveying valid alternatives. The Old Testament repeatedly rejects its contemporary pagan cultural milieu. This fact is clearly evident in the stern scriptural condemnation of idolatry, witchcraft and sorcery, in the unbending emphasis that Yahweh is the one and only living God, and in the irreducible distinction between true and false prophets.

But present-day thought increasingly challenges the historic evangelical emphasis on supercultural and transcultural divine revelation. Christian scholars are meshed in deep debate over such issues as cultural conditioning, contextualization and enculturation of the Bible. Their discussion goes far beyond the issue of scriptural inerrancy to question also the fact of propositional revelation and of transcultural divine disclosure. The crucial issue is no longer merely the danger of monocultural reduction of a transcultural revelation; instead, it involves comprehensive and diverse proposals for multicultural revisions of a biblical heritage now regarded as deeply rooted in ancient cultures. No flashpoint of contemporary religious dialogue bears more critically than this upon the significance of the Christian faith.

In the first third of this century it was Protestant modernism that spearheaded the discussion of culturally conditioned revelation. Modernists insisted that cultural factors modify all religious beliefs inherited from the past.

This neo-Protestant verdict had a twofold philosophical basis, namely, faith in evolutionary progress that elevates the present above the past, and confidence that scientific method empirically accredits sound beliefs. Modernists declared acceptable only those parts of the Bible and only those credal affirmations that can be validated by modern scientific criteria. They charged evangelical Christians with promoting and practicing an ancient culture-conditioned religion. While they agreed that the Bible commendably rejects animism and polytheism and much else that the modern world derides, modernists spurned the biblical doctrine of once-for-all revelation and redemption. The Bible's central role for miracle, they said, requires a prescientific worldview that breaches the all-pervading causal continuity demanded by modern scientism.

But if, as modernism believed, God is immanent in and revealed in the universal human cultural development, then why did the modernist consider himself as standing in a somewhat transcendent relation to culture? Why did the modernist regard himself, on the basis of contemporary insights, to be the definitive arbiter of religious reality? The answer, as William R. Hutchinson observes, lay in the fact that the modernist belief-cluster included not only "cultural immanentism" but also "a religiously-based progressivism" and "the conscious, intended adaptation of religious ideas to modern culture" (*The Modernist Impulse in American Protestantism,* p. 2). As modernists saw it, past sages accepted what was consonant with the age in which they lived as the standard of belief and behavior; the inspired biblical writers had likewise lacked truth valid for all time. The modernists so periodized history, however, that they considered their own dogmas not simply superior to all that had gone before, but as the very norm of civilized belief and conduct. Religious ideas, they held, were to be conformed ideally and finally to twentieth-century culture, not indeed to modern Asian or African culture, but to Western scientific culture in which God was thought to be specially present and active. Although past cultures had erected decisive roadblocks to religious progress, modern Euro-American culture was presumably overcoming all such obstacles.

The modernists exempted their own favored pronouncements from the cultural relativism that they elsewhere ascribed to religious conceptions.

They presupposed a providential convergence of the rise of modernism with the emerging kingdom of God. As they saw it, evolving culture was not corrupted or corruptive but merely incomplete; modernist education, legislation and socialization would soon facilitate the perfection of culture. Confidence that the wisdom of the ages had culminated in modernism encouraged modernists to exalt liberal theologians above biblical prophets and apostles and moreover to dignify them as consummatory agents in the divine regeneration of culture. By relegating all past revelatory beliefs to cultural contingency and elevating their own special tenets to a level of consciousness that transcends changing cultural embodiments, the modernists hoped to achieve the ultimate renewal and final conversion of culture.

Although some modernists still timidly declared the Christian revelation to be normative, they conformed it to modern culture; others, more boldly and consistently, retained only biblical fragments that they considered compatible with scientific empiricism. In either case the current mood conferred little assured survival value upon the past, since for both liberal Jewish thought and liberal Christian thought modern scientific culture became the intellectual frame in which the biblical heritage appeared inferior. As modernism advanced the empirical method to measure biblical religion and evaluate theological beliefs, it viewed even the Bible's noblest convictions, however irreducible to ancient cultural counterparts, as somehow dependent upon and rooted in ancient cultural contexts. Instead of allowing Judeo-Christian revelation to set an agenda for theological inquiry and perspective, modernism superimposed the empirical tradition of humanistic culture as the norm for all religious interpretation.

Modernists did not apply to their own teachings the principle of culture-dependence by which they overruled the finality of all past revelational claims. It remained for a cataclysmic culture-shock to ironically and unexpectedly challenge the modernists' exemption of their own views from culture-conditioning. The second World War, following fast upon the first, stunned liberal confidence in evolutionary progress. It also challenged the theory that modern culture is decisively revelatory of the divine; increasing signs of the decline of Western culture rendered questionable the modernist faith in God's radical immanence in culture and eroded confident expectation of an emerging Christian civilization nurtured by modernist theologians. Instead, new emphasis on man's all-pervasive sinfulness precipitated both the loss of historical optimism and a decline of faith in philosophical reasoning.

Because modernists projected their theories of an updated Christianity so vigorously, only gradually did the intellectual contradiction of those theories become apparent. But the supposed logic of the modernist position suffered increasing strain. Interjection of contemporary ideas into Christian beliefs led to an evolution-oriented eclipse of any significant doctrine of divine creation, to rejection of the divinity of Jesus Christ and to a "moral example" view of the atonement.

Liberals finally conceded that an empirical methodology requires assuming that all doctrines and moral principles are tentative; they were therefore forced to restate their asserted finality of Jesus with no reference to special metaphysical claims and in terms only of his life-transforming influence.

Neoorthodoxy aggressively attacked these pseudo-Christian commitments and soon pronounced the death of classic rationalistic modernism. Focusing attention on the dire moral predicament of mankind, it stressed the need for transcendent divine revelation and redemption. Tough-spirited modernists could reply, and with some reason, that neoorthodoxy reflected a cultural stance no less than did modernism, since its emphasis on radical transcendence involved no primary appeal to the objective authority of the Bible, but mirrored prevalent European philosophy. Necessary as it was to retreat from evolutionary utopianism, that retreat, said the modernists, need not require the abandonment of world-pervading divine immanence and of culture-conditioned revelation. Over against Barthianism with its one-sided emphasis only on special sporadic revelation, liberalism insisted both on universal revelation and on a variety of revelational modes; over against evangelical orthodoxy, liberalism refused to exempt even divine revelation from dependence on culture. The modernists therefore revised their view of God's disclosure in and through all cultural development by simply deleting their earlier assumption that earthly history merges progressively into the kingdom of God. At the same time they continued to deny the true extent of divine-human alienation; they reaffirmed an essential continuity between God and man that excludes miraculous revelation and redemption.

Evangelical Christianity insists that cultural development cannot be the source either of a sure revelation or of a final revelation; however progressive human culture may be at times, it reflects human sinfulness and remains under divine judgment. Cultural revelation is, in fact, a misnomer. Religious views are not to be commended simply because of their modernity or antiquity; whether past or contemporary, culture is not a source of ultimate religious truth.

When twentieth-century historical developments showed that even modernism's judgments were culture-skewed and untenable, the transcultural claims for Judeo-Christian revelation gained fresh prominence. Instead of stressing God's immanence in cultural development, evangelicals pointed to God's Word that confronts mankind as a higher authority than experience, and that calls even culture at its best to answerability before the Lord of history.

Evangelicals are fully aware that Scripture uses language and literary forms current in ancient times. But they deny that divine revelation is essentially conditioned by transitory cultural conceptions and patterns; they deny that the Bible teaches views of God, the cosmos, and human life that are simply borrowed from surrounding cultures. Evangelicals do not dispute the propriety of correlating Christianity with any and all truth adduced by philosophy and science, or even of seeking temporary tactical relationships between Christianity and culture. But conformity of basic

Christian tenets to the transitory *Zeitgeist* and ecclesial espousal of the mores of the day, is another matter.

Modern scholars refused to seriously reinvestigate the historic Judeo-Christian option, however. As a result critical thinkers today espouse an even more pervasive and comprehensive culture-dependence of revelation than did their counterparts earlier in this century. Phenomenological philosophers, for example, emphasize each knower's personal outlook and creative contribution to any and every cognitive claim. Humanistic anthropologists and positivistic sociologists insist that all religious and moral viewpoints are historically conditioned. Such humanistic and positivistic theory unreservedly repudiates the objective validity of Judeo-Christian theology. It considers futile and irrelevant the evangelical concern to avoid conforming a supposedly transcultural revelation to either the missioner's or receptor's particular cultural heritage. It belittles also modernism's ready culture-conditioning of all religious views except its own; not even the modernist who supposedly stands at the apex of evolutionary progress and arms himself with scientific methodology can therefore presume to escape the cultural noose. The current emphasis is that no one escapes culture conditioning; all biblical recipients of revelation, all who ever heard or translated that revelation, all who interpret it and who proclaim it to the world, as well as all who now hear and would share the message with yet others, are said to be necessarily conditioned by various worldviews in their perception and promulgation of external realities.

The result of this emphasis is a waning confidence in grammatico-historical interpretation and its goal of identifying a universally sharable meaning of the biblical text. Grammatico-historical exegesis cannot establish biblical theology as a comprehensive and authoritative summary of God's revelation, we are told, because the authority and meaning of the Gospel are not textual. Critics demean the longstanding evangelical emphasis on a universally valid theology expressed by all the biblical writers. We are asked to keep biblical representations in tension with the original writers' culturally-conditioned purpose, and to remember that our own perception of God's work, similarly culture-conditioned, must be continually reexpressed in new cultural forms as we address changing cultural contexts. We are told, in short, to demythologize the evangelical notion that God's truth can be expressed in fixed doctrinal formulas or in credal statements, and to consider such formulations as merely "pointers." We are exhorted to view Scripture as simply a call to faith, and to acknowledge personal faith as an inherent hermeneutical principle.

On the surface this bold summons to faith sounds heavenly-minded, but its result is nonevangelical and unorthodox, for it strips the Bible of any valid doctrinal system. While the supposed culture-conditioned and theologically conflicting statements of the prophets and the apostles present us with a call to obedience in the Spirit they leave us nonetheless with merely a "confessional" or fallible testimonial witness. Successive cultures, we are told, have impacted upon the ancient writers, bequeathing us a diversity of biblical theologies of which none is final. Neither prophetic revelation nor apostolic inspiration, we are told, escapes the conforming influence of an environing culture upon man's creaturely conceptions. Evangelical confidence in the comprehensive unity and universal validity of Bible doctrine is declared to be uninformed and unenlightened.

The evangelical view does not at all deny that mankind through the ages has been culture-dependent, or that human culture notably conditions even the religious history of a fallen and sinful race. No indictment of the culturally conditioned world religions is more devastating than Paul's letter to the Romans (1:21 ff.). But the biblical prophets and apostles not only warn Jews and Christians of the perilous consequences of cultural concessions, but they also emphasize by contrast the special heritage of redemptive revelation. The prophets and apostles insist, as Clark Pinnock remarks, that the inspired Scriptures and the finality of Jesus Christ "provide an Archimedian point in the flux of the human situation against which the flow of history may be measured and evaluated" (*Biblical Revelation,* p. 128).

But the new hermeneutic stresses that historical understanding demands a very different intellection of the past. It declares the whole revelatory and hermeneutical process to be culture-bound, whether it be divine disclosure at its loftiest heights, New Testament interpretation of the Old Testament, apostolic proclamation to the world, or our own understanding of the whole. Given this culture-relatedness of the Bible and of all human history, how can scriptural teaching be considered authoritative, we are asked. The new hermeneutic proposes to discover the decisive meaning of past texts for our times by existential immediacy, that is, by the contemporary recipient's internal awareness and response and creative contribution.

This approach is now often linked with an emphasis on Scripture's divine "intention" and with an appeal to the biblical writer's inner "intention." But if an ancient text has no fixed verbal meaning, or if its meaning is said to differ from age to age and from culture to culture, then the notion of understanding past texts is senseless. If external reality is not rationally comprehensible, and meaning is but internal and subjective, then one could not even pursue an ancient author's "intention," all the less so because our historical understanding is said in turn to creatively condition whatever we affirm. If, independently of the ancient texts, we have access to the "divine intention," it is misleading to associate such meaning with a discovery of the author's real intention. It is but a hoax on logical consistency and a miserable delusion to say that the sense of the text consists simply of its "relevance" for me on the assumption that what it means in encountering me in my cultural understanding is the only sense the text truly has, and that this sense is normative for other persons, and moreover echoes the inner intention of the original author.

No doubt each passing generation finds biblical elements specially significant for its own intellectual and cultural context. But unless the Bible's declared significance is intrinsic to the meaning of the text, interpretation has given way to spiritualization. E. D. Hirsch, Jr. remarks that "the point which ought to be grasped clearly is that a text cannot be made to speak to us until what it says has been understood. . . . The literary text (in spite of the semimystical claims made for its uniqueness) does not have a special ontological status which somehow absolves the reader from the demands universally imposed by all linguistic texts of every description" (*Validity in Interpretation*, p. 210). To insist on the present relevance of a text is one thing; to suspend its current vitality upon a rejection of objectively valid meaning is quite another. A text may have a somewhat different significance for different persons or times, or even at different moments in a person's life, but if the text itself has no inherent objective meaning then its import on any and every occasion is entirely subjective; in that case it is intrinsically meaningless and can just as appropriately signify its contrary meaning.

If by a culture-conditioned text one means not only its language and forms of communication but also the intellectual content, then the author's verbal intention cannot escape authorial fallibility, since culture-dependent teaching lacks finality. Only if an interpreter possesses a true grasp of the subject matter can he say that another author's meaning is either incomplete, distorted or false. But the dogma of culture-conditionedness automatically rules out claims to comprehensive knowledge and transcendent truth. In order to establish a writer's incompleteness or the fallibility and culture-conditionedness of his text, would not a critic have to claim not simply "more knowledge" than the ancient author had, both of his intention and of the culture of his day; would the critic indeed not also have to claim absolute knowledge? But if the critic is no less culture-conditioned than the original author, then all distinctions drain into relativity.

The current champion of universal culture-conditioning routinely implies that his own statements are somehow exempt from the limitations that he attaches to others' views. He refuses to apply the rule of restricted comprehension reciprocally to his own dogma about comprehensive culture-distortion. But since he disallows the modernist assumption that both evolutionary progress and scientific method lift him to a transcendent status that he denies to Judeo-Christian revelation, what culture-transcending platform has the advocate of the new hermeneutic for peering over and beyond the great wall of culture?

According to Martin Heidegger differences of cultural and historical epochs preclude any identity and continuity of meaning; personal significance presupposes the creative contribution of the knower. Heidegger's followers stress that the nature of time sets off past time as ontologically alien to the present. On this claim they ground the historicity of understanding, and insist that past meaning cannot be understood in the present. In that case, neither the evangelicals nor the modernists, nor the more radical secular critics, can recapture the authentic meaning of the Bible.

Heidegger's followers concede that living contemporaries escape the destructive consequences of this alien ontology of time; the living can intelligibly communicate among themselves in a common language. But if a time-gap between generations necessarily involves the discontinuity of meaning, why then not also the passing of a moment or of many moments? And if the passing of a few moments need not involve ontological alienation, why then should and must the lapse of many moments do so? If a time-span eradicates common meaning, post-Heideggerians had better not rely on publications to convey their intellectual claims from one generation to the next. In fact, even their effort to convey shared meaning to our present generation disputes a definitive role for historicity and personal creativity. The theory itself must be false in order to be true, and, if true, must be false. Heidegger's philosophy is often said to be antimetaphysical or nonmetaphysical, but it is no less metaphysical than Aristotelianism and no less controversial and debatable.

Even more pervasively influential than Heidegger's historicizing of meaning is the sociological relativizing of revealed truth and values. Many contemporary sociologists, especially secular humanists and other naturalists, imply that all cultural values and beliefs are of equal worth, and that none is final and absolute. But if we evaluate all cultural claims by the relativity theory we have no criteria for disputing the pretensions of any culture. Nor have we any way of validating the pretensions of modern humanism when it arbitrarily elevates its theory of cultural-relativity into an absolute.

The historicist and the humanist alike should be reminded that the insistence on universal cultural fallibility most appropriately begins at home, and that it would be the part of wisdom first to explore the culture-conditionedness of the critic who inconsistently confers privileged supremacy on his own philosophical theory. This ready disposition to impose cultural-historical conditioning on universal human experience stems, in fact, from uncritical culture-dependence in a generation addicted to historical relativism. The verdict that cultural influences have so skewed biblical teaching that it cannot serve as a standard for judging other views, has accommodated the stealthy entrenchment of transitory relativisms.

If indeed all truth and meaning are culturally conditioned, no basis remains for selectively exempting certain preferred biblical specifics. If we elevate culture-conditioning into a formative principle, and insist that biblical theology falls within a culture-relative context, then the principle of relativity to culture applies not only to this or that isolated passage—whether about the seriousness of sexual sins or the role of women in the church; it extends also to the scriptural teaching that "in Christ there is neither male nor female," or that we are to love God with our whole being and our neighbors as ourselves, or that it is sinful to covet a neighbor's wife or possessions. It will not do to exhibit certain doctrines as the special strength of biblical religion if we simultaneously dismiss other teachings on the basis of pervasive cultural dependence. Without universal truths no authentic Christian theology can be affirmed in any culture; so-called "relevant theological emphases" there may be, but not objectively valid theology. Without culture-transcendent propositional truth, "being a Christian" is compatible with unlimited theological diversity, a diversity that contradicts every orthodox affirmation in both the Scriptures and in the historic ecumenical creeds.

Orthodox evangelicals reject the premise that culture is a source or norm of revelational truth; rather, as they see it, culture is a social context in which transcendent revelation is to be applied and appropriated. Mediating theologians refuse fully to impose the secular principle of culture-conditioned revelation, and insist on at least some transcultural revelatory element. Sometimes they rather broadly and ambiguously define this transcultural factor as "the Gospel." This shifts primary attention away from the scriptural record, whose objective authority they reject as a canon of inspired propositional teaching.

All evangelicals acknowledge that Scripture conveys divine revelation in a concrete cultural context, that is, in a particular historical situation in language that is culturally related. They agree, moreover, that the text does not automatically impart its meaning but requires an interpreter familiar with the language, someone who mentally constructs the meaning of the given semantic units, and who brings some preunderstanding and presuppositions to the task.

Beyond these agreements differences soon become apparent. Some mediating evangelical exegetes contend that because revelation is "incarnational," that is, given in human history and language, it is therefore steeped in the cultural context of its time. God's "accommodation" to "culturally-conditioned" language, we are told, means that God speaks errantly even in Scripture. Yet if modern theologians can employ human language to tell us what is truly the case in matters of religious epistemology, it is strange, indeed, that God could not have done so. We are told, moreover, that God used the "thought-forms" of ancient cultures: this confusing term obscures the fact that in creation God himself gifts man universally with the categories of reason and morality. We have no reason to insist that today's forms of thought and laws of logic differ essentially from those of the past.

Critics all too often forget that biblical meaning is not derived by a simple word-by-word transfer of the linguistic sense of its culturally entrenched vocabulary. Meaning is extracted, rather, from the logical context in which Scripture or any other verbal communication is set. Words in themselves have no sure meaning; they are but symbols that gain conventional meaning, and their orderly use in sentences renders their specific meaning clear. Words derive their intended sense neither simply from their cultural use nor from etymology, but from a universe of discourse, that is, from sentences or propositions. James Barr's comments on the relation of language and culture are appropriate here. Concluding his book on *Biblical Words for Time* (pp. 206 f.), Barr writes: "I take it that theology is not identical with the environing culture, and thus the Hebrew-speaking culture of (let us say) the time of Jeremiah was not identical with the theology of that prophet. The words of the language, however, words like *love* and *God* and *time*, were common property to Jeremiah and the 'false' prophets, just as they later were to Paul and his opponents or to John and the Gnostics. It was the things they said with these words that were different." We may further illustrate the point that the same general culture can be used to support remarkably different philosophies and religions by noting that Maimonides, Aquinas and Spinoza each used Latin, but to express highly divergent positions. Barr continues: "If theology wishes to consider itself as other than identical with the culture in which it is set, it is fatal for it to maintain that all those who speak the same language think in the same way, or to maintain positions which tacitly imply this. Conversely, it is possible in a certain sense to maintain the unity of language and culture in such a way that one speaking the language will share the meanings which are part of the culture; but if one does this, and if one also takes the word as the unity of meaning and looks for context-free word-meanings, the meanings so discovered will in many cases be theologically equivocal."

God doubtless communicated his revelatory message to prophets and apostles within the limits of their conceptual comprehension, although at times they may not have fully grasped its significance. He addressed them, moreover, within their cultural milieu, whose worldview and lifeview they shared except as prior revelation had modified their perspective. But it is misleading and unjustifiable to say that divine revelation is limited to the cultural outlook. Today's exaggerated emphasis on contextualization reflects the influence of the social scientists, particularly of anthropologists, sociologists of religion and communications theorists and technicians, and poses some noteworthy dangers for theology. Simply because revelation is addressed within one's culture and is to be expressed and interpreted within that culture does not mean that divine revelation must be conformed to that culture. Culture is a complex of shared beliefs and customs, laws and morals. But to allow the prevailing cultural outlook to fix the limits of revelatory meaning and truth violates the scriptural emphasis on transcendent divine revelation.

In their day the inspired writers no doubt personally adhered to the prevalent outlook where revelation did not impinge on cultural concerns. The prophets and apostles were not divinely endowed with a systematically formulated world-and-life view alternative to their own cultural inheritance; in many respects they retained the limited and often fallacious theories of their time. But they often sharply condemned cultural principles and practices in the light of revelation, and where they expressly approved these they did so on the ground not of cultural tradition or heritage but of revelation. Where the writers do not teach cosmology, they speak in the common idiom of their day. The earth is said to stand secure on pillars (1 Sam. 2:8), for example, and Paul is caught up into the "third heaven" (2 Cor. 12:2). Such references do not however appeal to divine revelation to accredit a particular cosmology. If it is wrong for Christians to infer that the earth is round from the reference in Psalm 19 to the sun arching from one end of the earth to the other, why must the writers be thought to teach cosmological theory in passages that seem to suggest that the earth is flat, or that the universe is three-tiered? The phrase "heaven above, earth beneath, and water under the earth" may be merely a Hebrew expression of totality. Scripture does not impose outmoded theories of the structure and nature of the universe as doctrine. Must God limit himself to the "language meanings" of one's particular culture in order to convey revelational truth? In the culture context of the ancient Near East the very term God surely meant something very different for the Hebrews than it did for the Philistines, and any of the languages of the Near East could have expressed those differences.

On the surface it seems sensible to argue that we modern receptors of the message of revelation are culture-conditioned, and since all translators of the message were culture-conditioned, it is therefore futile to insist that the teaching of Scripture is not culture-conditioned. But this line of argument has far-reaching implications.

The culture-conditioning of translator and interpreter does not really require what the new hermeneutic maintains, namely, that every culture and generation must do its own exegesis anew. Relevant cultural application is clearly and obviously necessary; the expositor must always seek to apply revelation to dynamic cultural parallels. But if no fixed meaning exists from culture to culture and from generation to generation, then no decisive, authentic and authoritative meaning exists either for our time and place or for any other.

Even where we know a great deal about ancient cultures, present-day cultural prejudices can influence expositors to manipulate their appeal to culture-dependence in a way that deploys Scripture in support of privately cherished emphases. The current issue of the ministerial role of women is a case in point. Beyond all debate, Christ and the Bible ennobled women far above their status in nonbiblical society, whereas Western Christianity has for many years demoted the creative role of women in church and society due to a male-dominant culture pattern. Today a reactionary tendency promotes a feminist libertarianism whose inspiration comes, like male chauvinism, not from Scripture but from the secular mood. Culture-conditioned interpreters who champion contemporary feminism routinely charge that the Bible itself is culture-infected, and thereby merely compound secular misconceptions of subjection and liberation. Some critics claim that only the apostle Paul's Jewish rabbinic inheritance excluded any feminine priestly ministry and otherwise conditioned his doctrine concerning the role of women. Yet both in his pre-Christian years at Tarsus and in his spiritual encounters in Athens and Ephesus, Saul of Tarsus was aware of pagan cults that granted women a prominent role. Douglas Feaver observes that in the Athenian cult 95% of the priestly assistants were female ("Historical Development in the Priesthoods of Athens" in *Yale Classical Studies* 15, New Haven, Yale University Press, 1957, pp. 123–158). Could not Paul's restriction of the role of women in the church constitute more a rejection of Greek cultural practices than a perpetuation of Jewish prejudices, one that is grounded in revelation rather than in accommodation? Ancient historians note that the temple priestesses' children who were often dedicated for lifetime service, seldom knew the names of their fathers, and thus indicated the prevalence of temple prostitution. Paul was no stickler for rabbinic prejudices; after all, he stressed that Gentile Christians did not need to become cultural Jews in order to become Christian, whereas Peter held—until Paul corrected him—that Gentiles could enter the kingdom of God only through the door of Hebrew customs and ritual. Paul champions the equality of both men and women but he also brings both under the authority of the revealed will and purpose of God. He lifts the discussion of priesthood not only above the theme of masculinity and feminity, but also above that of the hierarchical status of symbolic mediators in order to underscore the universal priestly status of the entire believing community (1 Cor. 6:19). He sets both the termination of the male cultic priestly line and the restriction of the woman's role in the larger context of the priesthood of all believers.

Instead of conforming to cultural prejudices, the Bible strikingly and repeatedly departs from the contextual culture on major issues. In an age when pagans worshiped the planets and believed in many gods, the Genesis creation account, for example, focuses on the one sovereign God and identifies the entire universe as his creation. If this now frequently neglected narrative were for the first time discovered during a present-day archaeological excavation on Mount Sinai, the finding would be considered more significant than either the Rosetta Stone or the Dead Sea Scrolls. Consider, too, that in an age when Greek philosophy wholly excluded the bodily resurrection of mankind, and when even Jewish culture confined the hope of the resurrection to the future eschatological age, Jesus' followers affirmed his third-day resurrection and staked their lives on its factuality.

When modern intepreters declare biblical doctrine to be culture-dependent, or even judge it to be right or wrong, they move from interpretation to philosophical evaluation. The modern critic who offers to deliver the biblical writer from supposed enslavement to an ancient culture about which we have little independent knowledge, all too often forces upon the writer a current culture prejudice that he, the critic, himself brings to the text. Valid interpretation can hardly be achieved if one approaches the text with an advance assumption that those conditioned by contemporary culture can more truly say what a past writer has said because that writer was conditioned by his culture. Modern biblical criticism all too readily assigns a larger role to culture in the original formation of Scripture than it does to the Spirit of inspiration and confers on the modern critic, who covertly accommodates the Bible to alien beliefs, a special pneumatic capacity for defining revelational content. More often than not, pleas for enriching Christian faith by the insights of contemporary culture elevate modern prejudices to a position of prescriptive judgment on Christian doctrine and ethics.

Bibliography

Aalen, Sverre. "Glory/Honour/*Doxa.*" In *The New International Dictionary of New Testament Theology.* Vol. 2. Edited by Colin Brown. Grand Rapids: Zondervan Publishing House, 1976.

Adams, Marilyn McCord. "Is the Existence of God a 'Hard' Fact?" *Philosophical Review* 76 (1967): 492–503.

Albright, William F. *History, Archaeology and Christian Humanism.* New York: McGraw-Hill, 1969.

Albritton, Rogers. "Present Truth and Future Contingency." *Philosophical Review* 66 (1957): 29–46.

Alexander, Samuel. *Space, Time and Deity.* New York: The Macmillan Company, 1929.

Althaus, Paul. "Kenosis." In *Die Religion in Geschichte und Gegenwart.* Vol. 3. Cited by Jürgen Moltmann. *The Crucified God.* New York: Harper & Row, 1974.

Altizer, Thomas J. J. "Commentary." In *The Religious Situation: 1968.* Edited by Donald R. Cutler. Boston: Beacon Press, 1968.

Ames, Edward Scribner. *Religion.* New York: Henry Holt and Company, 1929.

Andrus, Hynum L. *God, Man and the Universe.* Foundations of the Millennial Kingdom of Christ. No. 1. Salt Lake City: Bookcraft, Inc., 1978.

Anselm. *Proslogium; Monologium; On Behalf of the Fool.* Translated by Sidney Norton Deane. Chicago: Open Court Publishing Co., 1958.

Appaswamy, A. J. *The Gospel and India's Heritage.* London and Madras: S.P.C.K., 1942.

Aquinas, Thomas. *De Veritate.*

———. *Summa Theologica.* 3 vols. New York: Benzinger Bros., 1947–48.

———. *Summa Theologiae.* Translated by Dominican Fathers of English Province. New York: Benzinger Inc., 1947.

Argyle, A. W. *God in the New Testament.* London: Hodder and Stoughton, 1965.

Aristotle. *The Works of Aristotle: Metaphysics.* Book 8. Translated by J. I. Beare. Edited by W. D. Ross and J. A. Smith. Oxford: Clarendon Press, 1928.

Arminius, James. "Disputation on 'The Nature of God.'" *The Writings of James Arminius.* Vol. 1. Grand Rapids: Baker Book House, 1956.

Augustine. *The City of God.*

———. *De Libero Arbitrio.* In *Augustine: Earlier Writings.* Translated by J. H. S. Burleigh. Philadelphia: Westminster Press, 1953.

———. *De Trinitate.*

———. *Fathers of the Church,* Vol. 45. Translated by V. J. Bourke. New York: The Catholic University of America Press, 1953.

———. "On Free Will." In *Augustine: Earlier Writings.* Vol. 3. Translated by J. H. S. Burleigh. Philadelphia: Westminster Press, The Library of Christian Classics, 1953.

Aulén, Gustaf. *Jesus in Contemporary Historical Research.* Translated by Ingalill H. Hjelm. Philadelphia: Fortress Press, 1976.

———. In *Revelation.* Edited by John Baillie and Hugh Martin. New York: The Macmillan Co., 1937.

———. *The Faith of the Christian Church.* Translated by Eric H. Wahlstrom and G. Everett Arden. Philadelphia: Fortress Press, 1960.

Baab, Otto. *The Theology of the Old Testament.* New York: Abingdon-Cokesbury, 1949.

Babbage, Charles. *The Ninth Bridgewater Treatise.* Reprint of 2nd ed. London: Frank Cass, 1967.

Baier, Johann. *Compendium Theologiae Positivae.* 3 vols. Edited with notes by Carl F. W. Walther. St. Louis: 1879.

Barnhart, J. E. "Incarnation and Process Philosophizing." *Religious Studies* (April 1967): 225–232.

Barr, James. *Biblical Words for Time.* 2nd rev. ed. London: SCM Press Ltd, 1969.

———. *Fundamentalism.* London: SCM Press Ltd, 1977; Philadelphia: Westminster Press, 1978.

———. *The Bible in the Modern World.* London: SCM Press Ltd; New York: Harper & Row, 1973.

Barrett, C. K. *The Gospel According to St. John.* London: S.P.C.K., 1967.

Barrett, William. *Irrational Man.* Garden City and New York: Doubleday and Company, Inc., 1958.

Barth, Karl. *Anselm: Fides Quaerens Intellectum; Anselm's Proof of the Existence of God in the Context of His Theological Scheme.* Translated by Ian W. Robertson. Richmond: John Knox Press, 1960.

———. *Church Dogmatics.* Edited by G. W. Bromiley and T. F. Torrance. Edinburgh: T. & T. Clark, 1936–1969; Naperville, IL: Alec R. Allenson, 1969.

———. *Epistle to the Romans.* Translated by E. C. Hoskyns. New York: Oxford University Press, 1933.

———. *The Humanity of God.* Richmond: John Knox Press, 1960.

———. *The Redeemer. The Work and Person of Jesus Christ.* New York and Nashville: Abingdon-Cokesbury Press, 1951.

Battles, Ford Lewis. "God Was Accommodating Himself to Human Capacity." *Interpretation* 31, No. 1 (January 1977): 19–38.

Bavinck, Herman. *The Doctrine of God.* Translated, edited, and outlined by William Hendricksen. Grand Rapids: Wm. B. Eerdmans, 1951.

Berkhof, Hendrikus. *The Doctrine of the Holy Spirit.* London: Epworth Press, 1965.

Berkhof, Louis. *Systematic Theology.* Grand Rapids: Wm. B. Eerdmans, 1946.

Bertocci, Peter A. *The Empirical Argument for God in Late British Thought.* Cambridge: Harvard University Press, 1938; Millwood, NY: Kraus, 1970.

———. *The Person God Is.* London: George Allen & Unwin Ltd.; New York: Humanities Press, Inc., 1970.

Blackstone, William T. *The Problem of Religious Knowledge.* Englewood Cliffs, NJ: Prentice-Hall, Inc., 1963.

Blamires, Harry. *Tyranny of Time: A Defence of Dogmatism.* London: S.P.C.K.; New York: Morehouse, 1965.

Bloesch, Donald. *Beyond Feminism and Patriarchalism.* (soon to be published).

———. *Essentials of Evangelical Theology.* Vol 1. *God, Authority, and Salvation.* Vol. 2. *Life, Ministry and Hope.* San Francisco: Harper & Row, 1978.

Boethius, *The Consolation of Philosophy.* Loeb Classical Library. Translated by Edward Kenner Rand. Cambridge: Harvard University Press, 1918.

Bowman, A. A. *A Sacramental Universe*. Princeton, NJ: Princeton University Press, 1939.

Bowne, Borden P. *Philosophy of Theism*. New York: Harper & Row, 1887.

————. *The Theory of Thought and Knowledge*. New York: Harper & Brothers, 1897.

Boyd, Robin H. S. *Khristavaita, A Theology for India*. Madras: Christian Literature Society, 1977.

Braaten, Carl E. *The Future of God. The Revolutionary Dynamics of Hope*. New York: Harper & Row, 1969.

Brabant, F. H. *Time and Eternity in Christian Thought*. London: Longmans, Green and Co., 1937.

Bradley, F. H. *Appearance and Reality*. New York: Oxford University Press, 1930.

Braithwaite, R. G. *An Empiricist's View of the Nature of Religious Belief*. Cambridge: Cambridge University Press, 1955.

Brandon, S. G. F. "Time as God and Devil." In *Bulletin of the John Rylands Library*. Vol. 67 (1964): 12–31.

Brasnett, Bertrand R. *The Suffering of the Impassible God*. London: S.P.C.K.; New York and Toronto: The Macmillan Company, 1928.

Bridgman, Percy W. *The Logic of Modern Physics*. 2nd ed. New York: The Macmillan Company, 1948.

Brightman, Edgar S. *The Finding of God*. New York: The Abingdon Press, 1931.

————. *Person and Reality*. An Introduction to Metaphysics. Edited by Peter A. Bertocci et al. New York: The Ronald Press, 1958.

————. "Personalism and Religious Education." In *Personalism in Theology*. Edited by Edgar S. Brightman. Boston: Boston University Press, 1943.

————. *Personalism in Theology*. A Symposium in honor of Albert C. Knudson. Edited by Edgar S. Brightman. Boston: Boston University Press, 1943.

————. *Personality and Religion*. New York: The Abingdon Press, 1943.

————. *Philosophy of Religion*. New York: Prentice-Hall, 1940.

————. *The Problem of God*. New York: The Abingdon Press, 1930.

————. "A Temporalist View of God." In *The Journal of Religion* (1932): 544–555.

Bring, Ragnar. *Dualismen hos Luther*. Lund: H. Ohlssons, 1929.

Brown, Raymond E. "Does the New Testament Call Jesus God?" *Theological Studies* 26 (1965): 560, n. 35.

Brown, Robert McAfee. *P. T. Forsyth: Prophet for Today*. Philadelphia: The Westminster Press, 1952.

Brueggemann, Walter. "Israel's Social Criticism and Yahweh's Sexuality." *Journal of the American Academy of Religion* 65, No. 3 (September 1977): 739–772.

Bruemmer, Vincent. *Transcendental Criticism and Christian Philosophy*. Frenecker: Vitgeverij Wever, 1961.

Brunner, Emil. *Christianity and Civilization. Foundations*. Vol. 1. Gifford Lectures, 1947. London: Charles Scribner's Sons, 1948.

————. *The Christian Doctrine of God*. Philadelphia: Westminster Press, 1950.

————. *Revelation and Reason*. Philadelphia: Westminster Press, 1946.

————. *Wahrheit als Begegnung*. Berlin: Im Furche-Verlag, 1938.

Buber, Martin. *I and Thou*. Translated by R. G. Smith. Edinburgh: T. & T. Clark, 1937; 2nd ed. New York: Charles Scribner's Sons, 1958.

————. *Kingship of God*. Translated by Richard Schedmann. London: George Allen & Unwin; New York: Harper & Row, 1967.

————. *The Prophetic Faith*. New York: The Macmillan Company, 1949.

Buchanan, Scott. *Possibility*. New York: Harcourt Brace & Company; London: Kegan Paul, Trench, Trübner and Co., 1947.

Bultmann, Rudolf. *The Gospel of John*. Translated by G. R. Beasley-Murray, et al. Philadelphia: Westminster Press, 1971.

————. *Kerygma and Myth*. Vol. 2. Translated by Reginald H. Fuller. London: S.P.C.K., 1962.

————. "Proginōskō." In *Theological Dictionary of the New Testament*. Edited by Gerhard Kittel and Gerhard Friedrich, 1:715.

——. *Theology of the New Testament.* 2 vols. Translated by Kendrick Grobel. New York: Charles Scribner's Sons. 1951, 1955.

——. "What Sense Is There to Speak of God?" In *The Christian Scholar* 43, No. 3 (Fall 1960): 213.

Burkitt, F. C. "On Romans ix.5 and Mark xiv.61." *Journal of Theological Studies.* 5 (April, 1904); 451–455.

Burnet, John. *Greek Philosophy: Thales to Plato.* London: Macmillan; New York: St. Martin's Press, 1968.

Burns, A. L. "Two Words for 'Time' in the New Testament." *Australian Biblical Review,* Vol. 3 (1953): 7–22.

Burtt, Edwin A. *Man Seeks the Divine.* New York: Harper & Brothers, 1957.

Buswell, J. Oliver, Jr. *A Systematic Theology of the Christian Religion.* Vol. 1. Grand Rapids: Zondervan Publishing House, 1962.

Caird, G. B. *The Apostolic Age.* London: Duckworth, 1955.

——. *Principalities and Powers.* Oxford: Clarendon Press, 1950.

Caird, John. *The Fundamental Ideas of Christianity.* Vol. 1. Glasgow: James Maclehose and Sons, 1899.

Calvin, John. *Institutes of the Christian Religion.* 2 vols. Edited by John T. McNeill. Translated by Ford Lewis Battles. Philadelphia: Westminster Press, 1960.

Camfield, F. W. *Reformation Old and New;* a tribute to Karl Barth. London: Lutterworth Press, 1947.

Camfield, F. W., ed. *Revelation and the Holy Spirit.* New York: Charles Scribner's Sons, 1934.

Campbell, C. A. *On Selfhood and Godhood.* New York: The Macmillan Company, 1950.

Čapek, Milič. "Change." In *The Encyclopedia of Philosophy.* Edited by Paul Edwards. New York: The Macmillan Company & The Free Press, 1967.

Carlson, Edgar M. *The Reinterpretation of Luther.* Philadelphia: Westminster Press, 1947.

Castañeda, Hector-Neri: "Omniscience and Indexical Reference." *The Journal of Philosophy* 64, No. 7 (April 13, 1967): 209 f.

Chakkarai, V. *Jesus the Avatar.* Madras: Christian Literature Society, 1932.

Champion, John B. *Personality and the Trinity.* New York: Fleming H. Revell Co., 1935.

Charnock, Stephen. *Discourses Upon the Existence and Attributes of God.* Vol 1. Philadelphia: Presbyterian Board of Publication, 1840.

Christ, Carol P., and Plaskow, Judith, eds. "What Became of God the Mother?" *Womanspirit Rising.* New York: Harper Forum Books, 1979.

Clark, Gordon H. *Behaviorism and Christianity.* Unpublished manuscript.

——. *A Christian View of Men and Things.* Grand Rapids: Wm. B. Eerdmans, 1952.

——. "Cosmic Time." In *Gordon Review* (February 1956): 94 ff.

——. *Karl Barth's Theological Method.* Nutley, NJ: Presbyterian and Reformed Publishing Co., 1963.

——. *The Philosophy of Gordon H. Clark. A Festschrift.* Edited by Ronald H. Nash. Philadelphia: Presbyterian and Reformed Publishing Co., 1968.

——. *Thales to Dewey.* Boston: Houghton Mifflin Company, 1957.

Clarke, Charles Newton. *The Christian Doctrine of God.* New York: Charles Scribner's Sons, 1909.

Clarke, Samuel. "Can God Do Evil?" In *Discourse Concerning the Being and Attributes of God, the Obligations of Natural Religion, and the Truth and Certainty of the Christian Revelation.* 2 vols., 5th ed. London: W. Botham, 5th ed. 1719.

Clarke, William Newton. *Can I Believe in God the Father?* New York: Charles Scribner's Sons, 1905.

Cobb, John B., Jr. *Christ in a Pluralistic Age.* Philadelphia: Westminster Press, 1975.

——. *A Christian Natural Theology.* Based on the Thought of Alfred North Whitehead. Philadelphia: Westminster Press, 1965.

Coburn, Robert. "Professor Malcolm on God." *Australasian Journal of Philosophy* 40–41 J (1962–63).

Cochrane, Arthur C. *The Existentialists and God.* Philadelphia: Westminster Press, 1956.

Collins, James. *God in Modern Philosophy.* Chicago: Henry Regnery Company, 1959.

Collins, Sheila D. "Toward a Feminist Theology." *The Christian Century* (August 2, 1972): 796–799.

Conner, W. T. *Revelation and God: An Introduction to Christian Doctrine.* Nashville: Broadman Press, 1936.

Cornford, F. M., trans. *The Republic of Plato.* Book V, 477. New York: Oxford University Press, 1950.

Cox, Harvey. *The Seduction of the Spirit.* New York: Simon and Schuster, 1973.

Cragg, Gerald R. *The Church and the Age of Reason*—1648–1789. New York: Atheneum, 1961.

Cullmann, Oscar. *Christus und die Zeit.* (*Christ and Time*). Zollikon-Zurich: Evangelischer Verlag A.G., 1946; Translated by Floyd V. Filson. New York: Westminster Press, 1950; London: SCM Press Ltd, 1951; rev. ed., 1962.

———. *Earliest Christian Confessions.* Translated by J. K. S. Reid. London: Lutterworth Press; Chicago: A. R. Allenson, 1949.

———. *Salvation in History.* London: SCM Press Ltd; New York: Harper & Row, 1967.

Cusanus, Nicholas. *Of Learned Ignorance.* Translated by G. Heron. New Haven: Yale University Press, 1949.

Daly, Mary. *Beyond God the Father.* Boston: Beacon Press, 1973.

———. *Gyn-Ecology, The Metaethics of Radical Feminism.* Boston: Beacon Press, 1978.

Delling, Gerhard. "*Kairos.*" In *Theological Dictionary of the New Testament.* Edited by Gerhard Kittel and Gerhard Friedrich, 3:461.

Derrick, Christopher. *Trimming the Ark: Catholic Attitudes and the Cult of Change.* New York: P. J. Kennedy & Sons, 1968.

Descartes, René. *Discourse on Method.* Vol. 6. Translated by L. Lafleur. New York: Liberal Arts Press, 1950.

———. *The Method, Meditations and Philosophy of Descartes.* Vol. 3: *Meditations.* Translated by John Veitch. New York: Tudor Publishing Co., n.d.

———. *Philosophical Writings.* Translated by Elizabeth Auscomb and Peter T. Geach. London: Nelson, 1954.

Dewey, John. *Experience and Nature.* La Salle, IL: Open Court Publishing House. 2nd ed., 1929.

———. *Logic: The Theory of Inquiry.* New York: Henry Holt & Co., 1938.

DeWolf, L. Harold. *The Religious Revolt Against Reason.* New York: Harper & Brothers, 1949.

———. *A Theology of the Living Church.* Rev. ed. New York: Harper & Row, 1960.

Dickson, Kwesi A. "Continuity and Discontinuity Between the Old Testament and African Life and Thought." In *Christianity in Independent Africa.* Edited by Edward Fashole-Luke et al. Bloomington: Indiana University Press, 1978.

Dodd, C. H. *The Interpretation of the Fourth Gospel.* Cambridge: Cambridge University Press, 1968.

Dooyeweerd, Herman. *New Critique of Theoretical Thought.* 4 vols. Philadelphia: Presbyterian and Reformed Publishing Company, 1953–58.

———. *In the Twilight of Western Thought.* Philadelphia: Presbyterian and Reformed Publishing Company, 1960.

Dorner, I. A. *History of Protestant Theology.* 2 vols. Edinburgh: T. & T. Clark, 1871.

Dunlap, Knight. *Religion: Its Functions in Human Life.* London: McGraw Hill, 1946.

Ebeling, Gerhard. "Time and Word." In *The Future of Our Religious Past, Essays in Honour of Rudolf Bultmann.* Edited by James M. Robinson. Translated by Charles E. Carlston and Robert P. Scharlemann. London: SCM Press Ltd, 1971.

Ebner, Ferdinand. *Das Wort und die geistigen Realitäten.* 2nd ed. Vienna: Thomas Morus Presse, 1952.

Edwards, Jonathan. *Freedom of the Will.* Edited by Paul Ramsey (Works of Jonathan Edwards ser., vol. 1). New Haven: Yale University Press, 1957.

Ehrenfeld, Davis. *The Arrogance of Humanism.* New York: Oxford University Press, 1978.

Eichrodt, Walther. "Heilsfahrung und Zeitverstandnis in Alten Testament." In *Theologische Zeitschrift.* Vol. 12 (1956): 103–125.

Elliot, Elisabeth. *Let Me Be a Woman.* Wheaton: Tyndale House, 1978.

Erasmus. *Epistolae vivorum obscurorum.* In *Opus Epistolarum.* Edited by P. S. Allen. Oxford: Clarendon Press, 1906.

Farley, Edward. *The Transcendence of God.* Philadelphia: Westminster Press, 1960.

Farnell, Lewis R. *The Attributes of God.* London: Oxford University Press, 1925.

Farrer, Austin. *Finite and Infinite.* 2nd ed. London: A. and C. Black Ltd., 1959.

———. *The Revelation of St. John the Divine.* Oxford: Clarendon Press, 1964.

Feaver, Douglas. "Historical Development in the Priesthoods of Athens." In *Yale Classical Studies.* Vol. 15. New Haven: Yale University Press, 1957.

Ferré, Frederick. "Analogy in Theology." In *The Encyclopedia of Philosophy,* Vol. 1. Editor in Chief, Paul Edwards. New York: The Macmillan Company & The Free Press; London: Collier-Macmillan Limited, 1967.

Flew, Antony and Macintyre, Alasdair., eds. *New Essays in Philosophical Theology.* London: SCM Press Ltd, 1955.

Flint, Robert. *On Theological, Biblical, and Other Subjects.* Edinburgh: William Blackwood and Sons, 1905.

Foerster, Werner. *"Kurios* in the New Testament." In *Theological Dictionary of the New Testament.* Edited by Gerhard Kittel and Gerhard Friedrich, 3:1086 ff.

Ford, Lewis. *The Lure of God.* Philadelphia: Fortress Press, 1978.

Foster, Randolph S. *God—Nature and Attributes.* New York: Eaton & Mains; Cincinnati: Curts & Jennings, 1897.

Frederick, Carl. *est: Playing the Game the New Way.* New York: Dell, 1974; New York: Delta Paperback, 1976.

Fromm, Erich. *The Art of Loving.* New York: Harper & Row, 1956.

———. *The Dogma of Christ.* New York: Holt, Rinehart and Winston, 1963.

———. *You Shall Be As Gods.* New York: Holt, Rinehart and Winston, 1966.

Gale, Richard M., ed. *The Philosophy of Time.* London: The Macmillan Company, 1968.

Galloway, G. *A Philosophy of Religion.* New York: Charles Scribner's Sons, 1914.

Garrigou-Lagrange, R. *God: His Existence and Nature.* 2 vols. Translated by B. Rose. St. Louis: Herder Book Company, 1934–6.

Gilkey, Langdon. *Naming the Whirlwind: The Renewal of God Language.* Indianapolis: Bobbs-Merrill, 1969.

Glanville, Joseph. *The Vanity of Dogmatizing.* New York: Columbia University Press, 1931.

Goldenberg, Naomi. *Changing of the Gods.* Boston: Beacon Press, 1979.

Gollwitzer, Helmut. *The Existence of God as Confessed by Faith.* Translated by James W. Leitch. Munich: Chr. Kaiser Verlag, 1964; Philadelphia: Westminster Press, 1965.

Green, Peter. *The Holy Ghost: The Comforter.* A Study of the Nature and Work of God the Holy Spirit. London-New York-Toronto: Longmans, Green and Co., 1933.

Greer, Germaine. *The Female Eunuch.* New York: Bantam Books, 1971.

Griffin, David R. *A Process Christology.* Philadelphia: Westminster Press, 1973.

Güntert, Hermann. *Grundfragen der Sprachwissenschaft.* Leipzig: Quele and Mener, 1925; rev. ed. A. Scherer, 1956.

Gunton, Colin. *Becoming and Being.* New York: Oxford University Press, 1978.

Gwatkin, H. M. *The Knowledge of God and its Historical Development.* Vol 2. Gifford Lectures. Edinburgh: T. & T. Clark, 1906; 2 ed., 1908.

Haering, Theodore. *The Christian Faith: A System of Dogmatics.* 2 vols. Translated by John Dickie and George Ferries. London and New York; Hodder & Stoughton, 1915.

Haldane, Viscount. *The Pathway to Reality.* London: E. P. Dutton & Co., 1926.

Hamilton, Kenneth. *The System and the Gospel. A Critique of Paul Tillich.* New York: The Macmillan Company; London: SCM Press Ltd, 1963.

Hamilton, Kenneth. *To Turn from Idols.* Grand Rapids: Wm. B. Eerdmans, 1973.

Harkness, Georgia. "Divine Sovereignty and Human Freedom." In *Personalism In Theology.* Edited by E. S. Brightman. Boston: Boston University Press, 1943.

Harnack, Adolf. *History of Dogma.* Vol. 1. Boston: Roberts Brothers, 1897.

Harrison, Everett F. "Glory." In Baker's *Dictionary of Theology.* Editor in chief, E. F. Harrison. Grand Rapids: Baker Book House, 1960, 1969.

————."The Use of DOXA in Greek Literature with Special Reference to the New Testament." Ph.D. dissertation, University of Pennsylvania, 1950.

Hartline, Beverly Karplus. "Double Hubble, Age in Trouble." *Science* (January 11, 1980): 167–169.

Hartshorne, Charles. *The Divine Relativity.* New Haven: Yale University Press, 1948.

————. *The Logic of Perfection and Other Essays in Neoclassical Metaphysics.* La Salle, IL: Open Court Publishing Co., 1962.

————. *Man's Vision of God and the Logic of Theism.* Chicago; New York: Willett Clark & Company, 1941.

————. "Tillich's Doctrine of God." *The Theology of Paul Tillich.* Edited by Charles W. Kegley and Robert W. Bretall. Vol. 1. New York: The Macmillan Company, 1952.

————. *The Transcendence of God.* A Study in Contemporary Philosophical Theology. Philadelphia: The Westminster Press, 1958.

————. "What Did Anselm Discover?" In *The Many-Faced Argument.* Edited by John Hick and Arthur McGill. London: Macmillan, 1968.

Hasker, William. "Mackay on Being a Responsible Mechanism," and "Reply to Donald Mackay." *Christian Scholars Review* Vol. 8, No. 2 (1978).

Hegel, G. W. F. *Lectures on the Philosophy of Religion.* 3 Vols. Translated by E. B. Speirs and J. B. Sanderson. New York: Humanities Press, 1968.

————. *Wissenschaft der Logik.* 2 vols. Translated by W. H. Johnson and L. G. Struthers. Nuremberg, 1812–13. *The Science of Logic.* 2 vols. Translated by A. V. Miller. New York: Humanities Press, 1969.

Heidegger, Martin. *Being and Time.* Translated by John Macquarrie and Edward Robinson. New York: Harper and Row, 1962.

Hengel, Martin. *The Son of God: The Origin of Christology and the History of Jewish-Hellenistic Religion.* Translated by John Bowden. Philadelphia: Fortress Press, 1976.

Henry, Carl F. H. *God, Revelation and Authority: God Who Speaks and Shows.* Vols. 1–4. Waco, TX: Word Books, 1976–79.

————, ed. *Horizons of Science: Christian Scholars Speak Out.* New York: Harper & Row, 1977.

————. *Notes on the Doctrine of God.* Boston: W. A. Wilde Company, 1948.

————. *The Influence of Personalistic Idealism on the Theology of A. H. Strong.* Wheaton, IL: Van Kampen Press, 1951.

————. *The Protestant Dilemma.* Grand Rapids: Wm. B. Eerdmans, 1949.

Hick, John H., and McGill, Arthur C., eds. *The Many-Faced Argument: Recent Studies in the Ontological Argument for the Existence of God.* New York: The Macmillan Company, 1967.

Hick, John. ed. *The Myth of God Incarnate.* Philadelphia: Westminster Press, 1977.

Hirsch, E. D., Jr. *Validity in Interpretation.* New Haven: Yale University Press, 1976.

Hodge, Charles. *Systematic Theology.* Vol. 1. New York: Charles Scribner's Sons, 1885.

Hodgson, Leonard. *The Doctrine of the Trinity.* London: Nisbet, 1963.

Hordern, William. *Speaking of God: The Nature and Purpose of Theological Language.* London: The Epworth Press, 1965.

Horkheimer, Max. *Eclipse of Reason.* New York: Oxford University Press, 1947.

Hughes, H. Maldwyn. *The Christian Idea of God.* New York: Charles Scribner's Sons, 1936.

Hughes, Philip Edgcumbe. *A Commentary on the Epistle to the Hebrews.* Grand Rapids: Wm. B. Eerdmans, 1977.

Hume, David. *Dialogues Concerning Natural Religion.* Edited by Norman Kemp. Indianapolis: Bobbs-Merrill Co., Inc., Liberal Arts Press, 1962.

———. *An Enquiry Concerning Human Understanding.* Indianapolis: Bobbs-Merrill Co., Inc., Liberal Arts Press, 1955.

Hutchinson, William R. *The Modernist Impulse in American Protestantism.* Cambridge, MA and London, England: Harvard University Press, 1976.

Illingworth, J. R. *Personality Human and Divine.* London: The Macmillan Company, 1896.

Inge, William R. *Personal Idealism and Mysticism.* London: Longmans, Green and Co., 1907, 1913, 1924.

International Standard Bible Encyclopedia, 5 vols. Edited by James Orr. Grand Rapids: Wm. B. Eerdmans, 1955.

Jaeger, Werner. *The Theology of the Early Greek Philosophers.* Gifford Lectures, 1936. Translated by Edward S. Robinson. London, Oxford, and New York: Clarendon Press, 1947.

James, William. "Does Consciousness Exist?" In *Essays in Radical Empiricism.* New York: Longmans, Green & Co., 1912.

———. *A Pluralistic Universe.* New York: Longmans & Green, 1909.

———. *The Varieties of Religious Experience:* A Study in Human Nature. Gifford Lectures 1901–1902. New York, London, Bombay and Calcutta: Longmans, Green & Co., 1902; New York: The Modern Library, n.d.

Jaspers, Karl. *Reason and Anti-Reason in Our Time.* New Haven: Yale University Press, 1952.

———. *Reason and Existenz.* New York: Noonday Press, 1955.

Jellema, Dirk. "Christianity and the 'New Faith'" *Christianity Today* 4, No. 19 (June 20, 1960): 11.

———. "The Rise of the Post-Modern Mind." *Christianity Today* 4, No. 16 (May 9, 1960): 13.

Jenni, Ernst. "Time." In *The Interpreter's Dictionary of the Bible.* Vol. 4. Edited by George A. Buttrick. New York and Nashville: Abingdon Press, 1962.

Jewett, Paul K. "Ebnerian Personalism." *Westminster Theological Journal,* Vol. XII, No. 3 (May 1952).

———. "The Holy Spirit as Female(?)." *The Reformed Journal* 28, Issue 24 (April 1978): 12.

Jirku, Anton. *Altorientalischer Kommentar zum Alten Testament.* Leipzig: A. Deichert, 1923.

Johnson, A. R. *The One and the Many in the Israelite Conception of God.* Cardiff: University of Wales, 1942.

Kaftan, Julius. *Dogmatik.* Freiburg: Mohr, 1897; Tübingen: Mohr, 3rd and 4th ed., 1901.

Kant, Immanuel. *Critique of Pure Reason.* Translated by F. Max Muller. New York: Doubleday and Co.; Anchor Books, 1955.

Kato, Byang. *Theological Pitfalls in Africa.* Kisumu, Kenya: Evangel Publishing House, 1975.

Kaufman, Gordon D. *Systematic Theology: A Historical Perspective.* New York: Charles Scribner's Sons, 1968.

Kelley, J. N. D. *Early Christian Creeds.* London: Longmans, 1960; rev. ed. New York: Harper & Row, 1978.

Kenny, Arthur. *Aquinas: A Collection of Critical Essays.* London: The Macmillan Company; New York: Doubleday and Company, Inc., 1969.

Kierkegaard, Søren. *Christian Discourses.* Translated by Walter Lowrie. London: Oxford University Press, 1939.

———. *Concluding Unscientific Postscript.* Translated by D. F. Swenson. Edited by Walter Lowrie. Princeton: Princeton University Press, 1941.

———. *Philosophical Fragments.* Translated by D. F. Swenson. Princeton: Princeton University Press, 1936, 1941.

Kittel, Gerhard. *"Doxa."* In *Theological Dictionary of the New Testament.* Edited by Gerhard Kittel and Gerhard Friedrich, 2:242.

Kittel, Gerhard, and Friedrich, Gerhard, eds. *Theological Dictionary of the New Testament.* 9 vols. Grand Rapids: Wm. B. Eerdmans, 1964–73. Abbreviated as *TDNT* in text.

Kleinknecht, Hermann. *"Theos:* The Greek Concept of God." In *Theological Dictionary of the New Testament.* Edited by Gerhard Kittel and Gerhard Friedrich, 3:78.

Kline, Leslie L. *The Sayings of Jesus in the Pseudo-Clementine Homilies.* Missoula: Society of Biblical Literature and Scholars Press, 1975.

Knapp, George Christian. *Lectures on Christian Theology.* Philadelphia: Thomas Wardle, 1845.

Kneale, William. "Time and Eternity in Theology." *Proceedings of the Aristotelian Society* (1960–61) 87–108.

Knight, G. A. F. *A Biblical Approach to the Doctrine of the Trinity.* Edinburgh: Oliver and Boyd Ltd., 1953.

Knox, John. "Epistle to the Romans." In *The Interpreter's Bible.* Vol. 9. New York: Abingdon Press, 1955.

Knudson, Albert C. *The Doctrine of God.* Nashville: Abingdon Press, 1930.

———. *The Doctrine of Redemption.* New York: Abingdon Press, 1933.

———. *The Philosophy of Personalism: A Study in the Metaphysics of Religion.* Reprint of 1927 ed. Millwood, NY: Kraus Reprint Co., 1968.

Koop, C. Everett., and Schaeffer, Francis A. *Whatever Happened to the Human Race?* Old Tappan, NJ: Fleming H. Revell Company, 1979.

Kretzmann, Norman. "Omniscience and Immutability." *The Journal of Philosophy* 63, No. 14 (July 14, 1966): 409–421.

Kuhn, Karl George. *"Theos:* The Rabbinic Terms for God." In *Theological Dictionary of the New Testament.* Edited by Gerhard Kittel and Gerhard Friedrich, 3:93.

Laeuchli, Samuel. *The Language of Faith.* New York: Abingdon Press, 1962.

Leach, Edmund. *A Runaway World?* New York: Oxford University Press; London: British Broadcasting Corporation, 1968.

Leitch, Addison H. "Omniscience." In *The Zondervan Pictorial Encyclopedia of the Bible.* Vol. 4. Merrill C. Tenney, gen. ed. Grand Rapids: Zondervan, 1975.

Levi, A. W. *Philosophy and the Modern World.* Bloomington: Indiana University Press, 1959.

Lewis, C. I. *Mind and the World-Order.* New York: Dover Publications, Inc., 1956.

Lewis, Edwin. *The Creator and the Adversary.* New York: Abingdon-Cokesbury Press, 1948.

Locke, John. *Locke's Essay Concerning Human Understanding.* Selections by Mary Whiton Calkins. Chicago and London: Open Court Publishing Co., 1933.

Lossky, Vladimir. *The Mystical Theology of the Eastern Church.* London: J. Clarke, 1957.

Lovejoy, Arthur O. *The Great Chain of Being.* A Study of the History of an Idea. Cambridge: Harvard University Press, 1936, 1970.

Lowry, Charles W. *The Trinity and Christian Devotion.* New York and London: Harper and Brothers, 1946.

Lyman, Eugene W. *Theology and Human Problems.* New York: Charles Scribner's Sons, 1910.

McConnell, Francis J. *The Christlike God.* New York: Abingdon Press, 1927.

McGill, Arthur C. "Recent Discussions of Anselm's Argument." In *The Many-Faced*

Argument. Edited by John Hick and Arthur McGill. London: The Macmillan Company, 1968.

Macintosh, Douglas Clyde. *The Problem of Religious Knowledge*. New York: Harper & Brothers, 1940.

———. *Theology as an Empirical Science*. New York: The Macmillan Company, 1919.

Mackay, Donald. *The Clock Work Image*. Downers Grove: Inter-Varsity Press, 1974.

McKeon, Richard. *Selections from Medieval Philosophers*. Vol. 1, Augustine to Albert the Great. Edited and translated, with introductory notes, by Richard McKeon. New York: Charles Scribner's Sons, 1929.

Mackinnon, Donald. *Borderlands of Theology and Other Essays*. London: Lutterworth Press, 1968.

McNeill, William H. "The Decline of the West." In *Solzhenitsyn at Harvard*. Edited by Ronald Berman. Washington, DC: Ethics and Public Policy Center, 1980.

———. "On Western Freedom." In *Solzhenitsyn at Harvard*. Edited by Ronald Berman. Washington D.C.: Ethics and Public Policy Center, 1980.

Macquarrie, John. *Principles of Christian Theology*. London: SCM Press Ltd, 1966.

McTaggart, J. M. E. *Some Dogmas of Religion*. 2nd ed. London: Longmans, Green and Co., 1930.

Machen, J. Gresham. *My Idea of God*. Edited by Joseph Fort Newton. Boston: Little, Brown and Company, 1926–27.

Marsh, John. *The Fullness of Time*. London: Nisbet & Co., Ltd.; New York: Harper & Brothers, 1952.

Marshall, I. Howard. *The Epistles of John*. In The New International Commentary on the New Testament. F. F. Bruce, gen. ed. Grand Rapids: Wm. B. Eerdmans, 1978.

Martin, H. V. *Kierkegaard: The Melancholy Dane*. New York: Philosophical Library, 1950.

Mascall, E. L. *Existence and Analogy*. New York: Longmans, Green and Co., Inc., 1949.

———. *He Who Is. A Study in Traditional Theism*. London: Darton, Longman & Todd, 1966.

———. *The Openness of Being*. Gifford Lectures, 1970–71. London: Darton, Longman and Todd Ltd., 1971.

Mathews, Shailer. *The Growth of the Idea of God*. New York: The Macmillan Company, 1931.

Matthews, W. R. *God in Christian Experience*. New York and London: Harper & Brothers Publishers, 1930.

———. *The Purpose of God*. London: Nisbet, 1935.

Mavrodes, George. "Some Puzzles Concerning Omnipotence." *The Philosophical Review* 72 (1963): 221–223.

Mbiti, John S. "Christianity and Traditional Religions in Africa." In *International Review of Missions* 63 (January 1974): 430–440.

Mencken, H. L. *Treatise on the Gods*. New York: Knopf, 1930, 1946; Blue Ribbon, 1932; Random House, 1963.

Mendelsohn, Jack. *Why I Am a Unitarian*. New York: Thomas Nelson and Sons, 1960.

Metzger, Bruce M. "The Punctuation of Romans 9:5." *Christ and Spirit in the New Testament*. Edited by Barnabas Lindars and Stephen S. Smalley. Cambridge: University Press, 1973.

Mill, John Stuart. *Three Essays on Religion*. London: Longmans, Green and Co., 1874.

Milmed, Bella K. *Kant and Current Philosophical Issues:* Some Modern Developments of His Theory of Knowledge. New York: University Press, 1961.

Miskotte, Kornelis H. *When the Gods Are Silent*. London: Collins, 1967.

Moffatt, James. *A Critical and Exegetical Commentary on the Epistle to the Hebrews*.

International Critical Commentary. Edinburgh: T. & T. Clark; Naperville, IL: Allenson, 1924.

Moltmann, Jürgen. *The Crucified God.* New York: Harper & Row, 1974.

Monod, Jacques. *Chance and Necessity.* New York: Vintage, 1971.

Montgomery, John Warwick. *Where is History Going?* Grand Rapids: Zondervan Publishing House, 1969.

Moore, G. E. *Philosophical Studies.* New York: Harcourt, 1922.

Moore, Peter, ed. "Man, Woman and the Priesthood of Christ." *Man, Woman, Priesthood.* Westminster, MD: Christian Classics, Inc., 1978.

Morgan, Marabel. *The Total Woman.* Old Tappan, NJ: Fleming H. Revell Company, 1973.

Morris, Leon. *The Gospel According to John.* The New International Commentary on the New Testament. F. F. Bruce, gen. ed. Grand Rapids: Wm. B. Eerdmans, 1971.

Moss, Claude Beaufort. *The Christian Faith: An Introduction to Dogmatic Theology.* London: S.P.C.K., 1954.

Moule, Charles F. D. *The Gospel According to Mark.* Cambridge: Cambridge University Press, 1965.

Mounce, Robert. *The Book of Revelation.* The New International Commentary on the New Testament. F. F. Bruce, gen. ed. Grand Rapids: Wm. B. Eerdmans, 1977.

Mueller, Max ed. *Sacred Books of the East.* 50 vols.

Murray, Bruce; Gulkis, Samuel; Edelson, Robert E. "Extraterrestrial Intelligence: An Observational Approach." *Science* Magazine 199 (February 3, 1978): 491.

Murray, John. *The Epistle to the Romans.* In The New International Commentary on the New Testament. F. F. Bruce, gen. ed. Grand Rapids: Wm. B. Eerdmans, 1973.

Nash, Ronald H. "Dooyeweerd and the Amsterdam Philosophy." *A Christian Critique of Philosophic Thought.* Grand Rapids: Zondervan Publishing House, 1962.

Neill, Stephen. *Christian Faith and Other Faiths.* London: Oxford University Press, 1961.

Niebuhr, Reinhold. *The Nature and Destiny of Man.* Gifford Lectures. Vol 1. New York: Charles Scribner's Sons, 1943.

Ogden, Schubert. The *Reality of God and other Essays.* London: SCM Press Ltd, 1967.

————. *Twentieth Century Religious Thought: The Frontiers of Philosophy and Theology, 1900–1960.* New York: Harper & Row, 1963.

Origen. *De Principiis.*

Otto, Rudolf. *Das Heilige* (The Idea of the Holy). Translated by J. W. Harvey. London: Oxford University Press, 1923.

Owen, H. P. "Infinity in Theology and Metaphysics." *The Encyclopedia of Philosophy.* Vol. 4. Editor-in-Chief Paul Edwards. New York: The Macmillan Company, 1967.

Pannenberg, Wolfhart. "The God of Hope." *Basic Questions in Theology.* Vol. 2. Translated by George H. Kehm. Philadelphia: Fortress Press, 1971.

————. "The Philosophical Concept of God." In *Basic Questions in Theology: Collected Essays.* Vol. 2. Translated by George H. Kehm. Philadelphia: Fortress Press, 1971.

————. "Speaking About God in the Face of Atheistic Criticism." In *The Idea of God and Human Freedom.* Translated by R. A. Wilson. Translation of "Reden von Gott angesichts atheistischer Kritik." In *Evangelischer Kommentare.* II., 1969; Philadelphia: The Westminster Press, 1973.

————. "Theology and the Kingdom of God." In *Theology and the Kingdom of God.* Edited by Richard John Neuhaus. Philadelphia: Westminster Press, 1969.

Paterson, W. P. *The Rule of Faith.* London: Hodder & Stoughton Limited, 1932.

Pennelhum, Terence. "Personal Identity." In *The Encyclopedia of Philosophy.* Vol. 6. Editor-in-Chief Paul Edwards. New York: The Macmillan Company & The Free Press, 1967.

Pieper, Francis. *Christian Dogmatics.* St. Louis: Concordia Publishing House, 1950.

Pike, James. *Time* 88, No. 2 (November 11, 1966).

Pike, Nelson. "Divine Omniscience and Voluntary Action." *Philosophical Review* 74, No. 1 (January 1965).

———. *God and Timelessness.* London: Routledge & Kegan Paul, 1970.

———. "Omnipotence and God's Ability to Sin." *American Philosophical Quarterly* 6, No. 5 (July 1969): 208.

Pinnock, Clark. *Biblical Revelation.* Chicago: Moody Press, 1971.

Plantinga, Alvin. *God, Freedom and Evil.* Grand Rapids: Wm. B. Eerdmans, 1978.

———. *God and Other Minds,* A Study of the Rational Justification of Belief in God. Ithaca: Cornell University Press, 1967, 1969, 1972.

———. "Necessary Being." In *Faith and Philosophy.* Edited by Alvin Plantinga. Grand Rapids: Wm. B. Eerdmans, 1964.

Plato. *The Republic of Plato.* Translated by F. M. Cornford. New York: Oxford University Press, 1945.

———. *The Works of Plato.* Translated by B. Jowett. New York: Tudor Publishing Company, n.d.

Pontifex, Mark. *Belief in the Trinity.* New York: Harper and Brothers, 1954.

Pringle-Pattison, A. Seth. *The Idea of God in the Light of Recent Philosophy.* Gifford Lectures 1912–13. New York: Oxford University Press, 1920.

Prior, Arthur. "The Formalities of Omniscience." *Philosophy* (1962): 124.

———. *Past, Present and Future.* Oxford: Clarendon Press, 1967.

Purdy, Richard A. *The Mormon Doctrine Concerning the Nature of God.* Master of Divinity thesis, Talbot Theological Seminary, 1973.

Quell, Gottfried. *"Kurios:* The Old Testament Name for God." In *Theological Dictionary of the New Testament.* Edited by Gerhard Kittel and Gerhard Friedrich, 3:1062.

———. *"Theos:* El and Elohim in the Old Testament." In *Theological Dictionary of the New Testament.* Edited by Gerhard Kittel and Gerhard Friedrich, 3:89.

Rahner, Karl. *Theological Investigations.* New York: Seabury Press, Crossroads Books, 1962.

Ramsey, A. M. *The Glory of God and the Transfiguration of Christ.* London: Longmans, Green and Co., 1949.

Randall, John Herman, and Randall, John Herman, Jr. *Religion and the Modern World.* New York: Frederick A. Stokes, 1929.

Reichenbach, Hans. *Experience and Prediction.* Chicago: University of Chicago Press, 1938.

———. *The Rise of Scientific Philosophy.* Berkeley and Los Angeles: University of California Press, 1938, 1951.

Richardson, Alan. "Time." In *A Theological Word Book of the Bible.* London: SCM Press Ltd, 1950.

Richardson, Cyril C. *The Doctrine of the Trinity.* New York-Nashville: Abingdon Press, 1958.

Ritschl, Albrecht. *Justification and Reconciliation.* Edinburgh: T. & T. Clark, 1900.

———. *Theologie und Metaphysik.* Translated and with introduction by Philip Hefner. Philadelphia: Fortress Press, 1972.

Robinson, H. Wheeler. *The Christian Experience of the Holy Spirit.* London: James Nisbet & Co., Ltd., 1928.

Robinson, John A. T. *Exploration into God.* Stanford: Stanford University Press, 1967.

Royden, A. Maude. *I Believe in God.* New York and London: Harper & Brothers Publishers, 1927.

Ryle, Gilbert. *The Concept of Mind.* New York: Barnes & Noble, 1949.

Santayana, George. *The Life of Reason.* New York: Charles Scribner's Sons, 1954.

Sartre, Jean-Paul. *Existentialism and Human Emotions.* New York: Philosophical Library, 1957.

Sasse, Hermann. "Aion." In *Theological Dictionary of the New Testament.* Edited by Gerhard Kittel and Gerhard Friedrich, 1:201.

Saunders, John Turk. "Of God and Freedom." *Philosophical Review* 75 (1966): 220 f.

Savage, C. Wade. "The Paradox of Stone." *Philosophical Review* 76 (1967): 74 ff.

Scanzoni, Letha, and Hardesty, Nancy. *All We're Meant to Be.* Waco: Word Books, 1975.

Schaeffer, Francis. *The God Who Is There.* London: Hodder and Stoughton, 1968.

Schaff, Philip. *Creeds of Christendom.* New York: Harper and Brothers, 1917.

Schleiermacher, Friedrich. *The Christian Faith.* New York: Harper & Row, Harper Torchbooks, 1963.

Schlesinger, Arthur. "The Solzhenitsyn We Refuse to See." *Washington Post* (June 25, 1978).

Schneider, Johannes. "Erchomai." In *Theological Dictionary of the New Testament.* Edited by Gerhard Kittel and Gerhard Friedrich, 2:668.

Schultz, Hans Jurgen. *Conversion to the World.* New York: Charles Scribner's Sons, 1967.

Schumacher, E. F. *Small Is Beautiful.* New York: Harper & Row, 1973.

Selbie, W. B. *The Fatherhood of God.* New York: Charles Scribner's Sons, 1936.

Shaw, D. W. D. *Who is God?* London: SCM Press Ltd, 1968.

Sheed, F. J. *God and the Human Condition.* New York: Sheed and Ward, 1966.

Sheed, W. G. T. *Dogmatic Theology.* Vol. 1. New York: Charles Scribner's Sons, 1888.

———. *History of Christian Doctrine.* Vol. 1. New York: Charles Scribner, 1863.

Sinclair, Upton. *The Profits of Religion.* London: Warner Laurie, 1936.

Skinner, B. F. *About Behaviorism.* New York: W. W. Norton & Co., 1924.

Slatte, Howard A. *Time and Its End.* New York: Vantage Press, 1962.

Smith, Henry B. *System of Christian Theology.* Edited by William S. Karr. New York: A. C. Armstrong and Son, 1892.

Smith, Huston. "Revolution in Western Thought." *The Saturday Evening Post* (August 26, 1961): 61.

Söderblom, Nathan. *Uppenbarelsreligion.* [The Nature of Revelation]. 2nd ed. Translated by Frederick E. Pamp. New York: Oxford University Press, 1933.

Sparrow-Simpson, W. J. *The Christian Doctrine of God.* London: Richard Flint & Co., 1906.

Spier, J. M. *Christianity and Existentialism.* Philadelphia: Presbyterian and Reformed Publishing Co., 1953.

Stace, W. T. *Time and Eternity.* Princeton: Princeton University Press, 1952.

Stählin, Leonhard. *Kant, Lotze, and Ritschl: A Critical Examination.* Edinburgh, T. & T. Clark, 1889.

Stauffer, Ethelbert. *"Theos."* In *Theological Dictionary of the New Testament.* Edited by Gerhard Kittel and Gerhard Friedrich, 3:100.

———. *"Theos:* The Uniqueness of God." In *Theological Dictionary of the New Testament.* Edited by Gerhard Kittel and Gerhard Friedrich, 3:94.

Steed, Christopher. *Divine Substance.* Oxford: Clarendon Press, 1977.

Stendahl, Krister. See Letters to the Editor. *Christianity Today* 20, No. 7 (January 2, 1976): 24.

Stiernotte, Alfred P. *God and Space-Time.* Deity in the Philosophy of Samuel Alexander. New York: Philosophical Library, 1964.

Stirling, James H. *Philosophy and Theology.* Gifford Lectures. Edinburgh: T. & T. Clark, 1890.

Stokers, Hendrik G. "Van Til's Theory of Knowledge." In *Jerusalem and Athens.* Edited by E. R. Geehan. Nutley, NJ: Presbyterian and Reformed Publishing Co., 1971.

Stone, C. D. *Should Trees Have Standing?* Los Altos, CA: William Kaufmann, 1974.

Strong, A. H. *Systematic Theology.* Vol. 1. Philadelphia: The Griffith & Rowland Press, 1907.

Sweeney, L. "Divine Infinity: 1150–1250." *The Modern Schoolman* 35 (1957–58): 38–51.

Taylor, Richard. "The Problem of Future Contingency." *Philosophical Review* 66 (1957): 1–28.

Temple, William. *Basic Convictions.* New York: Harper & Brothers, 1936.

———. *Readings in St. John's Gospel.* New York: St. Martin's Press, 1968.

Tennant, Frederick R. *Philosophical Theology.* Vol. 1. New York and Cambridge: Cambridge University Press, 1928.

Thayer, J. H. *A Greek-English Lexicon of the New Testament.* New York: American Book Company, 1889.

Thielicke, Helmut. *The Evangelical Faith.* Translated by Geoffrey W. Bromiley. Grand Rapids: Wm. B. Eerdmans, 1974.

Thomas, George F. *Protestant Thought in the Twentieth Century.* Edited by Arnold S. Nash. New York: The Macmillan Company, 1951.

———. *Religious Philosophies of the West.* New York: Charles Scribner's Sons, 1965.

Tillich, Paul. *Biblical Religion and the Search for Ultimate Reality.* Chicago: University of Chicago Press, 1964.

———. *The Courage to Be.* New Haven: Yale University Press, 1952.

———. *The Eternal Now.* New York: Charles Scribner's Sons, 1963.

———. *Systematic Theology.* 3 vols. Chicago: University of Chicago Press, 1951–1963.

———. *Theology of Culture.* Edited by Robert C. Kimball. New York: Oxford University Press, 1959.

Torrance, Thomas F. *Space, Time and Incarnation.* London: Oxford University Press, 1969.

———. *Theological Science.* London and New York: Oxford University Press, 1969.

Toulmin, Stephen. *An Examination of the Place of Reason in Ethics.* Cambridge: Cambridge University Press, 1950.

Tozer, A. W. *The Knowledge of the Holy.* New York: Harper & Brothers, 1961.

Trible, Phyllis. *God and the Rhetoric of Sexuality.* Philadelphia: Fortress Press, 1978.

Tupper, Frank E. *The Theology of Wolfhart Pannenburg.* Philadelphia: The Westminster Press, 1973.

Vaihinger, Hans. *The Philosophy of 'As If': A System of the Theoretical, Practical and Religious Fictions of Mankind.* Translated by C. K. Ogden. Boston: Routledge and Kegan Paul, 1935.

Van Buren, Paul M. *The Secular Meaning of the Gospel: An Original Inquiry.* New York: The Macmillan Company, 1963.

Van Til, Cornelius. *Junior Systematics.* Unpublished lecture notes.

Vaughan, Richard M. *The Significance of Personality.* New York: the Macmillan Company, 1930.

Vitz, Paul C. *Psychology as Religion: The Cult of Self-Worship.* Grand Rapids: Wm. B. Eerdmans, 1977.

Von Arnim, H. F. *Stoicorum veterum fragmenta.* 4 vols. Leipzig: 1903–1924; Stuttgart: B. G. Teubneri, 1968.

von Orelli, C. *Die hebräischen Synonyma der Zeit und Ewigkeit genetisch und Sprachvergleichend dargestellt.* Leipzig: A. Lorentz, 1871.

Vos, Geerhardus. "Omniscience." In *International Standard Bible Encyclopedia.* Vol. 4. Edited by James Orr.

Wainwright, Arthur W. *The Trinity in the New Testament.* London: S.P.C.K., 1962.

Warfield, B. B. "Trinity." In *International Standard Bible Encyclopedia.* 5 vols. Rev. ed. General editor James Orr. Grand Rapids: Wm. B. Eerdmans, 1955.

Watts, Leon. *Renewal* (September-October 1969): 13.

Webb, Clement C. J. *God and Personality.* Gifford Lectures, 1918. London: G. Allen & Unwin Ltd.; New York: The Macmillan Company, 1918.

———. *Religion and Theism.* Liverpool: Charles Scribner's Sons, 1934.

West, Charles C. "God-Man/Woman-Creation." Address to the American Theological Society, Princeton Theological Seminary, April 12, 1980.

Whitehead, Alfred North. *Process and Reality*. New York: The Macmillan Company, 1929.

———. *Process and Reality: An Essay in Cosmology*. Cambridge: Cambridge University Press, 1922.

———. *Religion in the Making*. New York: The Macmillan Company, 1926.

———. *Science and the Modern World*. New York: The Macmillan Company, 1925.

Wieman, Henry Nelson, and Meland, Bernard E. *American Philosophies of Religion*. Chicago-New York: Willett, Clark and Co., 1936.

Williams, Daniel Day. *The Spirit and the Forms of Love*. New York: Harper & Row, 1968.

———. "Tillich's Doctrine of God." *Philosophical Journal* 18 (1960–61): 41, 50.

Wisdom, John. *Paradox and Discovery*. Oxford: Basil Blackwell, 1965.

———. "The Metamorphosis of Metaphysics." In *Paradox and Discovery*. Oxford: Basil Blackwell, 1965; Berkeley: University of California Press, 1970.

Wiseman, Donald J. "Astrology." In *Baker's Dictionary of Christian Ethics*. Edited by Carl F. H. Henry. Grand Rapids: Baker Book House, 1973.

Wolff, Christian. *Theologia Naturalis methodo scientifica pertractata*. Vol. 1. Verona: Moroni, 1779.

Wolfson, H. A. *Philo*. Cambridge: Harvard University Press, 1947.

Wolterstorff, Nicholas. "God Everlasting." *God and the Good*. Clifton J. Orlebeke and Lewis B. Smedes, eds. Grand Rapids: Wm. B. Eerdmans, 1975.

Wunderlich, Lorenz. *The Half-Known God*. St. Louis: Concordia Publishing House, 1963.

Wyschogrod, Michael. *Kierkegaard and Heidegger: The Ontology of Existence*. New York: Humanities Press, 1954.

Person Index

Scripture Index

Old Testament

New Testament

Apocryphal and Other Extracanonical Works

Subject Index